'One of the most satisfying lives of a British monarch to be written in recent years, a book in the line of Neale's *Queen Elizabeth I* or Harold Nicolson's *George V*.' *New Statesman*

'Likely to become the standard biography. I have read it with the greatest pleasure . . . most illuminating about the King's personality and character.' *Sunday Telegraph*

'The foreword the Prince has, at his own suggestion, written to Mr Brooke's volume offers as lively and balanced a review of George III's character and misfortunes as any professional critic could offer . . . I am grateful to Mr Brooke for a virtual re-education in the period. He is extremely learned, acute and gifted with a sharp, clean style.' *Daily Telegraph*

'Likely to remain the standard work on the subject for a long time.' *The Economist*

John Brooke

Foreword by HRH The Prince of Wales

King George III

Panther

Granada Publishing Limited
Published in 1974 by Panther Books Ltd
Frogmore, St Albans, Herts AL2 2NF

First published in Great Britain by
Constable & Company Ltd 1972
Copyright © John Brooke 1972
Foreword copyright © HRH The Prince of Wales 1972
Made and printed in Great Britain by
Richard Clay (The Chaucer Press) Ltd
Bungay, Suffolk
Set in Monotype Times

To the memory of my beloved sister-in-law
YVONNE FRANCES CARROLL-VRDLOVEC,
née MARTIN
wife of MAJOR CHARLES CARROLL-VRDLOVEC, M.B.E.
Died 30 January 1970

FOREWORD

by

HRH THE PRINCE OF WALES

It was exactly a year ago that my interest was aroused in King George III as a result of reading a book and several pamphlets on the subject of his so-called insanity. I became fascinated in the whole life and personality of the King and explored the archives at Windsor as frequently as possible, reading through old correspondence and doctors' reports. It was while I was engaged in this pursuit that I met Mr John Brooke and had a long and intriguing conversation with him about the King and about the biography he was writing of the latter. We both agreed that George III had been unfairly maligned by historians and the writers of textbook history. This book, although by no means a whitewash of the King, attempts to portray him in a thoroughly human and sympathetic manner.

As human beings we suffer from an innate tendency to jump to conclusions; to judge people too quickly and to pronounce them failures or heroes without due consideration of the actual facts and ideals of the period. George III is a monarch who has gone down in history as 'the mad King'. If the average schoolchild remembers anything about history after leaving school he will remember that George III was mad. If he is American as well then madness is often given as a reason for the 'irrational' behaviour of the King towards the Colonists, making it necessary for them to declare independence. George III's cardinal error was that he 'failed' in history – he failed to retain the American colonies, and in the search to find a scapegoat for this national disaster the King became the obvious target. When in 1788 he suffered from the worst

7

attack of what is now believed by most doctors to be physical illness rather than manic depressive psychosis or psychiatric illness, contemporaries, followed by later writers, diarists and politicians, began to read insanity into many of the King's pronouncements and actions throughout his reign.

Modern medical knowledge and research have enabled doctors to study the physicians' reports on the King's health (which are immensely numerous and in great detail) in a different light and to produce diagnoses to show that the King's mental state during his attacks was in keeping with mental states due to infections, toxic processes and metabolic disturbances. Much has been written by learned scholars to the effect that George III was manic depressive, and suffered from sexual frustration, a difficult wife, and hideous family problems – all acting upon an inherently unstable character which finally gave way under the strain. If this was so why didn't the King 'go mad' far earlier than 1788? In that year he celebrated his fiftieth birthday and had apparently solved his long-standing political problems, with Pitt established firmly in the nation's confidence. Not only that. The Prince of Wales' debts had at last been settled and it was three years since the traumatic experience of finding that the Prince, in defiance of Acts of Parliament, had contracted a marriage with Mrs Fitzherbert – enough to crack any remotely unstable character. George III's illness does not appear to correspond to mania or hypomania. There was no feeling of well-being, euphoria or elation. He suffered terribly from various physical symptoms – such as abdominal and leg pains – and consequent mental anguish in the form of intense delirium – something which Dr Willis, the special 'mad doctor', in fact recognized and reported to the Privy Council.

After a study of the available evidence two present-day doctors with psychiatric training came to the conclusion that George III suffered from porphyria – an inheritable disease associated with recurrent toxic-confusional states. There has been long and furious argument amongst the medical and historical professions on the controversial subject of porphyria. I have read most of the correspondence in the *Times Literary Supplement* and in the *British Medical Journal*. The author of this biography, I know, is inclined to support the theory of porphyria. It does indeed seem to fit the symptoms, but the evidence is only suggestive, not conclusive. The recurrent toxic and confusional states suffered by the King could have been due to other physical causes such as infectious and metabolic disturbances. The observation of purple urine by itself is not sufficient proof; indeed, medical experience has shown that most cases of modern porphyria are precipitated by barbiturates – unheard of in the eighteenth century. But the important point is that the King suffered from attacks of a *physical* disease. There is no evidence that he was schizophrenic, or depressive, or that he suffered from syphilis of the central nervous system which, when untreated, is steadily progressive. Only in the last ten years of his life when, between the ages of seventy and eighty, deaf, blind, deserted by his family, surrounded only by 'mad doctors' and apothecaries who tied him up in strait waistcoats at the slightest sign of opposition to their will and banished him to the North side of Windsor Castle, did he show signs of mental decay associated with natural senility.

I think there can now be little doubt that George III suffered from periodic attacks of a metabolic illness. But, you may say, what difference does that make to the fact that the King was in some way mentally disturbed? Surely he was 'mad' whichever way you look at it? No. The subtle difference is that there was nothing wrong with his brain *before* the onset of the illness. The illness produced a mental state akin to the sort of delirium experienced by patients with very high fevers; patients who could in no way be labelled as mad either before or after their illness

9

and who had shown no previous signs of irrational and rather dotty behaviour.

The stigma of madness attached to the poor King has persisted far too long. It is high time that the veil of obscurity stifling the King's true personality, known and loved by his contemporaries, should be lifted. Mr Brooke's account of George III's life achieves this purpose. Instead of the old spectre of a monarch threatening the constitution by increasing the power of the Crown to the detriment of Parliament, there is revealed a man almost over-dedicated to his duty and to the defence of the British Constitution as he saw it. It was, after all, in George III's reign that the office of Prime Minister gradually evolved – thereby reducing the power of the Crown to the role of influential adviser.

As a young man George III was not particularly attractive and could almost be described as priggish. However, as he mellowed and gained experience his warmth and friendly interest in people – particularly evident at Windsor and Kew where he used to go walking and visiting alone, talking to his tenants and behaving as a natural and thoroughly civilized country gentleman – won him immense popularity. He was also a man with a marvellous sense of humour and fun, who inspired those who served him with a deep affection and loyalty. You have only to read Fanny Burney's diaries to discover that. At the height of one of the worst attacks of illness Dr Willis tried to make excuses for the ghastly treatment he was giving the King by saying: 'Sir, our Saviour himself went about healing the sick.' 'Yes, yes,' replied the King, 'but he had not £700 a year for it.'

Few have laboured harder at being a good King than George III. He cared and he was a genuine, honest person; qualities which quickly endeared the King to all classes of his subjects. The tragedy is that the American colonies never received a visit from him – if a royal tour had been a conceivable undertaking in the eighteenth century the leaders of the colonies might have understood him better. Perhaps Americans will soon come to see the true George III without bias and traditionally held opinions.

Nothing, I feel, sums up better the true effect that George III had on England than what Mrs Arbuthnot wrote after attending the King's funeral in 1820. His 'affectionate subjects' came 'to pay a last tribute of respect and to shed the tear of affection and gratitude over the grave of him who for 60 long years, had been the father of his people ' The father of his people.

Windsor Castle, April 1972

CONTENTS

LIST OF ILLUSTRATIONS

Frederick Lewis, Prince of Wales, by Philip Mercier
By permission of the National Portrait Gallery

Augusta, Princess of Wales, by Charles Philips
By permission of the National Portrait Gallery

John Stuart, 3rd Earl of Bute, by Sir Joshua
Reynolds
By permission of the National Portrait Gallery

William Henry, Duke of Gloucester, by Francis
Cotes
By gracious permission of Her Majesty The Queen

Queen Charlotte, 1782, by Thomas Gainsborough
By gracious permission of Her Majesty The Queen

Frederick, Lord North, by Nathaniel Dance
By permission of the National Portrait Gallery

Charles James Fox, by Karl Anton Hickel
By permission of the National Portrait Gallery

The castellated palace at Kew from a drawing by an
unknown artist
By gracious permission of Her Majesty The Queen

George, Prince of Wales, by Sir William Beechey
By gracious permission of Her Majesty The Queen

Frederick, Duke of York, by Sir Joshua Reynolds
By gracious permission of Her Majesty The Queen

King George III at Windsor, 1807, by Peter
Edward Stroehling
By gracious permission of Her Majesty The Queen

Queen Charlotte, 1807, by Peter Edward Stroehling
By gracious permission of Her Majesty The Queen

INTRODUCTION

In popular mythology King George III is known as the 'Mad King'. This is all most people know about him. Even well-read people know little more than that he was the King who 'gloried in the name of Britain' and lost the American colonies, who used to say 'What! what!' and thought Shakespeare 'sad stuff'. To Americans he is the King stigmatized in the Declaration of Independence as 'unfit to be the ruler of a free people'. His name has become a by-word for incompetence and stupidity. When a British newspaper wished to abuse a member of the recent Labour ministry it could think of no more devastating comment than that he was such a man as not even King George III would have appointed to the Cabinet.

There is, however, another side to the King. Each year thousands of people attend the annual exhibition of the Royal Academy. How many reflect that the Academy was founded by King George and that he paid the initial expenses out of his private purse? Each year thousands of American tourists walk through the King's Library in the British Museum. How many reflect that every book in that long and lofty gallery was purchased by King George as the nucleus of a national library? Each year thousands of visitors to the Science Museum see specimens from the King's collection of scientific instruments. How many reflect that he was the first King of Great Britain to study science as part of his education, that he maintained his own astronomical observatory, and patronized the greatest observational astronomer of all time? King George has good claims to be considered the most cultured monarch ever to sit on the throne of Great Britain. It is a sad commentary on the study of history as a liberal education that he should be remembered as the mad King who lost the American colonies and not as the lover of art, the

17

book collector, the patron of Herschel. Perhaps if he had collected mistresses instead of books he would have been a more popular figure with posterity. Debauchery reduces royalty to the lowest level, and people who would be disgusted or bored by a living rake find amusement in a dead one. How else can we account for the fascination which King Charles II has exercised over posterity?

During the last fifty years the reign of King George III has become a fashionable period of historical research. With the possible exception of King Charles I there is no British monarch whose conduct and character have been subjected to such critical and intensive scrutiny. With the sole exception of Queen Victoria there is no British monarch who has left such ample materials for the study of his conduct and character. The King's correspondence has been published almost in extenso and fills twelve large volumes. We know as much about King George as we can hope to know about any human being who has been dead for a hundred and fifty years. For information about his conduct and character we have no need to resort to the speculations of contemporaries or the theories of historians. We have but to clear our minds of cant and examine the facts.

The political history of the reign has been studied in detail. There is hardly a politician of consequence who has not been made the subject of a biography, hardly a political theme which has not been explored. The number of books written on the reign is beyond the capacity of any person to read. No scholar however diligent can keep pace with the manuscript collections which year by year are pouring into libraries and record repositories. The historian is in danger of being choked by superfluity of material. The period immediately following the King's accession was the chosen field of Sir Lewis Namier, perhaps the greatest historian of our time. Namier destroyed old legends about King George III (and also raised new ones). He stimulated the historical imagination, and sub-

18

sequent scholars were inspired to follow or provoked to oppose him. A corpus of research has been built up for the reign such as exists for no other period of British history. American scholars have made ample atonement for the injustice of the Declaration of Independence, and perhaps Anglo-American co-operation has reached its highest point in the study of the reign of King George. Such works as the *Yale Edition of Horace Walpole's Correspondence*, Professor Copeland's edition of the correspondence of Edmund Burke, or the great American editions of Boswell and Johnson, edited to a standard of scholarship previously unknown and unattainable, have rescued the eighteenth century from the dead hand of text-book history and restored it to life. We can now see the age as it really was, in all its magnificence and degradation, free from latter-day concepts and prejudices. We can see King George III against the background of his times.

Scholars today no longer accept the legends about the King which did duty for history fifty years ago. But the majority of people are not scholars and are unacquainted with the latest findings of historical scholarship. The visitor to Windsor Castle, who walks on the North Terrace where the King used to walk, beneath the windows of the room in which he died, will have formed his impressions of the King not from learned articles in the *English Historical Review* but from what he remembers having been taught at school. It takes a long time for the findings of scholarship to percolate to the level of school text-books, and even today children in Great Britain are taught legends about King George which every scholar knows to be false. The gap between the knowledge of the average man and woman and the knowledge of the scholar, in history as in science, is immense and is increasing year by year. Perhaps this does not matter in science but it does in history. It is the knowledge of the average man not the knowledge of the scholar which determines the image of a nation's past and its hopes for the future.

I have written this book for the average man not for the scholar, for those who take their ideas of history from illustrated magazines and television programmes rather than from the *English Historical Review*. I believe it is both possible and desirable to write history as Gibbon and Macaulay wrote it: so that the average man will understand it and the learned man will not despise it. This is what I have tried to do. Notes and references which are of interest only to the scholar are reserved for appendices. I have followed my invariable practice of going to original sources as much as possible, but like all scholars I am indebted to the work of my predecessors. I hope I have made proper acknowledgments to both the living and the dead.

Above all, I have tried to write a biography of King George and not a history of his reign. I am interested in the character of a man and the way he lived rather than in the events which took place around him. The technique of the biographer is like that of the detective of fiction: no fact however trivial is without value in reconstructing the life of his subject. I have tried to find the answers to such questions as these: what time did the King get up in the morning? did he shave himself or was he shaved by his valet? what did he have for breakfast? how did he spend his day? what did he like for dinner? when did he go to bed? Most biographies ignore such questions, either because there is insufficient information or else because they are considered below the dignity of biography. Yet if we are to understand human beings these trivial details of everyday life are of great interest, especially in the case of royalty whose life is so different from that of even the greatest of their subjects.

No man is an island. We are all connected with other people by ties of blood and marriage. We are all members of a family. I cannot conceive it possible to write the biography of any man without considering those who were nearest and dearest to him. I make no apology therefore for dealing at length with the King's relations with the members of his family. Yet in the biography of a monarch there must be a proper balance between his public and personal life. I have tried to keep this balance by writing about those public events on which King George felt deeply or with which he was personally concerned.

No one should attempt a biography unless he feels in sympathy with his subject. Yet the biographer should not become so identified with his subject that he can see no other point of view and instead of a biography produce a mere apologia. In writing this book I have kept in mind the words of King George to his future biographer – that 'the tongue of malice may not paint my intentions in those colours she admires, nor the sycophant extoll me beyond what I deserve'. King George was neither a great King nor a great man but he was a human being and not a cardboard figure of history. Kings are too often made the scapegoats for the sins of their subjects. It is as a human being, with his faults and follies, with the qualities which make people loved and disliked, that I wish to present him. That is what he himself would have wished.

I offer my dutiful thanks to Her Majesty The Queen for her gracious permission to consult and quote from the papers of King George III in the Royal Archives.

Mr Robert Mackworth-Young, Her Majesty's Librarian, has given me every assistance in his power and I am grateful for his many kindnesses. To Miss Jane Langton, Registrar of the Royal Archives, and her assistants during the time I worked there, Mrs Sheila de Bellaigue and Miss Julia Gandy, I have more obligations that I can well express.

Among living scholars of the reign of King George III the name of Professor Arthur Aspinall is outstanding. All historians of this period are indebted to him for his long and patient labours in the Royal Archives. Without his scholarly editions of the correspondence of King George III and King George IV this book could hardly have been attempted.

My friend Mr Hugh Murray Baillie has advised me on German affairs and on matters connected with the Court. I have drawn freely on his almost encyclopaedic knowledge of European royalty and have learnt from him far more than he will admit.

I have learnt much about American affairs from the researches of Mr Robert Chaffin of the University of Wisconsin.

Professor Ian R. Christie read the fifth chapter and saved me from many naive judgments and at least one downright howler. In a friendship of over twenty years we have discussed almost every aspect of King George III's reign and though we have often differed in opinion we have never quarrelled.

Mr Derek Jarrett allowed me to see the typescript of his article on the Regency Bill.

Dr Ida Macalpine read the first four chapters and pointed out many infelicities of style and expression. I am further indebted to her for her unfailing kindness and hospitality, and for her willingness to talk with me about King George III.

I have spent many happy hours talking with the late Mr Romney Sedgwick about King George III and Lord Bute.

Miss Marion Ward has advised me on French affairs, and undertook research to find where the King was when he received the news of his grandfather's accident.

Dr P. D. G. Thomas gave me a reference about the King's childhood.

Mr S. P. G. Ward gave me the transcript of a document in his possession relating to the King's last years.

I should like to thank Allen Lane, the Penguin Press, Dr Ida Macalpine and Dr Richard Hunter, the publishers and authors of *King George III and the Mad-Business* for permission to quote from their book, and Pantheon Books, Inc. for permission to do so in the United States of America.

Perhaps my greatest obligations are to a dead man. I learnt the technique of historical research from Sir Lewis Namier, and it was while walking with him through the King's Library in 1952 that I conceived the idea of writing this book. Namier and I differed on many points concerning the life and reign of King George III, but I always recognized that he was the master and I the pupil. Were he alive today, I do not think he would seriously disagree with this picture of King George III.

Chapter 1

THE HOUSE OF HANOVER

George William Frederick, later King George III of Great Britain and Ireland, Duke of Brunswick and Luneburg, Archtreasurer and Elector of the Holy Roman Empire, was born at Norfolk House, St James's Square, on 4 June 1738. According to the Julian calendar in use in Great Britain at the time he was born on 24 May. But after 1751, when Great Britain adopted the Gregorian calendar, King George followed contemporary usage and celebrated his birthday according to the new style. He was the second child and first son of his parents, Frederick Lewis, Prince of Wales, and Augusta, daughter of Frederick, Duke of Saxe Gotha.

His paternal grandfather King George II was the second of his line to wear the crown of Great Britain. His ancestors were at the beginning of the eighteenth century the rulers of a duchy in the north of Germany, part of the agglomeration of states large and small known to history as the Holy Roman Empire. The correct name of the duchy was Brunswick and Luneburg but it was generally known as Hanover after its principal town. Bounded on the east by Brandenburg Prussia and on the west by a number of smaller principalities, it was a country as yet almost unknown to the people of Great Britain. In the eighteenth century the Tory opposition to King George II's Whig governments used to refer to Hanover contemptuously as a petty German principality. Yet by German standards it was a state of considerable importance, for long the rival of Prussia for the supremacy of north Germany. Hanover was a factor in the European balance of power, and during the time of King William III and Marlborough had played its part in the wars against

Louis XIV of France. In 1692 Duke Ernest Augustus of Hanover, in return for his services to the house of Habsburg, was granted the rank of Elector and the office of Archtreasurer of the Holy Roman Empire. Hanover was thus elevated to a position in the Empire comparable to that of Prussia or Bavaria. And the consequence of the house of Hanover was further increased when in 1714 Duke Ernest's son and successor, George, succeeded to the throne of Great Britain.

A fortunate marriage determined the destiny of the house of Hanover. In 1658 Duke Ernest Augustus married Sophia, daughter of the deposed Frederick V, Elector Palatine, and granddaughter of King James VI of Scotland and I of England. The bride had little to recommend her in the way of dynastic pretensions. Her father had lost his throne as a result of his support of the Protestant cause in the Thirty Years War. Her mother was a sister of the unfortunate King Charles I of England and Scotland who had been brought to trial and executed by his rebellious subjects in 1649. The same year in which Princess Sophia married Duke Ernest Augustus witnessed the death of Oliver Cromwell, who had driven her mother's family out of Great Britain; but two years were yet to elapse before the Stuarts were to be recalled by a people sick of the Puritan attempt to impose the rule of righteousness. Assuredly Princess Sophia was no great matrimonial catch in 1658.

Despite the misfortunes which had befallen the Princess's family, she could boast that she came of a line which had always held true to the cause of Protestantism in a Europe which for over a century had been divided by rival religious allegiances. Duke Ernest Augustus was the ruler of a state which was overwhelmingly Protestant, and both the Princess's father and mother came from families distinguished among the leaders of the Protestant cause. The Princess's son, the future King George I of Great Britain and Ireland, was brought up in an authentic Protestant tradition. To that tradition he owed his throne. On that tradition his family built its future greatness. The Hanoverian monarchs, and not least King George III, never forgot that they had been summoned to Great Britain to maintain the Protestant establishment.

In the seventeenth century organized religion counted for a great deal with all classes of the population and formed much of the content of politics. Europe was divided into two great camps: Catholic and Protestant; and in each country the religion of the sovereign was an affair of state. Great Britain was firmly in the Protestant camp. Fear and hatred of Roman Catholicism, especially in the urban areas, was a powerful emotional force in politics. King James II, the last Catholic King, had aroused the distrust and opposition of both his English and Scottish subjects by his attempt to re-establish Roman Catholicism as the national religion. Few kings ever came to the throne with public opinion so much in their favour. No king ever surrendered his throne so greatly to the relief of his subjects. Had King James regarded his religion as his own private affair, neither to be imposed upon his subjects nor to be prescribed by them, he might have remained king to the end of his days and even have inaugurated an era of religious toleration. Perhaps then the future King George III would have been known to history as the Elector of Hanover and no more. But King James followed the fashion of his age and like his contemporary Louis XIV of France tried to make the religion of his people conform to that of their sovereign. The end could almost have been foreseen. The revolution of 1688 in England and Scotland was the rising of a Protestant people against a Catholic king. However divided the nation may have been before King James fled the country, there was unanimity on at least one point afterwards. English and Scots, Anglicans and Presbyterians, Whigs and Tories, though their differences in other respects were fundamental, concurred on this issue. Protestantism was the religion of the British people and the ruler of the British people must be a Protestant. The religion of the people was to determine the religion of the sovereign. The change was fundamental.

Thus the descendants of King James II who were brought up as Roman Catholics were excluded from their inheritance. The Act of Settlement of 1701 which regulated the succession provided that on the death of Queen Anne, the last Protestant monarch of the Stuart family, the throne was to descend to Sophia, wife of Ernest Augustus, Elector of Hanover, and her issue being Protestant. The native dynasty of the Stuarts was rejected because it was Roman Catholic. The foreign dynasty from Hanover was accepted because it was Protestant. By virtue of the Act of Settlement, the fundamental charter of the British monarchy, the Electress Sophia's son (Sophia herself having died a few weeks previously) succeeded on 1 August 1714 as King George I of Great Britain and Ireland.

In 1658 when Sophia, a princess in exile, gave her hand to Ernest Augustus, heir apparent to a duchy in the north of Germany, it could hardly have been foreseen that their son would one day succeed to the throne of the Stuarts or their issue outlast that of Bourbon and Habsburg as ruling dynasties. Yet so it has proved. The house of Stuart is extinct. The great royal families of the seventeenth century are in exile. Hanover itself has long been absorbed in Prussia. Even the concept of monarchy has vanished from all but a few European states. Yet the heiress of the Electress Sophia reigns in Great Britain.

King George I was fifty-three when he succeeded to the throne of Great Britain. The greater part of his life had been spent in Hanover, first as heir apparent then as ruler of the duchy. He had already passed the meridian of life when he was named in succession to the throne of Great Britain. His heart was wholly Hanoverian. Hanover was his native land; the roots of his family were in Hanover; and he ruled Hanover in right of his birth. When he landed at Greenwich on 30 September 1714, two months after he had succeeded to the crown, he landed in a foreign country. Of the language, customs, or people of his new realm he understood little. Though welcomed in England with demonstrations of rejoicing, he could have had few illusions about his popularity with his new subjects. The crowds who lined the streets of London to view his progress to St James's Palace paid their tribute not to the man but to what he symbolized. Perhaps in their heart of hearts many would have preferred to see the young man who lived in exile and styled himself James III ride in the coach which bore their new sovereign. King George I could count on no reserve of personal loyalty either to himself or to his family on which to draw during a time of trouble. He was King by virtue of an Act of the British Parliament which had regulated the conditions on which he and his family were to hold the throne. He had perforce to accommodate himself to the wishes of his subjects.

It could not have been easy for a gentleman of fifty-three to remove himself to a foreign country and accept the supreme responsibility for the conduct of their affairs. The fact that King George I made such a success of his new role indicates a quality of character in him which has rarely been appreciated. He rendered a great service to the British people which they were slow to acknowledge. Fortunately the King set great store on this new acquisition to his dignity, and was not to be rebuffed by failure to win a personal popularity which he would have deemed of little value. He was more concerned about his standing in European politics. The ruler of Hanover had but recently been admitted into the electoral college of the Holy Roman Empire and his position in Germany was still uncertain. The Crown of Great Britain gave him a weight and dignity he would not otherwise have possessed. The prestige of the British monarchy had never been higher. Britain had led the European coalition which had humbled the pride and power of France, and the memory was still fresh in Germany of how the Duke of Marlborough had marched from the Rhine to the Danube to win the battle of Blenheim and save the throne of the Habsburgs from their hereditary enemies. As Elector of Hanover King George I had fought under Marlborough's command, and one of the first acts of his reign was to restore Marlborough to his place of Captain-General of the British army. The British people may have cared little for King George I, but the King cared a great deal for the crown of Great Britain.

We may compare King George I's accession to the crown to that of a marriage contracted for family or financial reasons. The bridegroom was not in love with the bride – indeed he loved another; yet he wished the marriage to be fruitful if only that he could continue to enjoy his wife's dowry. He therefore made up his mind to live with her as comfortably as possible and after a while he almost got to like her. True, she had some strange ways to which he never really accustomed himself and a rather uncertain temper. But then he himself was not a model husband. Whenever the opportunity offered he liked to slip away to Germany to enjoy the embraces of his first love. His wife resented his desertion of her for another woman, yet was prepared to turn a blind eye to his infidelities provided they did not become too gross and provoke scandal among the neighbours. And so they jogged on from year to year – not a love match, but one resting on a solid basis of common interest.

Great Britain was territory which King George I had occupied but which he could always yield without great loss and retire to his base at Hanover. For in 1714 it was by no means certain how long he would remain King of Great Britain. His accession had been unopposed, but a number of his subjects were believed to be ready to welcome the Jacobite pretender and not make too strict inquiry into his religion – provided only that he could establish himself. Many who bowed to the King at his levee would have been equally ready to have bowed to James III; would have struggled to kiss his hand as their grandfathers had kissed the hand of King Charles II on his return from exile; would have solicited peerages or baronetcies according to their estimate of their quality – but who would not have risked lives or fortunes for his cause. Jacobitism could succeed only through success. Looking back from the distance of two hundred and fifty years it seems that King George I and his ministers exaggerated the danger of Jacobitism. But at the time no one could be sure. The long vista of history is deceptive. Nor are timely precautions to be despised because the danger they guard against never materializes. In the event there was no Jacobite restoration. But two armed rebellions were to take place before the Hanoverian monarchs felt secure upon the throne.

In the seventeenth century Great Britain had a reputation for political instability second to none. No people in Europe were so fickle. In 1714 there were men living who could remember the dethronement of James II and even the execution of Charles I. William III, the foremost statesman of his age, had hazarded everything to rescue the nation from Roman Catholicism and arbitrary government, yet had never succeeded in winning their affections. The English were at odds with the Scots and the dislike of each for the other was only exceeded by the hatred of both for the Irish. How could any monarch hope to govern such subjects? The throne of Great Britain was held on uncertain tenure and at the will of the British people. This, as the Hanoverian kings were quick to realize, was the best of all tenures.

It was once a commonplace of school history books to dismiss King George I as a German who cared for nothing British, could not speak the English language, and who had perforce to withdraw from the Cabinet and allow political power to devolve to his ministers. This is a false picture. The King's inability to speak English did not prevent him from communicating effectively with his ministers nor from keeping a firm control over foreign policy – the aspect of affairs in which he was most interested. He was not the man to allow power to slip through his hands by default. His experience in Hanover had not taught him the need to make himself popular with his subjects. Yet he strove to overcome the handicap of foreign birth and manners and to adapt himself to the conventions of British political life. In manner he was stiff and formal and could not unbend. Probably he was a shy man, unaccustomed to display himself in public and too old to learn the tricks of kingship which might win him a momentary popularity with the *bon ton* or the rabble of the metropolis – whose opinions, being vocal, have at all times counted for much with historians.

Perhaps it was too much to expect him at the age of fifty-three to assume the outward civilities proper to a British monarch. The smile, the bow, the easy act of condescension – a style of royal behaviour which came easily to the Stuarts but had to be learnt by the Hanoverians and could not be learnt in one generation – all this was lacking in King George I. Many a country squire came away from Whitehall flattered by an insincere smile from Charles II or James II and resolved to devote his life to the cause of the Stuart monarchy. Later, perhaps, reflecting in the bosom of his family, he may have doubted whether it was really prudent to hazard the future of his house and manors and broad acres on the dubious faith of a Stuart King. Years afterwards that smile would be remembered and contrasted favourably with the stiff bow he had received from the German gentleman who now sat on the throne of the Stuarts. A bumper would be drunk to the health of the king across the water. So many toasts to the health of that king! – provided always he remained across the water. But if he were ever to land in these islands then prudence rather than sentiment must dictate one's conduct. For who could trust the gratitude of a Stuart?

Such was the stuff of Jacobitism, at least in England. 'The Graces! the Graces! remember the Graces!', wrote Lord Chesterfield when exhorting his son to become the very model of a fine English gentleman. King George I lacked the graces and never became an English gentleman. This was remembered and counted against him. His real services to the British people were forgotten.

It is surprising how quickly the Hanoverian dynasty became acclimatized in Great Britain. The Stuarts, though they came from only over the border and spoke the same language as the English, never really settled in England. They ceased to be Scottish without becoming English. They were never British. At a time when events were working to draw the two peoples together, to heal age-long feuds, the Stuarts were an enemy to both and an obstacle to their union. On that union depended the future greatness and prosperity of the two nations. It had been achieved temporarily under Cromwell, the enemy of the Stuarts; solemnized under Queen Anne, the last of the Stuarts; it was consummated under King George, the successor of the Stuarts. Few political decisions consciously taken by the elected representatives of two proud and jealous nations have been so pregnant with consequences.

The very fact that King George I was a stranger, born in neither England nor Scotland, gave him an immense advantage over the native dynasty. He had no leaning to the one nation or the other, and no responsibility for the quarrels which divided them. He could not be accused of favouritism towards either. National distinctions meant little to him. He did not ask whether a man was born in England or Scotland but whether he was a supporter of the house of Hanover or the house of Stuart. This became the real political division during the reign of King George. National divisions were replaced by those of party: a gain to national unity. King George I was truly the first King of Great Britain.

In one other respect, hardly less critical than the difference between the two nations, the Hanoverian proved superior to the Stuart dynasty. The Hanoverians were more adept than the Stuarts at blending the traditional authority of the Crown with the increasing pretensions of Parliament, eventually to produce a system of government which has had no rival in the modern world for flexibility, honesty, and efficiency.

Monarchy had deep roots in both England and Scotland, but the idea of absolute monarchy uncontrolled by law or a representative assembly was unknown to either nation. The Stuarts had based their claim to the throne on hereditary succession and divine right, and had demanded the allegiance of their subjects as a religious obligation. Such a demand was a disservice both to monarchy and religion. On this basis there was no future for monarchy in Great Britain. The Hanoverians had no pretensions to the throne except by parliamentary right. Alone among the great European monarchies, they could boast that they held their crown by the free and deliberate consent of the elected representatives of their people. No king has ever had a better title to his crown than King George I.

Since the sixteenth century Parliament had been taking an increasing share in the government of the nation. And as the role of Parliament became of more consequence so it became more difficult to manage. Harmony between Crown and Parliament, at all times desirable, grew to be essential. Yet even the great Queen Elizabeth I, that consummate mistress of statecraft, had been compelled to deploy all her wiles and exert all her statesmanship to ensure the support of the House of Commons for her policy. 'Though God hath raised me high', she told her last parliament, 'yet this I account the glory of my Crown that I have reigned with your loves.' No Stuart could have pronounced these words. Such dignity and wisdom were beyond the capacities of her successors. King James I, a dominie enthroned, lectured his parliaments. King Charles I, with most of his father's faults and few of his virtues, tried to bully them. But none of the Stuarts, not even King Charles II, politically the most adroit and morally the most unscrupulous, was able to harness Parliament to the service of the Crown and the nation. Nor did King William III, though he owed his throne to a resolution of the House of Commons, ever learn the secret of how to win the confidence of that turbulent and refractory body. That secret seemed to be buried in the grave of the first Elizabeth. It was resurrected by the first George. The Hanoverians were the true heirs of the Tudors.

The revolution of 1688 had effected a fundamental change in the relations between Crown and Parliament. The Crown remained as it had always been the *fons et origo* of State authority. The King was still the effective head of government. William III assumed responsibility for the conduct of national policy just as James II had done. But whereas James II had tried to rule in defiance of Parliament, William III had to admit Parliament as a junior partner in the work of government. After 1688 Parliament met regularly every year, not as hitherto when it suited the convenience of the Crown. Through its control of finance the House of Commons had a veto over the conduct of the essential departments of state. Not a soldier could march, not a gun could be fired, not a ship could sail, until Parliament had first voted the money. In theory the conduct of foreign policy remained with the Crown and was no concern of Parliament. But in practice, since foreign policy could not be conducted independently of the state of the armed forces, Parliament had the decisive voice on issues affecting peace or war.

The Crown could declare war without the formal approval of Parliament (it did so both in 1914 and 1939) but only Parliament could raise the money. After 1688 there was a condominium in the essential departments of government between Crown and Parliament. Like two high-spirited horses yoked in harness, they had to pull together if the coach of state was not to be upset.

The game of parliamentary politics played according to British rules was new to the Elector of Hanover. What did he know of general elections, divisions in the House of Commons, Whigs and Tories? These things were unknown in Germany as indeed in most parts of Europe and some of them were but a recent innovation in Great Britain. Yet King George I mastered the rules and took to the game as if he had played it all his life. It may have been more by accident than design that he hit upon the secret of how to manage a troublesome and faction-ridden House of Commons – which not even the genius of King William III had been able to discover. Like most solutions to complex political problems it was in essence very simple once you had thought of it. All the Crown had to do was to give its confidence to some member of the House of Commons who could command the same degree of confidence from the House: to put its full influence at the disposal of its choice: to smile on his friends and frown on his enemies: and to remain loyal to him until such time as he should be disavowed by the House and no longer of use to the Crown.

The device of the office of Prime Minister – the man who was at the same time the Minister for the Crown in the House of Commons and the Minister for the House of Commons in the King's Closet – helped to establish a stable and civilized system of government in Great Britain. When King George I selected Sir Robert Walpole for his Prime Minister he could not foresee all the implications of his action. He did not realize that he had taken the first step towards anchoring the fortunes of his house

36

in the affections of his people. This, much more than the fact that the King absented himself from the deliberations of his ministers, is responsible for the growth of parliamentary government in Great Britain and the elevation of the Crown above party politics. Here was an expedient which reconciled the British people's traditional respect for monarchy with their wish to be ruled in accordance with the prevailing sense of the politically conscious part of the community. Here was a solution to the conditions of near anarchy which had bedevilled politics during the seventeenth century. Here was a political institution which could be adapted by subsequent generations to their own needs without having to resort to revolution or civil war. In the 250 years which have elapsed since the accession of the house of Hanover the social structure of Great Britain, the distribution of political power, the content of politics, and the sphere of government action, have changed beyond recognition. Yet monarchy and popular representation still go hand in hand. Greater men than King George I have achieved much less.

King George II succeeded his father in 1727 and died in 1760, having outlived his eldest son Frederick, Prince of Wales, by more than nine years.

The second monarch of the Hanoverian dynasty has received less than his due from historians. He was neither a great king nor an amiable man and he often appears a ridiculous and even contemptible figure. It was his lot in the early years of his reign to be surrounded by advisers of greater calibre than himself: his wife, Queen Caroline, perhaps the outstanding Queen Consort of modern times and worthy to rule in her own right; and his Prime Minister, Sir Robert Walpole, the shrewdest politician of his age. It became the fashion even in his lifetime to depict King George II as a stupid man, manipulated by minds sharper and cleverer than his own. Yet it is surely a sign of fundamental good sense that he allowed himself to be guided by two such clever politicians as Queen Caroline and Walpole. And it is often forgotten that for the greater part of his reign he was alone, having lost the Queen by death in 1737 and Walpole by parliamentary politics in 1742. During the years that followed he had to face an armed rebellion, two threats of invasion, and at least three serious parliamentary crises. Yet he surmounted them all: and when he died in 1760, in Horace Walpole's words 'crowned with honours and respected from success', there was sorrow in the hearts of those who had known him best. The aged Duke of Newcastle, who had served the King for almost the whole of his reign as Secretary of State and First Lord of the Treasury, mourned for him with true regret. 'I have lost the best King, the best master, and the best friend that subject ever had', he wrote. 'God knows what consequences it may have!'

Lord Hervey, an acute observer and for many years Vice-Chamberlain to King George II, describes him as a man whom it was much easier to hate than to love. He had none of that surface charm which endeared the Stuarts to the imagination of posterity. He was vain, irascible, impatient of opposition to his authority. He pretended to a dignity he did not possess and demanded respect without deserving it. There is something ludicrous in Hervey's description of the King stamping round St James's Palace, shouting 'Puppy! Scoundrel!' about any politician who had happened to have aroused his displeasure. Like his father and unlike his eldest son and grandson he had no intellectual interests and despised those who had. He was a selfish man and cared little for the feelings of others. Perhaps the only person he really loved was his wife, yet he was flagrantly unfaithful to her and boasted of his infidelities before her face.

The story of the house of Hanover during the reigns of the first three Georges – and consequently the political history of the nation – turns on the conflict between the King on the throne and the heir apparent, the King to come. This was repeated in each generation. King George I quarrelled with his son and forbade him the court. King George II quarrelled with Frederick, Prince of Wales, and also forbade him the court. After the Prince's death it seemed that the pattern might be broken, but as soon as the future King George III came of age he proceeded to quarrel with his grandfather. George, Prince of Wales, in his turn quarrelled with King George III. So it went on. Only when King George IV came to the throne and there was no Prince of Wales did this dismal cycle show signs of coming to an end.

This conflict is not peculiar to the house of Hanover. It is endemic in the history of monarchy. It can be traced back at least to the time of Constantine the Great, the first Christian Emperor of Rome, who put his eldest son to death; and perhaps even farther – to King David and Absalom. In the eighteenth century it is found in the ruling families of Prussia and Russia, accompanied with greater violence and hatred than was ever to be found in Great Britain. No one who has read the memoirs of Wilhelmina of Prussia, sister of Frederick the Great, will ever forget the terrible pages in which she tells how her father beat his son and compelled the future hero to watch the execution of his favourite. Such dreadful events never took place in England. In England there was the House of Commons to act as a bloodless arena for quarrelling politicians, a safety valve for the release of angry passions.

The conflict between successive generations is part of the law of life and a condition of human progress. That it should be so acute in ruling families is due not to any peculiar depravity in persons of royal blood but simply to circumstances inherent in personal monarchy. 'The experienced merit of a reigning monarch', writes Gibbon, 'is acknowledged by his subjects with reluctance, and frequently denied with partial and discontented murmurs; while, from the opening virtues of his successor, they fondly conceive the most unbounded hopes of private as well as public felicity.' We are discontented with what we have and hope for better in the future. Perhaps only the hope of a better future (the natural concomitant of the knowledge of a worse past) has kept the human species in existence.

When the sovereign was the real and responsible head of government the court was the centre of government. This is the position in the United States today, where there is an elected monarch, styled the President, with a court of personal advisers. In the great days of monarchy it was at court that decisions were taken. It was at court that appointments, honours, and profits were to be won. A statesman with a policy to pursue went to court, and having gained the favour of the monarch attracted dependants and followers. Those out of favour intrigued against the Minister and tried to enlist the heir apparent in their cause. Parties were formed at court long before they were known in Parliament, one enjoying the favour of the reigning monarch and the other centred round the heir apparent. In these circumstances it was difficult for the King and the heir apparent to avoid coming into conflict. In the great European monarchies these conflicts lasted as long as the monarchies themselves. In Great Britain they died out in the nineteenth century, when the centre of power shifted from court to Cabinet and when favour with Parliament or public opinion became the qualification for office.

In Continental monarchies the heir apparent had little influence apart from his reversionary interest. The day before his father died he was a nonentity: the day he succeeded to the throne he was the most powerful person in the state. But no action on his part short of rebellion could bring nearer the day of supreme power. Whatever the grievances, political, personal, or financial, of the heir apparent of France or Spain, he could do no more than bide his time and say with the character in Surtees's novel: 'If father would but die!'

The position of the Prince of Wales in Great Britain was far different from that of the Dauphin in France or the Prince of the Asturias in Spain. It is true that the British constitution allots no power to the Prince of Wales. His rank is second only to that of the sovereign, but in Great Britain no political authority is attached to rank. A Prince of Wales who is the eldest son of the sovereign is Duke of Cornwall by birth and as such possesses an appanage independent of the King. The Duchy of Cornwall holds large estates in the west of England and these counted for a great deal in the eighteenth century. It gave the Prince an income of his own, though not sufficient to enable him to maintain a separate court without an allowance from the King. It gave him political patronage and an interest in the parliamentary boroughs of Devon and Cornwall. A Prince of Wales who wished to take part in politics had places of profit and honour to offer to his followers and could assist them in their elections. He could form a party in the House of Commons. He could engage in opposition to the King's government. No Dauphin or Prince of the Asturias could do that. The Prince of Wales had a potential political consequence which was denied to the heirs of the great Continental monarchies.

Moreover, there was ready at hand for exploitation a source of discontent which the Prince of Wales could use to enhance his own popularity and depress that of the King – the personal connection between Great Britain and Hanover. The Stuart monarchs after they succeeded to the throne of England rarely visited their ancient kingdom of Scotland unless compelled by urgent political considerations. They preferred to remain in England, the wealthier country, and left Scotland to be governed by a regency. But the first two Hanoverian kings never forgot their German homeland and made no secret of their preference for Herrenhausen over St James's. Both made frequent and prolonged visits to Hanover. King George I died at Hanover and was buried there. King George II spent every alternate summer in Hanover and hated having to return to England. This preference for Hanover was deeply resented in Great Britain: and enabled a Prince of Wales, in opposition to his father, to bid for popular favour by posing as entirely British in his sympathies and opposed to Hanoverian influence.

There was a widespread belief in the early eighteenth century that the connection with Hanover was beneficial to Hanover and harmful to Great Britain. This was in the mind of Parliament when it regulated the succession. It was feared that a Hanoverian monarch, more sensitive to the interests of his native than of his adopted country, might be tempted to use the power and influence of Great Britain for purely German purposes. To guard against this, the Act of Settlement contained a clause by which Great Britain was not obliged to go to war in defence of Hanover without consent of Parliament. The two states, though ruled by the same sovereign, were to be entirely independent of each other. In theory it was possible for King George I in his capacity as King of Great Britain to declare war on himself in his capacity as Elector of Hanover. In practice such a Gilbertian situation was hardly likely to occur. Nor was it easy to imagine circumstances in which the interests of the two states could be so opposed to each other. In fact they were brought much closer together than perhaps either would have liked.

It may be doubted whether Hanover did not lose more than she gained when her Elector became King of Great Britain: and whether Great Britain did not gain more than she appreciated. Hanover was a Continental state at the mercy of more powerful neighbours. Great Britain was an insular state and a great power in her own right. By the union of the crowns Great Britain gained an ally in the event of becoming engaged in a European war and a source of mercenary troops. What did Hanover gain?

In any conflict which concerned Great Britain Hanover was certain to become involved. But Great Britain was not necessarily involved in any conflict which concerned Hanover.

Hanover occupied a delicate position in the political geography of north Germany. On her eastern frontier she was confronted by the powerful state of Brandenburg Prussia, concerned to establish a link with Prussian territories on the Rhine. A glance at the map of eighteenth-century Germany will show how geography had made Prussia and Hanover natural enemies. No Elector of Hanover could be indifferent to the threat from Prussia, and events in the nineteenth century were to show how real this threat was. During the lifetime of King George III Hanover was occupied by Prussia as part of Napoleon's settlement of Germany. In 1866, after the personal union between Great Britain and Hanover had been broken, Hanover took the losing side in the Austro-Prussian war; and as a result of the peace treaty, was absorbed into Prussia. In the eighteenth century, if ever Prussia and Great Britain were ranged on opposite sides in a European war (as they were during the War of the Austrian Succession and as they might have been during the Seven Years War) Hanover was in danger.

On her western frontiers Hanover was exposed to attack from France. The principalities of the Rhine were small and weak and unable to offer prolonged resistance to French arms. It is true that France had no quarrel with Hanover and no geographical considerations dictated the enmity of the two states. But it had been the aim of French policy since the days of Richelieu and Louis XIV to extend her frontiers northwards and eastwards at the expense of the Holy Roman Empire. And in a war with Great Britain it was good policy for France to attack her enemy by way of Hanover. Britain was an island, and provided she retained her naval superiority immune to conquest. France was a military power. Strategy dictated that she should wage war where her army could be used to the greatest advantage. And Great Britain's most vulnerable point was on the Rhine. Whatever the Act of Settlement might say, the British could not suffer such a diminution of the prestige of their sovereign as would follow a French occupation of Hanover. Hanover was involved willy-nilly in a war between Great Britain and her natural enemy, France. Great Britain was not necessarily involved in a war between Hanover and her natural enemy, Prussia.

Between the revolution of 1688 and the battle of Waterloo in 1815, Great Britain and France contested the supremacy of western Europe and the territories open to European penetration. Seven major wars, aggregating almost half the period, were waged between these two powers. These all followed the same strategical pattern. The British had the advantage on the sea: the French on land. The British conquered French islands in the West Indies, took toll of French shipping on the high seas, and established their supremacy in India and North America. The French sent their armies into the Low Countries and Germany and forced the British to fight on the Continent. France calculated that at the ensuing peace what she had lost outside Europe could be recovered by surrendering what she had gained in Europe. An island in the West Indies or a trading factory in India was fair exchange for a fortress in the Netherlands or a principality on the Rhine. The King of Great Britain's Hanoverian dominions became a counter in the game of European power politics.

The connection with Hanover was of benefit to Great Britain because it gave her access to a supply of mercenary soldiers. The British always found difficulty in raising an army in time of war. The army was the unpopular service, and a standing army in time of peace without consent of Parliament had been declared illegal by the Bill of Rights. The memory still remained of how Cromwell had imposed military rule on the three kingdoms, and the army was feared as a potential threat to freedom. Nor was this fear unjustified. Had any of the Stuart kings possessed an efficient army, the British monarchy might have become as absolute as the French and Parliament of as little consequence as the States-General. Only the Crown's inability to pay for a regular army had kept the British people free. British freedom was based on a hatred of militarism. Compulsory military service even for home defence was bitterly unpopular, and no government would have dared to propose conscription for overseas service. Conscription for the navy was different. The use of the press gang to recruit the navy was advocated by even the warmest defenders of civil liberty. The navy could be no threat to freedom. Conscription for the navy was a necessary measure for the defence of the realm. Conscription for the army was an infringement of the liberty of the subject.

As the British could not raise their own army they had to use mercenary troops. Sometimes they had to use mercenary generals. The army that triumphed under Marlborough at Blenheim contained more Dutch and Germans than British. The army that won the battle of Minden was commanded by a German. Without the aid of foreign mercenaries Great Britain could never have fought a Continental war. Even for the defence of the homeland mercenary troops were essential. When the Young Pretender marched into England in 1745 the Dutch were called upon to furnish a quota of troops for service in Great Britain. When France threatened invasion in 1756 an army was hired from Germany and stationed in the south of England.

Germany was the principal recruiting ground of the British army, and when King George II wanted soldiers he turned first to his Hanoverian dominions. He made a double profit on these transactions, gaining soldiers for Great Britain and money for Hanover. But it was galling to the pride of patriotic Britons that their King should have to enlist troops in Germany. Rather than admit the unpalatable truth – that sufficient troops could not be raised in Great Britain – recourse was had to the subterfuge that the army was used for purely Hanoverian purposes. In 1742, during the War of the Austrian Succession, the question of the employment of Hanoverian troops in British pay occasioned bitter debates in the House of Commons. William Pitt, the greatest orator of the age, 'thundered against the useless army in Flanders and the Hanoverian troops'. 'Neither justice nor policy', he declaimed, 'required us to engage in the quarrels of the Continent.' It was not the first time nor would it be the last that this cry was raised in the British Parliament.

These issues – the quarrel in the Royal Family, the connection with Hanover, and the use of foreign troops – formed the staple of politics during a great part of King George II's reign. They were still burning issues during the youth and early manhood of King George III. They determined his first political convictions. Long after they had ceased to be a source of contention in the House of Commons they shaped the course of politics.

King George II is seen at his worst in his dispute with his elder son, though in truth neither of the participants in this unsavoury episode comes out well. Those who engage in family quarrels rarely do. At this distance of time – over two hundred years – it is impossible to account for the bitterness engendered by this particular quarrel. There were differences about politics and disputes about money, but these do not explain the deep personal loathing between Frederick, Prince of Wales, and his parents. It is dreadful to read the words which Lord Hervey attributes to the King and Queen Caroline about their elder son. 'My dear first born', the Queen is reported to have said, 'is the greatest ass, and the greatest liar, and the greatest canaille, and the greatest beast, in the whole world, and I most heartily wish he was out of it.' And in her last illness she prepared for death in these terms: 'At least I shall have one comfort in having my eyes eternally closed – I shall never see that monster again.' What a way for a mother on her deathbed to speak of her son! The King refused to allow the Prince to visit his mother when she lay dying. 'Bid him go about his business,' he said to Hervey, 'for his poor mother is not in a condition to see him act his false, whining, cringing tricks now, nor am I in a humour to bear his impertinence; and bid him trouble me with no more messages, but get out of my house.' If we are to believe Hervey, these feelings were reciprocated by the Prince, who repeatedly sent messages during his mother's last illness to inquire if she were yet dead.

The Prince emerges from Hervey's memoirs as little less than a monster: undutiful to his parents; unfaithful to his mistresses; disloyal to his friends. He was 'profuse without liberality and avaricious without economy'; 'lewd without vigour'; with 'all the silly pride of grandeur and all the mean condescension of humility'; 'extremely amorous and extremely inconsistent'. Hervey's comparison of the Prince to Nero (from which these phrases are taken) occupies seventeen pages in the printed edition of the memoirs. It was written at the express request of the Queen, and was read to her over and over again until even its author grew tired of hearing his own work.

Is this a fair picture of the father of King George III? Perhaps it is unsafe to judge the Prince's character entirely by the evidence of Lord Hervey. The picture is dark: the phrasing reads like a literary exercise. The laboured antitheses ('profuse without liberality', 'avaricious without economy', 'lewd without vigour'), which the eighteenth century considered as the hallmark of a good literary style, were carefully thought out and meant to impress the reader. And though Hervey claims that he wrote without conscious malice, it is difficult not to feel that he deceived himself. Hervey and the Prince had once been good friends but they had quarrelled – partly over politics, more over a woman – and had become bitter enemies. A more favourable but still a critical portrait of the Prince is to be found in Horace Walpole's memoirs. 'His best quality', writes Walpole, 'was generosity': but against this he was insincere, indifferent to truth, and 'really childish'. Lord Chesterfield, who at one time was connected in politics with the Prince, describes him as 'more beloved for his affability and good nature than esteemed for his steadiness and conduct'. And the impression of the Prince we receive from the diary of Bubb Dodington, another of his followers, is not that of an able politician or a man of resolute mind.

The Prince was educated in Hanover and did not come to England until 1728, the year following his father's accession. In 1736 he married Augusta, daughter of the Duke of Saxe Gotha, a bride selected for him by the King. The marriage led to his estrangement from his parents. As a married man the Prince considered himself entitled to a higher allowance than the £50,000 a year he had been receiving as a bachelor. He claimed with considerable justification that he should receive the same allowance his father had received as Prince of Wales, £100,000 a year. When this was refused him, the Prince instigated his political friends to introduce a motion in the House of Commons for an address to the King to increase his allowance.

Demands for money always touched King George II on the raw. Any increase in the Prince's allowance would have to come out of the Civil List, which would mean less for the King. An appeal to Parliament was an open defiance of the King's authority as head of the Royal Family. The Prince had raised his standard and every Member of Parliament had to make his choice between father and son. The Queen was even more furious than the King. 'Look, there he goes,' she said to Hervey at about this time, catching sight of the Prince from her dressing-room window. 'That wretch! That villain! I wish the ground would open this moment and sink the monster to the lowest hole in Hell!' Her face was red with anger, and even Hervey, aware as he was of the Queen's hatred of her son, was astonished at her virulence.

When the motion came to be debated every device of parliamentary craft was used by both sides to whip up support. Bribes, promises, and threats were lavished on the government benches. The Prince was at a serious disadvantage. He could offer no bribes, only promises to be implemented far away in the future; and he had against him the greatest parliamentarian of the age. Sir Robert Walpole used all his art and skill, and the motion was defeated by a majority of only thirty votes.

The sequel four months later was the scandalous series of events attending the birth of the Prince's first child. These, more than anything else he ever said or did, have sullied his reputation with historians.

Despite evidence to the contrary, the Queen affected to believe that her son was impotent. When told that the Princess was pregnant, she expressed her fears that a suppositious child might be introduced into the Royal Family. The King and Queen wished the child to be born at Hampton Court, their country residence. The Prince, actuated apparently by no better motive than the wish to defy his parents, determined that the child should be born in London. At the dead of night, without informing the King or Queen, he removed his wife, already in labour, from Hampton Court to St James's Palace. There the baby was born without either of its grandparents being present. The child thus unceremoniously brought into the world was a girl – Princess Augusta, eldest sister of King George III, later wife of Ferdinand, Duke of Brunswick, and mother of Queen Caroline, the unfortunate consort of King George IV.

It is happily not the province of the biographer of King

George III to assess responsibility for this lamentable episode. Lord Hervey, who is our chief source for this as for so much else about the Prince, condemns his conduct in the strongest terms. It is a pity that we have no account from a witness sympathetic to the Prince. Making all allowance for malice on Hervey's part, the Prince emerges from this episode as irresponsible and childish, to say the least, only too willing to indulge his spite towards his parents at the expense of his wife and child. What man in his senses would convey a woman in childbirth from Hampton Court to London – in an eighteenth-century coach and along eighteenth-century roads? What did he hope to gain by this calculated insult to the King and Queen? They had the power to retaliate against him and were not slow to use it. A complete breach in the Royal Family followed. The Prince was ordered to remove himself and his family from St James's 'as soon as ever the safety and convenience of the Princess will permit'. A public announcement was made that whoever continued to pay their court to the Prince and Princess would not be received by the King and Queen. Did the King remember, when he authorized this announcement, that twenty years earlier he himself, then Prince of Wales, had been similarly forbade the court?

Thus excluded from the royal palaces, the Prince took the Duke of Norfolk's house in St James's Square: and it was here that his second child and first son, the future King George III, was born between six and seven in the morning of 4 June 1738. The baby was two months premature. Lord Egmont wrote in his diary:

The Princess of Wales was brought to bed of a boy, which the same night received private baptism, there being a doubt if he would live.

His Majesty took little notice of it, on account of the difference between him and His Royal Highness, only laughed and said the sadler's wife was brought to bed; alluding to the Prince being Governor of the Sadler's Company.

Thus Prince George came into the world: a sickly child, not expected to live; ignored by his grandfather the King; and born into an atmosphere of domestic strife.[1]

We know little of Prince George's earlier years. Like most children of the upper classes, both in his own age and for much later, he was suckled not by his mother but by a wet nurse – one Mary Smith. 'To her great attention', the King wrote on her death in 1773, 'my having been reared is greatly owing.' When he came to the throne he provided for her by appointing her to be his laundress, in which position she was succeeded by her daughter. We have one other glimpse of the King in his childhood. Mrs Campbell, wife of John Campbell, MP for Pembrokeshire, describes him at the age of four as 'a lovely child . . . as fat as Trub was at his age'. Evidently he had overcome the handicap of a premature birth.

Queen Caroline never saw her grandson. She died on 20 November 1737, six months before he was born. Her death did not heal the feud in the Royal Family. The Prince of Wales had been blooded to the sport of parliamentary hunting and was henceforth devoted to the chase. His pack took part in the opposition to his father's government, which finally triumphed when Sir Robert Walpole was forced to resign in 1742. It was the zenith of the Prince's career as a politician. So closely was the issue fought that for a few days Walpole's fate depended on the part the Prince would take, and the King was persuaded to offer him an increase in his allowance if he would change sides. The Prince refused the bribe and remained true to his allies. The King had to accept Walpole's resignation because Walpole was unable to retain his majority in the House of Commons. It was an omen for future kings. Forty years later Lord North reminded King George III 'that in this country the prince on the throne cannot with prudence oppose the deliberate resolution of the House of Commons'; and the will of the House of

Commons prevailed with King George III in 1782 as it had with his grandfather in 1742.

After a few uneasy years the King found a successor to Walpole in Henry Pelham, the former minister's leading disciple. The new regime differed little from the old. The ablest of the Prince's followers were given office and the Prince received an increase in his allowance. But he was ill at ease. As a supporter of the ministry he was not of the consequence he had been in opposition. His friends in office had perforce to transfer their political allegiance to their new master the King, and ceased to regard the Prince as their leader. In 1746 he changed sides, and at the general election of 1747 fought an expensive and unsuccessful campaign against the ministry. The last years of his life were spent in spiritless and pointless opposition. His party became the last refuge of the politically bankrupt. 'Poor Fred' earned his sobriquet because of his failure in politics.

In part his failure was the result of personal defects, but really it was inherent in circumstances. The battle was lost before it was begun. There was little that a Prince of Wales could gain besides financial concessions from engaging in opposition to his father's ministry: there was everything that he could lose, both on his own account and on that of his posterity. The spectacle of the Royal Family divided against itself was not dignified. A Prince of Wales who stooped to cultivate popular favour could only do harm to the Crown which he would one day inherit. The Crown suffered from the conflict between King and heir apparent. Whatever advantages either gained were fleeting and evanescent but monarchy as an institution always lost. It was a lesson ignored alike by all the Hanoverian kings.

While the Prince of Wales was engaged in parliamentary warfare, his brother William, Duke of Cumberland, fourteen years his junior, was serving with the British army on the Continent. In 1745 the task of suppressing the Jacobite rebellion was entrusted to the younger brother and the Prince's offer of service was declined. It must have been galling to the Prince to remain inactive in London while the Duke of Cumberland marched to meet the Pretender to their father's throne. Horace Walpole tells a story of this period which shows him in no heroic light. 'When the royal army lay before Carlisle, the Prince, at a great supper that he gave to his court and his favourites . . . had ordered for the dessert the representation of the citadel of Carlisle in paste, which he in person and the maids of honour bombarded with sugar plums.' Yet there is no reason to think that the Prince lacked courage or that he would not have risked his life equally with his brother. Perhaps if he had been entrusted with more responsibility he would have behaved with greater dignity. And if he had behaved with greater dignity he would have deserved more responsibility. But by 1745 it was too late. The breach with the King was beyond repair.

In the summer of 1747, while the result of the general election was yet undetermined, the Prince wrote to one of his followers:

Pray God, they have not a strong majority, or adieu to my children, this constitution, and to everything that is dear to me. My upright intentions are known to you, my duty to my father calls for it, one must redeem him out of those hands that have sullied the Crown and are very near to ruin all. I'll endeavour it, and I hope with my friends' assistance to rescue a second time this nation out of wicked hands.

Statements made by a politician at the height of a general election are not noted for temperance, and to ascribe unworthy motives to opponents is a defect not peculiar to politicians. But this was more than usually fatuous. 'The constitution in danger' was a favourite bogey with eighteenth-century politicians, and whenever a Prince of Wales went into opposition it was always to rescue the King out of the hands of wicked advisers. Forty years later the politicians clustered round the son of King George III mouthed the same claptrap. The 'wicked hands' whom the Prince claimed had 'sullied the Crown' were those of Henry Pelham and his brother the Duke of Newcastle, who had spent their lives in the service of the house of Hanover and stood to lose everything they possessed in the world should the dynasty fall. Did the Prince of Wales really believe this stuff? Was he serious in his fears for the future of his family? Or were those fears instilled into him by ambitious men? What were his 'upright intentions' and how did they differ from those of King George II? What did he intend to do when he mounted the throne?

These questions must be answered if we are to understand the political inheritance which the Prince bequeathed to his son. In so far as any answers can be given, they must be sought in his political testament. This is in the form of a letter addressed to Prince George, dated 13 January 1749, and though signed byt he Prince of Wales is not in his hand. It is a curious document. We do not know why the Prince should have decided to make his political testament at this time or indeed why he should have made one at all. When he put his name to this paper he was only 42 and his father 66. He must have expected to succeed his father within a few years. Yet an anticipation of premature death hangs over his words: 'I shall have no regret never to have worn the Crown, if you do but fill it worthily.' He left instructions that his testament should be read to his son from time to time after his death. It looks, therefore, as if the Prince expected to die before his father – unless this anticipation of premature death is a literary flourish, characteristic of the age.

The document is headed: 'Instructions for my son George, drawn by myself, for his good, that of my family, and for that of his people, according to the ideas of my grandfather, and best friend, George I.' It is not surprising that a son at odds with his father should profess respect for his grandfather: it is merely another way of demonstrating his hostility to his father. Yet the Prince's admiration for King George I seems to have been genuine, and he adopted from that King the plan of dissolving the personal union between Great Britain and Hanover. This had been recommended by King George I in his will, which had been suppressed by his successor. It was now revived by the Prince of Wales as a measure which would benefit both Great Britain and Hanover. 'This has always been my design', he wrote, 'and the latter years have still more convinced me of the wisdom of this project' – an obvious reference to opposition fears about 'Hanoverian measures' and the use of Hanoverian troops.

The only other concrete recommendation in the Prince's testament is that his son should live with economy and endeavour to reduce the national debt and the rate of interest. There was nothing original in this: Henry Pelham thought the same. In view of what was later alleged by Edmund Burke – that a plan to increase the prerogative had been conceived in the Prince's court– it should be noted that his testament contains no directions about the methods as distinct from the aims of his son's future government. There is nothing about abolishing parties: there could hardly be since the Prince was at this time the leader of a party; nor any suggestion that the authority of the Crown required to be strengthened. The Prince believed that his programme could be put into effect without any constitutional innovations. He did not advise his son to increase the authority of the Crown. He merely gave a general direction as to Prince George's moral conduct. 'When mankind will once be persuaded', he wrote, 'that you are just, humane, generous, and brave, you will be beloved by your people and respected by foreign powers.' The clear implication is that King George II was none of these things: hence the 'unsteady measures' which had 'sullied' his reign. The Prince of Wales saw the evils of his time in personal not political terms. It was not the

55

authority of the Crown that was at fault but the character of the King.

It must be presumed that the Prince's intentions were carried out and that Prince George was made acquainted with his father's political testament after his death. To what extent did it influence his ideas when he succeeded to the throne? Dislike of the connection with Hanover and demand for economy in government were the ruling prejudices of the Prince's party when he wrote his testament. Had the Prince lived he could not by himself have dissolved the union with Hanover, for the succession was regulated by the law of the Holy Roman Empire and could only be changed by agreement of the Empire. King George III began his reign with anti-Hanoverian sentiments, inherited from his father and strengthened by his tutor, but soon dropped them. He made no attempt to implement his father's plans respecting Hanover, and during his reign hostility to Hanover ceased to be an issue in British politics. As for the Prince's second point, it was undoubtedly desirable for the King to live with economy and no King tried harder than George III. But again this was a matter beyond the will of the sovereign. The enormous increase of the national debt during his reign was not due to personal extravagance or maladministration on his part but to the successive wars in which the nation became engaged. It was all very well for the Prince to advise his son 'that a good deal of the national debt must be paid off before England enters into a war', but the enemies of England might not be prepared to wait. Nor was an increase in the national debt, as it seemed to the Prince in 1749, the worst evil that could befall the nation.

In short, the Prince's testament was propaganda, not a realistic political programme, and was designed to suit the prejudices of his allies at the time. It was not without its influence on Prince George, but it was impossible to be put into practice.[2]

Had Frederick, Prince of Wales, never engaged in politics we might have had a better opinion of his character. He would have been spared the harsh criticism of Lord Hervey and Horace Walpole; and we might have learnt more of those aspects of his personality, mentioned only casually by contemporaries, which show him in a more favourable light. The follies and vices of royalty are always noted: their virtues are taken for granted and rarely receive recognition.[3]

There was much in the Prince's character which might have recommended him to posterity. He was the first prince of the Hanoverian dynasty to show any love for art or science. He was a discriminating collector of paintings, and two Van Dycks and a pair of landscapes by Rubens owe their places in the royal collection to his taste. George Vertue, the engraver and art historian, whose notebooks form the principal source of Horace Walpole's *Anecdotes of Painting in England*, paid tribute from personal knowledge to the Prince's 'affection and inclination to promote and encourage art and artists'. He shared the fashionable love of landscape gardening, which he practised at Kew. He planned a collection of exotic trees and plants, later developed by his widow and son into the Royal Botanic Gardens. He patronized men of letters and wrote verses. He was fond of music and an accomplished player on the violoncello. He dabbled in astronomy, and was a friend of John Theophilus Desaguliers, a progenitor of the planetarium. All of these interests were shared by his son, and perhaps King George III's intellectual curiosity was first roused by his father.

In domestic life the Prince seems to have been an affectionate husband and father, in both capacities superior to King George II. There is a great deal of contemporary gossip about his alleged love affairs. The eighteenth century revelled in scandalous stories about the great (so for that matter does the twentieth), and when the great are so inconsiderate as not to provide material for scandal

57

subsequent generations never fail to invent it. The Prince, however, was a most uxorious husband. In fourteen years of married life the Princess bore him nine children. King George III was well endowed with brothers and sisters, some of whom were to give him a great deal of trouble after he had succeeded to the throne.

The Prince was fond of amateur theatricals, and almost the earliest mention we have of King George III as a boy is when he took part in a performance of Addison's *Cato*. This play, a favourite with eighteenth-century theatregoers, was acted by a cast of children drawn from the court of the Prince of Wales before an audience largely composed of their proud parents. Prince George naturally took the part of the hero, the virtuous Marcus Portius Cato, and Prince Edward, his next brother, that of Juba, Cato's Numidian ally. The future Lord North, later King George III's Prime Minister during the unsuccessful American war, then a young man of seventeen, was one of the villains. The love interest was supplied by the Prince's eldest daughters, Princesses Augusta and Elizabeth. Horace Walpole, who was among the audience, was particularly impressed by the acting of Princess Elizabeth (who died aged nineteen in 1759), but says nothing of Prince George. We should not be surprised at this, for he was never a good actor. The following year Bubb Dodington saw a performance of *Jane Grey* acted by the Prince's children, but of this we have no detailed account.

Some half-dozen letters from the Prince to his children are extant.[4] They show his concern for their welfare and in particular for their progress at school. 'I have always wished you would come to like reading', he writes to Prince George on one occasion. 'It is only by that one forms oneself and one makes proper remarks of characters.' His eldest son was naturally his principal concern. 'Your hand, my dear George,' he writes, 'grows much better'; and again: 'Your German letter was a very good one, and I hope you'll know soon to write the letters too' (that is, to write the German script). Like all parents when parted from their children he sometimes had occasion to complain of their failure to write. 'I think you might have spared a quarter of an hour of your employments to please me in hearing of you', he wrote to his two eldest sons. 'Therefore for the future let one of you two always do it. Your sister has not forgot you, but has writ to you both. See how much more attentions she has than either of you, and those attentions (I have often told you) please and keep up mutual friendship.' The future King's great fault was his 'not caring enough to please'. It was a fault he tried hard in later years to overcome but never quite succeeded.

One year separated Prince George and Edward (later Duke of York), and the two boys were educated together. Their first tutor was the Reverend Francis Ayscough, who owed his appointment to his political connections (he had married the sister of George Lyttelton, one of the Prince's followers in the House of Commons). Ayscough's appointment was not regarded favourably by the King's ministers. He taught the boys English history and the elements of Christianity, and seems to have been neither a competent nor an inspiring tutor.

Horace Walpole is responsible for the story that at eleven years of age Prince George could not read English, which gave rise to the legend that the boy was badly educated. Prince Frederick's letters to his son are conclusive evidence that not only could he read and write English (and also German) at least by the age of eight, but also that he was taking some interest in public events. On 26 September 1747 Prince Frederick replied to a letter from his son and expressed himself as 'well pleased' with his comments on the conduct of the governor of Bergen-op-Zoom (who had surrendered the town to the French without putting up a fight). Prince George's first extant letter was written to the King on 23 June 1749 to thank his grandfather for nominating him a Knight of the Garter. The nomination had not been spontaneous, and the King had only been induced to name his grandson by pressure from the ministers and fear of censure from the opposition. The Bishop of Salisbury, chaplain of the Order, was sent to make the notification. 'The child, with great good sense,' writes Walpole, 'desired the bishop to give his duty and thanks and to assure the King that he should always obey him, but that as his father was out of town he could send no other answer.' The Prince was invested with the Order privately on 22 June, and the next day wrote to the King:

Sir,
I hope you will forgive me the liberty I take to thank Your Majesty for the honour you did me yesterday. It is my utmost wish and shall always be my study to deserve your paternal goodness and protection.
   I am with the greatest respect and submission,
    Sir,
      Your Majesty's most humble and most dutyfull subject,
      grandson, and servant,
               George

At the same time Prince George wrote another letter in German to Baron Munchausen, the Hanoverian Minister in London. The King sent both letters to the Duke of Newcastle, and they are now among the Newcastle Papers in the British Museum. No doubt they were corrected and approved by the Prince's tutor before being forwarded to the King, and the phraseology may not be entirely his own. But they are irrefutable proofs that he could write both English and German at the age of eleven.[5]

In September 1749 the Prince of Wales decided to put the education of his sons on a more formal basis. Lord North, father of the future Prime Minister, was declared governor to the boys and a second tutor appointed. The King, then in Hanover, was not informed of these arrangements and his consent was taken for granted. North was to have an additional salary of £1,000 a year (he already received £500 as a Lord of the Prince's Bedchamber), and his duties were 'to go about with Prince George and appear with him in public'. The new tutor, George Lewis Scott, had been recommended to the Prince by Lord Bolingbroke, and Henry Pelham thought him a man of 'exceeding good character' and a great improvement upon Ayscough. Ayscough was not discarded (he still continued responsible for Prince George's religious education), but henceforth he took second place to Scott. The Prince prescribed for his sons what seems by modern standards a pretty stiff time-table but was no more than what the eighteenth century thought proper for the education of young boys. Work dominated their day, and no time was left for idleness. They rose at seven and were in the schoolroom at eight. Lessons went on until twelve-thirty, and were followed by a play hour and by dinner at three. After dinner there were further lessons until supper at eight. The boys were to be in bed between nine and ten. The time-table was only varied on Sundays, when they were excused secular instruction in favour of attendance at church and religious teaching. This was Prince George's daily life as a boy.

In view of what was later alleged about Prince George being educated in Jacobite principles, it is as well to look a little more closely into the background of his new tutor. By family and upbringing George Lewis Scott was unimpeachably attached to the reigning dynasty. His father had been a diplomat and had served many years in Germany, where he became a friend of King George I before George I was King. Scott was born in Hanover; the Electress Sophia was his godmother; and he was given the Christian names of King George I. Though he may have obtained his post as the result of a recommendation from Bolingbroke, it could hardly have been for his Jacobite sympathies. In fact it would have been difficult to find a man with a more authentic Hanoverian background. In

61

addition (and this was probably why Bolingbroke recommended him) he was a scholar, a mathematician of some repute, and subsequently the friend of Johnson and Gibbon (Gibbon invited him to write the articles on science and mathematics for his periodical *Mémoires Littéraires*). From every point of view he was an ideal tutor, and the choice of Scott reflects credit on the Prince's good sense.

It was the last decision of any consequence that the Prince took. His death was sudden and unexpected. On 6 March 1751 he told Dodington that he had caught a cold, but this occasioned no particular comment. Walpole, writing to his friend Horace Mann in Florence on 13 March, mentioned that the King had been out of order but said nothing about the Prince. On 15 March he was reported out of danger, but still the illness continued. Dodington inquired after him at three o'clock in the afternoon of 20 March and was told that he was much better. He died at ten o'clock that night.

Ayscough broke the news to Prince George. The boy turned pale, laid his hand on his heart, and said: 'I feel something here, just as I did when I saw two workmen fall from the scaffold at Kew.'

Chapter 2

PRINCE OF WALES

The Prince's death was a political event of great consequence. His followers were deprived of their leader and lost all reason for their existence as a party. The opposition to the Pelham ministry collapsed overnight and politicians had to take their bearings afresh.

King George II was in his sixty-eighth year when his son died. Though in good health, he could not be expected to live many years longer and might die before his grandson reached his majority (at the age of eighteen). To avoid a regency, he would have to live to a greater age than any previous British monarch. And a regency, with the sovereign power exercised by deputy, was of all events the most to be feared. The Prince's death also raised the question of the education of the heir apparent. While the Prince lived that had been his responsibility: now that he was dead it became an affair of state. Prince George might be King within a few years. His reign might extend into the next century. His future conduct and the welfare of the nation would depend on the influences he imbibed during his adolescence. This was too important a matter to be left to chance. The schoolroom became a battleground between contending sets of politicians, with the favour of the future king as the prize of victory.

On the day following the Prince's death, his widow wrote to the King (the letter was written in French):[1]

The sorrow which overwhelms me does not make me the less sensible of the great goodness of Your Majesty. The only things, Sire, which can console me are the gracious assurances which Your Majesty has given me. I throw myself together with my children at your feet. We commend ourselves, Sire, to your paternal love and royal protection.

The King was not displeased to receive this letter. The news of the Prince's death had been a shock, yet he felt no sorrow for the loss of a son whom he hated. In King George II's eyes the Prince had been an undutiful son and his death was a blessing for the nation. But the King had no dislike for his daughter-in-law or grandchildren. No part of the blame for the Prince's sins could be laid upon them. The Princess had been a loyal wife, submissive at all times to her husband. Now she was a widow, with eight young children and within two months of giving birth to a ninth. Sympathy should be extended to her. King George II, who had been a harsh father, was prepared to be a tender father-in-law and grandfather. He was not by nature cruel, except when his fears or cupidity were aroused.

The King sent his daughter-in-law a kind message and went to see her. He tried to comfort her as well as he could. He told his two eldest grandsons that 'they must be brave boys, obedient to their mother, and deserve the fortune to which they were born'. He captivated Prince George, 'who said he should not be frightened any more with his grandpapa'. The Princess made it clear that her husband's politics were to be buried in his grave. She burnt his papers and ostentatiously declined to consult his political friends. She had never concerned herself with politics during his lifetime and it was too late to start now that he was dead. Her only care was for her children and especially for the boy who was now heir apparent.

Prince George succeeded automatically to his father's title of Duke of Edinburgh. On 20 April 1751, a month after his father's death, he was created Prince of Wales and Earl of Chester. These honours, together with the dukedom of Cornwall, had reverted to the Crown on the Prince's death. As heir apparent Prince George had a claim to the principality of Wales which could not be denied. But the dukedom of Cornwall is in remainder only to the eldest son of the sovereign, and Prince George, not being the son of a King, was never Duke of Cornwall. The King retained the revenues and patronage of the duchy for his own use.

In view of the King's age it was essential to make provision for the event of his death before his grandson had reached his majority. In the eighteenth century there was no general regency law and arrangements were made as need arose. On 26 April 1751 the King recommended to Parliament the appointment of the Princess of Wales as regent and guardian of her son. He would have preferred the Duke of Cumberland, but there was strong feeling against the Duke and his nomination would have met with serious opposition in Parliament. The choice of the Princess was based on feelings so natural as to command almost universal recognition, and since 1751 the right of the surviving parent to exercise the powers of regency on behalf of an infant sovereign has been the invariable rule. The Princess was to be assisted by a council composed of the Duke of Cumberland (the only prince of the blood of age), the great officers of state at the time of the King's death, and four others to be named by the King. Members of the council could be removed only by consent of the majority or of both Houses of Parliament; and certain acts of sovereignty (the dissolution of Parliament, the creation of peers, and the appointment of judges) could be exercised only with the advice of the council. These restrictions on the regent occasioned long and curiously academic debates in the House of Commons, in which Members vied with each other to display their constitutional learning.

The Princess offered no objections to this arrangement. She had won her main point: she, not the Duke of Cumberland, was to be regent. She had the good sense to see that to quarrel with the King and the ministers would benefit neither herself nor her son and would only strengthen the hands of the Duke's party. She was equally compliant with respect to the changes in the schoolroom. Neither King nor ministers were prepared to allow the heir apparent to be educated by tutors nominated by the late Prince of Wales and in sympathy with his politics. The delicate task of preparing the boy for kingship could be entrusted only to those who had the full confidence of the government. Lord North was replaced as governor by Lord Harcourt, an orthodox Whig; and Thomas Hayter, Bishop of Norwich and later of London, was appointed preceptor.

Neither was a wise appointment. Harcourt, though politically reliable and of fair character, was not a man of strong personality or of cultivated mind and was unlikely to appeal to a shy and intelligent boy. 'Minute and strict in trifles', writes Horace Walpole, he thought he had discharged his duty conscientiously 'if on no account he neglected to make the Prince turn out his toes'. The bishop has been described by Mr Sedgwick as 'a typical eighteenth-century ecclesiastical careerist': Walpole calls him ' sensible good-humoured gentleman', which is perhaps another way of saying the same thing. He was raised to the bench through the influence of the Duke of Newcastle and obtained translation to a richer see by a timely desertion of Newcastle in the next reign. Fifty years later King George III said that Harcourt was 'well intentioned, but wholly unfit for the situation in which he was placed'. Bishop Hayter, however, was 'an intriguing, unworthy man, more fitted to be a Jesuit than an English bishop', and the King considered that he was 'influenced in his conduct by the disappointment he met with in failing to get the archbishopric of Canterbury'.

The earl and the bishop were the titular heads of the Prince's household, but as with so many eighteenth-century appointments the work was mainly done by their deputies. Here, King and ministers chose well. Ayscough was dismissed and Scott confirmed as sub-preceptor; and Andrew Stone, Newcastle's under-secretary of state, was appointed sub-governor.

Stone was one of the ablest men in government service. The son of a Lombard Street goldsmith, he had been educated at Westminster and Christ Church; and was a close friend of William Murray, at this time Solicitor-General (and later as Lord Mansfield one of the greatest judges of modern times). Stone and Murray were Newcastle's confidential advisers, and Newcastle was the second man in the government. It was said of Stone, with reference to his influence over Newcastle and Newcastle's passion for trivialities, that the Duke of Newcastle did Andrew Stone's business while Andrew Stone did the Duke of Newcastle's. Stone's business in the household was to watch over the heir apparent on behalf of the Pelhams; and Newcastle believed 'there never were three properer persons' to supervise the education of a prince than Harcourt, the Bishop, and Stone. The King also had his liaison officer in the household in the person of James Cresset, the Princess's secretary, a man reputed skilled in the politics of the backstairs and persona grata with King and Princess. Thus both King and ministers had their spies about the Prince. All possible steps had been taken to prevent him from growing up disaffected to his grandfather's government. The Regency Act had been so framed that in the event of the King's death the Pelhams would retain their power during the minority. Both King and ministers had reason to be satisfied with the arrangements they had made.

Alas for the calculations of politicians! Despite all these precautions, within five years of Prince Frederick's death his son was at the head of a fresh opposition, more formidable than ever the Prince had been able to raise – so formidable that it brought to an end the Duke of Newcastle's thirty years' tenure of office and forced King George II to accept a minister prescribed to him by his grandson.[2]

The character of Augusta, Princess of Wales has generally been presented unsympathetically. During her son's reign she became one of the favourite targets of the London mob and gutter press, and although the grosser stories about her are no longer taken seriously some of the abuse heaped upon her still clings to her name. Even more damaging were the allegations made against her by Horace Walpole. Walpole describes her as a 'passionate, domineering woman', who conspired with her lover, the Earl of Bute, to take advantage of her son's inexperience and launch him on a policy designed to increase the prerogative of the Crown. He explained the political events of the first years of King George III's reign as due to the bad system of education laid down for him by the Pelhams and the bad system of politics which he pursued under the direction of his mother and his favourite. Whether this version of history be accepted depends largely on the view we take of the character and ambitions of the Princess.

The Princess was only seventeen when she came to England. She had not received a good education; she knew no one in this country; and she could not speak English. Her inexperience and innocence created a favourable impression, and neither the King nor Queen Caroline blamed her for their quarrel with Prince Frederick. According to Lord Hervey, she was at first kept in ignorance by her husband of the existence of this quarrel. Frederick, writes Hervey, 'used always to say a prince should never talk to any woman of politics, or make any use of a wife but to breed; and that he would never make the ridiculous figure his father had done in letting his wife govern him or meddle in business'. The Prince had been determined in all things to be different from his father. Whatever the King had done, the Prince would do the opposite. The King had always given his confidence to one minister – first Walpole, next Carteret, then Pelham. The Prince therefore would have no Prime Minister but would balance one adviser against another. The King had allowed his wife to talk to him about affairs of state. The

68

Prince therefore would never listen to any woman on politics. Just as he was determined not to be another King George II, so he would not allow his wife to become another Queen Caroline.

Horace Walpole's first impressions of the Princess had been favourable. In 1745 he believed that 'by all her quiet sense' she would turn out to be another Caroline. In this he was wrong, as twenty years later when he pictured her as a scheming ambitious woman. The Princess's quiet sense consisted in nothing more than total submission to her husband. This was the safest course she could pursue: it pleased the Prince, and the King would never blame her for submitting herself to her husband's authority. Her outstanding characteristic is that she had no character except what the Prince had stamped upon her during fourteen years of married life. Had she been a strong personality she would never have accepted the role for which he had destined her – a vehicle for producing child-ren and no more. She had no ambitions and lived for her husband and children. There was no idea in her head that had not been put there by the Prince, and these she had learnt by rote without understanding their import or relevance. She hated the King because the Prince had hated the King; she feared the Duke of Cumberland because the Prince had feared the Duke; she distrusted Pelham because the Prince had distrusted Pelham. Had her husband told her that the earth was flat or the moon was made out of cheese, she would have believed him.

Two factors shaped her conduct after the Prince's death: the fear that the King would die before her son came of age and that the Duke of Cumberland would usurp the throne.

Thanks to Lord Hervey, we know a good deal about the Prince's relations with his parents. But because Her-vey laid down his pen at the death of Queen Caroline and Horace Walpole did not begin his memoirs until the death of the Prince, we know much less of the Prince's relations with his brother. Yet the antipathy between the Prince and the Duke is perhaps of greater significance for King George III's adolescence than that between the Prince and the King.

The Duke of Cumberland was fourteen years younger than his brother. He was the favourite child of both his parents. Perhaps these two facts alone would have prevented any friendship between the brothers. But to jealousy and lack of sympathy, there was added suspicion and fear. The Duke was devoted to the army. In 1743, when only twenty-two, he had commanded a corps under his father at the battle of Dettingen – the last occasion on which a King of Great Britain has led his troops into action – and had been severely wounded. In the following year he took command of the British army in Flanders with the appointment of Captain-General, and in 1745 was recalled to England to defend his father's throne against the Jacobite pretender. At Culloden on 16 April 1746, the day after his twenty-fifth birthday, he crushed the last rebellion ever raised on British soil. For that he deserved well, both of the King and the Prince of Wales. But the Prince, whose offer of service had been refused, would have been more than human had he not felt envious of his brother's laurels.

For a brief space of time the Duke of Cumberland was a popular hero. But when the tide of popularity began to turn, his severities against the remnants of the Jacobite army after Culloden were remembered (they had not been noticed in England at the time) and he became 'Butcher Cumberland', the name by which he is known to posterity. It was not, however, because the Duke had slaughtered the Jacobite army that he became unpopular but because he tried to reform the British army.

The British army in the eighteenth century, as befitted a nation with a strong anti-militarist tradition, was an amateurish force. There was no effective central organization: no War Office in the modern sense; no staff system; no provision for officer training either for junior or higher ranks. The recruitment, discipline, and training of individual regiments was largely left to their commanding officers. The colonelcy of a regiment was a place of considerable profit and was usually held by a general officer. The King was the effective head of the army and decided all promotions and appointments. Except in time of war it was not usual to appoint a commander-in-chief or captain-general, and the Secretary at War was concerned solely with questions of finance or equipment and with transmitting the King's orders to the regiments. There was no body to do for the army what the board of Admiralty did for the navy. Many of the higher ranks were soldiers in name only, who had seen no service.

The Duke's appointment as Captain-General gave the army a professional head, whose authority was reinforced by his being the King's favourite son. On the conclusion of peace in 1748 he began a series of reforms designed to make the army a more efficient and professional force. Like all reformers, he encountered opposition from older men and established interests; and opposition within the army was buttressed by those outside who feared that a strong army would be a danger to constitutional liberty. If the nation had to have an army in time of peace (and many country gentlemen thought there was no need for one), then the smaller and less efficient the better. The Duke was a politician as well as a soldier. Henry Fox, Secretary at War in the Pelham ministry, was his right-hand man and political agent; and Fox acted as whip to a group of Members of Parliament, largely composed of army officers who looked to the Duke for professional advancement. At the general election of 1754, 49 regular army officers were returned to Parliament. With the Duke of Cumberland as master and Henry Fox as whipper-in, they formed a formidable parliamentary pack.

Prince Frederick had watched, first with jealousy and then with fear, the rise of his brother to an eminence of

71

power greater than his own. It had been degrading to have to stand aside while the Duke suppressed the rebellion, but it would be positively dangerous to allow him to increase his power to such a point that he might be able to ... to do what? Possessed of the favour of the King, the confidence of the army, and a large following in the House of Commons, what might not the Duke attempt? A military coup d'état on his father's death leading to a change in the succession was not beyond the bounds of possibility. Such fears were seriously entertained by Prince Frederick. And if this was a danger during the Prince's lifetime, how much more was it a danger now that he was dead and the heir apparent a boy of thirteen? 'The people had idly imagined', writes Horace Walpole, 'that advantage would be made of the youth of the Prince's children to raise the Duke to the throne. Nobody had doubted but he must be Protector if the King should die during their minority. All the precedents ran in his favour. ... No woman had ever yet been regent in a minority.' Hence the Princess's relief when the Duke of Cumberland was not named regent and her ready acceptance of the restrictions on her power. For if the King died and the Duke became regent, so ran her fears, not only her son's succession but even his life might be in danger.

It should be unnecessary to add that these apprehensions were totally without foundation. Though the Duke had no love for his brother and had felt no sorrow at his death, he was a man of honour and incapable of the action dreaded by the Princess. He had a high regard for the dignity of the Crown and the maintenance of the succession according to the rule of law. He felt slandered by suspicions which it was unworthy of his brother and sister-in-law to entertain. But he remained silent, too proud to defend himself against degrading accusations. Nor would the King, much as he hated Prince Frederick, have deprived the Prince or his son of their birthright.

Because there was no reality behind the Princess's fears

it does not follow that they can be dismissed as the obsessions of an hysterical woman and irrelevant to the life of King George III. On the contrary, they were deeply relevant. The nonsense people are apt to believe through fear or jealousy is as real as sense. King George III's story between his father's death and his own accession centres on fear of his uncle. How far the Princess had succeeded in infecting her son with this fear can be seen from a story told by Horace Walpole shortly after the Regency Bill became law:

Prince George making him [the Duke of Cumberland] a visit, asked to see his apartment, where there are few ornaments but arms. The Duke is neither curious nor magnificent. To amuse the boy, he took down a sword and drew it. The young Prince turned pale and trembled, and thought his uncle was going to murder him. The Duke was extremely shocked, and complained to the Princess of the impressions that had been instilled into the child against him.

But why be hard upon the Princess for her foolishness when sober and experienced politicians professed the same fears? Lord Chesterfield, at one time Secretary of State and Lord Lieutenant of Ireland, who prided himself on knowing the ways of the world, did not hesitate to compare the Duke of Cumberland to Richard III. In contemporary pamphlets this parallel was frequently drawn. Nor was it confined to the eighteenth century. Nearly a hundred years later the mother of the infant Princess Victoria had the same fear about another Duke of Cumberland. Whenever the sovereign or heir to the throne is under age, the 'wicked uncle' becomes an alarming figure. Richard III is a favourite bogey in the mythology of monarchy.

The honeymoon period between King and Princess did not last long. When Dodington went to see her in October 1752 he found her full of complaints. She told him that she was not deceived by the King's civility; referred to the Duke of Cumberland as 'her great, great fat friend'; and said that he and Princess Amelia (the King's unmarried daughter) were doing her 'all imaginable mischief' at St James's. She said this about the King:

She wished he were less civil, and put less of their money into his pocket: that he got full £30,000 per annum by the poor Prince's death: if he would but have given them the duchy of Cornwall, to have paid his debts. . . . Should resentments be carried beyond the grave? Should the innocent suffer? Was it becoming so great a King to leave his son's debts unpaid? and such inconsiderable ones?

Dodington slid away from the subject of the Prince's debts. He probably knew far more about them than the Princess (or at least how they had been incurred). He pointed out that it was impossible to 'new-make people'. The King had always been mean about money and always would be. Her best course would be to take no notice of it. 'She said she could not bear it, nor help sometimes giving the King to understand it in the strongest and most disagreeable light.' She then entered into another complaint about the King's intention to resume the lease of Carlton House, one of her husband's residences; and found fault with the ministers. 'What she could not excuse or forgive them for was their not doing something for the Prince's servants. That after so long a time and so many vacancies had happened, taking no notice of no one of them looked as if they had a studied design to keep old prejudices and resentments alive.' Dodington was in hearty agreement. As one of the Prince's courtiers he had lost his office at his master's death, and was only too anxious to make his way back into the King's favour.

The King's attitude towards his son's debts was not dictated solely by cupidity. In reserving to the Crown the revenues of the duchy of Cornwall, he set a precedent which was to be followed by King George III during the minority of his heir. In fact there was far more excuse for King George II than there was for King George III, for

King George II's heir never was Duke of Cornwall and was not entitled to the revenues of the duchy while King George III's was. Nor was it reasonable to expect the King to pay Prince Frederick's debts. Money owing to servants for wages or to tradesmen for goods supplied was paid in due course; but the King was not liable for debts his son had incurred for political purposes and he would have been foolish had he paid them. (King George III did not when he came to the throne.) Those who had lent money to the Prince or pledged their credit on his behalf did so in the expectation of repayment in the next reign in the form of influence, honours, or office. They gambled on what seemed a fairly safe speculation – the chance of the Prince outliving his father (and, what perhaps was not quite so safe, of his honouring his obligations). As matters turned out, they lost. But those who back the favourite for the Derby can hardly claim their money back if the horse is beaten by an outsider. To back the Prince of Wales against the King, as King George III's reign was to confirm, has always been a most dubious form of political speculation.

The Princess rarely spoke favourably of the King. She had been taught by her husband that the King was no more than the puppet of his ministers. Thus Dodington reported her conversation of 25 January 1753:

She said with much warmth that when they [the ministers] talked to her of the King she lost all patience; that she knew it was nothing; that in their great points she reckoned the King no more than one of the trees we walked by.

And again on 8 February:

That if they talked of the King, she was out of patience; 'twas as if they should tell her that her little Harry below [her son Henry, later Duke of Cumberland, then aged eight] would not do what was proper for him; that just so the King would splutter and make a bustle, but when they told him that it must be done from the necessity of his service, he must do it, as little Harry must when she came down.

If this is how the Princess talked of the King to her eldest son it is no wonder the boy grew up with little respect for his grandfather.[3]

In 1743 the Prince had taken a lease of Leicester House in Leicester Square, and in 1751 he settled his two eldest sons and their household in Savile House, next door to his own residence (roughly on the site of the present Empire cinema). After her husband's death the Princess continued to live at Leicester House with her younger children, while Prince George and Edward retained their separate establishment. Savile House remained Prince George's town residence until he succeeded to the throne. In the country he lived near his mother at Richmond Lodge, Kew. He took part in court ceremonies, and when the King was absent in Hanover assisted his mother at the weekly drawing rooms.

In May 1752 Lord Hardwicke, the Lord Chancellor, warned Newcastle, then with the King in Hanover, that all was not well at Savile House. On 21 November, three days after the King's return, Harcourt solicited an audience and requested permission to resign. He complained that his deputy, Stone, assisted by Scott and Cresset (all three of whom he described as 'creatures of Lord Boling-broke'), had arrogated to themselves the entire management of the two boys and that 'the tenor of it was such as led to the favouring persons and principles' for which Harcourt had 'a just abhorrence'. If this meant anything at all, it meant that the heir apparent was being educated in Jacobite principles. A few days later the King sent the Archbishop of Canterbury and the Lord Chancellor to obtain specific details of Harcourt's charges, only to be told that 'what he had to say was of a nature that made it improper to be said to anybody but the King'.

It is difficult to believe that a prince of the house of Hanover, only six years after the last Jacobite rebellion, would be receptive to Jacobite principles. It is equally difficult to believe that he could be taught such principles by men hand-picked by the King and the Pelhams for their political reliability. The accusation was tantamount to treason, and should never have been brought unless justified by the weightiest evidence. Yet neither Harcourt nor the bishop were able to produce any evidence. They did come out with a story that Prince George (or Edward – for the boy concerned differs according to different versions) had been discovered reading a Jacobite history of the revolution of 1688. But even this, flimsy though it was, was denied by the Princess.

Harcourt and the bishop however had not based their case upon facts. Like all who bring such charges they relied more on the extent to which they could frighten rather than convince. They broadened the charge to include teaching not only Jacobite but also Tory and 'arbitrary' principles of government, and rested their case on the known principles and characters of the subordinate officers of the household. Stone, it was alleged, if not a Jacobite himself was in contact with Jacobites. His friend Murray came of an undoubted Jacobite family. Scott must be presumed in sympathy with Jacobitism, since he had been recommended to his office by Bolingbroke. And if Stone and Scott were Jacobites then Cresset who consorted with them must also be one. Q.E.D. What need of further proof?

This was too much for the King. Even Newcastle who saw Jacobites under the bed (as late as 1762 when he resigned the Treasury he was paying for the services of an anti-Jacobite spy) could not swallow these fantastic allegations. If Stone, whom he had known intimately for over twenty years, or Murray, whom he had brought into Parliament and made Solicitor-General, or Scott, who had the Electress Sophia for godmother and had been named after King George I, or Cresset, who owed his appointment to the favour of King George II; if these men were Tories and Jacobites then no man in England, not even Newcastle himself, could be considered free from suspicion. The King refused categorically to believe the allegations of the governor and preceptor and accepted their resignations.

The real cause of the quarrel in Prince George's schoolroom had nothing to do with Jacobitism or the ideas of Lord Bolingbroke. It was a simple struggle for influence between Harcourt and the bishop, the ostensible heads of the household, and Stone and Scott, who did the work. Such disputes were always liable to occur in the households of princes, especially when the prince was heir apparent and future honours and fortunes might depend on his favour. The root cause was the eighteenth-century system of royal education which removed children at about the age of puberty from the direct control of their parents and placed them in a separate household. The nominal head of the household, standing *in loco parentis*, was the governor, who was always of an aristocratic family and in the case of the heir to the throne of at least the rank of earl. Joined in authority with him was the preceptor, responsible for the academic education of the children, usually a bishop or at any rate in holy orders. Subordinate to these were the sub-governor and subpreceptor; a treasurer, responsible for the finance of the household; specialist teachers for foreign languages, fencing, dancing, and riding; and personal servants and domestic staff. Two or more children of nearly the same age would be placed in the same household, as were Prince George and Edward and later the two eldest sons of King George III. Usually the children and their attendants lived in a separate house from their parents.

This system lasted in England until the time of the Prince Consort. Its obvious disadvantages were that it removed the children from the direct influence of their parents and from contact with other children of the same age. It created around them the atmosphere of a court, with all the disputes for precedence and influence which were usual at courts. It was difficult to find suitable people to undertake the responsibility for the education of royal children. The governor had to be a married man, of good character and principles, with no strong political connections, and willing to devote a large part of his time to residence with his charges. It was an irksome duty, and both King George II and King George III at different times had to exercise a good deal of persuasion to engage suitable governors. The choice of preceptor was somewhat easier, for education was an acknowledged responsibility of the clergy and service in a royal household was a certain claim to preferment. But the preceptor had other duties in his parish or diocese and could rarely give that constant attendance which was desirable. Thus both governor and preceptor tended to exercise only a nominal responsibility. The real influence devolved upon their subordinates who were more closely in touch with the children. Hence the repeated disputes, each of a similar pattern, in these establishments.

This is what happened in 1752. Harcourt had been absent most of the summer, attending to election business in Oxfordshire. The bishop was a remote figure, who tried to teach the boys logic and puzzled their mother almost as much as he did them. Lord Waldegrave, who succeeded Harcourt as governor, gives this explanation of the dispute:

The Bishop of Norwich, who, from having been the first chaplain to an archbishop, and afterwards chaplain at court, thought himself equally qualified to govern both Church and State, persuaded Harcourt, an honest, worthy man, but whose heart was better than his head, that they as governor and preceptor must be the sole directors of the young Prince, and that not even the Princess herself ought to have the least influence over him.

The bishop complained to the Princess that 'there were those about the Prince who set his Royal Highness against him' – almost the same complaint which Lord Holdernesse,

79

governor of the future King George IV, was to make to King George III in 1776.

According to Waldegrave, Harcourt, in his audience with the King, 'endeavoured to raise jealousies against the Princess, as secretly favouring the opposition formed by her late husband'. The Princess herself complained to Dodington that Harcourt had behaved ill to her, had not consulted her about the boys, and had spoken to them disrespectfully about their father 'as to send them to her almost ready to cry'. She knew nothing of their being taught arbitrary or dangerous principles, and felt hurt that Harcourt had raised the matter with the King without first informing her. She seemed to think that the whole affair was a plot against her, but the King 'was in a very good humour with her and the children and imputed nothing to them in this whole transaction'.

This ridiculous affair might have been no more than a storm in a teacup had it not been for the mischievous behaviour of Horace Walpole. From him stemmed the growth of a legend that King George III was educated by disciples of Bolingbroke in 'arbitrary' principles of government.

At the end of 1752 an 'anonymous memorial, pretended to have been signed by several noblemen and gentlemen of the first rank and fortune', but really written by Horace Walpole, was sent to 'five or six particular persons'. (These words are quoted from Walpole's memoirs, where he reveals himself as the author of the memorial.) It began with the statement, unexceptionable in itself, that 'the education of a Prince of Wales is an object of the utmost importance for the whole nation' and that 'it ought always to be entrusted to noblemen of the most unblemished honour and to prelates of the most distinguished virtue'. The 'misfortunes which this nation formerly suffered' under the Stuarts were owing to those princes being 'early initiated in maxims of arbitrary power'. It could not therefore fail to be a matter of concern that 'low men, who were originally improper for the high trust to which they were advanced', 'friends and pupils of the late Lord Bolingbroke', should be responsible for the education of the heir apparent. No names were mentioned, but a hint was thrown out of a conspiracy 'to overthrow the government and restore the exiled and arbitrary house of Stuart'.

Walpole does not explain his motives for circulating this extraordinary document. They were largely personal and such as he could not admit even in memoirs written solely for posterity. In a character sketch of himself written a few years later he tells us that he had 'a propensity to faction, and looked on the mischief of civil disturbance as a lively amusement'. He was discontented with the Pelhams for both personal and public reasons, and was endeavouring underhand to stir up opposition against them. He particularly disliked Stone and Murray, and it was against them that the anonymous memorial was chiefly directed.

It had more success in stirring up 'the mischief of civil disturbances' than its author could have expected. One copy was sent to Lord Ravensworth, a strong Whig but not a very sensible one, who took the accusations seriously. He remembered that he had heard stories from one Fawcett, a Northumberland attorney, to the effect that Stone and Murray and their common friend, Dr James Johnson, recently appointed Bishop of Gloucester, had twenty years earlier been accustomed to drink the Pretender's health. On the basis of this, Ravensworth posted to London to tell his tale to the ministry. Here it seemed was something substantial to back up the vague allegations of Lord Harcourt and Bishop Hayter. The King appointed a committee of the Privy Council to investigate the charges.

The committee met on 15 February 1753 and examined both Ravensworth and Fawcett in person. Ravensworth showed himself to be an honest though not particularly intelligent man, who had credulously swallowed stories which plain common sense should have made him doubt. Fawcett was uncomfortable and did not make a good impression: he twisted and turned, changed his story, and then admitted that after a lapse of twenty years he could not be really certain what had taken place. Stone, Murray, and Johnson denied the allegations, and the committee reported to the King that they were scandalous and malicious.

At this we might expect the matter to have ended. But at least two people continued to believe the charges contained in Walpole's memorial. One, not surprisingly, was Walpole himself, who in a passage of his *Memoirs of the Reign of King George III*, written nearly twenty years later, repeats the story that Stone, 'that dark and suspected friend of the Stuarts', and Murray, 'that dangerous man' and 'first disciple of Bolingbroke', were responsible for inspiring King George III with despotic ideas. The other, strangely, was the Princess. When Dodington went to see her on 29 March 1753 she expressed her pleasure that the affair had ended so well and praised the King's steadiness. Dodington said that he had always had a good opinion of Stone and was glad to see him put about Prince George, and was astonished to hear the Princess say that she had been frightened by the appointment. When asked why, she replied:

Because the Prince [Frederick] had always taught her to believe that he was a Jacobite, and that she firmly did believe it. That the Prince was convinced of it, and when things went ill abroad, used to say to her in passion, how could better be expected, when such a Jacobite as Stone was trusted?

The Princess's recollection of her husband's words is the best comment on this affair. In the 1750s 'Jacobite' had become a word of abuse, just as 'Bolshevist' and 'Fascist' have been at different times in the twentieth century. Whenever a Whig politician was 'in passion' he stigmatized his opponents as Jacobites, without necessarily meaning that they were supporters of the house of Stuart. The Princess, not understanding the ways of politicians, took her husband's abuse of Stone literally. This is all there is to the story that King George III was educated in 'Jacobite' or 'Tory' or 'arbitrary' principles of government.[4]

The Prince's new governor, Lord Waldegrave, accepted the office only 'at the earnest request of the King'.[5] At first sight, and considering the reasons for the change, it seemed an unsuitable choice. For Waldegrave came of an undoubted Jacobite family. His grandfather had not only been a Roman Catholic but had married an illegitimate daughter of King James II and had died in exile in France after the revolution. His son had conformed to the Church of England, had served King George I as Lord of the Bedchamber and King George II as ambassador, and had been rewarded with an earldom. James, 2nd Earl Waldegrave, the Prince's new governor, was high in favour with the King and had a 'very sincere esteem and friendship' for Henry Pelham. Despite his family background no suspicion of Jacobitism could be attached to him, and, perhaps fortunately for his historical reputation, he afterwards married Horace Walpole's favourite niece. Walpole gives an agreeable account of him. 'He was a man of pleasure, understood the Court, was firm in the King's favour, and at once undesirous of rising and afraid to fall. . . . A man of stricter honour, or of more reasonable sense, could not have been selected for the employment.' Forty years after Waldegrave's death King George III described him as a 'depraved worthless man', a harsh judgment, which is not borne out by contemporary evidence. He seems from his memoirs to have been a man of sense, who would have been a good choice had he succeeded in winning the affection and confidence of his charge. His colleague as preceptor was John Thomas,

Bishop of Peterborough, neither a noteworthy nor an objectionable choice.

Writing in 1758 Waldegrave thus describes the circumstances in which he assumed his appointment:

I had been appointed governor to the Prince of Wales towards the end of the year 1752, when Earl Harcourt resigned; and as my predecessor did not quit on the most amicable terms I was very kindly received.

I found his Royal Highness uncommonly full of princely prejudices, contracted in the nursery, and improved by the society of bedchamber women, and pages of the back-stairs.

As a right system of education seemed impracticable, the best which could be hoped for was to give him true notions of common things; to instruct him by conversation, rather than by books; and sometimes, under the disguise of amusement, to entice him to the pursuit of more laborious studies.

The next point I laboured was to preserve harmony and union in the Royal Family; and having free access to the Closet, I had frequent opportunities of doing good offices; was a very useful apologist whenever His Majesty was displeased with his grandson's shyness or want of attention; and never failed to notify even the most minute circumstance of the young Prince's behaviour which was likely to give satisfaction.

At first the Princess seemed well pleased with Waldegrave. She told Dodington in February 1753 that he was 'very well bred, very complaisant, and attentive, and the children liked him extremely'. Without any open hostility, there seems however to have been a certain tension in their relationship. Perhaps the Princess could never give her confidence to any man chosen by the King and perhaps Waldegrave realized and resented this. She told Dodington that she thought a governor was 'a sort of pageant, a man of quality for show'. If Waldegrave divined that this was her real notion of his duties, no wonder there was coolness between them.

'I stick to learning as the chief point', she said about the boys' education. And she was dissatisfied with the progress they were making. In October 1752, when Harcourt and Hayter were still in office, she had expressed the wish that the Prince 'were a little more forward and less childish at his age'. In February 1753, two months after the new regime had been established, she said to Dodington about the boys: 'You know how backward they were when we were together [i.e. during her husband's lifetime] and I am sure you don't think they are much improved since.'

These remarks, together with Walpole's statement that the Prince could not read English at the age of eleven, have been taken as evidence that the boy was dull, unresponsive to his teachers, and even mentally retarded. But Walpole's statement is demonstrably false, and the Princess's remarks must be taken in conjunction with those of Waldegrave. The Princess and Waldegrave agree in their estimate of the Prince. Waldegrave says that he was 'full of princely prejudices, contracted in the nursery, and improved by the society of bedchamber women': the Princess, that he was backward and childish for his age. These complaints refer not to his lack of intelligence or deficiency in learning but to his shyness and dislike of society. He was a lonely boy with no companion of his own age but his brother. Lady Louisa Stuart describes him when a boy as 'silent, modest, and easily abashed'. The Princess complained that he took to nobody but his brother, but it is difficult to see how he could take to anybody else so long as he never met anybody. King George III as a child lived in an adult world, the most terrible situation that can befall a child. Dodington hinted that it was much to be wished that he could meet 'more people of a certain knowledge of the world' and learn something of 'the general frame and nature of this government and constitution and of the general course and manner of business', but the Princess said that 'the young people of quality were so ill educated and so very vicious that they frightened her'. Dodington, very much a man of the

85

world, knew that the boy could hardly be other than childish under his present mode of life and that the risk of contamination by vicious people must be accepted if he were to learn something of humanity.

The reasons for his shyness are to be found in the behaviour of his parents. Lady Louisa Stuart, who as Bute's youngest daughter had the best opportunities of learning the facts about King George III's boyhood, tells us that Prince Edward was his parents' favourite son and that 'their preference of him to his eldest brother' was 'a feeling openly avowed'. Prince Edward was praised and petted; but, she writes, 'if the other ever faltered out an opinion, it was passed by unnoticed; sometimes knocked down at once with "Do hold your tongue, George: don't talk like a fool." ' If this is the way his father and mother talked to him, no wonder he was shy! Yet, Lady Louisa continued, he did not brood over it with sullenness. 'Pride and sharpness were not in him. It only tended to augment, perhaps create, the awkward hesitation we remember in that most excellent Prince; whose real good sense, innate rectitude, unspeakably kind heart, and genuine manliness of spirit, were overlooked in his youth, and indeed not fully appreciated till a much later time.'[6]

Everything we know about King George III as a man confirms this impression of his boyhood. As a man he preferred the company of a few close friends to a wider society. He chose as much as possible to live in the country rather than in London where he would have to meet people. He was shy with those he did not know and never knew what to say to those who bowed to him at his levee. As a boy this shyness was noticed unfavourably in view of the public position he would one day occupy. But even as a man and as King, he still lived a comparatively secluded life and he showed a degree of modesty rare in a monarch.

As to this intellectual attainments, we know that his father was dissatisfied with Ayscough, the boy's first tutor, and brought in Scott. Scott was a scholar, and under his tuition Prince George made reasonable progress. In addition to French and German (both of which he learnt to write tolerably well), he was soon learning Latin. He may even have begun Latin under Ayscough, though Ayscough's statement (as reported by Walpole) that he could make Latin verses is certainly false. He never advanced so far in Latin as to be able to tackle verse composition. But there are among his papers translations from Caesar and Sallust with corrections by his tutors, vocabularies of Latin words and phrases, rules for translation, etc. One of these exercises, dated 9 July 1753, a month after his fifteenth birthday, indicates that he must have been learning Latin for some considerable time. He seems to have progressed about as far as a boy of the same age would do today, and despite his insistence later that all his sons should learn Latin he became as bored with it as boys both before and after his time. The margins of some of his Latin exercises are adorned with drawings; and a translation from Caesar concludes with the words: 'Monsieur Caesar, je vous soite [souhaite] au diable'. There are among his papers vocabularies of Greek words and phrases with the Latin equivalents, but no translations from Greek.[7]

Scott taught him ancient history and British and European history as far as the War of the Austrian Succession (which ended only three years before Scott assumed his office). The Royal Archives contain the boy's essays on these subjects, with corrections in Scott's hand.[8] As would be expected from a tutor who was a mathematician and Fellow of the Royal Society, mathematics played a large part in the Prince's education. The problems set for his solution were practical ones, as can be seen from the following examples:[9]

At an election 357 persons voted; and the candidate chosen had a majority of 91. How many voted for each?

A general disposing his army into a square finds he has 204

men more than a perfect square; but increasing the side by one he will want 25 men to compleat the square. How many men had he?

A man dying left his wife with child, ordering by his will that if the child should prove a daughter then the wife should have ⅔rds and the daughter ⅓rd of the estate, but if it was a son then he should have ⅔rds and the mother ⅓rd. Now it happened that the mother was delivered of a son and daughter. How must the estate, which [was] £6,300 be divided between them?

Judging by his mathematical exercises which have survived, he did algebra and geometry not quite as far as the present ordinary level of the General Certificate of Education, and a little trigonometry. He was the first British King to study science as part of his education. Under Scott he did some elementary physics and chemistry, and in 1755 he undertook a course of 'natural and experimental philosophy' under Stephen Demainbray.[10]

There are seven large boxes of the Prince's essays and academic exercises in the Royal Archives.[11] Few are dated, but it is possible to make a rough distinction between the work he did while Scott was sub-preceptor and that after Bute had undertaken the charge of his education (in 1755, when the Prince was seventeen). This is partly based on the evidence of handwriting but more on the fact that Bute had the habit of annotating the Prince's work. We can therefore make an estimate of his academic attainments at the age of seventeen, the average age of a modern sixth-form boy. He had some knowledge of French and German (more than a boy of his age would have today), Latin, and the elements of Greek; a wide, but not detailed, knowledge of history; and some science and mathematics. He had learnt drawing and studied military fortification, and it is possible that while Scott was his tutor he developed his life-long interest in astronomy. We may also assume that he had been taught the history and doctrines of Christianity according to the creed of the Church of England. In addition, there were the social accomplishments of dancing, fencing, riding, and music (he learnt to play the harpsichord and the flute); and he had become interested in art and architecture. This was a much wider education than he would have received had he been born the son of a country gentleman and attended Eton or Westminster. Its most serious deficiency was one which could hardly be overcome at that period: his lack of contact with boys of his own age (apart from his brother) and his utter ignorance, except from books or what his tutors told him, of life outside the schoolroom and the Court. This is the position in which Bute found him in 1755: a boy of average intelligence and of more than average intellectual curiosity, but with no experience of the world, and intensely lonely.

We can now finally scotch the legend that King George III as a boy was dull, apathetic, lethargic, unteachable (all epithets which have been bestowed upon him by biographers and historians of his reign). Even had all his academic exercises been lost, we would still have the evidence of what he was as a man. He was only twenty-two when he succeeded to the Crown, and it was already well known that he was a lover of art, music, and literature. But the best evidence of his ability to profit from education is in the King's Library at the British Museum, evidence visible to the eyes of every visitor. From floor to ceiling this long and lofty gallery, built specially to house the collection, is lined with books from King George III's library which his son gave to the nation after his father's death. A man who collected books on such a scale must have had some interest in their contents. And his love of books and what books can give must have been one of the fruits of his education. George Lewis Scott and Andrew Stone implanted in their charge a love of learning, but it would never have flourished had not the soil been receptive.

King George III received at least as much academic education as was necessary to fit him for the throne. As will be seen later, he also acquired a correct conception of the British constitution and system of government. In these respects his grandfather and the Pelhams provided well for him. What they did not provide for, and what perhaps they could hardly foresee, were his emotional needs. The death of his father had laid upon him the burden that at any hour he might succeed to the Crown. It had put a boy of thirteen into his father's shoes. His mother, though she loved her children, lacked warmth and tenderness. His grandfather, though he professed kind intentions, was old and incapable of love. Prince Edward was no substitute for his father, and all his other relationships were on the plane of duty rather than affection. Prince George was responsive to those in authority over him, aware of the exalted position he would one day occupy, and longing for an older and more experienced person to guide and direct him as he imagined his father would have done. The King and his ministers had surrounded him with guardians who would keep him on the path of political rectitude. They were so concerned about the heir apparent that they forgot the growing boy. And even on the purely political plane their expectations were not fulfilled.

Before George III became King there was only one person outside his family for whom he had feelings of friendship. This was John Stuart, 3rd Earl of Bute, successively the King's tutor, friend, favourite, and Prime Minister, who directly and indirectly had a bigger influence over the course of his life than any other person. During the period of his political activity Bute suffered from a degree of obloquy which few British statesmen have ever had to endure, and it was only with the discovery of his private papers long after his death that a fair estimate of his character became possible.

Bute was born in 1713 and was twenty-five years older than the Prince – old enough to take the place of his father. He was brought up mainly in England, and made his entry into politics in 1737 as a representative peer of Scotland. His first brief venture was undistinguished. He is not known to have spoken in the House of Lords and he lost his seat in 1741. The next few years he spent in Scotland, where his estates though extensive were not remunerative. Lord Shelburne, who knew him well in middle life, describes him at this period as living in the Isle of Bute 'with as much pomp and as much uncomfortableness in his little domestic circle as if he had been king of the island, Lady Bute a forlorn queen, and his children slaves of a despotic tyrant'. He returned to England in 1746, so penurious that he could hardly afford to keep his carriage. But he went about in society, became acquainted with Frederick, Prince of Wales (they shared a love of amateur theatricals), and in 1750 was appointed one of the Prince's Lords of the Bedchamber. On the death of his patron Bute passed into obscurity. Dodington, whose diary forms the best record of the former Leicester House circle, mentions him only twice between the Prince's death and 1755, by which date he had become confidential political adviser to the Prince's widow.

The political situation at this time was delicate and in the opinion of the Princess dangerous. Henry Pelham, who had been first minister since 1743, had died in March 1754 and had been succeeded by his brother the Duke of Newcastle. Only two men were of sufficient stature to succeed Pelham as Leader of the House of Commons, the real source of his political power: William Pitt, Paymaster-General of the Forces, and Henry Fox, Secretary at War; and to both were formidable objections. Pitt was disliked by the King: Fox was disliked and feared by the Princess. Newcastle, nominal head of the ministry, was jealous of both. He hated to part with one jot of his power and certainly did not want to share it with one who would be at least his co-equal in authority. He offered Fox the lead in the Commons but declined to place the political patronage at his disposal; and when Fox refused the offer Newcastle put the lead into commission between Murray, now Attorney-General, and Sir Thomas Robinson, one of the Secretaries of State. By this arrangement he hoped to retain for himself the same supremacy in the ministry as had been held by his brother.

Unfortunately, neither Murray nor Robinson was equal to the task. Murray was an outstanding lawyer and a fine orator but lacked political courage. Robinson had spent most of his life in diplomacy and was a fish out of water in the House of Commons. Pitt and Fox, each with many more years' experience of Parliament, resented being superseded by men of inferior capacities. 'The Duke might as well send his jackboot to govern us', said Pitt scornfully; and putting aside their jealousies for the time he joined forces with Fox to make life unbearable for Newcastle and his lieutenants. This singular opposition was conducted from the front bench, for Pitt and Fox retained their offices and attacked the government spokesmen while professedly supporting the government.

By the spring of 1755 it was clear that this situation could continue no longer. Newcastle and the King would have to make their choice between Pitt and Fox. Events abroad were about to force a decision. War was approaching between Great Britain and France. Fighting had already broken out on the seas and in North America, and a fleet, said to be destined for an attack on the West Indies, was preparing in French ports. The King trembled for Hanover. His relations with Prussia, the ally of France, were not good, and in the event of an Anglo-French war he feared a Prussian attack on the electorate. In April 1755 he set out for Hanover to make arrangements for its defence.

On his previous visits to Germany (since the death of Queen Caroline) he had appointed a council of regency to exercise the authority of the Crown during his absence. Hitherto this council had never included members of the Royal Family. But in 1755, with war and perhaps invasion imminent, it would have been impossible to have excluded the Duke of Cumberland, Captain-General of the army. His appointment struck fear into the heart of the Princess. Perhaps she remembered having been told that King George I had died while on a visit to Hanover. If the King, now in his seventy-second year, should fail to return, what would be her position and that of her son? The Prince of Wales was still a year of being of age. By the Regency Act of 1751 the Princess would become regent. But if the King were to die in Hanover, who was to say the Act would be put into effect? Would the Duke step down and hand over his authority to the Princess? Would there not be a plausible pretext for retaining his position? Would it not be said that with the nation on the eve of war it was better that the powers of the Crown should be in the hands of a man and a soldier rather than in those of a woman? And had not the Duke the authority to bring this about? He was president of the regency council; his ally Fox, now Secretary of State, was also a member. Pitt had declared that during King George II's absence the Duke of Cumberland was virtually King with Fox as his Prime Minister. Suppose in the event of the King's death the Duke were to offer himself as regent on behalf of his nephew – who was to gainsay him? Could he not then arrange for the repeal of the Regency Act? Could not plausible reasons be found for setting aside the Prince of Wales from the succession? What had Richard III done in similar circumstances? These were the questions that tormented the Princess in the spring of 1755.

One man alone was able to help her. Pitt had been humiliated by the promotion of his rival to a secretary-ship of state and a seat on the regency council – which foreshadowed his further promotion to the lead of the House of Commons. An alliance between the Prince of Wales and Pitt was the obvious counterpoise to the Fox-Cumberland alliance. But who could forge it? The Princess had never taken part in politics and knew little of politicians. To whom could she turn in her hour of need? It was at this point that Bute came to her aid.

To form a just estimate of Bute's character, as Shelburne observed, is no easy matter. Yet Shelburne's own account, though that of a disillusioned man and written many years after their political separation, is the most discerning:

His bottom was that of any Scotch nobleman, proud, aristocratical, pompous, imposing, with a great deal of superficial knowledge such as is commonly met with in France and Scotland, chiefly upon matters of natural philosophy, mines, fossils, a smattering of mechanics, a little metaphysics, and a very false taste in everything. . . . He read a great deal, but it was chiefly out of the way books of science and pompous poetry. . . . He excelled most in writing, of which he appeared to have a great habit. He was insolent and cowardly. . . . He was rash and timid, accustomed to ask advice of different persons, but had not sense and sagacity to distinguish and digest, with a perpetual apprehension of being governed, which made him, when he followed any advice, always add something of his own in point of matter or manner, which sometimes took away the little good that was in it or changed the whole nature of it. He was always upon stilts, never natural except now and then upon the subject of women. He felt all the pleasure of power to consist in punishing or astonishing. . . . He could be pleasant in company when he let, and did not want for some good points, so much as for resolution and knowledge of the world to bring them into action. He excelled as far as I could observe in managing the interior of a court, and had an abundant share of art and hypocrisy.

Waldegrave, who had been supplanted by Bute and had no reason to love him, wrote about him in 1758:

There is an extraordinary appearance of wisdom, both in his look and manner of speaking; for whether the subject be serious or trifling, he is equally pompous, slow, and sententious.

Not contented with being wise, he would be thought a polite scholar, and a man of great erudition: but has the misfortune never to succeed, except with those who are exceeding ignorant. . . .

The late Prince of Wales, who was not overnice in the choice of ministers, used frequently to say that Bute was a fine showy man, who would make an excellent ambassador in a court where there was no business.

Both these characters of Bute present in essentials the same picture: that of a pedant, a man of learning without wisdom, eager to apply his knowledge to the business of politics and unacquainted with the real dispositions of mankind. Today we should describe him as a typical intellectual. He had far more learning than Waldegrave admits and his interest in science was remarkable at that period for a person of his class. But his learning instead of teaching him humility only added to his pride. 'You teach men to be kings,' says Caesar to the King of Egypt's tutor in Bernard Shaw's play. 'That is very clever of you.' Bute aspired to teach a boy how to become a king and sought in books the answer to the mystery of state-craft. He should never have gone to Court. His proper place was in an Oxford common room. He is the most finished example in British history of the don in politics.[12]

The Princess like many badly-educated people had an inordinate respect for learning and an exaggerated idea of what learning can do. She assumed that a man of such parts must be able to deal with the politicians. This is why she was impressed by Bute. Contemporary observers, who were not similarly impressed and did not know the facts, in their search for an explanation of why he had become the Princess's adviser could only assume that he was her lover. Waldegrave insinuates as much in his memoirs, and Walpole, who derived a good deal of his information from Waldegrave, declared at the end of his life that he had no more doubt of their being lovers than if he had caught them in the act. The story was current in London in the late 1750s and came to the ears of the Prince of Wales, and when Bute assumed office it was a favourite theme with the gutter press.

Two persons less likely to engage in a love affair than

Bute and the Princess could hardly be imagined. In 1755 Bute was forty-two, happily married to an attractive and devoted wife, and the father of a large family. He had never been suspected of gallantry. The Princess was thirty-six, the mother of nine children, and more famed for her discretion and good conduct than for her beauty or sexual charms. Everything we know of the character of either is evidence against a love affair. Had an affair existed it could hardly have been kept from the Prince, and we can be quite sure that he would have shown no favour to Bute had Bute been his mother's lover. Under the conditions of court life in the eighteenth century it was impossible for royalty to conduct a clandestine love affair. There were too many people in attendance who had opportunities of learning the facts. Such affairs when they existed were always conducted in the open simply because they could not be kept secret. The King's mistress was acknowledged and was an important figure at Court; and sometimes played a part in politics.

The decisive evidence however is to be found in the essays on history which the Prince wrote for Bute. These reflect Bute's teaching not only of history but of morality, and one of the lessons that Bute stresses over and over again is that Kings should avoid illicit sexual relations and beware of the influence of women in politics. Robert, son of William the Conqueror, is censured by the Prince because he was indolent and neglected his business for 'play, wine, and women'. The court of Henry II of France 'was famous for luxury, debauchery, and in short all sorts of vices that ruin great nations'. 'We hope we shall not be thought too hard', writes the Prince about Catherine de Medici, 'when we say that the fair sex in general are apt to fluctuate when concerned in public affairs.' An essay on Edward III was corrected by Bute to inculcate a moral lesson. It began originally: 'As Edward III was but fourteen, he had twelve guardians placed about him'. Bute crossed out the last three words and substituted: 'appointed him by Parliament, though in reality Mortimer, the Queen's favourite, governed the whole'. It would have been remarkable had Bute indeed been the Princess's lover that he should have gone out of his way to call his pupil's attention to such a close historical parallel as that between Mortimer and himself. To have done so suggests that he had an absolutely clear conscience about his own relations with the Princess. It is ironical that in the early years of the new reign Bute and the Princess were frequently attacked in satirical prints and newspapers under the guise of Mortimer and Queen Isabella.[13]

Bute's aim when he undertook the charge of the Prince's education was to teach the boy to avoid the follies and weaknesses of his grandfather. He saw that the Prince was shy and lonely, and he set out to do for him what he believed his father would have done had he lived. King George II's follies and weaknesses, so Prince Frederick had believed, had sprung from his dependence upon women – first, Queen Caroline, and next his mistress, Lady Yarmouth. The advent of Bute, far from strengthening the influence of the Princess over her son as was popularly believed, helped to wean him from her. Had the Princess really been politically ambitious and desirous of ruling through her son she would have turned against Bute and contrived to get rid of him. For Bute secured an influence over the Prince's mind which she could never have obtained. One lesson which Bute taught the Prince and which he never forgot was to beware of petticoat government. The Princess had no more influence over the politics of her son than she had had over those of her husband.

The King returned to England in the autumn of 1755 with two projects for his grandson, both of which met with the Prince's bitterest opposition.

While in Hanover the King had met the Duchess of Brunswick Wolfenbuttel and her two unmarried daughters. The house of Brunswick (as it was usually called) and the house of Hanover were branches of the same family, their territories were contiguous, and a matrimonial alliance between them was natural and proper. Brunswick was closely allied with Prussia, and such a match would facilitate a rapprochement with Frederick the Great and relieve the threat of a Prussian attack on Hanover. The King had been greatly impressed with the Duchess's second daughter Sophia Caroline, who was only a few months older than the Prince. 'He wished to make her his granddaughter', writes Waldegrave, 'being too old to make her his wife. I remember his telling me with great eagerness that had he been only twenty years younger she should never have been refused by a Prince of Wales but should at once have been Queen of England.'

The Prince of Wales was taught to believe that he was to be made a sacrifice, merely to gratify the King's private interests in the electorate of Hanover. The young Princess was most cruelly misrepresented; many even of her perfections were aggravated into faults; his Royal Highness implicitly believing every idle tale and improbable aspersion till his prejudice against her amounted to aversion itself.

It was commonly said that the Princess's opposition to the match was provoked by the wish to marry her son into her own family of Saxe Gotha.

Faced with resolute opposition, the King did not press the point. Relations between the Prince and his grandfather began to deteriorate, and political events pulled them farther apart. In October 1755 Fox and Newcastle concluded an alliance and Fox became leader of the House of Commons; and in November the King submitted to Parliament the treaties he had concluded with Russia and Hesse Cassel for the defence of Hanover. These provided for taking foreign troops into British pay and were unpopular even with some staunch government supporters. They gave Pitt and Bute a rallying cry: an opportunity to stand in defence of British against Hanoverian interests. In the debate in the House of Commons on 13 November, one of the most memorable of the century, Pitt delivered a great philippic against the Newcastle–Fox coalition and their Continental policy. The war, he declared, was undertaken for the 'long-injured, long-neglected, long-forgotten people of America', and it was not in the capacity of Great Britain to pay subsidies to foreign powers. 'He believed that within two years His Majesty would not be able to sleep in St James's for the cries of a bankrupt people.' Within two years Pitt, then Secretary of State, would be subsidizing a foreign power to an amount which Newcastle and Fox would never have dared to ask. But happily for all the future was concealed.

Pitt was dismissed. 'Goodnight, my dear Lord', he concluded his letter to Bute, telling him the news. 'I believe I shall sleep very quietly and wake as happy as any minister now in England. Heaven defend and prosper the great cause we have the glory to serve!' Pitt was the first martyr to that cause: the cause of Great Britain against Hanover, of constitutional liberty against military despotism, of a young Prince of Wales against an old King. To those who could remember Prince Frederick, this was merely another turn of the wheel in the cycle of opposition between King and heir apparent. There was nothing new under the sun, as Lord Chesterfield wittily observed, nor under the grandson either.[14]

In the political intrigues of this period, it is difficult to catch sight of the person of the Prince. In contemporary correspondence the party of the Prince of Wales was usually referred to as Leicester House – where the Princess lived – and it was assumed that the Princess directed the actions of her son. In fact Leicester House as a political term meant Bute and Pitt. The Princess, having secured a champion who she believed would effectively oppose the Duke of Cumberland and assert her son's rights, retired from a combat for which she knew she was unfit. The Prince, equally unfit because of his youth and inexperience, prepared to engage under the guidance of Bute; and at this period Pitt was content to be Bute's lieutenant and parliamentary spokesman. Their ideas on government and policy were as yet in harmony, and Pitt was an accomplished courtier when it suited him to be so. By the summer of 1756 Bute, though out of Parliament, was one of the most important politicians in the kingdom.

The Prince would come of age in June 1756, and in April the King referred to his ministers the question of his grandson's future provision. Strictly speaking he was not entitled to a separate establishment until he reached the age of twenty-one, but the cabinet, no doubt wishing to get him away from Bute, advised the King that the Prince should be given his own household. An allowance of £40,000 a year was proposed. Waldegrave was to be Groom of the Stole and head of the household; and the Prince and Prince Edward were to leave Savile House and reside at St James's. These proposals were approved by the King, and on 30 May communicated by Waldegrave to the Princess.

The Prince thanked the King for his kindness but requested permission to remain living next to his mother. 'Her happiness depends on their not being separated', he wrote, using the third-person style customary in correspondence of this nature, 'and anything so sensibly affecting his mother must prove extremely uneasy to him.' Nothing was said about Bute; but Waldegrave was told that it was expected that Bute would be named Groom of the Stole in the future establishment and that 'if *that* was not done the Prince should not look upon any persons to be appointed *by the King* as his servants'.

This took King and ministers by surprise. The King was reluctant to appoint Bute to any position of authority about the Prince, nor were the ministers pleased at the prospect. To be Groom of the Stole to the Prince of Wales was to have the reversion of first minister in the next reign. But what could Newcastle do? With the King in his seventy-third year, it would have been highly imprudent to incur the disfavour of the heir apparent. He had a delicate path to tread – to please the King without displeasing the Prince and to ingratiate himself with the Prince without losing favour with the King. Fortunately Newcastle was accustomed to this kind of situation. He had met with it frequently in election affairs. The obvious thing was to buy Bute off. Some 'proper mark of the King's favour' – a pension or a lucrative sinecure – might induce Bute to have the matter settled in accordance with the King's wishes. The offer was sent through the Duke of Argyll, Bute's uncle.

Bute however was not to be bought. 'My most ardent request', the Prince wrote to the King on 12 July 1756, this time using the first person, was that Bute should be Groom of the Stole. 'Nothing can make me happier or fill my mind with warmer gratitude than Your Majesty's gracious condescension in favour of a person whom early and long experience [his friendship for Bute had lasted about a year] has so naturally pointed out to my preference and of whose duty and zeal for Your Majesty I have the most certain knowledge.' Such a categorical demand was too much for Newcastle. The war was going badly. Minorca had been taken by the French; the nation was alarmed and indignant; and a parliamentary inquiry was threatened. Pitt was preparing to hurl his thunderbolts in the House of Commons. And if to all this there was to be added a breach in the Royal Family? Newcastle shivered in his shoes at the prospect that might be in store for him. He had no choice but to accede to Bute's demand for the first place in the Prince's household and to Pitt's demand for the first place in the House of Commons. The King gave in with bad grace. On 4 October the Prince was informed that Bute would be appointed Groom of the Stole and that he would be allowed to continue to live at Savile

House 'for the present' – a mere face-saver. A month later Newcastle resigned. The Duke of Devonshire succeeded him as head of the Treasury, with Pitt as Secretary of State and Leader of the House of Commons. Bute's triumph was complete. He had forced a Minister on the King. He had checked the power of the Duke of Cumberland.[15]

This protracted wrangle had been carried on by Bute in the name of the Prince of Wales. The Prince had signed the letters to the King but everyone believed they had been drafted for him by Bute. It is difficult to penetrate below the level of this formal correspondence and discover the Prince's real feelings. The nearest we can get comes from two brief glimpses in Waldegrave's memoirs. They are sufficient to show that he was not the prime mover in the transaction.

When the question of the Prince's establishment was first raised, Waldegrave was made to feel that his presence was no longer desired and that it would be better if he were to resign of his own accord. One evening after dinner the Prince engaged him in conversation, and 'with much hesitation and confusion' put this suggestion before him. The impression we derive from Waldegrave's account is of the Prince's awkwardness and gaucherie. He seemed to be repeating a lesson he had been made to get by heart. Certainly he showed no tact. He told Waldegrave that the head of his household must be a man in whom he could confide, and that 'unless he was gratified in this particular, he should consider all those who were placed about him as his enemies'. Waldegrave who had hitherto imagined himself in favour was deeply offended, and returned the Prince what he describes as an 'uncourtly answer' – no less than a hint about the Princess's alleged love affair with Bute. (Perhaps this was in King George III's mind in 1804 when he told Rose that Waldegrave was a 'depraved, worthless man'.) The Prince, continues Waldegrave, 'was much embarrassed, said little, and went immediately to his mother to give an account of what had passed'. Two days later (after time to consult Bute) the Princess apologized to Waldegrave and offered him the second place in the Prince's household, that of Master of the Horse. 'The Prince, who was present, assented to everything she said, but entered no further into the conversation.'

Our second glimpse of the Prince at this time comes from a letter Waldegrave wrote to Newcastle informing him of the Prince's reception of the news that the King had granted his request:

His Royal Highness was most extremely pleased. 'What! has the King granted both my requests? He has always been extremely good to me. If ever I have offended him I am sorry for it. It was not my own act or my own doing', and then was going on, which seemed to be that he was put upon it or influenced by others, but stopped and did not speak out.

Hardwicke, when told by Newcastle of this, commented:

I heartily wish the Prince had gone on with what he was about to say after the expression which dropped from him – *it was not my own act or my own doing*. The subsequent part might have been curious. . . . I am curious to know whether the Princess was present when the message was delivered to the Prince.

'He was alone', replied Newcastle, 'when my Lord Waldegrave first communicated to him the two messages and had his conversation with him upon them. The Prince was then in a rapture of joy, which has never appeared since.'

On 10 November 1756 a warrant was issued under the Privy Seal for an allowance of £40,000 a year to be paid to the Prince of Wales, £5,000 of which was for the use of Prince Edward.

How shall we explain Bute's influence over King George III? It was simply that Bute was the first person to treat him with kindness and affection. He broke through the shell of loneliness with which the boy was surrounded. After such a life as the Prince had led, it was certain that the first person who did this would win his confidence. Had he not been taught by his father and mother to despise the King and to fear the Duke of Cumberland, or had either of these been more tender or sympathetic towards the boy, he would never have become a rebel. He was not rebellious by nature: on the contrary, he was if anything too amenable to authority. But his mother loyally tried to carry out what she believed would have been her husband's wishes and the hand of Prince Frederick guided his son even after his death. Then, just as the Prince was approaching manhood, came Bute, a man of culture and learning, a former follower of his father, imbued with his ideas, sympathetic and encouraging. Here was a man in whom the Prince could confide, who would show him the way his father would have him tread. No wonder he put his trust in Bute! He was to tell things to Bute that he would never tell again to another human being – not even to his brother the Duke of Gloucester or his son the Duke of York, both of whom he dearly loved. The pity was that Bute was not content to be the King's friend. Unfortunately (not least for himself) he had ideas; he had ambitions; he aimed to be the Cardinal Fleury of Great Britain – the King's tutor who became Prime Minister.

This explanation of Bute's influence is strengthened by what we know of King George III as a boy. Though he had been given a sound education, he had gone unwillingly to school. Waldegrave writes of his want of application and extreme indolence, and in one of his early letters to Bute (25 March 1757) the Prince writes:

I am conscious of my own indolence. . . . I do here in the most solemn manner declare that I will entirely throw aside this my greatest enemy and that you shall instantly find a change. . . . I will employ all my time upon business and will be able for the future to give you an account of everything I read. . . . I am resolved in myself to take the resolute part, to act the man in everything, to repeat whatever I am to say with spirit and not blushing and afraid as I have hitherto.

This seems a strange confession for one who a few years later was noted for his industry and blamed for his obstinacy. As the biographer goes through the boxes in the Royal Archives containing the essays which the Prince wrote for his tutors, the fact of his youthful indolence becomes even more puzzling. Some of these essays extend to fifty folio sheets, every word in the Prince's hand. Surely this is evidence of industry not of indolence? Yet the testimony of Waldegrave and the Prince himself seems irrefutable.[16]

The paradox is not difficult to explain. His early indolence was psychological not organic, the inability to concentrate on his work rather than inherent dullness or lack of intelligence. All who have been concerned with education have met the child who refuses to learn or who learns only under pressure, and yet who under the direction of a sympathetic teacher blossoms out and astonishes those who have set him down as dull or lazy. What parent has not read with dismay the words 'could do better' or 'does not try' on his child's report sheet? What parent, inquiring about his child's unsatisfactory progress, has not been told that there is nothing really wrong with the boy but that he does not pay attention in class? That the Prince was a difficult pupil is easy to believe. The death of his father, the lack of warmth in his mother, the tension between her and his grandfather, the fear of his uncle, the incessant pressure upon him as to his future station – all these created a vein of unhappiness in his character which it was not easy to overcome. Waldegrave observed without understanding this. He writes: 'Whenever he is displeased, his anger does not break out with heat and violence [as did the King]; but he becomes sullen and silent, and retires to his closet; not to compose his mind by study or contemplation, but merely to indulge the melancholy enjoyment of his own ill humour.' He did not lose his temper but took to the sulks. Prince Edward was more open, more like his father and grandfather. Prince George had a good deal of his mother's passivity. He had to force himself to play his part in public and he never really enjoyed it.

None of those who knew him believed that he was dull or lacking in intelligence. 'His parts, though not excellent,' writes Waldegrave, 'will be found very tolerable, if ever they are properly exercised.' This was Bute's contribution to the development of his character. He took the boy and opened his mind. He encouraged his curiosity in the fields of art, literature, science, and politics; and the Prince began to learn on his own account because he wanted to learn. The indolent boy whom Waldegrave had known became the cultured monarch who patronized Herschel, founded the Royal Academy, and collected the King's Library.

In many ways Bute's influence over King George III was not conducive to his personal happiness or to the welfare of his people. Bute did not give him 'true notions of common things' – these he had to learn for himself and it took him a long time. The political instability of the early years of the reign which brought the King so much unhappiness was largely due to Bute. In after years the King regretted Bute and even persuaded himself that he had never wished to make Bute his minister. But it is to Bute's credit – and for this he has waited too long for acknowledgment – that he fanned a spark which grew into a flame and immeasurably enriched the King's life. How this happened we do not know. At the distance of two hundred years it is almost impossible to describe the progress of such an intensely personal relationship. The secrets of the human heart are not to be found in the archives. The things we really want to know about people are never put down on paper for the benefit of their biographers. Outside the sphere of music and literature, the deepest emotions are inarticulate.

* * *

Bute believed that the study of history would teach his pupil lessons of morality and statecraft which would guide his conduct when he came to the throne. He gave him a course of British history from the earliest times and followed this up with the histories of the leading European states. The Prince also studied the British political, legal, and fiscal systems and those of other countries; and learnt something of geography, agriculture, and commerce. He continued his mathematical studies (some of his exercises are corrected by Bute),[17] and Bute brought William Chambers to be his tutor in drawing and architecture. Whatever gaps there may have been in his education were fully remedied during this finishing period.

This was the method of teaching. The Prince first read up the prescribed subject or period of history and then discussed it with Bute. He then wrote an essay which Bute corrected and which formed the subject of a further discussion. Sometimes the work had to be done over again and a second essay written. Bute's corrections were not only of substance but of style and were strongly tinged with pedantry. An essay on Richard II which began with the sentence: 'Richard II succeeded his grandfather Edward III when he was but eleven years old', was altered by Bute to read: 'Richard II was but eleven years old when he succeeded his grandfather Edward III'. When the Prince wrote 'the King was greatly angered', Bute substituted 'provoked' for 'angered'; and the Prince's phrase 'begged him to call his grandfather to memory' was changed to 'begged him to call to mind his grandfather'. Spelling and punctuation were corrected, and in one essay where the Prince had used the ampersand he was made to write out the word in full.[18] Still, too much attention to detail is better than too little. The Prince received from Bute a much better education than if he had attended Oxford or Cambridge. Gibbon, who went up to Magdalen three years before Bute entered the Prince's household, would gladly have exchanged his tutor – the gentleman who 'remembered that he had a salary to receive and only forgot that he had a duty to perform' – for one so conscientious as Bute.

The Prince's essays are full of moral judgments on Kings and statesmen. An essay on Francis I of France contains this sentence:

A good Prince ought to make his passions subservient to the interest of his country, for all things are either good or bad for him as they regard his people; but Francis had been bred up with different sentiments from these, flattery the bane of all princes had poisoned his mind; he instead of regarding the affairs of his country, totally gave himself to pleasure, which was the reason all his military operations met with such frequent delays.

No doubt other examples to be avoided, of more recent date and nearer home, were pointed out, and he was reminded that the King had a mistress and the Duke of Cumberland was monstrously fat, allegedly from over-eating. The first duty of Kings was to lead a moral life and refrain from indulgence in sensual pleasures. It was no bad lesson to teach a young prince, and it was one King George III learnt well.

The King's duty to his subjects was founded in freedom. The King was the father of his people, the guardian of their rights and liberties. 'The pride, the glory of Britain, and the direct end of its constitution', wrote the Prince, 'is political liberty.' It would have gladdened the heart of John Hampden or Algernon Sidney to read such words in the hand of a British King. Andrea Doria was commended for giving freedom to the republic of Genoa – 'this great action must by all free people be looked on as the most excellent and truest sign of a great man'. Freedom of speech, he wrote in his essay on the British constitution, 'is not only the natural privilege of liberty but also its support and preservation, every man therefore here is allowed to declare his sentiments openly, to speak or write whatever is not prohibited by the laws'. His account of the British political system ends with the following sentence:

Thus have we created the noblest constitution the human mind is capable of framing, where the executive power is in the prince, the legislative in the nobility and the representatives of the people, and the judicial in the people and in some cases in the nobility, to whom there lies a final appeal from all other courts of judicature, where every man's life, liberty, and possessions are secure, where one part of the legislative body checks the other by the privilege of rejecting, both checked by the executive, as that is again by the legislative; all parts moving, and however they may follow the particular interest of their body, yet all uniting at the last for the public good.

Twenty-five years later King George III justified his dismissal of the Fox – North coalition with reference to this view of the constitution.

It is instructive to compare Bute's teaching on the constitution with the orthodox Whig interpretation as put forward by Horace Walpole. Walpole writes in his *Memoirs of the Reign of King George III*:

The legislature consists of the three branches of King, Lords, and Commons. Together they form our invaluable constitution, and each is a check on the other two. But it must be remembered at the same time that while any two are checking, the third is naturally aiming at extending and aggrandizing its power. The House of Commons has not seldom made this attempt like the rest. The Lords, as a permanent and as a proud body, more constantly aim at it; the Crown always.

Writing in the 1750s and on an historical basis the Prince laid particular emphasis on the freedom of the judicature. Walpole writing ten years later with reference to current events omitted all mention of the judges but stressed liberty of the press as 'a chief and material engine of freedom' – a point not overlooked by the Prince. But the fundamental ideas are the same: a balanced constitution, each branch with its separate functions and each acting as a check on the other two. This, so the eighteenth century believed, was the secret of British freedom. 'We may therefore infer from this long reign', the Prince wrote at the end of his essay on Edward III, 'that this people will never refuse anything to a sovereign who they know will be the defender of their liberties.' He would have agreed with Walpole's view of the constitution, but would have pointed out that during his reign it was the House of Commons not the Crown that was extending its power. And he would have been right.

His essays on the Civil War and the Revolution are the answer to the accusation that he was reared in arbitrary or high prerogative principles. Again, their theme is freedom: the freedom which the house of Hanover brought as contrasted with the despotism the house of Stuart hoped to establish. The essay on King James I is as hostile to that King as the most ardent Whig could desire. Charles I, wrote the Prince, 'had too high a notion of the regal power and thought that every opposition to it was rebellion'. His execution, the Prince correctly pointed out, was contrary to all law, and showed 'how far fury and enthusiasm can drive even so generous and humane a people'. King Charles's fall was brought about by his insincerity, his obstinacy, and his habit of 'being easily governed by his favourites'. James II was a tyrant and William III a liberator. The Prince ends his account of the Convention Parliament of William and Mary with the words:

The unhappy party divisions must ever give an honest man a most unfavourable opinion of these times, when the honour and dignity, the safety and tranquility, of the nation, were continually neglected for the little interested views of party; but however this Convention with all its blemishes saved the nation from the iron rod of arbitrary power. Let that palliate all defects, and though the constitution was not so well established as it might have been at this time, though sufficient care was not taken to keep the advantages of our insular situation, nor effectual bars put to Continental influence, let us still remember we stand in debt for our liberty and religion to the success of 1688.

The references to 'unhappy party divisions', 'our insular situation', and 'Continental influence' were prompted by Bute and had relevance to the current political situation. Otherwise these are the sentiments of Macaulay, most Whiggish of Whig historians, and the concluding words of the Prince's essay anticipate those in which Macaulay glorified the Revolution. In short, King George III was nurtured on the pure milk of Whiggism, flavoured by Bute. The flavour may have been sharp and astringent, but Walpole and Macaulay are incontrovertible witnesses to the purity of his Whig diet.*

There was a didactic purpose behind all Bute's teaching: he never forgot that he was not only the Prince's tutor but also his political adviser and future minister. He could hardly refrain from pointing the moral and adorning the tale. When the Prince wrote about William III: 'The King's conduct may be easily accounted for – to prefer the merit of present compliances to that of past obligations is not peculiar to a monarch', Bute added in the margin: ''Tis an ungrateful truth too often met with in ordinary life.'

Bute's alliance with Pitt was based on an anti-Hanoverian policy. 'Being thought an enemy to Hanover', as Waldegrave told the King, 'was the solid foundation of Pitt's popularity.' Pitt and Bute advocated a maritime and colonial instead of a Continental war, and pressed for the establishment of a national militia recruited by compulsory service instead of foreign and professional troops. These ideas are faithfully reflected in the Prince's essays. The military policy of Great Britain, he wrote, should be based on a navy 'equal if not superior to those of all other powers together, which must preserve it from invasion'. 'Numerous armies and strong fortresses are inconsistent

*See note 1, p. 608.

111

freedom', he declared, but a national militia would reconcile the nation to that army that shall be thought necessary to be kept on foot'. The real danger to British freedom was not France but the Duke of Cumberland.[19]

The King had unwillingly accepted Pitt, chafed beneath his yoke, and at the first convenient opportunity dismissed him. The decision was prompted by the Duke of Cumberland, who was about to set out for Germany to take command of the army formed for the defence of Hanover and was reluctant to leave his enemy in power in London. The King turned to Fox to form a new ministry. But Fox, though he hated Pitt and had rejoiced at his dismissal, lacked the courage to stand forward as the responsible head of the House of Commons. For three months there was an interregnum in which every possible political permutation was suggested: a period of intrigues and negotiations in which Bute as spokesman for the Prince of Wales took a leading part. At last in July 1757, Newcastle and Pitt – the one favoured by the King and the other by the Prince of Wales – joined hands to form a ministry which was destined to bring King George II's reign to an end in a blaze of glory.

The new ministry, so greatly derided when it was formed and so greatly regretted when it broke up, has been sometimes represented as a victory for Pitt, the energetic and popular war minister, over Newcastle, the distributor of parliamentary patronage. But in 1757 Pitt had yet to prove his ability to make war and over a year elapsed before the tide began to turn in Great Britain's favour. Pitt's strength arose not from his popularity – this the King could afford to ignore – but from the favour of the Prince of Wales. And at the very outset of the ministry an event occurred which greatly strengthened Pitt's position.

On 26 June 1757 the Duke of Cumberland, with an inferior army, was defeated by the French at Hastenbeck, and on 8 September concluded a convention which took

Hanover out of the war and left France free to advance farther into Germany. Perhaps this was the bitterest moment of King George II's life and he behaved in a manner which did him little credit. The Duke, who understood that he had received full powers to make the best terms he could for Hanover, returned to England to be overwhelmed with reproaches from his father. 'Here is my son,' said the King when the Duke attended his levee, 'who has ruined me and disgraced himself.' Pitt to his honour defended his enemy and told the King to his face that the Duke had full powers for what he had done. The Duke, too proud to make excuses, resigned his office of Captain-General and all his military appointments and passed into obscurity. For the remainder of the reign he was of no account in politics. The Princess need no longer fear him. Bute had achieved what he had set out to do. He could now look forward to a period of collaboration with Pitt in which their ideals of government would be realized, the King would quietly sink into old age and insignificance, and Bute would become the real ruler of the nation.

The King, however, showed no disposition to accept the role for which Bute had cast him. The Hanoverians were a tough breed. Although in his seventy-fourth year and with his eyesight failing, the King was far from senile and was not prepared to yield his authority to the surrogate of his grandson. On the contrary: Pitt found it necessary to trim his policy to suit the King's wishes. 'Mr Pitt won't do my German business', the King had said to Newcastle before Pitt took office. 'If he comes into your service, Sir', replied Newcastle, 'he must be told he must do Your Majesty's business.' And in fact Pitt did King George II's German business better than any minister had ever done.

The Seven Years War was really two wars, fought over different issues and neither necessarily connected with the other. In the east it was a war between Prussia and

Austria (aided until 1762 by Russia) for the possession of Silesia. In the west, it was a war between Great Britain and France for supremacy in America. Great Britain, who had been the ally of Austria in the previous war, was now the ally of Prussia, and France was the ally of her former enemy Austria.

After Hanover had declared her neutrality, the French thrust in the west was directed against Prussia's Rhenish provinces, and Frederick the Great had to wage war on two fronts. Pitt understood that the more France became committed to the Continental war against Prussia the fewer resources she would have for the colonial and maritime war against Great Britain. Disdaining to apologize for his former ideas, he turned right about face and became the foremost advocate of Continental war. Where Newcastle had trod timidly, Pitt plunged boldly. Prussia was given financial subsidies from Great Britain to an amount which Newcastle would hardly have dared to ask; Hanover re-entered the war; and an Anglo-German army was formed under the command of Duke Ferdinand of Brunswick to check the French invasion of Germany.

All this was disconcerting to Bute and the Prince of Wales. They could not deny that Hanover must be protected because Hanover had only been attacked as a result of the Anglo-French conflict. But was it really necessary to spend so much money on Continental warfare? What had become of Pitt's prophecy that the King would be unable to sleep in his bed because of the cries of a bankrupt people? Bute had forced Pitt on the King as an opponent of 'Hanoverian measures' and now Pitt was become an advocate for the very policy he had been put in to oppose. In truth, the alliance between Bute and Pitt could not survive Pitt's assumption of office. No man could serve two masters: the King and the Prince of Wales. Bute expected Pitt to communicate to him information about government policy and decisions, and refused to take account of the adjustments and compromises

114

Pitt had to make with his colleagues in the Cabinet. The end of their alliance came in December 1758 when Pitt notified Bute – but only *ex post facto* – of the decision to renew the subsidy treaty with Prussia. The Prince of Wales was offended that he had not been informed in advance, and wrote to Bute:

I suppose you agree with me in thinking that as Mr Pitt does not now chuse to communicate what is intended to be done but defers it till executed, he might save himself the trouble of sending at all, as I should hear only a few days later, as well as other people, what measures have been taken.

Indeed, my dearest friend, he treats both you and me with no more regard than he would do a parcel of children. He seems to forget that the day will come when he must expect to be treated according to his deserts.

Reading this letter, one wonders what King George III would have said thirty years later had the younger Pitt, then his Prime Minister, leaked government secrets to the Prince of Wales?

Bute drove the Prince hard, repeatedly taxing him with indolence and threatening to leave if he did not work harder. On 25 September 1758 the Prince promised 'to throw off that incomprehensible indolence, inattention and heedlessness that reigns within me', and as late as March 1760 he is still writing about his 'natural indolence'. His letters were written to please, and perhaps they reflect Bute's ideas more than his own. Bute's approval was the reward of the Prince's efforts: Bute's displeasure the worst punishment he could incur. The intense application to his duty which marks his mature years appears early in life, at the very time when he is abjectly confessing his indolence.[20]

'I will exactly follow your advice, without which I shall inevitably sink', the Prince wrote shortly after Bute had taken up his appointment. Even at this early stage of their friendship he was already looking forward to having Bute for Prime Minister when he came to the throne. In November 1757 he wrote: 'If you are but well and Providence assists us, England may yet be free and happy'; and in July 1758: 'What a pretty pickle I should be in a future day if I had not your sagacious counsels.' While Bute coveted the post of Prime Minister ('he panted for the Treasury', writes Shelburne), he knew with one part of his mind that he was unfit for the office. Ambition and fear struggled within him. When fear gained the upper hand, he reproached his pupil for his deficiencies; and the Prince had repeatedly to protest his devotion and willingness to submit to Bute in everything. In July 1756 he wrote:

I do in the same solemn manner declare that I will defend my friend and never use evasive answers, but will always tell him whatever is said against him, and will more and more show to the world the great friendship I have for him. . . .

I am young and unexperienced and want advice. I trust in your friendship which will assist me in all difficulties. . . .

I do hope you will from this instant banish all thoughts of leaving me. . . . I have often heard you say you don't think I shall have the same friendship for you when I am married as I now have. I shall never change in that, nor will I bear to be in the least deprived of your company.

After this, one would imagine that there would have been no need for further assurances. Yet the deeper Bute plunged into politics, the greater his doubts grew. The break with Pitt in December 1758 made the Prince write:

I have pretty much turned over in my thoughts the idea you had the other night of not accepting the Treasury in a future day. The more I reflect upon it the more I see the inevitable mischiefs that would arise from your taking such a step to this poor country and consequently to myself.

A few days later he wrote again:

Perhaps it is the fear you have I shall not speak firmly enough

116

to my ministers, or that I shall be staggered if they say any-thing unexpected. As to the former, I can with certainty assure [you] that they nor no one else shall see a want of steadiness either in my manner of acting or speaking, and as to the latter I may give fifty sorts of puts offs till I have with you thoroughly considered what part will be proper to be taken.

Bute practised a subtle form of moral blackmail with the Prince.

Together with assurances of everlasting devotion, the Prince's letters are full of adulation of Bute. In December 1758 he writes: 'I have in you a friend and an able man whose integrity and ability I should do great injustice if I did not look on them as great[ly] superior to any of the politicians.' Bute was a being far above the order of politicians. 'The longer I live', the Prince declared in July 1759, shortly after he had reached his twenty-first birth-day, 'the more I shall see how little trust can be placed in most men except yourself.' A month later he told Bute: 'You are the only man with whom one's reputation and honour can with safety be entrusted.' Hand in hand with gross flattery of Bute there is equally gross abuse of Bute's enemies. 'If I am but steady and have your assistance', the Prince wrote in December 1759, 'we may make them all smart for their ingratitude.' They were 'myrmidons of the blackest die' (June 1757), 'faithless men' (May 1760). 'I look on the majority of politicians', he told Bute, no doubt echoing what Bute had told him, 'as intent on their own private interests instead of that of the public.' New-castle was the King's 'knave and counsellor'. Pitt was sarcastically referred to as 'the great orator', and on different occasions as 'a true snake in the grass' and 'the blackest of hearts'. Even the King was not spared. 'The conduct of this old King', the Prince of Wales wrote in July 1759, 'makes me ashamed of being his grandson.' Hanover, which the King loved dearer than anything in life, was 'that horrid electorate, which has always lived upon the very vitals of this poor country'. In the last year

117

of his life the King was usually referred to by his grandson as 'the old man' and the wish for his death was but faintly disguised.

The grossest abuse was lavished on Pitt. The King would die shortly; Newcastle too was an old man; but Pitt might live a long time (he did in fact live another twenty years). In 1756 Bute had patronized Pitt and treated him with a certain *de haut en bas*. By 1759 Pitt was the idol of the nation, undisputed master of the House of Commons, and secure in the confidence of the King. He no longer needed Bute. He no longer showed that deference to Bute which Bute considered was his due. Bute's pride and vanity were hurt. His services had been scorned. His advice had been ignored. Had the war gone badly, Bute could have shown condescension and pity and extended the hand of help to the prodigal. But Great Britain had triumphed wherever she had waged war. The French had been driven out of India, Canada had become a British province, the French islands in the West Indies were either taken or were at the mercy of Great Britain, the British navy rode triumphant on the seas. No British war minister, not even the great Marlborough, had ever achieved such success. And Pitt had done all this not only without Bute but in defiance of Bute. This Bute could not forgive.

In the Prince's essays Bute's jealousy of Pitt's success in waging war appears in the form of concern for the national debt. The essays are full of such phrases as these: 'the heavy debt we now labour under'; 'thus in all probability it will continue until some great calamity and a total failure of public credit rescues the nation from the depression it now lies under': 'the enormous debt the nation labours under ... and the consequential increase of grievous taxes'; 'the enormous load of debt this nation now labours under'. At the end of the Prince's essay on the reign of Henry V, Bute added this paragraph in his own hand:

118

This was a glorious reign. Henry conquered France, but had he and his successors kept it Britain had been now a Gallic province, and notwithstanding the glory accrueing to the King and nation from their success, 'tis certain this conquest was by no means an equivalent for the vast sums expended in it and the quantity of blood spilt, and this the barons, notwithstanding their aversion to France, seemed to be sensible of.

Over and over again with monotonous regularity the Prince dwelt on the increase of the national debt, with the implication that this more than offset all the victories which had been gained. National bankruptcy would be some consolation to Bute for Pitt's success.[21]

Let us remember that these letters were written by a young man, but twenty-two when he succeeded to the throne, to the one friend whose good opinion he valued. It is distasteful to read such calumnies on those responsible for the conduct of the most successful war in British history. As no reproof is known to have come from Bute – and the repetition of these sentiments shows that no reproof ever did come – we must presume that these are what Bute wished to hear from his pupil. Was it fitting for the heir to the throne to write in this way about the most distinguished statesman of the age? Was it fitting of the Prince's tutor to encourage him? Bute could have reminded his pupil that Newcastle with all his weaknesses and follies had served the house of Hanover for more than forty years with unswerving loyalty and at the expense of his personal fortune. That Pitt with all his pride and aloofness had raised the nation from the depths of despair to the heights of glory. That the Prince would soon occupy the position which the King now held and would expect to be treated with that respect from his heir which he himself had so signally failed to show to his grandfather.

All these Bute could have told the Prince, yet did not. His failure marks the degree of his unfitness to be a prince's tutor. On the strictly academic plane, Bute was a

119

good teacher. He won the confidence of his pupil and encouraged him to learn. On the political plane, he taught the Prince no more than what were the accepted ideas about the British constitution. But on a higher plane – that of preparing the boy for kingship – he allowed his own vanity and jealousy to obscure the true interests of his pupil. He read with pleasure the letters in which the Prince flattered him and abused his enemies. He saw the Prince as undeveloped and malleable and he tried to shape his character. Under his direction the Prince became a tool to further Bute's ambition and to revenge himself on those who had outstripped him in the race for power. To the pride of birth and rank, Bute added a soul-destroying pride in his own intellectual powers and an undue contempt for those who disagreed with him.

Yet Bute had little more understanding of statecraft than the boy whom he undertook to teach. He had never sat in the House of Commons and for only four years in the House of Lords. He had never essayed the task of trying to win the confidence of his fellow citizens. He had no understanding of the compromises a statesman must make to implement his policy and no experience of having to defend his policy before a representative assembly. He saw politics in terms of abstract ideas which he equated with morality. Those who agreed with him were good men, those who did not were wicked. He failed to make allowances for human folly and human frailty. He failed to see that no politician is wholly good or wholly bad – that even the best do not neglect their personal interests and even the worst are not entirely oblivious to the public welfare. He failed to understand that the art of politics is the management of men and foreign affairs or finance merely its subject matter.

He imagined that all the evils which existed in the British political system were the result of human wickedness and could be cured by the accession of a sovereign of high moral character, conscious of his responsibilities and advised by a man of learning and virtue. In September 1759, on the death of the Prince's sister Princess Elizabeth, Bute wrote a letter of condolence to his pupil:

You are the second person in a most extensive polished empire; you will please God be the first. To act so supreme a part well is perhaps the height of human wisdom, and yet virtue, religion, joined to nobility of sentiment, will support a prince better and make a people happier than all the abilities of an Augustus with the heart of a Tiberius. The inference I draw from this is that a prince ought to endeavour in all his thoughts to excel his people in virtue, piety, generosity, nobility of sentiment; that when they have occasion to approach him they may do it with love and veneration; and feel he merits by his own virtue and not the fickle die of fortune the vast superiority he enjoys above them.

These were admirable sentiments which the Prince took to heart. His letters are full of repetitions of them. His sole ambition, he declared, was to restore 'my much loved country to her ancient state of liberty, of seeing her in time free from her present load of debts, and again famous for being the residence of true piety and virtue'. 'If vice and faction can be got the better of', he wrote on 11 August 1758, 'this nation will again appear in her ancient lustre'; and a few days later: 'Attempting with vigour to restore religion and virtue when I mount the throne, this great country will probably regain her ancient state of lustre.' One can be reasonably certain that any phrase which is repeated in the Prince's letters came originally from Bute.

Perhaps the best statement of Bute's political creed was that which the Prince put into his essay on the British political system:[22]

Let the day once come in which the banner of virtue, honour and liberty shall be displayed, that noble actions and generous sentiments shall lead to the royal favour, and prostitution of principle, venality and corruption meet their just reward, the honest citizen, the zealous patriot, will lift up their heads, all good men will unite in support of a government built on the firm foundations of liberty and virtue, and even the degenerate mercenary sons of slavery will suppress their thoughts, and worship outwardly the generous maxims of a prince, while they in secret detest his maxims and tremble at his virtues. Power, wealth, and honours still remain the favourite objects, but let the royal fiat change, the road revive, the long un-trodden path, and crowds of all denominations will soon frequent it, and a generous reformation will ensue. ... The prince once possessed of the nation's confidence, the people's love, will be feared and respected abroad, adored at home by mixing private economy with public magnificence. He will silence every clamour, be able to apply proper remedies to the heavy taxes that oppress the people, and lay a sure foundation for diminishing the enormous debt that weighs this country down and preys upon its vitals.

This was the path which King George III tried to follow through life. The wise may smile and with reason: the art of politics is not so simple. Yet despite countless disap-pointments and disillusionments at the hands of the politicians and even of his own sons, King George adhered to this simple creed and continued to set an example of morality and duty until he seems at times the guileless fool in the magic garden of eighteenth-century politics. And perhaps in the long run the nation gained from Bute's teaching and the King's practice.*

King George has been depicted as a neurotic and un-stable character, unable to adjust himself to reality, and his letters to Bute have been cited as evidence. Rather do they show Bute as unable to adjust himself to reality, as living in a world of fantasy. The Prince's error was in seeing mankind solely through Bute's eyes. His idealism, his anxiety to do his duty, his limited acquaintance with men – all these led him to Bute. Bute's piety, his concern for his pupil, his hatred of all that was mean and low in the politics of the time, completed the conquest. King

*See note 2, p. 608.

George III was slow to mature, but when he did he retained all that was sound in Bute's teaching and rejected all that was sententious and selfish. Bute, however, never grew up. The tragedy of this high-minded and well-meaning man – for despite the abuse lavished on him during his lifetime and the criticism heaped upon him since his death, Bute was both high-minded and well-meaning – is that of all who draw their understanding of humanity from books and are proud of their knowledge. He believed that because he had read history he could teach a boy how to become a King and that the example of piety in the monarch will induce virtue in the people. We should not be surprised that King George at the age of seventeen accepted this naive creed. Boys of seventeen today, with more opportunities of learning about the world than ever he had, accept creeds equally naive and far more dangerous. The wonder is that he outgrew it.

In February 1759 the Duke of Brunswick again raised the question of his daughter's marriage and the Prince of Wales again rejected it. 'Though there should not be another princess in Germany likely to make me happy', he wrote to Bute, 'I would never consent to take one out of that house.' After this no more was said.

On 4 June 1759 the Prince celebrated his twenty-first birthday, and on 13 November, at the opening of the session of Parliament, took his seat in the House of Lords. He was as yet little known even in the small circle of London society. Apart from formal appearances at Court and visits to the theatre and opera, he did not go out in London, but lived in private mostly at Kew. His younger brothers dined out and attended balls, and Prince Edward in particular became very popular. He was attractive to women and liked to flirt, and they felt flattered when a prince of the blood showed his attentions. But Prince Edward was no mere ladies' man. He had spirit and courage, and in the summer of 1758 obtained permission to serve on the expedition to St Malo. The following year, when the French invasion was expected, he made a long tour through the west of England; and on 13 July 1759 wrote to the Prince of Wales from Exeter:

I am led to lament very much that it is not convenient to you at present to take a tour, as it is impossible for you to imagine the effect it would have on all ranks of people, not one person in the country but would be proud of being first to shew his zeal and attachment to your person.[23]

A week later, on 20 July, the Prince wrote to offer his services to the King:

I beg leave to lay myself at Your Majesty's feet, humbly to offer up a petition in the success of which I feel extremely interested. While the country remained in tranquillity I thought my time best employed in acquiring a thorough knowledge of all matters peculiarly suited to my situation; but now that every part of the nation is arming for its defence, I cannot bear the thoughts of continuing in this inactive state. . . .

Permit me, therefore, humbly to request of Your Majesty to give me an opportunity of convincing the world that I am neither unworthy of my high situation nor of the blood that fills my veins. Your Majesty's known valour will diffuse its influence on my head and make the presence of your grandson an encouragement to your people, a terror to the enemy, and joined to his own resolution may in some measure supply his want of experience in military affairs, and enable him to support with dignity the post of danger, which he esteems the post of honour.

King and ministers were puzzled how to deal with this letter. 'The King asked me what answer he should return', wrote Newcastle, '*and said, he wants to be rising.*' Both Newcastle and the King believed that this was an application for the appointment of Commander-in-Chief, and Lady Yarmouth that it was prompted by fear that in the event of invasion the King would recall the Duke of Cumberland. The King referred the letter to the cabinet and instructed them to draft a reply for his approval.

It was delicate work; and between the surliness of the old King and the prickliness of the young Prince there was little room to manoeuvre. When no reply came after a week, the Prince wrote to Bute:

The King and those he has consulted have treated [me] with less regard than they would have dared to have done any Member of Parliament. I hope you will agree with me in thinking that if this just request is refused that for my own honour, dignity, and character, I may keep no measures with these counsellors who have not prevented the King treating me with such unheard of contempt.

Bute hastened to see Pitt and told him this was a matter the Prince had much at heart. Pitt was genuinely sympathetic and pleased that the Prince had offered his services. He pleaded with the cabinet that the King should be advised to return a kind answer. If the request met with a downright refusal 'every man in England would blame it, except those who were known to be attached to the Duke of Cumberland'. The King's reply, drafted by Pitt, Newcastle, and Holdernesse (Pitt's colleague as Secretary of State) was non-committal:

I received your letter which is a mark of duty to me, and have the highest satisfaction in your spirit and zeal for the defence of my kingdoms. It is my intention to give you on a proper occasion an opportunity of exerting them.

And this was how the Prince showed his respect to his grandfather:

You will see by His Majesty's letter [he wrote to Bute on 28 July] how shuffling it is and unworthy of a British monarch. The conduct of this old King makes me ashamed of being his grandson. He treats me in the same manner as his knave and counsellor the Duke of Newcastle does all people. For this answer by some may be looked upon as agreeing to my petition, by those who think further as an absolute refusal.

Bute complained to Pitt 'that something more was expected to be done', but did not say what. To his colleagues Pitt 'lamented the very recluse manner in which the Prince lived', and suggested that 'any occasion of bringing him out, of showing him, should be readily embraced'. 'He should never make his court to the Prince of Wales by proposing anything that could really affect the King's authority, but that he thought trifles were to be complied with.' It was impossible to appoint a young man of twenty-one with no previous military experience to the command of the army at a time when invasion was expected. But why should not the Prince accompany the Commander-in-Chief when he inspected the troops and learn something of military affairs under his guidance? Lord Ligonier, who had succeeded Cumberland, was a veteran of Marlborough's wars and would be an ideal instructor for the Prince. Pitt proposed 'that the King should order the Prince of Wales to review the regiments of Guards, to go to Chatham lines or the camp at Portsmouth, but always with Lord Ligonier', and afterwards to report to the King on the state of the troops.

Pitt pressed this on Newcastle. Newcastle, aware that it would be disliked by the King, consulted Lady Yarmouth who also urged it. Newcastle plucked up courage. 'At first I had an absolute negative', he wrote, 'with many pretty strong expressions' (the King could be direct in speech when annoyed). Newcastle persisted, but all he could get from the King was: 'Well, we will talk about it when you return from Sussex.' During the next few weeks the subject repeatedly crops up in Newcastle's notes for audiences with the King, but the King was so opposed to the idea that nothing could be done.

Pitt received no thanks from Bute or the Prince for what he had tried to do. His conduct was insolent, the Prince wrote to Bute: 'He has long shown a want of regard both of you, my dearest friend, and consequently of myself.' Bute did not tell the Prince – or if he did, failed to convince him – that Pitt had proposed a more suitable role for him than the command of the army, and that Newcastle had strained his credit with the King to serve the Prince. Bute did nothing to alleviate the bitterness in the Prince's soul. The deeper that bitterness grew, the more Bute rose in the Prince's esteem.[24]

On 30 July the Prince had an audience of the King, which in Newcastle's words lasted 'some seconds'. The King merely said that he would send for the Prince when the need arose and the Prince said nothing. He had the wild idea of offering himself as a volunteer to serve with the army as Prince Edward was with the navy. 'I really cannot remain immured at home like a girl', he wrote to Bute, 'whilst all my countrymen are preparing for the field and a brother younger than me allowed to go in quest of the enemy.' Prince Edward at that moment was on board the *Ramillies* in the squadron under the command of Rear-Admiral George Rodney which had been sent to Le Havre to destroy the French invasion barges. He wrote regularly to his brother about his experiences and his letters increased the Prince of Wales's jealousy and bitterness.

There can be no doubt that the Prince genuinely wished to serve his country. There can be equally no doubt that his application was prompted by Bute for political purposes. Less than twelve months later a similar application to serve by the Prince's second brother, Prince William Henry, met with the Prince's grave displeasure:

This is to acquaint you [the Prince wrote to Bute in April 1760] that my brother will presently call on you as he told me. He acquainted me that as I would not agree to his going in the army, I must permit him now to say that the reason he did not offer to go abroad was because I disapproved of it. I answered that as to his going abroad or ever being in the army, he very well knew I never would agree to it; and as to his publicly declaring I would not permit him, that I forbid him to bandy my name about. That he had again been set on by men who were his enemies, for that his conduct in this as well as the rest of his life was very different from what it ought to be towards

127

his eldest brother, who would be his King and who had always had too much tenderness for him.

The Prince could be as 'insolent' as Pitt when crossed. Forty years later, at an even graver crisis, another Prince of Wales asked permission of another King to go on active service; and the future King George IV received the same answer in 1798 from his father as the future King George III had received in 1759 from his grandfather. As Mr Romney Sedgwick remarks, this was a move 'which instinctively occurred to heirs apparent of the period as a means of embarrassing the government in a national emergency'. Which does not mean that Prince Frederick in 1745 or Prince George in 1759 or the Prince of Wales in 1798 were insincere in their wish to serve the nation.

In the last year of King George II's reign a succession of incidents occurred, each of which was seized upon by the Prince as a fresh cause of offence. When Lord George Sackville was dismissed the army and forbidden the Court for disobedience of orders at the battle of Minden, the Prince took up his cause and declared he would receive Sackville at his levee. But this was going too far, and Bute had the sense to see that public opinion was against Sackville and such a deliberate insult to the King would only bring discredit on the Prince. Again, when Lord Temple applied for the Garter without informing the Prince, this was considered as an unjustifiable instance of neglect. Henry Bilson Legge, Chancellor of the Exchequer, incurred the Prince's lasting enmity by daring to contest Hampshire against a candidate favoured by Bute. For this he was dismissed from office shortly after the Prince came to the throne – a piece of petty spite which reflects credit on neither Bute nor the Prince. In March 1760 the Prince was displeased when Prince Edward applied for a peerage without consulting him. 'Various slights and indignities are daily laid upon me', he wrote to

128

Bute in the spring of 1760, 'from people from whom I might have expected a different conduct. It is therefore impossible for me to bear them any longer, some public mark must be given of my disapproving it. I am ready to take any part my dearest friend can propose to me, the more active the better.' Really, one might almost conclude from this that the Prince was planning a coup d'etat against his grandfather! The spectacle of youth impatient to succeed age is not edifying. At no time in his long life does George III appear in a less pleasing light than during these last few months of his grandfather's reign.[24]

The Prince and Bute had many serious conversations during the winter of 1759–60 and politics was not always the subject of their talk. It may be that the Prince's increased bitterness towards the King and the ministers was the consequence of a crisis in his personal life. He had become conscious of the opposite sex. Scott had written of him at the age of eighteen that he had 'the greatest temptation to be gallant with the ladies, who lay themselves out in the most shamful manner to draw him in' – hitherto to no purpose. Three years later the temptation had increased, as he confessed to Bute:

You have often accused me of growing grave and thoughtful. It is entirely owing to a daily increasing admiration of the fair sex, which I am attempting with all the philosophy and resolution I am capable of to keep under. Princes when once in their hands make miserable figures. . . . When I have said this you will plainly feel how strong a struggle there is between the boiling youth of twenty-one years and prudence. The last I hope will ever keep the upper hand, indeed if I can weather it but a few years marriage will put a stop to this combat in my breast. I believe you will agree with me that application is the only aid I can give to reason, that by keeping the mind constantly employed is a likely means of preserving those passions in due subordination to it. Believe me, I will with the greatest assiduity attempt to make all that progress which your good counsels, if properly attended to, have reason to expect.

In November 1759 the Prince fell in love with Lady Sarah Lennox, sister of the Duke of Richmond and sister-in-law of Henry Fox. She was only fifteen and was making her first appearance at Court. She was a girl of great personal charms. 'She had the finest complexion, most beautiful hair, and prettiest person that ever was seen', wrote Fox. 'She is everything I can form to myself lovely', wrote the Prince to Bute.

I am daily grown unhappy, sleep has left me which never was before interrupted by reverse of fortune. I protest before God I never have had any improper thought with regard to her. I don't deny with often having flattered myself with hopes that one day or other you would consent to my raising her to a throne. Thus I mince nothing to you. The other day I heard it suggested as if the Duke of Marlborough made up to her. I shifted my grief till retired to my chamber, where I remained for several hours in the depth of despair. . . .

Having now laid the whole before you I submit my happiness to you who are the best of friends, whose friendship I value if possible above my love for the most charming of her sex; if you can give me no hopes how to be happy I surrender my fortune into your hands, and will keep my thoughts even from the dear object of my love, grieve in silence, and never trouble you more with this unhappy tale; for if I must either lose my friend or my love, I will give up the latter, for I esteem your friendship above every earthly joy.

He must have had a pretty good idea of what Bute would say, for he concluded his letter:

On the whole let me preserve your friendship, and though my heart should break, I shall have the happy reflexion in dying that I have not been altogether unworthy of the best of friends though unfortunate in other things.

Pray let me have a line from you tonight.

Bute replied immediately, promising to give the matter his most careful consideration but holding out no hopes:

Think, Sir, in the mean time, who you are, what is your birth right, what you wish to be, and prepare your mind with a resolution to hear the voice of truth, for such alone shall come from me, however painful the office, duty and friendship and a thousand other ties commands me, and I will obey though death looked me in the face.

Bute could never resist a touch of melodrama. But to his honour, he did tell the Prince the truth; and the Prince at no time of his life shrank from facing unpleasant truths.

The interest of my country ever shall be my first care, my own inclinations shall ever submit to it. I am born for the happiness or misery of a great nation, and consequently must often act contrary to my passions.

Here, in one sentence, is King George III's acceptance of his responsibilities as a constitutional monarch, of his duty to subordinate his personal feelings to the welfare of his subjects. Whatever mistakes Bute had made, he had given him a true idea of his constitutional position. There can be no doubt that in this particular case he gave good advice. The Prince would not have been happy with Lady Sarah nor she with him. It was an infatuation which he soon forgot: calf love. In the political situation of 1760 it would have been highly imprudent for him to have married a woman so closely connected with a leading politician as Lady Sarah was with Henry Fox. It would to begin with have immediately antagonized Pitt, and raised the darkest suspicions among those (and they were many) who regarded Fox not without reason as the most unscrupulous politician of the age. As events turned out, the Prince had quite sufficient political confusion to face when he came to the throne. But that confusion would have been worse confounded had he been the brother-in-law of Henry Fox and the Duke of Richmond.

'I should wish we could next summer', he wrote to Bute, after the idea of marrying Lady Sarah had been dropped, 'by some method or other get some account of the various princesses in Germany. That binds me to nothing, and would save a great deal of trouble when ever I consent to enter into those bonds.' Bute seems to have understood by this that the Prince intended to marry shortly, but the Prince set him straight:

I can never agree to alter my situation whilst this old man lives. I will rather undergo anything ever so disagreeable than put my trust in him for a single moment in an affair of such delicacy.

Everything had to wait for King George II's death.*

*See note 3, p. 609.

Chapter 3

POLITICAL APPRENTICESHIP

King George II died at Kensington Palace at about half-past seven in the morning of 25 October 1760. Death came to him swiftly and without warning. He had gone to bed the previous night in good health and spirits. In the morning he was awakened at his usual hour, drank his cup of chocolate, and went to make his toilet. His valet heard an unusual noise, returned to investigate, and found the King lying insensible on the floor. In falling he had cut his face against the edge of a bureau. A doctor was summoned and pronounced life extinct.[1]

At that moment the Prince of Wales, then at Kew, was setting out for his morning ride accompanied by some of his servants. They had crossed Kew Bridge and were making for Gunnersbury when they were overtaken by a messenger with a note from the King's valet informing the Prince that an accident had happened to the King.* Nothing was said of the King's death, which had not been confirmed when the messenger left Kensington. The Prince turned his horse's head and went back to Kew, giving for reason that the horse was lame; and at Kew he wrote a letter to Bute who was living close by. After relating the incident, the Prince concluded: 'I thought I had no time to lose in acquainting my dear friend of this. I have ordered all the servants that were out to be silent about what had passed as they value their employments, and shall wait till I hear from you to know what further must be done.' Hardly had this note been despatched when there arrived a letter from Princess Amelia to say that the King was dead. The new King immediately ordered his coach and set out to consult Bute.

*See note 4, p. 609.

October 25th was a Saturday, and most of the ministers had gone into the country for the week-end. The Duke of Newcastle was at Claremont, his seat at Esher in Surrey, and his closest colleague Lord Hardwicke was in Cambridgeshire. Pitt was the only cabinet minister in London and he too was about to depart for the country. His coach was standing at the door of his house in St James's Square (now the Royal Institute of International Affairs) when he received a summons from Lady Yarmouth to come at once to Kensington. There Pitt saw Princess Amelia and learnt of the King's death. His first action was to send messengers to all Privy Councillors in the neighbourhood of London summoning them to Kensington Palace, after which he drove to Kew. He saw Bute at about ten o'clock and the King an hour or so later, but nothing passed beyond formal condolences and compliments. The King 'with a grave and manly deportment', told Pitt that 'he felt how unequal he was to the load now come upon his youth, but that he doubted not he would have the assistance of all honest men, where unanimity was indispensably necessary at so critical a conjuncture'.

It is worth noting that Pitt was the first minister to see the new King and that he did so in response to a summons from the late King's mistress. Newcastle, on learning of King George II's death, had set out for Kensington, but was met by a messenger on the road and re-directed to Carlton House. Like Pitt, he saw Bute first, and only then was admitted into the King's presence. He described his reception in a letter to Hardwicke:

[The King] began by telling me that he desired to see me before he went to council, that he had always had a very good opinion of me; he knew my constant zeal for his family and my duty to his grandfather, which he thought would be pledges or proofs of my zeal for him. I said very truly that no one subject His Majesty had wished him more ease, honour, tranquillity, and success in the high station to which Providence had called him, and I can't think I shew my zeal to my

134

late royal master better than by contributing the little in my power to the ease and success of his grandson and successor. His Majesty said these remarkable words: 'My Lord Bute is your very good friend; he will tell you my thoughts at large', to which I only replied that I thought my Lord Bute was so.

Thus both Pitt and Newcastle were complimented by the King on the day of his accession and given to understand that their services would be valued in the new reign. Yet both were left in no doubt that Bute was to be the power behind the throne.

Everything went wrong on the first day of King George III's reign. Pitt had called the Privy Council to Kensington Palace, but the King decided that his first council should take place at his own residence, Savile House. Then, because his servants were at Kew, he changed the place of meeting to Carlton House, which since 1756 had been his mother's residence. (He avoided having the council at Kensington, where the late King's body lay, or at St James's.) What with orders and counter-orders considerable confusion resulted. The Duke of Cumberland, who had travelled up from Windsor, first went to Kensington, next to Savile House, and was finally re-directed to Carlton House. It was not until six o'clock in the evening that the Privy Council met to sign the proclamation of the King's accession and to hear his address.

This was the moment for which Bute had so long waited and for which he had so carefully prepared. He knew what had happened in 1727 when Sir Spencer Compton, King George II's minister designate, had been unable to draft the King's speech and had been compelled to ask for advice from his rival Sir Robert Walpole. Bute was determined not to be caught out. He had the King's address in his pocket, prepared well in advance, and during the day he had been able to give it the final revision. Before the Council met, the King showed it to Newcastle and the two Secretaries of State and ordered the Duke to read it aloud. 'Is there anything wrong in

135

point of form?' asked the King. 'We all bowed', continues Newcastle's account, 'and went out of the closet.' Then Pitt told Newcastle that he had not heard the address distinctly, particularly the last few words, and the Duke repeated them from memory.

This was the King's address as drafted by Bute:

The loss that I and the nation have sustained by the death of the King my grandfather would have been severely felt at any time, but coming at so critical a juncture, and so unexpected, it is by many circumstances augmented and the weight now falling upon me much increased: I feel my own insufficiency to support it as I wish: but animated by the tenderest affection for this my native country and depending on the advice, experience, and abilities of your Lordships, on the support and assistance of every honest man, I enter with cheerfulness into this arduous situation, and shall make it the business of my life to promote in everything the glory and happiness of these kingdoms, and to preserve and strengthen both the constitution in Church and State, and as I mount the throne in the midst of a bloody war, I shall endeavour to prosecute it in the manner most likely to bring an honourable and lasting peace.

In form there was nothing wrong with this draft: in substance there was to Pitt's mind a great deal. He objected to the last sentence, the one which he had desired Newcastle to repeat. After the King had read the address to the Privy Council, Pitt proposed that before it be published certain alterations should be made. He wanted the phrase 'a bloody war' changed to 'an expensive but just and necessary war' and the words 'in concert with our allies' added at the end. This would have transformed the address into a justification of Pitt's war policy and would have pledged Great Britain not to make peace without Prussia. Bute protested, asked why Pitt had not objected to the address when first read, and hinted that it was now too late to make changes. But Pitt was unexpectedly supported by his old antagonist Lord Mansfield, who said that as the address was in the King's hand he might alter it if he wished. No one was prepared to combat Pitt or to contradict the Lord Chief Justice. But it was only with extreme reluctance and under pressure from Bute that the King accepted the amendments.

Henry Fox criticized the conduct of the first Privy Council of King George III's reign, and complained 'that the use of form was never more seen than on this day'. But there appears to have been one glaring irregularity which neither Fox nor anyone else noticed. What was Bute doing there? He was not sworn a member of the Privy Council until 27 October, two days later, and had no right to be present at the meeting on the 25th. In fact the list of those who attended as published in the *London Gazette* the following day does not include Bute's name. Perhaps, though present at Carlton House, he did not attend the formal meeting of the Privy Council, and the altercation between Pitt and Bute took place after the council had ended. Whatever may be the explanation of Bute's presence, it was a constitutional irregularity and marked in the clearest possible way that Bute was to be the minister in the new reign.

It was past seven when the council ended, and Bute drew Pitt aside and asked to see him in private. He wanted to make a deal with Pitt, and proposed that they should 'bury in oblivion all that was past' and work together for the good of the King and the nation. He professed to have laid aside all thought of becoming head of the Treasury – he wished merely to be a 'private man', the King's personal friend and confidential adviser. He would enter upon business with Pitt 'with the same spirit as if nothing had ever interrupted their friendship', and he even declared his approbation of Pitt's conduct of the war.

Had Bute really understood Pitt's character, he would have known that this was quite the wrong approach. Pitt was not to be won by reminiscences of past friendship or assurances of future support. A bully himself, he was amenable only to a bigger bully. He told Bute plainly that his 'advancement to the management of the affairs of this country would not be for His Majesty's service'. Of himself, Pitt said:

He must act as an independent minister or not at all, that his politics were like his religion which would admit of no accommodation. That if the system of the war was to undergo the least change or shadow of a change he could no longer be of any service. . . .

Thus Pitt set the course he was to follow during the next few years. They parted, each displeased with the other. For Bute it had been a bad day.

The best hope of political stability at the outset of the new reign lay in an alliance between Bute, the minister of the King, and Pitt, the minister of the House of Commons. But such an alliance demanded compromises and adjustments on both sides, and these Pitt was not willing to make. It would not have been easy to have worked with Bute, but every statesman has to work with colleagues with whom, given a free choice, he would gladly dispense, and compromises and adjustments are part of the art of statesmanship. Pitt refused even to make the attempt. He insisted that the war should be conducted as it had been under the late reign, irrespective of changing circumstances, the views of his colleagues or even of the King. He would be 'an independent minister'. What was this but a demand that he should be master, his colleagues subordinates, and the King a cipher? Under any system of government those in charge of a nation's affairs have to work together as a team. Pitt bears a heavy share of responsibility for the political confusion of the early years of King George III's reign. It is a sad commentary on his statesmanship.[2]

Bute then requested Newcastle to remain as head of the Treasury. Newcastle first pleaded his age; next, consulted his friends, hoping that their avowed opinions would accord with his real wishes; and finally, after having been assured by Bute of his support, agreed to remain. Bute was declared Groom of the Stole and a member of the cabinet. His position as 'favourite and adviser' (the phrase of the Duke of Devonshire) was recognized by all. 'Lord Bute told Mr Pitt', Devonshire wrote in his diary two days after the King had succeeded to the throne, 'that the King would have no [cabinet] meetings at which [Bute] was not present and that for the future everything should be considered and debated in his presence, and then His Majesty would determine as he thought proper.' In February 1761 Bute said to Lord Temple: 'I suppose your Lordship does not mean to look upon me as a bare Groom of the Stole — the King will have it otherwise.' To which Temple replied: 'I look upon you as a minister, and desire to act with you as such.' In place of the Newcastle–Pitt Coalition, uneasy enough at the best of times, there succeeded the coalition of Newcastle, Pitt, and Bute, a triple-headed monstrosity, each partner of which was jealous of the other two.

The cards were stacked in Bute's favour, had he known how to play the game. Newcastle, despite his protestations, was anxious to keep his place. He had been in office almost continuously since the accession of the house of Hanover. Office was his delight and his passion. He could not imagine life without it. Unlike Pitt, it was not the responsibility but the appearance of power which he craved. Bute could not have had a more accommodating ally. 'Trifles pleased him', wrote the King to Bute, reporting a conversation with Devonshire about Newcastle. 'A little seeming good humour from me, and your telling him things before he hears them from others, are the sure maxims to keep him in order, for nothing is so hateful to him as the thoughts of retiring.' (The King was already learning things from other sources than Bute.) Moreover, Newcastle was sixty-seven in 1760 and could not expect many more years of active political life. An alliance between Newcastle and Bute directed against Pitt would have been entirely to Bute's advantage. Bute would have taken over Newcastle's empire without fuss or bother.

Bute, in Shelburne's words, 'felt all the pleasure of power to consist in punishing or astonishing'. What was to be done now his pupil was King and himself one of the most powerful men in the nation, he had no idea. Before the King came to the throne he had complained of the responsibilities facing him. 'Why am I doomed to climb ambition's steep and rocky height', he had written to a friend, 'who early in life had the meanest opinion of politicians?' And in March 1763, when he resigned the office he would never have held but for the favour of the King, he told Fox: 'The end of my labours was solemnly determined even before I undertook them.' 'The theatricals which had originally introduced him to Leicester House', writes Sir Lewis Namier, 'were his proper element: sense of reality he had none.' It is difficult not to feel for the King, young, inexperienced, and naive, trapped between Pitt who coveted power for a purpose and Bute who coveted power for the purpose of renouncing it, with Newcastle flitting between them like an *ignis fatuus* – all light and little substance.

Bute understood neither his own interest nor that of the King. When Devonshire told him that so long as the war lasted Pitt could not be dispensed with and therefore some management should be held towards him, Bute answered: 'My Lord, I would not for the world the King should hear such language, he would not bear it a moment.' 'Not bear it!' replied Devonshire, with the good sense of a sound Whig. 'He must bear it! Every King must make use of human means to attain human ends or his affairs will go to ruin.' Here was the authentic voice of Whiggism explaining the facts of political life to the theorist and speculator. The King began to learn these when he renounced Lady Sarah Lennox and the next few years were to teach him more. But Bute never learnt them. He explained to Devonshire that he did not mean that the

King would not listen to advice or 'be told what means were necessary for his service, but that he would not suffer to have his prerogative touched in so tender a point as to be told who he was to speak to'. The damage had been done however, and the legend of King George III's high prerogative notions was on its way to becoming part of Whig mythology.

Things were not running as Bute had expected, and the King had not been on the throne a month before he had to defend himself against the reproaches of his favourite.

He [Bute] seemed last night to blame me for not taking a more spirited part [wrote the King]. Let him with justice say whether I have not from the first day of my mounting the throne wished for his consent to get rid of those who are unwilling to do their duty. Was I not very adverse to the altering my declaration? and I plainly see that if every ill humour of a certain man [Pitt] is to be soothed, that in less than a couple of months I shall be irretrievably in his fetters; a state of bondage that an old man of seventy odd groaned and that twenty-two ought to risk everything rather than submit.

It is difficult to know precisely when the King began to become disillusioned with Bute. More than forty years later he gave George Rose an account of the events of the first day of his reign, which shows to what extent in 1804 he wished to obliterate from his mind the recollection of his friendship with Bute. According to this, when the King learnt of his grandfather's death he warned his mother 'in the warmest manner to say nothing on the subject to Lord Bute, lest he should entertain some notion of endeavouring to be placed in a political situation'. Newcastle and Devonshire were blamed for bringing Bute into the Cabinet as a counterpoise to Pitt, against the wishes of the King who claimed he had a low opinion of Bute's political ability. The King remarked that Newcastle had suggested Bute for Secretary of State but forgot it was at his own prompting. As we have seen, the first thing he did when he heard of his grandfather's death was to consult Bute. The King's conversation with Rose in 1804 shows the power of the human mind to forget what is distasteful. It took the King at least six years to realize Bute's incapacity, though the knowledge must have been growing on him for some time. And perhaps the first seeds of doubt were sown in the early days of the reign.

On 26 October, the day following his accession, George III was proclaimed King by Garter King of Arms at Savile House, Charing Cross, Temple Bar, Cheapside, and the Royal Exchange, under the style 'George the Third, by the Grace of God King of Great Britain, France, and Ireland, Defender of the Faith, and so forth'. The British claim to the throne of France, which dated back to Edward III and had long since been abandoned, still appeared in the royal style, while the King's German dignities were left to be inferred.*

The King made a good impression in public. He had grace and dignity and none of the surliness which his grandfather had sometimes shown. 'His person is tall and full of dignity', wrote Horace Walpole, 'his countenance florid and good-natured; his manner is graceful and obliging; he expresses no warmth, nor resentment against anybody; at most, coldness.' Walpole professed no good opinion of royalty, but admitted that the King seemed 'the most amiable young man in the world'. A few weeks after his accession he was thrown from his horse and bruised his head and shoulders, but insisted on going to the theatre that night as usual.

To the Duke of Cumberland, the dreaded ogre of his boyhood, the King was particularly gracious, a courtesy which the Duke appreciated. He told the Duke that it was his wish to live well with all his family and that it would not be his fault if this were not so. He would not allow his brother Prince Edward (now Duke of York and heir presumptive) to be mentioned in the prayer for the Royal

*See note 5, p. 610.

Family because the Duke of York would have had precedence over his uncle. The funeral of King George II was conducted with respect and reverence (the King according to custom not being present). He told Devonshire 'that he should resent any neglect shown to the late King just the same as was done to himself'. King George II's testamentary dispositions were scrupulously carried out, and a large sum of money destined for Lady Yarmouth was placed in her hands.

King George III was the first unmarried monarch to ascend the throne since the restoration of Charles II, and there was naturally much speculation about his choice of a bride. This was restricted by both British and German law. The Act of Settlement laid down that the King could not marry a Roman Catholic, and the law of the Holy Roman Empire decreed that as Elector of Hanover he must marry into a princely house. The King therefore looked to Germany for a bride and shortly after his accession began to make inquiries about suitable princesses. The task was entrusted to Baron Munchhausen, Hanoverian representative in London, and his brother, one of the King's ministers in Hanover. The strictest secrecy was enjoined and kept. Bute was the only British minister consulted. The cabinet knew nothing of what was going on until the King announced his choice. It seems likely that the Princess Dowager was kept informed but her advice was neither asked nor proffered. The King kept the business in his own hands and his choice was entirely his own.[3]

The principal qualities the King desired in his bride were a pleasant disposition, a good understanding, and the ability to bear children. He did not ask for beauty, though no doubt other things being equal he would have preferred a pretty to a plain woman. He did not want a wife with intellectual interests and above all he did not want a wife with a disposition to meddle in politics. There was to be no petticoat government during his reign. With

143

these criteria in mind, a list of nubile German Protestant princesses was compiled in Hanover and sent over for the King's consideration. It contained six names. Princess Charlotte of Mecklenburg Strelitz, the eventual choice, was not among them.

Bute's comment on seeing the list was that he would like the King to select one of the princesses of the house of Brandenburg. Brandenburg was connected politically and dynastically with the house of Brunswick, and such a choice would facilitate a match between the Hereditary Prince of Brunswick and the King's sister, Princess Augusta – a match which would be popular in England, and which in fact took place three years later. The King remarked only on the Princess of Saxe Gotha, his mother's niece and his own cousin. She was said to be fond of 'philosophy', and the King said that he did not wish to marry a woman of such tastes. Bute thus favoured a connection with the house of Brunswick on which King George II had set his heart, while the King rejected an alliance with his mother's family. The incident illustrates how little influence the Princess Dowager had over her son's choice.

The list was returned and Munchhausen was asked for more information. On 20 November 1760 he added two further names: the Princess of Denmark, who was however believed to be already promised; and the Princess of Mecklenburg Strelitz, of whom he knew nothing. The future Queen Charlotte appeared at the end of the list almost as an afterthought, and very much an outsider in the matrimonial stakes.

The King now drew up a short list. The Princess of Anhalt Dessau was rejected because her grandfather had married an apothecary's daughter, and this mésalliance might introduce a complication into the succession of her issue to any state of the Empire. (The King, though he 'gloried in the name of Britain', took care to select a bride who would be acceptable in Germany.) The Princess of

144

Brandenburg, her first cousin and Bute's choice, was rejected for the same reason. It was also said that her mother had been imprisoned after having an affair with a courier. Princess Frederica of Saxe Gotha, the King's cousin, besides being addicted to 'philosophy' was deformed and thought to be unable to bear children (she died unmarried in 1776 at the age of thirty-five). After these three had been struck out, the field was restricted to four runners: the princesses of Brandenburg Schwedt, Hesse Darmstadt, Brunswick Wolfenbuttel, and Mecklenburg Strelitz. Again, the future Queen was placed bottom of the list. Munchhausen considered that she had been brought up at too small a court to qualify for the position of Queen of Great Britain. Of these four, the Princess of Brunswick, sister of the girl whom the King had rejected in 1755, was virtually ruled out because of her age – she was only fifteen. Brandenburg Schwedt and Hesse Darmstadt now became the favourites, and the King asked Munchhausen to send an emissary on whose judgment he could thoroughly depend to report on Philippina of Brandenburg.

The report was unfavourable. Princess Philippina was described as good-looking but obstinate and ill-tempered. She was struck off the list. It took some time to procure reports on the remaining princesses, for Caroline of Hesse Darmstadt lived in Alsace, then under French occupation and Mecklenburg was some distance from Hanover. 'The King's longing and impatience increase daily', wrote Munchhausen to his brother; and he intimated that if a favourable report were received of Princess Caroline she would be awarded the golden apple.

The first report was favourable. 'If my dearest friend is contented with what he sees', wrote the King to Bute on 27 April 1761, 'I own I am, and should be for settling this as soon as possible. The worst thing to my liking is her size.' But it soon transpired that there were worse things. Her father was eccentric, to say the least, and she herself 'stubborn and ill-tempered to the greatest degree, in short, much the same character as the Princess of Schwedt.' There was now no one left but Charlotte of Mecklenburg, and though she had been described as no beauty all the reports of her character were favourable. 'I own 'tis not in every particular as I could wish', wrote the King when transmitting to Bute the report on Princess Charlotte, 'but yet I am resolved to fix here. The family of the Princess of Darmstadt has given me such melancholy thoughts of what may perhaps be in the blood.'

In June 1761 the King decided to send a messenger to the court of Mecklenburg to prepare the way for the formal demand of Princess Charlotte's hand. For this office Bute selected one of his followers, David Graeme, who though of a Jacobite family had long shown his loyalty to the house of Hanover. Not a rumour of his errand leaked out. Afterwards, when the marriage had been announced, the story was told that Graeme had been sent on a mission to the Protestant courts of Germany to select a bride for the King. David Hume, the historian, is reported to have congratulated Graeme with reference to his Jacobite antecedents 'on having exchanged the dangerous employment of making Kings for the more lucrative province of making Queens'. But in truth Graeme was no more than a messenger. He bore a letter from the Princess Dowager to the Duchess of Mecklenburg intimating that the King was considering a match with her daughter. It was an informal approach which did not commit the King. If the response were unfavourable, he could withdraw without loss of dignity: if accepted, an ambassador would be sent to make the demand in form.

Of course the proposal was accepted, but the Duchess felt bound to point out that her daughter had been brought up in the Lutheran Church. This caused no difficulty, since the Princess expressed her willingness to conform to the Church of England and the King was advised that she could do so without straining her conscience. He

146

was eager for the marriage to take place as soon as possible and certainly in time for Princess Charlotte to be crowned with him in September. He wrote to Bute at the end of June:

How disagreeable would it not be for a young person to appear, almost at her first arrival, in Westminster Abbey, and go through all that ceremony. Besides, contrary winds might detain her, and consequently force that august ceremony to be suspended, which would be very irregular, and disappoint thousands who will be flocking on this occasion to London. Indeed, she ought to be above a month here before that day that she may have a little recovered that bashfulness which is beautiful in a young lady on her first appearance.

On 8 July the Privy Council was summoned to hear the King's declaration of his intended marriage. It took them all by surprise. Walpole says that it was expected the meeting had to do with the peace negotiations with France. Lord Harcourt – the same who had been the King's governor and had brought charges of Jacobitism against Stone and Scott – was appointed Ambassador to Mecklenburg to demand the Princess's hand. A party of ladies, headed by the Duchesses of Ancaster and Hamilton, was named to escort her to England.

The King hoped that his bride would be ready to set out by 1 August. She was to bring no servants other than one or two *femmes de chambre*, 'for by my own experience', wrote the King, 'these women meddle much more than they ought to do'. (He had learnt something since the days when Waldegrave thought him full of 'princely prejudices' contracted in the society of bedchamber women.) Graeme was instructed to ascertain her measurements so that her wedding clothes could be made in England. But delays intervened. On 12 July Princess Charlotte's mother died. 'Man is ever liable to checks', wrote the King to Bute, 'my dearest friend will be sensible how great mine is on this occasion. I should be quite knocked down, were not the Duke of Mecklenburgh [the Princess's

brother] ready to do anything that we may here propose.'
On 20 July the King caught chicken pox. But nothing
diminished his ardour. A tress of Princess Charlotte's hair
sent over by Graeme 'of a very fine dark colour and very
soft' gave him great pleasure.

The journey from Mecklenburg to England took at least
a fortnight and longer if the winds were contrary. The
Princess and her escort were ten days at sea, and it was
not until 7 September that the King learnt they had
landed safely at Harwich. That night he wrote to Bute:

I cannot go to rest without thanking my dearest friend for his
most kind congratulations [on the Princess's arrival]. Indeed,
I now think my domestic happiness in my own power. I am
overjoyed to the greatest degree and very impatient for that
minute that joins me to her, I hope for my life. I cannot too
much return my sincere and humble acknowledgments to my
Creator for this greatest blessing that he has been pleased to
point out to me.

I have now but one wish as a public man and that is that He
will make her fruitful that I may have the happiness of instill-
ing those sentiments of love to this dear country and its laws to
my successor which my most dear friend has ever uniformly
laid down before me.

It is said that Queen Charlotte spent part of her time on
the voyage playing the harpsichord and learnt to play
'God save the King'. She spent her first night in England
at Witham, near Chelmsford, in Essex, at the house of
Lord Abercorn. The next morning, 8 September, she
resumed her journey to London. The *Annual Register*
reported her progress:

On the road she was extremely courteous to an incredible
number of spectators on horse and foot gathered on this
occasion, showing herself, and bowing to all who seemed
desirous of seeing her, and ordering the coach to go extremely
slow through the towns and villages as she passed, that as
many as would might have a full view of her.

148

The procession stopped once on the journey, at Romford, where the Princess drank coffee and entered the King's coach which had been sent to meet her. She arrived at St James's Palace at three in the afternoon. The Duke of York was waiting to hand her out of the coach and to lead her to the King. They met in the garden. The Princess prepared to make her curtsey but the King raised her up, embraced her, and took her into the palace to meet his mother and the rest of the Royal Family. She dined privately with them (she must have been hungry, for she had eaten little or nothing since breakfast); was dressed (one wonders if any adjustments had to be made to her clothes at the last minute?); and took her place in the bridal procession to the Chapel Royal, just across the road from the palace. She was escorted by the King's brothers, the Duke of York and Prince William (later Duke of Gloucester), her train borne by her bridesmaids, ten unmarried daughters of dukes and earls. She trembled as she walked, and the Duke said (apparently in French): 'Courage, Princess, Courage.'[4] The marriage took place about nine o'clock in the evening. The ceremony was performed by the Archbishop of Canterbury and the bride was given away by the Duke of Cumberland. Afterwards, the King and Queen attended the drawing room where the guests had assembled, and while supper was being prepared the Queen played and sang on the harpsichord. They did not retire until between two and three in the morning. The next day there was a drawing room at which people were presented to the Queen, and in the evening a ball.

It says a good deal for Queen Charlotte's character that she was able to play her part so successfully in these ceremonies. She was after all only seventeen. She had come to a foreign country whose language she did not speak to be married to a man she did not know. She was put into a dress she had never seen (surely a most provoking experience for any woman on her wedding day?) The difficulties of communication alone were tremendous, for though she could talk to the King in French or German she presumably had to be coached by her ladies in the few words of English necessary for the marriage service. She did not have the advantage of commanding beauty. Yet all accounts agree that she behaved with dignity and grace. She must have been well brought up. She must also have been physically strong to go through such a day and consummate the marriage at three o'clock in the morning.

To a generation accustomed to a romantic view of courtship and marriage this story may seem strange. But the eighteenth century did not expect too much from life. Perhaps this is the great difference between that period and our own. The mere absence of physical pain in an age when drugs and anaesthetics were unknown was a blessing, and if to good health was added worldly comfort it was unreasonable to expect a romantic love. The eighteenth century took a practical view of marriage. Rank or wealth were important factors in selecting one's partner: the ability to live comfortably together and the pleasures of a family were the fruits of a happy marriage. King George and Queen Charlotte did not fall in love and marry: they married and fell in love. The marriage was a success because each partner determined that it should be.

The King was fortunate in that he did not have to marry for political or dynastic reasons. Within limits he could choose his wife himself. He took pains to learn what he could of her character, and since beauty was not a decisive consideration it did not matter that he had not seen her. For Queen Charlotte, a marriage with the King of Great Britain was beyond her most sanguine expectations. She came from one of the smaller royal families of Germany. She was endowed with neither wealth nor beauty. To what could she look forward in life? At best, to marriage with the ruler of a state as small as Mecklenburg or a cadet of one of the larger German princely houses. Her future husband (and almost any husband was better than

150

a lonely spinsterhood on an inadequate income) might be vicious or depraved, a worn-out voluptuary or a near-imbecile youth. These were her prospects in 1761 when she learnt that she was to marry the leading Protestant monarch in Europe, young, handsome, of good character, rich, secure, established. She must have been the envy of every princess in Germany! 'Oh, my sweetest Lizzy!' exclaimed Mrs Bennet, when she learnt that her daughter was to marry the rich and handsome Mr Darcy. 'How rich and how great you will be! What pin-money, what jewels, what carriages you will have!' What must the Princess and her mother have felt when Colonel Graeme arrived with his message from the King of Great Britain?

On 22 September 1761 King George and Queen Charlotte were crowned in Westminster Abbey. The King never forgot that solemn ceremony and observed the oath he took to the end of his reign. Together with the pomp and pageantry there was a certain simplicity, consonant with the style of the age and the character of the King. The King and Queen came from St James's Palace to Westminster Hall in sedan chairs, like ordinary citizens going to the theatre. Places near Westminster Hall and the Abbey commanded prices as high for the period as they did in 1953. The front seats in the galleries of the Abbey cost ten guineas each, and a house overlooking the route the procession was to take was hired for the day at a thousand guineas. The procession set out from Westminster Hall at eleven in the morning but it was not until 1.30 that the King and Queen entered the Abbey and not until 3.30 that the King was crowned. Then came the coronation banquet, and at 10 p.m. the King and Queen returned to St. James's as unobtrusively as they had set out. Contemporary accounts do not notice what to us seems most noteworthy about the coronation of 1761, namely how long the ceremonies lasted and how tired the King and Queen must have been at the end of the day.

*   *   *

151

The political events of the early years of George III's reign have long been matter of dispute among historians. It is doubtful if there is a comparable period of British history which has been analyzed in such detail or another King whose motives have been so minutely dissected. It was once the fashion (for there are fashions in the writing of history as in everything else) to regard King George III as inaugurating a new system of government (or reviving an old system) in which the Crown strove for a greater personal responsibility than had been the case under his predecessor. During the King's lifetime some of his critics went even further and charged him with behaving in an unconstitutional manner. Walpole wrote of a plan 'to raise the standard of prerogative', and Burke of a court cabal 'designed to secure to the Crown the unlimited and uncontrolled use of its own vast influence'. Some laid the blame for the King's intentions on Bute: others on the Princess Dowager: and there was a third school of thought which believed that the King got his ideas on government from reading Lord Bolingbroke, the lapsed Jacobite who wrote about the Patriot King. Historians wrote about King George III's system of 'personal government', of 'secret influence', 'an experiment in benevolent despotism', or 'an attempt to restore royal power'. Generations of British schoolchildren were brought up to believe that the King had been told by his mother 'to be a King' and that Great Britain lost the American colonies in consequence of his following her advice.*

Forty years ago the publication of the King's early correspondence and the discovery of Bute's papers stimulated a new line of research. Sir Lewis Namier described the working of the electoral system about the middle of the century and wrote the political history of the first two years of the reign in minute detail. Mr Romney Sedgwick published the King's letters to Bute and told the story of

*See note 6, p. 611.

their relationship. The result of this research was to present a different picture of the eighteenth-century system of government and the role of the Crown. Instead of 'the able attempt of George III to recover the powers of the Crown', Mr Sedgwick considered that the King had merely carried on 'to the best of his more than limited ability, the system of government which he had inherited from his predecessors'. After thirty years' work on the period, this was Namier's considered verdict on the King: 'What I have never been able to find is the man arrogating power to himself, the ambitious schemer out to dominate, the intriguer dealing in an underhand fashion with his ministers.'

The debate continues. We shall not be able to understand George III as King until we first understand the man. The flaw in so much historical writing about the reign has been the failure to see him as a human being.

Two days after his accession the new King issued a proclamation 'requiring all persons being in office of authority or government at the decease of the late King, to proceed in the execution of their respective offices for six months unless sooner removed'. This was the usual procedure at the beginning of a new reign but it meant nothing. Changes were in the air. An old and tired King had been succeeded by a young and fresh one. In the eighteenth century the accession of a new King was an event of political importance comparable today to the assumption of office by a new President of the United States. The form of government remained the same, but changes were to be expected among the leading personnel and a new direction given to policy. No one in the United States in 1969 expected President Nixon to retain former President Johnson's confidential advisers. In the same way, no one in Great Britain in 1760 expected King George III to retain the men who had advised King George II. Every Prince of Wales had his minister designate, and prudent men with an eye to the future would make their

153

court to 'the one the King had marked out for his favourite'. It was not unconstitutional for the King to wish to turn out Newcastle and Pitt and replace them by Bute. It did not indicate a hoisting of the standard of prerogative or the workings of a court cabal. It was merely the normal change to be expected at the demise of a King. It was of course highly imprudent, as it is always imprudent to dismiss those responsible for the conduct of a successful policy. This was why it did not happen.

Perhaps Bute in his heart of hearts would have preferred to remain the favourite without responsibility rather than become the responsible minister. He oscillated between the wish for power and the fear of responsibility. In 1758 he had frightened the King with the idea of 'not accepting the Treasury in a future day'; when that day came he told Pitt that he had given up all thoughts of the Treasury. Did he consult the King before he made his overture to Pitt on the night of 25 October? It seems unlikely. One of the lessons the King had been taught by Bute was to beware of favourites; and at the beginning of the reign Munchhausen, with the cordial agreement of the British ministers, had advised the King to act for himself. The King was resolved that if Bute was to have influence, then Bute must bear responsibility. Two days after his accession the King appointed Bute to the cabinet, and in March 1761 he became Secretary of State for the Northern Department. At the general election that month he entered the House of Lords as one of the representative peers for Scotland.

During the first two years of the reign the personal influence of the Crown was at a lower ebb than at any time within living memory. The King, faithful to his promise when Prince of Wales, consulted Bute on everything and invariably accepted his advice. The most trivial matters were referred to Bute. In November 1761 the King consulted him about the seating arrangements at the banquet which the City of London were giving for the

Royal Family and who were to be invited to a private ball at court:

As to the two ladies [the King wrote] I wish for Lady C. Russell and Lady J. Stewart. I would ask my dearest friend's opinion who must send to the dancers, and whether it is absolutely necessary for the Duke of Manchester [Lord Chamberlain to the Queen] or any one else to attend. Also whether he does not think it infinitely properer that none of the family should be partners. I own to me it appears very like a nursery when brothers and sisters, except where form requires it, dance together.

I ask for an answer in the course of the evening that I may know my dearest friend's opinion on the questions I have stated to him and any others that may occur to him on this affair.

The King like any monarch had to learn his business, but when he wrote this letter he had already been a year on the throne. At no later period of his reign did he ever consult a minister on such matters. Bute maintained the attitude of a tutor to his pupil even when his pupil was King. The following letter to Bute, probably written about the turn of the years 1761–2, shows how little their relationship had changed. In the absence of Bute's letter to which this was a reply it is impossible to explain all the references or say what it was in the King's conduct which had displeased Bute.

The frankness with which my dearest friend has wrote to me is the greatest sign of that attachment he has invariably professed to me. I will therefore with equal openness answer it.

I am above denying that I have often dropped things that have made me uneasy on recollection, but mean to be more cautious for the future. . . .

As to what is thrown out of my not taking the pains I used to do, there my conscience is at ease, for I have never looked so much into the state of this country since on the throne as of late. . . .

As to what my dearest friend says of the quick changes in

155

Administrations from the fluctuations of men's conduct in this kingdom in particular, this is often before my eyes though a very unpleasing thought.

I thank my dearest friend for his hint of not taking notice of men of quality; though I do not recollect its ever having happened yet it will make me more cautious lest it should at any time be the case.

Nothing can astonish me more than that any one should accuse me of all people of loving foreign fashions, whom I own rather incline too much to the John Bull and am apt to despise what I am not accustomed to. . . .

Newcastle and Devonshire agreed that Bute meant to be master, but thought him 'not only ignorant of business but visionary' with 'no plan of administration or even thought of the practicability of effecting it'. The King talked of reformation and purging out corruption but his idea of reformation was confined to being as different as possible from his predecessor. King George II had cared more for Hanover than for Great Britain: King George III spoke of Hanover as 'that horrid electorate', and with his own hand inserted in the draft of his speech to his first Parliament the words 'Born and educated in this country, I glory in the name of Britain'.* King George II had kept a mistress: King George III lived in chastity, and a week after his accession issued a proclamation 'for the encouragement of piety and virtue, and for the preventing and punishing vice, profaneness, and immorality'. King George II's ministers, so his successor had been taught to believe, were corrupt: King George III refused to allow any government money to be spent on subsidizing candidates at the general election. Even in the matter of his residence he deliberately differed from his grandfather. King George II had lived at St James's Palace, and when in the country at Kensington and Hampton Court: King George III bought a new house in London (the Queen's House, now incorporated in Buckingham Palace) and

*See note 7, p. 612.

used St James's only for Court ceremonies. He abandoned Kensington and Hampton Court and made Kew
and Windsor his country residences. He tried to put into
practice the measures recommended by his father. He
lived with economy (though he did not succeed in keeping
out of debt), and accepted a fixed sum for his Civil List
(which his father had promised to do when he came to the
throne). In short, he carried on his father's feud with his
grandfather even after his grandfather's death. The re-
placement of King George II's ministers by men of his
own choice was merely the culmination of this feud.
Frederick, Prince of Wales, was amply revenged on his
father by his son.

In November 1760 the King wrote to Bute:

I am happy to think that I have [at] the present the real love of
my subjects, and lay it down for certain that if I do not show
them that I will not permit ministers to trample on me, that my
subjects will in time come to esteem me unworthy of the Crown
I wear.

The change in the tone of government between the last
years of King George II and the early years of his successor is largely explained by the difference between seventy-
seven and twenty-two years of age. In the last years of his
life the late King had relaxed his hold on the reins of
government. He was old and almost blind: the war was
going well: he was satisfied with his ministers. It was time
for him to take his ease. To him there succeeded a young
man eager for work, burning to put into practice ideas
which had long been cherished in the study and the
library, and knowing little of how government really
worked. 'I could hardly help smiling', wrote Newcastle,
when told that the King 'had a notion of not being
governed . . . by his minister or ministers as the late King
had been'. He remembered how self-willed King George
II could be, how he and Pitt had tried in vain to persuade
him to give his grandson the opportunity of acquiring

157

military experience. King George II had never been governed by any minister as his grandson was by Bute. Experience taught the King what Bute could never have taught him: that kingship like every other trade has to be learnt by practice, and that politicians are much like other men – neither so good nor so bad as our ideas lead us to imagine.

Some years after his accession (probably about 1766) the King began to write an apologia for his political conduct, intended for the instruction of his son.[5] After mentioning the criticisms which had been made of him by disappointed politicians, he wrote:

This has made me undertake to write down my own transactions which I call Heaven to witness I mean without partiality to myself fairly to state, that whenever God of his infinite goodness shall call me out of this world the tongue of malice may not paint my intentions in those colours she admires, nor the sycophant extoll me beyond what I deserve. I do not pretend to any superior abilitys, but will give place to no one in meaning to preserve the freedom, happiness and glory of my dominions, and all their inhabitants, and to fulfill the duty to my God and my neighbour in the most extended sense. That I have erred is undoubted, otherwise I should not be human, but I flatter myself all unprejudiced persons will be convinced that whenever I have failed it has been from the head not the heart.

If all the papers of King George III had been destroyed except this one document, we would still possess the key to understanding his character: his humility, based on a deep religious faith. It is impossible to imagine any of his contemporaries on the thrones of Europe writing of themselves in this strain. There can be no doubt of the King's sincerity in a paper written solely for the eyes of his son. Unfortunately, this document, though it exists in three states, is incomplete, and we do not have the King's detailed account of the events of the early years of his reign.

Yet one sentence, in which he describes the political situation when he came to the throne, is of great interest:

The ministry continued and consequently the war, alliances, and home affairs bore the same face; the only difference of conduct I adopted was to put an end to those unhappy distinctions of party called Whigs and Tories, by declaring that I would countenance every man that supported my Administration and concurred in that form of government which had been so wisely established by the Revolution.

Whatever his intentions, the King did not 'put an end to those unhappy distinctions of party'. He thought of politics in terms of the past, of what they had been in the days of his father: the real state of affairs in 1760 was different from what he imagined it to be. 'The moment of his accession was fortunate beyond example', wrote Horace Walpole. 'The extinction of parties had not waited for, but preceded, the dawn of his reign.' This however turned out to be not altogether the blessing that the King and Walpole assumed. There were more serious evils in the body politic than 'the unhappy distinctions of party'.

The divisions between Whig and Tory owed their origin to differences during the last quarter of the seventeenth century about religion and the succession to the throne. Many years before George III became King, these had become confused and obliterated. With the failure of Jacobitism, the Tories ceased to have any cohesion or raison d'être. Most of their leaders and men of ambition went over to the Whigs, and the rank and file remained in sullen opposition to what they called Hanoverian measures. In 1754 there were about a hundred Members of Parliament who could still be called Tories. But they did not act together as a party, they did not acknowledge any leader, and they failed to provide an effective opposition to the Whig ministry. They even disclaimed the name of Tory, which was used only by Whigs and generally as a term of derision. It was not the Tories whom Newcastle feared but the dissident Whigs.

The position of the Whigs in the last years of King George II's reign was well described by Waldegrave:

When the Hanover succession took place, the Whigs became the possessors of all the great offices and other lucrative employments; since which time, instead of quarrelling with the prerogative, they have been the champions of every administration.

However, they have not always been united in one body, under one general, like a regular and well-disciplined army; but may more aptly be compared to an alliance of different clans, fighting in the same cause, professing the same principles, but influenced and guided by their different chieftains.

If the old Tory party was dead by 1760, the old Whig party was moribund. It had achieved its aims. Its principles had been generally accepted by the nation. Its rival chieftains fought each other for the spoils of office, and where political issues arose these were generally of an ad hoc nature. Rarely were they questions of principle. The main body of the Whigs were content to follow whichever of their leaders found favour with the Crown. Party had degenerated into faction.

It was not the King but Pitt who put an end to 'the unhappy distinctions of party'. He rescued the Tories from opprobrium and eased their return to court. When he made his stand against subsidy treaties in 1755 he identified himself with Tory ideas and Tory prejudices. Here was a Whig politician who professed to share their concern for economy and their anti-Hanoverian views. When he came into office he appealed to their patriotism. He pressed for the establishment of a national militia and encouraged the Tories to accept commissions. They flocked to the colours, the first time some of them had taken the oath of allegiance to a Hanoverian King. Pitt was sometimes able to do little jobs for them and he favoured public measures in which they were interested. As one peer put it, the constellation was in the ascendant under the influence of which the Tories might hope to receive favours. King George II and Newcastle, both old men who could remember the time when the Tories were no better than Jacobites, grumbled but acquiesced.

The accession of King George III completed the process of reconciling the Tories to the dynasty. Here was a new King, young and gracious, born in this country and guiltless of the past. The Tories went to the King's levee and kissed his hand. Some even accepted Court appointments. On 5 December 1760 Newcastle was scandalized to learn that five Tories had been appointed to the King's Bedchamber. With typical ungraciousness, Bute had failed to inform him in advance and the Duke only learnt of it accidentally while visiting Lady Yarmouth. He complained bitterly that 'the Whigs were given up', threatened to resign, yet allowed himself to be smoothed down. To his friends he explained that he only remained in office 'for the service of the Whigs'. But who were Whigs and who were Tories it was becoming increasingly difficult to say.

The King like most of his subjects regarded party distinctions as a disturbing element in national life. They prevented the growth of national unity and were especially dangerous in time of war. But the reconciliation of the Tories and the disintegration of the Whigs did not end party distinctions. It merely led to their revival as personal factions, with no national appeal and no political vision. The story of their struggles is the political history of the first ten years of the reign. It is not an edifying story. The King set his face against government by faction. He wished to be King of all his people, not merely King of the Whigs as his grandfather had been. He struggled to preserve his independence from faction: not to extend his prerogative but to defend it. On the whole he was successful, but he could not prevent the re-emergence of party in a more lasting form.

Marriage, and the birth of his first son the following year, increased the King's self-assurance. He remained devoted

161

to Bute, but began to act on his own account and became less inclined to accept Bute's advice unquestioningly. Political events soon added their spur.

In the spring of 1761 peace negotiations opened between Great Britain and France. These soon revealed the British cabinet at odds with itself. Pitt wanted a peace which would consolidate all Britain's gains and leave France impotent as a colonial power. Nor was he prepared to make peace until Frederick the Great had been satisfied. Newcastle was anxious for peace above all things and periodically asserted that the nation was not in a financial condition to carry on the war much longer. Bute hovered between the two: he wanted peace as much as did Newcastle, but he feared lest too many concessions to France would increase Pitt's popularity. In the event the negotiations broke down and France secretly concluded a convention with Spain. Pitt learnt of this and proposed to declare war on Spain. The cabinet was unanimous against him, and on 5 October 1761 Pitt and Lord Temple resigned. The King rewarded his services with a pension of £3,000 a year for his life and his son's and a peerage for his wife. It was no more than Pitt had deserved, and the King thought it a small price to pay for being rid of him.

Pitt's resignation did not make matters in the cabinet any easier. It soon became clear that he had been right and that war with Spain could not be avoided. 'This fresh enemy makes my heart bleed for my poor country', wrote the King to Bute on 14 November 1761. 'I think unless we can get rid of our expence *somewhere* it will be impossible to bear up when a new power attacks us.' The obvious place where to reduce British commitments was Germany. 'Though I have subjects who will suffer immensely [i.e. in Hanover] whenever this kingdom withdraws its protection from thence', the King wrote on 6 January 1762, 'yet so superior is my love to this my native country over any private interest of my own that I cannot help wishing that an end was put to that enormous expence by ordering our troops home.' He had no liking for Frederick the Great – 'that too ambitious monarch', 'that proud overbearing prince', as he described him – and wished to see the withdrawal of the British subsidy to Prussia. This became the issue between Bute and Newcastle: and when the question of voting further credit for the continuance of the war in Germany came up, the King looked forward eagerly to Newcastle's resignation. 'The successor I have long had in my eye to the Duke of Newcastle', he wrote coyly to Bute, 'is a man void of his dirty arts who will think of mine and his country's good, not of jobs. If my dearest friend does not know him by this character, I will add that he now holds the seals and lives in South Audley Street [where Bute lived].'

Again Bute hesitated, as he had done in March 1761. 'The thought of his not accepting the Treasury', wrote the King to his friend on 19 May, 'or of his retiring, chill my blood. Is this a moment for despondency? No, for vigour and the day is our's.' He brushed aside Bute's excuse of 'ignorance in business' and the difficulty of finding a suitable Chancellor of the Exchequer. 'Take the Treasury and numbers will be with you.' Perhaps at this point he began to have doubts about Bute's political courage. King George could see no reason for hesitation. He rarely could, nor did he sympathize with those who did. Basically, he was a stronger character than Bute and he did not easily abandon a course of action he had once assumed. But he was twenty-five years younger than Bute; and there was in him all the naivety, the lack of political realism, natural at his age.

Bute had to face a divided cabinet and a House of Commons elected while Newcastle was head of the Treasury. He was uncertain of both. Peace negotiations had been reopened, and in August had reached the stage when it became necessary to appoint a British plenipotentiary to Paris. The Duke of Bedford who was

163

selected for this office was the leader of the 'peace at any price' school; and though the King raised no objection to his appointment at the time, he later expressed dissatisfaction with Bedford's conduct. Lord Egremont, Secretary of State for the Southern Department, who was in charge of the negotiations, and his brother-in-law George Grenville, leader of the House of Commons – the men who would have to defend the treaty in Parliament – were less inclined than the ambassador to make concessions. Bute again found himself in the unhappy position of a mediator between two groups of intransigents. The King, more eager for peace than perhaps Bute would have liked, was 'much hurt' when the news of the British capture of Havana threatened to delay the conclusion of the treaty with Spain. He was indefatigable in lobbying politicians in support of the ministry. The Duke of Cumberland was 'much pleased' at being asked to stand godfather to the King's first child and at being informed in advance of the terms of the draft treaty which Bedford was taking to France. Newcastle was in good humour and confessed candidly that 'the state of our finances required peace'. Those who professed objections were treated coldly by the King (at least so he says in his letters to Bute). But the farther the negotiations proceeded, the more the tensions in the cabinet increased. By October Egremont and Grenville were threatening resignation and Bute was at his wit's end how to control his unruly team. He was now beginning to realize that the real art of politics was the management of men: a truth the King had yet to learn.

Bute was conscious that he would have to bear the supreme responsibility: that all who had a grievance, whether public or personal, would turn on him. 'I feel most sensibly', he wrote to Egremont on 26 July 1762, 'that I am, from the King's known goodness to me, to stand at mark for the long train of calamities that the continuation of this war brings in my view.' And for the disappointments which peace would bring. He was cons-

164

cious also of his bitter unpopularity with the London mob, and he could hardly appear in the streets without insult being offered to him. Above all there was the menace of Pitt, waiting to pounce upon the treaty when it should reach the House of Commons. As a peer Bute could not manage the Commons, and Grenville was both inexperienced and untrustworthy. The ministry must be strengthened before Parliament met. But to whom could Bute turn? In his extremity he advised the King to recall Newcastle. But Newcastle had no wish to act as a lightning conductor to avert the approaching storm from Bute's head. Then Bute resolved upon a desperate expedient, no less than the appointment of Henry Fox to a seat in the cabinet and the lead in the House of Commons.

Ever since the formation of the Newcastle–Pitt coalition in 1757 Fox had been politically speaking on the sidelines. He had held the lucrative office of Paymaster-General of the Forces from which he had accumulated a large fortune, but he had been entirely without political influence. The withdrawal of his patron, the Duke of Cumberland, had further lessened his political stature. Fox had to stand by while Pitt, the man he hated most in this world, achieved such triumphs as Great Britain had never known. There was bitter jealousy and hatred in his heart – against Newcastle who had thrown him over, against Pitt who had supplanted him. He bided his time, and waited for the reversal of fortune which would surely come with the accession of the new King. When it came, he could not resist the opportunity to take his revenge. He was able, well acquainted with the House, and not afraid to do deeds from which Bute would have shrunk. From Bute's point of view he was the ideal choice for a lightning conductor.

This was the turning point in the King's friendship with Bute. For the first time he hesitated to accept Bute's advice on a political matter. He had been reluctant to accept Bute's advice to recall Newcastle. But Fox! the foremost exponent of the 'loaves and fishes' school of politics! the man who stood for all that King George had been taught to abhor! 'Probably more than any other statesman even of his period', writes Namier, 'Fox thought of power and employment primarily in terms of patronage and profit.' What would become of the plans of reformation which Bute had talked about at Kew, which the King had written about in his essays, if Fox took over the House of Commons? Was he the man to inaugurate a reign of virtue? 'The seeing him at the head of the House of Commons', the King wrote the subsequent year, 'was very unpleasant to me: but I consented to it as that was the only means of getting my dear friend to proceed this winter in the Treasury.' To the King, Fox was 'void of principles'. The King was not wrong.

There was a personal reason for the King's dislike of Fox. In March 1761, when the King had been considering the claims of the various German princesses, he had given a hint to Lady Susan Fox-Strangways about his approaching marriage. Lady Susan was the niece of Henry Fox and the cousin and close friend of Lady Sarah Lennox, the King's first love. She was a girl of a highly romantic disposition – in plain words, a very silly girl – who shortly afterwards concluded a runaway marriage greatly to the embarrassment of her family, with an impecunious Irish actor. The King's conversation with Lady Susan had related to the prospect of having her cousin as bridesmaid at the approaching wedding, but was taken in a very different sense. Every word the King said, every gesture, every look, was reported to Fox, and was made to bear an interpretation conformable to Lady Susan's romantic inclinations and Fox's ambitions. He conceived the idea of using Lady Sarah as a means of ingratiating himself with the King. Why should not the King marry a subject? Henry VIII and James II had done. Any suggestion to the contrary was merely 'ridiculous German pride'. But if for dynastic reasons he was obliged to marry a woman of

166

royal blood, why should he not take a mistress? Every King of England for the last hundred years had done so. Everybody knew (or at least everybody believed) that the Duchess of Kendal, mistress of King George I, and the Countess of Yarmouth, mistress of King George II, had exercised great political influence during the reigns of those kings. Who knew this better than the Earl of Ilchester, Fox's brother and Lady Susan's father, who owed his peerage to a judicious bribe given to King George II's mistress? Why should not Lady Sarah Lennox become the Madame de Pompadour of King George III? And why should not Henry Fox become the power behind the throne?

At the end of March Lady Sarah fell from her horse and broke her leg. By the time she returned to London, at the end of May, the King had fixed his choice on Princess Charlotte and Colonel Graeme was preparing to set out on his mission to Mecklenburg. All this of course was unknown to Fox. He imagined that the King was as yet unengaged and he set his plan in motion. Lady Sarah was instructed to appear regularly at court and the King was carefully watched. He coloured when he saw her, talked graciously to her, asked her to stand by his chair. All these signs, which Fox saw or imagined he saw, were taken as undoubted proofs that the King was in love with Lady Sarah. Tutored by her uncle, Lady Sarah tried to make herself as attractive as possible to the King. 'She appeared every morning', writes Horace Walpole, 'at Holland House [Fox's residence in Kensington], in a field close to the great road (where the King passed on horseback) in a fancied habit making hay.'

Fox's scheme did not escape observation. His friend Horace Walpole knew what was going on, and gives it as his opinion that Fox would not have been 'scrupulous or delicate' about the terms of the union between the King and Lady Sarah. If Walpole knew, we may be sure that others did too and it would not be long before something

167

would be said to the King. In fact, the King knew the whole plot. In a letter to Bute, shortly after his marriage, he writes:

Nothing can astonish me more than that any one should accuse me of all people of loving foreign fashions, whom I own rather incline too much to the John Bull. . . . But I see the source of this accusation. Many who flattered themselves to make their way through some mistress to me, seeing themselves entirely disappointed by that attachment I have for her to whom I am wedded, out of rage and despair spread such reports.

Many years later the King told Rose 'that his memory was a good one, and that what he did not *forget* he could not *forgive*'. He neither forgot nor forgave Fox's scheme to make Lady Sarah Lennox his mistress. In order to keep Bute in the Treasury, he was compelled to take Fox as Leader of the House of Commons; but he never abated his dislike of him and in later years transferred that dislike to Fox's son. Fox rendered outstanding services to the King in the winter of 1762–3, and duly received the peerage he had been promised. But the earldom, which he coveted above all, was denied him. Bute always acknowledged his gratitude to Fox but could not obtain for him an earldom. No effort by Grafton or Walpole in the winter of 1766–7, a time when the King was dependent on these two for the stability of his administration, could gain this favour for Fox. 'I cannot help asking myself', Fox wrote to a friend in January 1768, '. . . why I am in such disgrace with the King? Have I deserved it? I am now the only mark left of irrevocable displeasure, and I vow to God I cannot guess why.' He had forgotten what the King never forgave.

Lady Sarah was not in love with the King and soon got over her disappointment at not becoming Queen. Her subsequent adventures confirm the impression that she would not have been happy with him. In 1762 she married Sir Charles Bunbury, from whom she was divorced in

1776 for adultery and desertion. Her second marriage was more fortunate, and she became the mother of a large and devoted family. Her first husband is remembered today in widely different capacities: as a prison reformer, one of the pallbearers at Dr Johnson's funeral, a steward of the Jockey Club, and the first winner of the Derby. It is said that Bunbury and the 12th Earl of Derby drew lots as to who should give his name to the race and that Derby won. Had fortune not determined otherwise, the blue riband of the British turf might have bestowed a vicarious immortality on King George III's first love.

In September 1762 the draft of the preliminary treaty of peace reached England and was communicated by the King to the Duke of Cumberland. 'Nothing could be more personally gracious to the Duke than the King was during the whole audience, which lasted a full hour.' The Duke objected to several points of the proposed treaty; and in the account of the audience which he gave to Lord Hardwicke 'said that upon some points of the articles the objections were begun by the King and insisted upon by His Majesty in full as strong a manner as they could be by the Duke'. Great Britain did not obtain all she had claimed, but to press for all her claims might have meant another year of war. It was worth making some sacrifices for peace – an opinion which was subsequently shared by the politically conscious part of the nation.

It was the treaty with Spain, in particular the question of an equivalent to Great Britain for the capture of Havana, that led to the renewed crisis in the ministry, the appointment of Fox, and the almost total collapse of Bute. Bute saw himself surrounded by enemies. He not only panicked but infected the King with his fears, and induced him to believe that the stability of his Crown depended on the House of Commons endorsing the treaty. He tried to inveigle Newcastle into sharing the responsibility, and when he failed advised the King to summon the Duke of Devonshire to the cabinet meeting which was to consider the final terms of peace. Devonshire was not ex officio a member of the cabinet and had ceased to attend meetings when Newcastle resigned. His presence at this particular meeting was desired only in order to commit the potential opposition to support the treaty. His refusal to attend was taken by the King as a personal affront, and by Bute as a sign that Devonshire was plotting with Newcastle and the Duke of Cumberland to overturn him.

In this atmosphere of suspicion and intrigue, created by Bute out of fear, the King behaved foolishly. On 28 October, on his way from Kew to London, he overtook Devonshire and Newcastle proceeding in the same direction. Bute had told him of a 'great meeting' of Newcastle's friends to be held that day and the King jumped to the conclusion that Devonshire was coming to London to concert measures of opposition with Newcastle. (He was in fact only passing through London on his way to Chatsworth.) On his arrival at St James's Palace, the King wrote to Bute: 'How it galls that I meet the Duke of Devonshire still bearing the wand! If he should come today . . . he shall not leave the closet as Chamberlain.' Shortly after one o'clock Devonshire waited on the King to take his leave before going into the country. 'I ordered the page to tell him I would not see him', wrote the King to Bute, 'on which he bid him ask me with whom he should leave his wand. . . . I said he would receive my orders. . . . On the Duke of Devonshire's going away he said to the page, "God bless you, it will be very long before you see me here again." ' Devonshire's dismissal was followed by the resignation of his relations. On 31 October the Duke's brother, Lord George Cavendish, came to resign his place of Comptroller of the Household. The King was sulky and at first said nothing. 'At last he burst out', wrote Cavendish to Newcastle, ' "If a person wants to resign his staff, I don't desire he should keep it I

170

am sure", gave his head a toss back, and retired towards the window to set the staff down.' Four days later, at a meeting of the Privy Council, the King called for the Council book and with his own hand struck out the name of the Duke of Devonshire.

Few things in King George III's long life show him in so poor a light. Devonshire was not without blame and the King had reason to be annoyed with him. It would have been more proper had Devonshire either attended the cabinet when summoned or offered his resignation. But the punishment was out of proportion to the offence. Dismissal from the Privy Council was rare, and was usually reserved for those in systematic opposition to the Crown or for even more serious offences. The last case was that of Lord George Sackville in 1760 for disobedience of military orders at the battle of Minden. It should not have been inflicted on grounds of suspicion alone, and on a man whose family had given loyal service to the Hanoverian dynasty over three generations and who had never once voted in opposition. The only excuse for the King's petulance is that he was young, impatient, and frightened. Perhaps behind his behaviour we can recognize the influence of the pedant who felt all the pleasure of power to consist in punishing or astonishing. We do not know what advice Bute gave, but the King had warned him a week before that he intended to dismiss Devonshire and Bute appears to have offered no objection. Possibly he could not have restrained the King even had he wished. He had too thoroughly infected his pupil with his own fears. 'The sword is drawn', the King wrote on 3 November 1762, 'vigour and violence are the only means of ending this audacious faction.' Anyone would imagine from the way he wrote that the country was on the brink of civil war.

Devonshire's dismissal was the pretext for which Newcastle had been waiting. He set to work to rally his friends and put out feelers to Pitt and the Duke of Cumberland.

171

'It is hardly credible that the Duke of Cumberland will choose to take so offensive a step', wrote the King. 'If he does, he shall be treated as he deserves.' The news that the treaty had been signed reached England on 8 November, and the King was disconcerted at the concessions Bedford had made. 'It grieves me much he ever went there', he wrote. 'A man of more coolness and less jealousy in his temper would have done the business in half the time.' But on the whole the King was satisfied with the treaty. 'I think it a noble peace. . . . What thanks ought not to be given to my d. friend for this great service to his country. Had he not sometimes been rough with his colleagues, we had [not] been in the situation of signing.' It was now Fox's business to get the treaty through the House of Commons, and it was a stimulus to his labours to pay off old scores against Newcastle and Pitt. Members of Parliament were lobbied and asked for their opinions, and Fox found there was an overwhelming majority in favour of the treaty. Pitt, an opponent *à l'outrance*, had few supporters. Newcastle, a pacifist at heart, had no moral basis from which to attack the treaty, and soon found that the friends of his power were now the friends of Bute. The story told by Walpole (and fifty years later by Wraxall) that Fox employed bribery to persuade the House of Commons to accept the treaty is untrue. The treaty was generally acceptable and there was no need for bribery. The nation was tired of war, and all the aims for which Great Britain had begun the war had been achieved. In any case there was not the money for bribery; nor was the House of Commons in 1762, any more than it is today, amenable to bribery. All Fox had to do was to employ the engines of parliamentary persuasion just as a leader of the House of Commons does today. By the first week in December he was able to assure Bute that the majority was certain.

At this moment, with victory in sight, Bute informed the King that he wished to resign his office and revert to court employment. He would cease to be a responsible minister and become an irresponsible favourite. The King was taken aback. He had not expected this. 'It overturns all the thoughts that alone have kept up my spirits in these bad times.' He replied to Bute:

I own I had flattered myself when peace was once established that my d. friend would have assisted me in purging out corruption, and in those measures that no man but he that has the prince's real affection can go through. Then, when we were both dead, our memories would have been respected and esteemed to the end of time.

'Remember what Fox formerly said', concluded the King. 'We will give Lord Bute a Garter and a court employment and then we may do as we please.' But Bute was no longer concerned with purging out corruption or ensuring that his name would be esteemed to the end of time. Fear oppressed him. On 25 November, on his way to the opening of Parliament, he was hissed and pelted by the mob, and if the Guards had not been summoned his life would have been in danger. The King rode to Parliament in his new state coach (the same in which Queen Elizabeth II rides today), and the crowds that assembled to see him were greater than at the coronation. He too was insulted, but he cared nothing for the mob. Forty years later he told Rose how he had rebuked Bute when his friend had tried to dissuade him from going to the theatre that night. King George III never lacked courage.

At this point we must recall the words of Shelburne about Bute: 'He was insolent and cowardly . . . he was rash and timid . . . he was ready to abandon his nearest friend if attacked. . . .' What Bute feared in November 1762 was not defeat in the House of Commons but assassination by the London mob. Incredible as it may seem, he really believed that the mob had been hired by his political opponents and that his life was in danger. Moreover, he managed to convince the King that this was so. 'How bad are not men grown', wrote the King, 'when their minds can harbour an instant the thought of assassination.' To safeguard his friend's life, he was prepared to recall Pitt to office. 'I am ready to put any plan in execution', he wrote on the evening of the meeting of Parliament, 'to rid my dear friend of apprehensions that must every hour attend him, and shall be most happy if the changing his situation shelters him from what there is at present too much reason to fear.' The belief that there was a plot to assassinate his friend explains the King's invectives against his subjects at this time – 'This is I believe the wickedest age that ever was seen' – 'this ungrateful people' – 'the greed that this age is cursed with'.

It sounds fantastic that such beliefs could be seriously entertained by the King and his minister. But it is not more fantastic to believe that Newcastle and Pitt plotted in 1762 to set the London mob on to Bute than to believe in 1755 that the Duke of Cumberland plotted to murder his nephew and usurp the throne. Yet the King and Bute had certainly believed that about the Duke. And there was an element of reality in Bute's fantasy. Every unpopular minister in the eighteenth century risked attack from the London mob. It was an occupational hazard of the trade, as criticism by the press is today. In 1765 the Duke of Bedford's house was assaulted and soldiers had to be sent to guard his family. In 1771 Lord North was attacked on his way to Parliament, his coach destroyed, and he himself only saved from death by the intervention of two opposition Members of Parliament. In 1785, after his unpopular shop tax, the younger Pitt dared not return to his official residence in Downing Street for fear of the mob who were after his blood. The London mob was an unpleasant reality: what was fantastic was Bute's belief that the mob had been spirited up by his political opponents.

From Parliament Bute had nothing to fear. The House of Commons approved the treaty by 319 votes to 65. The

174

opposition was routed; and Fox proceeded to take his revenge. Bute gave him a free hand and he took full advantage of it. Newcastle and his followers were stripped of their offices and every man connected with them turned out of his employment. 'A more severe political persecution never raged', writes Walpole. So complete was the purge that the King began to have doubts. Was it really necessary to go to this extent? 'No man should be dismissed', he wrote to Bute on 18 January 1763, 'unless others besides the Foxes declare them to be of that denomination.' Three days later he wrote about a suggested army appointment which had been inspired by Fox: 'If my dear friend looks on it as a thing absolutely necessary for government I will do it . . .'; and about an ecclesiastical appointment: 'I don't think Mr Fox very likely to recommend a man that will do honour to that sacred profession.' By now Bute was no more than nominal minister. The effective control of government was in Fox. The King knew it, yet could not bring himself to face the truth about his friend.

'The angel Gabriel could not at present govern this country', wrote Bute on 30 January 1763, 'but by means too long practised and such as my soul abhors.' This declared his unfitness for the task. He pleaded the state of his health as the reason for his resignation – 'the eternal unpleasant labour of the mind, and the impossibility of finding hours for exercise and proper medicine, the little time I get for sleep, the little I ever enjoy even when abed' – what Prime Minister could not plead similar excuses? In March Bute confessed to the King that he was 'heartily sick of his situation' and recommended Fox as his successor.

This brought the King up with a jolt. At once all Bute's ideals were exposed. Fox as Leader of the House of Commons had been bad enough, but Fox as Prime Minister! – this was too much. ' 'Tis not prejudice', he wrote to Bute, 'but aversion to his whole mode of

175

government.... Has this whole winter been any thing else but a scene of corruption? and I am persuaded were he the acting [i.e. real] minister this would appear in more ways than he is now able to accomplish.' Even the judicial bench would be filled by 'wretches that are unfit to decide the properties of free men because they can be the means of acquiring a vote in Parliament'. Bute may have abandoned his hopes of purging out corruption but the King had not. If Fox's elevation to the Treasury was the only solution Bute could propose, the King declared he would accept it. But, he wrote, 'I own from the moment he comes in I shall not feel myself interested in public affairs and shall feel rejoiced whenever I can see a glimmering hope of getting quit of him'. Even after this categorical declaration and with a full knowledge of what Fox had done and tried to do, Bute still offered him the Treasury.

Fox declined the supreme responsibility, as he had done in 1757, ostensibly because of his wife's objections but really because he was afraid. ('Mr Fox', writes Shelburne, 'was not formed to be a man *sui juris*, else he would have been so.') Instead he recommended Grenville, and after a good deal of negotiating Bute formed a ministry with Grenville as First Lord of the Treasury and Leader of the House of Commons. Grenville was allowed some say in the disposal of minor offices, but all the key appointments were filled by Bute. Even the members of the Treasury Board over which Grenville was to preside were named by Bute. When the ministry was formed, Grenville had an audience of the King and was given his instructions. He was told that the King had accepted him as minister on Bute's advice and as such he would be supported. (Nothing was said of his own qualifications for the office, and he was given to understand that these were not highly esteemed.) Fox's friends must be treated with the 'greatest kindness'; the country gentlemen must receive 'every degree of regard'; and Bute's brother, James Stuart Mackenzie, must continue to control the patronage of

Scotland. The King declaimed vigorously against New-castle and Pitt 'who had behaved so scandalously' (pre-sumably by conspiring against Bute), and declared he would rather yield his throne than admit them to office. (He was to make many similar declarations about other ministers in the years to come.) Grenville was meek and submissive and acknowledged his obligations to Bute – 'to which', wrote the King, 'I made him not the least compliment'.

Bute took no office, though the King wished him to become Lord Chamberlain; and after the ministry had been formed, left London for a cure at Harrogate. He took with him assurances of the King's inviolate attach-ment. The King professed contempt for his new ministers. 'I care not one farthing for these men I have now to do with', he wrote. They were grasping, greedy, and ungrate-ful, particularly Grenville, who had hardly assumed office when he began badgering the King for a rich sinecure for his family. (On Bute's advice the King granted the re-quest.) 'All those I employ are mean in their manners of thinking as well as their actions.' 'They forget what they owe me, but I shall not, therefore sooner or later they shall suffer for it.' Such was the way the King wrote about them. A trivial error by Grenville (he forgot to make an appointment for Lord le Despenser to kiss hands for his peerage) was visited by the King with a disproportionate degree of anger. 'I mean to reprimand Grenville myself', he wrote to Bute on 27 April 1763; and the next day: 'I spoke pretty strongly to him of his neglect . . . for which he made a million of excuses.' In successive letters he wrote of Grenville's 'tiresome manner' and 'selfish dis-position'. All this held out no prospect of long life to the new ministry.

It seems that the King vented his disillusionment with Bute on the head of the luckless Grenville. Bute was still his 'dear friend', and despite all the evidence of his in-capacity the King continued to depend upon him. The

Grenville ministry was intended as a mere façade. Bute was to remain the power behind the throne and final authority would rest with him. 'I shall never meet with a friend in business again', the King wrote. Grenville drew up the King's speech at the end of the session, and was ordered to send it to Bute for his approval. The patronage of Scotland remained with Bute, and the King intimated that ecclesiastical patronage would be placed at his disposal. The ministers were to be reduced to the level of clerks. 'I shall . . . without regret change my tools whenever they act contrary to my service', the King wrote on 14 April 1763. He told Bute on the eve of his departure for Harrogate: 'Thank God I have a friend, and that is what few princes can boast of except myself. That comforts me and makes me look on my ministers as my tools solely in my public capacity.' Above all things the King must preserve his independence – that is, his right to be dependent on Bute. 'My honour and everything that is dear to me depends on not getting men over me' – always, of course, excepting Bute.

This situation could not possibly continue. However much the King may have disliked Grenville, he was the King's choice. No pressure had been put upon the King by the House of Commons to take Grenville as his minister. He had done so of his own free will, acting on the advice of Bute. Once having done so, he was obliged to give Grenville his full political confidence. It was Grenville who had to accept responsibility to Parliament for the measures of government. No self-respecting minister could endure to have an irresponsible favourite placed over his head. If ever King George III can be accused of behaving in an unconstitutional manner it is during the first few months of the Grenville ministry.

Bute could remain the King's private friend only on condition that he did not interfere in politics. The days were long past when a favourite could govern Great Britain. The confidence of the Crown must go hand in hand with the power of the Crown. Bute had had his innings and had run himself out. He must now retire to the pavilion and make way for the next man. That, however, is what he did not do.

Between the resignation of Bute in April 1763 and the appointment of North in January 1770, five men held the office of first minister: Grenville, the Duke of Cumberland, the Marquess of Rockingham, Pitt (now Earl of Chatham), and the Duke of Grafton. This was a marked contrast from King George II's reign, when there were only six ministries during more than thirty years. The eighteenth century did not like short-lived ministries or the stresses and strains involved in the frequent turnover of ministers. They were regarded as an unhealthy sign in the body politic, a symptom of that dread disease faction. The cry was for unity and stability, for a ministry which comprehended the best men of all parties; and even politicians who played the party game felt bound to render lip-service to the ideal of a national ministry. Every age has its cant in politics, which is none the less taken seriously. The King shared this feeling, yet he must take part of the blame for the period of instability which followed Bute's resignation. This arose from his youth, inexperience, and dependence on Bute. Basically the trouble was that though Bute left office he did not leave politics and his influence continued – first as favourite and next as bogey man. Each minister in turn strove to occupy the position Bute had held and to enjoy the authority with the King which Bute had enjoyed. It was only when the bonds which connected the King to Bute weakened and the King had learnt to stand on his own feet politically that a stable situation became possible.

The Grenville ministry got off to a bad start. Within a matter of weeks it became involved in the case of the notorious John Wilkes, which brought on a prolonged parliamentary crisis and almost led to the ministry's defeat in the House of Commons. In July, before Wilkes's case had come before the House, the King told Grenville that he wished to strengthen the ministry by recalling Newcastle and Hardwicke – the very men whom only a few weeks before he had declared he would rather yield his throne than employ again. Grenville immediately suspected that this was Bute's doing and expressed the strongest objections. But the King went ahead, only to find that Hardwicke refused to return to office except as 'a party and upon a plan concerted with Mr Pitt and the great Whig lords' – in other words, only if Grenville were to retire. The King consulted Bute who seems to have advised him against this demand, and for the time being the idea was dropped.

In August 1763 the sudden death of Lord Egremont gave the King an opening to reconstruct the ministry, and Bute was ordered to begin negotiations with Pitt. Grenville expressed his 'surprise and concern' and 'declared strongly that it was absolutely contrary to his advice and opinion'. He reminded the King of his repeated declarations that he would not recall Pitt and of his promise to support the ministry. The next day (27 August) when Grenville went to the Queen's House he found Pitt closeted with the King, and to his humiliation had to wait two hours before being called for his audience. His account concludes:

The King held pretty near the same language as before, took no notice of Mr Pitt's having been with him, and in less than twenty minutes bowed to Mr Grenville [to signify that the audience was over], told him it was late, and, as he was going out of the room, said with emotion, 'Good morrow, Mr Grenville', and repeated it a second time, which was a phrase he had never used to him before.

Grenville left under the impression that his days in office were numbered.[6]

The next day, a Sunday, Grenville was summoned to

the Queen's House for eight o'clock in the evening. The time indicated some urgency, for the King rarely saw his ministers after dinner. Grenville found the King 'in the greatest agitation'. Pitt had proposed that Temple should become head of the Treasury and himself Secretary of State; Newcastle and his friends were to return to office, Devonshire to be again Lord Chamberlain (and presumably re-admitted to the Privy Council); and substantial changes to be made among the minor offices. In short, Pitt proposed a return to the Pitt Newcastle coalition of King George II's time, not merely as to men but as to measures. 'He strongly arraigned the peace', said it must be 'ameliorated', and hinted at his wish for closer relations with Prussia. The King had been staggered at what Grenville calls the unreasonableness of these demands, and he now requested Grenville to remain in office. The account in Grenville's diary continues:

[The King] gave [Grenville] the fullest assurances of every support and every strength that he could give him towards carrying his business into execution: that it was necessary the direction should be in one man's hands only, and he meant it should be in his; that he had no right after what had passed to expect a compliance with this proposal, but that he hoped for it, from the zeal, attachment, and love with which he had hitherto served him.

Grenville was gratified to hear this, professed his devotion to the King's service, but stipulated that no 'secret influence' should be allowed to prevail against the responsible ministers (the first time that his ominous phrase was used to the King). The King said that Bute wished to retire altogether (which was true – he had only intervened at the King's request), and that 'he would absent himself from the King for a time till an administration firmly established should leave no room for jealousy against him'.

Grenville was now the man of the hour. His career is an

interesting study of how a man of no outstanding abilities may rise to the top through sheer persistence, hard work, and a measure of good fortune. When King George III came to the throne no one could foresee that within three years Grenville would be his first minister. For the first twenty years of his political life Grenville had been no more than the younger brother of the rich, proud and overbearing Lord Temple, and brother-in-law of the domineering genius William Pitt. For years he had writhed beneath their patronage, kept down far below his natural level, until the new reign enabled him to stand on his own feet. He broke with his family and threw in his lot with Bute. But Bute was equally patronizing. In his correspondence with the King he refers to Grenville as 'George', and the use of a man's Christian name in the eighteenth century did not indicate a high degree of respect. Grenville was used by Bute to suit his own political convenience. He was first elevated to the leadership of the House of Commons and then summarily demoted to make way for Fox. In April 1763 he found himself transferred to the highest political office. Hardly was he settled into his place when there came the negotiation with Pitt and the opportunity for Grenville to kick away the ladder up which he had climbed.

It is a melancholy truth that men who rise suddenly in life are invariably ungrateful to their benefactors. There is an irresistible temptation to break with those who have known us when we were poor or humble. In justice to Grenville, it must be said that he would not have made an effective minister had he remained in the shadow of Bute. And he knew himself to be abler than Bute. Though unversed in foreign affairs (which he wisely left to others), he was a master of finance – the first business of the House of Commons – and soon commanded the confidence of the House. Considering the difficulties he faced, it is astonishing how quickly and surely he established his ministry. He had to overcome the hostility of the King, the patronage of Bute, the enmity of Pitt. In 1763 he had no following in Parliament. Yet in 1765 all the power of the Crown, aided by the Duke of Cumberland, was barely sufficient to eject him; and though he never again held office, no man in politics was more respected.

Grenville's relations with the King are full of interest to the student of human nature in politics. They would make the theme of a political novel, if another Trollope or another Disraeli could be found to do justice to the eighteenth century. The King began by treating Grenville with hauteur. Grenville remained humble and suppliant until Bute left London. Just as the King was beginning to appreciate Grenville, he met with such demands from his minister as no King could be expected to endure. In the end, though Grenville was the ablest man in the House of Commons and did the King's business better than any minister before the days of the younger Pitt, the King came to dislike him more than any other politician. And Grenville never understood why.

Grenville's first task was to make sure that Bute never again interfered in public affairs; his second, to strengthen his parliamentary position and ensure his own primacy. Almost immediately there was a renewal of tension with the King. Bute had held the office of Keeper of the Privy Purse which he now resigned, and the King proposed to appoint Sir William Breton. The office was entirely non-political and concerned the management of the King's private income. (Today it is at the disposal of the sovereign, not on the advice of the Prime Minister.) Bute had held it not as minister but as the King's friend. Breton, his designated successor, was also a private friend, and a former courtier of the King's father: he had been one of the party out riding with the King when he received the news of his grandfather's accident. From Grenville's point of view he was unsuitable because he was not a Member of Parliament and his appointment would not strengthen Grenville's position in the House of Commons.

He was also too closely connected with Bute, and his appointment might suggest that Bute's influence persisted. Grenville suggested Lord Guilford, the King's first governor (who had a son, Lord North, in the House of Commons); the King demurred; whereupon Grenville proposed that he should take the office himself and hold it without salary. He was intent on obtaining for himself all the authority Bute had held. The King heard his complaints 'with impatience and emotion', and 'claimed the right of disposing of an office so immediately about his own person'. Still Grenville persisted (one of the things the King came to dislike most about him was that he would never take no for an answer), until at last the King broke out: 'Good God! Mr Grenville, am I to be suspected after all I have done?' At these words Grenville gave way. 'The King seemed pleased', he noted in his diary, 'to have got rid of this matter according to his wishes.' But Grenville was not pleased.

Nor was he pleased to learn that the King had decided without consulting him to make the same allowance for his Privy Purse as he had done under Bute. This again was a private matter and no concern of the First Lord of the Treasury. But Grenville wished to bring the Privy Purse under Treasury control as were other departments of Crown finance – which would have made the Crown totally dependent on the House of Commons.

To strengthen the ministry Grenville, with the King's consent, offered the presidency of the Council to the Duke of Bedford. This brought an accession of about twenty votes in the House of Commons. Grenville himself, Lord Halifax and Lord Sandwich, the Secretaries of State, and Bedford, formed the inner circle of the cabinet, but were by no means a united body. There was considerable jealousy as to who should recommend to offices – like all good Whigs, they understood that the real business of government was the distribution of patronage. Had the King been politically ambitious or adroit he might have

184

taken advantage of these jealousies, played off one minister against another, and asserted his own supremacy. Instead, he threw the game into Grenville's hands. 'The King told Mr Grenville', runs the entry in Grenville's diary for 15 September 1763, '. . . that . . . he meant to take Mr Grenville's recommendations and his alone . . . for that he meant that all graces should be done through Mr Grenville alone, but that this conversation was only to be between His Majesty and Mr Grenville, as it would not be prudent to tell it to the other ministers.' As Leader of the House of Commons Grenville enforced his right to recommend to House of Commons appointments, and the King stood by him until Grenville grossly overplayed his hand.

There was no difference of political opinion between Grenville and the King. On the two great political issues which confronted the ministry – the prosecution of Wilkes and the taxation of America – King and minister thought alike. There was in fact much to draw them together, for Grenville had a concern for economy which like that of the King amounted almost to parsimony. But no agreement on political issues can overcome personal dislike. Grenville's favourite occupation, says Walpole, was talking, and 'brevity was not his failing'. Even Thomas Pitt, his cousin, admirer, and devoted political adherent, describes him as 'to a proverb tedious'. 'He was diffuse and argumentative', writes Pitt, 'and never had done with a subject after he had convinced your judgment till he had wearied your attention.' Henry Fox, so sharp and so clever at seeing the weaknesses of men, put his finger on the trouble. The King could not bear Grenville's self-righteousness and verbosity. 'A dose, so large, and so nauseous, often repeated, was too much for anybody's stomach.' The King, with natural good manners, always let his ministers have their say in their private audiences. Grenville went on and on and seemed as if he would never stop. 'When he has wearied me for two hours', said the King, 'he looks at his watch to see if he may not tire me for an hour more.' What hours of boredom the King must have had to endure listening to Grenville, generally at the end of a long and tiring afternoon at court!

The King might have put up with Grenville's tediousness had he not been so greedy of money and grasping of power. While preaching economy, Grenville took care to provide for his family at the expense of the nation. Yet when the King wished to spend money on his private comforts, Grenville became the Treasury watch-dog. Here is an example recorded by Walpole:

When His Majesty took in a portion of the Green Park to form a new garden for Buckingham House, the fields on the opposite side of the road were to be sold: the price, twenty thousand pounds. This sum Grenville refused to issue from the Treasury. The ground was sold to builders; and a new row of houses, each of which overlooked the King in his private walks, were erected to his great annoyance.

In 1801, when the King was recovering from the second attack of his illness, it is noted that as he walked in his garden he was overlooked from the windows of the houses in Grosvenor Place.

The King lived most of the week at Kew, where Bute also had a house. In order to be able to spy on the King and make sure that he was not caballing with Bute, Grenville petitioned for a grant of New Lodge in Richmond Park – and did not scruple to enlist Bute to plead his cause. It was by such conduct that Grenville made himself obnoxious to the King.

On the political level Grenville grasped at the right to appoint to every office that became vacant. In 1764, on the death of Hogarth, the King proposed to abolish the office of Court Painter. Grenville objected and told Thomas Worsley, in whose department the office fell, that if anyone presumed to speak to the King on patronage business without Grenville's consent 'he would not serve an hour'. This incident made a deep impression on the King. He mentions it in the memorandum he drew up to explain his conduct towards the Grenville ministry, and according to Bute it was 'the original cause of the King's displeasure with Mr Grenville'. There was a perpetual dispute between Grenville and Stuart Mackenzie, Bute's brother, about Scottish patronage. In April 1764 the King wrote to Bute about the appointment of a judge in Scotland:

I am glad there has been this struggle of the ministers for I will show them who recommends Scotch offices. I have ever declared Mr Mackenzie for that department, I will settle that matter instantly, and if they have not understood my orders on this occasion it is not for want of explaining the thing clearly.

And at the end of the letter: 'As I understand my dear friend has settled with Mackenzie the judge, I will hasten the execution of it.'

Bute then was still influential if he could control Scottish appointments. To this extent Grenville's complaints had substance. He was Leader of the House of Commons, and it was intolerable that a portion of the patronage of the House should lie outside his control. The dispute over Bute's influence lay in the field of patronage, not policy. On issues of policy Bute could not have interfered even had he wished: these were the business of the cabinet. Patronage was another matter: here Bute could interfere. In theory all offices under the Crown were at the disposal of the sovereign. But in practice there had to be a modus vivendi between King and minister. The King had to recognize that in general patronage must be distributed with a view to gaining parliamentary support; the minister had to recognize that in some areas (primarily court, Church, and army) the King must be allowed to appoint irrespective of parliamentary considerations. The trouble with Grenville was that he would allow the King no say; and whenever his recommendations met with objections, immediately set these down to the influence of Bute. He could never forget that it was through Bute that he had received his office; that he had been Bute's very humble servant and follower; and that Bute had addressed him as 'Dear George' instead of 'Dear Sir'. The King did his best to assure Grenville that Bute was 'a private man and meant to remain so'. Grenville did not believe him. 'Mr Grenville', his diary runs, 'answered him with great civility and no overstrained professions.' He knew that Bute continued to see the King, and he was as jealous of his power as a lover of his mistress.

Matters came to a head after the King's illness in the spring of 1765. Apart from an attack of chicken pox in July 1761 and a brief illness a year later (of which the main symptoms were pain in the breast and a cough), the King had enjoyed good health. In 1765, however, he was ill intermittently from January to April. On 18 January he was reported to have a 'violent cold' with pain in the breast for which he was blooded. On 25 February he was blooded again and kept his bed 'with a feverish cold'. On 3 March there was a return of fever and pain in the breast. But he was not so ill as to be unable to transact business, and Grenville and the other ministers saw him regularly. Rumours circulated that he had a tendency to consumption, and Lord Holland (the former Henry Fox) told Walpole that he believed the King would not live a year.

On 3 April the King was sufficiently recovered to be able to resume his levee, which Grenville attended. He writes in his diary:

Mr Grenville went afterwards to the King in his closet. His Majesty told him that, before he spoke upon any other subject, he desired to apprize him of one of a very serious nature – viz. a bill of Regency, which he had thought upon during his illness, but would not enter upon until he was quite well and able to appear.

He asked Grenville to convene the cabinet to discuss the matter. In general he approved of the Act of 1751 but wished for one fundamental change: that he himself should have the power of naming the Regent 'without specifying the particular person in the Act of Parliament'. Grenville bowed, 'expressed his general approbation of the King's goodness in thinking of a Regency', and proceeded to other business. He did not tell the King his real thoughts.[7]

All Grenville's suspicions were roused, as well they might be. The proposal to reserve to the King the right to nominate the Regent was unprecedented. In all previous Acts the Regent had been named. Why did not the King follow former practice? The natural choice for Regent and guardian of the infant King in the event of the demise of the Crown would be the Queen, the surviving parent. No one would object to the Queen as Regent. Why then was she not appointed? Was this a device to enable the King to name his mother without the odium of an open nomination? Was this Bute's method of making sure that his influence would continue even in the event of the King's death? These were the suspicions that filled the minds of Grenville and his colleagues, and it must be admitted that the King had given some grounds for them.

The Regency Bill is a curious and misunderstood episode in King George III's life. Two points must be made clear at once. First, the bill provided only for the event of the King's death, not for his incapacity. It would hardly be necessary to state this obvious fact were it not that it has generally been believed that the King's illness in 1765 was accompanied by symptoms of insanity, and some historians have declared that the Regency Bill provided against the event of a future attack. As will be shown later, the story of the King's insanity in 1765 is pure myth and was unknown to contemporaries. Secondly, there is no evidence that Bute was consulted on the bill. It seems to have been entirely the King's own idea and was put

189

into legal shape by Lord Mansfield. The Regency Bill, far from demonstrating the influence of Bute as Grenville supposed, was a sign that the King was about to throw off Bute's influence.

If it was the King's intention from the beginning to appoint the Queen Regent, which seems to have been the case and which was in fact done, why was she not named in the bill? Had there been an open nomination the bill would have had an easy passage through Parliament and all suspicion of Bute would have been avoided. Perhaps there was a purely legal objection. The Queen could not exercise the powers of Regency until she came of age which would not be until after the bill had become law. But the real reason was the one the King gave to Grenville, who did not believe it – to prevent any 'faction or uneasiness' in the Royal Family. It was not his mother about whom the King was concerned but his brother Edward, Duke of York, who stood in 1765 precisely where the Duke of Cumberland had stood in 1751 – the nearest adult male in succession to the throne. As such it might be held that he had a better claim to the Regency than that of a woman born outside the kingdom. Relations between the King and the Duke of York were not good. The King disapproved of his brother's mode of life and something like jealousy had replaced the affection of their younger days. The King would not appoint the Duke Regent and leave to him the charge of his son's upbringing. He did not want the Duke to be on the council formed to advise the Regent, until the Duke of Cumberland persuaded him that to omit the Royal Dukes would give offence. But though determined to exclude his brother as far as possible, he had no wish to parade openly the ill feeling between them. There had been far too many quarrels in the Royal Family already. Hence the reason why he did not tell Grenville what was in his mind and why he desired the nomination of Regent to be kept secret. When the time came he named the Queen, and the Princess

Dowager in the event of her death. The inclusion of the Princess is explicable only on the assumption that she was named in order to exclude the Duke of York, for to become Regent she would have to outlive both her son and daughter-in-law – a highly unlikely event. The Regency Bill was framed not to let the Princess in as Grenville feared but to keep the Duke of York out. It is another example in the history of monarchy of fear of the 'wicked uncle'.

All this, however, was unknown to Grenville, and the King said nothing to enlighten him. He regarded the bill as a family affair: Grenville as a political measure. Consequently neither understood the other. Grenville failed to realize the King's obsession with the Duke of York, and the King failed to realize Grenville's obsession with Bute. The result was an elaborate game in which the King and the politicians were at cross purposes.

When Grenville expressed his doubts about the proposal to reserve the nomination of the Regent and hinted that it would meet with opposition in Parliament, the King was bewildered. 'Mr Grenville', he said, 'you have more than once thrown out an idea of this being attended with some difficulty. . . . Is that your opinion and from whence does it arise?' But all Grenville would say was 'that he believed it would be much more secure' to name the Regent. He described the King as 'agitated and embarrassed' and uncertain what to do, but gave him no help.

The bill was introduced in the House of Lords, where a motion to address the King to name the Regent was rejected by 89 votes to 31. This was followed by a prolonged discussion on the legal aspects of the bill. The choice of Regent was to be limited to the Queen 'or any other person of the Royal Family usually residing in Great Britain'. But who was of the Royal Family? Did it consist only of those in remainder to the Crown? If so, the Princess Dowager was not a member and was ineligible to become Regent. Only British subjects could hold office under the Crown. Was the Queen a British subject by virtue of her marriage though no formal act of naturalization had passed? These and other questions puzzled the King, who had no head for legal distinctions. It was suggested to him, apparently by Lord Halifax, that matters would go much easier if he were to agree to the omission of the Princess Dowager. Since the King had no intention of naming his mother as Regent he saw no objection to this proposal, and himself suggested the addition of the words 'born in England' which effectively excluded her. The bill thus amended passed the Lords and was sent down to the Commons.

Horace Walpole's account of the bill represents the ministers as taking advantage of the King's inexperience to induce him to put a public slight upon his mother. But Walpole was convinced that the Princess was aiming at the Regency, whereas all the evidence suggests that she was totally uninterested in the bill. The Lords' amendment was in fact a slight on the Princess, and it is evidence of the King's naivety and inexperience that he did not realize this until it was pointed out to him by the Lord Chancellor. When Grenville was admitted into the closet, 'the King coloured, and, with great emotion, said that he had something to speak to him upon, which gave him the greatest uneasiness, which was the mark of disregard shown to the Princess of Wales, his mother, by the words which excluded her alone from the Regency' (he was obviously embarrassed at not having seen this before). Lord Chancellor Northington had represented (correctly) 'that many people were much offended by it' and (incorrectly) 'that a motion against it would be made by the opposition'. Could not Grenville propose in the House of Commons the re-insertion of the Princess's name? No, Grenville could not.

Mr Grenville then endeavoured to show His Majesty how impossible it was for him to propose the alteration: that His

Majesty's Secretary of State [Halifax] having, with his authority, proposed those words which excluded Her Royal Highness, how could his Chancellor of the Exchequer [Grenville] by the same authority propose the adding her name? That people must and would suppose that either the one or the other had mistaken His Majesty.

All this, Grenville went on to say, would never have happened if only the King had agreed to name the Regent in the bill. If only the King had listened to Grenville, how easy things would have been! Of course Grenville was perfectly right. But he did not know that it was the King's wish to exclude the Duke of York which had brought him into this unpleasant situation. 'The King was in the utmost degree of agitation and emotion, even to tears.'

In the House of Commons on 9 May John Morton, a former member of Frederick, Prince of Wales's party, moved to re-insert the Princess's name. He did so without authority from the Princess, simply in order to repair what he considered to have been a public slight upon her. Grenville saw that no opposition could be offered by the ministry, and the amendment was carried without a division. On the report stage the next day some wild spirits among the opposition moved to delete the amendment and were beaten by 167 votes to 37. Thus the bill became law in the form proposed by the King: and after giving it his assent the King signed an instrument nominating the Queen as Regent and in the event of her death the Princess Dowager.

It had been a difficult time for King George. He had barely recovered from his illness when he proposed the Regency Bill, and he might not have done so had he realized the difficulties that confronted him. He did not enjoy being involved in political and legal discussions and these had been more than usually tiresome and complex. But before the bill had gone through he had inaugurated a ministerial crisis which was to cause him even greater anxiety, to determine much of his future attitude towards

193

politicians, and to reveal him as the veriest political simpleton.

On 13 May 1765 an apparently innocuous bill for raising the duties on the importation of Italian silks was rejected in the House of Lords, largely through the opposition of the Duke of Bedford. 'It happened', writes Walpole, 'that the silk manufacture was at a low ebb, and many weavers in Spitalfields were unemployed.' On 14 May a body of weavers, estimated at about four thousand strong, marched to Kew to petition the King to relieve their distress. The Queen who was six months pregnant was alarmed, but no disturbance took place and the King promised he would do what he could for them. The next day, 'uneasy and very much disturbed', he mentioned the matter to Grenville and pressed him 'very earnestly to see what could be done'. That afternoon when the King went to the House of Lords to give his assent to the Regency Bill he was followed by a large mob. The Duke of Bedford was hissed and pelted and a large stone was flung into his carriage which cut his hand and bruised his temple. These events touched off the worst riots which London had known for many years. It was against this background that the King opened negotiations for changing his administration.

The first hint the King gave of his intention was on 7 April when he summoned the Duke of Cumberland to the Queen's House to hear the provisions of the Regency Bill. The King had not seen his uncle in private for three years, and the Duke had been extremely ill during the winter. The wound in his knee, received at Dettingen, had broken out, and he had been compelled to undergo a painful operation. Indeed at one time the rumour ran that he was dead.

The King began the audience by telling the Duke that he had summoned him to the Queen's House to save him the trouble of climbing the stairs at St James's – and also, perhaps, that their meeting might not attract undue attention. For this audience was not a mere mark of courtesy on the King's part. Contrary to his usual custom, he prepared notes of what he wished to say. He intended to tell the Duke 'according as he shall express himself . . . that I have not reason to be satisfied with some of the people I employ'. But the conversation did not get so far. 'I did perceive', writes the Duke in his account, 'or at least I thought I did, that His Majesty had still more on his mind to communicate; but I did not think it respectful to endeavour to know more fully what was in the King's mind.'

It is not surprising that the King hesitated to open himself to his uncle, for the Duke had been more or less in opposition ever since the peace treaty. That the King should choose to confide in him after all that had passed between them indicates the depth of his feelings about his ministers. But in whom else could he confide? He had promised to exclude Bute from political affairs, and after the fiasco of August 1763 he could not again employ Bute as a political negotiator. He was on bad terms with his eldest brother and reluctant to entrust him with political secrets. It only remained to swallow his pride and send for the Duke of Cumberland. He could not have done better. The Duke had a respect for the dignity and honour of the Crown and would not see it disgraced. He had disliked his nephew's dependence on Bute, but now that Bute was no longer of account he was willing to let bygones be bygones. In his time of trial, the King found that his 'wicked uncle' was really a benevolent uncle who stood by him in his distress.

The Duke absented himself from Parliament while the Regency Bill was under discussion and went to Newmarket for the spring meeting. There he had a conversation with Lord Northumberland, the retiring Lord Lieutenant of Ireland, apparently by accident but really by the King's command, in which Northumberland gave the

Duke to understand that the King was displeased with his ministers. Further conversations took place in London, but the Duke was loath to take part in political negotiations until the Regency Bill had been completed. At last, late in the evening of 13 May, the day the bill received its final reading, Northumberland came to the Duke 'by His Majesty's order' with a commission to negotiate with Pitt and Newcastle for the formation of a 'strong and lasting ministry'. Northumberland himself was to be head of the Treasury, Pitt Secretary of State, and Newcastle either Lord President of the Council or Lord Privy Seal. Of the Grenville cabinet only Lord Egmont, First Lord of the Admiralty, was set down to retain his office, though it is probable the King also intended to keep the Lord Chancellor Northington. The Duke discussed these arrangements with Newcastle and Rockingham the next day, and arranged to send his political agent, Lord Albemarle, to see Pitt at Hayes.

Northumberland's instructions were to preserve the 'utmost secrecy and celerity'. But it was impossible to prevent rumours from leaking out, and as early as 9 May Bedford had spoken 'very strongly' to the King about 'the reports which were got about of an intended change'. On 16 May Grenville taxed the King squarely with planning to change the ministry, and the King was confused and embarrassed. 'Mr Grenville, I will speak to you another time about that,' he said. 'I promise you I will speak to you; you may depend upon it I will speak to you.' At this point the silk weavers' riots boiled up. On 17 May Bedford's house in Bloomsbury Square was attacked by a mob and troops had to be summoned. Walpole writes:

As was foreseen, the rioters in prodigious numbers assaulted the house in the evening, and began to pull down the wall of the court; but the great gates being thrown open, the party of horse appeared, and sallying out, while the Riot Act was read, rode round Bloomsbury Square, slashing and trampling on the mob, and dispersing them. . . . In the mean time a party of the

196

rioters had passed to the back of the house, and were forcing their way through the garden, when fortunately fifty more horse arriving in the very critical instant, the house was saved, and perhaps the lives of all that were in it.

The King was detained at Kew with a recurrence of his illness, and from there directed the movement of troops into London. On 18 May another great crowd assembled outside Bedford House, but according to Grenville 'more from curiosity than from anything else' and no attack was made. Still, the ministry believed that the danger was not over; and Halifax recommended the appointment of the popular hero, the Marquess of Granby, to the command of the army. Granby, he wrote, 'might save the lives of these deluded wretches, which may be exposed and sacrificed by another commander equally well-intentioned but less a favourite of the people'. This was an obvious hit at the Duke of Cumberland: and drew from the King a gesture of confidence in his uncle the strongest that he could make – no less than an invitation to the Duke to resume his former appointment of Captain-General. The Duke was touched. His nephew was of the right breed after all. (The Hanoverian Kings were always reluctant to confide the command of the army outside the Royal Family.) 'I don't imagine these reports ought to break a moment of Your Majesty's rest', the Duke wrote. 'I wish to God you had no more formidable enemies than these poor wretches.' He believed that the danger from the rioters had been exaggerated by the ministry in order to put pressure on the King, and that the situation was not so serious as to demand the appointment of a Captain-General. Halifax asked in the House of Lords who could dare to advise the dismissal of 'so great and deserving a man' as the Duke of Bedford and 'make him a victim to the rage of the populace'. The mob was at the door, said Grenville in the Commons, and no government to suppress it. Stories were told that the mob had threatened to pull down every mercer's shop in London and level Bedford House to the ground. Alarmist these stories may have been, but such things could happen as was shown fifteen years later during the Gordon riots. The King was hurt at the slander that he had remained at Kew through fear and declared that if need arose he would put himself at the head of the army.

Meanwhile the negotiations with Pitt had broken down. Newcastle and his friends were willing to return to office provided Pitt would take the lead. But Pitt was coy. He stayed in the country and returned discouraging answers to the Duke of Cumberland's emissaries. On Sunday, 19 May, at the King's request, the Duke went to Hayes to talk face to face with Pitt – an unprecedented act of condescension on the part of a Royal Duke. He had been given plenipotentiary powers from the King to agree to all Pitt's terms – even to his demand for an alliance with Prussia, which it must have cost the King many a pang to accept. Temple was to become First Lord of the Treasury with Pitt as Secretary of State and in charge of foreign affairs. But Pitt, in the modern idiom, 'played it cool'. He talked about his ill health and said that he could not come into office while Bute remained influential about the King. This was humbug. He knew perfectly well that the Duke of Cumberland's presence at Hayes was proof that Bute's reign was over. For five hours the Duke used every argument and gave every assurance. He might as well have talked to a brick wall. Pitt was always proof against the call of duty where he saw nothing to his own advantage. Sadly the Duke returned to London and vowed 'that in the future he would ever be the King's man'.

There was nothing left for the King but to make the best terms he could with the ministers. Those terms would be hard. Grenville's vanity was hurt, and he took immediate revenge by lectures in the closet of even more intolerable length. The peppery Duke of Bedford was indignant at having been kept two days a prisoner in his own house. He told the King to his face that Bute 'was the exciter of this mob, that he was at the bottom of it'. Halifax in the Lords openly referred to Bute as 'an evil counsellor about the King'. Grenville observed that the mob was 'well disciplined' and had obviously been paid for its work. Bute was hoisted with his own petard. In 1762 he had accused Newcastle and Pitt of instigating the mob that had attacked him on his way to the House of Lords. Now in 1765 he himself was the victim of an equally foolish and unfounded accusation. Thus the wheel turns round. Fear of the mob was endemic throughout the eighteenth century, and whenever the mob gathered it was always supposed to have been spirited up by some politician for his own purposes.

The ministers now had the King at their mercy. King George had been foolish. He had been foolish to confide the government to a favourite: foolish to continue with his favourite after Grenville had become minister: foolish not to admit Grenville into his confidence about the Regency Bill: foolish to antagonize his ministers before he was certain of their successors. But however foolish he had been, he did not deserve the humiliation which Grenville was about to inflict upon him. When the King received Grenville on 21 May he had to eat the humblest of humble pie. According to Grenville's diary, he told his minister 'that he had a design to change his government but not the part which was under his care' – which if correctly reported was untrue. It seems that almost at the last moment the King was desperately trying to divide his ministers, an expedient which might have occurred to him before had he been the Machiavellian character depicted by some contemporaries. He praised Grenville, but said there had been 'slackness, inability, precipitation, and neglect' on the part of Grenville's colleagues – an unfair accusation about the most efficient ministry which governed England during the first twenty years of the King's reign. He denied that Bute had any responsibility for what had happened, and Grenville replied in effect that he did not believe him. The King concluded by requesting Grenville to remain in office. Grenville answered that he must first consult his colleagues.

At eight o'clock that evening the ministers met at Bedford House, now free from the attentions of the mob. There were present at this unique cabinet meeting (if such it can be called): Grenville, Bedford, Halifax, Sandwich, and Northington. Egmont, the other regular member of the cabinet, who had taken the King's part throughout the crisis, was either not invited or refused to attend. The King was impatient to learn the result of their deliberations and at 9.15 wrote a note to Grenville – 'I am surprised that you are not yet come, when you knew it was my orders to be attended this evening. I expect you therefore to come the moment you receive this.' In the twelve large volumes of George III's correspondence there is no other letter written in quite so peremptory a style. Grenville left the meeting and hastened to the Queen's House. 'What conditions do you mean to ask?' inquired the King. Grenville replied that they had not yet finished their deliberations, but that he could at least tell the King that they must have the 'strongest assurances' that Bute must never again have anything to do with his affairs and that Mackenzie must no longer 'hold up the standard of ministry for Lord Bute in Scotland'. The King asked what else? Grenville said that they were to meet again the following morning to complete the list of demands. All he could say at present was that however hard these might appear they were not so hard as Pitt would have imposed. He concluded with a warning that there must also be an understanding about the position of the Duke of Cumberland. Thus Grenville proscribed at the same time both Bute and the Duke – an ironical commentary on the last years of King George II's reign! Grenville's account of his audience ends: 'The King in the course of the conversation repeated several times that he was an honest man, and that he hoped Mr Grenville thought he was so.'

Hardly had Grenville gone, when the Duke of Cumberland was announced. He brought the news that Pitt had finally declined and that Newcastle and his friends would not come in without him. In an audience that lasted till one o'clock in the morning, he managed to convince the King (and the King must have required a great deal of convincing for the audience to be prolonged to so late an hour) that there was no alternative but to accept Grenville's terms, whatever they might be. The next day, 22 May, at twelve noon, Grenville presented them in full. They comprised, in addition to those respecting Bute and Mackenzie, the appointment of Granby as commander-in-chief, the dismissal of Lord Holland from the Pay Office, and the appointment of a Lord Lieutenant of Ireland 'by the full approbation and recommendation of the ministers'. To put an additional bite on the King, Grenville informed him that he had that morning been reconciled to his brother Lord Temple. He concluded with the warning that these terms were 'absolutely sine qua non'. 'The King said he would consider of them, and give Mr Grenville his answer in the evening.'

The burden of kingship lay heavy on the 26-year-old King that day. During the course of the afternoon and evening he gave audiences to the Lord Chancellor, the Duke of Cumberland (an hour's conversation), Bedford, Granby (another hour), Egmont (two hours), and then followed further talks with the Duke and the Chancellor. By the time he sent for Grenville at eleven at night he must have been almost worn out. He had not been in bed until one that morning: he had risen at his usual hour of seven: and since then had given no less than eight audiences – each one long, critical, and presenting a different point of view. Mental stress apart, there was the sheer physical fatigue of this day and the effort of remembering and evaluating what each person had said. And finally, at eleven at night, he had to face the voluble and self-righteous George Grenville. Kings are not more than ordinary men. They are not gifted with superhuman powers of body or of mind. They require the same number of hours for sleep, for relaxation, for refreshment as other people do. King George had not yet recovered from a serious illness. Let us pause for a moment and consider not the King but the man, faced with such a day's labour. The King never forgot the twenty-second of May 1765. It was a traumatic experience in his life. He vowed never again to submit to another like it.

The King persuaded Granby, who was an easy-going man and had not solicited the appointment, to decline the command of the army. The other demands he granted without demur, except only Mackenzie's dismissal. He was ready to divest Mackenzie of the control of Scottish patronage, but begged that he should be allowed to retain the sinecure office of Lord Privy Seal of Scotland which the King had promised him for life. He told Grenville:

He saw evidently they were not satisfied with his parting with his power, but that nothing would content him but his parting with his honour too – bid him take notice what he told him – and earnestly and in great anger bid him take notice of this – more than once – that he had forced him to part with his honour – that as a King for the safety of his people he must submit – but that nothing induced him to this but the danger of the crisis.

These are the words the King himself told Egmont he had used to Grenville. In Grenville's diary there is simply the sentence: 'The King complained bitterly of the hardship put upon him in making him dismiss Mr Mackenzie.' Self-centred and insensitive to the feelings of others, Grenville never realized the affront he gave to the King in the matter of Mackenzie. King George III was a simple man with a simple code of honour and nothing hurt him so much as to be forced to break his word. The wish to reinstate Mackenzie had an influence on his politics during the next few months far beyond its intrinsic importance. In time the King learnt to forgive all his minis-

202

ters for their conduct on 22 May 1765 – except Grenville. Bedford was taken back into favour, Halifax again became Secretary of State, Sandwich was First Lord of the Admiralty for eleven years. But for Grenville, the man who had insisted on the dismissal of Mackenzie, there was no forgiveness. In July 1767 the King told a friend of Horace Walpole that 'he had rather see the Devil in his closet than Mr Grenville'. From 22 May 1765 to the day of Grenville's death on 13 November 1770 the King's politics revolved round two aims: first to get Grenville out of office, and next, to make sure he never came back. And he never did.

On 24 May Grenville found the King 'very gloomy and with an air of great dissatisfaction', and the doctors were ordered to attend. The King told one of them that he had not slept for more than two hours a night for several days. He felt so weak and depressed that he asked Grenville for permission to go into the country – an astonishing act of abasement for a King, which it would be impossible to believe were it not recorded by Grenville in his diary:

His Majesty asked Mr Grenville if he might not go that night into the country, for he felt that he wanted the air. Mr Grenville said by all means, and he was glad to hear that His Majesty intended it, as he thought it would do him good.

At Kew on Sunday, 26 May, the King was so unwell 'that he did not chuse to take the Sacrament that day' and the usual drawing room was cancelled. It is against the background of a serious physical illness, which deprived the King of sleep and left him weak, that we ought to see the events of May 1765.

The ultimatum of 22 May was merely the first of the demands the ministers intended to make. 'Rigby [Bedford's political agent] swore a great oath', writes Walpole, 'that the King should not have power to appoint one of his own footmen.' Grenville was the master now and proceeded to crack the whip. On 29 May, when the King was sufficiently recovered to be able to resume his levees, Grenville asked him to appoint a friend of Bedford to the office of Master of the Horse to the Queen. Ill and humiliated though the King was, he still had the spirit to refuse this recommendation. He told Grenville that this was not an office at the disposal of the ministry. It was a court employment about the Queen and the Queen should appoint whom she pleased. Grenville bowed and acquiesced. But a few days later he came again with a request to recommend to a military employment equally beyond the disposal of the First Lord of the Treasury. Newcastle would hardly have dared to make such an application to King George II. 'The King's countenance is certainly calmer and his manner civiller than it was', Grenville wrote on 7 June, 'but Mr Grenville has no reason to think it proceeds from anything but disguise.' The ministers knew that they were tolerated only because the King had no alternative. And so they decided to bring matters to a test and stake their future on one throw.

On 12 June Bedford, who was about to go to Woburn for a few weeks, sought an audience to clear up outstanding business in his office – and also to bring the King finally to heel. The ministers had approved a paper which Bedford read to the King, complaining of his failure to show them the 'countenance and support' he had promised and charging him with continuing to consult Bute. It was worded in the strongest, indeed most disrespectful manner, and contained something very like a threat against Bute:

Is not the King, in his retirement [i.e., when he was at Kew], beset with avowed enemies? Is not the Earl of Bute, representing the ministers in a bad light to the King, either by himself or his emissaries, interfering at least indirectly in public counsels?

Does not this favourite, by interfering in this manner, and not daring to take a responsible employment, risk the utmost hazard to himself and, which is of more consequence, risk the King's quiet and the safety of the public?

Bedford concluded by beseeching (or rather, commanding) the King 'to permit his authority and his favour and countenance to go together' and by giving him a month to make up his mind. To add to the offence, Bedford told everyone what he had said and in a matter of days the audience was the talk of every drawing room in London.

'You will, my dear Lord', the King wrote to Northington after this audience, 'easily conceive what indignation I felt at so very offensive a declaration, yet I mastered my temper and we parted with cool civility.' No King could accept such a remonstrance from his ministers. Had King George yielded to this second ultimatum he would have become a mere *roi fainéant* with Grenville as his mayor of the palace. He would have been despised by his family, by his people, by every King in Europe, by the very men who governed him. He would have betrayed the inheritance which it was his duty to preserve and hand on to his successor. Eighteen years later another minister was to attempt where Grenville had failed, and Charles James Fox was to learn in 1783 what Grenville had learnt in 1765 – that the nation would support the King in defence of his prerogative.

The Duke of Cumberland was again commissioned to sound Pitt, and if Pitt again refused, to try to form a ministry from 'those worthy men', the Duke of Newcastle and his friends. 'For they are men who have principles', wrote the King, 'and therefore cannot approve of seeing the Crown dictated to by low men.' What a change from the way he had written about Newcastle a few years earlier! On 19 June Pitt saw the King for three hours. The King's notes for this audience are a revealing document. He assured Pitt that Bute would not interfere. 'I will pledge my word there is not a man in England on whose friendship you may more fully depend.' Pitt knew this by the very fact of the Duke of Cumberland undertaking the office of negotiator. The King then begged Pitt not to dismiss those friends of Bute who still remained in office. 'Why will you wish to turn out men that it would sting me to the quick if I could be brought to part with them? Take them under you, whom they will not support the less firmly for having proved themselves attached to me.' Pitt knew this also. 'You can name me no Whig families', continued the King, 'that shall not have my countenance, but where Tories come to me on Whig principles let us take them.' Who knew this better than Pitt, who had himself taken Tories on Whig principles and had done more than any man to reconcile the Tories to the Hanoverian dynasty? On one point only did the King have reservations – Pitt's wish for an alliance with Prussia. 'The ramming Austria deeper with France', he wrote in his notes, 'and kindling a new war by unnecessary alliances are things I can neither answer to my God nor to my conscience.'

But the negotiations were not broken off on an issue of policy. Men not measures dictated Pitt's conduct. The ostensible reason he gave for refusing to form a ministry in June 1765 was Temple's refusal to take the Treasury. The real reason was that the offer had come to him through the Duke of Cumberland, and that had he accepted he would have been compelled to rely on the support of those who professed allegiance to the Duke. Pitt would have no mediator between himself and the throne. Had he taken office in August 1763 he would have been obliged to Bute: had he taken office in June 1765 he would have been obliged to the Duke of Cumberland. And Pitt would be obliged to no man. With him it must be *ego et rex meus*.

And so the Duke was entrusted with the formation of the new ministry. He had considerable difficulty in doing so, for some of Newcastle's friends would not serve without Pitt and all were as suspicious of Bute as ever Grenville or Bedford were. At the head of the Treasury the Duke placed the Marquess of Rockingham, one of his racing friends; and the Duke of Grafton, another Newmarket associate, became Secretary of State. The other Secretary of State, and Leader of the House of Commons, was General Henry Seymour Conway, who had been the Duke's aide-de-camp at Fontenoy and Culloden. Newcastle and Winchilsea, old men with but a few years to live, and Northington and Egmont, survivors from the Grenville ministry but primarily attached to the King, completed the cabinet. The Duke himself held no office but presided at Cabinet meetings and was the real Prime Minister.

The new government, known to history as the Rockingham administration, was a constitutional anomaly. It is the strangest cabinet in British history. It is the only one to be presided over by a Royal Duke. It is the only one formed round the principal members of the Jockey Club. Apart from Conway, who had served for a few years as Secretary to the Lord Lieutenant of Ireland, none of the men who filled the three principal departments of state had ever before held political office. The King had escaped from the control of Grenville only to fall under that of his uncle. The man who in 1755 had been depicted to him as a potential Richard III, to combat whose influence the Princess Dowager had summoned Bute to Leicester House – 'Viceroy' Cumberland and his three inexperienced and incompetent lieutenants now governed England! Our history knows no stranger irony.[8]

Chapter 4

THE YEARS OF CONFUSION

The Duke of Cumberland died on 31 October 1765, at the age of only forty-four. His death could hardly have happened at a more untimely moment. The ministers were deprived of their leader before they had met Parliament and before he had had time to weld them into a team. Had the Duke lived even twelve months longer the political history of King George III's reign would have been different. The difficulties which arose between the King and his ministers would have been smoothed over and their asperity against Bute toned down. The Duke, as Horace Walpole saw, could speak to the King with an authority and favour denied to the ministers. 'He could have interposed in their behalf, or could have bent them to necessary submission to the Crown, which no other man in England was capable of doing.' Had the Duke remained at their head, they might have become the strong and stable ministry which the King desired and the confusion of the following years might have been avoided. Deprived of his lead, his incapable lieutenants floundered and ran the ship on the rocks.

When the Duke died, Newcastle told the King that 'there was a chasm which must be supplied'. The ministry must secure additional strength to face the opposition that would be raised in Parliament, certainly by Grenville, possibly by Pitt. The King wished his ministers to make a firm alliance with Bute's party. This included some of the ablest men in the House of Commons, though none of the first rank; and now that their erstwhile leader was unable to protect them, they were desirous of attaching themselves directly to government. But the Rockinghams, like the Grenvilles, though with much less reason, were

208

haunted by the shade of Bute. Grenville, after all, had some reason to complain of Bute, though his suspicions were exaggerated. But Newcastle's and Rockingham's suspicions were beyond all reason. Was it to be imagined that the Duke of Cumberland, the man whom Bute had sworn to destroy as a political figure, would form and preside over a cabinet if his enemy still remained influential with the King? The fact that the King had turned to the Duke to help him get rid of Grenville was evidence that he no longer entertained confidence in Bute. Now that the Duke was dead, the Rockinghams must put their trust in the King. They must accept his assurances that Bute was no more than a private friend. They must defer to the King's feelings. Nothing could have established their ministry on a firmer basis than restoring Mackenzie to his office. This would have relieved the King of a weight on his conscience and have won them his goodwill. But this, despite all the Duke of Cumberland's authority, they resolutely refused to do. They treated Bute as if he were a pariah – one absolutely beyond the pale, with whom no contact should be made – and they extended this treatment to all who had any connection, however distant, with Bute. To give one example: they proscribed the Earl of Northumberland, a good courtier if ever there was one, simply because Northumberland's son had married Bute's daughter. The Rockinghams prided themselves on what they called their 'consistency', which with foolish people means that once you have said a thing you must adhere to it for evermore. Like servants out of place, they were intensely concerned for their characters, and they felt that their characters would be damned for all time if they ever bestowed a favour on one of Bute's friends. They began by distrusting the King and they ended by wondering why the King distrusted them. The proper relationship of confidence between King and ministers, which the Duke of Cumberland would have fostered and developed, was never achieved by his lieutenants. It would have required a higher degree of statesmanship than either Newcastle or Rockingham possessed. Or King George III.

The ministers hoped to fill the chasm made by the Duke's death by taking in Pitt. On this there was a difference of opinion which split the cabinet and eventually wrecked the ministry. Rockingham and Newcastle wanted Pitt as an ally, an accession to the existing ministry, and expected him to recognize their pre-eminence. Grafton and Conway (in so far as Conway could ever make up his mind) wanted Pitt as their leader. They regarded the existing ministry as a mere substitute for the one Pitt had been unable to form, to be dissolved whenever Pitt found it convenient to take office. Egmont and Northington ostentatiously dissociated themselves from their colleagues and professed allegiance only to the Crown.

The King was anxious above all to keep out Grenville. He wished the ministry to continue because the only alternative seemed to be one dominated by Grenville. Shortly before his dismissal Grenville had been reconciled to his brother, Temple, and this reconciliation had also involved Pitt. To all appearances Pitt was governed by Temple, otherwise why should he be unable to take office when Temple refused the Treasury? If the King were to make another overture to Pitt, as the ministers wished, would not Pitt insist that not only Temple but also Grenville should take office with him? The spectre of 'the family', as the King described the brothers and their brother-in-law, haunted him like a nightmare. Grenville by himself had been bad enough. Only after a political crisis lasting two months and only by calling in the Duke of Cumberland had the King managed to get the upper hand. But Grenville and Pitt together! Who could stand against them in the House of Commons? Certainly not Conway, the present Leader of the House, who was already half way to becoming Pitt's man. Grenville and Pitt in office together would give the King the law. Grenville

210

would insist on recommending to every employment in the gift of the Crown: Pitt would insist on an aggressive foreign policy. And if the King should ever again be brought to the situation he was in on 22 May 1765, who would do for him what the Duke of Cumberland had then done? Only Rockingham and his colleagues stood between the King and 'the family'. The King had no high opinion of the talents of his ministers and he resented their suspicions of Bute, yet he was ready to stand by them because the alternative was so dreadful. He deferred to their wishes, declined to see Bute in private, and for a time ceased to correspond with him. So long as the Rockinghams were able to do his business he would support them; but if it came to the point that they were unable to carry on, it was for the King not Rockingham to decide what other arrangements should be made.

The situation was made more complicated and critical by the introduction of a political issue fraught with tremendous consequences, although at the time these were not realized by either King or politicians. In 1764 Grenville had announced his intention to raise a revenue from the colonies, which took practical shape the following year in the famous Stamp Act. The measure had aroused little interest in Great Britain. The most momentous act of the Grenville ministry is not mentioned in the correspondence between the King and his minister. No such indifference existed in America. Hardly had the new ministers settled into their departments when news began to arrive of the hostile reception given to the Stamp Act in the mainland colonies. By the end of the year it was clear that it could be implemented only by military force. What was to be done? There were insufficient troops in America to compel obedience. To send more would involve expense, nor could they be easily found. And was it wise to attempt to enforce a measure which had roused so much hostility? Opposition to the Stamp Act was not confined to America. British merchants were suffering

211

from the embargo which the Americans had laid on trade with Great Britain and were loudly demanding that something must be done. On the other hand, it was bad policy to repeal an Act of Parliament before it had been given a fair trial. All taxes were unpopular, but it was no reason to repeal a tax simply because those who had to pay disliked doing so. To make matters worse, the Americans not merely objected to the tax: they objected even more to the principle behind it – to the right of the British Parliament to raise taxes on America. They saw themselves in the position of John Hampden confronted with the demand for ship money. The Stamp Act had raised the issue of the constitutional relations between Great Britain and her colonies. These were some of the questions – dangerous and far-reaching in their implications – which faced the Rockingham ministry at the end of 1765.

A politician's attitude depends largely on whether he views affairs from the point of view of government or opposition. This is the fundamental difference, and it is not cynicism to contend that power makes politics. Had Grenville still been minister when news of the riots in America reached England, he might have adopted a less uncompromising attitude. Had it been his responsibility to enforce the Stamp Act, he might have been willing to make concessions. Now that he was out of office and a measure which he had promoted was being attacked, he rose to its defence. The difficulties of enforcement and the possible consequences of a constitutional dispute with the colonies did not concern him. He would not have to deal with them. The Rockinghams, however, who had no responsibility for the Stamp Act, saw no reason to run into trouble by attempting to enforce an unpopular measure not of their creation. They did not disagree with the principle behind the Act. They felt it only fair to expect the Americans to make a contribution towards the cost of their government. They saw no reason why the British taxpayer (already sufficiently burdened by the

Seven Years War) should be further burdened for the sake of America. They held it as axiomatic that the authority of the British Parliament extended over all in allegiance to the Crown, and that the House of Commons had the same right to tax the citizens of Boston as it had to tax the citizens of London. But whether it was wise to exercise this right, or to do so in a manner to which the Americans so strongly objected, was another question. The most acute political divisions rarely arise over issues of principle, but more frequently over the application of principles which are generally accepted to concrete political situations. Grenville, who was responsible for the Stamp Act but would not be responsible for its enforcement, wished it to be enforced. Rockingham, who had not been responsible for the Stamp Act but who would be responsible for its enforcement, wished it to be repealed. This was the difference between them.

Since the Duke of Cumberland's death the ministers had been pressing the King to allow them to open negotiations with Pitt. 'I constantly told them', the King wrote, 'that I had three times in vain attempted that measure: that it could never again arise from me: that Mr Pitt had declared the last time he was with me that he must for ever retire.' What, then, was the point of sending for him again? But Rockingham, faced with the problem of framing an American policy for the meeting of Parliament, was anxious to hear Pitt's opinions. 'To which I replied', wrote the King, 'that they might consult whom they pleased, but that I had no share in the affair.' Accordingly, on 5 January 1766, Rockingham told the King that the ministers had sent an emissary to Bath (where Pitt had gone in the hope of alleviating his gout) not only to learn Pitt's views on America but also to find out the terms on which he would be prepared to take office. This was entirely unauthorized and contrary to the King's express declaration. It was both foolish and pointless. It was foolish, because it told Pitt the ministry were

213

in need of his assistance and encouraged him to pitch his terms high; it was pointless, because it produced no reply of any service. To the first question Pitt answered that he would give his opinions on America only to the King or to Parliament. To the second he returned a rigmarole of an answer, the sense of which was that he could take office only if asked to form a ministry. 'I immediately said', wrote the King, very sensibly, 'that as to the first part it was refusing to answer the question they had asked, as to the second that I had nothing to do with Mr Pitt's ideas about government when not asked by me.'

It seemed that the cabinet was about to break up. Grafton threatened to resign if a further effort were not made to secure Pitt, and Conway showed signs of being prepared to follow him. No ministry, least of all one so weak in parliamentary talents, could survive the loss of its principal spokesmen in both Houses. At this point the King did a foolish thing. Under the impression that within a few days he might be left without a ministry and be forced to capitulate to 'the family', he resumed his confidential correspondence with Bute.

Bute had been hurt at the King's refusal to see him and had contrived that the King should be aware of his feelings. The King responded; and on 10 January wrote Bute a long letter, appealing for the support of his followers (whom Bute had ostentatiously declared were not his but the King's):

I own I should think I had great reason to complain if those of my friends that are still in office tried to overturn those I employ; for then they would be acting towards me the very part I have met with from all, that is making disturbance that they may profit by it.

At the same time he undid much of the good that this appeal might have produced:

As to my friends differing from ministers where they think their honour and conscience requires it, that I not only think right but am of opinion it is their duty to act so; nay, I think that it is also incumbent on my dear friend to act entirely so also.

This was telling Bute that he and his friends could vote against the ministry's American policy, and that those who held office would not suffer in consequence. King George was not always so accommodating to tender consciences. He had not been so over the peace treaty; he had not been so when he had urged the dismissal of General Conway for voting according to his conscience on the question of general warrants; he was not to be so with those who voted against his ministers during the American war. He usually demanded, not without reason, that Members of Parliament who held office should vote with the government or forfeit their places. This was the old Whig tradition, the tradition of Sir Robert Walpole who had never hesitated to turn out a man who voted against him. Nor would the King have been so accommodating on this occasion had he not believed that the ministry was on the verge of dissolution. 'All I desire', he wrote to Egmont on 11 January, 'is that they will act firmly till the arduous business of the American colonies is over, then I can stand upon my own feet.' Perhaps also he was uneasy at Bute's reproaches and wished to placate him. The relationship between a master and a pupil is not easily dissolved.

The ministers continued to press for another approach to Pitt, and on 18 January, sorely against his inclination, the King authorized Grafton and Rockingham to put two questions to Pitt: whether he was disposed to come into office, and whether a further refusal from Temple would prevent his accepting. Pitt returned flattering professions and talked nonsense. No man, he declared, was more desirous to serve the King: the present ministers were the only ones with whom he could act: unfortunately, there must be many removals which would displease those who were turned out: 'yet that if a single man was discontented

215

the whole could not efficaciously take place'. About Temple he was evasive. Temple must be offered the Treasury: if Temple demanded that Grenville should be given office, Pitt could not serve: and he declined to say what he would do if Temple again refused. Yet behind this gallimaufry there was meaning and sense. Pitt was trying to convey to the King without putting it into plain language (and except when abusing his opponents Pitt never used plain language) that when the American business was over he was ready to form a ministry without his brothers-in-law. Unfortunately the King was a plain man, not apt to look beyond the obvious meaning of words. He failed to take the hint. All that he understood was that Pitt wished to dissolve the Rockingham ministry. And he was pledged to support the Rockingham ministry so long as they were able to do his business. He owed this at least to his uncle. 'I had ever declared I would support them', he told Grafton, 'that therefore I now called upon them as men of honour to do their part.' Let there be an end of this kow-towing to Pitt.

The ministry now proceeded to submit their American policy. It was not a matter on which the King could easily determine. No King of the Hanoverian dynasty could see without concern the authority of Parliament meet with contempt and defiance. It was the duty of the Crown to see that the laws were obeyed, and it was almost instinctive for King George to wish to have the Stamp Act enforced. But it was represented to him that the tax was a heavy burden on the colonies: that it was an unwise measure, as unpopular in Great Britain as in America: and that there were other ways of raising a revenue to which the Americans would not object. When the King suggested modification of the Stamp Act to meet legitimate complaints, he was told there was no alternative between enforcement and repeal; and that the cabinet meant to make their American policy an issue of confidence. On this they would stand or fall. If the repeal of the Stamp Act was carried, they would remain in office. If it was defeated, they must resign. This decided the King. Faced with the choice between Rockingham and the repeal of the Stamp Act or Grenville and its enforcement, he preferred Rockingham, little as he esteemed him as a minister and despite the doubts he entertained about Rockingham's policy. After all, it was merely a dispute about means. On the great end to be achieved – the raising a revenue from the colonies with a view to their good government and firm subjection to the mother country – there could be no disagreement.

On 2 February, the day before the American resolutions were to be introduced into the House of Lords, the King gave audience to Rockingham; and the next day wrote to the Lord Chancellor:

I gave him [Rockingham] every light I could as to the difficulties they will have to struggle with. He called on my promise at all times of not giving up administration whilst they thought they could act. By this you are fully apprised of the part they will take this day, which I believe will prove a fatal day to them. This hour is perhaps one of the most critical ever known in this country; but I hope Providence will steer me through it with honour and at the same time in whatever manner may in the end be most to the advantage of this (from various factions) much injured country.

The King did not say that some of the difficulties Rockingham would have to encounter were due to his own ill-advised letter to Bute. It was a pity that Rockingham had not talked to the King earlier. Perhaps in that case the King would not have given Bute's friends permission to vote against the ministry

On 4 February the ministry was defeated in the Lords on an amendment to their resolutions (not essential to their policy). 'It is the fullest proof', wrote Rockingham, 'of what Lord Rockingham has in duty been obliged to inform His Majesty was to be expected.' No wonder Rockingham was gloomy. The Lords, unlike the Commons, were politically the creatures of the Crown, and it was almost unknown for a ministry to be defeated in the House of Lords. Rockingham was sensitive about his own position, for he cut an inglorious figure in the House, having spoken but once since Parliament met. The cabinet considered whether or not to resign, but decided instead to obtain an *éclaircissement* from the King. They could not go on if it was believed that the King was opposed to their American legislation. Newcastle asked him point blank if he was for the repeal of the Stamp Act, and the King answered: 'Yes, I am now. I was not for it at first, but now I am convinced or think that is necessary.' 'In that case', said Newcastle, 'I hope Your Majesty will let your servants know your opinion upon it.' His account continues:

His Majesty was pleased to say, he had done so. 'But what can I say when they tell me they can't in conscience vote for the repeal?' To which I replied, 'Conscience, Sir, is too often influenced in favour of persons and things, and that courts have ways of letting their opinion be known.'

Newcastle had been a party manager too long to have much use for conscience in politics. In time the King was to learn the truth of his remarks. But having once given his servants permission to vote according to their convictions, he could not turn right about face and order them to vote with the ministry. He said he would speak to his courtiers 'but did not imagine that he would be able to do much'. Newcastle concluded by warning him against Bute. But the King had already realized how little dependence could be had on Bute. If only the Rockinghams had not insisted on consulting Pitt, if only they had restored Mackenzie to his place, perhaps the King would no longer have felt the need to confide in Bute.

On 6 February the ministry was again defeated in the Lords after a debate in which Bute spoke against them. But what happened in the Lords was of little importance.

It was in the Commons that their fate would be decided. On 7 February, before the first debate, Rockingham obtained permission to inform Members of Parliament that the King was for the repeal, and that day the ministers won a great triumph. Grenville's motion for an address to enforce the Stamp Act was lost by 274 votes to 134. This was a bigger majority than even the most optimistic government supporter had expected, and it could not have been obtained without the use of the King's name. The first round in a parliamentary contest was nearly always decisive, and it was now certain that the repeal of the Stamp Act would go through.

Rockingham's use of the King's name worked against the impression produced by Bute's speech that the King was hostile to repeal. For the first time the King and Bute had openly taken opposite sides on a political issue. The Rockinghams should have seen this as a sign that Bute no longer governed the King. A few days later this became absolutely clear. Rockingham in his eagerness to make the King's opinion known had misrepresented it. He had omitted to say that the King was for repeal as an alternative to enforcement but that he would prefer modification to either extreme. When this became known, Bedford, through the Duke of York, conveyed a message to the King that if modification rather than repeal was the King's wish he would be happy to lend his assistance. The King replied to his brother (18 February 1766):

I have carefully considered the memorandum you this day delivered to me of what the Duke of Bedford had dropped to you. I have never refused any man of quality an audience who has desired it, but as all the Duke of Bedford said can only be looked on as an intimation that he is willing to attend me by way of offering his advice and assistance in regard to the Stamp Act, I cannot take notice of it as I do not think it constitutional for the Crown personally to interfere in measures which it has thought proper to refer to the advice of Parliament.

The King was not pleased at the Duke of York's interference, nor, after what had happened last June, was he willing to receive Bedford in his closet.

Historians have made much of what they allege to be King George's failure to give the Rockingham ministry adequate support, and Horace Walpole charges the King with having encouraged opposition to his ministers. The truth is that the Rockinghams could not have lasted a month without the King's support; that he deferred to their advice against his own convictions; and once they had determined to make the repeal of the Stamp Act an issue of confidence he did all he could to repair his initial blunder. It was not the King who despaired of the ministry but the ministers themselves. After the repeal of the Stamp Act, it was incumbent on them to acquire additional strength – not in numbers of votes but in debating talent. As far as numbers were concerned they had little cause to worry. On their American legislation, a controversial issue on which many Members of Parliament who were not in regular opposition had voted against government, they never had a majority of less than 100 in the House of Commons. Grenville's majority on general warrants never exceeded 50. Here was a foundation for a strong and lasting ministry. Had the ministers gone boldly about their business, had they not been obsessed by fears of Bute and hopes of Pitt (both equally unfounded), they might have gained the confidence of the King and rendered themselves impregnable in Parliament. Grenville, from a position even less favourable than that of Rockingham, had shown what could be done by character and resolution, and had he not made himself obnoxious to the King might have remained minister to the end of his days. But character and resolution were wanting in the leaders of the Rockingham ministry. Rockingham resembled Grenville only in his determination to make himself obnoxious to the King.

Pitt was becoming impatient for office. On 14 April he

launched a bitter attack against the ministry on a matter of no consequence. Conway hastened to smooth him down and Grafton revived the project of making him head of the ministry. But Rockingham had become tired of Pitt's tantrums and refused to run after him any longer. On this Grafton declared that he could not remain a member of a cabinet 'that set Mr Pitt at defiance' and submitted his resignation. Once again all was in confusion.

All the King could now expect of his ministers was that they would somehow or other hold together until the end of the session, which would give him time to make other arrangements – 'Else the absurdity of men', he wrote on 1 May, 'will force me into accepting *the family*, than which there is nothing I would not rather submit to.' If only the Rockinghams would make a firm alliance with Bute's friends! Really, the King asked very little. He did not ask for any of Bute's friends to be taken into the cabinet. All that was necessary was for two or three to be given sinecures or minor places of business – just sufficient to show that those who had been associated with Bute should no longer be debarred from preferment. The King looked upon the restoration of Mackenzie as a matter of justice and of his own honour and not the object of a political bargain. But when the matter was raised in the cabinet, the ministers shook their heads. Rockingham and Conway thought it might be possible to find a place for Mackenzie; Newcastle doubted even this. All (except Northington and Egmont) agreed 'that adding any more of Lord Bute's friends in great offices would be construed by all the world as if they were acting their parts only under his patronage which was what they neither could nor would submit to do'. The Rockinghams did not see that the best way to combat Bute's influence was to win over his friends, most of whom were anxious to desert a leader who could no longer be of service to them. Pitt did this a few months later, at the expense of a promotion in the peerage and three offices of dignity and profit but no

221

political importance. Rockingham's failure to do so marks the level of his political ineptitude.

On 3 May the King wrote a long letter to Bute, his first since January, perhaps the most revealing in their whole correspondence. 'I cannot bear tormenting you', he began, 'with the many grievances I have when I can possibly keep them to myself.' Since Bute's resignation three years ago there had been one prolonged political crisis, and the King had had about as much as he could stand. Possibly there had been a recrudescence of his illness of the previous year. 'I can neither eat nor sleep', he told Bute, 'nothing pleases me but musing on my cruel situation.' He had changed little since the days when Waldegrave noted how he would retire to his study 'to indulge the melancholy enjoyment of his own ill humor'. By temperament he was no politician. He did not possess the vanity, the desire for the limelight, the need to project his personality to other people, which distinguishes alike the politician and actor. He liked a placid life, a life of order and routine, doing the same things at the same time each day, a dull life. His aspirations when he began his reign were moral rather than political, and by 1766 they had dwindled into little more than the wish for a settled ministry of almost any political complexion provided that it did not include George Grenville. He disliked emotional scenes, and did not know how to deal with a political crisis. 'If I am to continue the life of agitation I have these three years', he wrote to Bute, 'the next year there will be a council [of] regency to assist in that undertaking.' He had no one but Bute to assist him, no one in whom he could confide, and he was surrounded by suspicious men who watched his every move. He could not write to Bute without taking precautions against their correspondence being discovered. Bute's letters had to be addressed to the Princess Dowager, and the King was not certain whether even members of his own family were not spying on him. 'All this I beg may be trusted to no living soul', he concluded his letter, 'shews how cautious we must be, pity your unhappy friend for indeed he deserves it.'

The King's object in writing was to find out, if the ministry were unable to continue longer, whether a new one could be formed from Bute's friends without resort to Pitt or Grenville. Bute gave this scheme no encouragement, and left the King nothing to hope for except that somehow or other the Rockinghams would manage to carry on. For the vacant office of Secretary of State they proposed the Duke of Richmond, a young man of thirty, formerly a supporter of Bute and Grenville but as Conway's son-in-law now deemed to be thoroughly reliable. The King protested at Richmond's lack of experience; in addition, he greatly disliked Richmond who had behaved badly to him at the beginning of the reign. But Rockingham declared he could not remain in office unless Richmond were appointed, and of course this settled the matter. The last straw came when the ministers refused to undertake some parliamentary business concerning the King's family. On the Duke of Cumberland's death the King had promised his brothers that he would apply to Parliament to divide the Duke's allowance of £25,000 a year between them, each brother to receive £8,000. The matter had been postponed because of the pressure of American business, and now Rockingham declared that because of the lateness of the session it would have to be postponed until next year. 'He wants now to make me break my word [the very offence Grenville had committed]', wrote the King to Egmont on 28 May, 'which I cannot do. On my telling him this day that opposition, if they found ministry silent, would propose it, he said then it must be withstood. I on that sharply replied that no man of honour could have advised a measure and then reject it because taken up by adversaries.' (Obviously King George did not understand party politics.) Even Horace Walpole, devoted though he was to Conway, told him what fools the ministers were. 'For God's sake', Walpole said, 'satisfy the King and the princes on this point; but you are so unfit to be ministers that I advise you to find some plausible and popular excuse afterwards to resign.'

'My prudence is now exhausted', wrote the King to Egmont on 28 May. 'I am inclined to take any step that will preserve my honour.' The step he was to take was shortly to be indicated. Bute had failed him; Rockingham was a man of straw; Pitt alone was left. If only he could be certain that Pitt was not connected with Grenville! Pitt was a master of the politics of the back stairs and had kept his ear close to the ground. His friend Camden, Chief Justice of the Common Pleas, was in touch with Northington, the Lord Chancellor. There was a professional cama-raderie between lawyers which overrode political differences, and Camden and Northington were disposed to work together for the King's ease and their own advantage. Camden wanted the Great Seal, and Northington was not averse to yielding it provided he were assured of adequate compensation. In the event he had no reason to complain. Pitt, always lavish to those who fell in with his ambition, loaded Northington to an extent which the King later admitted was shameful. In return, Northington undertook to convince the King that Pitt had broken with his brothers-in-law and to find a plausible pretext for dismissing the ministry. Once the King was convinced that Pitt was prepared to form a ministry 'of the best of all parties and an exclusion to no descriptions' (except of course Grenville and his friends), the rest was easy. The King had learnt at least one lesson from the events of the previous year – that he should not be off with the old ministry until he was on with the new.[1]

The King had not been in touch with Bute since the beginning of May, and Bute knew nothing of the events which had culminated in the decision to send for Pitt. On 12 July, the day the King saw Pitt, he wrote a long letter to

Bute, almost the last in their correspondence, explaining the reasons for his decision:

My resolution is to try through Mr Pitt to build an administration on as general a basis as the times will permit; to see as many of those gentlemen who were contrary to my inclinations removed reinstated, particularly Mr Mackenzie; in short to see you, my dear friend, once quit of the unmerited abuse you have so long suffered and openly appearing as my private friend. . . . I now hope God is giving me this line to extricate this country out of faction.

Alas for the vanity of human wishes! The decision to send for Pitt did not 'extricate this country out of faction': if anything it plunged the nation deeper into faction. But it had one consequence the King had not expected. It ended irretrievably the friendship between himself and Bute.[2]

At first everything seemed to augur well. Pitt's intention to form a ministry which should transcend and obliterate party distinctions accorded with the King's wishes. But the time was long past, if indeed it had ever existed, when this could be attempted with any prospect of success. Party divisions, though not as yet based on ideological lines, were too deep-rooted to be eradicated. Indeed, had there been genuine ideological differences Pitt's task might have been easier, for men will disclaim their political ideals more readily than their political connections. Personal divisions in politics are more bitter than those arising from party feeling. Conservative can work with Labour and Democrat with Republican – indeed they have to, otherwise representative government would be impossible; but nothing can overcome the jealousy and dislike of one man for another and no pain is so bitter as that of disappointed ambition. Despite what romantic poets have written, disappointments in love can be borne provided adequate substitutes are available; but there is no substitute available for the man who has been disappointed of becoming Prime Minister or President. Juliet was a more than adequate substitute for Rosaline, but the governorship of New York is poor compensation for the man who hoped to become President of the United States. 'The parliamentary cabals which divided the court during the first twelve years of George III', wrote Lord Holland, grandson of Henry and nephew of Charles James Fox, 'being mere struggles for favour and power, created more real blood and personal rancour between individuals than the great questions of policy and principle which arose on the American and French wars.' This was the atmosphere in which Pitt essayed his impossible task.

He took the Rockinghams as the basis of his ministry. Newcastle and Rockingham were dismissed (Pitt would have no one in his cabinet who had previously served as head of administration). Conway, despite his obvious deficiencies, was retained as Leader of the House of Commons. Grafton was made First Lord of the Treasury, an office he tried to avoid and for which he knew himself to be unfit; the brilliant, irresponsible, and treacherous Charles Townshend became Chancellor of the Exchequer; and Lord Shelburne, whom the King and nearly everyone else disliked, the other Secretary of State. Two serving officers were brought into the cabinet as heads of the army and navy: both distinguished in their professional capacities but neither of cabinet calibre. The Lord Chancellor, Camden, was a mere shadow of Pitt; and the Lord President, Northington, was superannuated. This was not a cabinet for taking decisions: it was a cabinet designed to register Pitt's edicts.

Pitt's crowning act of folly was his decision to enter the House of Lords as Earl of Chatham. His health was so bad that he could no longer bear the heat and fatigue of the House of Commons, and he wished to found a great aristocratic family. Yet it was a mistake to abandon the arena where he had achieved greatness and which had made him great. The House of Commons was the *fons et origo* of his political strength. Pitt, 'the great commoner', in the House of Lords was like Samson shorn of his locks. Great Britain could not be governed from the House of Lords. With all his pride and folly William Pitt had been a great statesman: perhaps the greatest the British Isles had known since Oliver Cromwell ruled three kingdoms with the aid of the New Model Army. But the Earl of Chatham was no more than the shade of that which once was great.

Outside the cabinet, Chatham (as he must now be called) attempted to pick and choose from the different factions. He retained most of Rockingham's people; seduced two of Grenville's friends; and tried in vain to win the Bedfords by an offer to Lord Gower, the Duke's brother-in-law. But in general the Bedford and Grenville parties stood aloof. Mackenzie was restored to his place but without the control of Scottish patronage. Two of Bute's friends were given office and hopes held out to the rest. The Earl of Northumberland was promoted to a dukedom. On such terms Bute's friends were cheaply gained. But Bute was discontented. He was not informed of the reinstatement of his brother, and greatly to his annoyance found that Chatham treated him no differently from Grenville or Rockingham – that is to say, he ignored him. Chatham intended to break all parties, Bute's as well as Grenville's and Rockingham's; and though Bute protested that he was not the leader of a party, that his friends were not his but the King's, nobody believed him. Bute was hurt at not being consulted. 'My heart is half broke and my health ruined', he wrote to the King, 'with the unmerited barbarous treatment I have received.' He besought his former pupil to be allowed 'in this most humiliated situation to possess your friendship independent of your power'. But perhaps he knew that he asked for the impossible. Bute could have been the King's friend only if he had renounced the quest for political power. Now it was too late. Having once been in the political arena, he was forever suspected of political ambitions; and a constitutional sovereign cannot afford to take his friends from among the ranks of the politicians. The ideals with which Bute had inspired the King, in the days when the King was young and in fear of the Duke of Cumberland, had turned sour. The King had learnt how wrong Bute had been about the Duke. There was no longer any basis for his friendship with Bute.

After King George's death his son, the Duke of York, told Charles Greville what he had learnt from his father of the King's last meeting with Bute.* The story, as it appears in Greville's journal, is as follows:

Yesterday [13 December 1826] the Duke told me that the late King was walking with him one day at Kew, and His Majesty said, 'The world tells many lies, and here is one instance. I am said to have held frequent communication with Lord Bute, and the last time I ever saw or spoke to him was in that pavilion in the year 1764.' The King went over to breakfast with his mother, the Princess Dowager, and she took him aside and said, 'There is somebody here who wishes very much to speak to you.' 'Who is it?' 'Lord Bute.' 'Good God, mamma! how could you bring him here? It is impossible for me to hold any communication with Lord Bute in this manner.' However, he did see him, when Lord Bute made a violent attack upon him for having abandoned and neglected him. The King replied that he could not, in justice to his ministers, hold any communication with him unknown to them, when Lord Bute said that he would never see the King again. The King became angry in his turn, and said, 'Then, my Lord, be it so, and remember from henceforth we never meet again.' And from that day he never beheld Lord Bute nor had any communication with him.

If we assume that 1764 is a mistake for 1766, the above may well be a reasonably correct though probably dramatized account. Bute went abroad in 1769, and spent the next few years travelling in search of health and spirits. He took no further part in politics and his correspon-

*See note 8, p. 612.

228

dence with the King practically ceased. The King's last known letter to Bute was written sometime between 1770 and 1776. Although the King still addressed Bute as 'my dear friend', he refused his request for a peerage for his son and recommended him to apply to Lord North in the usual manner. The ashes of their friendship were cold. When Bute died in 1792, his son delicately conveyed to the King the information that he possessed his sovereign's letters – 'an accurate investigation of my late father's affairs', he wrote, 'has brought to my knowledge the numerous delicate and uncommon obligations in which he stood endebted to his King' – and he appealed for help in his embarrassed financial condition. The King was very kind to the family. But he appears to have destroyed all the letters he had received from Bute, and he tried to obliterate from his mind the memory of Bute's influence.

None of King George III's ministers, not even Bute, enjoyed quite the degree of support accorded to Chatham. The King felt that he had at last found a minister who could quell the political turmoil, and resolved that Chatham should have no reason to complain (as Grenville and Rockingham had done) of lack of support from the Crown. He submitted himself to Chatham as completely as he had to the Duke of Cumberland the year before, and for a brief period Chatham exercised an authority such as no Prime Minister has ever known. The King raised no objection to Chatham's favourite project of an alliance with Prussia, and Chatham initiated negotiations without bothering to consult the cabinet. The King was always reluctant to increase the peerage but at Chatham's recommendation he created three dukedoms – apart from those bestowed on members of the Royal Family, the only dukedoms created during an active reign of more than fifty years. Every recommendation Chatham made, whether concerning policy or patronage, was accepted by the King without demur. The Duke of

Cumberland was dead and Bute out of favour and there was no one between Chatham and the throne.

Chatham had grandiose plans both in the fields of foreign and domestic policy. In addition to the alliance with Prussia and Russia, he proposed a parliamentary inquiry into the affairs of the East India Company, a delicate matter which was bound to arouse controversy and opposition. Of even greater consequence were relations with the American colonies, to which Chatham paid surprisingly little attention. The echoes of the Stamp Act were still reverberating in America, and the spirit of opposition to the authority of the British Parliament had been roused. Even in his greatest days it would have required all Chatham's statesmanship to achieve his aims. But his strength was sapped by age and ill health; his statesmanship, triumphant in war, was dim in time of peace; and he had renounced his control of Parliament when he left the House of Commons. The strange malady which overtook him in the winter of 1766 threw the ministry into confusion and brought back the political anarchy which the King so dreaded.

In December 1766, after Parliament had adjourned for the Christmas recess, Chatham went to Bath. When the session opened, he was too unwell to attend. 'I am mortified', wrote the King to Grafton on 17 January 1767, 'that Lord Chatham is prevented by a severe fit of the gout from coming to town. . . . I desire you will let him know how sincerely I feel also for what his mind as well as body suffers at this time.' Affairs in London, deprived of Chatham's attention, went ill. 'The Earl of Chatham is at Bath', wrote one of his opponents on 27 January, 'and consequently the King's administration has got the gout and hobbles terribly.' On 16 February Chatham began his journey to London, but was taken ill on the way and had to put up at an inn at Marlborough. For a fortnight he lay there, his body crippled and his mind disturbed, while the cabinet, which was never meant to act without him, fell into confusion. Conway and Townshend went into open rebellion and declared against the East Indian inquiry, and in the House of Commons the ministry suffered a humiliating defeat on an opposition motion to reduce the land tax.

Like a good general, the King strove to restore order and discipline into the ranks of his ministers. He aligned himself solidly behind Chatham's India policy and encouraged Grafton not to despond at the ministry's defeat. 'In this world these things will happen', he wrote, 'therefore rest assured that it will if possible stimulate me to act with greater vigour.' On Chatham's arrival in London the King renewed his promise of support and his confidence in his minister's firmness. For if Chatham, armed with all the authority of the Crown, could not restore stability to the ministry, who could? If Chatham failed him, on whom could he depend?

The King's loyalty to his minister is the more noteworthy because personally he did not like Chatham. Few people did. The King felt uncomfortable with him. He disliked Chatham's rhetorical language and exaggerated compliments, and was lost in the atmosphere of mystery in which Chatham seemed to envelop his thoughts. Though the King exacted all the respect due to the Crown, he did not care for fine words or unctuous flattery. Chatham could not write a simple letter of business without 'laying himself at His Majesty's feet', professing his 'humble duty and submission', or thanking the King for his 'exceeding condescension and transcendent goodness'. No other minister used this sort of language, and it conveyed to the King a hint of insincerity. There was too much of the style of Uriah Heep about Chatham to please King George. The King often commented on the clarity or otherwise of the despatches submitted to him. What could he make, however, of this sentence (typical of many), which appears in Chatham's letter of 7 March 1767: 'The preposterous union of clashing factions will not, till things change their nature, outweigh and finally overbear the honest sense of the nation, dutifully attached to a most benignant sovereign, pursuing nothing but the welfare and happiness of his people'? If Chatham had anything to say, could he not say it in fewer words and in language that could be more easily understood? But that was not Chatham's way. He was, says Shelburne, 'always acting, always made up, and never natural'; and the King who liked plain speech and common honesty could not understand him.

There can be no question but that Chatham's gout (or whatever disease it was) was genuine and not the product of hypochondria. He had been afflicted with it for many years, and it says much for his strength of mind that he was able to overcome intense bodily pain and physical incapacity. But at the same time he extracted advantage from it and deliberately cultivated the image of the suffering patriot. The King had little sympathy with invalids. To Northington, another sufferer from the gout, he wrote on 2 February, with obvious reference to Chatham: 'I was agreeably surprised this day with hearing that you arrived last night in town. . . . Your resolution is superior to that of others afflicted with the gout.' When Chatham finally arrived on the evening of 2 March he was too ill to see the King, and wrote next day:

Lord Chatham begs to be permitted to lay himself with all duty and submission at the King's feet, and to pour out a heart overflowing with the most reverential and warm sense of His Majesty's infinite condescension. He intreats most humbly to renew the tender of his devoted services, grieving to think how feeble they are, every hour more and more animated by the truly royal magnanimity of His Majesty. . . .

He is most unhappy still to continue out of a condition to attend His Majesty's most gracious presence.

He saw the King on 12 March, received renewed assurances of the fullest support, and forthwith disappeared into seclusion. Not for more than two years – on 7 July

1769 – did he again appear at court. Although he retained his office until October 1768, from March 1767 his unwilling deputy, Grafton, was de facto minister.

For the first few weeks of Chatham's absence the King waited patiently for his recovery. He wrote to Chatham on 30 April 1767:

I am desirous you should thoroughly be acquainted with my sentiments on the present unfortunate state of your health, as I imagine it may be of use in removing any anxiety that the want of it might occasion. I embrace this opportunity of assuring you that I am fully persuaded of your zeal and attachment to my service, and that nothing but the weight of your disorder prevents your taking the vigorous part your heart at all times prompts you to. . . . The Duke of Grafton and Lord Bristol know that I have avoided sending to you lest it should only hurry you, and that through their means and that of Dr Addington [Chatham's physician] I have received constant accounts of the progress of your fever.

This simple and straightforward account of the King's feelings evoked the following in the true Chatham style:

Lord Chatham most humbly begs leave to lay himself with all duty and submission at the King's feet and to offer the most ardent acknowledgments for His Majesty's infinite condescension and humanity towards a devoted servant. He trusts that His Majesty's goodness will receive with indulgence these imperfect expressions of a heart overflowing with the deepest veneration and gratitude.

With such letters as these the King had to be content.

By the end of May, however, his patience was running short. He had been sadly disappointed in Chatham. Instead of the stable government for which he had hoped, all was chaos and confusion. Although the ministry retained a comfortable majority in the Commons, one of its spokesmen (Conway) was in opposition to its American policy and the other (Townshend) to its Indian policy. The spectacle of cabinet ministers speaking against each other in the House could only bring the ministry into contempt. Bad as the situation was in the Commons, it was worse in the Lords. There the unfortunate Duke of Grafton had to defend the citadel almost alone against a formidable array of debating talent and an even more formidable array of silent peers. In two divisions at the end of May the ministry scraped through with majorities of only four and three. Even the bishops, normally reliable enough, began to turn against them; and in one division, greatly to the King's annoyance, the Duke of York voted with the opposition. The Bedfords, Grenvilles, and Rockinghams seemed to have sunk their differences in their determination to bring down the ministry. If Conway, who was under pressure from his old friends to resign, should accede to their wish there would be nothing to stand between the King and a triumphant opposition. The King could then expect another day of humiliation like 22 May 1765. And this was the ministry that was to extricate the country out of faction, to end party divisions! This was the ministry recommended to the King by the City of London!

At the end of May Grafton's morale broke. He was in a difficult and uncomfortable position as acting head of a government whose chief was incommunicado yet retained his authority. He could take no steps to strengthen the ministry without Chatham's consent. Yet Chatham declared himself unfit for business and refused to see his deputy. At this point the King took matters into his own hands and offered to visit Chatham himself. His letter of 30 May deserves extensive quotation, not only because it shows his resolution to support his ministry but also that he was beginning to learn to act for himself. The experience of the last two years had taught him that he could not rely on a Bute, a Duke of Cumberland, or a Chatham, to do for him work which he found personally distasteful.

'No one', the King's letter began, 'has more cautiously avoided writing to you than myself during your late indisposition; but the moment is so extremely critical that

234

I cannot possibly delay it any longer.' The narrow majorities in the House of Lords, the 'great coldness' of Shelburne, the 'avowed enmity' of Townshend, the resolution of Conway to retire, threatened the continuance of the ministry.

My firmness [the King continued] is not dismayed by these unpleasant appearances, for, from the hour you entered into office I have uniformly relied on your firmness to act in defiance to that hydra faction, who has never appeared to the height it now does till within these few weeks. Though your relations [the Grenvilles], the Bedfords, and the Rockinghams are joined with intention to storm my closet, yet if I was mean enough to submit they own they would not join in forming an administration, therefore nothing but confusion could be obtained.

Grafton was on the point of resignation 'unless you would see him and give him encouragement'.

Your duty and affection for my person, your own honour, call on you to make an effort. Five minutes conversation with you would raise his spirits for his heart is good; mine, I thank Heaven, want no rousing; my love to my country as well as what I owe to my own character and to my family prompt me not to yield to faction. Be firm, and you will find me amply ready to take as active a part as the hour seems to require. Though none of my ministers stand by me, I cannot truckle.

This letter induced Chatham to receive Grafton. As a result of their talks Grafton agreed to remain as acting minister and received authority to take what measures he considered necessary to strengthen the ministry. 'I observed', writes Grafton in his autobiography, 'that a junction with the Bedfords or the Rockinghams appeared to be the only steps that could now be effectual.' Chatham indicated his preference for the Bedfords.

There now began a complicated series of negotiations between the ministry and the opposition parties which lasted most of June and July. The ministry's aim was to break the combined opposition by attaching at least one of the parties to the court. The King had no preference between Bedford and Rockingham but refused to receive Grenville again as a minister. Grafton began by approaching the Bedfords as the party favoured by Chatham, but found that the opposition intended to stand by each other. Rockingham, acting on their behalf, assumed that the ministry was at an end and that he was invited to form a new one. There followed an elaborate fencing match in which Grafton, seconded by Horace Walpole, who for a brief period played a decisive part in his country's history, tried to get Rockingham to state his terms.

The King was correct in describing the opposition as faction. Their union was not based on principle. On American policy they were deeply divided, less by plans for the future than by memories of the past. Bedford and Grenville could not renounce the Stamp Act: Rockingham could not forget that he was the minister who had repealed the Stamp Act. There was no basis for common political action between the three parties except the will to drive out Chatham and for each to grab as large a share as it could of the spoils of office. Walpole told Conway on 18 July:

That the nation was now quiet and satisfied; and that all sober men, not ranked in any faction, would not bear to see the King taken prisoner. That all men saw through the pretences of the several factions; that all danger of arbitrary power was over ... but that another danger was growing upon us, a danger I had always feared as much as the power of the Crown – danger from aristocracy and from those confederacies of great lords.

When the Duke of Richmond told Walpole that the opposition would not retain Camden as Lord Chancellor because he was the King's man (he was in fact one of Chatham's most devoted followers and went with him into opposition in 1770) – 'I asked', writes Walpole, 'if they expected that every man should depend on King

236

Rockingham, and nobody on King George?' And Walpole records another conversation he had with Conway about the same time. 'I told him there were many independent men who would not sit still and see the closet taken by storm. No, he replied, it was what he himself and the Rockinghams had come in two years before to prevent.'

The negotiations yielded no immediate profit to the court in an accession of votes but they did have the desired effect. They broke the combined opposition. Bedford and Rockingham quarrelled about who should lead the House of Commons and each party declared itself free to follow its own course. It had only been necessary, as Walpole forecast, to give the opposition sufficient rope and it would surely destroy itself. The outlook for the ministry brightened when Townshend died suddenly. He had always been a disturbing element, yet too powerful to be dismissed. Lord North, who succeeded as Chancellor of the Exchequer, was a man with whom it was difficult to quarrel. His entry into the cabinet smoothed personal relations and increased the ministry's debating strength. In December Grafton bought off the Bedfords and put his ministry on a firm foundation.

During the course of these events the King had remained loyal to Chatham. There was no intention to displace him. On 25 June the King wrote to his ailing minister:

I am thoroughly resolved to encounter any difficulties rather than yield to faction. This is so congenial with your ideas that I am thoroughly persuaded your own feelings will make you take an active part at this hour, which will not only give lustre and ease to the subsequent years of my reign but will raise the reputation of your own political life in times of inward faction even above it in the late memorable war. Such ends to be obtained would almost awaken the great men of this country of former ages, therefore must oblige you to cast aside any remains of your late indisposition.

237

It was a remarkable letter, with its reference to the war (when the King had described Chatham as 'the blackest of hearts') and its hint at the end that Chatham could overcome his malady by an effort of will. Chatham represented that his health was so broken 'as renders at present application of mind totally impossible', but on 2 July the King made a further effort to rouse him:

I earnestly call upon you to lay before me a plan and also to speak to those you shall propose for the most responsible offices. You owe this to me, to your country, and to those who have embarked in administration with you. If after this you again decline taking an active part, I shall then lie under a necessity of taking steps that nothing but the situation I am left in could have obliged me to.

Once more there is the suggestion that Chatham was not so ill as he was given out to be. Only after hearing from Chatham's solicitor, Thomas Nuthall, who visited him on 5 August and found him not only in a deep melancholy but also with 'a good deal of fever upon him', did the King become really convinced. 'The seeing a man who has appeared in so very great a light', he wrote to Camden, 'fall into such a situation is an abasement of human nature.'

The entry of the Bedfords into the ministry and the appointment of North to succeed Conway as Leader of the House of Commons shifted the centre of gravity of the cabinet away from Chatham's friends. It became even more of a hotch-potch than it had been before. On one point all were agreed – King, Bedfords, and Chathamites all disliked Shelburne. It is difficult to understand why Shelburne should have been so unpopular (unless he deliberately set out to imitate Chatham), but it is a fact that few people could tolerate him for long. Grafton wanted him out and the King saw him as an obstacle to unity. But Grafton was reluctant to dismiss a man who had been appointed to office by Chatham, and tried by

238

snubs and slights to force Shelburne to resign. In October 1768, egged on by the King and the Bedfords, he at last steeled himself for the deed. First he deemed it wise to seek an interview with Lady Chatham (Chatham himself being still incommunicado) to explain to her, for the benefit of her husband, the reasons for this step. The issue justified Grafton's forebodings. On 12 October Chatham requested permission to resign.

'Though I have within these eight years', wrote the King to Grafton, 'met with enough to prevent my being surprised at any thing that may happen, yet I cannot conceal the not having expected the letter you received the last evening from Lord Chatham.' To Chatham himself he wrote:

I think I have a right to insist on your remaining in my service, for I with pleasure look forward to the time of your recovery when I may have your assistance in resisting the torrent of factions this country so much labours under. . . . Therefore I again repeat it, you must not think of retiring but of doing that that may be most conducive to your health and to my seeing you take a public share in my affairs.

Chatham's reply, apparently the last letter he ever wrote to the King, must be given in full:

Penetrated with the high honour of Your Majesty's gracious commands, my affliction is infinite to be constrained by absolute necessity from illness to lay myself again at Your Majesty's feet for compassion. My health is so broken that I feel all chance of recovery will be entirely precluded by my continuing to hold the Privy Seal, totally disabled as I still am from assisting in Your Majesty's councils. Under this load of unhappiness, I will not despair of Your Majesty's pardon while I again supplicate on my knees Your Majesty's mercy and most humbly implore Your Majesty's royal permission to resign that high office.

Should it please God to restore me to health, every moment of my life will be at Your Majesty's devotion, in the mean time the most gracious thought Your Majesty deigns to express of my recovery is my best consolation.

Sixty years ago Lord Rosebery pointed out how difficult it is to write the life of Chatham. 'It is difficult because of the artificial atmosphere in which he thought it well to envelop himself, and because the rare glimpses which are obtainable of the real man reveal a nature so complex, so violent, and so repressed.' The task is no easier today. This complex, violent, and repressed character is as much an enigma to us as he was to King George III. The King accepted his resignation, and Grafton became head of the ministry.*

The most exciting political events of the early years of the reign – though this is not how the King would have described them – were certain incidents in the career of John Wilkes, M.P. for Aylesbury and later for Middlesex. These might almost have formed the subject matter of a long, rambling eighteenth-century novel after the fashion of *Tom Jones* or *Peregrine Pickle* with some such title as 'The life and surprising adventures of John Wilkes, gentleman'. Wilkes first appears in history as a martyr for the cause of the freedom of the press, next for the rights of electors to choose freely their Members of Parliament, and lastly as a successful agitator for the liberty to publish reports of parliamentary proceedings. Yet no man was less disposed to suffer martyrdom and no martyr cared so little for the cause for which he suffered. Wilkes was a jolly blackguard, fond of his bottle and his whore, with a taste for scholarship and good conversation, and out for what he could get. No man was better company at the dinner table. 'He has inexhaustible spirits', wrote Gibbon who dined with him in 1762, 'infinite wit and humour, and a great deal of knowledge . . . his conversation full of blasphemy and bawdy.' James Harris, a most respectable man, conceded that Wilkes had 'a constant flow of mirth and humour', though his sentiments and morals tended 'to the profligate and debauched'. Boswell, who shared

*See note 9, p. 612.

240

Wilkes's taste for wine and women and his reverence for learning and literature, wrote about his 'constant felicity' – 'He has an elasticity of mind that nothing can crush.' Even Dr Johnson, than whom no man could have been more prejudiced against Wilkes, found him good company at dinner. 'Jack has great variety of talk, Jack is a scholar, and Jack has the manners of a gentleman', said Johnson after their celebrated meeting at Dilly's dinner table in 1776. In short, Wilkes was a man it was impossible to dislike and undesirable to take seriously. King George contrived to do both.

Like many eighteenth-century Members of Parliament who did not come from the aristocratic or landed classes (and like many who did), Wilkes habitually lived above his income. He entered Parliament in 1757, after two expensive election contests. Men in his position naturally tried to touch the government till, but Wilkes is almost unique in the eighteenth century in having achieved a competence out of opposition. At the beginning of the reign he set up in journalism, and in 1762 launched his notorious newspaper *The North Briton*. This was violently anti-government, anti-Bute, and anti-Scot. It catered for the lower middle classes of London, with whom the Scot played the part of scapegoat assigned by later generations to the Jew. In the popular satires of the day the Scot is always depicted as a lean and lanky figure, speaking an uncouth dialect, a Jacobite at heart, with a train of hungry dependants all looking for provision at the expense of honest John Bull.[3] Baiting the Scots was Wilkes's trade, and there were many who welcomed the goods he had to offer. Wilkes had the knack which marks the good journalist of being able to put into words what is in the minds of his readers – and was bold enough to do so. Whether he believed what he wrote is immaterial – the point is, his readers did. It was broadly and coarsely suggested in *The North Briton* that Bute owed his influence with the King to his being the lover of the Princess Dowager. The King himself was treated with respect (except that he appeared as the dupe of his mother and her paramour). When Bute resigned, Wilkes transferred his hostility to the Grenvilles and depicted them as the mere tools of Bute. In the notorious number 45 of *The North Briton*, published on 23 April 1763, Grenville was accused of putting a lie into the King's Speech and Bute of having bribed the House of Commons to ratify the peace treaty.

Liberty of the press was held on precarious tenure in the eighteenth century. The literate classes were few in numbers; the circulation of newspapers was tiny; and journalism was a trade rather than a profession – merely an adjunct to the business of printing or bookselling. Most newspaper proprietors tried to sell themselves to the government or the opposition. Responsibility, the essential corollary to the freedom of the press, was not yet a mark of journalism. Politicians today are sometimes accused of being unduly sensitive to criticism by the press, but no twentieth-century politician has ever been abused as Bute and Grenville were by *The North Briton*. The use of violent and inflammable language was commonplace and the boundary between what was tolerable and what was defamatory was ill defined. A public man today who feels himself injured by the press has a remedy in the law of libel, but no such remedy was possible for an eighteenth-century politician. The preservation of the good name of public men devolved upon the State, and a journalist who attacked the government might find himself charged with sedition.

No reputable politician defended *The North Briton*. Pitt, whose policy it professed to support, described it as a 'licentious' and 'criminal' publication. No one was surprised when Wilkes was arrested for publishing a seditious libel in number 45. He had been asking for it for some time, and the only wonder was why government had allowed him to go so far. No one doubted that he was guilty. To this hardly any defence was made. But there were

242

grave doubts on the legality of his arrest. Was he protected by his privilege as a Member of Parliament against arrest for seditious libel, and could he be arrested for this or any other offence on a general warrant? These were matters of constitutional significance, far more important than what happened to Wilkes. They were to become matters of acute controversy.

Wilkes, released on habeas corpus, skipped to France to avoid punishment, and was expelled the House of Commons with only one dissentient voice. The opposition were glad to see him go. They were now free to challenge government on the legal aspects of his arrest without having to defend the man and excuse his conduct. General warrants gave them a cause which they badly needed. The eighteenth century was acutely sensitive to matters of procedure and liked to see things done according to law. Grenville did not argue the legality of general warrants, but pointed out that there were plenty of precedents for their use and that the question was one for the courts of law not the House of Commons. But many Members of Parliament who normally supported government felt unable to go with Grenville on this issue. In the decisive division of 18 February 1764, after a debate which lasted from three o'clock in the afternoon until five the following morning, Grenville carried a motion to adjourn by only 14 votes in a house of 450 Members. The debate had shown the House in its best light: alert to possible infringements of the constitution; concerned for the rights of the subject, even of a man so unpopular as Wilkes; and above all independent and incorruptible.

King George was little concerned in this. It was the business of the ministers not of the King. He had approved of the decision to prosecute Wilkes, whom he regarded as a thoroughly worthless individual. His dislike was increased by the discovery of an obscene and blasphemous poem which Wilkes had printed at his private press. To the reproach of faction and the offence of libel Wilkes had now added the crime of impiety. The King hoped he would be suitably punished. But for the manner of Wilkes's arrest, the use of a general warrant, and the seizure of his papers, the King was not responsible. These had been decided by the ministers, acting on the highest legal advice. The King hardly appreciated the significance of the controversy over general warrants and could not enter into the merits of the arguments – subtle, involved, and full of chicanery. To him the matter appeared simple, and he failed to see any danger to freedom in the mode of arresting a man undoubtedly guilty of libel and blasphemy. Greatly as he was beginning to dislike Grenville, he deemed it his duty to support Grenville in his parliamentary battle. In one matter he went possibly further than Grenville might have done, for he dismissed two Members of Parliament who were army officers from their regiments because they voted against government on this issue. (One of them was the same General Conway who became Secretary of State under the Duke of Cumberland in July 1765.) On matters of policy, Grenville had no cause to reproach the King.

In February 1768 Wilkes returned to England. He was in no doubt as to what awaited him. In his absence he had been outlawed and found guilty of blasphemy and libel, and he must now face his punishment. But his resources were at an end, and the longer he stayed abroad the more likely he was to be forgotten in England. And Wilkes could not afford to remain forgotten. He did not wish to live in exile the rest of his life, dependent on charity. Better try his luck again in England. 'What the Devil have I to do with prudence?' he said. '. . . I must raise a dust or starve in a gaol.' And so he came back, unabashed, impenitent, as jaunty as ever, and resolved to raise a dust. And so he did: in fact he raised a positive storm.

At first the government took no action against him. Grafton, who had been one of Wilkes's sympathizers in

1763, was reluctant to embroil himself. But he was soon compelled to intervene. Parliament was dissolved on 11 March 1768, and at the general election Wilkes offered himself as a candidate for London. He came bottom of the poll. The next day he announced his candidature for Middlesex. It seemed impossible that he could succeed. He had no property in the county, no money, no time to canvass the electorate, and no political programme. To the astonishment of all (perhaps even of himself) he was returned head of the poll. 'It is really an extraordinary event', wrote Benjamin Franklin, who was in England at the time, 'to see an outlaw and exile, of bad personal character, not worth a farthing . . . immediately carrying it for the principal county.' On 20 April, now a Member of Parliament, Wilkes surrendered himself to the King's Bench to receive sentence for his conviction. He was fined £1,000, and sentenced to twenty-two months' imprisonment.

It is not difficult to imagine how scandalized the King was by these events. Was it proper that a man serving sentence for libel and blasphemy should be allowed to sit in the House of Commons? Grafton and Camden agreed with the King, and the cabinet decided in principle that Wilkes should be expelled the House. The lawyers and the experts on parliamentary procedure were consulted, and Conway and North were deputed to inform the principal government spokesmen in the Commons of the cabinet's decision. On 25 April the King wrote to North:

Though entirely confiding in your attachment to my person, as well as in your hatred of every lawless proceeding, yet I think it highly proper to apprize you that the expulsion of Mr Wilkes appears to be very essential and must be effected; and that I make no doubt when you lay this affair with your usual precision before the meeting of the gentlemen of the House of Commons this evening, it will meet with the required unanimity and vigour. . . . If there is any man capable of forgetting his criminal writings, I think his speech in the court of King's

245

Bench on Wednesday last reason enough for to go as far as possible to expel him; for he declared number 45 a paper that the author ought to *glory in* and the blasphemous poem a mere *ludicrous production*.

The meeting 'turned out pretty well', wrote North to Grafton, though most of those present disliked the idea of expelling Wilkes twice for the same offence. They need not have worried: Wilkes was to give plenty of cause for expulsion. But hardly anyone thought of asking what would happen if having been expelled Wilkes were to be re-elected. This, which became the crux of the matter, was never seriously considered.

Wilkes's election triggered off a series of riots in London even more extensive than those of 1765. Two days before the election, Boswell, travelling from London to Oxford, noted the enthusiasm for 'Wilkes and liberty' – the slogan with which his name began to be commemorated. By five o'clock on the morning of the election a mob had taken possession of all roads leading to Brentford, where the poll was held; and no one was allowed to pass who did not wear Wilkes's favour in his hat. (Grafton in his autobiography suggests that intimidation of voters was one reason for Wilkes's success.) In the evening there were riots in London. Windows were broken in houses which were not lit up in honour of Wilkes, but the mob was elated rather than incensed and no lives were lost.

Worse was to come. On the day of the opening of the new Parliament, 10 May, a great crowd assembled outside the House of Lords, 'clamouring for Wilkes and liberty'. Another mob attempted to break open the King's Bench prison in Southwark and rescue Wilkes. Troops had to be summoned, fighting took place, and a man was killed. But Wilkes was not the only (or perhaps the principal) grievance of the London populace that spring. There was acute economic distress among the labouring classes; and the crowd outside Parliament not only shouted

'Wilkes and liberty' but that 'bread and beer were too dear and that it was as well to be hanged as starved'. The seamen went on strike for higher wages, refused to allow ships to leave the port of London, and marched to Parliament in a body to demand redress of grievances. They were opposed by the coal heavers, who had been thrown out of work by the seamen's strike, and fierce fighting took place between the two groups. Several people were killed, and for a few days parts of London were in a state little less than civil war.

When we read the great letter writers of this period – and the eighteenth century was rich in this most personal form of literature – we get the impression of a civilized and cultivated upper class, secure in rank and wealth, and able to indulge their taste for culture or frivolity without the need to earn a living. But this in a way is a false picture. Civilized and cultivated though the upper classes may have been, they were living, as they very well knew, on the slopes of a volcano which might erupt at any time. There were many gradations in the social structure between the very rich and the poor, but at the bottom was a vast amorphous mass for whom life was a constant struggle with few pleasures except drink and violence. Especially was this so in London, where the poor lived in indescribable conditions of wretchedness and where their concentration in a small area gave them strength and made them feared. The fine ladies and gentlemen whom we meet in the pages of Horace Walpole or Fanny Burney, exquisitely dressed, exquisitely mannered, discussing politics or literature with refinement and good taste, had the fear of what they called 'the mob' constantly in their minds. It was dangerous to go into certain parts of London well dressed. When the mob were out celebrating it was prudent to light up your house and celebrate with them: when the mob were angry it was prudent to appease them with free beer. Otherwise you stood in danger of having your fine clothes bespattered with mud or your

247

windows broken or your coach overturned. For violence was the pleasure of the mob. In the twentieth century people watch television: in the eighteenth century they watched public executions. In the twentieth century people demonstrate in Trafalgar Square: in the eighteenth century they rioted at elections. No one could be certain what the mob would do in a time of unemployment or economic distress. The first duty of an eighteenth century government was to keep the mob quiet – or in more dignified terms, to preserve law and order. And the primary responsibility for this lay with the King.

The resources for preserving law and order were inadequate. Eighteenth-century civilization rested on an insecure basis. There was no proper police force; and although in times of trouble magistrates were authorized to call for the help of the army, they were reluctant to do so. Such action might result in legal proceedings, and no reliance could be placed on the justice of a London jury. Nor were soldiers always available or in adequate numbers. 'There are in reality', wrote the King in May 1768, 'so few troops in the country that there is constantly a degree of difficulty in providing troops on the daily calls the civil magistrates are obliged to make in these very licentious days.' The nation's distrust of a standing army rendered the upper classes of London peculiarly liable to the attentions of the mob.

These facts were in the King's mind when he wrote about 'the licentiousness of the age', 'these very licentious days', or 'the evils of a daily increasing licentiousness' – all phrases from his letters at this time. As he saw it, the conduct of Wilkes increased the danger of serious disturbances. That one man, bankrupt, profligate, and insolent, should be able to rouse the mob, with the resulting damage to lives and property, seemed to the King intolerable. Not only must the government restore law and order, but it must eradicate the root of the evil. If the chief offender were not punished, the authority of government would be at an end. Wilkes must be expelled the House of Commons. It was a measure, wrote the King (27 January 1769), 'whereon almost my Crown depends'.

It did not of course occur to the King or his ministers – or to the opposition – that these riots were in part the consequence of economic distress among the London poor and that it was the duty of government to alleviate distress. Such action was beyond the contemplation of any eighteenth-century government. God had so made the world that there were rich and poor, and though common humanity demanded that the poor should not be left to die of starvation there was little the government could do to alleviate their lot. Had the King and his ministers attempted any such measures, they would have been accused of truckling to the mob. The duty of government was negative not positive: to suppress disorder not to relieve distress. The old Duke of Newcastle, now almost at the end of his life of service to the Hanoverian dynasty, thoroughly approved of what the King had done:

It is certainly necessary [he wrote on 13 May 1768] to encourage the civil magistrate to support his authority; for if that is not done, we must be either governed by a mad, lawless mob, or the peace be preserved only by a military force; both of which are unknown to our constitution: and therefore every honest man who wishes well to it ought to exert himself in the support of the civil magistrate.

The complaint the opposition made when Parliament met was not that the government had been too severe with the rioters but that it had not been severe enough.

Throughout the Wilkes affair the King was governed by the advice of his ministers. When Wilkes sent him a letter, couched in respectful terms and beseeching a pardon, he had refused to receive it. How could he, a constitutional King, interfere in a matter that was before the courts of law? When Wilkes was elected to Parliament, the King had taken the opinion of the cabinet. 'I am persuaded', writes Grafton, 'that His Majesty would readily have approved, in this case, whatever measure his principal servants had recommended.' The cabinet's decision was reached after careful thought and study of the precedents. Had Wilkes not given further offence by a libel on Lord Weymouth, the Secretary of State who had authorized the employment of troops in St George's Fields on 10 May, it might not have been possible to expel him. The motion for expulsion was carried on 3 February 1769 by 219 votes to 137. So far the House had not exceeded its powers or done anything grossly objectionable. Whether it was wise to exercise its power was another matter. It would probably have been better to have left Wilkes alone. After twenty-two months in prison he might well have been forgotten. To make a martyr of him could only increase his consequence. But the point must be made, because it is frequently ignored, that the expulsion of Wilkes was perfectly legal and no more than he deserved.

From now on matters descended from the plane of the serious to that of the farcical. On 16 February Wilkes was again elected for Middlesex, this time without opposition, and the next day was again expelled. There followed a further election and a further expulsion, and a resolution by the House that Wilkes was incapable of being elected into the existing Parliament. Wilkes ignored this resolution; and there might have been no end to this cycle of expulsion and re-election, for Wilkes completely controlled Middlesex and no freeholder could be got to oppose him, had not a rash and intrepid volunteer come forward. In an evil hour for his fame, Grafton promised government support to Henry Lawes Luttrell, an army officer, M.P. for Bossiney, who had already signalized his dislike of Wilkes. He was by no means a good candidate: an Irishman, of an unpopular family, without an acre of property in the county; but he was the only one the ministry could get. The freeholders on the government side were so cowed and Luttrell was so unpopular that he received only 296 votes as against 1,143 for Wilkes. The House of Commons thereupon resolved that Wilkes, having been declared incapable of sitting in the existing Parliament, was not duly elected, and pronounced Luttrell M.P. for Middlesex.

Thus ended, at least for a time, what the King described as 'this unpleasant business'. It had been his duty to enforce the law and to maintain the rights and privileges of the House of Commons. He was now being asked by the opposition to dissolve Parliament on the grounds that the House of Commons had acted illegally. What had been the constant complaint against the Stuart Kings but that they had tried to restrict the privileges of the Commons? King George could fairly claim that he had done no more than his duty as a constitutional monarch. But if the House of Commons had its rights and privileges, so also had the electors of Middlesex. It was not for the House to say whom the electors should or should not choose as their Member of Parliament. Only the law of the land, not a resolution of the House of Commons, could disqualify Wilkes from sitting in Parliament. Despite his offences, Wilkes was not disqualified by statute. (As a matter of strict fact he was, because he did not possess the necessary property qualification, but then neither did many of those who voted against him.) If it once came to be accepted that the House had a right to exclude any Member who had given offence, there was an end of representative government. The House would degenerate into an assembly nominated by the will of the majority and Great Britain's boasted constitution would be no more. This, so the opposition argued, was the real point at stake; and they were right. In declaring Luttrell to be the duly elected Member, the House had infringed the privileges of the freeholders of Middlesex and by implication those of every elector in the country. It was an act of aggression against the people – but by the House of Commons, not the Crown. It was the first great

251

example in the reign of the increasing pretensions of the House of Commons.

That the King should not have recognized the constitutional principles at stake is not surprising. Neither did Grafton, Camden, or Conway – all three members of the cabinet which determined upon the expulsion of Wilkes and the seating of Luttrell. All three had voted against the Grenville ministry on general warrants. Grafton had visited Wilkes when imprisoned in the Tower of London; Camden had been the judge who had decided that Wilkes was protected by privilege and had ordered his release on habeas corpus; Conway had been dismissed from his regiment and his place in the Bedchamber because of his vote on general warrants. All three were disciples of Chatham, the friend of constitutional freedom. They were the King's principal advisers, and the King had done nothing except on the advice of his responsible ministers. If these men, who had shown themselves sensitive to constitutional issues and could not be accused of prejudice against Wilkes, failed to see what was at stake on the Middlesex election is it any wonder that King George did not?

Nor can it be contended that there was any undue influence by the Crown over the House of Commons. A study of the division lists shows that Members voted according to their convictions. As on general warrants, there was a sizable minority of government supporters who were not prepared to go with them on this issue. The motion for declaring Wilkes's attack on Lord Weymouth a seditious libel was carried by a majority of 103; that for his expulsion by 82; but the resolution for the seating of Luttrell by only 54. Plainly there was a number of Members who were prepared to admit that Wilkes deserved censure, even that he should be expelled the House, but were not willing to accept Luttrell as the duly elected Member for Middlesex. Even so late in the life of this Parliament as 1773, though the matter had by then been debated ad nauseam, a motion against the decision on the Middlesex election was defeated by only 50 votes in a house of over 350. In the spring of 1774, when the government was carrying every question on its American policy by overwhelming majorities in a bored and indifferent House, it was hard pressed on the Middlesex election. In February 1774 it had a majority of only 59 in a House of 353 Members. The next month the Boston Port Bill received its second reading without a single Member walking into the lobby against it; and on 19 April only 49 Members could be got to support the repeal of the tea duty, on which Burke delivered one of his most celebrated speeches. America counted for less than Middlesex in the scale of national importance, for the obvious reason that the people of Middlesex voted for Members of Parliament and the people of America did not. The truth is that the Middlesex election was a complicated issue with strong arguments on both sides. That the House was wrong according to modern doctrine is beside the point. The real point is that the House was honest.[4]

The long parliamentary struggle over the Middlesex election was a triumph for Lord North, Leader of the House of Commons since December 1767.

The King had not been fortunate in his ministers. Apart from Bute, there had been no one with whom he could talk freely or with whom he felt at ease. His latest, the Duke of Grafton, was touchy and irritable, disliked his office, and neglected his work for racing and a kept woman. Looking back, we can see that the King was in search of a minister who could stand to him in the same relation as Sir Robert Walpole or Henry Pelham had to King George II. The dominant political problem of the first ten years of the reign was the quest for a minister who could command the confidence of both the Crown and the House of Commons. More by luck than design, yet with a touch of shrewd judgment, the King found his man in Lord North.

North started in politics as a protégé of Newcastle. His father had been Frederick, Prince of Wales's choice for Prince George's governor in 1751, but on Prince Frederick's death the Pelhams had replaced him by Lord Harcourt and consoled him with an earldom. The future King and the future minister had known each other as boys, and had acted together in the juvenile production of Addison's *Cato* at Leicester House. But boyhood acquaintance was not responsible for North's favour with the King. North had attached himself to King George II's ministers and had risen slowly in the hierarchy of office. In the early 1760s he was known as a useful junior minister and a competent debater, but without any pronounced political allegiance and of no domineering genius. When he entered the cabinet as Chancellor of the Exchequer in 1767, no one was enthusiastic for the appointment yet no one criticized it. It seemed the obvious choice. North got to the top just by being around and in default of anyone better.

If we could bring back to life the great parliamentarians of the eighteenth century perhaps there is no one who would give us greater pleasure than Lord North. Chatham would be a bore; Burke's speeches are better read than heard; Fox would be insipid apart from the cut and thrust of debate. But the sight of North being interviewed on television would be sheer joy. We should smile at his appearance on the screen – the 'large prominent eyes that rolled about to no purpose', the 'wide mouth, thick lips, and inflated visage', the 'deep untunable voice', the 'air of a blind trumpeter' (such is Walpole's description); and wonder how a man with such unprepossessing features got to the top. When the interviewer began to ask the sort of awkward questions television interviewers delight to put to politicians in the hope of catching them out, we should admire the skill with which North evaded the

254

traps set for him and turned the tables on his pursuer. After a while, reluctantly at first, we should begin to feel that here was a man we could trust: not a man of great intellectual powers or commanding oratory, not a Gladstone or a Churchill, but a man very much like ourselves, absurd sometimes but always entertaining and human and with ideas and feelings similar to our own. North came close to being the ideal democratic statesman. He never said anything that could not readily be understood; he never appeared cleverer than the average man; and he was acutely sensitive to public opinion. He was the Stanley Baldwin or Clement Attlee of his age.

If North had been no more than a clever politician he would not have commanded the universal respect he enjoyed. The twenty years or so which succeeded the accession of King George III was the golden age of the House of Commons. A man who entered Parliament with North would have heard the elder Pitt at the height of his powers. He would have witnessed the debut of Burke, the greatest intellect ever to be applied to the practice of parliamentary politics; of Charles Fox, the inspirer of the Liberal party of the nineteenth century; of the younger Pitt, the spiritual ancestor of the modern Conservative party. Within a period of thirty years he would have heard the elder Pitt's 'Rhône and Saône' speech, Charles Townshend's 'champagne speech', and Sheridan's great oration on the princesses of Oude. In the life of Parliament which has now lasted for over seven hundred years it is doubtful if there is another period so rich in great speakers. A man who could lead the House of Commons which had known the elder Pitt, and could do so with Burke, Fox, and the younger Pitt ranged against him, was of no ordinary abilities.

The secret of North's success with the House of Commons and with the King was his immense personal charm. Wraxall, who knew him well, writes that it was impossible to experience dullness in his society. 'If they turned out

Lord North tomorrow', wrote Gibbon in 1775, 'they would still leave him one of the best companions in the kingdom.' Gibbon was fastidious and discriminating, of intellectual tastes and not disposed to suffer fools gladly. He would not have sat down at North's dinner table merely because North was Prime Minister and there was good food and drink. There must have been good talk and good company to please Gibbon. But these social attractions, which count for so much in the judgments we make about people, are almost impossible to transmit to posterity by the printed word and in consequence are apt to be undervalued by historians. From the incomplete summaries of debates in the House of Commons we can get some impression of what North was like as Leader of the House, but there was no Boswell seated at the table at 10 Downing Street and North's after-dinner conversation is lost to us for ever. In the management of men, the real business of the politician, social qualities count for as much as political ideas. Historical characters are no mere vehicles for ideas but creatures of flesh and blood like ourselves. The man who pleases, who makes himself agreeable, whose society is sought after and enjoyed, will command a greater influence than the bore. Nowhere is this more so than in the House of Commons. Men of all political opinions enjoyed North's society and even his bitterest opponents could not help liking him.

In the eighteenth century the relations between the King and his Prime Minister were on a more personal basis than they are today. Today, as in the eighteenth century, the Prime Minister is the Sovereign's confidential adviser. But he is not for that reason the Sovereign's personal friend. Their relationship is political not personal. The Prime Minister owes his office not to the choice of the Sovereign but to the fact that he can command a majority in the House of Commons. He forfeits his position when he loses his majority. No amount of personal feeling on the part of Sovereign or Prime Minister can fundamentally change their relationship, though it may make it easier or more difficult for them to work together. But in the eighteenth century the element of personal feeling was all-important. The King spent long hours in private talks with his Prime Minister. They saw each other four or five times a week – much more frequently than the Sovereign sees the Prime Minister today. Much business concerning the Royal Family and the King's finances, which today is handled by the private secretary to the Sovereign, was in the eighteenth century the concern of the Prime Minister. There was no party system to relieve the King of the necessity to exercise a personal judgment in his choice of a Prime Minister. The Prime Minister did not owe his position to the fact that he could command a majority in the House of Commons. He owed his majority in the House of Commons to the fact that he could command the confidence of the King. Grenville's majority deserted him when he ceased to be Prime Minister. Rockingham acquired a majority when he became Prime Minister. If public business was not to suffer, King and Prime Minister must be on friendly terms. Apart from Bute, King George had liked none of his ministers. We know how much he disliked Grenville. Rockingham, though Grenville's superior in courtesy and consideration, was diffident and reserved, a poor man of business, and not an entertaining companion in the closet. Chatham was pompous, long-winded, oracular, and difficult to understand: Grafton was fidgety and touchy, and showed too plainly how much he disliked his employment. The King could talk to none of these men with the ease and familiarity which his grandfather had shown towards Sir Robert Walpole. And a King must be able to talk easily and familiarly with someone. What a blessing North must have been – intelligent, affable, cultivated, amusing, and never forgetful of the difference between Sovereign and Prime Minister.

In the summer of 1769 there were signs that another

257

political crisis was about to develop. On 7 July Chatham appeared in public for the first time since his illness, more than two years previously, and had a long talk with the King after the levee. He expressed his disapproval of the ministry's policy towards the East India Company and over the case of Wilkes; said it was doubtful if his health would ever allow him to attend Parliament again (he had been saying this for the last seven years); 'but if it did, and if he should give his dissent to any measure, hoped that His Majesty would be indulgent enough to believe that it would not arise from any personal consideration'. The King knew Chatham too well not to understand what this meant, and as the summer advanced the signs of Chatham's intentions multiplied. He was again reconciled to his brothers-in-law (they had quarrelled once more when Chatham had taken office), and began to exercise a persuasive influence on those of his followers who remained in the cabinet. The King grew uneasy about Camden and may even have had his fears about Grafton. Perhaps the award of the Garter to Grafton in September 1769 was designed to confirm him in office. For if Chatham went into opposition and Grafton followed him the King would again be at the mercy of faction triumphant.

And he very nearly was. On the first day of the session (9 January 1770) amendments to the Address were moved in both Houses demanding an inquiry into grievances, the principal one being the Commons' decision on the Middlesex election. In the Lords Chatham was supported by Camden, speaking from the Woolsack; in the Commons Lord Granby, Commander-in-Chief, declared that he repented of his vote on the Middlesex election. The spectacle of two Cabinet ministers supporting a motion of censure on the ministry of which they were members was unprecedented in the annals of Parliament. It was more: it was scandalous. It was a reflection on the integrity of public men which the King, who had no high opinion of the morality of politicians, felt deeply. If

258

Camden and Grafton had disagreed with the cabinet's handling of the Wilkes affair, why had they not resigned? Such would have been the honourable course. This was the course which had been taken by Chatham in 1761 when he found himself opposed to his colleagues on the policy to be pursued towards Spain. Why had not Camden and Grafton followed the example of the great statesman whom they professed to idolize? Their resignation or at least the threat of it might have induced the cabinet to take a different attitude. But to cling to office against their principles and then to resign at the moment which would best suit the convenience of the opposition was despicable. Few of the followers of Chatham were men of character. Had they been, they would not have been followers of Chatham.

Again the King prepared to fight in defence of the constitution. Neither the Bill of Rights nor the Act of Settlement gave power to one House of Parliament to prescribe to the Crown who should be Prime Minister. Who was Chatham that he should dictate to King George III? He had a majority in neither House of Parliament. If there were to be a general election tomorrow, Chatham could not obtain a majority unless he were first appointed a minister of the Crown. The King had followed the advice of his ministers and the cabinet which had advised him was composed of men nominated by Chatham. Throughout this tiresome business he had followed the strict path of constitutional rectitude. He was now entitled to claim that Parliament should stand by him as he had stood by Parliament.

The King offered the Great Seal to Charles Yorke, son of Lord Chancellor Hardwicke. Yorke's great ambition was to sit in his father's place in the House of Lords, yet his political connections were with the Rockinghams and he hesitated to take office in a ministry that seemed on the brink of dissolution. The King had no patience with hesitation at such a moment, and told Yorke that if he refused this time he should never again have the offer. What with the King's threats, his brother's warnings, and Rockingham's reproaches, poor Yorke hardly knew which way to turn. After three days' agony of mind and body he kissed hands, went home, and took to his bed. On 20 January he died. Rumour had it that he had committed suicide in an agony of remorse; but contemporary accounts by his wife and brother indicate that he died a natural death, probably from the bursting of a blood vessel. It is not cynical to doubt whether any politician can feel remorse about accepting office. One might as well ask whether a business man feels remorse when his shares increase in value or a civil servant when promoted in his department. It is not success, but failure, that leads men to commit suicide.

The ministry was now without a Lord Chancellor. The day following Yorke's death there came an even greater blow when Grafton requested permission to resign the Treasury. Nothing that the King could say would induce him to remain. In his autobiography, written thirty years later, Grafton assigns as the reason for his resignation his isolation in the cabinet after Camden and Granby had left. To the King it was an act of cowardice, and he always referred to the Duke's 'desertion' of him at the moment of crisis. For Grafton's resignation stripped the King of his last line of defence. He was now reduced to the position he had held on 22 May 1765 when the Grenville ministry presented their ultimatum. Within the space of a week, three cabinet ministers had resigned. How could the ministry continue without a Lord Chancellor and a head of the Treasury? On 22 January, Conway found the King 'in the utmost distress'. Horace Walpole wrote, with a touch of sympathy for the King:

Conway hinted at trying Lord Rockingham; but the King said he knew the disposition of Lord Rockingham and his friends, and would not hear of them. He was as thoroughly averse to Lord Chatham: both, he said, were engaged to dissolve the

Parliament; but he would abdicate his Crown sooner. 'Yes', continued the King, laying his hand on his sword, 'I will have recourse to this sooner than yield to a dissolution.' He talked of trying to go on if Lord North would put himself at the head of the Treasury.

That day the King invited North to become head of the Treasury and leader of the ministry. North asked for time to consider the offer. He wished to see how events went in the House of Commons. On 25 January an opposition motion of censure was defeated by 224 votes to 180. It was not a large majority but it was sufficient: if opposition could not win in this division they could not win at all. On 28 January North accepted. He was to remain in office until 20 March 1782.

On 31 January the opposition renewed their motion in a slightly different form and were beaten by 226 to 186. 'I am greatly rejoiced at the conclusion of the debate', wrote the King to North. 'A majority of 40 at this particular crisis, considering it is upon the old ground that has been at least ten times before the House, is a very favourable auspice in your taking the lead in administration. Believe me, a little spirit will soon restore a degree of order in my service.' On 28 February, on a motion respecting the debts on the Civil List (about which the House was particularly sensitive) the ministry's majority rose to 97. 'The seeing that the majority constantly increases gives me great pleasure', wrote the King. By the end of 1770 the opposition had quarrelled and Rockingham and Chatham were on the worst of terms. The dispute with Spain over the Falkland Islands which the King had feared would lead to war was concluded to the advantage of Great Britain, and on 13 February 1771 the Commons approved the convention with Spain by 275 votes to 157. North's authority in the House was now established beyond doubt. He was the minister who commanded the confidence of both Crown and House of Commons: the heir of Sir Robert Walpole and Henry

Pelham: an authentic Whig. He was the minister for whom King George had been searching since the resignation of Bute.

The King had been proved right. It had, after all, only needed 'a little spirit'.

It has been necessary to consider in some detail the political events of the first ten years of King George III's reign because these have largely influenced the judgments that have been made of his aims and character. These were the years when the King served his apprenticeship, and the experience he gained determined his way of handling politicians and political problems. This was to be put to the test when the crisis of American affairs broke upon the nation in 1774. A candid review of the period from 1760 to 1770 will acquit the King of the charges of attempting to increase the royal prerogative or to return to a more personal form of government. But it will leave us in doubt whether he was by temperament and inclination suited to the business of politics.

It is sometimes assumed that Kings are born with a taste for politics and an interest in government or else that they inherit these with their crowns. A little knowledge of human nature will show that this is not so. During the last two hundred years perhaps only Queen Victoria among British monarchs had a real interest in politics. The others performed a duty, for the most part conscientiously and honestly, but one they would not have attempted had they been born in a private station.

Had King George been born a country gentleman, he would have followed Candide's advice and cultivated his garden without taking much interest in politics. But he grew up with the knowledge that he would one day have to shoulder the burden of kingship and the fear that he would prove inadequate to the task. He succeeded to the throne with less experience of life than any of his predecessors for over a hundred years. He succeeded at a younger age than any previous monarch since Edward VI in 1547. King George II was of mature years when he became King. George I and William III were already experienced rulers. Queen Anne had been brought up among the shifting and tortuous politics of the later Stuart period. James II and Charles II had felt the sharp sting of adversity. Compared with these, King George III in 1760 was almost a babe in arms. 'I am young and unexperienced', he had written to Bute in 1756, 'and want advice'; and he was not much older nor more experienced when he became King. Unlike his predecessors, he served his apprenticeship to kingcraft after, not before, he succeeded to the throne. King George had to learn the hard way, and we should not be too severe upon him for his mistakes.

His friendship for Bute did not arise from a desire to increase his power. Had he been grasping of power, he would never have trusted a favourite. Every man isolated on the lone summit of supreme authority – whether King, Prime Minister, or President – requires a confidant. There is a passage in Lord Davidson's memoirs, written in 1937 for Neville Chamberlain, which explains the King's need for Bute:[5]

It is essential to have the friendship of someone outside the cabinet whose loyalty and discretion is beyond question, in whose judgment the Prime Minister has faith, with whom he can discuss his innermost thoughts, talk nonsense, try out new ideas and even discuss his colleagues. In short, a confidant from whom no secrets are hid.

Bute served this purpose for the young King George as Lord Melbourne did for the young Queen Victoria. Had Bute been able to remain outside of politics, much of the confusion of the early years would have been avoided. But under eighteenth-century conditions Bute had to become a politician – a role for which he was ill-equipped and which disqualified him for that of the King's confidant.

A monarch also needs a mediator between himself and the politicians. Under King George I, this role had been filled by the King's mistress, the Duchess of Kendal; under King George II, first by Queen Caroline, and after her death by Lady Yarmouth. In the nineteenth and twentieth centuries the task of mediator became the function of the private secretary to the Sovereign. The development of this office has been a potent factor in easing the relations between the Sovereign and the politicians and placing them upon an impersonal basis. The private secretary is appointed by the Sovereign but not from among the ranks of the politicians. He is the servant of the Sovereign, not of the ministry. Yet he is the confidant of both and the mediator between them. His task is to ensure that relations between the Sovereign, who is irremovable, and the Prime Minister, who is removable at the will of the electorate, are at all times harmonious irrespective of the political complexion of the ministry. Both Sovereign and Prime Minister can speak freely to him. Each can say to him what perhaps they would not wish to say to the other. He can soften asperities and convey thoughts and feelings which it is not desirable to express in a formal manner. Had there been someone to do for King George III and Grenville what General Ponsonby did for Queen Victoria and Gladstone perhaps there might never have been the crisis of 22 May 1765.

King George had to conduct his affairs face to face with his ministers. Alone among monarchs of the modern period he had neither mistress nor private secretary, and Queen Charlotte was not able to attempt the role which had been accomplished with success by Queen Caroline. There was no one to act as a buffer between the King and the ministers. The element of personal feeling could never be absent from their relationship.

The office of Prime Minister did not exist in the eighteenth century though the term is frequently used. During the first years of the King's reign the Duke of Cumberland and Chatham came nearest to holding this office, yet neither were Prime Ministers in the modern sense. Their authority stemmed from the fact that they enjoyed the confidence of the Crown, not of the electorate as does a modern Prime Minister. They were favourites in the tradition of Bute. The key post in government was the person styled by contemporaries 'the minister in the House of Commons'. Except for short periods and under exceptional circumstances, it was almost impossible to conduct government unless the principal minister, the head of the Treasury, was a member of the House of Commons. When the head of the Treasury was a peer, the ministry had a short life. When he was a commoner, nothing short of a total loss of confidence on the part of the Crown or the House of Commons could remove him. The great ministers of the eighteenth century – Walpole, Pelham, North, Pitt – were all commoners. It is the paradox of that aristocratic age that the supreme office could never be held by a member of the House of Lords. A peer was all very well as Secretary of State or Lord Chamberlain – in fact the whole cabinet could be composed of peers – provided only the head of the Treasury was a member of the House of Commons. It did not matter what happened in the House of Lords. Their boasted independence was a myth. They were creatures of the Crown. The only sources of political power in Great Britain were the Crown and the House of Commons, and the man who commanded the greatest power was he who enjoyed the confidence of both.

If only Bute, who enjoyed the friendship of the King, had been a member of the House of Commons! – if only Grenville, who was a member of the House of Commons, could have won the confidence of the King ! – so many of the problems which have puzzled historians about the early years of the King's reign would have been avoided. In normal circumstances there was no need for a Prime Minister in the eighteenth century. The range of governmental activity was restricted, there was no party system or mass electorate, and no necessity for anything like a government policy. Each minister reported to the King on the affairs of his department and when the King wished for advice he deferred to the collective wisdom of the cabinet. It was only in time of war that it became necessary to have one minister to co-ordinate all the activities of government to an overwhelming purpose. The office of Prime Minister arose from the needs of war not of peace, for it is only in war or when war is imminent that men begin to appreciate the need for government.

In Lord North the King had found an efficient Leader of the House of Commons. He had solved the political problem which faced him when he came to the throne. Because of his youth and inexperience it had taken him longer than it ought to have done. But he had solved it at last. He could now afford to relax and take his ease, free from worry about politics or the House of Commons – until the advent of another war and the need for a Prime Minister.

Chapter 5

REBELLION IN AMERICA

To Americans and British alike King George III will always be remembered as the King who lost the American colonies. This is for most people the chief political event of his reign and the one with which he is most closely identified. His reputation has suffered grievously in consequence. This is not surprising in America. The Declaration of Independence of the United States names the King as the principal culprit in the quarrel with the mother country. 'The history of the present King of Great Britain', so runs the Declaration, 'is a history of repeated injuries and usurpations' – eighteen of which are specified. 'He has refused his assent to laws the most wholesome and necessary for the public good. . . . He has obstructed the administration of justice. . . . He has erected a multitude of new offices. . . . He has plundered our seas, ravaged our coasts, burnt our towns. . . . He has excited domestic insurrections amongst us. . . .' These are a few of the crimes laid to the account of King George in the Declaration of Independence. 'A prince', the indictment concludes, 'whose character is thus marked by every act which may define a tyrant, is unfit to be the ruler of a free people.' In the mythology of American history King George III is the would-be tyrant whose wicked plans were foiled by the courage and resistance of the American people. He is the scapegoat for the act of rebellion.

Nor has he received more sympathetic treatment in Great Britain. In the nineteenth century when imperialism became an article of the British political creed, the loss of the American colonies was seen as a national disaster without precedent in British history. It was the one exception to that uniform record of success which the British

267

had been taught to believe was their reward for having renounced Popery and embraced freedom. The reaction to the loss of the colonies in the governing class took two forms. First, a persistent denigration of American life and culture. The word 'Yankee' in Victorian England came to stand for everything that was brash and vulgar. 'Yankee boasting', 'Yankee bounce', 'Yankee democracy' were familiar terms of abuse, and they helped to maintain the illusion that British civilization was superior to American. Some such assurance was needed, for by the middle of the century the British were becoming uneasily aware that the United States was growing into a great power. Perhaps one day the United States might be able to meddle with the affairs of the British Empire – to menace Canada, for example, or to lend aid and encouragement to revolutionary elements in Ireland. These were threats which Great Britain could not look upon with indifference. It was time the Yankees were taken down a peg. There were some in England who saw with grim pleasure the United States drift into a civil war which could only weaken the republic – a fit punishment for the ungrateful people who had renounced the British Empire. Two words may describe this reaction to the loss of the American colonies: sour grapes.

Secondly, it was desirable to transfer the responsibility for the loss of the colonies to a suitable scapegoat. In an age when democracy was increasing its demands the British governing class had to preserve its reputation for political wisdom. And who more suitable than King George III for the role of scapegoat? He was King when the colonies were lost and he was singled out in the Declaration of Independence as the great object of American opprobrium. A hundred years or so after its signature, the British began to reflect that what they had once considered a treasonable document might be a paean in praise of liberty. Ireland excepted, there might be something to be said for the principles enshrined in the Declaration. If only King George had listened to Edmund Burke and Charles James Fox instead of George Grenville and Lord North! Obviously, it was all the fault of the King not of the British nation – a foolish and mad King, attempting to increase his power and ruling through corrupt Ministers. The Americans had been right to rebel. How many books have been written on this theme? In the mythology of British history King George III is the scapegoat for the failure of imperialism. The Americans have charged him with tyranny, the British with corruption. In the literal sense, he has had the worst of both worlds.

Today, nearly two hundred years after the signature of the Declaration of Independence, we can see the events which led to the foundation of the United States in a more rational light. A great deal of the jealousy and fear felt by each nation for the other has disappeared. They have participated as allies in two world wars. The political climate has changed beyond recognition. The British Empire is a thing of the past and few Britons mourn its disappearance. Americans no longer suspect British imperialism: Britons no longer fear the United States as a potential enemy in a future war. The loss of the American colonies is no longer regretted as a reproach to the prestige of a governing class which is now extinct. Few people today are so naive as to equate monarchy with tyranny or republicanism with virtue. We have seen in our own time kings who were models of every democratic virtue and tribunes of the people who established tyrannies beyond the ken of former ages. We have been liberated from the passions of our ancestors. The dead past need no longer afflict us like a festering sore. It is now possible to consider King George III's part in the American war free from the emotions which obsessed good patriots and historians concerned to serve the cause of patriotism. Let us put aside Thomas Jefferson and Charles James Fox and see King George III as he really was.

Many and various were the causes of the movement which historians have denominated the American revolution. Perhaps we shall understand these better if we give the movement a more fitting name. It was not a revolution in the sense in which France experienced a revolution in the eighteenth century or Russia in the twentieth. It did not lead to the emergence of a new governing class with new principles of government. It was a rebellion, like that of the Dutch against the King of Spain in the sixteenth century or the Israelites against the Pharaoh of Egypt as narrated in the Book of Exodus. It was the assertion by a colonial people of its right to self-government: the first great nationalist rising of modern times: the prototype of the rising of the Irish nation against Great Britain, of the South American nations against Spain, and of many others in Europe, Africa, and Asia. The Declaration of Independence marks the emergence of nationalism as a force in modern history.

Reared in the principles of Whiggism, it is not surprising that King George and the British governing class failed to understand what was at stake in their dispute with the colonies. The world has much for which it should be grateful to the Whigs. The era of Whig civilization, which lasted in Great Britain for roughly a hundred years after the revolution of 1688, with all its deficiencies and blemishes produced the most tolerant and least oppressive form of government which western man has known. The fundamental basis of Whiggism was the Protestant establishment: the supremacy of State over Church. It did not matter what form Church government took – it was episcopal in England, presbyterian in Scotland – provided the Church was national and the State supreme. Roman Catholicism, a religion based on an international organization and claiming authority over the State, was inimical to Whiggism; and in Roman Catholic countries in the eighteenth and nineteenth centuries there arose a bastard form of Whiggism designed to combat the authority of the Church. Whiggism was anti-clerical and tolerant, for persecution is an attribute of the clergy rather than of the laity – of those whose profession it is to believe rather than of those whose interest it is to conform.

Whiggism was based on a civilian organization of society. It assumed the right of the politically conscious members of society to exercise the responsibilities of government and to receive in return the rewards of government. The Whigs did not believe all men were created equal: a proposition demonstrably false. They did believe that all men were endowed with certain inalienable rights which it was the duty of government to preserve. Government was the concern of the propertied class, who had the greater stake in society; and those excluded from a share in government because they lacked property were also exempt from the burdens of government – the need to perform military service and to pay direct taxation. It was when these burdens began to be extended from the propertied to the non-propertied class – during the great war against Napoleon – that the Whig system of government broke down. Whiggism assumed that men were capable of looking after their own affairs without the assistance of the State (perhaps this was the greatest flaw in Whig theory), and that State intervention was an exceptional not a normal incidence of life. Government existed for limited and defined purposes: to protect life and property; to conduct foreign policy; and to ensure an orderly distribution of the favours of the Crown to those who did the work of the Crown. 'Providence has so ordered the world', wrote Shelburne in his autobiography, 'that very little government is necessary.'

Whiggism therefore was both anti-clerical and anti-militarist. It was tolerant and pacific. And considering the misery which has generally resulted when either the clerical or military professions have been allowed to dominate government, we may perhaps consider that of all the theories of government which the ingenuity of man has devised Whiggism has done least harm and achieved most good. It was the most lukewarm of political theories and appealed least to the imagination. For that very reason it was best calculated to govern mankind in peace and amity. Unlike other political theories, it contained within itself the seeds of something greater. Because of its tolerance, it favoured the growth of scientific ideas; because of its pacifism, it favoured the spread of international understanding. It may be that the future of humanity will depend on how we learn to adapt the principles of Whiggism to the modern world.

Whiggism was not a creed for export. It never took root in Ireland (though Ireland if left to herself might have evolved her own form of Whiggism as the United States did); and the record of the British in Ireland is the greatest stain on Whig civilization. It was in effect confined to Great Britain, the only Protestant power in Europe which was an island and had no need to maintain a standing army for its defence. In its origins Whiggism was insular and defensive; but like all creeds born in an atmosphere of persecution once its principles were generally accepted it became aggressive and expansive. The extinction of Jacobitism and Great Britain's success in the Seven Years War led to the emergence of an imperialist form of Whiggism which destroyed the original creed.

The old Whigs valued colonies because they were of advantage to the mother country. To Walpole, Pelham, and Newcastle colonies were a source of raw materials which could not be produced in Great Britain and a market for British exports. They were places where undesirable characters could be accommodated without expense to the British tax-payer: convicted felons; younger sons without a provision; eccentric offspring of the governing class who had made England too hot to hold them. It never occurred to the old Whigs that it was desirable to spread the principles of their creed – what has been called in the twentieth century the British way and purpose – to lands of which they knew little and cared less. Ireland of course was a special case, because the possession of Ireland was deemed essential to the defence of Great Britain and many of the Whig aristocrats owned property in Ireland. Whiggism had to be upheld in Ireland by force of arms. But in general the Whigs were not imperialists. It was William Pitt, who at best was no more than half a Whig, who conceived the idea that the more of the map that was painted red the better for mankind. Under Pitt's inspiration the theory was propagated that it was desirable to acquire colonies in order to spread the gospel according to the revolution of 1688 to the un-converted parts of the world. To the economic motive for colonization was now added a missionary zeal. Pitt, the first imperialist in modern British history, dug the grave of the Whigs. Britain was no longer to be a European, but an imperial, power.

The Seven Years War in the west had originated in disputes between Great Britain and France in North America, and had found the British colonies ill supported by the mother country and ill prepared to organize their defence. Newcastle's foreign policy had been concerned with erecting barriers to French influence in Europe not to French aggression in America. It was Pitt who under-took to plead the cause of the Americans. 'The present war', he declared in his great speech of 13 November 1755, 'was undertaken for the long-injured, long-neglec-ted, long-forgotten people of America.' He defended the policy of subsidizing Frederick the Great and sending a British army to the Continent not as Newcastle would have done – because this reduced the power of France in Europe – but because it reduced the power of France in America. 'America had been conquered in Germany', Pitt told the House of Commons on 13 November 1761. Newcastle was a good European, who had been brought up to believe that it behoved Great Britain to pay attention to the balance of power on the Continent. But as the Seven Years War drew to a close, with Britain triumphant in every quarter of the globe, interest began to swing away from Europe towards the empire the British had acquired in India and America. The era of British imperialism had begun. Two hundred years later, when the British had abandoned their empire and had become disillusioned with imperialism, they began to swing back towards Europe. Perhaps in the long run Newcastle was wiser than Pitt.

Hardly had peace been concluded in 1763 before the British government began to consider what King George called 'that greatest and most necessary of all schemes, the settlement of America'. The newly acquired territories must be absorbed into the old empire, and the whole must be organized for defence and profit. The colonies must be brought firmly under the control of the mother country just as Ireland had been in the previous century. There must be a judiciary and revenue service independent of the colonial assemblies and responsible to the central government. Troops must be stationed permanently in the colonies to guard against a recrudescence of French aggression (and also to make sure that the colonists remained amenable to British authority). 'An extensive empire', wrote Gibbon in *The Decline and Fall*, 'must be supported by a refined system of policy and oppression; in the centre, an absolute power, prompt in action, and rich in resources; a swift and easy communication with the extreme parts; fortifications to check the first effort of rebellion: a regular administration to protect and punish; and a well-disciplined army to inspire fear, without provoking discontent and despair.' Gibbon wrote this passage about the empire of Charlemagne but perhaps he had that of King George III in mind. This ideal of empire has fascinated all imperialists from Diocletian to Stalin. It was not peculiar to Great Britain in the eighteenth century. Nor was it a subject of controversy.

Pitt and Bute, the King and Grenville, were agreed on aims and principles. Their differences were over methods and priorities. Newcastle almost alone, representative of a fast-diminishing generation of old Whigs, had doubts about the new imperialist policy. He remembered Sir Robert Walpole's remark that sleeping dogs should not be disturbed. But few troubled themselves about what Newcastle thought. He was an old man and had had his day.

The new policy would be expensive; and it seemed to the British only reasonable that the colonies should pay for their own government and defence. Ireland did, so why not America? Late in 1762 the British government began to consider ways and means of raising a revenue from the colonies. This was a matter which required much deliberation and should not be too hastily introduced. When Charles Townshend precipitately raised it in the House of Commons, he drew down upon himself a rebuke from the King. 'This subject was new to none', the King wrote to Bute, 'having been thought of this whole winter. All ought to have declared that next session some tax will be laid before the House, but that it requires much information before a proper one can be stated.' On 4 March 1763 Bute's Ministry introduced the first instalment of their imperial plan. The Secretary at War informed the House of Commons that the government intended to maintain a standing army in the American colonies. At first the expense of this army would be met by the British taxpayer but eventually it would be paid for by the Americans themselves. The opposition raised no objection. Pitt, making one of his infrequent appearances in the House, gave the plan his approval. His only criticism was that the number of 10,000 troops to be stationed in the colonies was too small. He feared that the peace would not be of long duration, that France would soon be in a position to renew the war, and that Great Britain ought to be prepared. Government and opposition were agreed on the policy of maintaining an army in America, and it was Pitt, the declared friend of America, who pressed for an increase in the size of the army.

To the Americans a military establishment was at best a nuisance. What need had they of soldiers? Now that Canada had been ceded to Great Britain they no longer feared the power of France, and they felt perfectly capable of dealing with the Indians without the aid of regular troops. It occurred to no one in Great Britain that the colonial assemblies, the representatives of the American people, should be consulted about the proposed military establishment. It was regarded as axiomatic that colonies were subordinate to the mother country. Why consult the colonial assemblies about a matter which was within the sphere of the imperial government? Even so late as 1774 Edmund Burke, who had uniformly opposed the policy which was driving the colonies towards rebellion, did not deny that on imperial questions the authority of the Parliament of Great Britain was supreme. Parliament, he declared in his celebrated speech on American taxation (19 April 1774), 'as from the throne of Heaven . . . superintends all the several inferior legislatures, and guides and controls them all.' Surely the British government was entitled to assume that the defence of the empire was an imperial question on which the authority of Parliament ought to be supreme? This was a proposition which no British politician could deny without denying the idea of empire. But from it the British drew conclusions which no American could accept without being disloyal to the idea of America.

The Americans prided themselves on their British extraction. They shared the Whig view of government which prevailed in Great Britain. They paid homage to the Bill of Rights, the Act of Settlement, the Hanoverian succession and all the other household gods in the Whig pantheon. But they did so with a certain mental reservation and they evolved for themselves their own form of Whiggism. They believed that the liberties guaranteed by

276

the Bill of Rights were the heritage of Americans as well as Britons and were a bulwark against the tyranny of Parliament as well as against the tyranny of the Crown. They accepted the authority of Parliament because it was not exerted too onerously against them. But they could not accept that their own parliaments – the colonial assemblies – should be annihilated and rendered as of no account. This is what would have happened had they allowed the House of Commons to dictate their military establishment and to prescribe the taxes necessary for its support. *Exercitus facit imperatorem* – the ultimate source of power in any state lies in those who control the armed forces. The ultimate source of power of any representative assembly is the power of the purse – who pays for the army? – and once that power is lost the assembly becomes feeble and ineffective. Had the House of Commons yielded to the ambition of the Stuart kings for a revenue independent of Parliament they would have become as impotent as the States-General of France and Charles I as absolute as Louis XIV. Had the American assemblies yielded to the will of the British Parliament they would have been reduced to the status of county councils. They would have had no authority of their own, only such as was delegated to them by the imperial Parliament. Thus it was that the conflict between Great Britain and America, which was really a conflict over control of the armed forces, came to be fought over the issue of taxation. It is said that love makes the world go round. But in politics it is money that counts. It is not the hand that rocks the cradle that rules the world but the hand that raises the tattoo.

What was or what was not an onerous exertion of authority depended from which side of the Atlantic it was viewed. What might be considered in London as 'a just exertion of the rights of the mother country' could be viewed in Boston or New York or Philadelphia as 'an intolerable invasion of our liberties'. We shall not understand the events leading to the American rebellion if we view them as incidents in a conflict between right and wrong. That is how they have too often been seen by American nationalists and British imperialists, anxious to justify the behaviour of their countrymen. The truth is that each nation had some right on its side but a great deal more of wrong. The British were not prepared to grant to the Americans the liberties won by the Bill of Rights and the Americans were not prepared to grant to their Negro slaves or Indian neighbours the rights they claimed from the British. Historical events can rarely be judged by the standards of a pure and austere morality. Imperialism may be a discredited creed in the twentieth century but it is not for that reason an immoral system of government. It is a stage in the evolution of a nation like adolescence in the life history of an individual. If we were as far in time from the empire of King George III as we are from that of Augustus or Justinian we should see its virtues more clearly.

It is not with right or wrong that history is concerned but with success or failure. The race may not always be to the swift nor the battle to the strong but the judgment of history is always to the successful. Thus historians have been almost unanimous in condemning the policy of the British government because that policy failed. It is sometimes suggested that the separation of the two nations was a tragedy, an event which did harm to humanity and which might have been prevented had the British shown more statesmanship. If only the King had been less obstinate or Lord North more firm, if Grenville had not introduced his stamp tax or Townshend his customs duties, or if half a dozen other imponderables had not happened as they did, perhaps the United States might today be part of the Commonwealth. Had the two great Anglo-Saxon powers remained politically united, so this argument runs, the course of history would have been changed. There might never have been a First World War: there might never have been a Hitler or a Stalin.

All this is stuff. If there is one event in history which can truly be described as inevitable it is the political separation between Great Britain and her American colonies. What was not inevitable was the way by which separation came about. It need not have taken place over the issue of taxation: it need not have taken place as the result of war. War and the aftermath of war – the behaviour of the British army towards the American civilian population, the behaviour of Congress towards those Americans who remained loyal to Great Britain – embittered feeling between the two nations. The hostile attitude each had assumed towards the other long persisted. It was long before the United States outgrew the stage of insular and prickly nationalism: it was long before Great Britain outgrew the stage of aggressive imperialism. When the two nations became allies in the Second World War each insensibly reverted to the position they had held in 1776, and Franklin Roosevelt became an advocate for the right of self-determination and Winston Churchill for the authority of empire. We may sometimes wonder whether men ever learn from history.

If we could forget our pride in the past, if we could renounce the legacy of bitterness and jealousy which followed the American war, we might admit that political separation was of advantage to both nations. Had the colonies remained subject to the British Crown they would have been 'cabined, cribbed, confined'. Great Britain also would have suffered by the connection. She would not have been able to work out her own problems in her own way. She would have been dependent on her more powerful children. Who in Great Britain during the American Civil War was not relieved that the United States was an independent nation? Who in Great Britain in 1917 and 1941 did not rejoice that the United States was a great and powerful nation?

* * *

Despite changes of ministry, the British government pursued a consistent policy towards the colonies. However much the politicians might disagree over ways and means, there was no disagreement in principle over the grand design of imperial policy. The three main points – a standing army, a permanent civil service, a colonial revenue – were never forgotten. Bute introduced the plan of maintaining an army in the colonies. Grenville introduced the stamp tax as a means of raising a revenue. Rockingham, unable to enforce the Stamp Act, decided to repeal it; but affirmed the right of the British Parliament to legislate for the colonies in all cases whatsoever – which included the right to levy taxes. Hardly had Chatham taken office when his cabinet began searching for new ways of raising a revenue to which the Americans would not object. Chatham insisted that the colonies should obey the Mutiny Act and make provision for the troops stationed in America – which, since this took money out of the pockets of the colonists, was an indirect form of taxation. Charles Townshend, his Chancellor of the Exchequer, introduced port duties, founded a commission of customs at Boston, and announced the government's intention to render colonial officials and judges independent of the assemblies. Each ministry in its separate way did something to forward the grand design. Like a sailing ship faced with a heavy wind, the British government tacked one way and then another but always headed in the same direction.

The King had no doubt that they were going in the right direction. Grenville in his final audience on 10 July 1765 besought the King 'as he valued his own safety, not to suffer any one to advise him to separate or draw the line between his British and American dominions'. By this Grenville meant that the King should maintain the rights of the British Parliament against those of his American subjects. The King hardly needed the warning. He held his throne by a parliamentary title and no King after the revolution of 1688 could pursue a policy against the will of Parliament. To deny the competency of Parliament to legislate for the entire British empire was to deny the Bill of Rights. King George had been too well educated in the principles of the British constitution not to know where his duty lay.

It was not the King's business to determine the tactics of the grand design. That was the concern of his ministers. When the Rockingham ministry took office and the first protests against British imperialism were heard from America, the King, still in dread of Grenville, was disposed to throw the blame for the disturbances on his late ministers. On 17 December 1765 he wrote sarcastically about 'the great care the last Administration took by the wise regulations they made for putting the Stamp Act in execution'. He favoured the amendment of the Act to meet any 'just grievances' from America; but when told by Rockingham that there was no alternative between enforcement, which could only be done by the army, and repeal, he declared in favour of repeal. In later years the King became convinced that the repeal of the Stamp Act had been a mistake. 'The fatal compliance in 1766', he wrote, had 'encouraged the Americans annually to increase in their pretensions' to the point of 'that thorough independency which one state has of another'. In May 1777, at the height of the war, he wrote of the 'too great lenity of this country' towards the colonies which 'increased their pride and encouraged them to rebel'. It has not been fashionable to credit King George III with any great extent of political vision, but on the repeal of the Stamp Act he was wiser than his ministers. If the British Parliament intended to maintain their claim to tax the colonies, the correct policy would have been to have amended the Stamp Act – if necessary, by reducing the tax to a purely nominal one – rather than to have repealed it. Repeal was a virtual acknowledgment that Great Britain's position was untenable and a victory for the colonial idea that they could not be taxed without their consent. If Parliament were prepared to admit this, what was the point of the Declaratory Act? If Parliament were not prepared to admit it, what was the point of repealing the Stamp Act? If by riots and demonstrations the Americans could effect the repeal of the Stamp Act, then by similar means they might hope to effect the repeal of any Act of Parliament which they deemed obnoxious.

The King believed that 'the unhappy factions' which divided the House of Commons prevented the framing of a proper policy for America. There can be no doubt that he was right. Despite what ministers said in Parliament, the real reason why the Stamp Act was repealed was their wish to cultivate Pitt. We should not be deluded into thinking that the Rockingham cabinet sympathized with American claims. Had the Duke of Cumberland lived another six months there would have been no repeal of the Stamp Act. He would never have allowed his cabinet to drift into a policy of appeasement.

After 1766 the British government pursued what was for them a conciliatory policy. They wished to do nothing which would provoke the Americans. Within the framework of imperialism, they were restrained rather than precipitate; and Lord North, though no statesman, handled a difficult situation with tact and won public sympathy for his policy. But relations with the colonies grew worse. Granted two postulates – that Great Britain was bent on a policy of imperialism which would deny to the Americans the rights of nationhood, and that the Americans were no longer willing to be treated as colonists but demanded self-determination and if need be were prepared to fight for it – it is difficult to see how war could have been avoided. Either Great Britain or America must yield and neither would yield except to force. The real charge against the British government is not that they unnecessarily provoked war but that they did not make preparations for war while the Americans were yet weak.

From a military point of view it would have been better for Great Britain to have taken up arms in 1766 rather than in 1775. The true *casus belli* was the Stamp Act, not the Boston Tea Party. This was the first challenge to British authority, and the future would depend on how the first challenge was met. In 1766 the colonies were unprepared for war and there were deep differences between them. In 1775 they had learnt to sink their differences in face of the common enemy. In 1766 it would hardly have been possible for America to have concluded an alliance with France. In 1775 this was the obvious policy for both countries, flattering alike to the ambition of France and the pride of America. What delayed the outbreak of war, and thus placed the British at a serious military disadvantage, was their reluctance to use force and their refusal to admit that it could be a solution to their dispute with the colonies. In 1766 British political opinion was not prepared to go to war to enforce the Stamp Act. American political opinion was prepared to face the danger of rebellion rather than accept the Stamp Act. The policy of appeasement – the refusal to make war until there is no alternative between war and national disgrace – so much applauded in 1938, so much condemned in 1940, has a long pedigree in British history.

Let us now see affairs from the American point of view. Each year that followed after 1765 brought further evidence of British hostility and hastened the day when the colonists would finally realize (and how many of them had not already realized it in their heart of hearts?) that America would never be free until America was independent. Yet there had to be a long process of degeneration in Anglo-American relations before the American farmer and merchant, labourer and apprentice, girded on his sword or shouldered his musket and prepared to encounter the professional army of King George and the mercenary troops he had hired from Germany. During this period both nations drew on their common heritage.

The reluctance to face reality was common to Great Britain and America. Appeasement rather than war has always appeared to both nations the true solution to international disputes.

There was a great deal of ambivalence in the attitude of both nations which led to charges of insincerity and hypocrisy. The British, with few notable exceptions, never faced up to the consequences of their imperial policy. They seem never to have realized that their grand design would be destructive of American freedom, the greatest legacy the British had bequeathed to America. Each party leader blamed his rivals for the deterioration in Anglo-American relations without reflecting that he had contributed his own share. The Americans while repeatedly acknowledging the supreme authority of the British Parliament always found good reasons for refusing to accept that authority in specific cases, Parliament, so they argued, could not tax the colonies because the colonies were not represented in Parliament and it was a fundamental principle of the British constitution that no man could be taxed without his consent signified by his representatives. True: but then if Parliament could not tax the colonies Parliament had no authority over the colonies, for the power of a representative assembly stems from its control of taxation. Pressed to their logical conclusion the American claims admitted the supremacy of the Crown over the colonies and denied that of Parliament. 'The sovereignty of the Crown I understand', wrote Benjamin Franklin. 'The sovereignty of Parliament I do not understand. . . . We have the same King but not the same legislature.' The fathers of the American republic were the heirs of the Tory tradition in British politics, and perhaps the only true Tories in the world today are to be found in the United States. Which may account for the otherwise surprising fact that we sometimes meet Americans, especially from the east coast states formerly under British rule, who are far more monarchical than the average Briton. All this is hard on King George III, who was pilloried in the Declaration of Independence for supporting the sovereignty of Parliament and refusing to become King of America.

For nearly ten years after the repeal of the Stamp Act the two nations engaged in a prolonged boxing match. The details of that period do not concern the biography of King George. Each hurt the other; each grew more embittered and angry towards the other; but both kept their heavy punches in reserve and were reluctant to risk a knock-out blow. Yet everything was moving towards a predestined end. All British policy led to the punitive legislation of 1774 and the destruction of political freedom in the colonies: all American resistance led to the Declaration of Independence. The Boston Tea Party brought matters to a head. Here was a defiance of authority which the British government could not afford to ignore. Here was an act of rebellion which the Americans could not afford to disclaim. The Boston Tea Party was an event in history like Hitler's occupation of Prague – something that was bound to happen sooner or later, which everyone except its author had feared and sought to evade, and which when it came was welcomed as an end to cant and pretence and appeasement.

What was King George's part in these events?[1] To judge from his correspondence it was small. The problem of America was not that which most concerned the King during the years from 1768 to 1774. The search for a stable ministry, Wilkes and the Middlesex election, the troubles of the Royal Family, the day-to-day business of court functions – these occupied more of his time and thoughts than America. He had no ideas on American policy beyond the general wish, shared by his subjects, to maintain British supremacy over the colonies. He judged each question as it arose on its merits and tried to be fair to both nations. If he showed any partiality it was

285

towards America. He felt that if America manifested an inclination to obedience Great Britain should be generous. In 1766 he was reluctant to use troops to enforce the Stamp Act and in 1769 he opposed the more extreme suggestions of his ministers towards Massachusetts Bay.

When the Boston Tea Party turned the world upside down the King agreed with North that stern action must be taken. He took pains to inform himself of the state of affairs in America from those who might be expected to know. On 4 February 1774 he gave audience to General Gage who was on leave from his appointment as commander-in-chief in North America. 'He says they will be lions whilst we are lambs', the King wrote to North, 'but if we take the resolute part they will undoubtedly prove very meek.' On 1 July he summoned Thomas Hutchinson, late governor of Massachusetts Bay, for a confidential conversation, and was pleased to learn that 'the people of Boston seem much dispirited'. Hutchinson gave it as his opinion that the punitive legislation of the spring was wise and necessary and would soon bring the colonists to 'a speedy submission'. At the same time Edward Gibbon was seeking to learn the facts of the situation from experts on America, and was reaching conclusions similar to those of the King. 'I am more and more convinced', he wrote on 31 January 1775, 'that we have both the right and the power on our side, and that, though the effort may be accompanied with some melancholy circumstances, we are now arrived at the decisive moment of persevering or of losing forever both our trade and empire.' And on 8 February: 'I am more and more convinced that with firmness all may go well; yet I sometimes doubt Lord North' – a sentence that could well have been written by the King. Gibbon was then hard at work on the first volume of *The Decline and Fall of the Roman Empire*. If a knowledge of history can help men towards an understanding of current politics, then surely Gibbon should have realized the truth? When the most learned historian of the age was wrong about America we should not be too hard on King George.

Spring ripened into summer; the Continental Congress was summoned to meet at Philadelphia; and the colonies showed no disposition to come to heel. A conciliatory gesture from Massachusetts Bay might have softened the attitude of the British government; but it never came. The Americans were resolved not to yield an inch in their opposition to the punitive legislation. 'The die is now cast', the King wrote on 11 September 1774, 'the colonies must either submit or triumph. I do not wish to come to severer measures, but we must not retreat; by coolness and an unremitted pursuit of the measures that have been adopted I trust they will come to submit.' Gibbon would have approved: this was the teaching of history. 'The New England governments are in a state of rebellion', the King declared on 18 November. 'Blows must decide whether they are to be subject to this country or independent.' He had made up his mind that civil war was inevitable and faced the prospect with a good conscience and sober confidence. 'Where violence is with resolution repelled it commonly yields', he wrote on 15 February 1775, 'and I own though a thorough friend to holding out the olive branch, I have not the smallest doubt that if it does not succeed that when once vigorous measures appear to be the only means left of bringing the Americans to a due submission to the mother country the colonies will submit.'

The King could conceive of no middle way for the colonies between independence and unconditional submission. He did not understand that it is the business of politicians to find a modus vivendi between two unacceptable solutions. He saw politics as an extension of morals and always in terms of black and white. 'I know I am doing my duty and therefore can never wish to retract', he wrote in July 1775. The idea that 'the legislature has no right to tax the colonies' would always be opposed by him as tending to annihilate 'one of the essential rights of a supreme legislature'. The claims put forward by the colonies were such 'that it would be better totally to abandon them than to admit a single shadow of them to be admitted'. This was what Benjamin Franklin had meant when he said that he understood the sovereignty of the Crown but not the sovereignty of Parliament. 'I am fighting the battle of the legislature', the King wrote on 10 September 1775, '. . . therefore am ready to stand every attack of ever so dangerous a kind with the firmness that honesty and attachment to the constitution will support.' It was not the right of the Crown but the right of Parliament that was at stake. It was not the Crown but Parliament that was encroaching on the liberties of America. For more than a hundred and fifty years Parliament had been jealous of the power of the Crown. King George III had been accused of attempting to increase his power. Here was his opportunity to show how well he had learnt the lessons of history. He would not repeat the mistake of the Stuart Kings, and take advantage of the dispute between his subjects in Great Britain and his subjects in America in order to increase his own power. He would be the defender of the constitution: the protector of the rights of Parliament. Both Gibbon and King George tried to resolve the American problem in the light of their knowledge of history. History is not always a safe guide.

'Countries should always be governed by the will of the governed', said Charles James Fox in the debate on the repeal of the tea duty (19 April 1774). It is a proof of Fox's wisdom that he realized this fundamental truth of politics long before the rest of his fellow countrymen. The King had been taught to believe that Great Britain should be governed by the will of the British people. But no one had ever told him that America should be governed by the will of the American people, and the idea was antipathetic to the political thought of his age. Even Edmund Burke, who criticized so severely the policy of the King's ministers and pleaded so eloquently on behalf of the colonies, did not countenance this idea. Nor in subsequent years was Burke willing to grant self-government to Ireland or at the time of the French Revolution to admit the demand of the French nation to be governed by the will of the governed. Why should we expect King George to be superior in understanding to Edmund Burke? It was long before Great Britain learnt to accept Fox's principle. Few Englishmen in the nineteenth century desired to see Ireland governed by the will of the Irish people: hardly anyone believed it possible to govern India by the will of the Indian people. Indeed, we may go even further and ask how far Fox's principle is accepted in the world today?

It is undesirable that a constitutional monarch should be in advance of his people. It is unreasonable to expect him to be in advance of the greatest intellects of his age. The British government's American policy had the full support of public opinion. The punitive legislation of 1774 aroused little opposition in the House of Commons, and at no time did so many as a hundred Members go into the lobby against the government. Lord North was entitled to claim as he did in later years that the nation was behind him on the measures which led to the American rebellion.

Let us suppose that King George had been gifted with supreme political wisdom: that he had heeded the great truth spoken by Burke that 'magnanimity in politics is not seldom the truest vision': that in 1774 he had felt towards the American nation as Gladstone did towards the Irish nation in 1886. In that case he might have been impelled to dismiss North, to call Chatham or Rockingham to power, to dissolve Parliament, to employ the influence of the Crown to secure a House of Commons favourable towards conciliation with America, if need be to promote a reform of Parliament. Measures like these might have retained for Great Britain the formal and temporary

289

allegiance of the colonies. Even this is by no means certain; for the rule of democracy can be as arrogant and chauvinistic as the rule of property and the extension of the right of voting by no means ensures the predominance of statesmanship and vision. But such changes would have new-modelled the British constitution and the King would have been no longer a constitutional monarch but an enlightened despot. Instead of a process of gradual adjustment to new circumstances and ideas, as took place in the nineteenth century, Great Britain would have undergone a revolution and a revolution brought about by the Crown.

We may be thankful that King George III was not a statesman. It is not desirable that a constitutional King should be a statesman. Statesmanship is the prerogative of ministers not of monarchs. It is better for a nation to be governed by a George III than by a Frederick the Great or a Joseph II. Happy the nation that numbers no great men among its Kings! The ideal constitutional monarch should in the quality of his mind be no greater than the average of his politically conscious subjects: he should share their ideals, their prejudices, perhaps even their follies: and should act as a brake on change rather than as a stimulant. He should appeal to the common of mankind. It was fortunate for Great Britain that King George III did not attempt to find a solution of the American problem independent of the House of Commons. For that he deserved well of his people. Far from reproaching him for having lost the American colonies, subsequent generations should be grateful that he preserved the British constitution with all its possibilities of peaceful change. America was a small price to pay for that blessing.

On 26 July 1775, a month after the battle of Bunker Hill and a year before the Declaration of Independence, North warned the King that 'the war is now grown to such a height that it must be treated as a foreign war'. The King needed no warning. He had already taken steps to augment the army. It was the general opinion of army officers and colonial governors who had served in America that the colonists would not make good soldiers, that they lacked discipline, and would be unable to encounter a regular army in the field. One officer boasted in the House of Commons that with 5,000 regular troops he could march from one end of America to the other. But this arrogance was not shared by the government in London or by the military commanders in America. They believed that it would need a considerable effort to subdue the colonies and that Great Britain would have to bestir herself. The King faced the prospect of war with sober confidence but with no illusions.

One of the three major-generals sent to America in the summer of 1775 was John Burgoyne, famous in history as the commander of the British army which surrendered at Saratoga in October 1777 – the 'gentlemanly Johnny' of Bernard Shaw's play *The Devil's Disciple*. But the Burgoyne of Shaw's imagination – witty, urbane, with no belief in the cause for which he was fighting, who prepared to hang a man with the same courtesy he would have shown when inviting an earl's daughter to dance a minuet – is not the Burgoyne of history. The real Burgoyne was a sterner character, much more of a soldier and much less of a gentleman. He was appalled at the state of unpreparedness of the British army in America and advised the King to wage war *à l'outrance* in order to achieve a quick victory. He recommended a large army in New York and another in Canada; a body of Indians should be enlisted: arms should be provided for the Negro slaves to overawe the southern colonies: and a fleet should be sent to blockade the coast. 'This might possibly do the business in one campaign', wrote Burgoyne. But his advice struck a chill to North's heart. 'The cause of Great Britain is not yet sufficiently popular', he told the King on

291

23 August 1775. The House of Commons was complacent and might be unwilling to vote large sums for an extensive war. And was this really the best way to bring back a deluded people to their allegiance? The time-honoured methods of making a donkey go were to beat him with a stick and to dangle a carrot under his nose. The Americans, so it seemed to the King and North, in their unreasonableness and obstinacy had behaved much like donkeys and should be treated as such. A large army in the colonies in the spring of 1776 would be the stick to beat the American donkey. An offer of conciliation, which would yield something and yet preserve the essential authority of Parliament, would be the carrot. Even this offer, unacceptable though it was to America, was too much for some of North's supporters. 'An idea struck several gentlemen', North reported the debate to the King, 'that it was too great a concession, and we were likely to lose several friends, but their wavering was a strong proof that the disposition of the House independent of any ministerial connection is to maintain the authority of Great Britain over America.' The King approved his minister's policy. 'It shews what is expected', he wrote, 'and gives up no right.'

Thus coercion and conciliation – the stick and the carrot – went hand in hand. There was something to be said for Burgoyne's proposals. Once a nation is resolved to make war, it is better to do so with vigour and get it over as quickly as possible. *Blitzkrieg* is the only sensible method of making war. A prolonged war rarely brings the political advantages expected and always brings disadvantages which were not expected. Had Great Britain been in a position to make war in the summer of 1775, and had she been prepared to do so ruthlessly and brutally, it is just possible that the rebellion would have been crushed at the outset. In that event George Washington would have ended his life on Tower Hill as did the Jacobite rebels of 1745, and King George III, Lord North, and General Burgoyne would have acquired a reputation for statesmanship which they did not deserve. Such is the respect which history pays to force when it is successful.

Men and money are the sinews of war, and in the eighteenth century the British government found it difficult to raise either. Of the two, money was probably the easier to get, provided money was plentiful and the Treasury offered a sufficiently high rate of interest. Men were always more difficult to raise, for though the British labouring classes were poor their standard of living was higher than in any other European country and they were rarely driven by hunger to enlist in the army. There were many people in Great Britain in the summer of 1775 – both high and low – who shared the King's belief in the justice of the cause but were not prepared to risk their fortunes or lives on the outcome of the war. The responsibility for raising money devolved on North: for raising soldiers, on the King.

The King turned to Germany, the traditional recruiting ground of the British army. Soldiers were easier to find in Germany and they came cheaper. In August 1775 five regiments of Hanoverians were taken into British pay. 'The present transaction', the King wrote to North on 4 August, 'is a clear and handsome loan of five battalions ... for which I claim nothing but to be reimbursed all expenses.' Though the King had 'gloried in the name of Britain' and had once described Hanover as 'that horrid electorate', he was not prepared to see Hanover suffer in a quarrel which concerned Great Britain alone. The rights of Parliament were the stakes and Parliament must pay the entrance fee or forfeit the race. The Landgrave of Hesse Cassel, the King's uncle, offered a regiment, which was gladly accepted; and troops were hired from other German princely houses connected with the Royal Family. Brunswick Wolfenbuttel and Mecklenburg Strelitz contributed their quota; and Catherine of Russia was asked to help but sent a rude reply. 'She has not had the civility to answer in her own hand', the King wrote to North on 3 November, 'and has thrown out some expressions that may be civil to a Russian ear but certainly not to more civilized ones.' However desperate his need for troops, the King was not prepared to infringe the laws of the Holy Roman Empire which forbade recruiting for foreign armies. It was one thing to pay a German prince for the hire of his troops. It was quite another to send recruiting sergeants into his territories to bribe or intimidate potential soldiers. When this suggestion was made to the King (not by his ministers) he rejected it flatly. It would be 'turning me into a kidnapper', he wrote to North on 14 November 1775, 'which I can not think a very honourable occupation'. Rather than imitate the conduct of Frederick the Great, King George preferred to delay recruiting his mercenary troops.

On 26 August 1775 the King wrote to North:

The misfortune is that at the beginning of this American business there has been an unwillingness to augment the army and navy. I proposed early in the summer the sending beating orders to Ireland, this was objected to in the cabinet; if it had then been adopted the army would have been at least two or three thousand men stronger at this hour.

The King wished to complete the 'old corps', that is bring the existing regiments up to their proper strength. This was the cheapest way of increasing the army and also the most efficient, for recruits would serve side by side with trained soldiers. He suggested to North (10 September 1775) that if 'the nobility and gentry of property could be persuaded separately in their parishes to give half of a guinea in addition to the levy money for the encouragement of each of their parishioners enlisting in the army, that would be doing a real service'. On 25 September he wrote again:

Are the London merchants so thoroughly absorbed in their private interests not to feel what they owe to the constitution which has enriched them, that they do not either show their willingness to support either by an address or what I should like better a subscription to furnish many comforts to the army in Ireland.

From the City of London, whose politics from the beginning of the reign had been opposed to the Court and which was now dominated by Wilkes and his friends, the King could expect little. But in general the war was not popular, and North was despondent about the prospect of recruiting a sufficient army. 'The ardor of the nation in this cause', he wrote to the King on 26 November 1775, 'has not hitherto arisen to the pitch one could wish, and it is certain should be encouraged wherever it appears.'

The King set his face against raising new regiments, at least until the existing regiments were brought up to strength. 'I am certain', he replied to North on 28 November, 'nothing could give such real grounds of disgust to the army as the raising additional new corps.' Raising new regiments was not only a more expensive way of recruiting but it gave occasion to jobbery. The 'nobility and gentry of property', who were the army's recruiting agents, expected to nominate to commissions in the regiments they raised, and would use this privilege to provide for their friends and relations and to strengthen their electoral interest. Officers were promoted out of their turn and newly-commissioned officers given rank above the heads of those already in the service. At the end of the war when the regiment was disbanded they would expect to receive half pay – a further source of expense.

The King was torn between the need to increase the army and his wish to be fair to regular officers. As the hopes of a quick victory receded and the demand for more troops became pressing, he had to yield in his principles. In December 1777, after Burgoyne's surrender at Saratoga, he was 'much pleased' by the offer of some gentlemen in the neighbourhood of Manchester to raise 1,000 men. But 'if they apply for the recommendation of too many of the officers', he wrote to North on 9 December, 'or for very extraordinary advanced rank to those of their friends to be advanced from other corps ... it will give such general disgust to the army and in particular to those serving in America that it would be more disserviceable than advantageous'. He suggested that the men should be raised first and no commissions should be granted until the regiment was complete. (There had been many cases of men joining the army for the levy money and afterwards deserting.) A similar proposal from the corporation of Liverpool was accepted on the understanding that no application should be made for a commission above the rank of captain. Then came a request for a gross job: the promotion of a captain to the rank of lieutenant-colonel. At this the King dug in his heels. He wrote to North on 29 December 1777:

I yesterday mentioned that I can never think of giving Captain Stanley the rank of lieutenant-colonel, the utmost that I could be brought to and that reluctantly would be that of major. ... Though you are not a military man, you can easily see what a strange medley this Liverpool regiment will be unless some officer of experience is put at the head of it to train and discipline the corps. ...

By an unwearied attention to the services of officers I flatter myself I have their goodwill, which would be totally destroyed if I was giving way to every job that noblemen are wishing for their relations, not the service of their country.

No doubt patriotism had stimulated the corporation to raise a regiment but politics was not without its influence. Liverpool was a parliamentary borough with a large electorate, and its politics turned on the conflict between the corporation and an independent party. A judicious distribution of commissions would strengthen the corporation's interest and help to win back control of the borough which had been lost at the previous general election. The fact that the corporation supported North's ministry and the independents opposed the American war

296

did not influence the King. He would not allow politics to prevail over the interests of the army.

Scotland was a poor country in the eighteenth century and the army a more popular service than in England. In Scotland even more than in England recruiting was an instrument of politics, and commissions were a great bait for the minor gentry and landless classes. After Saratoga there was a rush to the colours in Scotland and the King grew alarmed at the request for jobs. When the city of Edinburgh proposed to raise a regiment, he wrote to North (15 January 1778):

The immense number of new corps [in Scotland] has given promotion to one part of my kingdom in preferment to the rest. If the gentlemen would be persuaded to turn their proposal into completing the old Scotch corps in the service it would be much more advantageous. . . .

I hope Lord North will do his utmost to prevent the forming any more offers of new corps. They will instead of being of utility only perplex and totally annihilate all chance of completing the regular forces, which alone in time of need can be depended upon; particularly in England the raising corps would be total destruction to the army.

It was useless to protest. If the army was to be increased it must be on terms acceptable to those who did the recruiting. All the King could do was to veto the grosser and more scandalous jobs. Lord Macleod, son of the Jacobite Earl of Cromartie who had been attainted after the rebellion of 1745, offered to raise a regiment provided he were appointed its colonel. The King protested that Macleod had never served in the British army and could not be placed above officers who were senior to him – but of course he was. Without the head of the Macleods as its commanding officer there would have been no Macleod regiment. The King refused a similar offer from the Earl of Dunmore. 'The principle on which I go', he wrote, 'is that no man is to get above one step and he quitted the army several years ago and only as a captain.' The Duke of Gordon, anxious to rehabilitate his scapegrace brother Lord William Gordon (who had seduced George III's first love, Lady Sarah Lennox), offered to raise a regiment with Lord William as its commander. The King wrote to North (29 December 1777):

I can never think of giving Lord W. Gordon the rank of lieutenant-colonel. His first coming into the army was on the raising Major-General Morris's corps [in 1759], with which he never served. He had for a short time a company in the 25th regiment. Not liking his duty, he sold out while the regiment was at Minorca, therefore has not the smallest claim to military rank.

Lord William was persuaded to relinquish his military pretensions for a sinecure, but the Gordon regiment was not raised by the Duke.

Admirable though it was, the King's wish to avoid jobbery in the army was not conducive to military success. If he had not been so concerned to be fair to the officers of the old corps Great Britain might have won the American war. The urgent need for Great Britain in the summer of 1775 was to have a large army in America by the following spring. If the American rebellion was to be crushed, it would have to be crushed at the outset. The longer it lasted the more organized and efficient the Americans would become and the greater would be the danger of foreign intervention. Great Britain could not expect to lose the first campaign and yet win the war: if she lost the first campaign she would almost certainly lose the war. The leisurely methods of making war to which the British had become accustomed in Europe would not do in America. After Lexington every available regiment of the old corps should have been sent to America and a new army recruited in Great Britain to act as a source of reinforcements. The militia should have been embodied (which was not done until 1778), and officers and men encouraged to transfer to the regular army. This is what Frederick the Great would have done. He would not have cared about breaking the laws of the Holy Roman Empire or promoting officers out of their turn provided he got the troops he wanted. He would not have hesitated to have burnt Boston or New York, to have roused the Indians or armed the Negroes. He would have waged ruthless war: and after victory would have governed the colonists as a conquered people.

King George could not do this. He was a constitutional King, accustomed to accept the advice of his ministers, not an enlightened despot. His ministers could go no faster than Parliament and public opinion permitted. Nor could they treat subjects in revolt as a foreign enemy. In the event they did not go fast enough, and in their anxiety to avoid expense (always a source of concern to eighteenth-century governments) ignored the King's opinion and delayed the recruiting drive. When it came in 1777 it was too late. Had the cities of Manchester and Liverpool or the Earl of Dunmore and the Duke of Gordon been prepared to raise troops in 1775 as they did in 1777, and had the King been prepared to lower his standards for the commissioning of officers, there might have been a large British army in America in the spring of 1776. But by the end of 1777 no effort that the British could make would have been sufficient. The Americans had compelled a British army to surrender in the field and it could only be a question of time before France and Spain intervened on their side. Whatever the issue of the war, the aims of British imperialism would not be realized. America had become a nation, and the authority of Great Britain was lost for ever.

'We must show that the English lion when roused has not only his wonted resolution but has added the swiftness of the race horse', wrote the King on 11 January 1776. But the horse was slow to start, and even when it got going it plodded along more like a selling plater than a potential classic winner. In March 1776 the British withdrew from

Boston. Then events seemed to turn in their favour. The American expedition into Canada was repulsed; in July 1776 General Howe captured New York; and in September 1777 followed this up with the occupation of Philadelphia. Howe inflicted several defeats on Washington's army but failed to bring the American commander to decisive action. Instead of the quick victory for which the British had hoped and which was in truth their only hope of victory, the war was fought at the leisurely pace of a campaign in the Low Countries. 'Have you realized', says the American officer to Burgoyne in Shaw's play, 'that though you may occupy towns and win battles, you cannot conquer a nation?' In the first two years of fighting the Americans suffered more defeats than the British, but this was not the decisive factor. With infinite skill Washington manoeuvred to keep his army in being as a fighting force and no crack appeared in the American resolve to maintain their independence.

The turning point came in October 1777 when Burgoyne surrendered at Saratoga. As a military event this was of no great consequence. It was a reverse, but not the great military disaster that Leipzig was to Napoleon or Stalingrad to Hitler. The bulk of the British army in America was still undefeated. But the political effects of Saratoga were out of all proportion. The British had built great hopes on the campaign of 1777. They had put into the field the largest army ever sent from Great Britain. Burgoyne had started from Canada brimful of confidence. This was his great opportunity to win military glory. After capturing Ticonderoga in June he had issued a bombastic and vainglorious proclamation in which he threatened to spread ruin and devastation through the northern colonies. Four months later he had to eat his words. The boost to American morale was immense. The decaying French monarchy had been watching the war with close interest and the British government was uncomfortably aware that the French were ready to pounce as soon as they saw that the British were trapped. The King advised North that nothing should be done to provoke France. But the Americans had been assiduously cultivating the French, and there was little the British government could do to prevent French intervention. And if France intervened, Spain would certainly follow. 'My mind is perfectly prepared to meet what I should certainly think a very unhappy event', wrote the King on 7 January 1778, 'from the consciousness that I have scrupulously attempted to avoid, and that without one single grievance France chooses to be the aggressor.' In March 1778 Great Britain broke off diplomatic relations and France openly intervened on the American side.

The King faced the defeat of Saratoga with courage and resolution. It was 'very serious but not without remedy', he wrote on 4 December 1777. It was clear, he told North on 13 January 1778, that without an army which it was beyond the power of Great Britain to raise offensive operations in America must be abandoned. 'A war at sea is the only wise plan.' Great Britain should hold what she had in America, defend Canada and the West Indies, and trust to the long-term effects of blockade. These were not the King's ideas but those of Lord Amherst, who put them before the cabinet on 17 January. But the cabinet was reluctant to accept the plan. Too much had been staked on the policy of subjugating the colonies by offensive warfare. Perhaps North could not forget – or feared the House of Commons would not forget – his declaration of 2 May 1774 that Great Britain had no reason to dread the strength of the colonies. A responsible minister cannot eat his words so easily as a general and policy cannot be reversed overnight. The secret of making war as North realized is to keep the confidence of those who are paying for the war. The House of Commons demanded victory in America and victory in America they must have. This was no time to reduce the strength of the army in the colonies. It would be admitting that the aims of the government were unattainable, that the government had been wrong and the opposition right. No responsible minister can make admissions such as these and hope to retain his authority. The King could advocate a defensive war in America but his minister could not.

On 18 January the cabinet advised the King that a further three battalions should be sent to America, one of them if possible to be drawn from the old corps. The King was reluctant to accept this advice. 'I cannot help saying', he wrote to North the next day, 'that nothing can be more detrimental in case of a European war than the idea of sending in our present weak state another old corps out of Great Britain; but I will not object on this occasion.' It would have been better if he had vetoed the proposal. The old corps was the strength of the British army. They were trained and disciplined soldiers. No reliance could be placed on the newly-raised regiments. Was it wise at this juncture to send more of Britain's best troops on a wild-goose chase in America, perhaps to share the fate of those who had marched so confidently with Burgoyne?

But North was in no state to consider matters objectively. Faced with the news of Saratoga and the prospect of a French war, he panicked. He was less concerned with policy or strategy than with his own position in the House of Commons. He had always thought of himself as Leader of the House rather than as Prime Minister and he was acutely sensitive to parliamentary opinion. The House would insist on inquiring into the causes of Burgoyne's failure. There would be recriminations, criticisms, charges; and North flinched from the prospect of facing angry and disillusioned Members. Some offer of accommodation must be made to America, which Congress would doubtless reject but which would enable North to tell the House that he had done his best to bring about an honourable solution of the conflict. If Parliament insisted on maintaining its pretensions, North could then call upon them for further efforts. He proposed to give up the right of taxation, to repeal the punitive legislation of 1774, and even to amend the Declaratory Act. He was prepared to concede everything Congress should ask short of recognizing the independence of the United States: the one condition which Congress was resolved to exact. He knew how distasteful these proposals would be to his followers in the House of Commons, how much they would lower him in the estimation of the House; and he begged the King to release him from his office.

The King was taken aback. 'You are my sheet anchor', he had told North in November 1775; when others had 'shamefully' deserted the King's service, North had stood firm. If he was to leave now, who could take his place? Memories of 22 May 1765 were in his mind – that dreadful day when he had been compelled to yield to George Grenville and humbly to ask his minister's leave to go into the country. If North were to resign, the opposition would be as hard upon him as ever Grenville had been. Charles James Fox, their leader in the House of Commons, had private reasons of his own for disliking the King and would rejoice at the opportunity of humiliating him. 'I should have been greatly hurt', the King wrote to North (31 January 1778), 'at the inclination expressed by you to retire, had I not known that however you may now and then be inclined to despond yet that you have too much personal affection for me and sense of honour to allow such a thought to take any hold on your mind.' He advised North to consult the cabinet and the principal government speakers in the House of Commons before taking a decision on his conciliatory proposals. His letter continued:

Perhaps this is the minute of all others that you ought to be the least in a hurry to produce any plan of that kind, for every letter from France adds to the appearance of a speedy declaration of war. Should that event happen, it might perhaps be wise to strengthen the forces in Canada, the Floridas, and Nova Scotia, withdraw the rest from North America and without loss of time employ them in attacking New Orleans and the French and Spanish West India possessions. Success in those parts would repay us the great expenses incurred. We must at the same time continue destroying the trade and ports of the rebellious colonies, and thus soon bring both contests to a conclusion; and this country, having its attention diverted to a fresh object, would be in a better temper to subscribe to such terms as Administration might think advisable to offer America, who on her part will at such a time be more ready to treat than at the present hour.

On 3 February the King wrote again:

Should a French [war] be our fate, I trust you will concur with me in the only means of making it successful, the withdrawing the greatest part of the [troops] from America and employing them against the French and Spanish settlements, but if we are to be carrying on a land war against the rebels and against those two powers it must be feeble in all parts and consequently unsuccessful.

An accurate prophecy of what was to happen in the next four years!

There was good sense behind the King's proposals. Great Britain's military position in the spring of 1778 was strong and her resources by no means exhausted. What was needed was a great national effort, comparable to that of 1759, aimed at the critical points of French power in the West Indies and on the sea. The best way to weaken the spirit of American independence was to strike hard and decisive blows against France. A defeat inflicted on France would be felt in America. In the spring of 1778 the capture of a West Indian island would have been a greater success for Britain than the capture of Philadelphia, and victory over the French navy more than compensated for surrender at Saratoga. A war directed primarily against France would have aroused patriotic feeling in Great Britain and won the approval of those who sympathized with the American cause. A civil war would have been turned into a national war.

For this there had to be a strong united cabinet, headed by a minister able to concentrate the national effort on making war. North's cabinet was neither strong nor united. It was a cabinet of departments, not a team. No single man was in charge of the conduct of the war and there was no one to co-ordinate the activities of government. In short, there was no Prime Minister. North was leader of the House of Commons but not leader of the cabinet.

Since the revolution of 1688 British government had been geared to movements of opinion within the House of Commons. In time of peace this was a blessing, for it meant that public opinion could exert its influence on policy. In time of war it came close to being a disaster. The House of Commons is no body for deciding the policy or strategy of a great war. If war is to be conducted efficiently the House of Commons has to play a subordinate role. All successful war ministers – Chatham in 1757, Palmerston in 1855, Lloyd George in 1916, Churchill in 1940 – have been thrust on the Commons by backstairs intrigues. None of them would have been appointed by a free vote in the House. In each case the men who controlled the Commons had to be replaced by others, less sensitive to the moods of the House but of tougher fibre, and prepared to appeal if necessary against Parliament to the nation at large. North was too good a leader of the Commons to become a great war minister. He knew this himself. He wrote to the King on 5 May 1778:

Your Majesty's service requires a man of great abilities, and who is confident of his abilities, who can choose decisively, and carry his determinations authoritatively into execution. Such should be the character of your ruling Minister, and there should be one capable of forming wise plans and of combining and connecting the whole force and operations of government. I am certainly not such a man.

The cabinet understood the need but looked in vain to North. 'Damn him!' said Lord Chancellor Thurlow in an unguarded moment in 1780, '. . . nothing can goad him forward, he is the very clog that loads everything.' Lord George Germain, who had no reason to love Chatham and whose political future was bound up with the success of the war, wrote in 1779:

Do what you will, nothing will avail till Lord North will adopt a system, pursue it with firmness, and oblige every department of government to act under his directions. . . . I know no other receipt [but the one] Lord Chatham had last war. All was languid and every department had its forms and difficulties. He raised them all, and by activity alone succeeded in every attempt.

But North could not do what Chatham had done.

He became so depressed that his usual good judgment deserted him and he fell a prey to absurd fears. On 15 March 1778 he declared to the King: 'The present Ministry can not continue a fortnight as it is, and there is nothing which seems so likely to stem the first violence of the torrent as sending to Lord Chatham. If His Majesty can not consent to that . . . he is afraid the whole system will break up.' In fact the Ministry was in no danger and was to last another four years; while Chatham, now nearly seventy, had long lost his vigour and even if the King had sent for him could not have formed a cabinet which would have lasted twelve months. But the King had no intention of sending for Chatham: he had had quite sufficient of that overbearing and unpredictable genius. Nor would he again put himself at the mercy of any clique of politicians: he wanted no repetition of 22 May 1765. He replied to North: 'No advantage to this country nor personal danger can ever make me address myself to Lord Chatham or any other branch of the Opposition. Honestly I would rather lose the Crown I now wear than bear the ignominy of possessing it under their shackles.' And the next day: 'It is not private pique but an opinion formed on an experience of a reign of now seventeen years that makes me resolve to run any personal risk rather than submit to Opposition.' Had he done so he would have become what he believed his grandfather to have been – a King in chains. No consideration in life shall make me stoop to Opposition', he told North on 17 March. '... I will rather risk my Crown than do what I think personally disgraceful. . . . It is impossible that the nation shall not stand by me. If they will not, they shall have another King.'

Something had to be done about North, who was now working himself up into a state of hysteria. On 17 March he begged the King in heart-rending terms to release him. 'Capital punishment itself', he wrote, 'is, in Lord North's opinion, preferable to that constant anguish of mind which he feels from the consideration that his continuance in office is ruining His Majesty's affairs. . . . His former incapacity is so much aggravated by his present distress of mind that he will soon be totally unfit for the performance of any ministerial duty.' Those who knew North best understood that this was a mood that came upon him frequently, genuine and distressing to himself and his friends, but which would pass away. The King understood North's difficulties (and also how much North himself was responsible for them), and encouraged him to strengthen the ministry by taking in members of the opposition. 'My sole wish', he wrote, 'is to keep you at the head of the Treasury and as my confidential Minister. That end obtained, I am willing through your channel to accept any description of person that will come devotedly to the support of your Administration.' He did not object to Chatham entering the Cabinet provided he came as a colleague of North and not as the leader of the Ministry. He was prepared to waive all personal prejudices against individuals. But he declined to negotiate with the Opposition – 'I have had enough of personal negotiations', he wrote; and as in July 1767 insisted that any negotiations North should undertake should be on the basis of strengthening an existing Ministry not forming a new one.

To go cap in hand to the politicians, as he had had to do to Grenville in 1765 and to Chatham in 1766, was the road to disaster:

Men of less principle and honesty than I pretend to may look on public measures and opinions as a game. I always act from conviction, and certainly never can say but that I am shocked at the base arts all these men have used, therefore cannot go towards them. If they will come to your assistance I will accept them.

The note of self-approbation in this passage reminds us of what Waldegrave wrote about the King as a boy – that he had 'rather too much attention to the sins of his neighbour'. The attitude expressed in the phrase 'Thank God, I am not as other men are' was common in the eighteenth century, and Rockingham and Chatham were quite as self-righteous as King George. The King's criticism of the Opposition leaders though harsh was not devoid of truth. The principles on which North had acted and which had brought on the American war had been enunciated before his time by Rockingham and Chatham. Rockingham had promoted the Declaratory Act which had confirmed Great Britain's supremacy over her colonies 'in all cases whatsoever'. Chatham had stated in the House of Commons during the debates on the repeal of the Stamp Act that if America should again resist British authority 'he would second a resolution of the most vigorous nature to compel her with every man and every ship in this country'. North had merely tried to enforce what Chatham and Rockingham had declared must be enforced. If ideas are the determinants of history Rockingham and Chatham were equally responsible with North for the conflict. To the King, who did not regard 'public measures and opinions' as a game, there was something hypocritical in the attitude of the Opposition leaders. He did not understand the difference between the ideas which a politician may profess in opposition and the practical measures he may be compelled to take when in office. He did not understand the compromises and adjustments which have to be made before ideas can be translated into reality, and how they change in the process. In short, King George was no politician. He was still in 1778 the idealist he had been when he studied under Bute at Kew.

North, however, was a politician, and he knew it would be useless to invite Chatham or Rockingham to serve under himself or either to serve under the other. 'Lord Chatham must be the head of any Administration in which he acts', he told the King on 19 March 1778, 'and it would be vain and useless to expect him on any other footing.' His pleadings became so urgent that on 22 March the King asked him a straight question:

If I will not by your advice take the step I look on as disgraceful to myself and destruction to my country and family, are you resolved, agreeable to the example of the Duke of Grafton, at the hour of danger to desert me?

North's reply was equivocal:

Lord North never thought himself in any degree equal to his situation thus, accordingly, in much quieter times, repeatedly requested His Majesty's permission to withdraw. His Majesty, by his constant refusal of that permission, has continued Lord North in office till the times are become more arduous and difficult, and Lord North consequently more unequal to his situation. . . .

Lord North has no intention at this moment to quit his place, but as to performing the duties of it, he has neither time nor capacity to enable him to go through them. He, therefore, most earnestly supplicates the King to choose a leader for the Administration out of some other quarter, if not out of the Opposition, as his affairs must suffer if so much dependence is had upon Lord North.

His attitude towards the war was profoundly pessimistic:

The condition of this country . . . is deplorable. It is totally unequal to a war with Spain, France, and America, and will,

Lord North fears, be over matched if the contention is only with the house of Bourbon. . . . Great Britain will suffer more in the war than her enemies . . . by an enormous expense which will ruin her and will not in any degree be repaid by the most brilliant victories. Great Britain will undo herself while she thinks of punishing France.

On almost every point of this appreciation North was wrong. It would have astonished Washington or Vergennes had they learnt of the desponding view of Great Britain's military prospects taken by her first Minister. The King, who did not despond easily and thought the country's condition by no means deplorable, knew that little in the way of energetic action could be expected from a man in this frame of mind. He agreed to release North at the end of the session, and instructed him to make the necessary re-arrangements in the law department of the Ministry.

It soon appeared that North was not so anxious to retire as he had professed to be. He wrote to the King on 30 March:

He will, if His Majesty should really find it necessary to detain him longer than the end of the session, continue, let his situation be ever so weary, till His Majesty is able to arrange his servants in the manner the most agreeable to himself and the most advantageous to the public.

The King was touched, and offered his help in expediting the arrangements. North replied with a renewal of his wish not to put the King to any trouble. 'He will sacrifice every personal consideration to His Majesty's service in which he will die rather than abandon His Majesty.'

A month went by, and North did nothing about the changes necessary to effect his release. The King began to wonder whether his Minister was really sincere in his wish to retire. In May 1778 he went to Portsmouth to inspect the fleet, and while there received a most pathetic letter from North. A few phrases will show the state of his mind:

Nothing can prevent the utmost confusion and distress but a material change in the Ministry. . . . My disgrace is in a manner certain whether I continue in office or leave it. . . . I never could nor can decide between different opinions. . . . My mind, always weak, is now ten times weaker than it was. . . . Let me die disgraced, for that I can not now avoid, but let me not go to the grave with the guilt of having been the ruin of my King and country.

All this because Charles Fox had attacked him in the House of Commons! There was no more likelihood of North's disgrace than of his imminent death. It was not the ill success of the war that distressed him but his own position in Parliament. 'I feel myself losing every day the good opinion and confidence of the House of Commons', he had written in a revealing phrase. This in fact was not so, but it was true that the Opposition gained strength and confidence after Saratoga. Fox now began to show those powers which made him one of the greatest parliamentarians of the century, and an opposition in which Burke held only the second place was formidable indeed. North had to fight the Ministry's battle almost alone. Thurlow was about to depart for the Lords, Wedderburn was discontented and sulky, and Germain had never shown the parts he had possessed before his disgrace. North never forgot that his standing in politics depended on his command of the House of Commons. Without that he was nobody. But in 1778 there was a long time to go before he lost it.

'The present situation of the country is arduous but far from desperate', he wrote on 10 May 1778. Six weeks earlier he had declared that it was deplorable. On 11 May he told the King that 'his strength, his spirits, and his capacity are so exhausted that it will be impossible to keep him any longer in his present situation without the certain ruin of the country'. Six weeks earlier he had declared that he was ready to serve to the end of the session or till the King had formed a new Ministry. And

311

in those six weeks he had taken no step to forward the law changes. What could be done with a man who changed his mind so rapidly, who veered from optimism to pessimism and back again within a few weeks with no explanation for his alteration of mood? What could be done with a man who had abandoned hope of victory and had lost faith in the cause for which he was fighting? At least the King would try. On his return from Portsmouth, determined to have it out with his Minister, he summoned North to the Queen's House for Sunday evening, 10 May.

Perhaps it would have been better if the King had agreed to release North. A man who frankly admits himself to be unequal to his office should never be allowed to continue. But if North retired, who was to take his place? This was the question that tormented the King. There was no one on the Government benches of North's stature: no one who could repel the attacks of Fox and Burke as North did night after night: no one who could labour as North laboured and still preserve his geniality and good temper and the respect and liking of the House. The independent Members of Parliament, on whose votes the Ministry depended, were devoted to North; and however despondent he may have been in his letters to the King he rarely showed despondency in the House of Commons. There were some in the Cabinet who could have been replaced with advantage. But North was irreplaceable. He stood alone. Even those who criticized him most bitterly confessed that they could not find another to take his place.

Had the King allowed North to resign, within a month he would have had to capitulate to a triumphant Opposition and to have suffered again the humiliation of May 1765. The only alternative to North was Charles Fox. It was not personal pride, nor dislike of Fox, nor even his resolve to maintain the independence of the Crown, that made King George strive to retain North as his Minister. It was his conviction that the policy associated with North

312

was acceptable to political opinion while that advocated by Fox was not. Despite the defeat at Saratoga the nation was strong in support of the principles which had provoked the Americans into rebellion. Recruiting for the army was never so high as in the months following Saratoga. The British were not to be deflected from their purpose by one defeat in a subsidiary theatre of war. In the summer of 1778 a motion for discontinuing the war in America (a motion that was carried in February 1782) would have been overwhelmingly defeated in the House of Commons.

Had the Opposition been called to office in 1778 they would have insisted as they did in 1782 that the King should recognize the independence of the United States. This would have been the right policy. But it was not a policy which would have commended itself to political opinion. It would have had to be forced upon the nation. It was one thing to recognize American independence in 1783 after seven years of war had failed to subdue the Americans. It would have been quite another in 1778 when Great Britain's position was strong and the issue doubtful. A nation can submit to defeat in war. War is an uncertain business and right does not always prevail. But no nation can deliberately perform an act of humiliation except under pressure of overwhelming force. There are times in history when a course of action once begun – foolishly, perhaps, and without thought of the consequences – must be pursued to the end. Had the nations of Europe in 1914 foreseen the slaughter of the next four years there would have been no war. Had the British in 1774 foreseen the strength of the American resolution to maintain their freedom there would have been no Boston Port Act or Massachusetts Regulating Act. By 1778 it was too late. Great Britain was like a motorist caught in a traffic jam, unable to advance, unable to get out, doomed to wait until events took their course.

It is time to scotch the legend that North was no more

than a tool of the royal will who continued to retain his place only because of pressure from the King. This does not do justice to the complexity of North's character or to the King's feelings for his Minister. North was sincere when he told the King he wished to resign and also when he took no steps towards effecting his resignation. He wanted at the same time the pleasures of office and the pleasures of retirement. When office became a burden he longed for retirement, and when retirement seemed at hand office became desirable. 'You want to retire', wrote the King on 19 May 1778, 'and yet will not take the first step towards enabling me to arrange matters that I may acquiesce in your request.' North was like a woman who longs to be seduced and yet to retain her chastity. Because he was easy-going and good-tempered he gave the appearance of being unambitious. Yet when he took the Exchequer in 1767 he stipulated for a seat in the cabinet and when he resigned in 1782 he declined to consider retiring to the House of Lords. Like Newcastle under whom he had served his apprenticeship he was both ambitious and afraid of responsibility. Perhaps he was happiest during the period of the Fox–North coalition, when he held the balance of power in the House of Commons and surrendered the lead to Fox.

North's family was not rich by the standards of eighteenth-century nobility. He had a large family, and was dependent for his income on the salary of his office and an inadequate allowance from his father. A politician in his day had to meet considerable expenses out of his own pocket. No Prime Minister made money out of politics and most of them left office poorer than when they kissed hands. In September 1777 John Robinson, North's Secretary to the Treasury, drew the King's attention to the state of North's finances and suggested that North's moods of depression arose from worrying about his debts. Robinson had advised North to speak to the King, but 'delicacy' and 'natural reservedness' had prevented him.

314

The King knew what it was to be in debt. He had been in that state for practically the whole of his reign and had just been relieved by Parliament. He took Robinson's hint and wrote to North (19 September 1777):

You have at times dropped to me that you had been in debt ever since your first settling in life, and that you had never been able to get out of that difficulty. I therefore must insist that you will now state to me whether 12 or £15,000 will not set your affairs in order, if it will, nay if £20,000 is necessary, I am resolved you shall have no other person concerned in freeing them but myself. . . . You know me very ill if you do not think that of all the letters I have ever wrote to you this one gives me the most pleasure, and I want no other return but your being convinced that I love you as a man of worth as I esteem you as a minister. Your conduct at a critical moment I never can forget, and am glad that by your ability and the kindness of Parliament I am enabled to give you this mark of my affection, which is the only one I have yet been able to perform; but trust some of the employments for life will in time become vacant that I may reward your family.

Not since the days of Bute had the King written to a minister in terms of friendship. North was moved, as much by the King's words as by the offer to pay his debts. 'His Majesty's constant goodness', he replied, 'encourages him to hope that he imputes the innumerable errors and defects of his administration solely to his want of ability to execute an employment which he undertook at His Majesty's command and to which he had never the vanity to aspire.' The sum concerned amounted to £20,000 and was paid out of the secret service account.

In May 1778 the place of Lord Warden of the Cinque Ports became vacant. It was, wrote North to the King, 'always the favourite object of my ambition'. The King was delighted to be able to oblige his Minister and offered North the place at a salary of £4,000 a year. But not even to oblige North would he give the place for life. 'I daily find', he wrote, 'the evil of having put so many employments out of the power of the Crown, and for the rest of my life I will not confer any in that mode but where constant practice has made it matter of course.' In addition, he promised North the first tellership of the Exchequer that became vacant – a place for life, one of the richest sinecures in the gift of the Crown, rarely worth less than £10,000 a year and even more valuable in time of war. There was nothing of special favour in this. It was customary for a Prime Minister who had no large fortune of his own to provide for his family while in office. Sir Robert Walpole had endowed his sons with sinecures, and George Grenville had obtained a tellership of the Exchequer for his second son (then a boy of eight) and a pension for himself when he left office. (It was with the proceeds of this sinecure that Thomas Grenville amassed the collection of books known as the Grenville Library, which he afterwards presented to the British Museum.) The promise of the tellership was not a bribe to induce North to remain but a reward for services rendered – 'I am anxious to give that to your family whether you remain or not in your present situation', wrote the King. Still, it had the effect of making North more receptive to the advantages of office. 'In return to His Majesty's gracious declaration', North replied on 23 May 1778, '. . . Lord North thinks it his duty to repeat that though his earnest wish certainly is to retire, yet he is ready to continue in his present office as long as His Majesty deems it for his service that he should continue there.'

Had North really wished to resign, had his feelings been always such as he represented them in moments of depression, he would never have accepted these favours from the King. He wanted to remain in office and to throw the responsibility for his remaining on to the King. He wishes, wrote Charles Jenkinson on 1 December 1779, 'that he may have it to say to the world that he is ready to retire, but that Your Majesty insists on his continuing in his present situation'. That way he could declare with a clear conscience that it would not be his fault if Great Britain lost her American colonies. From 1778 onwards his letters are full of declarations of his unfitness for office – and also of his intention to stay if the King should wish. On 14 November 1778 he wrote to the King:

As His Majesty is bent against every alteration of Administration, he will continue to submit to every personal distress he suffers from his situation, hoping from His Majesty's goodness and justice that after having ventured so freely and frequently to deliver his opinion no part of the mischiefs which the public will probably suffer from Lord North's continuance in office will be imputed to him.

And on 21 January 1782, when it was clear that Great Britain would have to recognize the independence of the United States, North reminded the King:

I am very sensible how unfit I have always been, and how much more unfit I am now to decide in matters of nicety and difficulty, and if I had not repeatedly laid before Your Majesty my incapacity, and humbly advised Your Majesty more than once a year during the past ten years to place your affairs in other hands, I should take to myself a much greater share of the blame for what Your Majesty's service has suffered by my indecision.

'He is too fond of having it believed that he continues in office contrary to his inclinations', wrote Jenkinson. North made no secret of his wish to resign – he told it to his colleagues, to the Opposition leaders, to all the world – and he succeeded in convincing himself and posterity that he remained only because the King had laid his commands upon him.

'His labours are immense', wrote Jenkinson on 19 May 1780, 'and such as few constitutions could bear.' He was head of the Cabinet and primarily responsible for Government policy, leader of the House of Commons, and finance Minister – a combination of responsibilities which brought the younger Pitt, to whom public business

317

was the joy of life, to a premature grave. Besides the conduct of the war, he had on his hands grave problems affecting Ireland and India; and it is a remarkable tribute to North's character that he did so well under such heavy burdens. No statesman in our history has been so underrated. He could never have been a good Prime Minister because he lacked the qualities of hardness and callousness essential to the office – 'A Prime Minister', said Lord Attlee, 'must be a good butcher.' He was too soft-hearted and could never say no to an applicant, and like Newcastle he got himself into difficulties by making promises which he could not fulfil. Men soon found that the best way to get anything out of North was to bully and badger him, to make his life a misery until he complied; and he suffered torments from the importunities and reproaches of selfish and ambitious colleagues.

The King understood his minister. He wrote to North on 2 June 1778:

The greatest part of your difficulties arise from entering too far with others in plans of business but particularly arrangements of employments without fairly stating your sentiments unto me. If on the contrary you sounded my opinion first you would save much trouble and vexation to both of us, and where can you repose your undigested thoughts more safely than in the breast of one who has ever treated you more as his friend than Minister?

The King placed more patronage at North's disposal than he had done for any minister since Bute, and even consulted him about appointments in the Church and at Court – patronage which he usually reserved to himself. North could complain of lack of support from his colleagues but never from the King. The King wrote to him on 14 November 1778:

From the hour of Lord North's so handsomely devoting himself on the retreat of the Duke of Grafton, I have never had a political thought which I have not communicated unto him,

318

have accepted of persons highly disagreeable to me because he thought they would be of advantage to his conducting public affairs, and have yielded to measures my own opinion did no quite approve.

North was reluctant to confide in the King, and during the last three years of the Administration the King learnt more of what was going on in government from subordinate Ministers than from North. To relieve North of work he was unable or unwilling to do, the King attempted to take a more active part in government. In May 1778 he went to Portsmouth to inspect the fleet, and tried to infuse into the administration of the navy some of his own energy. A squadron was about to depart for America to meet the French. On 5 May the King wrote to North from Portsmouth dockyard:

I intended to have left this place on Thursday morning, but found on visiting the fleet at Spithead this day that several of the ships intended to be part of Vice-Admiral Byron's squadron could not fix which day they would sail. I have therefore given notice . . . that I shall not leave Portsmouth until Rear-Admiral Parker is sailed . . . this has put great alacrity into all of them. Sir Hugh Palliser has since told me privately that my taking that step will make them sail many days sooner than they would else. . . . I have no object but to be of use, if that is answered I am completely happy.

On 25 October he besought North to ensure a good attendance of Government supporters at the opening of Parliament, and when North did nothing about it wrote again on 2 November: 'I therefore must insist on your laying thoughts on that subject before the Cabinet at your meeting on Thursday, and I have just wrote to the two Secretaries of State to acquaint them you have my directions for that purpose.' And with reference to possible defaulters from the Government ranks, the King added: 'My disapprobation shall be shewn in the fullest manner to those who swerve from their duty.'

319

'The times require vigour', wrote the King on 14 November 1778, 'or the state will be ruined.' His most spectacular action came in the summer of 1779, when events seemed to be moving towards a crisis such as Great Britain had not known since the accession of the dynasty.[2] In the House of Commons matters were going from bad to worse, and North, tormented by the importunities of ambitious colleagues and heart-broken at the death of a favourite child, seemed to be losing his grip. There was discord between the naval and military commanders and their political superiors, each blaming the other for the ill success of the war. The quarrel between Admirals Keppel and Palliser arising from the indecisive battle off Ushant in the summer of 1778 had introduced political divisions among the higher ranks of the navy. The Cabinet was at sixes and sevens, disposed to agree only on the insufficiency of North as their leader. The Opposition had refused all invitations to join the Ministry. Spain had entered the conflict and Ireland showed a disposition to follow America and throw off the yoke of Great Britain. One historian of this period (Sir Herbert Butterfield, in his book *George III, Lord North and the People*) has described the British government at the end of 1778 as exhibiting 'a spectacle rarely, if ever, equalled in the course of centuries' for weakness and inefficiency. Every reader of the King's correspondence will be inclined to agree with this judgment. So also must affairs have appeared to an outsider shortly before the Chamberlain Ministry fell in 1940. Yet neither in 1779 nor in 1940 was Great Britain reduced so low as she appeared to be.

The morale of the nation was unbroken. Despondency existed only in the higher echelons of government, and in the highest of all there was no despondency. On 11 June 1779 the King wrote a long letter to North:

I should think it the greatest instance of the many I have met with of ingratitude and injustice, if it could be supposed that any man in my dominions more ardently desired the restora-

320

1 Frederick Lewis, Prince of Wales, *by Philip Mercier*

2 Augusta, Princess of Wales, *by Charles Philips*

3 John Stuart, 3rd Earl of Bute, *by Sir Joshua Reynolds*

4 William Henry, Duke of Gloucester, *by Francis Cotes*

5 *opposite*, Queen Charlotte, 1782, *by Thomas Gainsborough*

6 Frederick, Lord North, *by Nathaniel Dance*

7 Charles James Fox, *by Karl Anton Hickel*

8 The castellated palace at Kew, *by an unknown artist*

9 George, Prince of Wales, *by Sir William Beechey*

10 Frederick, Duke of York, *by Sir Joshua Reynolds*

11 King George III at Windsor, 1807, *by Peter Edward Stroehling*

12 Queen Charlotte, 1807, *by Peter Edward Stroehling*

tion of peace and solid happiness in every part of this empire than I do. There is no personal sacrifice I could not readily yield for so desirable an object, but at the same time no inclination to get out of the present difficulties, which certainly keep my mind very far from a state of ease, can incline me to enter into what I look upon as the destruction of the Empire. I have heard Lord North frequently drop that the advantages to be gained by this contest could never repay the expence. I own that let any war be ever so successful they will find as in the last that it has impoverished the State, enriched individuals, and perhaps raised the name only of the conquerors, but this is only weighing such events in the scale of a tradesman behind his counter. It is necessary for those in the station it has pleased Divine Providence to place me in to weigh whether expences though very great are not sometimes necessary to prevent what might be more ruinous to a country than the loss of money. The present contest with America I cannot help seeing as the most serious in which any country was ever engaged. It contains such a train of consequences that they must be examined to feel its real weight. Whether the laying a tax was deserving all the evils that have arisen from it, I should suppose no man could allege that without being more fit for Bedlam than a seat in the senate; but step by step the demands of America have risen – independence is their object, that certainly is one that every man not willing to sacrifice every object to a *momentary and inglorious* peace must concur with me in thinking that this country can never submit to. Should America succeed in that the West Indies must follow them.... Ireland would soon follow the same plan and be a separate state. Then this island would be a poor island indeed, for reduced in her trade merchants would retire with their wealth to climates more to their advantage, and shoals of manufacturers would leave this country for the new Empire. ... Consequently this country has but one sensible, one great line to follow, the being ever ready to make peace when to be obtained without submitting to terms that in their consequence must annihilate this empire, and with firmness to make every effort to deserve success.

The King had changed his mind within the previous few months about the possibility of waging defensive war in America. He had submitted to the advice of his Ministers. An Opposition motion to concentrate the war effort against the house of Bourbon – the policy which the King had advocated in February 1778 – was opposed by North in the House of Commons. The King shared the almost universal delusion that the possession of colonies was essential for British trade and prosperity and that without America Great Britain would cease to be a great nation. 'We can but escape by concessions and disgrace', wrote Horace Walpole, an opponent of the American war, a month before the King's letter to North, 'and when we attain peace, the terms will prove that parliamentary majorities have voted away the wisdom, glory, and power of the nation.' Robert Nugent, a Government Member, said in the House of Commons after Saratoga:

The contest now was not whether America should be dependent on the British Parliament, but whether Great Britain or America should be independent. Both could not be so, for such would be the power of that vast continent across the Atlantic that was her independence established this island must expect to be made a dependent province.

The King also shared the widespread illusion about the power and stability of France. It came as a great shock to the eighteenth century when revolution broke out in 1789 in France, for France was considered the European nation most immune to revolution. Yet for many years before 1789 the French monarchy was in decay. With every advantage on her side, she did not achieve her aims during the American war, and the combined Franco-Spanish attempt to invade England was a disaster nearly as great as the armada of 1588. Even under North's weak leadership Great Britain held her own against the hostility or hostile neutrality of half Europe. The King was right in his belief that with resolution and courage in her leaders she would have fared even better. When we compare the state of government in Great Britain with that in France or Spain or even in the enlightened despotisms of Prussia and Russia, we are astonished not by Britain's weakness but by her strength. Less than ten years after Walpole had despaired of British glory, the younger Pitt, without any fundamental change in the system of government and despite the loss of America, had raised the nation to be the leading power in Europe.

'The issue of a crisis', wrote Sir Lewis Namier, 'depends not so much on its magnitude as on the courage and resolution with which it is met.' On 21 June 1779 King George summoned his Cabinet to the Queen's House (an unprecedented event in his reign), and spoke to them for half an hour on the state of affairs. He 'declared to God he had never harboured a thought of injuring the constitution or abridging his people's liberties'. He had not been responsible for the war, but once it had broken out he felt it his duty to support his Ministers to the utmost of his power. In return he now expected 'firmness and support' from his Ministers. 'It was his resolution to part with his life rather than suffer his dominions to be dismembered.' He was willing to admit any man to office if it would strengthen the Ministry, but 'I will expect to see it signed under his hand that he is resolved to keep the Empire entire'. Sir Winston Churchill said that he did not become Prime Minister in order to preside over the dissolution of the British Empire. Neither did King George become King in order to surrender the American colonies.

'If others will not be active, I must drive', the King wrote to Lord Sandwich, First Lord of the Admiralty. During the invasion crisis of 1779 he paid particular attention to the disposition and efficiency of the fleet. He succeeded in getting the Admiralty to revise the orders sent to the fleet in a more offensive spirit, and when the Channel squadron put into harbour he ordered Sandwich to Portsmouth to make sure they got out as soon as possible. By repeated adjurations he encouraged North not to lose heart. 'I do not despair that . . . the provinces will

323

even now submit', he wrote on 22 June; and on 5 September: 'The hand of Providence seems to be taking a part in our favour.' Although England was threatened with invasion, the idea of offensive warfare must not be abandoned: 'It is by bold and manly efforts nations have been preserved, not pursuing alone the line of home defence.' There is a touch of the Churchillian spirit about King George in the autumn of 1779.

The King could encourage or reprimand, could advise or inspire, his Ministers; but he could not direct the war. Strategy was the business of the Cabinet, and the King always deferred, even against his opinion, to their advice. He had neither the experience nor the time to interfere in the routine of office. He knew his place in the system of government and he kept to it. It is ironical that posterity should accuse the King of wishing to be his own Prime Minister, of trying to direct the war, when the real charge against him is that he did not attempt these roles. Had he done so Great Britain would have been in a more favourable military position in the winter of 1779. Had the King's advice been taken to begin recruiting in the spring of 1775, Great Britain might have had an adequate army in America the following year. Had the King's advice been taken in 1778 Great Britain might have evolved a coherent and sensible strategy. To take decisions there must be leadership. North's character was not that of a leader, and King George III was too faithful to the principles of the constitution to assume an authority which was not his by right.

Hitherto the Opposition had been mainly concerned with the alleged misconduct of the war and had directed their attack on the ministers. But in the autumn of 1779 there began a movement of protest which involved criticisms of the Crown and even of the King himself. It was the more serious because it was not inspired by the Opposition as a move in the parliamentary game but was an independent and spontaneous protest by the landed class against what they regarded as extravagance and corruption in government. On 30 December 1779 a meeting of Yorkshire country gentlemen, summoned by the Rev Christopher Wyvill, a North Riding squire, voted a petition to Parliament demanding an inquiry into 'the gross abuses in the expenditure of public money' and pressing for the reduction of 'exorbitant emoluments' and the abolition of 'sinecure places and unmerited pensions'. North need not be unduly alarmed at the opposition of Fox and Burke: they were professional politicians playing the party game. What Wilkes and the City of London thought was of little account: a political movement in Great Britain only becomes serious when it commands the support of the provinces. But it was cause for alarm when a protest came from the class that paid the land tax in the first county of England. Not the conduct but the system of government was about to be attacked.

To understand the events which followed the York meeting – the spread of the petitioning movement throughout Great Britain, the favourable reception accorded to Burke's economical reform bill, the acceptance by the House of Commons of Dunning's motion that 'the influence of the Crown has increased, is increasing, and ought to be diminished' (26 April 1780) – we must enter upon the subject of the finances of the Crown. Unless we understand the financial difficulties in which the King was involved we shall not understand his character and especially his conduct towards his sons. It is commonly held that sex is the key to the understanding of character. This may be so, but sex is a matter so intimate that it is rarely revealed to the biographer. We have to make do with the materials available to us and we are on surer ground when we deal with money. If we understand a man's financial affairs we shall know a great deal about him. For King George there is ample information and no need to guess.

In the eighteenth century the finances of the Crown and the finances of government were inextricably intertwined. They were regulated by the old doctrine that 'the King should live of his own' – that is that the expenses of court and government (which were regarded as the same) should be met out of the hereditary revenues of the Crown and should not require application to Parliament. In an economy based on the ownership of land the King was regarded as the first of landowners, and like other landowners was expected to regulate his expenses according to his income. In practice this was possible only in time of peace and not always then. War required extraordinary expenditure, which compelled the Crown to seek the aid of Parliament and thus gave Parliament a degree of control over the policy of the Crown. It was the inability of the Stuart Kings to live of their own which stimulated the pretensions of Parliament. James I and Charles I could have maintained their prerogatives only by avoiding war or domestic insurrection.

In 1697 affairs were put upon a more regular footing. Henceforth, at the beginning of each reign the Crown was granted a Civil List which was held to be sufficient to cover all the expenses of civil government. In return the Crown was relieved of the expenses of the armed forces. These were voted by Parliament each year under the separate heads of navy, army, and ordnance, and were raised by taxation. Thus Parliament maintained its control over defence and foreign policy: the essential departments of the State.[3]

In 1714 King George I was granted a Civil List of £700,000 a year for himself and £100,000 for the Prince of Wales, and it was provided that if the product of the hereditary revenues exceeded these sums the surplus was to go to the public. In 1727 King George II received the most generous financial provision that has ever been given to a British sovereign in modern times. This was the great service Sir Robert Walpole performed for the King at his accession, and which enabled Walpole, contrary to the forecasts of all the political tipsters, to retain his office. The King was granted the full sum of the hereditary revenues, subject to a provision for the Prince of Wales. At first this was £50,000 a year, but it was understood that when the Prince married his allowance would be increased to £100,000 – the sum his father had received as Prince of Wales. This was not done until 1742, five years after the Prince had married; and it was the King's delay in making proper financial provision for his son that led to the great quarrel between them. The Prince had good reason to complain: for King George II, with the largest income ever granted to a British sovereign, had made the stingiest provision for his heir apparent. During the last ten years of the reign the Civil List averaged £823,000 a year, and in the last year amounted to £876,000.

In the seventeenth and eighteenth centuries – and perhaps later – the British monarchy was run on the cheap, and no King apart from George II received an income adequate to the dignity of the Crown. The traditional role of the House of Commons was to prevent extravagance and to ensure that the Crown should be financially dependent upon Parliament. At all times in history the propertied classes have disliked paying taxes for the support of government, and in the eighteenth century this was elevated to the level of a political principle. The country gentlemen disliked the existence of government and thought the less there was of it the better. There must be an army to protect property and guard against invasion, but was it necessary to maintain one so large as to be a menace to freedom? And was it necessary to maintain a large court to provide places and pensions for greedy courtiers, men sometimes without pedigree even, at the expense of honest and deserving country gentlemen? Was it for this that the land tax (the eighteenth-century equivalent of the income tax) was raised to the iniquitous figure of four shillings in the pound? 'Peace and two shillings till we must have four is my whole system of politics', wrote 'honest Jack White', an old-fashioned Whig country gentleman, to Newcastle on 30 June 1755. Rents were falling, the prices of agricultural produce were falling – but the land tax was rising; and if things went on at this rate the country gentlemen would be ruined! Such were the feelings of the landed class, Whig or Tory alike, as expressed in debate after debate in the House of Commons. King George III had considerable sympathy with them.

The complaint is familiar today though the words in which it is expressed are different. In the eighteenth century the word 'courtier' was one of opprobrium to the landed class just as 'bureaucrat' is to some people today; and the twentieth-century demand to reduce the number of civil servants is paralleled by the eighteenth-century demand to reduce the number of courtiers, placemen, and pensioners. This meant extending parliamentary control over the Civil List. Hence Wyvill's movement was directed not so much against ministers as against the Crown. And due to circumstances of its own creation the Crown was ill fitted to defend itself.

In 1747 Frederick, Prince of Wales, abandoned the attitude of armed neutrality he had held since 1742 and came out into open opposition against his father's ministry. To secure the support of the Tories at the general election he drafted a programme which he declared he would put into effect when he succeeded to the Crown. Most of its points were innocuous or impracticable and were soon forgotten. The last one, however, was important. 'His Royal Highness further promises to accept of no more, if offered him, than £800,000 for his Civil List per annum.' Thus the Prince proposed to revert to the Civil List as settled for his grandfather, King George I, whom he professed to admire. Whether he was sincere in this proposal or whether he included it merely to cajole the Tories, whether had he succeeded to the Crown he

328

would really have accepted a fixed Civil List and have renounced the extra revenue enjoyed by King George II, are questions which cannot be answered. It is perhaps significant that in his political testament, though he advises his son to live with economy and reduce the National Debt, he says nothing about this proposal for a fixed Civil List.

Unfortunately for King George III, one man took it seriously and regarded it as a promise that must be redeemed. And because Bute took it seriously so also did the King. The first legislative act of the reign gave the King a Civil List of £800,000 and surrendered the hereditary revenues to the public. From the point of view of the Crown this was the most disastrous step that could have been taken. King George II in the last year of his life had enjoyed an income of £876,000. King George III, with greater calls upon him than upon his grandfather, was to have an income of only £800,000. The Royal Family was increasing. The King had three brothers who would soon be of age and would have to be provided for. He had two sisters who would require portions when they married. There were the expenses of a Coronation. Royal jewels would have to be bought (King George II had left his to the Duke of Cumberland, who sold them to King George III for £54,000). The King refused to live in the late King's palaces and bought a new house in London. He would wish to marry (another source of expense), the Queen would require an allowance, and the children to be educated. There were many items of extraordinary expense at the beginning of a reign, all of which could not be met out of the surplus left by King George II. Even King George II, rich and parsimonious, had sometimes found it difficult to make both ends meet. Yet King George III bound himself to do so, with greater obligations than his grandfather and less money to meet them.

We may pause here and reflect that had Bute and the King entertained the high prerogative notions ascribed to

329

them they would never have accepted a Civil List which made it certain that the Crown would have to apply for relief to Parliament. If the power of the Crown was to be increased an independent income was essential. We may also consider how little Bute understood of finance. During the years following the Peace of Paris prices rose rapidly, and in an age of inflation the King had to live on a fixed income. No wonder he fell into debt! The contrast between his financial position as it was and as it might have been is startling. As the hereditary revenues were based on the produce of the customs and Post Office, they increased with the growth of trade and commerce. It has been estimated that had the King accepted the Civil List of his grandfather, by 1777 his income would have been over £1,000,000 a year and by the end of the century nearly £2,000,000. Perhaps with such an income, he might have been more ready to forgive the extravagance of his sons and much of the friction which developed in the Royal Family would have been avoided. It is certain that he would have been in a better position to resist the demand of Parliament for control over the expenditure of the Crown.

By 1769 the debt on the Civil List amounted to £513,000 and it was impossible to avoid any longer an application for relief to Parliament. During the debates in the House of Commons some harsh words were said and many suspicions aired as to how this debt had accumulated. 'Considering the system of economy established in His Majesty's domestic concerns', said one Member, 'he ought not to be in this situation.' It was broadly hinted that there had been not only mismanagement but also corruption: that the debt had been incurred, as another Member put it, 'to influence the freedom of this House'. Yet the House agreed without a division to vote the money to pay the debt. In 1777 a further application to Parliament was necessary, and the opportunity was taken to ask for an increase of the Civil

List to £900,000 a year. This time the House of Commons was not so compliant. The increase of the Civil List was agreed to by a majority of only 28 votes (137 v. 109), and some Members who were normally supporters of the ministry and even personal friends of North abstained from voting. The Speaker, when presenting the bill for the Royal assent, reminded the King that at a time of public distress, when the nation was 'labouring under burthens almost too heavy to be borne' (a typical example of eighteenth-century exaggeration), his faithful Commons had granted the Crown not only 'a large present supply, but also a very great additional revenue – great beyond example – great beyond Your Majesty's highest expense'. The House voted its thanks to the Speaker and ordered his speech to be printed.

The King was not offended by this rebuke. He felt it was deserved. He acknowledged the House had come to his assistance 'in a very handsome manner'. He was concerned at the disgraceful state of his finances – the Civil List of Ireland was also in arrears – and at his inability to live upon his income. His father had recommended him to live frugally and not get into debt and he had failed. Yet far from being extravagant he had consistently practised economy – even parsimony. Like Gladstone he considered thrift as a moral virtue and waste as a vice. His economy was a constant theme for satire. It was hard to be satirized in prints as a miser and to be criticized in the House of Commons as a spendthrift.

Nothing in King George's life more illustrates his unpretentiousness than his attitude towards his financial affairs. In 1760 he could have had financial security for the asking. Had he demanded the settlement of the Civil List granted to his grandfather, neither Pitt nor Newcastle would have objected. Pitt, who never wished to stint the Crown and was always lavish with money, would have deemed King George II's Civil List a precedent for King George III. Newcastle, a true Whig, would have sunk his doubts to ingratiate himself with the new King. The Tory country gentlemen, enchanted with the King's person and manner and the welcome he gave them at Court, would have acquiesced without a murmur. There never was a King in British history who had such an opportunity to make himself independent of Parliament as King George III. Yet he refused to do so for the sake of a principle and to fulfil his father's promise.

The attitude taken by a later and unsympathetic generation towards the King's debts may be illustrated by a passage from the article on the King in the *Dictionary of National Biography*:

The income settled on the Crown, swelled as it was by the profits of the duchies of Cornwall and Lancaster and revenues from Scotland, Ireland, and other sources, was sufficient for all ordinary needs, and far more than sufficient for a King who lived so simply. . . . Much waste went on, as was abundantly proved in 1777, but large sums were no doubt spent in corruption of various kinds.

There are at least two false statements in this passage; and even in 1890, when this article appeared, there was abundant material about the King's financial affairs and no need to guess how his debts had arisen. The Civil List accounts were laid before the House of Commons and are printed in the Journals, and the originals have long been available in the Public Record Office. If waste and corruption are to be assigned as the causes of the King's debts, it must be explained how they continued to grow under the younger Pitt, an undeniably careful and uncorrupt minister, as well as under North, an allegedly corrupt one. To ascertain the real causes we must examine how the King spent his money.

The main source of Crown income was the Civil List of England and Wales. There were separate Civil Lists for Scotland, Ireland, and the Isle of Man, and also the Hanoverian revenues, but the income derived from these sources was spent entirely where it was raised. There were also some smaller sources of income of which the most considerable was that from the Duchy of Lancaster. The Civil List for England and Wales had to provide for the expense of government (apart from the armed forces) and the Court, allowances to members of the Royal Family (each of whom kept his or her own court), and the King's private income (the Privy Purse). In theory it was for the King to decide how the money was to be divided between these different services – 'It is Your Majesty's own money', Newcastle once told King George II, 'you may do with it what you please.' In practice the division was regulated by custom and precedent, and only the amounts set aside for the Royal Family were decided by the King himself. King George III fixed his Privy Purse at £48,000 a year, which in 1777 he increased to £60,000. Grenville, when First Lord of the Treasury, seems to have thought the original figure too high (King George II's Privy Purse had been £36,000). But the Treasury, though it had the overall management of the Civil List, had nothing to do with the Privy Purse. This was in charge of the Keeper, appointed by the King and responsible to him alone. One of Grenville's complaints against the King was that he was not appointed Keeper of the Privy Purse as Bute had been, and it seems to have been Grenville's wish to assert Treasury control over the Privy Purse. But the Duke of York wrote in 1818:[4]

The Privy Purse, together with the revenues of the duchy of Lancaster, has ever been considered as the private property of the Sovereign of these realms, perfectly at his own disposal and free from the control and cognizance of Parliament. Even in the worst of times, and when the Crown has been under the necessity of applying to Parliament for the debts of the Civil List to a great amount, the most violent demagogue never attempted to utter a word about the Privy Purse or to ask for any report concerning it.

When the Civil List accounts were presented to the House

of Commons no details were given of payments under the Privy Purse, only the lump sums issued each year.

The greatest part of Civil List expenditure was on government and Court. Government expenses included the salaries of ministers, civil servants, ambassadors, judges, and all in government service; pensions and allowances, some merited, some granted by former sovereigns, some the fruit of successful jobbery; and a great many other payments of different kinds. To give some examples: in 1760–61 the King gave £500 for the relief of foreign Protestants and £52,285 towards the expenses of the Foundling Hospital; in 1761–62, £438 to the college of New York (later Columbia University); in 1763–64, £1,059 to the Emperor of Morocco and £533 to the Bey of Algiers (bribes to prevent piracy in the Mediterranean); in 1764–65, £5,000 for paving the streets of Westminster and £2,000 towards printing the Journals of the House of Commons; in 1766–67, £52 to Chelsea water works for supplying the Treasury with water; in 1767–68, £1,000 to the poor of London. At Court, the chief expenses were the salaries and maintenance of the courtiers. It was part of the perquisites of a courtier that he was fed and lodged (and sometimes clothed) at the King's expense, and this had to be done in a style befitting his rank. Fanny Burney, though her position in the Queen's household was comparatively humble, had her private footman and the use of a coach. The King lived a homely and simple life, and the Court was maintained not for his personal vanity but for the dignity of the monarchy and the nation. It would reflect on the nation if the Court of Great Britain was outshone by those of the Continental monarchies. After the heavy expenses occasioned by the Coronation and the King's marriage, Court expenditure was reduced except for wages and the cost of food and drink – two items that reflected the inflation of the age.

In all this there was no corruption but a good deal of waste and inefficiency. The system of administration and finance was antiquated and obsolete. The Court was a survival of the more lavish courts of Tudor and Stuart times when the King lived more in public than did the Hanoverian monarchs. There were too many sinecures in the government service, the duties of which were either performed by lowly paid deputies or no longer performed at all. To give one example, by no means the most notorious. Horace Walpole and his brother shared a sinecure in the customs which gave them a joint income of over £1,800 a year: the salaries of their deputies and clerks who did the work came to £650. At Court there were too many people doing too little work. The King had about a dozen Lords of the Bedchamber, all peers or courtesy lords, who took it in turn to go into waiting when the King appeared in public. Each had £1,000 a year for one month's attendance out of the twelve. There were twelve Grooms of the Bedchamber at £500 a year, Members of Parliament or former Members, to assist the Lords. There was a Board of Green Cloth (eight members at £1,000 a year), which did little work; and Masters of Buckhounds, Staghounds and Foxhounds (£2,000), who did none except to sign their names.

All these were considered the proper perquisites of the governing class. Another source of waste was the traditional habit of the governing class of quartering its dependants and poor relations upon the Crown. Allied to this was the practice of giving former civil servants or courtiers, men who had done good work and performed loyal services, sinecures in lieu of retirement pensions. Under King George II Claudius Amyand had been appointed Keeper of His Majesty's Libraries at £200 a year. This was a nominal office (the King did not care for books and presented his library to the British Museum), and was used to provide retirement pay for a former undersecretary of state. King George III, who did care for books, appointed his own librarian and paid him a salary out of the Privy Purse, thus paying for two librarians and receiving service from only one. No office was ever allowed to fall into disuse, even when there were no longer any duties attached to it. In the seventeenth century there was a royal palace at Newmarket. By the time of King George III this was in ruins, but the office of Housekeeper at Newmarket still existed and Martha Bonfoy, widow, appears in the Civil List accounts under that title at £150 a year. It was considered right and proper for the Crown to provide for men of rank or quality who had fallen upon evil days. Lord Somerville managed to get £800 a year out of the King's Civil List, though how or why is not clear since he is said to have left over £50,000 in the funds.

The habit of touching the Crown, as Bertie Wooster would have said, extended from individuals to corporate bodies. In 1765 the King paid £120 to defray the expenses of the dinners of the magistrates of Westminster. The corporation of Macclesfield got £50 a year for the services of a preacher, doing rather better than the University of Oxford who got only £20 for the same purpose (and far better than Cambridge who got only £10). The magistrates of Westminster could afford to pay for their own dinners and Oxford and Cambridge for their own preachers – but why do so if the money could be got out of the Crown? Even members of the Royal Family were not above touching the King. Edward, Duke of York, was not so poor or extravagant as to be unable to pay the £35 demanded by the College of Arms as fees for the creation of his dukedom – but why do so if the King was willing to pay? In the seventeenth century Kings touched subjects for the King's evil: in the eighteenth century subjects touched Kings for the subjects' good.

Long before the birth of King George the bounty of the Crown was being used by politicians to recruit a parliamentary following. It was the standing complaint of politicians in opposition (but forgotten when they were in office) that Members of Parliament were influenced in their voting by the fact or prospect of office. To some

336

extent this was true: office has always exerted an influence over the conduct of Members and always will. But it does not follow that Members are corrupt. William Jolliffe, an independent and crotchety follower of Lord North, said in the House of Commons in 1778:

In questions of small importance, if every man was to follow his own caprice, no government could last a day, the business of this empire would be anarchy and confusion; but when the fate of thousands is at stake, when millions may be wasted and an empire lost, he ill deserves to sit here who can from any motive sacrifice his opinion. It is not in the power of the Crown to bribe a man of property on such occasions.

Most Members of Parliament in the eighteenth century were men of property, and the salaries and pensions offered by the Crown were hardly sufficient to tempt them to sell their independence. 'Bribery', as Namier pointed out, 'to be really effective has to be widespread and open; it has to be the custom of the land and cease to dishonour its recipients.' In a simple economy such as that of the eighteenth century it would have been difficult to bribe without everybody knowing. In the complex commercial society of the twentieth century, where so much wealth is held in the form of shares and there are so many devices for concealing real ownership, it would be possible to bribe Members of Parliament. In the eighteenth century it was not. And even if it had been, it could not have been done on £800,000 a year.

There remains a further source of possible corruption: the secret service account or private account as it is sometimes called. This was the perennial bogey of the country gentlemen, because, like the Privy Purse, detailed accounts were never submitted to Parliament. 'Legends naturally surround all secret service', wrote Namier, who scotched this particular legend forty years ago. 'Its very name inspires fear and distrust and stimulates men's imaginations.' Today it stimulates legends which perhaps even the genius of Namier could not scotch – of James

Bond-like creatures, licensed to kill and to indulge in indiscriminate sexual intercourse, and of stern-faced figures in Kensington, posing as honest business men and weaving plots of labyrinthine subtlety. In the eighteenth century the legends were less titillating but equally far-fetched. To the eighteenth-century country gentleman the words 'secret service' conjured up visions of anonymous acolytes from the Treasury slipping bank notes into the pockets of Members of Parliament as they walked through the division lobby or visiting the constituencies to distribute bags of guineas among the 'honest and independent'. William Dowdeswell, himself a country gentleman, said in the debate on the Civil List debts (28 February 1769):

There is another part of the account which I should wish to have for my own satisfaction. . . . The attention of every man is fixed upon the vast expenses of the secret service. Let us know what it is.

It might be imagined from this that secret service expenses had risen considerably during the reign of King George III. In fact they had not. During the last eight years of the previous reign the average annual expenditure on secret service had been about £51,000: in the first eight years of King George III it was just over £60,000. But if Dowdeswell really wished to know how the secret service money was spent he had but to ask his political leader, Lord Rockingham, who had in his possession the accounts from 1765–66 – the period of his own Ministry, when Dowdeswell was Chancellor of the Exchequer. (They are now among Rockingham's papers in Sheffield City Library.) There was no great mystery about the secret service fund. The responsibility for distributing the money devolved on the First Lord of the Treasury, and every ex-First Lord or Secretary of the Treasury knew how it was spent.

Secret service money as its name implies was used to

meet State expenditure that had to be kept secret. The greater part of it was spent on bribing foreign politicians, paying for the services of spies, and for the costs of the secret department of the Post Office which opened and deciphered diplomatic correspondence. (All letters sent through the post in the eighteenth century were liable to be opened and read – a practice not confined to Great Britain.) King George III thought that money spent in this way was largely thrown away and liable to misinterpretation. In 1771 he wrote about a proposal to bribe the court of Sweden:

As there is no public mode of obtaining the money that is expended in that corruption it must be taken from my Civil List, consequently new debts incurred, and when I apply to Parliament for relieving me an odium cast on myself and Ministry as if the money had been expended in bribing Parliament.

Nor had he too high an opinion of the spies employed by the British government in France during the American war. 'I have read through the very voluminous and undigested letters from Mr Wentworth [chief British agent in Paris]', he wrote in January 1778, 'whose productions I confess it is hard labour to wade through'; and he thought the reports of Nathaniel Parker Forth, another agent in Paris, no more trustworthy than the newspapers – 'those daily productions of untruths'. Spies always seemed to imagine that they were paid for their reports at so much a word, and if they had no information they invented it. They were credulous, ill-informed, and of doubtful moral character. The King disliked having to resort to corruption and espionage.

The secret service account was also used to provide pensions for bankrupts and poor people. As the pensions were secret they could not be seized by creditors nor were they subject to taxation. Former servants of the Royal Family (George Lewis Scott was one), literary men such as Dr Johnson, and poor relations of wealthy families were taken care of in this way. Strict secrecy was not always observed – everyone for instance, knew about Dr Johnson's pension and it was even mentioned in debate in the House of Commons. Newcastle used the secret service fund to accommodate importunate Members of Parliament for whom he could not find places, but during King George III's reign the number of Members on the list decreased and in 1782 there were only three. In the previous reign it was also used to finance government candidates at elections, but under King George III this was done from the Privy Purse.

The King worked the system he had inherited from his predecessors as best he could. He did not attempt to reform it (his experience with Bute had taught him the folly of trying to be a reforming monarch) nor did he use it for corruption. He was aware of the possibility of abuses which he tried conscientiously to avoid. He was most contrite when in 1770 he inadvertently broke his promise to the Irish Parliament not to grant any further pensions for life. He set his face against downright jobbery, but, as he told North, the demands of ministers sometimes forced him to sanction appointments he did not quite approve. He cut down the establishments of his sons to set an example of economy. The true solution to the problem of Crown indebtedness, however, was not in personal economy by the King. It lay in three directions: an increase of revenue, a reform of Court and administration, and the separation of the finances of the monarchy from those of the State. The revenue increased automatically as a result of the increase in national wealth and the discovery that higher taxation was not necessarily inconsistent with national prosperity. Reform took longer to achieve. The first steps were taken under North, something was done by Burke and more by the younger Pitt, but it was not until the days of Peel and Gladstone that the new financial and administrative structure was complete. Reform had to be preceded and accompanied by a change in public morality, part of what Wilberforce called 'the reformation of manners', which transformed British social life at the turn of the century and in which the King had a share. Economy in government expenditure became the greatest of public virtues, and it ceased to be the fashion for the governing class to provide for itself at the expense of the Crown and the nation. The third change – the separation of the finances of the monarchy from those of the State – did not happen until the reign of King William IV.

How did King George handle his own financial affairs?[5] The King's personal income during the first seventeen years of his reign was about £53,000 a year. It consisted of £48,000 from the Civil List (the Privy Purse), about £5,000 from the Duchy of Lancaster, and the profits of the King's farms at Richmond. One farm (Marsh Gate Farm) was let at a rent of £30 a year, and the other (Richmond Farm) was managed on the King's behalf. This brought in a small but steadily increasing income. For the last quarter of 1766 the profits of Richmond Farm were only £27 2s but by the last quarter of 1771 they had increased to £74 5s. In that year the King's two farms brought him £300 – a trivial amount compared with his expenses, but sufficient to show that had he been born in a private station he could have made a tolerable living from the land. The King was not only a practical farmer but a farmer who made a profit.

In later years, especially after he made Windsor his principal country home, he considerably increased his personal property. He gave up Richmond Farm and cultivated three farms in Windsor Great Park, which he used mainly for experiments in stock breeding. He took Marsh Gate Farm into his own hands and also acquired other property: seven houses in Windsor (three on Castle Hill, two in St Alban's Street, one in High Street, and one in

Sheet Street); a public house and three small tenements in Pimlico, near the Queen's House; Gloucester Lodge (where he resided) and four other houses in Weymouth. He was also lord of the manors of Egham and Winkfield, near Windsor. All these had been acquired out of his personal income, and were his private property not the property of the Crown. Because of the gaps in the Privy Purse accounts it is impossible to say what income the King derived from his personal property. When his affairs were taken into the hands of trustees in 1811, some of this property was sold and over £7,000 paid into the King's private account. Even so, the greater part remained. It seems probable that in 1811 he was deriving an income of not less than £2,000 a year from his private property and perhaps a good deal more. And to the capital which he owned in farms and houses must be added his art collections and his library, property which brought in no income but which could only increase in value.[6]

The instructions which the King drew up for the conduct of the Privy Purse show the care he devoted to his affairs:[7]

The pensions and salaries to be paid on the 25th of March, 24th of June, 29th of September and 25th of December.

The bills to be delivered to the Clerk of the Privy Purse on the 1st of April, 1st of July, 1st of October, and 1st of January. After he has examined the sums he must immediately carry them to the Privy Purse for his inspection, who will after this order the payment of them. The Privy Purse will then bring to me the quarterly accounts agreeable to the form prescribed accompanied with the vouchers, which after having kept a day or two I shall return and sign the account as his discharge. The copy of the account for my use to be delivered at the same time the account is brought.

The Privy Purse when he has received the money at the Exchequer for the month must bring me a short state of the monthly account with a copy for my use. When he has my leave of absence he will direct his clerks to bring that state. I shall then signify what money he is to bring to me, which he shall add to the papers which I shall sign, and when I pass the quarterly account he is to return the monthly papers that they may be destroyed.

Coutts in the Strand is the banker I have ever employed for the Privy Purse.

Everything must be precise and in order; there must be no waste or extravagance; and the King must know at any time how much money he had and how much he owed. He could hardly avoid debts on the Civil List but he would have none on the Privy Purse. Had King George been a business man he would never have made a fortune for he was afraid to take risks and too much concerned to keep out of debt. But he would have paid his way and maintained his family in a comfortable state. Had the national finances been conducted on the principles on which the King conducted his own the country gentlemen would have had little cause for complaint. They would have recognized in King George one of themselves – the first country gentleman of England.

The biggest charge on the Privy Purse, about £6,000 a year, was for salaries and retirement pensions for the King's personal servants – those who were not provided for in official positions at Court. They ranged from £300 a year to Richard Dalton, the King's librarian, to £25 a year to the women who nursed the King's children. All who retired in the King's service received pensions, and pensions were provided for the widows of former servants and sometimes for the children if they were in poor circumstances. The King also took upon himself the charges of pensions for servants of deceased members of the Royal Family, and those who could not be accommodated on the Privy Purse were put upon the secret service list. Individually these pensions were not large. Few were above £100 a year: the lowest was the £7 10s a year which appears in the accounts for 1816 opposite the words 'rat-catcher's widow'. They were paid to people who were of no account politically and are unknown to posterity, but whose services over the years had conduced to the comfort and ease of the Royal Family. In assessing the real value of these salaries and pensions it should be remembered that free board and lodging were usually provided in addition. No one who served King George well was forgotten.[8]

Each year the King distributed Christmas and New Year presents. To the upper servants he made personal gifts: to the lower he gave money. The total for the lower servants in the accounts for 1765–66 (the only year for which we have a complete list) amounts to £327 3s 6d. Guineas or half-guineas (or in some cases two guineas) were given to the man who made the King's chocolate, who lit the fires, who powdered the King's wigs, who brought the monthly bills of mortality in the City of London, who cleaned the locks in Kensington Palace, to the woman who cleaned the stairs, who brought the King the bi-weekly issues of the *London Gazette*. The names of these people are not given and most of them must have been casual labour. Other payments are in the nature of tips. The attendants at the King's boxes in the three London theatres received four guineas each, the bill stickers one guinea. Each new year the King gave five guineas to the drummers of each regiment of Foot Guards and Horse Guards.[9]

The Privy Purse accounts, like those of the Civil List, contain a great many payments which the King had to meet by tradition and custom. Although he had begun his reign by professing his dislike of Hanover, he continued the practice of his grandfather and paid for the expenses of the Hanoverian chancery out of the Privy Purse. The salary of the Hanoverian Minister in London, together with those of his clerks and assistants, the charges for office accommodation, postage, etc. cost the King £5,000 a year.[10] It was a privilege of courtiers to request the King and Queen to be god-parents of their children; and on these occasions the baptismal fees were paid by

the King on a graduated scale ranging from 40 guineas
for the child of a duke to 15 guineas for the child of a
commoner who was not a member of the Privy Council.[11]
A sedan chair (the usual method of travelling in London
in the early years of the reign) cost the King a guinea a
time. The boys of Christ's Hospital were given eight
guineas each New Year's Day; the German Protestant
mission to India ten guineas; the beadle of the Honourable Artillery Company five guineas. The King paid £10
each time he went to the theatre and £20 when he attended
the opera or oratorio. The churches of three London
parishes (St Martin's in the Fields, St Margaret's, and
Kensington) had the privilege of ringing their bells on the
King's birthday. For this they received three guineas each,
and ten parishes in the neighbourhood of Richmond two
guineas. Twelve times a year, at the festivals of the
Church, the King made an offering of five guineas; and
five guineas each time he took the Sacrament.[12]

The most important aspect of the Privy Purse accounts
is the light they throw on the character of King George.
No man is a hypocrite in his pleasures, said Johnson; and
no man spends money on things he does not like. A large
proportion of the King's income was spent on books,
works of art, and music. In 1766 bills to booksellers and
bookbinders came to £1,030, in 1767 to £1,713. Three
entries in 1768 (4 April, 4 July, 9 December) record payment to 'various booksellers' of £356 8s 4d, £405 14s 8d,
and £103 13s 9d. The King was a particularly good customer of Tom Davies, who introduced Boswell to Johnson and whose shop in Covent Garden was the scene of
their first meeting. Francis Barnard, who procured Johnson his audience with the King in 1767, was the chief
buyer. He regularly attended London auction sales, and
he or his son travelled to the Continent in search of books
for the royal library. British diplomatic missions were
instructed to inform the King of outstanding sales in the
countries to which they were accredited. The King did not

aspire to be a patron of literature, but he subsidized the production of Joseph Edmondson's learned peerage of England to the extent of £236. He was an assiduous reader of newspapers, the bill for which came to about £40 a year.

The names of some of the great artists of the period appear in the accounts. On 7 December 1763 the King paid Reynolds £210 for a portrait of Bute, and on 3 February 1769 £378 to Allan Ramsay for portraits of himself, the Queen, and their two eldest children. The Royal Academy, which the King founded in 1769, was subsidized out of the Privy Purse and cost £911 during the first year. Alexander Cumming, the great clock maker, received £1,178 0s 6d on 14 February 1765 for a barometrical clock (now in Buckingham Palace), and on 5 July 1765 Christopher Pinchbeck was paid £1,042 for another clock. In February 1764 the King bought three harpsichords at a cost of £278 10s, and in April 1767 an organ for the Queen for £241 10s. The annual cost of tuning the harpsichords and organs (the King also had one) came to £45. The King employed two men to copy music for him: Mr Tweed, who copied *The Messiah* in full score in 1766 for seven guineas; and Mr Simpson, whose expenses for copying music in 1767 came to £22 16s. Scientific instrument makers also figure in the accounts (though Herschel, the greatest of all, was yet to come); and the Queen kept a private zoo in St James's Park, consisting of an elephant and a zebra, which cost the King over £100 a year.

One further source of expense remains to be accounted for. Each month the King received into his own hands a sum of money, which varied according to the balance in the Privy Purse but which on an average from 1763 to 1772 (the years for which the surviving accounts run) amounted to £27,500 a year. How this money was spent we cannot be absolutely sure, for since it was paid direct to the King only the gross sums appear monthly in the accounts. It certainly could not have been used to pay the normal bills which were never settled by the King personally. There was in fact only one purpose for which the King would ever want money. Lady Mary Coke was told in 1769 by Lady Charlotte Finch, governess of the royal children and an intimate friend of Queen Charlotte, 'that the sums of money he gives in private charities is prodigious'. In 1782, when Parliament was about to regulate the Civil List, the King protested against any diminution of his Privy Purse, 'the only fund from whence I pay every act of private benevolence' – 'those acts of benevolence', as he described his charitable distributions, 'which alone make the station bearable'. There are no expenses of this nature in the Privy Purse or any other accounts. The only fund King George had for private charity was the money he received personally: £27,500 a year, more than half his income.

A word must be said about Queen Charlotte's finances.[13] She had her own court, with her Lord Chamberlain, Master of the Horse, Mistress of the Robes, together with their servants and attendants – a replica in miniature of the King's court; whose salaries and expenses had to be paid for out of the Queen's allowance. This was originally £40,000 a year, and was increased to £50,000 on the birth of the Prince of Wales. This was just about sufficient to enable her to pay her way in 1762. She was not extravagant, and after paying all salaries and expenses she had between £6,000 and £7,000 for her Privy Purse. But as her family increased so did her expenses. The boys were a charge upon her until the age of puberty, when they became the responsibility of the King; and the girls until they were twenty-one. The more children that were born to her the more nurses, seamstresses, laundresses, teachers, governesses, etc who had to be employed in the royal nursery; and an income which was sufficient to support one child would hardly do when there were fifteen. The Princess Royal told Lady Elgin in 1802 that for long the

347

Queen could not afford to employ an English teacher for her daughters, and that the duty had been undertaken by Lady Charlotte Finch.[14] In 1778 the Queen's expenses began to exceed her income, and the annual deficit threatened to swallow up her savings. The King gave her £6,000, but this was only a stop-gap measure; and in 1786 she had to ask for an increased allowance. The King asked Lord Ailesbury, the Queen's Treasurer: 'What was it coming to and when would it be better?'; to which Ailesbury replied: 'It was likely to be worse rather than better as the princesses grew up, and that several young ladies were more attended than them.' Pitt gave the Queen £12,000 from the Civil List and her allowance was increased to £58,000 a year. By then the boys were off her hands, but the girls were growing up and required more money than when they were children.

In 1792 the Queen's expenses were £66,901 – a deficit of over £8,000. On 26 October 1793 she wrote to Ailesbury, begging him to advise her about her financial position. She was ready to do anything he recommended, short of asking the King for more money. She protested that she was not extravagant, that she did everything she could to keep the bills down and even stinted her daughters, but that in her position it did not become her to be too parsimonious:

The bills I know are high this quarter but etiquette will have it so, for the quantity of lace and linen I am in duty bound to have and the clothes are far more than I want, nay I assure you than ever I wear, and some years ago I meant and wished to have less and change seldomer but was advised against it on account of the noise it would make amongst the Bedchamber women, and if you knew of how little I want of what I must buy you would yourself say that the arrangement made for me was hard.

Fine ladies in the eighteenth century (and for long afterwards) were at the mercy of their servants, who expected to succeed to their mistresses' clothes and did not like it if the dresses were worn until they became out of fashion. Readers of *Vanity Fair* will remember how annoyed the coachman was when Amelia Sedley gave her gowns to Becky Sharp instead of to her maid. 'The truth is', writes Thackeray, 'he was attached to the lady's maid in question, and indignant that she should have been robbed of her perquisites.' The Queen had to have new gowns each year whether she wanted them or not in order that her Bedchamber women should not be robbed of their perquisites. A generation unaccustomed to domestic service will never know how much servants made out of their masters and mistresses in the great days.

It does not appear how the Queen got out of her embarrassments in 1793. Things became easier for her when the King was able to make a separate provision for his daughters. But until 1812 she had to manage on the income of £58,000 a year which she had been given as long ago as 1786.

Chapter 6

POLITICAL CRISIS

The spring session of 1780 was marked by the attempt of the opposition, aided by a powerful and well-organized agitation out of doors, to carry Burke's economical reform bill. The bill was undoubtedly popular, and attracted the support of many independent Members of Parliament who were not normally hostile to government. Although it was eventually dropped, the opposition scored a moral victory; and on 6 April 1780 they carried against government a motion by Dunning that 'the influence of the Crown has increased, is increasing, and ought to be diminished'. North took this as a sign that he no longer possessed the confidence of the House, and wrote to the King:

If I had not for four years past apprised Your Majesty that this event would happen, and if I had not made it my constant prayer that I might be allowed to quit Your Majesty's service, I should feel very unhappy now at what has happened and may further be expected.

The King would not admit that the motion was levelled personally against North. He believed the opposition had aimed their censure at himself, and he met their charges with confidence and a good conscience. 'A little time will I am certain open the eyes of several who have been led on farther than they intended', he wrote on 11 April. On 24 April a further motion by Dunning that Parliament should not be prorogued until grievances had been redressed was defeated by a majority of 51. The King seemed to have been proved right. Parliament had made a gesture and had declined to implement it. But the success of Dunning's first motion was a warning which it was dangerous to ignore. If the war dragged on or went badly, Parliament might not be so accommodating.

The King was mistaken in thinking that Dunning's motion was aimed at himself. It was not the personal authority of the King which the House of Commons wished to see diminished but the influence of the government over the House. Yet that influence, far from increasing, was less in 1780 than when the King came to the throne.[1] There were fewer placemen and government contractors in the House, and party feeling had stimulated the growth of a large and compact opposition. The number of government boroughs had decreased, and in one borough (Orford) the King had voluntarily surrendered the Crown influence to a private patron (something which King George II would never have done). At the general election of 1780 North had fewer seats at his command than Newcastle had in 1761, and the days were long past when the ministry could decide election petitions in favour of its own supporters. It was not the influence of the Crown that was increasing but the pretensions of the House of Commons. The great political controversies of the reign (the Middlesex election and the dispute with the colonies) were concerned with the privileges and powers of the House of Commons. The Crown's inability to live upon its income had enabled the House of Commons to encroach into the sphere of royal finance. The delicate balance of the constitution, in which the eighteenth century took so much pride, was being tilted towards the side of Parliament.

In June came the Gordon riots; and for a week London was at the mercy of an enraged, fanatical, and destructive mob. This was a confirmation of all the King had feared during the Wilkes riots ten years earlier. The Americans had set the example of mob rousing in the name of liberty, and the British were now following in the name of religion. Many stories are told of the King's coolness during those terrible days. He kept his head and did his

351

duty. 'My attachment is to the laws and security of my country', he wrote, 'and to the protection of the lives and properties of all my subjects.' If Lord George Gordon, a man of no consequence in the House of Commons, could rouse the mob by pandering to their bigotry and communal hatred, what could not others do? The event of the riots confirmed the King's belief that 'violence if met by firmness is commonly repelled'.

The summer of 1780 seemed to mark the turning point in the fortunes of North's ministry.[2] The British had switched the impetus of their attack in America to the southern colonies, and the capture of Charleston in May appeared to confirm the wisdom of this strategy. It was believed that there were great numbers of loyalists prepared to rally to the British cause if only they could be assured of aid and protection. The general election in September seemed to promise a House of Commons more favourable to the ministry. Burke's economical reform bill was revived and defeated. Yet the outlook was more threatening than these appearances promised. Holland was added to the number of Great Britain's enemies; the Armed Neutrality, led by Catherine II of Russia, maintained a hostile attitude to the British claim of search on the seas; and the advance in the southern colonies slowed down. On 3 November 1781, while the Cabinet was anxiously expecting news from America, the King wrote to North:

I feel the justness of our cause; I put the greatest confidence in valour of both navy and army and above all in the assistance of Divine Providence. The moment is certainly anxious. The die is now cast whether this shall be a great empire or the least dignified of the European states. The object is certainly worth struggling for and I trust the nation is equally determined with myself to meet the conclusion with firmness.

The news for which all were waiting reached London on 25 November, two days before the meeting of Parliament.

It was bad. Cornwallis, with the bulk of the British field army in America, had surrendered to Washington at Yorktown.

Yet the King did not despair. Yorktown was a defeat greater than Saratoga, but it was not the end. Saratoga had stiffened the British resolve to win the war: might not Yorktown do the same? But he realized that the plan of the war must be changed, that it was no longer possible to conduct offensive operations in America, and he accepted the cabinet's advice that no further reinforcements should be sent. His mind flew back to his earlier plans. 'Fluctuating counsels', he wrote, 'and taking up measures without connecting them with the whole of this complicated war, must make us weak in every part.' This did not mean that the British should abandon their claim to sovereignty, and the King was determined not to acknowledge the independence of the United States. He wrote to North on 21 January 1782:

I shall never lose an opportunity of declaring that no consideration shall ever make me in the smallest degree an instrument in a measure that I am confident would annihilate the rank in which this British empire stands among the European states, and would render my situation in this country below continuing an object to me.

The King was deceived by the notion that Great Britain had become a world power through the acquisition of colonies and would cease to be one if she lost them. The reverse was the truth: Great Britain had acquired an empire because she had become a world power and she would remain one after she had lost the American colonies. The King lived to see his error; but the British delusion of lasting greatness based on imperial rule was not scotched by the Declaration of Independence.

Yorktown was more than a military defeat: it was a disaster. It broke the morale of the governing class and paralyzed the national will to make war. What was the point of continuing the struggle? The colonies could not be recovered without an army, and even if they were it was certain no revenue would be obtained from America. Any sovereignty Great Britain might retain over the United States would be purely nominal. The cabinet was almost unanimous in believing that American independence must be recognized, and the House of Commons was fast coming round to the idea that North's ministry was too compromised by the war to be able to make peace. On 22 February General Conway's motion against the further prosecution of the war in America was lost by only one vote and on the 27th a similar motion was carried by 19 votes. A week later the House agreed without a division to a resolution condemning as enemies to the country all who should advise the continuance of the war 'for the purpose of reducing the colonies to obedience by force'. The House of Commons had renounced the policy it had adopted in 1774, and North advised the King that the ministry could continue no longer.

The King was 'much hurt' at the success of Conway's motion and 'mortified' at the prospect of losing North. He commissioned the Lord Chancellor to sound Gower and Weymouth – members of the former Bedford party – as to their willingness to resume office. He was prepared to accept 'such others of any party they may think right to recommend',

the basis of public measures being founded on keeping what is in our present possession in North America, and attempting by a negotiation with any separate provinces or districts to detach them from France, even upon any plan of their own, provided they remain separate states.

At first sight it seems that the King was prepared to recognize the independence of individual provinces but not of the United States, a proposal which stood no chance of being accepted by Congress. But the words 'on any plan of their own' implied recognition of the United

States, and by the expression 'provided they remain separate states' the King meant provided they did not become satellites of France. He was haunted by the fear that the colonies could not maintain themselves as an independent nation and would be drawn into the French orbit. If that should happen, for how long would Great Britain be able to retain Canada and her possessions in the West Indies? A Franco-American power would dominate North America just as Spain and Portugal did South America, and the whole continent would be closed to British trade. It was not pride that made King George reluctant to recognize American independence but concern for the commerce and prosperity of Great Britain. He exaggerated the influence France would possess over the United States and under-estimated the strength of American nationalism, but there were solid reasons for his fear. No one in 1782 could foresee that in ten years' time France would be in the grip of revolution, and the men who had urged Louis XVI to make war on Great Britain would be pensioners of King George.

The motion of 27 February tied the hands of the British government in the forthcoming negotiation. There were many issues besides independence to be settled. What were to be the boundaries of the new state? Were the United States to include the interior lands which had been allotted to Canada by the Quebec Act? What was to happen to those Americans who had suffered for their loyalty to Great Britain? There were some in Congress who hoped to include Nova Scotia and Canada within the United States: there were few who were sympathetic to the Loyalists. If Congress proved stubborn on these issues what could Great Britain do? After the resolution of 27 February it would be impossible to renew the war. And what if Congress should refuse to make peace until the demands of France and Spain had been satisfied? The British would then have no recourse but to appeal to the clemency of their former subjects. It seemed to the King

355

that Parliament had thrown away the one strong card in the British hand.

On 28 February North introduced a bill to enable the government to make peace with the colonies. Possibly it was shortly after this that the King began seriously to think of abdication. He drew up a declaration, apparently to be submitted to Parliament, resigning the Crown to the Prince of Wales:

His Majesty during the twenty-one years he has sat on the throne of Great Britain has had no object so much at heart as the maintenance of the British constitution, of which the difficulties he has at times met with from his scrupulous attachment to the rights of Parliament are sufficient proofs.

His Majesty is convinced that the sudden change of sentiments of one branch of the legislature has totally incapacitated him from either conducting the war with effect or from obtaining any peace but on conditions which would prove destructive to the commerce as well as essential rights of the British nation.

His Majesty therefore with much sorrow finds he can be of no further utility to his native country which drives him to the painful step of quitting it for ever.

In consequence of which intention His Majesty resigns the Crown of Great Britain and the dominions appertaining thereto to his dearly beloved son and lawful successor George Prince of Wales, whose endeavours for the prosperity of the British empire he hopes may prove more successful.

We do not know what induced the King to change his mind. Certainly it was not because of any improvement in the parliamentary situation. All attempts to strengthen the government had failed, and on 8 March the House of Commons rejected a motion of censure against North's ministry by only ten votes. At 6.50 the next morning the King wrote to North:

Lord North may easily conceive that I am much hurt at the appearance of yesterday in the House of Commons and at his opinion that it is totally impossible to conduct public business

356

any longer. This leads so much after the trials I have made of late to my taking so decisive a step that I certainly must maturely deliberate before I can return any answer.

The King took two days to deliberate; and then instructed Lord Chancellor Thurlow to approach the opposition leaders with the offer of a coalition 'of the best of all parties in point of private characters and abilities'. Thurlow applied first to Rockingham, the leader of the largest opposition party, who fourteen years earlier had tried to form just the sort of ministry the King now envisaged. But times had changed since 1767. Rockingham now had a political programme. He demanded that the King must recognize American independence and accept measures designed to reduce the influence of the Crown. Rockingham also made it clear that he must be given a free hand to form a ministry and that no one who had been associated with what he called 'a sort of secret system, from which many attributed all the evils of the reign', would be allowed to retain office. These points being accepted by the King, Rockingham would expect to receive his commission to form a ministry. In short, the King must eat humble pie as he had been made to do by Grenville in May 1765. Ironically, Rockingham was the man who in 1765 had stepped forward under the aegis of the Duke of Cumberland to rescue the King from Grenville.

No King could accept such terms except under overwhelming pressure. It was not long in coming. On 15 March, the day after Rockingham had presented his ultimatum, North escaped defeat on a motion of no confidence by only nine votes. 'I am resolved', wrote the King to North on hearing the result of the division, 'not to throw myself into the hands of opposition at all events, and shall certainly if things go as they seem to lead know what my conscience as well as honour dictates as the only way left for me.' And to Thurlow: 'The changing from one party to another can answer no real good. Besides I

357

must then give up my principles and my honour, which I value above my Crown.' A further motion of censure was threatened for 20 March, and on the 18th North told the King that the end had come. A group of independent country gentlemen who had hitherto supported the ministry had informed him that they could do so no longer. With such a narrow majority, the withdrawal of even a handful of the ministry's supporters would ensure its defeat. 'Your Majesty is well apprised', North continued, 'that in this country the Prince on the Throne cannot with prudence oppose the deliberate resolution of the House of Commons.' There could be no disputing this proposition. The King submitted with bad grace. He wrote to North:

After having yesterday in the most solemn manner assured you that my sentiments of honour will not permit me to send for any of the leaders of opposition and personally treat with them I could not but be hurt at your letter of last night. Every man must be the sole judge of his feelings, therefore whatever you or any man can say on that subject has no avail with me.

Till I have heard what the Chancellor has done from his own mouth I shall not take any step, and if you resign before I have decided what I will do you will certainly for ever forfeit my regard.

On 20 March North announced his resignation to the House of Commons and the next day the King offered Shelburne the lead in a new ministry.

The King had declared over and over again that he would never recognize American independence and would never invite the opposition to form a ministry. In the end he had to do both, and the result of his repeated refusals was that he was suspected of insincerity and was in a worse political position in March 1782 than he would have been had he submitted earlier. His conduct has been invariably censured as impolitic, and historians have written about his obstinacy and refusal to face reality. They had the advantage of knowing what happened afterwards. Such knowledge, as Namier wrote, 'is a marvellous stimulant to cogent reasoning and astute deductions'. Historians are always wiser than statesmen – on paper.

The difference between what King George called firmness and his critics obstinacy depends on our point of view and knowledge of subsequent events. To give one example. In the summer of 1940 Germany was supreme in Europe. France had been defeated, Italy had entered the war against Great Britain, Japan and Russia were unfriendly, the United States sympathetic but neutral. What hope had Great Britain of achieving the aims for which she had gone to war in 1939? Was it not the part of true statesmanship to accept reality, recognize German hegemony, and make peace while there was still a chance of obtaining reasonable terms? At this moment Churchill with the full support of Parliament and the nation declared the British resolve to continue the war until Nazism had been extirpated. Today we praise his firmness and courage. But if events had gone the other way (as well they might) would we not condemn his obstinacy and refusal to face reality? Without attempting to compare King George with Churchill, there is a parallel between the state of Great Britain in 1782 and in 1940. The difference between the conduct of the King and Churchill is not obstinacy and firmness but failure and success.

It is not the King's obstinacy that is noteworthy but his willingness to compromise. Repeatedly during the American conflict he submitted to the opinions of his ministers against his better judgment: in 1766 on the repeal of the Stamp Act, in 1775 on the need to mobilize, in 1778 on the conciliation commission. 'I will never make my inclinations alone nor even my own opinions the sole rule of my conduct in public measures', he had written to Thurlow in 1779. '. . . I will at all times consult my ministers and place in them as entire a confidence as the nature of this government can be supposed to require of me.' When the House of Commons declared against the continuance of the American war, the King accepted their decision unpalatable though it was. When it became clear that North could no longer maintain his majority in the House, the King opened negotiations with the opposition. But he would not yield until forced and he did so unwillingly. 'What George III had never learnt', wrote Namier, 'was to give in with grace.' How many of us can? North's resignation ushered in a political crisis which was to last for two years and to try the King severely.[3] The search for a minister who could command the confidence of both the Crown and the House of Commons as North had done ended only with the victory of the younger Pitt at the general election of 1784. During these two years there were four ministries – the first three (Rockingham, Shelburne, and the Fox–North coalition) each lasting only a a few months, the fourth (the younger Pitt), which began as the weakest ministry of the century, without a majority in the House of Commons, lasting for seventeen years. A recent historian of this period (Dr John Cannon in his book *The Fox–North Coalition*) describes it as 'the political and constitutional climax of the reign'. This is the point of view of the historian, concerned to trace the evolution of the party system and the growth of constitutional monarchy. But there is another way of looking at these events, that of the biographer, who sees them as the climax of the personal antipathy between King George and Charles James Fox and is interested in the revelations of character. Both points of view are equally relevant and we should not lose sight of either. To a remarkable extent events during this period were determined by a conflict of personalities. There would probably have been a political crisis on the resignation of North whoever had been appointed his successor, but that crisis was embittered and prolonged by the personal feeling between the King and Fox.

Next to his attitude during the American war, the King's relations with Fox have done most to prejudice subsequent generations against him. Almost every historian of this period has written of Fox with admiration. He was one of the greatest men in an age when greatness was abundant. Though he held high office for only two short periods, he became the inspirer of the Whig party of the nineteenth century, in Macaulay's words 'the greatest parliamentary defender of civil and religious liberty'. When these ideals had triumphed and had been accepted as part of the fabric of British political life (and we sometimes forget how long it took), Fox was honoured as their advocate. As late as the 1840s there were still men active in politics who had known and worked with Fox and were carrying the torch for him, while King George was honoured only by a fast diminishing generation of ultra Tories.

The King's hatred of Fox was equalled by Fox's hatred of the King. Their feeling for each other was no mere personal dislike, no mere antipathy of character and temperament. Nor was it based upon political differences, for during his first years in Parliament Fox was a supporter of the King's ministry and had held junior office under North. He had made himself unpopular with the opposition by his stand against Wilkes's election for Middlesex, and it seemed that he was destined to become North's first lieutenant and eventual successor. The origin of the ill feeling between the King and Fox is to be found in the events of the early years of the reign and in the part played by Fox's father, Lord Holland.

Charles Fox was the favourite child of a fond and indulgent father: adored, petted, and spoilt. No whim was too idle to be gratified. The stories told about Charles's childhood – how he was allowed to wallow in a large bowl of cream and how his father built a wall for him at Holland House so that the boy could see it knocked down – show Holland's adoration of his brilliant son. In his eyes the boy could do no wrong. While still at school he was admitted into the circle of his father's friends and conversed with them as an equal. When only nineteen Holland bought a seat for him in the House of Commons, and shortly after his twenty-first birthday Charles was given office. He was obviously destined for a great political career in which he would accomplish all his father had failed to accomplish and revenge all the injuries which embittered his father's old age. Holland would be justified in his son. Charles Fox took into politics the fatal legacy of his father's enmities.

Foremost among these enemies was the King. In the winter of 1762, when Grenville was terrified at the prospect of having to face Pitt in the House of Commons and Bute was at his wits' end how to get the Treaty of Paris through the House, Holland had undertaken the lead and saved the ministry. Bute acknowledged that without Holland he could never have remained at the Treasury that winter. For this Holland deserved well of the King. Instead, he considered he had been treated ungratefully. True, the King had kept his word and raised Holland to the peerage. But he had received with indifference, perhaps with pleasure, the Grenville's ministry's demand for Holland's dismissal from the Pay Office. Then Holland had suffered the mortification of seeing Pitt, the man he hated most, placed above him in the House of Lords. It became an obsession with him to obtain an earldom. He enlisted the help of Grafton, then First Lord of the Treasury. But the King was inflexible. He had done what he promised and would do no more. Court favour was to be forever denied to Holland. Holland wrote bitterly to Charles (24 July 1767):

I was at court yesterday. . . . I had as much to say as any man ever had, and *said* it. I saw obstinate, determined denial, without any reason given; nor had I any occasion to follow your advice, *to take a shuffling answer for a denial*; for I was not flattered even by a shuffling, promising answer, but told it

362

would be very inconvenient to do it now, without being told why (and the Duke of Grafton says he does not know of one promise nor does he think it unreasonable), or when there would come a time when it might not be inconvenient.

'Of all court service know the common lot,
  Today, 'tis done, tomorrow 'tis forgot.'

Don't ever, Charles, make any exception, or trust as I did. Well! I may thank myself, and have nothing to do but to forget it. I trust I shall, for after all what does it signify?

But it did signify. It warped and embittered his soul. Holland could not transmit an earldom to his children as Chatham could, but he did transmit the story of the King's ingratitude and the duty of revenging it.

Charles Fox was not a dutiful son. Spoilt children rarely are. He added to his father's cares by his addiction to gambling, and compelled Holland to liquidate part of the enormous fortune he had made out of the Pay Office to pay his debts. Though insensitive to his father's softer feelings, he was acutely sensitive to his father's vendettas. Holland had married the Duke of Richmond's daughter without her parents' consent, and had taken a leading part in the opposition to Lord Hardwicke's Marriage Act which prohibited runaway marriages. Whenever the repeal or amendment of the Marriage Act was proposed in the House of Commons (it is remarkable how much this eminently sensible measure was disliked), Charles Fox always rose to oppose the Act just as his father had done. In 1772 he resigned his seat at the Admiralty Board in order to oppose the Royal Marriage Act which gave the King control over the marriages of the Royal Family. Any limitation on the right to marry freely was like a red rag to a bull to Charles Fox. But of all Holland's vendettas the one which Charles took up with most zest was that against the King.

Whenever the King was mentioned in conversation, Fox could hardly restrain himself from passionate and indiscreet denunciations. 'It is intolerable', he wrote in

363

September 1781, 'that it should be in the power of one blockhead to do so much mischief.' To his intimates (and to those not so intimate) he spoke of the King as 'Satan' – an expression, wrote George Selwyn in 1782, 'which he seems fond of and has used to others'. On the day he received the seals as Foreign Secretary he said to Lord Carmarthen: 'Certainly things look well, but he (meaning the King) will die soon, and that will be best of all.' What a thing for an incoming Secretary of State to say about his sovereign! And to say it to a former Lord of the King's Bedchamber, who eighteen months later was to succeed Fox as Foreign Secretary! Fox must have been mad to have talked of the King in this way – to Selwyn, an inveterate 'King's man', concerned for the safety of his sinecures – to Carmarthen, so soon to become a political opponent. If he said these things to Selwyn and Carmarthen we may be sure he said them to others and that they were reported to the King. The King saw all the leading politicians at his levees and all the women of fashion at his drawing rooms. He never refused a private audience to a man or woman of rank. He heard all the gossip of London society and knew all that was said of him in political circles. Fox had many enemies, and it was easy for those who were anxious to ingratiate themselves with the King to drop a word into his ear. Fox made no secret of his hatred for the King and his wish for the King's death, and the King knew all that Fox felt about him. This fact must be borne in mind when we judge the King's conduct. It was not politics which led King George to proscribe Fox. It was not differing ideas of the function of the Crown or the role of party in the state. Burke shared Fox's ideas. He had been in opposition longer than Fox; and when Fox was still a follower of Lord North, Burke had put forward the concept of party which Fox now professed. But Burke would have cut out his tongue rather than speak in public about the King as Fox did.

364

Fox was so much the slave of his passions as to be blind to all considerations of political advantage or plain common sense. He was, wrote Selwyn, 'so intoxicated with the all sufficiency, as he imagines, of his parts' as 'never to put himself under the disagreeable restraint of one minute'. This was a bitter comment by a disillusioned friend but it points to the cause of Fox's failure. Conscious of great parts, convinced that once in office he would soon make himself master of the House of Commons, he held the King's favour in contempt. For one who believed that public opinion should be the sole source of political power he was strangely indifferent to what people thought about him. 'The essential defect of his character', wrote Philip Francis, 'and the cause of all his failures, strange as it may seem, was that he had no heart.' This judgment is echoed by Selwyn:

Charles, I am persuaded, would have no consideration on earth but for what was useful to his own ends. You have heard me say that I thought he had no malice or rancour; I think so still and am sure of it. But I think he has no feeling, neither, for anyone but himself.

What else could be expected of a spoilt child?

To understand the King's hatred of Fox we must again recall the early events of the reign and the expressions the King had used about Fox's father in his letters to Bute. He had written of his 'personal dislike' of Holland, of Holland's 'bad character', of his aversion to Holland's 'whole mode of government'. The dreadful winter of 1762–63 when Holland had managed the House of Commons for Bute had been nothing but 'a scene of corruption'. After twenty years' experience of politics the King might have been expected to have forgiven Holland for his 'mode of government'. It was after all not very different from the system which North and every other eighteenth-century minister had to practise. The King had learnt much since the days when he had dreamt of inaugurating a reign of virtue. In 1782 he was no longer the artless boy who had sat at the feet of Bute.

'And yet the old schooling sticks, the old grey eyes
Are peeping o'er my shoulder as I work.'

He had an ideal of government which was not that of Holland or Charles Fox: in which neither jobbery nor party feeling found a place.

Even had the King been able to forgive Holland his jobbery, he could not have forgiven Holland's attempt to impose a mistress upon him. The affair of Lady Sarah Lennox was an irremovable barrier between Holland and the earldom. Yet the King might not have visited the sins of the father upon the son (he did not in the case of the two Pitts) had not Charles Fox been the type of son he most disliked – too much like his own first-born. As a young man Fox was the idol of the gilded youth of London: the centre of a group of hard-drinking, high-gambling, free-living young aristocrats, more than a little contemptuous of the manners and morals of their elders. He had, in his own words, 'a natural partiality towards rebels'. 'That young man', the King wrote in 1774, 'has so thoroughly cast off every principle of common honour and honesty that he must become as contemptuous as he is odious.'

It must be remembered that until Fox became Secretary of State in 1782 the King rarely met him and never in private. His knowledge of Fox's character was based on what he read in the newspapers and what people told him. Fox was a man it was easy to hate but difficult to dislike. It was easy to hate his public image because he took so little care to make it attractive: it was difficult to dislike him when meeting him face to face. His immense personal charm which captivated men so different as Burke, Johnson, and Wilberforce was never experienced by the King. He never knew the real Fox. Nor did Fox know the real King George. He only knew the King of Whig legend, concerned to increase his personal power through corruption and secret influence. He only knew the distorted image of the King transmitted to him by his father.

On North's resignation, the King sent for Shelburne and offered him the lead. Shelburne was compelled to decline. He knew he could not form a ministry without the support of the Rockingham party, and that Rockingham would refuse to take office unless he were given the Treasury and the ostensible lead. The King had no choice but to accept Rockingham's terms. But at the outset he scored a tactical victory. He refused to see Rockingham, but conducted all negotiations through Shelburne and made it clear that Shelburne was to be treated as co-Premier. Rockingham and Shelburne were to recommend jointly to all appointments and these were to be submitted to the King through Shelburne. There was a division of power: Rockingham had the Treasury, Fox the lead in the House of Commons, and Shelburne the confidence of the King. This was not a system that could last long. To maintain stability, the confidence of the Crown must go hand in hand with the power of the Crown. The King had said harsh things of Shelburne in the past, on one occasion referring to him as 'the Jesuit of Berkeley Square'; but now Shelburne appeared as the defender of the Crown against a triumphant opposition – a role he was not indisposed to play. Shelburne was the King's last card in his game with Fox, and as events soon proved a card of low value.

Fox and Rockingham ran the King hard. They had many mouths to feed and many old scores to settle. The King wrote to North on 27 March:

At last the fatal day is come which the misfortunes of the times and the sudden change of sentiments of the House of Commons have drove me to, of changing the ministry and a more general removal of other persons than I believe was ever known before. I have to the last fought for individuals but the number I have saved except my Bedchamber is incredibly few. You would hardly believe that even the Duke of Montagu was strongly run at, but I declared I would sooner let confusion follow than part with the late governor of my sons and so unexceptionable a man.

Only Thurlow of the old cabinet was left, and almost every place whether of business or dignity was demanded by the new ministers for their friends. It pained the King to have to turn out his old friend Lord Ailesbury from the lord lieutenancy of Wiltshire to make way for a nominee of Rockingham. Two peerages were created at the recommendation of ministers and the three vacant Garters demanded. One went to Shelburne; one to the Duke of Richmond, who had insulted the King in his closet at the beginning of the reign and had not been to Court for years; and the third to the Duke of Devonshire, a young man who made no mark in public life but who was closely connected with Rockingham. To accommodate these the King had to refuse Lord Dartmouth, North's stepbrother, a deeply religious man who had served ten years as Colonial Secretary and Lord Privy Seal. There was a spirit of vindictiveness towards the fallen ministers unknown since the days of Grenville, and only with great difficulty did the King manage to secure retiring pensions for North and Robinson.

Legislation designed to reduce the influence of the Crown went through Parliament with little opposition. The King feared that the ministers would seize the opportunity to impose Treasury control over the Privy Purse, but this seems never to have been their intention. There were in effect three measures: the disfranchisement of officers of the customs and excise; an Act to incapacitate government contractors from sitting in the House of Commons; and Burke's Civil List Act, designed to reduce government expenditure and prevent the Civil List from running into debt. The King accepted all three measures, and suggested a number of improvements to Burke's Act. 'The greatest savings that can be made in the household', he wrote, 'as to the number of useless places is in the department of the Chamberlain where no reform has as yet been made.' He was concerned that the limitation of the pension list should not extend 'to the not providing for those who by services of twenty or thirty years are disabled from continuing ... or have had any accident to disable them, and are not in circumstances to maintain themselves'. He was careful to safeguard the rights of the Crown, and commented on the proposal that the expense of the Board of Works and the household should be controlled by the Treasury:

I certainly wish, where the dignity of the Crown or my own convenience or amusement is not concerned, to be as economical as possible, and shall not object to the Treasury being the judges of the propriety of the estimates, whilst I am to be the sole judge of the necessity of the business being done if it regards my own amusement or convenience.

The King was not prepared to allow his ministers control over Crown expenditure. It was not the Crown but the nation which had run into debt.

Economical reform did not produce the results its sponsors expected, largely because they expected too much. They exaggerated the influence of government over the House of Commons, and assumed it was this, not public opinion, which had kept them so long out of office. Economical reform did not inaugurate the bloodless revolution which Fox expected. It effected no essential change in the system of government. It reduced the government interest in elections though to what extent is doubtful – this had been decreasing ever since the King's accession and would have decreased further even without economical reform. It became more difficult to provide for Members of Parliament who wanted the prestige and emoluments but not the labour or responsibility of office. 'The source of pensions is absolutely stopped', wrote Gibbon in July 1783, himself a solicitor for something good, 'and a double list of candidates is impatient and clamorous for half the number of desirable places.' Deprived of his seat at the Board of Trade, which had been abolished by Burke's Act, Gibbon was forced to retire to Lausanne, there to complete *The Decline and Fall of the Roman Empire* – an unexpected result of economical reform.

Another unexpected – indeed paradoxical – result was that economical reform by reducing the influence of the Crown increased the power of the King. By reducing the number of places available to Members of Parliament, it increased the value of honours. Office was usually bestowed according to ministerial advice; but although ministers could advise the King on the creation of peerages, the doctrine was not yet accepted that the King could act only on ministerial advice. By keeping the creation of peerages in his own hands, King George had an invaluable weapon which he used to good effect during the following months.

Burke's arrangements for ensuring that the Civil List did not run into debt were unworkable and had to be modified. With fewer obligations, and under the charge of a minister undeniably able and ostentatiously uncorrupt, the Civil List continued to pile up debts. Twenty years after Burke's Act had become law the debt was over £1,000,000. Burke's Act did nothing towards solving the problem of Crown indebtedness, for it was based on an incorrect postulate – that the Civil List, when stripped of the means of corruption, was sufficient for the normal purposes of government. Burke did not abolish all sinecures – indeed he defended their use as a reward for services rendered, and shortly after his bill became law he himself was in search of a sinecure. Thus a great opportunity was missed to reform the system of court and government. In fairness to Burke it should be said that he had no such aim in view. He contended that there was nothing fundamentally wrong with the system. Even if he had intended a thorough reformation, he lacked the time and the knowledge. Reform was to be a matter of years not of months, a slow process forced upon the nation by conscience and the demands of war. Burke had a genius for labour, but even he could not tackle at the same time reform in Great Britain and in India.

Yet some abuses were rectified and a new spirit was abroad. The old system was no longer defended by prescription and men no longer feared reform as the prelude to revolution. Burke conferred a great advantage on King George. He liberated the Crown from the suspicion of corruption and increased its moral stature. The personal power of the King as distinct from the political influence of the Crown depended on the character of the monarch and the respect in which he was held by his people. After 1782 King George could no longer be accused of bribing Members of Parliament. His personal authority was greater in the last thirty years of his reign than in the previous twenty. It was so great that had he not been followed by two incapable successors and a young and inexperienced girl, the nineteenth century might have witnessed a reversion to a more monarchical system of government. The Albertine monarchy of the 1840s and 1850s regained much of the prestige which had been lost by King George IV and King William IV, and the power of the Crown remained substantial until Queen Victoria's immense energies were sapped by old age. In 1894, at the age of 74, she exercised for the last time in the history of the monarchy the prerogative for which her grandfather had so strenuously contended – the right to choose her Prime Minister without the advice of the politicians. There was much of King George III in Queen Victoria, and he would have been proud of his granddaughter.

So it may be said that the King achieved something like the reign of virtue he had dreamt of when he studied under Bute at Kew. 'The prince once possessed of the nation's confidence, the people's love', he had written in

371

his youthful essay on the British political system, 'will be feared and respected abroad, adored at home by mixing private economy with public magnificence.' Thirty years later his dream came true. It came true by devious means, not always approved of and sometimes actively resisted by the King. Great Britain was a monarchy, not as Fox thought a republic presided over by a monarch. The Crown in Parliament was omnipotent in Great Britain but not – as the American war showed – in those territories of the Crown outside Great Britain. King George accepted Parliament as an equal partner with the Crown in this condominium and won his personal and constitutional duel with Fox. Fox depreciated the authority of the Crown; underestimated its strength in popular affections; and lost.

The Rockingham–Shelburne ministry was a strange throwback to the past. It was haunted by the ghost of Chatham and obsessed by the memories of old feuds. Of the cabinet of eleven, five had served under Chatham and another five had been prominent in the opposition to his ministry. Only Fox had entered politics since the days of Chatham. This was not a cabinet fit to take decisions, yet strong and decisive action was never more necessary. Although fighting had ended in America, war was still being waged against France, Spain, and Holland; affairs in India were in a critical state; and Ireland seemed about to follow America and throw off her dependence on Great Britain. Yet the cabinet was at sixes and sevens. Rockingham and Shelburne quarrelled over patronage and Fox and Shelburne over the conduct of peace negotiations. Fox and the Rockinghams wished to make an immediate recognition of American independence, partly on principle (they had advocated this since 1778) and partly in the hope of detaching the United States from France. Shelburne and the Chathamites held that independence should be conceded only as a condition of peace. The issue was complicated by Fox's dislike of Shelburne (another of Holland's old feuds which his son had taken over) and by the fact that each was conducting separate negotiations: Fox as Foreign Secretary with France, Shelburne as Home and Colonial Secretary with the former colonies.

The King retired into his shell and sulked, indulging 'the melancholy enjoyment of his own ill humour'. He declared he had nothing to say about the peace negotiations and would leave them entirely to his ministers. They had made it impossible to continue the war and must now make the best peace they could. But as the rift between Shelburne and Fox deepened and Shelburne set out to ingratiate himself with the King, the King threw his weight behind him. 'Common sense tells me', he wrote, 'that if unconditional independence is granted we cannot ever expect any understanding with America, for then we have given up the whole and have nothing to give for what we want from thence. Independence is certainly an unpleasant gift at best, but then it must be for such conditions of peace as may justify it.' 'Peace is the object of my heart', he declared, 'if it can be obtained without forfeiting the honour and essential rights of my kingdom'; and he never ceased to regret the Commons' resolution of 27 February. 'For every difficulty in concluding peace', he told Fox in July 1783, 'this country has alone to blame itself. After the extraordinary and never to be forgot vote of February 1782 and the hurry for negotiation that ensued, it is no wonder our enemies seeing our spirit so fallen have taken advantage of it.'

The independence of the United States was a fact: all the British government had to decide was when and how to recognize it. On 23 May Fox submitted a cabinet recommendation that independence should be recognized 'in the first instance, instead of making it a condition of a general treaty'. Two days later Shelburne informed the King that independence was to be conceded only as a condition of peace. Perhaps it is possible to explain this discrepancy without resorting to the supposition that either Fox or Shelburne had deliberately deceived the King. Anyone who has ever sat on a committee, whether it be the cabinet or a parochial church council, will know how difficult it is to reach a decision and how much more difficult for members to recollect what decision they have reached. In the Rockingham–Shelburne cabinet this difficulty was increased by the absence of an effective chairman and the fact that at least three members were congenitally incapable of holding a firm line on any political issue. For a month Fox and Shelburne proceeded in different directions until on 30 June the cabinet came down in favour of Shelburne. Fox at once declared that he would resign.

While these dissensions were taking place the ostensible head of the ministry lay on his deathbed. Rockingham had never enjoyed good health, the burden of office had enfeebled his constitution, and he fell a victim to the influenza epidemic which swept Europe in the spring of 1782. Even had he lived it is doubtful if the ministry could have survived much longer. Before it was realized how serious Rockingham's illness was, Shelburne and the King were making plans for a new cabinet, and on the evening of Rockingham's death the King offered Shelburne the Treasury 'with the fullest political confidence'. He wanted a ministry on a 'broad bottom', to include all parties. But he could not expect and perhaps did not desire the cooperation of the Rockinghams. Fox and Lord John Cavendish resigned and there were other resignations outside the cabinet. Still, sufficient of the Rockinghams remained to give the ministry the appearance of being drawn from all parties. But it was a hotch-potch ministry.

The King had won the first round. Fox was out and the Rockingham party split. But the odds were heavily in favour of Fox. Shelburne was handicapped by being in the House of Lords and by having no one of Fox's stature to lead the Commons. He was even more handicapped by his character. Though undeniably able and as his auto-biography shows of remarkable insight, he was unpopular and distrusted. Like his great master Chatham whom he imitated he was incapable of working with other men, and few who served under Shelburne wished to repeat the experience. Though he flattered the King and followed Chatham in decrying the idea of government by party, he was too devious and subtle for King George. The King never understood him (how many did?) and never liked him. Still, he gave him loyal support. Shelburne was by no means the ideal minister but he was infinitely prefer-able to Fox.

At this point the spotlight switches to North. Since his resignation North had lain low. He retained a consider-able following in the House of Commons, sufficient to give the game to whichever side he favoured. Almost at the same time Shelburne and Fox put out feelers for his support, and the fallen minister was in the happy position of being caressed and courted by the very men who had threatened him with impeachment and declared his con-tinuance in office a disaster for the nation. North relished the humour of the situation, but was too wise and too timid to commit himself until he saw the way clear. Parliament had risen for the summer recess and peace negotiations were still in progress. North preferred to hold his hand until he saw what sort of peace Shelburne was able to make.

It was not likely to be a good one. After the resolution of 27 February Great Britain had no alternative but to recognize the independence of the United States, to con-cede the back lands formerly part of Canada, and to accept fair promises (never meant to be implemented) in favour of the loyalists. With regard to France and Spain there was more room to manoeuvre. The King in his anxiety for peace was prepared to cede Gibraltar to Spain,

375

which he scornfully described as 'this proud fortress' – the 'source of another war or at least of a constant lurking enmity'. Gibraltar was a cause of expense not of profit to Great Britain. How much better to exchange it for an island in the West Indies! 'It has been my purpose', the King wrote on 11 December 1782, 'ever since peace has been on the carpet to get rid of ideal advantages for those that by a good administration may prove solid ones to this country.' When the draft treaty was laid before him he wrote to Lord Grantham, Fox's successor as Foreign Secretary:

The more I reflect on the want of sailors and soldiers to enable us to carry on with any probability of advantage the war against so many enemies . . . the more I thank Providence for having through so many difficulties, among which the want of union and zeal at home is not to be omitted, enabled so good a peace with France, Spain, and I trust soon with the Dutch, to be concluded.

It was doubtful if the House of Commons would agree.

Everything now depended on North, and on 7 August 1782 the King wrote to his former minister:

Lord North has so often whilst in office assured me that whenever I would consent to his retiring he would give the most cordial support to such an administration as I might approve of, that I should not think I either acted properly to my own affairs or placed that confidence in his declarations if I did not express my strongest wishes that he will give the most active support the next session of Parliament to the administration formed with my thorough approbation on the death of Lord Rockingham, and that during the recess he will call on the country gentlemen who certainly have great attention for him to come early and shew their countenance, by which I may be enabled to keep the constitution from being entirely annihilated, which must be the case if Mr Fox and his associates are not withstood. Many strange scenes have occurred in this country but none more so than the present contest. It is no less than whether the sole direction of my kingdoms shall be trusted in the hands of Mr Fox.

North's reply was cautious. He would not commit himself until the peace terms were known nor could he answer for men who were independent of both government and opposition. The King was displeased and suspected North of hanging back for political reasons. This was less than fair to North, who was concerned for his public reputation and determined not to contradict the principles he had professed when in office. North also had a grievance which did not induce him to consider favourably any request from the King.[4]

On the day North resigned, the King had assured him: 'I ever did and ever shall look on you as a friend as well as faithful servant.' But this feeling did not last long. The King was in an irritable mood in the summer of 1782, a prey to self-righteousness and self-pity. He felt the need for a scapegoat on whom he could discharge his malaise, and North became the unlucky victim. He was always slap-dash in doing business, though perfectly honest and above corruption, and had been careless about the secret service accounts. When these were submitted, the King wrote in high indignation:

I must express my astonishment at the quarterly account books of the secret service being only made up to the 5th of April 1780, consequently that two years are as yet not stated. I cannot help saying it is a most shameful piece of neglect I ever knew. No business can ever be admitted as an excuse for not doing that; if every sum received had instantly been set down, as well as every article paid, this could not have happened. The Duke of Grafton never let a month elapse after the quarter without getting the book finished and delivering it.

When the King came to examine North's election accounts, he found further reason to be annoyed. To finance the general election of 1780 North had borrowed from Henry and Robert Drummond, the bankers, £30,000 at 5 per cent interest. The loan had been incurred by North personally but on the instructions of the

377

King and for government business. When he left office
neither principal nor interest had been paid. It should
have been paid from the election account which the King
financed by monthly contributions of £1,000 from the
Privy Purse, but no payments had been made into the
election account since February 1781. Possibly North had
neglected to ask the King for the money or else the King
wanted it for other purposes. The only way North could
see of liquidating the debt was to pay £13,000 by retro-
spective contributions to the election account (£1,000 for
each month since February 1781). This would leave about
£22,000 yet to pay (including a debt to North of £2,754),
which the ex-minister suggested might be met out of the
Privy Purse.

The King was dumbfounded at this unexpected demand. With the Rockingham ministry about to make
stringent inquiries into Crown expenditure, how could he
hope to find £35,000 for an election debt? North should
have taken care to collect the monthly £1,000 for the
election fund and paid the remainder out of the secret
service account. Now it was too late. The new Treasury
would certainly not authorize payment from the secret
service account. And if they found out that the King had
been financing elections from his Privy Purse they might
revive Grenville's demand for Treasury control over the
Privy Purse. The King undertook to pay 'by degrees' the
£13,000 that should have come from the election account
and repudiated the remainder of the debt. The remaining
£17,000 due to the Drummonds, plus the accumulated
interest on the whole sum, North must pay from his own
pocket.

When every possible censure has been passed on
North's carelessness, it must be said that he did not deserve this treatment from the King. King George was
more than unsympathetic: he was unjust. Although North
was legally responsible for the money, the King had a
moral responsibility which he could not shake off merely

because North had failed to keep him informed. The money had been borrowed on the King's account and Drummond's would never have lent it had they not known that it was for the King's service. The best that can be said for the King is that he was so upset at the loss of the colonies and the change of ministry that he allowed a legitimate complaint to pervert him into an act of gross injustice. The result was that North's gratitude to the King for paying his debts and for favours done to himself and his family was replaced by a sense of grievance. And in the end the King had to pay after all for North did not have the money. 'It was not owing to inaccuracy in me', the King wrote to Henry Drummond on 24 October 1784, when apologizing for the delay in payment, 'but the most barefaced fraud on the part of Lord North.' This was untrue; but by then North had given occasion for other and more serious complaints.

It is impossible to say how far the King's behaviour over the election debt influenced North's political conduct at the beginning of 1783. Probably North would have joined Fox in any case. He was proscribed by Shelburne, or rather by Shelburne's Chancellor of the Exchequer William Pitt (son of the great Chatham), who declared he would never sit in the cabinet with North. Moreover there were solid political advantages to be gained from an alliance with Fox. North was strongly opposed to parliamentary reform, and by joining Fox he could put a veto on a measure which he regarded as dangerous to the constitution. Fox's party was rich in parliamentary talent and North's ablest friends urged him in that direction. A Fox–North coalition offered every prospect of a stable ministry and North felt there ought to be an end to political controversy over dead issues. The American colonies were lost and there was little point in arguing who had been responsible. The past could not be undone; what was now needed was economy, reasonable reform, and national unity. These aims were more likely to be achieved by joining Fox than by supporting Shelburne out of office. On 14 February 1783 Fox and North met and soon came to an understanding. They would unite to defeat Shelburne and then form a ministry themselves. As to the constitutional rights of the Crown – 'The King ought to be treated with all sort of respect and attention', said North, 'but the appearance of power is all that a King of this country can have.' Fox, who intended to have all the substance of power, agreed. Did North really believe this? Was this dictum based upon his recent unhappy experiences with the King and the debt of £22,000 which had been unfairly saddled upon him and which he could not pay? Or did North say this just to please Fox? Whatever the answer, this was not a correct statement of constitutional practice. But it was an accurate forecast of what Fox intended.

On 17 February during the debate on the treaty Fox announced the existence of the coalition in words which were long remembered and used against him:

It is neither wise nor noble to keep up animosities for ever. It is not my nature to bear malice or to live in ill will. My friendships are perpetual, my enmities are not so. *Amicitiae sempiternae, inimicitiae placabiles.* . . . The American war and the American question is at an end . . . and it is therefore wise and candid to put an end also to the ill will, the animosity, the rancour and the feuds which it occasioned.

Perhaps only Fox would have had the courage and candour to make such a declaration, and perhaps it would have been wiser had he not done so.

The division was taken in the early hours of 18 February and resulted in a defeat for Shelburne's ministry by 224 votes to 208. The King had so little expected this that he assumed from the letter announcing the division that the ministry had won. On 22 February on a motion directly censuring the treaty the ministry was again beaten, and on the 24th Shelburne submitted his resignation. There could be no gainsaying the fact that opinion in the House of Commons was against him.

'I am sorry it has been my lot', the King wrote, 'to reign in the most profligate age and when the most unnatural and factious coalition seems to have taken place.' He reverted to his attitude of the previous year. 'No consideration shall make me throw myself into the hands of any party.' There must be a coalition not merely of Fox and North but of 'the best of all' – a non-party ministry. The King first offered the Treasury to Pitt, who declined; and then summoned North and authorized him to talk with Fox. He was not opposed to having Fox and his friends in the cabinet provided they would accept the lead of an independent peer unconnected with party. Fox answered that he could not serve unless the Duke of Portland, Rockingham's successor as titular head of the party, were appointed First Lord of the Treasury. The King broke off the negotiations and cast his net wider, but could find no one to encounter Fox and North in the House of Commons. In his despair he reverted to the idea of abdication and composed a speech to be delivered to the House of Lords. Then he thought better of it and on 12 March accepted Fox's terms.

Up to this point Fox had played his hand well. His demands were not unreasonable. In the difficult situation following the American war it was essential to have a strong united ministry possessing the confidence of both the Crown and the House of Commons. Fox was entitled to demand that his colleagues should be in general agreement with his policy and to ask for assurances that he enjoyed the political confidence of the Crown. If these had been all his demands he might have won over the King. They were no more than Pitt asked and received a year later. The King was sensible of the nation's need, and on several occasions during his reign had accepted ministers who were personally obnoxious to him because they could be of service. In 1765 he had delegated the authority of the Crown to the Duke of Cumberland; in 1766 he had given Chatham virtually a free hand. After pronouncing anathemas against Newcastle, Sandwich, Richmond, Shelburne, and half a dozen others of cabinet stature (to say nothing of lesser lights), he had yet admitted them to his service when they could be of use. He had demonstrated over and over again that he was prepared to put the public good before his personal feelings. There was no political reason why he should not have done so in 1783. Some sort of coalition was inevitable, and that between Fox and North was no more unprincipled than one between Shelburne and North (which the King had favoured). When Fox declared in the House of Commons that bygones should be bygones he was speaking plain common sense.

But it was not enough for Fox to have his political demands accepted by the King. The King must also be humiliated. Only thus could Fox avenge his father's wrongs and satisfy his hatred of the King. The King must be allowed no say in the formation of the ministry. There must be no member of the cabinet who did not owe political allegiance to either Fox or North. Patronage and policy must be at Fox's disposal. 'The appearance of power' was to be all the King should have. In effect, King George must abdicate in favour of King Fox. 'Put not your trust in princes', had been Holland's advice to his son; and Fox neither expected nor desired the confidence of the King. It is difficult to see how any eighteenth-century ministry could last long without a reasonable degree of confidence between the King and his first minister. Fox had an immensely strong hand in the spring of 1783. Instead of being content with a reasonable return, his personal dislike of the King led him to overplay it. He went for grand slam when he should have been satisfied with game. He played his hand like a gambler.

The one hope the King had of avoiding the coalition

was that Fox and North should quarrel about the disposal of offices. This they did but quickly patched up their quarrel. On 17 March Portland informed North, in a letter to be transmitted to the King, that he was prepared to form a ministry and expected to receive the King's commands in person. He continued with words whose significance was not lost on the King:

If it is His Majesty's pleasure to place me at the head of the Treasury, it is impossible to suppose that he means to withhold from me any part of his confidence, but it is very necessary that the publick should be convinced of that circumstance, and that I should be authorized to speak to those whose assistance may be thought necessary to apply for, in such a manner as may satisfy them of my being possessed of the means of fulfilling the engagements I may propose to them.

On 21 March Portland attended at the Queen's House with a list of the proposed seven members of the cabinet. The King refused to look at it. 'I had declared', he wrote, 'that I must see and examine the whole plan of arrangements before I could give any opinion on particular parts of it.' Portland expostulated, 'began to grow warm', and said that this showed a want of confidence in him. A further audience on 23 March also ended in deadlock. It was in vain that Portland explained that he had not yet prepared a complete list of all appointments. The King should have confidence in the cabinet and trust that whatever they proposed would be for his service. This, replied the King, 'was asking more than any man above forty could engage to do'. He insisted on his right to see the 'plan of arrangement'.

Unless the King could find an alternative minister for the House of Commons all this was merely postponing the evil day. The country had now been without a ministry for four weeks, grave and urgent problems were awaiting decision, and the House of Commons was growing impatient. Pitt was again approached, hesitated, and again declined. Every possible suggestion was considered

383

and found to be impracticable. 'I am the more pressing to attempt to catch at anything', the King wrote to Thurlow on 28 March, 'as I feel if someone will not assist me I must within a couple of days take the step I have so often hinted to you.' A message to Parliament announcing his abdication and a letter to the Prince of Wales were already prepared. 'The first time I appeared as your sovereign in this place', the message begins, 'now above twenty-two years, I had the pleasing hope that being born among you I might have proved the happy instrument of conciliating all parties and thus collecting to the service of the State the most respectable and most able persons this kingdom produced.' This had been his constant aim; but 'by the obstinacy of a powerful party that has long publicly manifested a resolution not to aid in the service of the empire unless the whole executive management of affairs is thrown entirely into its hands' it had become impossible. 'My obedience to the oath I took at my coronation prevents my exceeding the powers vested in me, or submitting to be a cipher in the trammels of any self-created band.' He had therefore decided to abdicate the throne of Great Britain and to retire to Hanover, 'the original patrimony of my ancestors'. He concluded with a dignified, indeed noble, farewell:

You may depend on my arduous attention to educate my children in the paths of religion, virtue and every other good principle that may render them if ever called in any line to the service of Great Britain, not unworthy of the kindness they may hereafter meet with from a people whom collective I shall ever love.

May that all wise Providence who can direct the inmost thoughts as well as actions of men give my son and successor not only every assistance in guiding his conduct, but restore that sense of religious and moral duties in this kingdom to the want of which every evil that has arisen owes its source; and may I to the latest hour of my life, though now resolved for ever to quit this island, have the comfort of hearing that the endeavours of my son, though they cannot be more sincere than mine have been, for the prosperity of Great Britain, may be crowned with better sucess.

As one reads this speech one wonders what would have been the reaction of Parliament had it actually been delivered. It must be remembered that the majority of the Lords and Commons knew little of what had been happening in the last few weeks except through sources hostile to the King. They did not know, for example, that as early as 3 March the King had agreed to Fox's return to office, and that on 12 March he had accepted Fox's demand for Portland as head of the Treasury. They did not know of the dispute between the two partners of the coalition or of Fox's wish to humiliate the King. Had Fox's aim been no more than he described it to the House of Commons – to induce the King to accept a minister not 'by his personal favour alone, but by the public voice, by the sense of his Parliament, and the sense of his people' – it might have been achieved weeks before.

On the evening of 1 April the King submitted. He sent for North and told him the cabinet could kiss hands the next day, 'after which the Duke of Portland and he should plan the arrangements of employments'. 'I have withstood it', he wrote to Lord Temple, 'till not a single man is willing to come to my assistance and till the House of Commons has taken every step but insisting on this faction by name being elected ministers.' He concluded with words that boded no long life to the ministers:

A ministry which I have avowedly attempted to avoid by calling on every other description of men, cannot be supposed to have either my favour or confidence and as such I shall most certainly refuse any honours that may be asked by them . . . I hope many months will not elapse before the Grenvilles, the Pitts, and other men of abilities and character will relieve me from a situation that nothing but the supposition that no other means remained of preventing the public finances from being materially affected would have compelled me to submit to.

2 April 1783, when Fox kissed hands, was a day of humiliation for King George comparable only in its misery to 22 May 1765. Students of the ironical in history will not fail to notice that in 1783 the King appealed for deliverance to the son of the man who had presented the ultimatum of 1765.

Yet the King had two invaluable weapons, as yet unused, that were ultimately to bring him victory. The first was the power to create peerages. The dispute between the King and Portland over the 'plan of arrangements' was not concerned with offices but with peerages. The King never interfered in the minor appointments to a ministry, and having accepted the cabinet he was not likely to quarrel with the coalition about who should be appointed to the Boards of Treasury or Admiralty. He could not swallow the camel and strain at the gnat. When Portland told the King on 17 March that he must be 'possessed of the means of fulfilling the engagements' he had made to his followers, he was asking for authority to promise peerages. At his first audience as head of the Treasury he asked a dukedom for Lord Hertford and a marquessate for Lord Fitzwilliam – one from each party which composed the coalition. 'I declined entering on that subject', wrote the King. He did well to say nothing. Had Fox been able to demonstrate to his followers that he could appoint to the peerage as well as recommend to office, the coalition would have been in for life. But hard as he had pressed the King, he could not advance his pretensions so far. He could not stand up in the House of Commons and declare he was unable to serve because the King had refused a dukedom to Lord Hertford. So long as the King kept the creation of peerages in his own hand, the coalition's tenure of office was uncertain.

The second weapon was even more deadly. Fox had appealed to the King to choose his ministers according to 'the sense of Parliament', to 'the sense of his people'. Parliament had pronounced in favour of Fox. But what if

King George were to exercise his prerogative to dissolve Parliament and appeal to the highest court of all – to 'the sense of his people'?

The coalition offered a prospect of stable government such as Great Britain had not know since the outbreak of the American rebellion. If only Fox could avoid George Grenville's mistakes, he might hope to obtain the political if not the personal confidence of the King. North had advised Fox when they concluded their alliance that the King 'ought to be treated with all sort of respect and attention', and Fox intended to follow this advice. A fortnight after taking office (16 April 1783) he wrote to the King:

Mr Fox hopes that Your Majesty will not think him presumptuous or improperly intruding upon Your Majesty with professions, if he begs leave most humbly to implore Your Majesty to believe that both the Duke of Portland and he have nothing so much at heart as to conduct Your Majesty's affairs, both with respect to measures and to persons, in the manner that may give Your Majesty the most satisfaction, and that, whenever Your Majesty will be graciously pleased to condescend even to hint your inclinations upon any subject, that it will be the study of Your Majesty's ministers to show how truly sensible they are of Your Majesty's goodness.

The King docketed the letter: 'No answer'. He waited to see how far Fox's practice would follow his professions. He did not have to wait long. Fox could never resist the urge to take the part of the rebel, whether as a son against his father or a people against its sovereign. When the King and the Prince of Wales quarrelled, Fox, the spoilt child, forgot his duty to the King and instinctively took the side of the Prince.

The King's two eldest sons, George, Prince of Wales (later King George IV) and Prince Frederick (later Duke of York) were born within just over a year of each other and were brought up together. At first they were under the charge of Lady Charlotte Finch, governess of the royal children, but in 1771 the King took them away from Lady Charlotte and gave them their own household. They were rather young for it – the Prince was not yet nine, while the King himself had been twelve when he had been put into the hands of tutors. The King invited Lord Holdernesse, formerly Pitt's colleague as Secretary of State, to be their governor. 'I am in the fifty-third year of my age', he told the King, 'and can not expect that my infirmities will diminish or my talents increase at that time of life.'[5] The young princes were not the most tractable of boys and seem to have led their governor something of a dance. In 1774 Holdernesse's health broke down and he was obliged to go for a long tour to the Continent. Some of the letters he wrote to his charges during the year he was abroad have survived.[6] They show how conscientiously he took his duties; they are full of the most irreproachable moral sentiments and abound with good advice; they would have delighted the King but his sons must have found them dull reading. The boys began to find out what an old stick their governor was, and when Holdernesse returned he discovered he had lost all influence over his pupils. 'I have not obtained that share of the young princes' confidence', he complained to the King on 26 April 1776, 'which alone could enable me to be of use to them.'[7]

The King now faced the same difficulty his grandfather had faced in 1752 and which was almost unavoidable under the eighteenth-century system of royal education – how to find suitable persons for a difficult and laborious task. He turned first to Lord Bruce, whom he had long known and esteemed: a man of blameless private life, devoted to the Church of England, and little interested in politics. But Bruce was no more fitted to bring up young boys than his predecessor, and only strong pressure from the King induced him to accept. The King was so grateful that he promised him an earldom – one of the few instances during the reign of a peerage being conferred without solicitation.

Richard Hurd, Bishop of Lichfield, the new preceptor, was the King's favourite on the episcopal bench and a personal friend. He was a scholar whose editions of Horace won the praise of Gibbon, a humanitarian and philanthropist, a vigorous apologist for the Church of England, and no politician. But the King's respect for learning was not shared by his sons, and Hurd was no more successful as preceptor than Bruce was as governor. The outstanding appointment in the new household was George Hotham, the sub-governor. In the difficult years that lay ahead Hotham proved an able and devoted servant to both King and Prince of Wales, and the Prince would have done well had he listened more to his advice.

Hardly had the household been set up than Bruce backed out, pleading the distress his appointment had caused his wife. 'I have met with some severe blows', the King wrote, 'but this is perhaps the strongest I have ever received.'[8] He turned to Bruce's elder brother, the Duke of Montagu. 'I can not help feeling', wrote North, 'that the Duke of Montagu will grow tired of the confinement and necessary attention of his employment, and put His Majesty again to the inconvenience of a change.'[9] To make sure he did not, the King offered him an earldom with remainder to his daughter, an honour that Montagu had long coveted. 'I soon persuaded him', the King wrote, 'of the distress this occasioned, and that being caused by his family he was in duty as well as in honour bound to extricate me out of it by accepting the post himself.' And when Montagu did so – 'I instantly carried him to the Queen that there might be a witness of his having accepted.'[10] When a man had to be dragooned in this way it was hardly likely that he would give satisfactory service.

The King told the new governor that he wished his sons to be brought up 'as examples to the rising generation'.[11] Their daily timetable was similar to that of himself as a

389

boy. They rose at seven-thirty and were in the school-room at eight. From then until eight in the evening with intervals for exercise and dinner they were with their tutors. After supper they were to read by themselves 'and give an account of what they have read to the sub-preceptor'. Apart from an hour on alternate days, no time was set for play or recreation. Sunday was a day of rest, with attendance at church, at court, and religious instruction.[12]

A modern educationist will no doubt shake his head and say this was no way to bring up young boys. No wonder they turned out as they did! It was however the only way the King knew, the way he himself had been educated. The eighteenth century was impressed with the disposition of young people to get into trouble if left to themselves and believed it best to regulate their lives. The King accepted without question the conventional ideas of his age just as most people do today. He wished his children to grow up with a sense of duty and service, first to God and then to their country; and he tried to set them a standard at which to aim. But neither the Prince of Wales nor Prince Frederick was as docile as their father had been and neither became an example to the rising generation. King George's educational method was a failure. And perhaps any method he could have tried would have been equally a failure.

The hostility between the King and the Prince of Wales began early. The Duke of Kent, the King's fourth son (father of the future Queen Victoria) wrote in 1809 that 'from his earliest years my eldest brother was his mother's favourite, my second brother his father's';[13] and the Prince told Lord Malmesbury in 1785 that his father hated him and had done since he was seven. This statement should not be taken as objective truth. The Prince was highly exasperated with his father at the time and was trying to win Malmesbury's support. But there can be no doubt that the Duke of York was the King's favourite son and yet that this did not lessen the affection between the brothers.

In 1780 the Prince reached his eighteenth year and the King gave him a separate establishment but not an independent income – a half-way stage between adolescence and manhood. He was uneasy about his son and felt that he was not yet sufficiently mature to be given full independence (as the King had been at the same age). In a letter of 14 August 1780 he chided the Prince for lack of progress in his studies, 'love of dissipation' ('for some months ... trumpeted in the public papers'), and inattention to the duties of religion. Yet the tone of his letter was friendly, indeed cordial; and the King appealed to his son to help him support the heavy burden of kingship:

The numberless trials and constant torments I meet with in public life must certainly affect any man. . . . The experience of now near twenty years has convinced me that however long it may please the Almighty to extend my days, yet I have no reason to expect any diminution of my public anxiety. Where am I therefore to turn for comfort but into the bosom of my own family?

'I wish more and more to have you as a friend', he wrote on 22 November 1780, 'and in that light to guide you, rather than with the authority of a parent.' He laid down certain restrictions on the Prince's conduct. He was not to go to masquerades (no reader of *Pamela* or *Peregrine Pickle* will fail to understand why), nor to 'balls or assemblies at private houses, which has never been the custom for Princes of Wales'. Yet far from putting leading strings on his son, the King gave him more liberty than most fathers at the time would have done. As events showed, he gave him too much. By the date the King wrote this letter the Prince already had a mistress.

He had fallen a victim to the worst type of woman. Mary Robinson was an actress and society prostitute, and was determined to make as much as she could from her connection with the Prince. She got from him a promissory note for £20,000 (to be paid when he came of age), and to put a further bite on him threatened to publish his letters. As the Prince had no money he had to confess the affair to the King, who authorized the payment of £5,000 from the secret service account for the recovery of the letters. 'I am happy to say', wrote the King, with that touch of self-approbation which he could never resist, 'that I never was personally engaged in such a transaction which perhaps makes me feel this the stronger.' The King did not know that Fox had been called in to recover the promissory note, which the Prince's inamorata had surrendered for an annuity to herself and her daughter.

Prince Frederick also had a mistress, but he had conducted his affair more circumspectly. He had made no foolish promises nor spent any money on her. Perhaps being the favourite son he was less inclined to offend his father. Prince Frederick had his way to make in the world. He had been placed in the army, and in December 1780 left for Hanover to complete his military training. Deprived of the steadying influence of his brother, the Prince of Wales went from bad to worse. The King, who now began to confide in his second son, wrote to him on 13 March 1781 with the news that the Prince had been ill with 'a most violent irruption':

Thank Heaven it seems now nearly over and if he will take this as a warning may save his life. . . . He has undoubtedly both in eating and drinking been much too free, every one of his family [i.e. his household] were surprised at it from the first time they dined with him. Indeed his behaviour is not such as to gain credit with the world. A buck is a *mauvais ton* for a young gentleman and shews a want of education, but in a prince it is much worse. God never made distinctions of rank but that with it is expected a propriety of behaviour should ensue.

Gerard Lake, the Prince's equerry, shortly before leaving

for active service in America in January 1781, also gave him good advice:

I think your great good nature is liable to be imposed upon by people who have not the smallest pretensions to your civility or attention, and who will presume upon that goodness and become troublesome to you. . . . A knowledge of the world and of men is very necessary and the most difficult to be acquired. . . . It is the more so for you, as the retired and private education unavoidably chalked out for a prince has prevented you from knowing so much of them as young men who have reaped the benefit of a publick school.

Here was another difficulty which attended the education of royal children and which was not solved until our own time. It was impossible in the eighteenth century to send them to school, and yet if they never met other children on equal terms they would be slow to acquire 'knowledge of the world and of men'. Royalty inevitably attracted toadeaters and flatterers concerned to profit from the connection. The King knew that his own upbringing had been too sheltered. He had made a favourite of the first man who had been kind to him; and how fortunate he was to find such a friend as Bute who was genuinely concerned for the King's welfare. But perhaps if he had known more of men he would not have become so dependent on Bute and many of the troubles of the early years of the reign would have been avoided. The King tried to ensure that his own children should neither live too sheltered nor be given their independence too soon. He placed his hopes for the future on their religious training and the example of their parents. But the Prince of Wales was a difficult son.

The Prince was weak. He could never resist temptation, whether a woman offering her body or a dealer offering a picture at an extravagant price. He was foolish, and cared only for the momentary gratification of his pleasures. He was vain and cowardly and no trust could be placed in his word. He was uninfluenced by religious feelings. Yet he

393

was charming and plausible and because of this and his position as heir to the throne never lacked friends. He was more sociable than his father and an entertaining companion at the dinner table. It took time to understand the King. It was much easier to like the Prince and much easier to become disillusioned with him.

Shortly before the Prince reached his nineteenth birthday, he seduced (or was seduced by – it is not clear who took the initiative) Madame Hardenberg, wife of a Hanoverian officer living in London – later as Prince von Hardenberg one of the restorers of the Prussian monarchy after Jena. 'How I love her!' he wrote to Frederick. 'How I would sacrifice every earthly thing to her! By Heavens, I shall go distracted! My brain will split!' (He was to write similar nonsense about other women.) Her husband found out and took her to the Continent, and the Prince formed the wild notion of following them and sent Lord Southampton, his Groom of the Stole, to ask the King's permission to go abroad. The story reached the newspapers and the Prince confessed it to his mother with permission to inform the King. 'You know our father's stern disposition', the Prince wrote to Prince Frederick, 'everything that was shocking is to be expected from him.' It is difficult to see what else was to be expected from him at the revelation of his son's intrigue with the wife of one of his officers.

The King was more hurt than angry. He replied to the Prince on 6 May 1781:

Do read over the letter I wrote to you a few days after your last birthday, and the one in December previous to the appointment of your family. You confessed they gave you pleasure and satisfied you. Examine yourself and see how far your conduct has been conformable to them, and then draw your conclusion whether you must not give me many an uneasy moment. I wish to live with you as a friend, but then by your behaviour you must deserve it. If I did not state these things I should not fulfill my duty either to my God or to my country. I say as little as possible from an hope that your reason will begin to act. Whenever it does, I do not doubt but instead of pain you will give me pleasure.

'Nothing you can do can long be a secret', he reminded the Prince, 'the very companions of your follies ever repeat what happens.' Instead of being the means 'of restoring decency in this kingdom', the Prince was bringing discredit on the monarchy.

When you read this carefully over, you will find an affectionate father trying to save his son from perdition; one who knows any evil you have acquired is not owing to bad example at home, who wishes you may become worthy of the situation that Divine Providence probably intends for you, who knows you are not wanting in natural talents if you will exert them, and hopes you have an heart to feel what is owing to those who have from your tenderest infancy treated you with kindness, and are desirous of continuing it.

'The King is excessively cross and ill-tempered', wrote the Prince to his brother on 18 September 1781, '. . . we are not upon the very best terms.' 'For God's sake', replied Prince Frederick, 'do everything which you can to keep well with him. Consider he is vexed enough in publick affairs. It is therefore your business not to make that still worse.' The King's short temper during the last weeks of the North ministry may have arisen as much from the behaviour of the Prince of Wales as from the opposition.

By the time the Prince had reached his twentieth birthday he had committed every folly but one. He had not yet engaged in politics in opposition to his father. But the urge to follow the family tradition was irresistible. 'The new administration [that of Rockingham and Shelburne] seem to wish me better than the former one', he wrote to Prince Frederick on 10 May 1782; and by the end of the year he had enlisted under Fox's banner. It was as natural for Fox to take the part of the Prince against the King as it was for the Prince to go into opposition. Thus the establishment of the coalition in office was a political victory for the Prince of Wales as well as for Fox.

The Prince looked to the ministry to forward his interests. He would come of age in August 1783, and the King referred the question of his financial establishment to the cabinet. The Prince was extravagant and already in debt and wanted as large an income as possible. The cabinet's first proposal was that he should be given £100,000 a year: about £12,000 from the revenues of the Duchy of Cornwall, and the remainder to be voted by Parliament. This would give him a larger income than any previous unmarried Prince of Wales. The King had received only £35,000; Frederick, Prince of Wales's allowance had been £50,000 as a bachelor, and had only been increased to £100,000 five years after his marriage. Had precedents been followed, the Prince would have been granted £50,000 (plus the Duchy of Cornwall revenues) with an assurance that this would be increased to £100,000 on his marriage.

There were reasons why the King was disposed to accept the cabinet's recommendations. During the Prince's minority the revenues of the Duchy of Cornwall had been paid into the secret service account. The King had followed the precedent of his grandfather who during King George III's minority had appropriated the revenues of the duchy for the service of government. But King George III, not being the son of the sovereign, never was Duke of Cornwall and had no claim to its revenues. The Prince of Wales was Duke of Cornwall from his birth and was entitled by right to the revenues of the duchy.

If the King had treated Prince Frederick the same way, the Prince of Wales would have had less cause for complaint. Prince Frederick also had an independent income, derived from the secularized bishopric of Osnabruck in the Holy Roman Empire to which he had been appointed by his father in 1764. But the King had not appropriated these revenues: they had been allowed to accumulate, and when Prince Frederick came of age in 1784 were handed over to him as a lump sum. The King had used the Prince of Wales's income, which was derived from the Crown, for the service of the Crown, but not Prince Frederick's income, which was derived from the Holy Roman Empire. Thus the Prince of Wales could fairly lay claim to a higher income than was warranted by precedent.

At first the King demurred to the cabinet's proposal and asked them to reconsider it. He thought £100,000 was too much for an unmarried Prince of Wales, especially when taxation was high after an unsuccessful war. Portland replied that the cabinet considered it possible to propose this sum to Parliament on the understanding that it was not to be increased when the Prince married and that he was to receive no initial grant for buying or furnishing a house. This the King accepted. Carlton House, where his mother had lived (and where the King had held the first Privy Council of his reign) was unoccupied and would do very well as a town house. There was no country house available, but apartments would be reserved for the Prince in Windsor Castle.

But the cabinet were having second thoughts. At least two members – North and Lord John Cavendish, Chancellor of the Exchequer – thought it unwise, when new and unpopular taxation had recently been imposed, to suggest to Parliament so large a sum as £100,000. After allowing for the Duchy revenues, Parliament was being asked to provide £88,000 a year. It would facilitate the business in the House of Commons if the King would contribute £50,000 from the Civil List leaving only £38,000 as Parliament's share. Perhaps the money might be made up to the King in some other way. This was the purport of a long, embarrassed, and extremely confused letter which Portland sent to the King on 15 June.

'It is impossible for me to find words expressive enough of my indignation and astonishment', began the King's reply. Having never liked the plan of the larger income, he was glad of an excuse to get out of it. He had only consented to it on the understanding that Parliament was to provide the money. But if the money was to come from the Civil List then the King would determine how much the Prince should get. He reverted to his original idea – £50,000 from the Civil List and £12,000 from the Duchy – which would still give the Prince £27,000 a year more than he had received as Prince of Wales. The unlucky Portland received the vials of the King's wrath.

Believe me [the King wrote to North] no consideration can ever make me either forget or forgive what has passed, and the public shall know how well founded the principles of economy are in those who have so loudly preached it up, who have most shamefully on that supposed principle diminished the peace establishment, yet, where they think it will answer their own wicked purposes, are ready to be most barefacedly lavish.

The next day the King apologized to Portland. His conduct, he said, had been 'in every respect unwarranted and perfectly unjustifiable', and was to be attributed to 'the unfortunate event of the American war' which had 'soured and ruined his temper'. Though the King did not say so, the conduct of the Prince of Wales had soured and ruined it even more. In the end a compromise was arranged, with the King having the best of it. The Prince received £50,000 a year from the Civil List, and Parliament made a grant of £60,000 to pay the Prince's debts (estimated at £29,000) and to cover the expense of furnishing Carlton House.

Perhaps no episode in Fox's life is more revealing of his character. It was folly to take the part of the Prince of Wales against the King : it was madness when the cabinet was not behind him. How could Fox possibly hope to force his plan on the King when his Chancellor of the Exchequer would not support him? On the first dispute in the Royal Family, Fox forgot the professions he had made to the King and instinctively took the part of the son against the father. 'I beg leave to repeat again', he wrote to the Prince, 'that I think myself bound by every principle of honour as well of gratitude to take whatever part your Royal Highness chuses to prescribe me in this business.' In short, he regarded himself as responsible to the Prince of Wales, not to the King, and was prepared to stake the future of the ministry on the event. He had now to be got off his promise, and the Duchess of Devonshire was employed to request the Prince to release Fox.

In a dutiful letter the Prince promised his father 'as far as it lays in my power . . . not to exceed my income'. The King replied that 'not a single word shall be mentioned... relative to any past unhappy misunderstandings'.[14]

It is just possible (but only just) that had it not been for Fox's attitude towards the Prince's establishment the King might have learnt to accept the coalition. 'Though in states as well as in men', he wrote pointedly to Fox on 7 September 1783 (the letter concerned France's delay in signing the definitive treaty), 'where dislike has once arose, I never expect to see cordiality.' There could be no cordiality between King George and Fox but there might have been tolerable relations. The last hope vanished when Fox took the part of the Prince of Wales against the King.

Yet it was impossible to dismiss Fox. Who could be found to take his place? Pitt had twice been tried and had twice refused. The King poured out his troubles to Temple but Temple could not help him. Fox's successor must be in the House of Commons. The King spent an unhappy summer, mourning the death of his four-year-old son Prince Octavius and brooding over his political misfortunes.

Now that peace had been concluded and a modus vivendi reached with Ireland (to last, however, for only a few years) India was the most urgent problem facing the government. This was so novel and complex that it had been repeatedly shelved by successive ministries. North's Regulating Act of 1773, which first established a system of government for the British territories in India, had proved defective. North had never found time to rectify it; and his successors were too occupied with reform and the aftermath of the American war to be able to think about India. The problem was complicated by the fact that these territories were not the possessions of the Crown but of a chartered company – an association of business men and investors, concerned primarily to make a profit and pay a dividend. Some way must be found to harmonize the happiness of Bengal peasants with the financial interests of London merchants. India must no longer be a 'plundered land', a prey to every adventurer concerned to make the fortune he did not deserve in his own country. Abuses must be remedied and prevented, delinquents must be punished, and the government of India must become responsible. These were the principles behind Fox's India Bill. It is to the honour of Fox and his colleagues that in framing their bill they thought more of the happiness and good government of India than of their own political advantage.

The bill was not the ideal solution to the problem of India. It was so concerned to prevent government from doing evil that it left government little power to do good. It gave insufficient authority to those who had to do the work in India and assumed that it was possible to govern from London territories three thousand miles away. But these were not the objections raised against the bill by its opponents. The chief point which struck contemporaries was the proposal to transfer the political responsibilities of the East India Company to a body of commissioners sitting in London, appointed first by Parliament and subsequently by the Crown. All were named in the bill; all were Members of Parliament; all were supporters of the coalition. Lord Fitzwilliam, Portland's friend and Rockingham's heir, was to be head of the commission.

Instantly the cry was raised that the patronage of India was to be taken from the Company and given to Fox. He would become the greatest subject in Europe! possessed of a greater power to reward dependants than the King himself! so powerful that the Crown would not be able to remove him! These were the bogeys conjured up in the popular imagination by the bill's opponents. 'God forbid that the patronage of India should go to the Crown, but shall it go to Charles Fox? Is he a man of such virtue?' Rarely was the bill considered on its merits, but almost always as a political manoeuvre by Fox to increase his power.

This was hard on Fox, who had made an honest attempt to grapple with an intractable problem. He knew that the bill involved grave political risks and these he deliberately took. Whatever the bill's defects it had one supreme merit: it introduced the principle on which all future legislation was to be based – that Parliament must assume ultimate responsibility for the government of India. But Fox with his usual maladroitness had given handles to his enemies. He made it appear that the bill was being rushed through Parliament. It was introduced at the dead time of the parliamentary year – the pre-Christmas session, which many country gentlemen did not attend and which was usually reserved only for routine government business. The proposals for the appointment of commissioners seemed designed to enhance Fox's personal power. Why were they to be appointed by Parliament and not by the Crown? The King rarely concerned himself with House of Commons patronage, and had the bill become law he could hardly have refused to accept Fox's recommendations. But Fox could never resist the temptation to score off the Crown even when no political advantage was to be gained.

The bill could not have been introduced without the consent of the Crown and there is no reason to think that the King disapproved of the measure. He never bothered

401

with the details of legislation submitted to him. These were the business of his ministers. He was concerned with principles not with their translation into practice, and the principles behind the India Bill were those he had long advocated. In 1773 he had told North that 'a continual inspection from Parliament' into the affairs of the East India Company could alone 'save it from destruction'. This was precisely what Fox's bill proposed to do. The King disapproved of the conduct of the nabobs – the 'fleecers of the East Indies' as he called them – quite as much as Fox or Burke. In 1773 he had agreed with Fox that Clive should be censured for his conduct in India: in 1781 he had agreed with Burke that Hastings should be recalled. Fox's India Bill was a measure after the King's own heart. It was not the bill he disliked but its author.

Pitt and his friends mustered in strength against the bill and were resoundingly defeated. The second reading in the Commons was carried by 229 votes to 120. Fox had won a triumph. It now seemed certain that the bill would pass. No eighteenth-century ministry was ever defeated in the Lords on a measure of confidence. The passage of the bill would consolidate Fox's power and enable him to approach the King again on the question of peerages. This time it would be difficult for the King to refuse. And with the political confidence of the King and the personal friendship of the heir apparent, Fox's position would be unchallengeable. On 9 December the bill received its first reading in the Lords, as Portland reported to the King 'without a word of objection or obstruction from either side of the House'. Only a few more jumps to clear and Fox was home and dry. The political punters who had backed the favourite were already in line for their winnings.

Almost home and dry – but not quite! The duty of the House of Lords according to the King was 'the preventing either of the other two branches of the legislature from encroaching on the other'. This was orthodox Whig doc-

402

trine. But in practice the House of Lords fulfilled no such exalted function. It was no more than the creature of the Crown. The Crown alone could create or promote peers, could nominate or translate bishops; and these functions had not as yet been usurped by the ministers. Fox and his friends had been so intent on reducing the influence of the Crown over the House of Commons that they had forgotten about its influence over the House of Lords. The King had given a hint to the peers when he had refused Fox's recommendations; he had given a hint to the bishops when during the interregnum between Shelburne and the coalition he had nominated an Archbishop of Canterbury. But more than hints were required before the Lords would do their duty. The King's opposition to his ministers had to be made clear. Nearly ten months had elapsed since the coalition had forced itself upon the King, and during most of that period the peers had been absent from London and unaware of the King's feelings. The episode of the Prince of Wales's establishment never became public and was known to few. When the peers returned in November and Fox brought in a bill consonant to the King's feelings they naturally assumed that he had won the King round just as Shelburne had the previous year. The King's intervention in the House of Lords against the India Bill can only be understood if we remember that the majority of peers did not know of his wish to be rid of Fox.

Perhaps the silliest thing Fox did in April 1783 was to turn out Thurlow. The Lord Chancellor as head of the law and 'keeper of the King's conscience' held a privileged position in the eighteenth-century cabinet, and King George was apt to look to his Chancellors for disinterested advice. Fox seems to have feared that Thurlow would become the King's agent in the cabinet, but with proper handling he might have become Fox's agent in the closet. In office, Thurlow would have tried to reconcile Fox to the King; out of office, he intrigued for Fox's

403

dismissal. On 1 December he presented a memorandum to the King and suggested that the Lords should be informed of his feelings 'in a manner which would make it impossible to pretend a doubt of it'. In plain words, the Lords should be ordered to vote against the India Bill.

This was all very well, but it would be disastrous to provoke a crisis with the coalition until there was an alternative ministry to take their place. This was the lesson the King had learnt from the events of 1765 – never to be off with the old ministry until he was on with the new. Was Pitt now ready to serve? Thurlow had good reason for thinking he was. Thurlow's memorandum had been drawn up in collaboration with Temple, Pitt's cousin, who knew Pitt's mind. But Pitt would first have to be assured that the King would stand by him. How could the King communicate with Pitt without arousing the suspicions of his ministers? Thurlow thought he knew a way.[15]

The communication was carried on through Lord Clarendon, Chancellor of the Duchy of Lancaster in the North ministry, and Count Alvensleben, Hanoverian Minister in London. Pitt received the assurance he sought. John Robinson, North's Secretary to the Treasury, who knew the House of Commons better than any man, prepared a survey to show how the House would behave in the event of a change of ministry and satisfied Pitt that he could command a majority. An analysis was made of the House of Lords, and again Pitt received confirmation that provided the King stood by him he would be supported by the upper house. Comforted by these assurances, Pitt decided to embark. At the age of only twenty-four, with his political life in front of him, he placed his confidence in King George. And King George placed his confidence in Pitt. Neither could have ventured without the other.

On 11 December the King authorized Temple to inform the peers that 'whoever voted for the India Bill were not only not his friends but he should consider them as his enemies'. The first division in the Lords, on a motion to adjourn, was taken in the early hours of 16 December and resulted in a defeat for the coalition by 69 to 57. Temple had been given too little time to canvass the peers, and many were not aware that the King wished the bill to be rejected. Among those who voted for the bill were eight bishops, five Lords of the Bedchamber, seven Scottish representative peers, and the Prince of Wales. How many of these would have gone against the King's opinion had it been generally known? Certainly not the Prince, who whatever his good wishes for the coalition was not prepared to provoke an open breach with his father. He apologized for his vote and received a kind message from the King in reply.

On 17 December the bill was rejected on second reading by 75 to 57. One of those who helped to increase the majority was Lord Stormont, Lord President of the Council, whose inclusion in the cabinet had occasioned the dispute between Fox and North and delayed the formation of the ministry. The King sent him a short note of regret:

Things are so situated that I cannot but change the present administration. I can easily conceive that Lord Stormont cannot immediately take a share in a new one; but after his handsome conduct before he accepted the Presidency of the Council, I should not do justice to my feelings if I did not thus express to him my sorrow at his being out of my service.

At 43 minutes past 10 in the evening of 18 December the King wrote to North:

Lord North is by this required to send me the seals of his department, and to acquaint Mr Fox to send those of the foreign department. Mr Frazer on Mr Nepean [the undersecretaries] will be the proper channel of delivering them to me this night. I choose this method as audiences on such occasions must be unpleasant.

The next day Pitt kissed hands as First Lord of the Treasury and Chancellor of the Exchequer and Temple as Secretary of State.

The King's intervention against the India Bill has generally been considered as unconstitutional. Judged by the nineteenth-century interpretation of the constitution it certainly was. Even in the eighteenth century it was accepted doctrine that the King's opinion should not be used to influence debate in Parliament, and King George had subscribed to this view. 'I do not think it constitutional', he had written in 1766, 'for the Crown personally to interfere in measures it has thought proper to refer to the advice of Parliament.' But this convention, like the similar one that the King could do no wrong (which the lawyers accepted as true and the politicians knew to be false), was no more than a parliamentary convenience designed to prevent personal criticism of the King in debate. King George II had never hesitated to make clear his opinions about a measure. Walpole writes about the Habeas Corpus Bill of 1759:

The King talked openly at his levee against the bill; and it was understood to be offensive to him to vote for the extension of it. He was King; he did not desire to reduce the prerogative lower than it had been delivered to him.

With the change of a word or two, this might be King George III on the India Bill. Moreover, politicians never scrupled to let the King's opinion be known when it suited their purpose. Rockingham had promoted the repeal of the Stamp Act by informing Members of Parliament that the King favoured the measure. It was accepted practice for the King to indicate to Members of Parliament at his levee his approval or disapproval of their political conduct. What was unusual in 1783 was that the King intervened *against* his ministers, and that Temple was authorized to speak on his behalf. This was necessary because of the shortness of time and because it was generally believed that the King approved the bill. And so he did, considered on its merits. It was only on 10 December, when Pitt definitely accepted, that the King could let it be known that he wished for the defeat of the ministry. When the Prince of Wales did not know his father's real wishes we may be sure there were many others who shared his ignorance.

It may be doubted whether the Crown can ever behave unconstitutionally. Unconstitutional behaviour is like treason—

Treason doth never prosper: what's the reason?
For if it prosper, none dare call it treason.

When unconstitutional behaviour prospers, it is no longer unconstitutional. What is or what is not constitutional depends on what the Crown can get away with. King George III got away with his action on the India Bill in 1783. Queen Victoria, who disliked Gladstone almost as much as her grandfather had disliked Fox, could not have got away with similar action on the Home Rule Bill in 1886. But Queen Victoria had her own way of letting her opinions be known. We must judge King George by the constitutional ideas of his day not by those of a hundred years later. And a good case can be made for saying that the bill itself was unconstitutional since it violated the rights of property which it was the duty of Parliament to preserve.

Whether unconstitutional or not, the King's conduct was certainly unscrupulous. The ministers were entitled to complain that he had given no hint of his opposition to the bill until it reached the House of Lords. 'We are beat in the House of Lords', Fox wrote, 'by such treachery on the part of the King and such meanness on the part of his friends . . . as one could not expect either from him or them.' His bitterness was natural but scarcely justified. He had played the game hard. He had taken the part of the Prince of Wales against the King. He had tried to reduce the Crown to a mere nominal authority. He could hardly complain if the King hit back at him with the only weapon he had. The true justification of the King's conduct in 1783 is that he believed himself to be fighting for his political existence against an unscrupulous opponent. In such a contest no holds are barred.

Fox, however, was not yet beaten. The game had only reached half-time, and though the King had taken the lead it still seemed possible for Fox to win. It was one thing to dismiss the coalition: it was another to establish Pitt in office against a hostile House of Commons. Fox carried two resolutions in the House: that it was 'a high crime and misdemeanour' to report the King's opinion for the purpose of influencing debate, and that any minister who advised the dissolution of Parliament was 'an enemy to his country'. 'We are so strong', Fox wrote (this was before Pitt had taken office), 'that nobody can undertake without madness: if they do, I think we shall destroy them almost as soon as they are formed.'

At first it seemed that he might be right. Pitt had great difficulty in forming a cabinet. Few were willing to join what Mrs Crewe, the Whig hostess, described as a 'mince-pie administration', fit only to last the festive season. Thurlow resumed the great seal, but four members of Shelburne's cabinet declined office. Pitt made a tentative, half-hearted approach to Fox for an accommodation but Fox refused to listen. Then, on 22 December, came an event which might have upset everything. Temple, who had shared with Pitt and Thurlow responsibility for the plot against the coalition and was to lead for the new ministry in the House of Lords, suddenly resigned. His reasons are obscure. It has been contended that he was afraid of impeachment for having carried the King's message to the Lords, and also that his resignation was in protest against Pitt's refusal to dissolve Parliament immediately. Whatever his reasons, he was badly frightened, and his withdrawal staggered both the King and Pitt. Five years later, when Temple had resumed office as Lord Lieutenant of Ireland, the King had still not forgiven his 'base conduct' in 1783. Fortunately Parliament was about to rise for the Christmas recess and ministers were given a breathing space. But when Parliament reassembled on 12 January 1784, though the cabinet had by then been completed and some of those who had refused to serve had come round, Pitt was still despondent. It was all very well for Carmarthen and Richmond to say that ministers would disgrace themselves if they were to give up now, but Pitt almost alone had to wage the battle in the House of Commons. There Fox commanded and his troops were unbroken. Their morale was high and they looked forward to routing 'master Billy' and King George.

In truth the defeat of the coalition was certain, provided the King and Pitt kept their heads and acted with courage and prudence. They had but to employ the two irresistible weapons of the Crown and Fox's horde would be scattered. The first was used at once. Peerages were granted to three of the biggest boroughmongers (Edward Eliot, Sir James Lowther, and the Duke of Northumberland) – a demonstration to all who were ambitious of social advancement that their interest lay in deserting Fox. The second weapon – the dissolution of Parliament – was delayed for various reasons. Pitt and Fox were in negotiation with a group of independent country gentlemen who were anxious to bring about a union between the two leaders. Had this been successful it would have resulted in a ministry 'on the most comprehensive lines', without party basis, which the King had always professed to wish. But Fox had so blotted his copybook that rather than have him return in any capacity whatsoever the King was prepared to abandon his cherished political ideal. He pressed for a speedy dissolution, and on 26 January summoned the cabinet to the Queen's House. 'His

Majesty', writes Carmarthen (now Foreign Secretary), 'in a well-conceived speech of some length, and in different parts of which he appeared much agitated, expressed his wish upon all occasions to observe the true principles of the constitution as the sole rules of his conduct. He . . . declared a fixed and unalterable resolution on no account to be put bound hand and foot into the hands of Mr Fox; that rather than submit to that he would quit the kingdom for ever.'

For almost three months Pitt was in a minority in the House of Commons and suffered defeat after defeat. His India Bill, meant to replace that of Fox, was rejected. Motions were passed and addresses voted calling for his resignation and censuring him for remaining in office without the confidence of the House. Pitt simply ignored them. Having now recovered from his bout of despondency, his coolness and courage were admirable. Had he faltered or taken fright, all would have been lost. But like the little pig in the song he had built his house of stone, and the big bad wolf could huff and puff as much as he liked but could not blow it down. Pitt was sure of the King and there was nothing Fox could do. He had one weapon in his armoury – to refuse supplies, and that weapon he dared not use. His followers would have deserted him. It would have been a declaration of civil war.

It could not be denied that for a minister to retain office without a majority in the House of Commons was – to say the least – a most unusual proceeding. The King justified himself by the old Whig view of the constitution he had learnt as a boy:

The times are of the most serious nature; the political struggle is not as formerly between two factions for power, but it is no less than whether a desperate faction shall not reduce the sovereign to a mere tool in its hands. Though I have too much principle ever to infringe the rights of others, yet that must ever equally prevent my submitting to the executive power being in any other hands than where the constitution has placed it. . . . My cause . . . is that of the constitution as fixed at the Revolution, and to the support of which my family was invited to mount the throne.

To this Fox would have replied by recalling North's words to the King in March 1782 – 'In this country the prince on the throne cannot with prudence oppose the deliberate resolution of the House of Commons.' 'What sort of a government', Fox asked in the House on 1 March, 'could take place on a principle which did not imply the confidence of the House?'

The answer was: no government. But the weakness in Fox's argument was that the House of Commons could only prescribe a minister to the Crown when it was supported by political opinion in the nation. Queen Victoria could not have dismissed Gladstone as King George III dismissed Fox because Gladstone's majority in the House reflected a majority in the nation. Fox's did not. Pitt and the King could appeal against the House of Commons to the nation and there could be little doubt of the result. The coalition had been based on the understanding that nothing further remained to be done to reduce the influence of the Crown. Yet the strength of the Crown for electoral purposes remained almost untouched. The King had an election fund: Fox had none; the King had an electoral organization: Fox had to improvise one; the King could offer peerages to boroughmongers in return for the nomination to their seats: Fox could only make promises and appeal to past obligations; the King had places to offer Members of Parliament: Fox could offer only places in reversion. We should not be surprised that Fox was defeated at the general election of 1784. The surprise is that so many of his followers stood by him when his cause was hopeless. It illustrates an aspect of his character which the King never knew.

The voice of the nation now began to be heard. Addresses were reaching St James's from the constituencies expressing approval of the King's action and support for Pitt. The City of London took the lead – the first time in the reign the City had ever commended the King's political conduct. John Wilkes, the firebrand of 1768, whom the King had once declared he disliked more than any man living, accepted £2,000 from the King's electoral fund towards his expenses in Middlesex. An address from Westminster, Fox's own constituency, was signed by 8,000 voters. The number of addresses in support of the King and Pitt was greater than on any previous political question. The same pattern was repeated at the general election. In the open constituencies, where public opinion could express itself, wherever there was a choice of candidates the decision was invariably given for those who supported Pitt. Sir Charles Bunbury was returned at every general election for Suffolk between 1761 and 1807 with one exception – 1784, when he stood as a Foxite, beaten in the words of the *Ipswich Journal* by 'the determined sense of the freeholders . . . to oppose the friends of the coalition'. Thomas William Coke of Holkham, who had attached himself to Fox on his first entering Parliament, represented Norfolk for almost fifty years. His sole defeat was in 1784, when he received so little support that he was unable to go to the poll. Fox himself scraped home for Westminster after a prolonged scrutiny, and until it was decided sat as representative of a pocket constituency in Scotland.

The election results most worthy of note came from Yorkshire. The county of Yorkshire, with about 20,000 voters, was the largest constituency in Great Britain, and York, the county town, one of the largest urban constituencies. Here if anywhere public opinion counted. Yorkshiremen were proud of their independence: unlike Londoners, they did not follow the mob; unlike the Scots, they did not follow their social superiors. Yorkshire neither engaged in factious opposition nor gave a compliant support to the measures of the Crown. From Yorkshire had begun the movement for economical reform; Yorkshire was the home of Lord Rockingham, whose political mantle Fox had inherited. At the general election of 1780 Rockingham had secured the return of Members in his interest for both county and borough. Lord Fitzwilliam, his nephew, had inherited every acre his uncle had possessed in Yorkshire. But the freeholders of Yorkshire denied to the follower of Fox what they had cheerfully granted to the Yorkshire landowner. Fitzwilliam's candidates for the county were unable to start against an address in support of Pitt and a subscription of over £18,000 raised on behalf of their opponents. His candidates for York, one of whom was Lord John Cavendish, the coalition's Chancellor of the Exchequer, were beaten.

Yorkshire also supplied the reason for Fox's defeat. This was much more than a matter of electoral management. Had there been universal suffrage in Great Britain in 1784 Fox would have been defeated even more decisively than he was under the system of restricted voting. Lord Fauconberg, speaking in the Castle Yard at York on 25 March, placed before the electors the real issue: 'Whether is George III or Charles Fox to reign?' There could be no doubt of the answer. The King had learnt as a youth 'that this people will never refuse anything to a sovereign who they know will be the defender of their liberties'. Was it to be expected, Walpole had asked in 1767, 'that every man should depend on King Rockingham and nobody on King George?' Was every man in 1784 to depend on King Fox? 'People . . . have no idea', wrote one of Fitzwilliam's electoral agents, 'but that Mr Fox wants to get the better of the King and be the Lord Protector'; and another agent reported: 'The trading part of the county are almost unanimous . . . against taking from the King what they look upon to be necessary in him for the preservation of the true constitution.' The comparison between Fox and Cromwell was frequently made and not as a compliment to Fox.

413

Fox had pursued his vendetta against the King without a thought of public opinion. He did not realize the immense hold the monarchy had on popular affections and how unfavourably his public image compared with that of King George. In popular estimation Fox was a desperate adventurer, a gambler who played for high stakes in politics as he had done at faro, who never went to church and lived with a kept woman. King George was careful, sober, pious, and chaste. Fox was a man of the metropolis, one of those wicked London rakes one read about in novels who cheated young gentlemen of their inheritance and young girls of their virtue. King George was a country gentleman who delighted in farming and field sports. Who would not rather see the government confided to King George than to Fox? The comparison was unfair to Fox, who had out-lived his youthful follies, but it was the public image of the man and the public image of a politician counts for at least as much as his real personality. Perhaps in the last analysis the difference was this: Fox was a spoilt child who had trod the primrose path; the King a child scorned by his parents and brought up the hard way. It is not surprising that King George III proved himself 'the man of the people'.

Chapter 7

THE KING AND HIS FAMILY

All discussion of King George III's character must begin with his belief in God. This is the fundamental fact about him. His 'trust in divine Providence', repeated over and over again in his letters, was no mere form of words. It was a simple man's expression of a living faith. He began and ended each day with prayer. When Prince Frederick was leaving for Germany in 1780 the King gave him a copy of the Bible. 'When you know it is my last request before your departure', he told his son, 'I trust you will every morning and evening read in this book, and I am convinced you will soon feel the comfort I do from that constant practice. It will at least twice in the day give an opportunity of self examination without which even with the best intentions you cannot avoid much evil.'[1] To Prince Augustus, who shared his interest in science, he wrote on 18 December 1787:

Your lessons on natural history will if possible raise your ideas of the wisdom and goodness of the All Mighty in the formation of every atom contained within this terrestrial globe, and when one reflects how small a part that takes of the celestial bodies we know, and consequently how many objects he has probably had equally to attend to, yet how small is that of his many attributes, the knowing how ungratefully man has behaved towards him he has from nothing placed him in so superior a station in the creation, and yet that his goodness shall have been so unbounded as to have sent his only son to suffer death on the cross for the redemption of man – this consideration must warm the heart of every one who possesses the smallest spark of gratitude, and be the cause of the strongest resolutions to obey his laws.

The King was exemplary in his attention to the observances of religion. When the Royal Family was at

Windsor or in London divine service was held in the King's private chapel every morning at eight o'clock. (There was no chapel at Kew.) On Sundays the King and Queen attended morning service – in London at the Chapel Royal, in Windsor at St George's Chapel ('the cathedral', as it was usually referred to by the Royal Family). They never went to evening service. Eighteenth-century services lasted about two hours, and the length of an eighteenth-century sermon would try the patience of a modern congregation. The King became a connoisseur of sermons. 'He liked none but what were plain and unadorned', he told Fanny Burney; and he judged the fitness of clergymen for preferment by his impressions of their preaching. Twelve times a year he took Holy Communion. On these days the usual Sunday drawing room was cancelled and during the preceding week the King and Queen did not visit the theatre. Sunday was always kept as a special day. The Queen read a sermon in English or German to her daughters, and there was no game of cards in the evening.

The King was no theologian and no bigot. He was bound by law and his coronation oath to maintain the privileged position of the Church of England but he had no wish to persecute Dissenters or Roman Catholics. Equally he had no inclination to relieve them of civil disabilities imposed by law. 'It is the duty of ministers', he told North in 1772, 'as much as possible to prevent any alterations in so essential a part of the constitution as everything that relates to religion.' The Church of England was as much a part of the constitution as the Crown or Parliament and it should be preserved unimpaired. Even the annual observance of Charles I's execution as a day of national humiliation – hardly a matter which meant much to a Hanoverian monarch – seemed to the King worth preserving. 'It will keep many worthy men in good humour', he wrote, 'besides the abolition of the day would not be very delicate.'

Waldegrave had written of him as a boy: 'His religion is free from all hypocrisy, but is not of the most charitable sort; he has rather too much attention to the sins of his neighbour.' In later years this took the form of denunciations of 'this selfish and unprincipled age' and lamentations that he had been born to reign in 'the most profligate age'. His study of history should have taught him that every age is selfish, unprincipled, and profligate in its own peculiar way, and the eighteenth century was no worse than any other. 'There exists in human nature', wrote Gibbon, 'a strong propensity to depreciate the advantages and to magnify the evils of the present times.' The King was not exempt from this defect.

The King frequently appealed to the rectitude of his intentions, yet he was neither smug nor self-satisfied. 'No one should be above confessing when they have been mistaken', he wrote to Prince Augustus on 21 July 1786, apologizing for having accused him unjustly of not having written. King George could admit that he had been in the wrong, which few sovereigns of this period could. He did so to Portland in 1783 and to Henry Dundas in 1801. At Dundas's house at Wimbledon the King toasted him as the man responsible for the expedition to Egypt the previous year, which at the time the King had opposed. 'In my opinion', the King said, 'when a person has been perfectly in the wrong, the most just and honourable thing for him to do is to acknowledge it publicly.' King George might be tenacious of his opinions but he had no belief in his infallibility. At his coronation he took off his crown before receiving the sacrament. Before God he was no more than an ordinary mortal. He had a deep sense of reverence and humility and a consciousness of his own limitations.

The foundations of the King's personal happiness were securely rooted in a comfortable marriage. If he had searched the length and breadth of Europe he could not

417

have found a woman who suited him better than Princess Charlotte of Mecklenberg-Strelitz. 'The more I see of the world the happier I am that she is in England', wrote the King's sister Augusta, Hereditary Princess of Brunswick in 1770, 'for none of these ladies would have done for you.' The King loved three people deeply: his brother William, Duke of Gloucester; his son Frederick, Duke of York; and the Queen. Of these he loved the Queen the best. In 1804, after more than forty years of marriage, when he was approaching his seventieth year and recovering from his third attack of illness, he gave the Queen a copy of the opinions of the physicians on his case docketed with the words: 'To be deposited with the former ones with the Queen of my heart'. She had a special place in his affections to which no other could aspire.

His love did not take the form of confiding in her or looking to her for advice. It was only after his illness in 1788 that he began to talk to her about politics, in which she was profoundly uninterested. He was no King George II nor she another Queen Caroline. The King never forgot Bute's warnings against petticoat government. He did not admit his wife as an equal partner in their marriage but as a coadjutor. She accepted her position cheerfully because she shared his ideals. When the King quarrelled with the Prince of Wales, her sympathies were with her favourite son yet she never allowed her husband to become aware of her feelings. She was more than a little in awe of him. When she fell into debt in 1793 she was reluctant to ask him for more money. Her letters to him are written in the formal style of an eighteenth-century wife to her husband. She addressed him as 'Sir' and ended 'your very affectionate friend and wife'. He wrote to her 'Dearest Charlotte' and ended 'your loving husband'.

Yet Queen Charlotte was no negative character. In her own way she was as strong as her husband. Her sphere was restricted but within that sphere she was supreme.

The King left the management of his daughters entirely to her and she ruled them like a martinet. When the King fell ill for the last time in 1811 and there had to be a new establishment for the Royal Family, she fought the Treasury tooth and nail for a favourable financial settlement for herself and her daughters. During the years when George III was King in name only she maintained the high standards and dignity which the King had laid down for the Royal Family. She would do nothing of which he would have disapproved. She quarrelled with her son Ernest, Duke of Cumberland, himself a formidable person, because he married a woman, her own niece, who had been divorced from a previous husband. Her children understood her strength of character and her sons adored her. She was respected by all and never more than when she was on her own.

Physically she was a strong woman. She bore the King fifteen children (for more than half the first twenty years of her married life she was pregnant), and died at the age of seventy-four. When she was betrothed to the King in 1761 the French Resident at Hamburg sent his court an appreciation of her character. Her education, he wrote, had been entirely neglected; but she had a good heart, was well-meaning and charitable, and kind to her dependants. She lacked worldly wisdom, did not know the value of money, had no understanding of politics, and spoke French badly. But though the French Resident did not notice them she had qualities which far outshone these defects: the will to please and the ability to learn. She had interests which enabled her to become a true wife and companion to the King. She was fond of music and shared the King's enthusiasm for Handel. She loved needlework; and she became a collector, particularly of furniture and pottery. She read widely in modern literature, in English, French, and German. She could talk intelligently about Madame de Genlis and could quote Madame de Sévigné. Her library, formed solely for her own use and her daughters', was sold after her death for £5,615 – a large sum in 1819 for a private library. Queen Charlotte would have disliked being called a bluestocking but she was unquestionably a cultured woman.

Nineteenth-century historians had nothing to say about the King's sexual life: twentieth-century historians have said too much. When psychoanalysis became fashionable, historians began to use it as a tool to explore the minds of their characters. But psychoanalysis is no substitute for accurate investigation of facts, and psychoanalysis imperfectly understood is a will o' the wisp that may lead the best historians into the grossest absurdities. The King became a victim of the popular delusion that all mental disturbances are to be explained in terms of sexual maladjustment. It could not be denied that he was faithful to his wife: hence, it was argued, he must be repressed, and only his rigid standards of morality prevented him from fulfilling his unconscious wish to sleep with other women. One distinguished historian diagnosed his illness as in part the result of his 'resolute fidelity to a hideous Queen' and another has described him as a 'sexually timid, if nonetheless passionate man'. As one reads these historians one cannot help but think that once again the King has had the worst of both worlds. Had he taken a mistress, as Kings George I and II did, the nineteenth-century historian would have counted it against him, and have cited his licentiousness as a cause of his illness. Because he was faithful to his wife the twentieth-century historian has deduced that he must have been repressed, and in our age sexual repression is deemed as great an evil as licentiousness was to the Victorians.

'Diligence and accuracy', wrote Gibbon, the model of historians, 'are the only merits which an historical writer may ascribe to himself.' They are certainly the capital virtues. One ounce of fact is worth a ton of speculation. Before we theorise about the King's sexual life, let us examine the facts. They are few, as they must necessarily be for any historical character. The fact that he was faithful to his wife indicates a standard of morality for which he should be praised not condemned. The fact that he had fifteen children by her indicates that he was a passionate man. The fact that he continued to make love to her twenty years after their marriage indicates that he found satisfaction in her embraces. This is all we know about the King's sexual life and probably all we shall ever know.

It is untrue to describe Queen Charlotte as 'hideous', which implies that she had some physical deformity. Walpole writes about her at the time of her marriage: 'She is not tall, nor a beauty; pale, and very thin, but looks sensible and is genteel. Her hair is darkish and fine, her forehead low, her nose very well, except the nostrils spreading too wide; her mouth has the same fault, but her teeth are good.' Sophie von la Roche in 1786 thought she had 'beautiful eyes' and a 'beautiful expression'. Her worst defect was her mouth, which clearly appears in Ramsay's portrait. But in other portraits (those by Zoffany in 1767 and by Gainsborough in 1781) this is not so obvious, and the betrothal picture by Ziesenis (if indeed it is Queen Charlotte) is a charming study of a young girl. That she was no beauty or even downright plain we may well believe, but there is a world of difference between a plain woman and a hideous one. Nor is a woman's sexual attractiveness dependent upon her physical appearance.

Their first child, the future George IV, was born on 12 August 1762, and within a week of his birth was created Prince of Wales. Further children followed until 1780, with an interval of no more than eighteen months between each; and the last child, Princess Amelia, was born in 1783. During the early years, before the family had increased so much and when the children were yet small, the King and Queen took them with them when they moved between Kew and London, but as they grew older they lived mainly at Kew under the charge of Lady

421

Charlotte Finch, their governess. Little treats were arranged for them on their birthdays. The Prince of Wales's first Christmas present from his parents (in 1763, when he was only a year old) was 'a little ring of a single brilliant', engraved with the letters GP, which he afterwards gave to Lady Charlotte. In 1766, on the Prince's fourth birthday, a fancy dress party was held at Richmond Lodge. The Prince 'danced a hornpipe in a sailor's dress', his brother Prince Frederick appeared as harlequin, and Prince William (then the baby of the family – he was one year old) was dressed as a 'madamoiselle'. There was a concert in the garden, and a boat race on the Thames which the children watched from the terrace. In January 1767 the Prince of Wales was taken by his parents to the theatre for the first time; and in February to the opera, where Lady Mary Coke noted that he 'behaved like an angel, seemed much amused, and not in the least tired when it was ended'.[2]

The King was fond of children and delighted in their company. He preferred girls, and it is questionable if he understood or sympathized with adolescent boys. Lady Mary Coke tells a story about the birth of Princess Augusta, the King's second daughter, in 1768:

Doctor Hunter, knowing how anxious the King was that it should prove a princess, thought he had better prepare him for it, and said to His Majesty, 'I think, Sir, whoever sees those lovely princes above stairs must be glad to have another', to which His Majesty answered, 'Doctor Hunter, I did not think I could have been angry with you, but I am; and I say, whoever sees that lovely child the Princess Royal above stairs must wish to have the fellow to her.'

When away from his family, he longed to hear about the children. On 24 April 1778, when the King was at Chatham, the Queen wrote to him:

Mary [their fourth daughter, then in her second year] is very anxious to see Your Majesty. She desired me to call *Dear Papa*, but after telling her that could not be she desired to be lifted up, and she called for at least half an hour *Papa coming, now Papa come,* but seeing she was disappointed by not receiving an answer I desired her to tell me what I should say to the King in case I should write, and she answered Minny say *Goody Papa, poor Papa.*

'The children are, thank God, all in perfect health', the Queen wrote on 19 August 1781, when the King was visiting the fleet at the Nore, 'and present both their love and duty to you. Octavius in particular wishes much to be with Papa *on board a horse* but not on board a ship.'[3]

The rate of infant mortality in the eighteenth century was appalling by the standards of present-day western civilization, and the deaths of young children were accepted as a dispensation of Providence beyond human control. The King and Queen were fortunate in that only two of their children died in infancy. The first child to die, 'dear little Alfred', was taken ill during the last winter of the American war, and during the early months of 1782 his health was a source of constant anxiety. When he died on 20 August 1782, the King felt the event deeply but perhaps more on the Queen's account than his own. The death of Prince Octavius the following year (3 May 1783) hurt him more. 'Had you known what a sweet child he was', wrote the Prince of Wales to Prince Frederick, 'you would have felt his death as severely as I did.' 'My mind is far from at ease', the King wrote to Prince William on 14 June. 'It has pleased the Almighty to put an end very unexpectedly of the most amiable as well as attached child a parent could have.' At a time when he was distressed by political events (this letter was written during the dispute with the coalition about the Prince of Wales's establishment) the King's thoughts were full of his dead child. 'There will be no Heaven for me', he said, 'if Octavius is not there.'

The King's mother, the Princess Dowager of Wales, survived her husband more than twenty years and died of cancer of the throat in 1772 at the age of fifty-two.

Little would need to be said about her after her son succeeded to the throne were it not for the nonsense talked by contemporaries. She lived a retired life, at Carlton House in London and Kew Palace in the country. In 1770 she visited the Continent to see her daughters, the Princess of Brunswick and the Queen of Denmark. Walpole tells us that when the King succeeded she asked for the title of Princess Mother which was denied her for lack of a precedent, but there is no evidence in the correspondence of Bute or the King to substantiate the story. She had little influence over her son and none in politics. Yet so late as 1771, when she was dying of cancer, the most ridiculous stories were told about her in the newspapers, and what is even more ridiculous were believed by otherwise knowledgeable men. Even the Duke of Newcastle, who should have known better, thought that he detected her influence during the Chatham ministry. Chatham himself, on his return to health and opposition, spoke in the House of Lords of a secret influence exerted against him when he was in office and dropped a broad hint that he suspected the Princess to have been at the bottom of it. James Townsend, a Radical Member of Parliament, declared in the House of Commons on 25 March 1771 that 'he thought the Princess Dowager of Wales was the real cause of all the calamities which had befallen this country for these last ten unfortunate years, and that an inquiry should be made into her Royal Highness's conduct'. Horace Walpole was so obsessed with the Princess that he chose the date of her death (an event of no importance in history) as the logical place at which to end his memoirs of King George III's reign.

It is time that justice was done to this much maligned lady. The facts are not difficult to ascertain. After the death of her husband she lived a pious and chaste life and during the reign of her son she was of no consequence in politics. She did her best to be a loyal wife to her husband and a good mother to her children. Let her rest in peace.

On three evenings a week (Sunday, Tuesday, and Friday) the King and Queen visited the Princess. She came to them on Wednesday. During the last years of her life, as the disease overcame her, she became querulous and difficult. 'My mother', the King wrote to the Duke of Gloucester on 12 November 1771, '. . . I am sorry to say visibly loses ground, and it is impossible you can figure to yourself how much she is reduced since you went abroad.'[4] On 19 November he told his brother that 'her speech grows less intelligible, she hourly emaciates, and has dreadful faintings towards night, which must soon put an end to a situation that it is almost cruel to wish to see her long continue in'.[5] When she realized she was dying, she asked for her daughter Princess Augusta to be with her. 'If I thought this could be a thing of long duration', the King wrote to his brother-in-law on 22 November 1771, 'I should have opposed it. . . . I much doubt whether she can live a fortnight.'[6] Princess Augusta came and remained with her mother to the end. The Princess kept her normal routine until the last day of her life. When the King and Queen came to see her on the evening of 7 February 1772 she insisted on getting up and being dressed to receive them. By then she was unable to speak. 'We had the melancholy scene of knowing she could not last', wrote the King, 'but that it must not be taken notice of as she did not choose to think so.'[7] She went to bed at her usual hour and the King and Queen remained in the house all night. At six in the morning her lady-in-waiting went to her room and found her dead. She was buried in Westminster Abbey on 13 February. There were disgraceful scenes at her funeral. 'The mob huzzaed for joy', wrote Walpole, 'and treated her memory with much disrespect.' And not only the mob.

The King's elder sister Princess Augusta (whose birth in 1737 had occasioned the great quarrel between Frederick, Prince of Wales and King George II) was married in 1764 to the Hereditary Prince of Brunswick. This was a popular match in Great Britain where the Prince was known as one of the allied commanders in the Seven Years War, but it was unfortunate for the Princess. Her husband was a difficult character and was flagrantly unfaithful to her. She bore his treatment with dignity and refused to complain. She kept up a regular correspondence with the King in English and French, and wrote of her husband's kindness and how much she loved him. 'May I say though he is my husband', she wrote on 11 December 1769, 'that I never knew anybody with a more real good heart. You know he is sensible and clever. In short, he is monstrously fond of me and I am a happy woman.'[8] But the Princess's family was not deceived. When she came to England in 1771 to nurse her mother, the King (who disliked the Prince) wrote to the Duke of Gloucester: 'She seems much graver than formerly, and I should rather think by her whole manner that it goes on but coldly between her and the Hereditary Prince, though she has not dropped the most distant hint of it.'[9] On 31 March 1774 the King's younger sister Caroline Matilda, Queen of Denmark, wrote to him:[10]

Your mentioning my sister in your last letter gives me an opportunity of doing the same. She says that the Prince's humour grows every day worse, and that since the beginning of his illness she finds a great alteration in him towards her. She does everything in her power that it should not appear in public, and has always so many attentions for him that it is impossible to remark that they are not well together.

Princess Augusta was consoled by the kindness and sympathy of her brother and her letters are full of expressions of her affection and gratitude. Here is one, dated 18 May 1803:[11]

My dearest brother,
    You are too good to me in sending me these religious books.

I shall read them with double pleasure as they come from you. I hope that you will live long and happily, to be a blessing to all around you. The comfort you now are to your old, faithful and attached sister. I should be a sad creature did I not feel the truest gratitude and the most sincere affection for all the continued kindness and friendship that time nor absence has not eradicated.

Her husband died in 1806 of wounds received at the battle of Auerstedt. Brunswick was occupied by the French and incorporated by Napoleon in his puppet kingdom of Westphalia. The Duchess then in her seventieth year was reduced almost to poverty. She had nothing but her husband's collection of coins and antiques which she begged the King to sell for her in England. The King sent a frigate to bring her home, gave pensions to her and her three sons, and settled her in a house at Blackheath. Here on 19 September 1807 brother and sister met for the first time for thirty-six years: the Duchess an almost penniless refugee, the King blind and crippled with disease. How much suffering had both endured since the days when they had played together as children at Kew! 'My dearest brother', the Duchess wrote on 24 February 1808, 'all my letters can be nothing but thanks. . . .'; and on 2 March: 'Indeed you are a father to all.'[12] She died in 1813. Her eldest son was 'Brunswick's fated chieftain' who was killed at Quatre Bras, her daughter the ill-fated wife of King George IV.

The King's other sister Princess Caroline Matilda was destined for even greater unhappiness. She was the baby of the family, a posthumous child, and was married in 1766 at the age of only fifteen to her first cousin Christian VII of Denmark. A more wretched husband could not have been found in the whole of European royalty. Christian was debauched, diseased, and almost an imbecile. There could be no happiness with such a man. Queen Caroline Matilda sought sympathy from Struensee, the court physician, and became his mistress. Even more unfortunately, she became involved in his political schemes.

The King had not been happy about the marriage. His sister was young, and he had heard stories about the King of Denmark – though not the whole truth. On the eve of her departure he wrote to her: 'I think I can no way so essentially show Caroline my real affection for her than in giving her a few hints that may perhaps be a means of preserving her from the precipices into which she may also very probably fall.'[13] He cautioned her against meddling in politics and advised her to show proper respect to her husband's mother and grandmother. But it would have taken a stronger character than Princess Caroline to escape the dangers in store for her. The Duke of Gloucester, who visited Denmark in 1769, found her in low spirits,[14] and it is hardly surprising that she allowed herself to be seduced by Struensee. It was not sex, however, but politics which brought about her downfall. The Danes might have condoned her adultery had it not been for Struensee's reforming projects which offended some of the first families in the kingdom. Using the authority of the King, whom he had made subservient to his will, he pushed his plans too fast and too far; and Queen Caroline was involved in his downfall. King George, unaware of the full facts but apprehensive of the way events were going, repeatedly warned her to take care but to no avail. On 17 January 1772 Struensee was arrested and Queen Caroline deprived of her children and sent to a fortress.

The party that had seized power in Denmark was bent on her divorce, and King George demanded that she should be returned to his protection and her marriage portion repaid. 'I . . . trust', he wrote to Princess Augusta on 8 May 1772, 'that by mildness she will be brought back to the amiable character she had before perverted by a wicked and contemptible court.'[15] A fleet was equipped and sent to Danish waters. The Danes allowed Queen

Caroline to go to Celle, in her brother's Hanoverian dominions, but refused to allow her to take her children. At Celle she was treated as a Queen and a daughter of England, and her brother sent instructions that everything should be done to make her comfortable and happy. 'Dear sister', he wrote on 23 June 1772, 'continue that circumspection in your behaviour that has gained great credit during your misfortunes. It is the most effectual means of showing what a blessing you might have been if those that had surrounded you had possessed any principle of honour and integrity.'[16]

But Queen Caroline was not happy. She fretted about her children, and dreamt of a revolution in Denmark which would restore her to the throne. King George besought her to put these ideas away from her.[17]

Your letters seem to point out how much Denmark still employs your mind. As far as relates to the health, education, and welfare of your children, I shall undoubtedly take every method of satisfying your curiosity, but any farther than that can only serve to keep your mind in a state of disquietude that can never be of any advantage and must be detrimental to your health. Whenever the present horrid people that manage that kingdom are either removed by death or the intrigues of some new party, it cannot avail anything in your favour; but your leading an exemplary life will by degrees turn the cry in your favour and will hereafter make your son step forward in defence of his mother. I doubt but many dissatisfied people will try to make up to you, but I trust you will not give ear to their proposals. Others will be encouraged by the Danish court to sound you with no other view but to pry into your thoughts. Believe me, dear sister, the only dignified as well as safe part for you is to give up all thoughts of that country, at least till your children can be in a situation to come to your assistance.

In 1775 a party in Denmark put out feelers to the Queen for the countenance of her name in an attempt to overthrow the regime. The negotiation was conducted through Nathaniel William Wraxall, subsequently author of memoirs which contain valuable information about politics in Great Britain and a great deal of tittle-tattle about the courts of Europe. Wraxall came to England, but the King refused to have anything to do with the scheme.

My dearest sister [he wrote on 23 April 1775] it is not by calling myself an honest or an honourable man that I can deserve either of those epithets, but by a correct conduct; for to get you safely out of Denmark I certainly said I would not assist in getting you back to that kingdom. What I said I will scrupulously fulfill. . . . Indeed, I cannot, dear sister, say any more than if the Danish nobility shall at any time bring the King to recall you with that eclat and dignity that alone can make it advisable for you to return to his kingdom, I shall not only not prevent your going but support those who have been accessory to it; but from what I have declared I cannot either enter farther into the affair or be entrusted with the plan on which they mean to act.[18]

When the King wrote this letter his sister was seriously ill. She never returned to Denmark and never saw her children again, and she died a month later at the age of only twenty-four.

In 1785 the Danish court suggested to the King that his eldest daughter, the Princess Royal, should marry her cousin, Queen Caroline's son. The King was not attracted by the idea. 'After the treatment my late sister received', he wrote, 'no one in my house can be desirous of the alliance.'[19] He preferred to wait until he had received confirmation of the Prince's good character, and the suggestion came to nothing.

Three of the King's brothers lived to adult age: Edward, Duke of York; William, Duke of Gloucester; and Henry, Duke of Cumberland. Each caused him a good deal of worry and concern.

The Duke of York was radically different from the King in character and temperament and after they grew up there was little sympathy between them. The Duke was sociable and fond of pleasure and had no intellectual interests. He lived in the company of rakes, enjoyed playing foolish practical jokes, and developed a mischievous disposition to meddle in politics. 'He was silly, frivolous, and heartless', wrote Lady Louisa Stuart, 'void alike of steadiness and principle; a libertine in his practice, and in society one of those incessant characters who must by necessity utter a vast deal of nonsense.'[20] Still, he had some reason to be dissatisfied with his brother's conduct towards him.

Shortly after the King succeeded there came a vacancy in the bishopric of Osnabruck. This was an ecclesiastical state in the Holy Roman Empire, part Catholic part Protestant, whose territories adjoined Hanover. By the Treaty of Westphalia the right of nomination lay alternately in the Roman Catholic chapter and the house of Hanover, and in 1761 it was the Protestant turn. The bishop need not be a Catholic or even in orders. A Protestant Bishop had no ecclesiastical functions but was simply the executive head of the state and the receiver of its revenues, and the house of Hanover used its right of nomination to provide for a junior member of the family. In 1715, when it was the last Protestant turn, King George I had appointed his brother; and in 1761 the Duke of York as the eldest of the King's brothers had the strongest claim. King George not only passed him over but delayed the nomination for two years until the birth of his second son. Lady Mary Coke, partial though she was to the King, commented unfavourably on the appointment. 'It seems a hardship upon his brothers', she wrote, 'and may be a loss to the family, as His Majesty has not the second nomination, and the life of a new born child is very uncertain.' It was in fact a slight to the Duke of York and was resented accordingly.

The Duke lost an independent appanage worth about £20,000 a year. The King tried to compensate him by a gift of £16,000 for the purchase of a house, and on the

431

Duke of Cumberland's death in 1765 obtained permission from Parliament to divide the late Duke's income between his brothers. The Duke of York was not short of money, but could not forget the slight which had been placed upon him. In common with his brothers he disliked the King's dependence on Bute and probably took no pains to hide his feelings. In 1765 the King tried to exclude him from the Council of Regency. In 1766 the Duke became associated with the Bedford party, then in opposition, and in 1767, greatly to the King's annoyance, voted against Administration in the House of Lords. Lady Mary Coke, who fancied that the Duke was in love with her, noted in June 1767 that the King treated his brother coldly in public. The King was not sorry to see the Duke leave for a tour on the Continent. After visiting Paris, where he was received by Louis XV, he went to Marseilles, and was taken ill at Monaco. On 9 September 1767, when he knew himself to be dying, he dictated a pathetic letter to his next brother the Duke of Gloucester:[21]

The weak state I find myself in induces me, whilst it still may be in my power, to desire you to pay my last weak duties to the King, and if at any time I should have incurred his displeasure, I hope the generosity of his temper will at least make him forgive my unheeded past conduct which is all at present I have it in my power to offer.

The Duke died on 17 September. 'The King was most seriously grieved for the loss of his brother', wrote a contemporary, 'and literally almost cried his eyes out.'[22]

William, Duke of Gloucester, the next brother, was five years younger than the King. This age difference prevented any close friendship between them as boys and their intimacy only developed after Bute's withdrawal. The Duke of Gloucester had poor health, was weak and gentle by nature, and uninterested in politics. The King responded to his brother's need for protection and learnt to care for him more than for any other member of his family. 'You are the only friend to whom I can unbosom every thought', he told the Duke in November 1771.[23] The Duke found the British climate disagreeable and travelled extensively on the Continent. In 1769 he visited his sister the Queen of Denmark and in 1770 accompanied his mother on her visit to Germany. In 1771 while travelling in Italy he was taken seriously ill. The King sent out three of his personal physicians and for some weeks lived in the expectation of his brother's death. On 9 November he wrote to the Duke:[24]

It is impossible to express the joy I have felt ever since the arrival of Hunter [the courier] on Thursday; for I own the letters of the 18th ultimo which I received on Tuesday had possessed my mind with the greatest grief. I expected no other account than that Heaven had taken you from me, though thanks to God my mind is now at ease. I can scarcely relate what I have suffered without tears, but this has only taught me how much I love you. . . .

The Queen has desired me to express the sincere part she takes in your recovery and there is not a child that can speak that did not when I returned here [Richmond Lodge] last night give marks of their unaffected joy which has been general among all ranks of people.

The King's youngest brother Henry, Duke of Cumberland, was the black sheep of the family. As a young man he ran after women and sometimes caught them. The Duchess of Norfolk was shocked to see him riding in his carriage in Hyde Park with his mistress – 'I believe he is the first of the Royal Family', wrote Lady Mary Coke, 'that ever carried their mistress in the royal equipage.' In 1768 he was said to be attached to Lady Sarah Bunbury; and the foolish Lady Craven, later Margravine of Brandenburg Anspach, claims in her memoirs that Cumberland was 'very partial' to her and that 'his partiality in time extended to love'. He seems to have been attracted by married women and it was this which brought him into trouble. In 1770 he was named by Lord Grosvenor in an

433

action for criminal conversation (the eighteenth-century expression for adultery) and was cast in damages for £10,000. The Duke's letters to Lady Grosvenor were read in court and were retailed round London. Cumberland had to ask the King for a loan of £13,000 to pay the damages and costs and it was only with great difficulty that North was able to raise the sum from the Civil List. 'This takes a heavy load off me', the King wrote to North on 5 November 1770, 'though I can not enough express how much I feel at being in the least concerned in an affair that my way of thinking has ever taught me to behold as highly improper, but I flatter myself the truths I have thought it incumbent to utter may be of some use in his future conduct.'[25]

A year later, on 1 November 1771, the Duke called on his brother at Richmond Lodge.[26] He was not a frequent visitor to the King's country home and the King was surprised to see him. The brothers went for a walk in the woods surrounding the house and for a time Cumberland talked freely and apparently without constraint on indifferent subjects. Suddenly he stopped, pulled out a paper from his pocket, and asked the King to read it. To the King's consternation it was a formal letter from the Duke announcing his marriage to Ann Horton. What followed is best described in the King's own words:

After walking for some minutes in silence to smother my feelings, I without passion spoke to him to the following effect. That I could not believe he had taken the step in the paper, to which he answered that he would never tell me an untruth. Upon which I continued that if that was the case it would only be wasting my time to put before him the reason that any of his family must have stated if he had placed confidence in them previous to his taking this disgraceful step. . . . That to the indelicate method of notifying this to me, I hoped he would not add the cruelty of speaking to my mother in her bad state of health. That though it would be a terrible task on me, yet for her ease I would break it to her. I told him as the step was taken I could give him no advice, for that he had irretrievably ruined himself. But that it appeared to me that after such a disgraceful conduct any country was preferable to his own.

Two days later the Duke and his bride embarked for Calais.

Ann Horton was a widow, aged twenty-seven at the time of her second marriage and two years older than the Duke of Cumberland. She was the daughter of Simon Luttrell, Lord Irnham, head of an old Irish family, who sat in the Irish House of Lords and British House of Commons and was politically important in both countries. He had obtained his Irish barony from Grafton, and played his political cards so well that he got a viscountcy from North and an earldom from the younger Pitt. He was not a man of good character. Junius calls him 'this hoary lecher', and Lady Louisa Stuart was expressing contemporary opinion when she described him as 'the greatest reprobate in England'. He was hardly a fit person to be father-in-law to a member of the Royal Family, and the marriage soon became the jest of London. The opposition exulted in the fact that Irnham's eldest son and Ann's brother was the same Henry Lawes Luttrell who had stood as government candidate for Middlesex in 1769. John Wilkes was amply revenged on King George.

The King's objections did not arise from the person of the Duchess or the character of her father. Had she been the richest heiress in England and the daughter of the most respectable duke, he would still have objected to the match. He stated his reasons in a letter to the Duke of Gloucester:[27]

In any country a prince marrying a subject is looked upon as dishonourable, nay in Germany the children of such a marriage cannot succeed to any territories; but here, where the Crown is but too little respected, it must be big with the greatest mischiefs. Civil wars would by such measures be again coming in this country, those of the Yorks and Lancasters were greatly owing to intermarriages with the nobility. I must therefore on the first occasion show my resentment. I have children who must know what they have to expect if they could follow so infamous an example.

The comparison with the Wars of the Roses was hardly relevant to eighteenth-century conditions. The Duke of Cumberland, had he been able to argue his case, could have pointed to the example of Henry VIII who had four times married a subject. In the late seventeenth century James II when Duke of York had married a subject, and the two daughters of that marriage had sat on the throne of England. Even King George himself had wished to marry a subject until dissuaded by Bute. But historical precedents meant little. In the Europe of King George III's day no prince of a great monarchy could do what the Duke of Cumberland had done without loss of dignity and esteem. The position of Parliament in the British constitution made it undesirable for a member of the Royal Family to marry a subject. In the sixteenth and seventeenth centuries when Parliament met infrequently and at the will of the Crown such marriages were not objectionable. In the nineteenth century, when the Crown became elevated above party politics and the influence of the great aristocratic families over the House of Commons had declined, the marriages of the Royal Family ceased to have any political significance. In 1871, a hundred years after the Duke of Cumberland had married Ann Horton, a daughter of Queen Victoria married a son of the Duke of Argyll with the Queen's consent and blessing. No political interest was affected: neither government nor opposition gained or lost a single vote. The eighteenth century was an intermediate period between royal and parliamentary government. When Ann Horton was Duchess of Cumberland, five members of her family (her father and four brothers) sat in the House of Commons, and the marriage had (or what was almost the same, might be suspected to have) political consequences. King George wished his family to be above reproach, in politics as well as in morals.

The eighteenth century was an hierarchical society and distinctions of rank were preserved and valued. The family not the individual was the real unit of social organization. A younger son of an aristocratic or gentry family would not marry without the consent of the head of his family. The King had been treated with less respect than a Duke of Bedford or a Duke of Devonshire. In no family was this deference more desirable than in the Royal Family. The Duke of Cumberland had no income of his own, except what he received from the Civil List and the King's favour. He was entirely dependent on his brother. He was expected to maintain a style of living appropriate to a member of the Royal Family. He had to hold his court, to have his gentlemen of the bedchamber, equerries, grooms, and pages, all of whom were provided with salaries out of the Duke's allowance. When he married his wife would have to have her ladies and to live in a style consonant to her husband. The Duke's income (about £15,000 a year) was sufficient to support his state while he remained single but would not do when he married. The Duke was well aware that the King would not agree to his marriage with Ann Horton. He had therefore married her without the King's consent and now looked to the King for provision for his wife.

'The more I reflect on his conduct', the King wrote to his mother, 'the more I see it as his inevitable ruin and as a disgrace to the whole family.'[28] It was of course a legal marriage and any children born of it would be in succession to the throne. But the King was determined not to recognize his brother's wife as a member of the Royal Family. He sent a message to the Duke: 'That if he would never mention the step he had taken and would not make Mrs Horton publickly take his name I would again receive him, but if he did not agree to this I would never have any communication with him.'[29] The Duke refused to put a

437

public mark of indignity upon his wife by denying her the rank and station she had won by her marriage. His reply to the King showed more dignity and character than any other action of his life.[30] Perhaps Ann Horton had put some backbone into him. The King commented sourly: 'I am sorry to say it seems the performance of a Newgate attorney. I now wash my hands of the whole affair, and shall have no farther intercourse with him.'[31] An announcement was made that those who paid their court to the Duke and Duchess would not be received by the King and Queen.

What was done could not be undone but at least the King could make sure that nothing of the same kind ever happened again. He could protect his sons against designing women though it was too late to protect his brother. The Royal Marriage Act of 1772 made it illegal for any member of the Royal Family to marry without previous consent of the Crown; declared future marriages contracted without such consent to be null and void; and imposed penalties upon all assisting at such marriages. The issue of princesses who married into foreign families were exempt from the Act, and there was a proviso that anyone above the age of twenty-five could marry without consent of the Crown provided he or she gave twelve months' notice in advance and neither House of Parliament declared their disapprobation. The Act applied to all descendants of King George II, and is still in force today.

The Royal Marriage Act was the personal measure of the King: apart from the Regency Act of 1765 the only legislative enactment which he proposed during the whole course of his reign. It was drafted by Lord Mansfield, and submitted to the cabinet for their approval where it was not relished. North consulted his aides in the House of Commons and learnt that he would have a hard fight on his hands. Gibbon was probably expressing the general opinion when he described it as 'a most odious law'. 'I do not remember', he wrote, 'ever to have seen so general a concurrence of all ranks, parties and professions of men. Administration themselves are the reluctant executioners, but the King will be obeyed and the bill is universally considered as his.' Even the House of Lords, usually subservient to the Crown, gave the bill a cold reception. The King wrote to North on 26 February 1772 after the second reading in the Lords:

I do expect every nerve to be strained to carry the bill through both Houses with a becoming firmness, for it is not a question that immediately relates to Administration but personally to myself, therefore I have a right to expect a hearty support from everyone in my service and shall remember defaulters.

The progress of the bill through the House of Commons is the most convincing proof of the independence of the House. Despite the knowledge that the bill was the King's personal measure and his threats to dismiss placemen who opposed it, many who normally supported government did not fear to voice their objections. Nor was anyone dismissed. One junior minister (Richard Sutton, undersecretary of state) voted against the principle of the bill yet was allowed to retain his office. On the Royal Marriage Bill the King's bark was worse than his bite. Perhaps he hesitated to do for himself what he would have done for his ministers.

On the first division in committee – on an amendment which denied the right of the Crown to regulate the marriages of the Royal Family – the government majority was only 36. 'I wish a list could be prepared', the King wrote to North, 'of those that went away and those that deserted to the minority that would be a rule for my conduct in the drawing room tomorrow.' The committee stage, where every clause was debated almost word for word, was a fine opportunity for those Members who prided themselves on their historical or constitutional learning. The ministry's majority varied from clause to clause and none could be certain from day to day if there would be a majority. On an amendment to limit the bill for the duration of the King's life the government's majority sank to 18. North steered his way with infinite skill through the quicksands and jagged rocks which barred his passage, and established himself as the ablest leader of the House of Commons since Sir Robert Walpole. 'I look on your abilities', the King wrote on 18 March, 'and the zeal you have shown in conducting this bill through the different stages as the means that have brought it thus and that will crown it with success.' The third reading was carried on 24 March by 168 votes to 115. At the end of the session the King conferred the Garter on North, the first time since 1726 that the Garter had been given to a member of the House of Commons.

Long before the Duke of Cumberland's marriage there had been rumours in London society that the Duke of Gloucester was secretly married to Maria, dowager Lady Waldegrave, widow of the King's former governor. Lady Mary Coke heard the story as early as August 1766 but could not make up her mind to believe it. She thought it likely that the Duke was living with Lady Waldegrave but was he really married to her? Lady Charlotte Finch assured Lady Mary that the King was quite easy about these rumours and that the Duke of Gloucester had promised his brother he would never marry Lady Waldegrave. Throughout the affair of the Duke of Cumberland's marriage the King had written regularly to the Duke of Gloucester, then in Italy, and had confided everything to him. The Duke had appeared to share the King's views of their brother's conduct. It had been, he wrote to the King 22 November 1771, 'a series of follies and inconsistencies'. 'His behaviour in this last instance', the Duke of Gloucester wrote on 20 December, 'is inexcusable and weak beyond measure. He has got into very bad hands, and we know is easily led to any thing. I own I greatly fear for some subsequent follies. . . . But

440

he never did act for himself, and certainly does not now.'[32]
After receiving these letters the King could hardly doubt
that the rumours of the Duke of Gloucester's marriage
were untrue. The Duke surely could not have censured
his brother's conduct in such terms if he himself were also
married to a subject.

What then must King George have felt when he received this letter from the Duke of Gloucester, dated
13 September 1772?[33]

I am grieved much at finding myself obliged to acquaint Your
Majesty with a thing which must be so disagreable to you; but
I think the world being so much acquainted with my marriage,
whilst Your Majesty is still supposed to be ignorant of it, is
neither decent nor right. I will not pretend to justify the action:
it is now six years since, being in September sixty-six, and I
hope you will believe, Sir, it would never have been made
publick had it not been for a variety of accidents which have
made it necessary for me now to declare it to you.

The fact was the Duchess was pregnant.

The revelation of the Duke of Gloucester's marriage
hurt the King deeply. It was bad enough that the Duke of
Cumberland should marry a subject. But that the Duke of
Gloucester, the King's favourite brother, the one person
to whom he confided everything, should not only have
been secretly married for six years but should have led the
King to believe otherwise, was something King George
had not expected and which he felt he did not deserve.
The last year had been nothing but a series of domestic
calamities – the Duke of Cumberland's marriage, the
Queen of Denmark's disgrace, the illness of the Princess
Dowager – but this was the one the King found hardest
to bear. Yet he treated the Duke of Gloucester with much
less rancour than he had done the Duke of Cumberland.
He 'must be displeased', wrote the Duchess (as Lady
Waldegrave will now be styled), 'but his behaviour has
been such upon the occasion that we have all the reason

441

in the world to be grateful to him.' He could only do with
the Duke of Gloucester as he had with the Duke of
Cumberland, and offer him the alternative of a left-
handed marriage or of acknowledging his wife and being
forbidden the court. Like his brother, the Duke of
Gloucester declined to conceal his marriage. The King
and his brother parted in sorrow and without anger, but
their amity did not last long.

According to Lady Louisa Stuart, the edict against
visiting the Dukes of Cumberland and Gloucester was
not strictly enforced. 'It overawed people for the first
month; in the second they stole a visit to Gloucester or
Cumberland House, went to court early in the third, and,
being spoken to as usual, troubled their heads no more
about the matter. It soon grew a dead letter, which nobody pretended to mind but the household, the ministers,
and their wives.' The Dukes of Gloucester and Cumberland were made much of by the opposition – 'a cheap and
safe way', writes Lady Louisa, 'of showing disrespect to
the Crown'. 'Never were princesses so reverenced and
Royal Highnessed by patriots.' 'Well!' said Princess
Amelia, King George II's surviving daughter, 'to talk no
more of my nephews and their women. . . .'

Lady Louisa describes the difference in the behaviour
of the two duchesses:

The Duchess of Gloucester maintained a degree of state,
approved of by the Duke, that gave some stiffness to her parties, which were commonly rather select. Unbounded freedom
reigned at Cumberland House, as its mistress, laughing forms
and etiquettes to scorn, was better pleased that tag, rag, and
bobtail (pardon the vulgar phrase) should flock in, than that
numbers should ever be wanting.

The Duchess of Cumberland's sister, Lady Elizabeth
Luttrell,

more precisely what the Regent Orleans entitled a roué than
one would have thought it practicable that anything clad in

petticoats could be, governed the family with a high hand, marshalled the gaming table, gathered round her the men, and led the way in ridiculing the King and Queen. . . . A mighty scope for satire was afforded by the Queen's wide mouth and occasionally imperfect English, as well as by the King's trick of saying What! what! his ill-made coats, and general anti-pathy to the fashion. But the marks preferably aimed at were his *virtues*; his freedom from vice as a man; his discourage-ment of it as a sovereign . . . beyond all his religious *prejudices* – that is to say, his sincere piety and humble reliance upon God. Nothing of this scoffing kind passed at Gloucester House: the Duke respected himself and his brother too much to permit it, and the Duchess, however sore on her own ac-count, saw nothing ridiculous in conjugal fidelity, nor yet in going to church and saying one's prayers.

Yet Ann Horton was a good wife to the Duke of Cumberland. She kept him straight – after his marriage he never looked at another woman – and she did her best to prevent him making a fool of himself in politics. It was not her fault if she failed. It was otherwise with the Duchess of Gloucester. Maria Gloucester was the illegiti-mate daughter of Sir Edward Walpole, Horace Walpole's elder brother, and one of the most beautiful women of her age. She had three daughters by her first husband and was seven years older than her second. She was proud, over-bearing, avaricious, and shrewish; and though she be-haved with more decorum than her sister-in-law she led her husband an unhappy life. The King diagnosed vanity as the leading element in her character and he was not far wrong. So early as October 1772 the Princess of Bruns-wick told the King that their brother no longer loved his wife and regretted their marriage.[34] Ann Horton may not have been the ideal wife for the Duke of Cumberland but at least she made him happy. Maria Gloucester made her husband miserable.

In May 1773 the Duchess of Gloucester gave birth to her first child by the Duke, and two further children fol-lowed (one of whom died in infancy). The Duke's health did not improve, in 1775 he had to go abroad again, and in 1777 he was believed to be dying. He was naturally concerned about the future of his wife and children, and in 1774 when the Duchess was expecting their second child asked the King to provide for them. The King returned an official answer through the Secretary of State that he did not think proper to apply to Parliament for the Duke's children while his own were as yet unprovided for. As for the Duchess, 'His Majesty was pleased to say he could give no answer at all.' Lord Rochford who conveyed this message was instructed to inform the Duke orally that his children would be taken care of.

The Duke was offended by this reply and the Duchess more so. The King's refusal to acknowledge her as a member of the Royal Family galled her vanity and she threw fuel on the fire of her husband's resentment. He gathered round him a knot of politicians who were in opposition to North's ministry, and in June 1774 voted in the House of Lords against the Quebec Bill. In January 1775 he made a further application for financial provision, and threw out the hint that if the King did nothing one of Gloucester's friends would raise the matter in the House of Commons. The King wrote to North:

I cannot deny that on the subject of the Duke of Gloucester my heart is wounded. I have ever loved him with the fondness one bears to a child than a brother. His whole conduct from the time of his publishing what I must ever think a highly disgraceful step has tended to make the breach wider. I cannot therefore bring myself on a repetition of this application to give him hopes of a future establishment for his children, which would only bring on a fresh altercation about his wife whom I can never think of placing in a situation to answer her extreme pride and vanity. Should he be so ill advised as to have a provision for her and the children moved in Parliament, the line of conduct to be held is plain as my conduct is proper. I am not unwilling that the whole world may know it, and all the answer to be given by my minister [is] that it is natural the

King should not apply to Parliament for provision for the children of a younger branch of his family when he has not as yet done it for his own numerous offspring, and totally avoid mentioning the lady. So far for the public; but for yourself I am certain you know my way of thinking too well to doubt that should any accident happen to the Duke I shall certainly take care of his children.

The Duke would have been wiser to have trusted his brother rather than listened to his wife. Nothing could be done until the debts on the Civil List had been paid and when the time came the King was not ungenerous. In 1777 Parliament voted that in the event of the King's death each of his younger sons should receive £10,000 a year and each daughter £6,000, while the allowances for the Duke of Gloucester's children were fixed at £8,000 for his son and £4,000 for his daughter. In 1787, when the Duke's son was about to go up to Cambridge the King gave his father a further £4,000 a year. On the Duke's death his son's allowance was increased to £14,000 and his sister's to £5,000 with the promise of a further £2,000 on her mother's death.

This financial settlement relieved the Duke of Gloucester's mind and led to a reconciliation with the King. The King wished the Duke of Cumberland to be included, but the younger Duke had not made matters easy by engaging in politics. 'The whole political sentiments and conduct of the Duke of Cumberland are so very adverse to what I think right', the King wrote on 9 May 1780, 'that any intercourse between us could only be of a cold and distant kind and consequently very unpleasant.'[35] The event of the Gordon riots was used to bring about a reconciliation but the King insisted that this was not to include his brothers' wives. He wrote to the Duke of Gloucester on 9 June:[36]

I wish to be on the best terms with my brother and that we may not disagree, therefore when we meet I hope it will be

445

understood that nothing is to be mentioned in the conversation between us about the Duchess of Gloucester.

I shall be happy at any time to see the Duke of Gloucester's children.

According to Horace Walpole the Duke of Gloucester put the letter into the fire and said 'It is not fit that this letter should ever be seen.' Perhaps the Duchess was watching him. The Duke went to the King who in Walpole's words 'wept over him, and told him he had ever loved him the best of his family, and hoped to see him often.' 'The King heard with great patience very strong things the Duke said to him.' At least this is what the Duke of Gloucester told the Duchess and her uncle Horace, but whatever these 'strong things' were they did not induce the King to change his mind about the Duchess. Henceforth relations between the brothers were cordial. 'I am grown a very old gentleman [he was 36]', the Duke of Gloucester wrote to the King from Weymouth on 25 September 1780, 'and content myself with trying to shoot, I do not say shooting.'[37]

During the next few years the Duke became better acquainted with his wife's character. By 1786 their relations had almost reached breaking point and shortly afterwards the Duke took a mistress. When a middle-aged man who has never engaged in gallantry takes a mistress it is a sure sign that his wife has ceased to love him. Perhaps she had never loved him, but only coveted the rank and station of being his wife and when these were refused her turned against him. In 1787 the Duke opened his heart to the King and told him about the Duchess's 'very unfortunate turn of mind and temper'.[38]

I have told her that if she lets the children from this time alone, and behaves more respectfully to me before the world, she may still remain in my house, though so long since as when my daughter was but a year old she threatened me with leaving me. I hope Your Majesty will forgive my troubling you with

446

all this detail but my heart is very full. I am indeed severely punished for my juvenile indiscretion by the very ungrateful return I receive at home.

We know little of the Duke's later relations with his wife. He died on 25 August 1805. The King, who was not expecting his death, wrote to the Duke's son:

My dear nephew, It is with the utmost concern I have received the letter brought by Mr Vincent acquainting me of the death of my excellent brother. It is impossible for me at present to add more than that you and every part of his family shall feel the affection I had for him.

'The poor King is singularly affected with it', wrote the Duke of Kent. At the request of the Duchess the Duke was buried in St George's Chapel, Windsor. The King treated the Duke's children as his own and his acerbity towards the Duchess diminished. He wrote kindly about her in letters to her son and when she died sent her children his condolences. She was buried with her second husband. At least in death she was granted the style of Her Royal Highness.

The King's later relations with the Duke and Duchess of Cumberland were not happy. They had no children. When the Prince of Wales began to go out in society he resorted to Cumberland House, and there learnt to drink, wench, and gamble. Prince Frederick deplored the influence the Duke of Cumberland had over his brother. 'You cannot stand this kind of life', he wrote, '. . . I have no doubt that he means you exceedingly well, but believe me, he is not the best adviser you can follow.' During the political crisis of 1783–4 Cumberland was strong for the coalition – 'our friends', as he called them, but the Duchess warned the Prince of Wales of the dangers of becoming a party man. 'I ever was of opinion', she wrote on 27 December 1783, 'that the prerogative of the Crown ought not to be diminished and every struggle for power in the present inauspicious season of republicanism is

447

dangerous to monarchy.'[39] A few years were to show the truth of these words.

During the last years of his life the Duke of Cumberland was financially embarrassed and spent much time abroad. 'Until I am clear', he wrote on 8 February 1786, 'England must be the most improper place in the world for me.' When he died in 1790 the Duke of Clarence wrote to the Prince of Wales:

Poor fellow, he certainly had the best heart in the world. I am glad to hear by Frederick the King was so much hurt. But, my dear brother, the Duchess is to be pitied. Her conduct by all accounts was exemplary: indeed her goodness has been manifested on all occasions.

The Duke left nothing but debts and the King offered his widow a pension of £4,000 a year. This was considered by the Prince of Wales to be a 'shabby proposal'. 'It is totally impossible for her', he wrote, 'as his brother's wife to exist, so far from living, in the manner she ought to do upon so very incompetent an income.' £4,000 a year was a comfortable income for a widow with no children, but it would not enable the Duchess to pay her husband's debts and support her in the style of a Royal Highness. The King maintained his rigour towards the Duchess and refused to recognize her as a member of the Royal Family. She spent the last years of her life on the Continent, a lonely and pathetic creature.

Ever since the great fire which destroyed Whitehall Palace in 1698, St James's had been the London residence of the monarchy. Accordingly, after his grandfather's death, the King left Savile House and went to live at St James's Palace. But he had no intention of making his permanent home there. He refused to live in any of the palaces King George II had occupied, and abandoned Kensington and Hampton Court, his grandfather's country residences, in favour of Kew. There is a story that King George III disliked Hampton Court because his grandfather had once boxed his ears there. In 1770 when a fire broke out at Hampton Court the King told Lord Hertford he would not have been sorry had the palace been burnt down. Equally the King disliked St James's, 'this dust trap' as he once called it. It was too close to the centre of London and too open to the London mob. After 1762 he used it only for court ceremonies and as a home for his younger sons. King George was the first British monarch to make a distinction between his court and his home, between his public and his private life. St James's became the King's place of business: his London home was the Queen's House.

The Queen's House, or Buckingham House as it had formerly been called, stood on the site now occupied by Buckingham Palace.[40] It had been the town residence of the Dukes of Buckingham and when King George came to the throne was the property of the illegitimate son of the last Duke. Lord Carnarvon, one of the King's Lords of the Bedchamber, is said to have suggested it as a suitable residence for the King. It was out of the centre of London, surrounded by fields, and yet within easy access of St James's. The King bought it out of the Privy Purse at a cost of £28,000. Furniture and pictures were taken from Hampton Court and Kensington for the new residence, and the King and Queen moved in during the summer of 1762. All their children apart from the Prince of Wales were born there.

It is possible that the King bought the house as temporary accommodation until a new one could be built. It was not large enough for a royal palace and as the King's family increased it became too small to lodge all the children. There are designs by Thomas Wright for a new palace in St James's Park,[41] but if it was ever the King's intention to build in London he soon abandoned the idea. The King's plans for a new palace at Kew and for restoring Windsor Castle did not allow him to spend money in

London. In 1775 an Act of Parliament transferred the property to the Queen for her life in exchange for Somerset House, her original dower house, which the King had given to his newly founded Royal Academy of Arts. Extra rooms were added to house the King's collections, but it was left to King George IV to begin the building of a new palace in London.

The palace at Kew, variously known as Kew Palace, the White House, or the Old Palace, adjoined the river Thames and was not ten miles from Charing Cross.[42] It had been the country home of the King's parents, and was held on lease from the family of Capel, Earls of Essex. Frederick, Prince of Wales, had enlarged the house and cultivated the gardens; and after his death his widow, advised by Bute, developed her husband's collection of plants later to become the Royal Botanic Gardens. The King as Prince of Wales lived at Richmond Lodge, a smaller house near that of his mother. Here he learnt the news of his grandfather's death and here he set up his country home after his marriage. On the death of his mother in 1772 he moved to the White House and in 1782 bought the freehold. But the White House like the Queen's House in London was too small for a growing family. Another house, the Dutch House, just across the road from the White House, was used as a nursery for the royal children. In 1773 the Prince of Wales and Prince Frederick with their tutors and servants were lodged in the Dutch House, while the other boys as they grew up were placed in houses round Kew Green. The girls lived with their parents at the White House, until in 1802, when all the children had grown up, it was pulled down and the King and Queen moved into the Dutch House. Queen Charlotte continued to live in the Dutch House during the King's last illness, and it was here, on 17 November 1818, that she died.

There was thus a small colony of royal residences at Kew but no palace big enough to house the whole family.

About 1784 the King began to build a new palace on the site of Richmond Lodge, by the banks of the Thames opposite to Brentford. This was the famous 'castellated palace', designed by James Wyatt in the Gothic style. The King wrote about it to his daughter the Princess Royal on 26 September 1803:[43]

I am building at Richmond. It advances but slowly partly owing to a certain want of diligence in Wyatt and partly to the present want of workmen. . . . I never thought I should have adopted Gothic instead of Grecian architecture, but the bad taste of the last forty years has so entirely corrupted the professors of the latter I have taken to the former from thinking Wyatt perfect in that style, of which my house will I trust be a good example.

'This extraordinary exercise in late Georgian Baronial', as it is described in the guide to Kew Palace, was not regarded favourably by contemporaries. Queen Charlotte tried to dissuade the King from attempting it. Wraxall compared it to the Bastille, built on the worst possible site. 'The foundation is in a bog close to the Thames and the principal object within its view is the dirty town of Brentford.' Wraxall was no judge of architecture but he reflected what people felt about King George's castellated palace. Mr John Charlton, author of the excellent guide to Kew Palace, gives us some idea of what it would have been:

It appears to have consisted of a large central keep with round towers at the angles and projecting staircase turrets. It was surrounded by a great courtyard enclosed by a high curtain wall with large square angle towers, smaller interval towers, also square, and a three-storey gatehouse towards the Dutch House with another, less elaborate, towards the river. The central keep was apparently of four and the courtyard build ings of three storeys. It is obvious that the building, if completed, would have been highly inconvenient and uncomfortable.

It was never completed, and what remained of the King's folly was pulled down in 1828.

451

The King was more fortunate in his building at Windsor.[44] The origins of Windsor Castle can be traced back to William the Conqueror and there is no building in Europe which has so long a record of habitation by a ruling family. Kings of England from the twelfth to the seventeenth centuries had adorned and improved Windsor Castle. In the fourteenth century Edward III had founded the Order of the Garter, and in the fifteenth century St George's Chapel was built. Windsor Castle was the favourite residence of Queen Anne; and it was here, overlooking the North Terrace, a few steps from the room in which King George III was to die, that she received the news of Marlborough's victory at Blenheim. After her death the Castle fell into neglect. It was too far from London to make a convenient royal residence and the first two Georges preferred to live at Hampton Court. During their reigns old servants of the Royal Family were quartered in various buildings of the Castle and no attempt was made to maintain the fabric. King George III rescued it from this state of neglect.

History is in every stone of Windor Castle. The names of the buildings – Norman Gateway, King Edward III Tower, King Henry VIII gate – are witnesses to its antiquity. King George had a greater feeling for the past than his immediate predecessors. They belonged of a new dynasty which had supplanted an old one and there was a parvenu touch about them. He was an established monarch, the latest in a line of Kings which went back over seven hundred years. He was the heir of a tradition and felt the continuity with his mediaeval predecessors. Although his taste in architecture inclined to the classical, he shared the emotions behind the Gothic revival.

It was Queen Charlotte who brought the King to Windsor. In 1775 the house in the Castle grounds where Queen Anne had lived became vacant and Queen Charlotte asked it for herself. The Queen's Lodge as it became known stood on the south side of the Castle, near to what is now the King George IV Gate. To accommodate the Royal Family, Sir William Chambers built a long barrack-like extension to the house. Even then it was not big enough. In 1777 the Queen bought a neighbouring house from the Duke of St Albans which had been granted to his ancestress Nell Gwynne. This, the Lower Lodge as it was called, became the residence of the younger princesses and their attendants. The cost of making these two houses habitable came to over £40,000.

The King's first letter from Windsor is dated 22 August 1777. At first he intended only to stay there occasionally when he was out hunting and it was too late to return to Kew. But the charms of the place grew upon him and by 1780 he was spending more time at Windsor than at Kew. The King liked informality, and at Windsor he was not King but a plain country squire. The Castle grounds then as now were open to the public and King George met the common people of England at Windsor as he could never have done in London. Charles Knight, the son of a Windsor bookseller, remembered as a boy seeing the King in his father's shop, 'a quiet, good-humoured gentleman in a long blue coat', turning over the latest publications like any other customer. He took pleasure in watching the boys playing cricket or flying their kites in the park. 'Many a time', writes Knight, 'had he bidden us good morning when we were hunting for mushrooms in the early dew and he was returning from his dairy to his eight o'clock breakfast. Everyone knew that most respectable and amiable of country squires, and His Majesty knew everyone.' On fine summer evenings the King and Queen would walk arm-in-arm, their daughters and attendants following, passing by the Round Tower and emerging on to the North Terrace, described in a Windsor guide of 1782 as 'the noblest walk in Europe'. The King and Queen would stop and talk to people, not courtiers or politicians, but the ordinary people of Windsor who had gone to pay their respects to their squire. It was the same at Kew, where the Royal Family lived as 'the simplest country gentlefolks' and where they walked in the village without any attendants.

Under King George Windsor became truly a royal borough. The King invented the Windsor uniform, 'in blue and gold turned up with red', which was worn by the gentlemen in his service and which it became an object of ambition to wear. He looked after the interests of its citizens and contributed towards their amenities. He gave £1,000 towards paving the streets; increased the value of the living and presented the parish church with an organ from St George's Chapel; and built a hospital for sick soldiers on a plot of land presented by the corporation. In 1793 he helped Windsor to get a theatre and was a frequent attender. His patronage of the local shops, wrote the Windsor guide for 1792, had 'excited a spirit of industry and emulation in the different tradesmen, who vie with each other in the improvement of their shops, and in the quality and cheapness of their various commodities'. He bought property in the town and two adjoining manors, and farmed in the Great Park. He revived the royal interest in the politics of Windsor, and from 1780 onwards recommended one of the borough's two Members of Parliament.[45]

Sir William Chambers had advised the King that the Castle could not be made habitable without enormous expense, and the King preferred to give priority to the restoration of St George's Chapel. Repairs and alterations were made to the altar and the choir; a new organ was built; and the King commissioned his favourite painter, Benjamin West, to design four stained glass windows. With scant regard for antiquity the original stone tracery of the great east window over the altar was demolished to make way for a stained glass representation of the Resurrection. 'In the centre compartment', writes the Windsor guide, 'among the host of cherubim and seraphim, is a portrait of Prince Octavius.' This was paid for by the

King and the Knights of the Garter, the King paying much the larger share. The restoration of St George's Chapel cost about £20,000, of which the chapter paid £5,800 and the King the remainder. By the end of the reign St George's had superseded Westminster Abbey as the place of burial for members of the Royal Family.

In 1786 the state apartments in Windsor Castle had been restored to order. In that year the King and Queen entertained the Duke and Duchess of Milan at Windsor. 'We dined at the lower apartments in the Castle', wrote the Queen, 'and went to the Lodge after dinner. By seven we returned to the Castle, where we met the company which was invited upon the occasion, had the concert at the great guard room, and supped in St George's Hall.' When the restoration of St George's Chapel was completed, the King employed Wyatt to convert the buildings round the upper ward of the Castle into the Gothic style and to construct a series of private apartments. The King's apartments – a bedroom, sitting-room, and a room for his servant – overlooked the North Terrace and faced towards Eton. On 2 November 1804 the Royal Family left the Queen's Lodge and took up their residence in the Castle. To Queen Charlotte the change was not welcome. It was all very well for King George to live in a room which rarely received the sun and without even a carpet on the floor (the King disliked carpets which he said harboured dust). He was a man of the simplest tastes but the Queen liked a little comfort in her old age. 'I have changed from a very comfortable and warm habitation', she wrote, 'to the coldest house, rooms, and passages that ever existed.'

'I am no architect', the King once told Benjamin West. Nor was he much of a builder. King George IV was to spend an enormous amount of money on building but at least he left something for it. Though Carlton House has been demolished, the Royal Pavilion at Brighton and the upper ward at Windsor are monuments to his taste. King

George III spent much less than his son but most of it was frittered away, and it was not until he had been on the throne for over forty years that he had a palace large enough to house his family. If he had devoted his energies to one object only – the restoration of Windsor Castle or the new palace at Kew – he might have achieved something permanent. As it was he left nothing memorable. Those who love Hampton Court can never quite forgive him for having abandoned it as a royal residence, but he must be given credit for bringing the Royal Family back to Windsor.

The King's affection for Eton College began before he went to live at Windsor.[46] His first visit to the school was in 1762 and from then onwards hardly a year passed without the King and Queen paying a visit. He became well known to masters and boys, and took a deep interest in the customs and traditions of the school. In time he came to think of himself as an Etonian. 'You Westminsters must now look to yourselves', he said to Lord Onslow in 1801, 'or we shall get ahead of you very soon.' The Eton custom of celebrating 4 June, the King's birthday, began during his lifetime.

It is generally taken for granted that the principal residence of a monarch must be in the capital city of his kingdom. This was not so with King George. 'I certainly see as little of London as I possibly can', the King wrote in 1785, 'and am never a volunteer there.' His dislike of London was partly because of his fondness for country life, and partly a result of the abuse he and his mother had encountered from the mob during the early years of the reign. He used the Queen's House as a *pied à terre*, only staying the night there for a particular reason such as a visit to the theatre which made it too late to get back to Kew or Windsor. Even in the 1790s when he was approaching his sixtieth year, after a long and tiring day at court, he would take a hasty dinner at the Queen's House, mount his horse, and ride the twenty miles to Windsor.

London was his place of business but Kew and Windsor were his homes. King George was the first commuter.

King George was a tall, well-built man, in later life inclining to stoutness, with a good leg – a quality as much admired in a man in the eighteenth century as it is in a woman today. The only record of his weight is that on 14 February 1789 he weighed 12 stone 3 pounds. But this was at the end of his long illness when he was much reduced. In normal health he must have weighed much more, probably about 14 stone. The most prominent features of his face were a high forehead, protruding eyes, a large nose, thick lips, and a dimpled chin. It is possible that even as a young man he suffered from defective vision, and as he grew older and his eyesight worse he acquired a bent and peering look. His complexion was ruddy. His face was not handsome but he had a steady and open expression which commanded respect, and he carried himself well in public. Throughout his active life he followed the fashion of his youth, already becoming out of date when he succeeded to the throne, of shaving his head and wearing a wig – not the full-bottomed wig in vogue during the earlier years of the century but a small one which came down to the lobes of his ears. Fanny Burney thought his voice 'particularly full and fine', and Boswell, who heard him deliver the speech from the throne on 25 November 1762, wrote that he spoke with 'dignity, delicacy, and ease'. He cared little for clothes or for fashion, and dressed much the same as an old man as he had when young.

The King led a regular and active life.[47] He rose at about six, and shaved himself. Once dressed, his first business was to deal with any correspondence that had arrived during the night, and there are several of his letters written before seven a.m. He once summoned Sir Charles Thompson to attend him at the unfashionable hour of eight in the morning. Unless the weather was very bad he always took a ride before breakfast, and often rode after breakfast with one or more of his brothers or sons. At the Queen's House he had a manège built in which he could ride indoors during bad weather. In the early years of the reign the King and Queen breakfasted together, and when the children were small they were allowed to visit their parents after the meal. Later they breakfasted separately, the Queen at nine and the King earlier. We do not know what they had for breakfast, except that the King drank tea and the Queen coffee.

The rest of the day's programme depended on whether the King was in London or in the country. If in London he would go to his study for an hour or so after breakfast, and about midday would leave for St James's to attend the levee or drawing room. The usual time of dinner was four but the King often dined much later. If the levee was full it might be five or six before he got back to the Queen's House. On these days the Queen did not wait for him but dined alone or with her daughters at the usual time. Dinner was strictly a family meal. In the early years of their marriage the King and Queen dined alone, or occasionally with the Princess Dowager or one of the King's brothers as their guest. In later years they were joined by their daughters and by any of their sons who happened to be staying in the house. But except when foreign royalty visited them or on special occasions such as the Prince of Wales's birthday the King and Queen never gave dinner parties. Lord North and William Pitt, who between them were the King's first minister for over thirty years, seem never to have had a meal with their sovereign. In the country the King and Queen occasionally dined out but hardly ever in London.

After dinner the King retired to his study and rejoined the Queen at about seven for tea. The evening was spent in various ways. On at least two evenings in the week the King and Queen used to visit the Princess Dowager. On Thursdays they went to the theatre, on Saturdays to the opera, and they regularly attended the concerts of the Ancient Music Society in the Society's rooms in Tottenham Court Road. Most evenings they spent at home, listening to music and playing at cards. Queen Charlotte was fond of cards while King George disliked anything that savoured of gambling. At the beginning of his reign he stopped the practice of playing hazard at court on Twelfth Night, and the card parties which King George II had enjoyed did not appeal to his grandson. But the Queen coaxed him into allowing cards to return. In 1768 Lady Mary Coke noted that the King and Queen played at 'whisk', a game which had only recently been introduced into England, with Lady Effingham and Lady Charlotte Finch. Both were close friends. Lady Effingham was familiarly addressed as 'Effy' by the King and Queen and was always summoned to be with the Queen in her confinements, and Lady Charlotte was the first friend the Queen made in England. In this familiar society the King relaxed, and for a few hours put such tiresome people as George Grenville and the Earl of Chatham out of his mind.

When the girls grew up they joined their parents for the evening and with them came a group of courtiers, personal friends of the King and Queen. Colonel Goldsworthy and Major Price would be there, and the Courtowns, Lord Ailesbury, the Weymouths – names familiar to the reader of Fanny Burney. The card tables were set up, and whist or commerce was played to the accompaniment of background music from the royal band. It is a scene reminiscent of that at Dingley Dell when Mr Pickwick honoured the 'solemn observance' of whist and the young people enjoyed a round game. We do not know whether any money was staked and it seems probable that they played only for love, certainly not for the high sums that changed hands at King George II's or Princess Amelia's card parties. There is a report however that they played *vingt-et-un* – the old army game of 'pontoon' –

which can hardly be played except for some stakes; and they also played at commerce, reverse, and other games long since forgotten. There was no card-playing on Sundays, Good Friday, Christmas Day, or the anniversary of King Charles I's execution (30 January).

The game ended at about ten and was followed by supper. This was the one meal at which the King and Queen regularly had guests. The eighteenth-century supper was an elaborate meal – no mere affair of a few sandwiches and a cup of tea – but the royal suppers did not last long and the King and Queen were usually in bed by eleven or twelve at the latest. King George disliked late hours. The King and Queen had separate apartments which communicated by a private staircase, but they slept together.

Balls were held on the birthdays of members of the Royal Family. The Queen's birthday which was on 18 May, within a fortnight of the King's, was officially celebrated on 18 January, but there was often a private ball for the Royal Family on the actual day. In 1789 when the King and Queen were at Weymouth they celebrated the anniversary of their wedding by giving a ball for their daughters. Thirty-two guests were invited and the ball ended at 2.45 in the morning. Another ball at Windsor Castle on 6 January 1794 began at 9, was broken off for supper at 12, and ended at 3.30 a.m. At 10 the King was out riding as usual. The Queen's birthday ball on 19 May 1794 (held on that day because the 18th was a Sunday) did not end until 4 a.m. The Queen stayed in bed the next morning, but at 9.30 the King was on his horse about to set off for Kew. He once told Wyatt that six hours' sleep was enough for a man, seven for a woman, and eight for a fool. But often these balls did not last much beyond midnight. They were small affairs, attended only by a few close friends of the Royal Family, mostly middle-aged couples. As a young man the King enjoyed dancing. At the ball given for the King of Denmark in September 1768 he was in great spirits and 'did not retire until after four o'clock in the morning'. In middle age he left dancing to younger people and preferred his rubber of whist.

There is a pleasant cosy touch about the King's domestic life. On Sundays when cards were forbidden he would play chess or backgammon with one of his equerries. Sometimes in the interval between arriving home and dinner he would bring his papers into the Queen's room where she sat sewing and sign some of the innumerable public documents which required his signature. He would get up himself and put coal on the fire rather than ring for a servant. His servants and attendants were devoted to him and the King appreciated their devotion. Lord Ailesbury wrote in 1786 about the visit of the Archduke and Archduchess of Milan to Windsor: 'The King last night thanked those that had done their duty so well about the entertainments, for which they had such short notice for their services, and succeeding so well.'

Christmas was celebrated as a solemn religious festival, not as an occasion for merrymaking. The entry in the Queen's diary for 25 December 1789 describes a typical Christmas Day with the Royal Family:

We breakfasted at nine and at ten we went to our rooms. I read to the princesses a sermon for the day and prayers for the sacrament. At twelve we went to church. The Rev. Dr Fisher read prayers and the Bishop of Salisbury preached and gave the sacrament. We returned half hour after two, then dressed. At four the younger princesses came and dined with us. We staid below till six then went upstairs and read proper service for the day till the King came. Again sacred music. Did not play. Lady Courtown came at eight, we parted at ten, supped, and retired at eleven

The next day the King went hunting and did not get back until five.

The eighteenth century was a great age for eating and drinking, at least for the quantity consumed at meals. 'We sat down thirty people', wrote Prince William in 1786, describing a dinner party he had attended. 'Few got up sober, for we were at the table and bottle seven hours and a half.' Dinner parties were exclusively male affairs, and without the refining influence of feminine society were apt to degenerate into orgies. The King in this as in so many other matters was out of touch with contemporary fashion. He told Fanny Burney in 1785 that 'the fault of his constitution was a tendency to excessive fat, which he kept, however, in order, by the most vigorous exercise, and the strictest attention to a simple diet'. 'I prefer eating plain and little to growing diseased and infirm.' Had he lived in the twentieth century he would have been an avid student of those diet sheets which are a feature of women's magazines.

Lunch was a meal unknown to the eighteenth century, and the King ate nothing between breakfast at nine and dinner at four. His dinner was a simple affair: soup, meat and one vegetable, and fruit. He was fond of mutton which he liked with turnips or beetroot, and the traditional English dish of roast beef was reserved for Sundays. He seems not to have cared for venison, a popular dish with the upper classes. He liked salads and fresh fruit, and if it was made into a tart he would eat the fruit and leave the pastry. He drank sparingly, never more than three or four glasses of wine at a meal and that often mixed with water. He never drank spirits. He was a great tea drinker, and when visiting would prefer a cup of tea to a glass of wine. Often he would go without supper, and if he had the meal it was usually a little fruit or eggs and bread and butter. In 1786 at the supper for the Archduke and Archduchess of Milan he ate only apple compote. When the King and Queen paid a visit lavish hospitality was prepared for them and usually declined. On their visit to Whitbread's brewery in 1787 the King 'stood all the time and eat only bread and butter'. The Queen said how good the brown bread was and the King cut a slice for Lord Ailesbury. 'We drank nothing', wrote Ailesbury in his diary. 'Queen and princesses had tea and strawberries, etc.' It was not etiquette for the attendants to eat in the presence of the Royal Family. Fanny Burney, who visited Oxford with the King and Queen in 1786, describes the cold collation which was provided in Christ Church. After getting up early in the morning (it took two hours to dress her hair – one wonders how long it took to dress the Queen's), listening to long orations in the Sheldonian, tramping round the colleges, Fanny felt hungry; and elaborate subterfuges were made for her and the other attendants to have a snack without the King noticing. Not that the King would have minded. He would have laughed at the sight of Fanny tucking surreptitiously into a wing of cold chicken but the dons would have been scandalized. Etiquette had to be observed, not because King George stood upon his dignity but because the dons stood upon theirs.

Hunting was the King's favourite recreation. Every day in the country he went out after breakfast and did not return until dinner. No day was too long for him, and like Lord Scamperdale 'the distance could never be too great provided the pace corresponded'. When he drove his daughters in his phaeton he sometimes frightened them by the speed at which he urged the horses. He would have stayed out as long as the light lasted but the Queen liked him to be home early. At the end of a long day with the hounds he would drink nothing but barley water, which once provoked an expression of humorous disgust from Goldsworthy who would have liked something stronger. Fanny Burney was warned not to go near Windsor on the King's hunting days for all the inns would be full of people going to the hunt – 'we heard of nothing but the King and royal huntsmen and huntswomen'. The King was often accompanied by his brothers or sons. He preferred stag to fox hunting because the chase lasted longer, but after his illness in 1788 when he was advised to take less exercise (advice which he ignored) he also indulged in the less exacting sport of hare hunting. Occasionally he took a toss, as in 1782 when his horse ran away with him and threw him against a gate.

The King's reign witnessed the development of horse racing into an organized sport, with a set of rules and something like a code of conduct. The Prince of Wales and the Duke of York both ran racing stables, and the Prince won the Derby in 1788. But in general their experiences on the turf were unfortunate, and in 1792 the Prince decided to sell his horses. The King did not keep a racing stable but he liked to watch racing (the Queen thought a horse race 'a vulgar business'). He used to go occasionally to Epsom and regularly attended at least one day of the Ascot June meeting. He gave a plate of a hundred guineas to be run for by horses who had hunted with his hounds, and had a road built from Windsor Castle to the race track. But the development of the Ascot June meeting into the present-day Royal Ascot belongs to the reign of King George IV. The King never went to Newmarket, where the gambling was high and the practices dubious.

He must have been a superb horseman and physically fit. On their journeys the Queen and her daughters travelled by coach, but the King rode on horseback and only in the foulest weather could he be induced to enter the coach. In 1804 at the age of 66 he rode ten miles with George Rose through the New Forest to keep a dinner engagement in one of the heaviest downpours of rain Rose had known. In 1788, just before his illness, while travelling from Windsor to London he got off his horse and walked twelve miles – 'which is more than the Prince of Wales can do, young as he is', wrote Anthony Storer. He seemed impervious to cold. Lord Glenbervie describes a conversation with him in 1804 on the terrace at Weymouth. A cold damp wind blew, Glenbervie shivered and his teeth chattereed, but the King went on talking and seemed not to feel it. He took few precautions as regards his health and hated being fussed over by doctors.

He admired physical courage and endurance. In 1804 while the Royal Family was journeying from George Rose's house in the New Forest to Southampton, Princess Amelia, then aged twenty-one, was thrown from her horse and badly shaken. The King refused to allow her to enter the coach but insisted that she should ride on. Rose suggested that she should return, which 'provoked a quickness from His Majesty that I experienced in no other instance. He observed that he could not bear that any of his family should want courage.' 'I thank God', the King continued, 'there is but one of my children who wants courage – and I will not name him, because he is to succeed me.' 'I own', wrote Rose, 'I was deeply pained by the observation.' Unfortunately it was true.

At all times in history it has been the duty of monarchs to show themselves to their subjects. A cloistered and fugitive King will soon be no King at all. The way this has been done varies from age to age with social conditions and technical changes. The progresses of Queen Elizabeth I from country house to country house and the Christmas appearances of Queen Elizabeth II on television serve the same purpose – that of allowing the people to see their sovereign. The difference is that in the sixteenth century the governing class counted for more than the mass of the population. In the twentieth century there is no governing class, and science has made it possible for the sovereign to speak to all her subjects at the same time.

Under the ancien régime in France access to the sovereign was the right of every subject. 'Familiarity has never harmed a King of France' it was said, and British visitors to Paris were surprised to see the common people as well as the aristocracy admitted to the antechambers of Versailles. In Great Britain in the eighteenth century access to the sovereign was reserved to the governing class and was accorded through the system of levees and drawing rooms. In this respect the constitutional monarchy of

Great Britain was less democratic than the theoretically absolute monarchy of France.[48]

Twice a week, on Wednesdays and Fridays, the King held a levee at St James's Palace. During the session of Parliament there was also a levee on Mondays but after the King's illness in 1788 this was given up. The levee was for men only. Anyone could attend provided he wore court dress (which in effect restricted attendance to the upper classes) and anyone could be presented to the King provided he could find someone to make the presentation. Drawing rooms were held on Thursdays and Sundays. These were attended by both King and Queen and were open to both sexes.

For certain people regular attendance at levees and drawing rooms was virtually compulsory: members of the Royal Family, ministers, Members of Parliament friendly to the government, and foreign ambassadors. Lady Mary Coke once arrived late for a drawing room and found herself crushed into a corner with Chatham, Lord Chancellor Northington, and two bishops. These people were not expected to attend every levee but absence was sometimes noticed and censured. The King once reprimanded the Prince of Wales because he skipped a levee to go fox hunting, and North and Pitt generally sent an apology to the King if they were unable to attend. The King excused ministers in advance if he knew they would find it difficult to attend because of official or parliamentary business. When a Member of Parliament ceased to attend at Court it was a sign that he was about to go into opposition. In addition to the official classes there were others who wished to pay their duty to the King. A country gentleman, up to London for a few weeks with his wife and family, would request the favour of his Member of Parliament or Lord Lieutenant. Army officers were presented by their colonels, parsons by their bishops, and foreigners by their ambassadors.

The levee usually began at twelve. On his arrival at St

James's the King was escorted to the state bedchamber, and dressed in levee clothes by the Lord of the Bedchamber in waiting, supervised by the Groom of the Stole. It was the custom in the eighteenth century for royalty to be waited upon on formal occasions by their nobility, who performed services which in later ages would be the responsibility of a valet or a maid. To put on the King's shirt or the Queen's petticoat was a privilege of rank and office and jealously guarded. It was a survival of the days when the highest post in the state was that of the person closest to the King. In Great Britain the King was dressed in private and the general public was not admitted to the state bed-chamber as in France.

When the King was dressed, he entered the privy chamber. The right to access to the privy chamber was restricted to those who held or had held high office. As the King passed through the doors to the presence chamber were thrown open. The gentlemen attending the levee formed a circle round the two rooms. At the entrance of the King conversation ceased. The King went to the first man on his right hand. A bow was given and returned. The King said a few words and received a few words in reply; another bow, also returned; and the King passed on to the next man and so round the circle. There was no obligation to stay to the end of the levee and people usually went away after the King had spoken to them.

It was King George's custom to speak to all who attended and if he failed to do so it was taken as a sign of his displeasure. In 1767 he deliberately refused to speak to the Duke of York after the Duke had voted against the Grafton ministry. George Selwyn wrote on one occasion: 'Lord Cholmondeley complains that the other day, when he went to the King's levee, he was not spoke to, and talks of having an audience and explanation.' In 1770, when the King inadvertently failed to speak to Madame de Welderen, wife of the Dutch Minister, she looked 'very

467

furious', as if, writes Lady Mary Coke, 'she could have made the States declare war against the King for the omission'. In 1788 when the King wanted to get away quickly for a concert at Windsor he told Lord Ailesbury that he would only say yes or no to people at the levee. Even so, it was not until 7.15 that he was able to leave London. In later years the strain of having to talk to everybody became too much for him. Lord Chancellor Eldon advised him to sit at the levee, to which the King replied: 'No, I cannot sit, for there are so many persons coming to these levees who ought not to come, who ought never to be admitted, the only way I have of not speaking to them is to walk on.' The levee was becoming more frequented and the King was now in his sixties. After 1788 the number of levees was cut down to one or two a week but they still constituted a heavy burden on the King's time and energy. In 1794, although he spent part of the summer at Weymouth where no levees were held, he made nearly a hundred appearances at Court. He ceased altogether to hold levees when he became blind.

Every gesture, every expression of the King's face, was noted by the political quidnuncs and its implications eagerly discussed. The length of time the King spent in conversation with a politician was an index of how far he was in favour. When the King had no more to say to Newcastle than to ask if he was going to Claremont, Newcastle was offended. In 1782, when the King failed to ask Lord Lincoln about his relation Sir Henry Clinton, then commander-in-chief in America, it was assumed that he was dissatisfied with Clinton's conduct of military operations. In 1765 when the opposition leaders were received favourably by the King it was a sign that the Grenville ministry was on the way out, and the cool reception the King gave to Fox in 1782 told observers that Fox's tenure of office would not be long. With Members of Parliament a kind or a harsh word at the levee could do a great deal.

468

Most people when first presented to royalty are tongue-tied as to what they should say. They do not realize that royalty may be equally tongue-tied as to what to say to them. When King George was confronted at his levee with a country gentleman of whom he had never heard, shy and ill at ease in the unaccustomed surroundings of the court, what was he to say? Yet he had to say something, and what he said might be remembered and treasured for years. The type of Squire Bramble in *Humphrey Clinker*, a country gentleman of two or three thousand a year, might visit court only once in a lifetime. The King generally asked questions about where his visitor lived, who his neighbours were, what was the harvest like in that part of the country. The conversation was commonplace but it pleased. The King had a good memory and an aptitude for recognizing people, and they felt flattered when he showed acquaintance with their family or other circumstances which they imagined were not known to him. He developed the art of putting people at their ease. The Tories who came to court at the beginning of the reign were weaned from their Jacobitism as much by the King's affability and good manners as by any sympathy with his political ideas. The republican Walpole and the High Tory Johnson have alike paid tribute to the King's courtesy. 'I find it does a man good to be talked to by his sovereign', said Johnson, and there were many who felt the same.

All this had to be learnt. It did not come easily to the shy boy who had been rebuked by his parents when he tried to take part in conversation. It needed an effort by the King. The wits made fun of his habit of ending his remarks with 'What? what?' This method of questioning people was developed for use at court in order to get them to talk. Conversation cannot be carried on by one person alone, and etiquette demanded that the King must introduce the topic. When Fanny Burney first went to court she was told by Mrs Delany:

I do beg of you, when the Queen or King speaks to you, not to answer with mere monosyllables. The Queen often complains to me of the difficulty with which she can get any conversation, as she not only always has to start the subjects, but, commonly, entirely to support them: and she says there is nothing she so much loves as conversation, and nothing she finds so hard to get.

But when Fanny met the King she was so awestruck that she could say nothing. He entered the room (in the house he had given to Mrs Delany at Windsor) without being announced, opening the door himself, and at first Fanny did not realize who he was. He knew her as the author of a popular and admired novel, as a friend of Johnson and a member of the Streatham circle. He wanted to hear her talk about literature, to find out how she came to write *Evelina* and what she was writing now. He had to question her in order to get her to talk, and even then she said little more than 'Yes, Sir' and 'No, Sir'. She could not agree with what he said about Mrs Siddons but she dared not contradict him, and so the conversation never got going. Johnson at his meeting with the King in 1767 was more self-assured and did not need bringing out. But Johnson was an acknowledged figure in literature and many years older than the King. In time Fanny also learnt to talk freely with him.

It was easy to talk to him. He was interested in so many things and above all in people and how they lived. He was never pompous or stilted, he enjoyed a joke, and loved to chaff his equerries. He did not think it beneath his dignity to talk with the meanest of his subjects. There are many stories told about King George, the truth of which it is impossible to determine, but all of the same nature. He is said once to have met a boy in Windsor Great Park. 'Who are you?' asked the King. 'I be pig boy', replied the lad, 'but I don't work. They don't want lads here. All this belongs hereabouts to Georgy.' 'Pray, who is Georgy?' 'He be King and lives at the Castle, but he does no good for me.' The King found him a job on one of his farms. There is another story of his meeting an old woman working alone in a field near Weymouth. When asked where her companions were, she said they had gone to see the King. 'And why did not you go with them?' 'Because I have five children to provide for and cannot afford to lose a day's work.' 'Then,' said the King, slipping her a guinea, 'you may tell your companions that the King came to see you.' There are too many stories of this kind for there not be a basic truth behind them: that the King could talk freely and easily with any class of his subjects without lowering his dignity. Such stories have never been told about King George II or King George IV.

Horace Walpole has an anecdote about a wealthy American merchant who said: 'They say King George is a very honest fellow; I should like to smoke a pipe with him.' Perhaps the fundamental reason why Great Britain lost the American colonies was that King George and Queen Charlotte never visited America. Had they done so, had the King met the ordinary American as he met the ordinary Englishman, the concept of monarchy in America would have become a living reality. The King would have appeared among them as their King instead of being a distant symbol of the authority of Great Britain. He would not have cared for the Boston radicals any more than he did for those of London, but perhaps there might have been some who like Wilkes himself would have forgotten their radicalism. The merchants of Massachusetts, the planters of Virginia, the shopkeepers of Pennsylvania, would have struggled to kiss the King's hand with as little decorum as did the Oxford dons in 1786, and King George would have cared as little for their ignorance of etiquette. There would have been addresses and illuminations, the King would have knighted mayors and councillors, and the most considerable men would have aspired to the honours of the peerage. The idea of such a visit in the eighteenth century was almost impossible, and had it been made and repeated the British would have grown as jealous of America as they had been of Hanover during the previous reign. No member of the Royal Family visited America before the separation, and the Americans like the Irish never felt the magic of monarchy.

The King learnt all the gossip of London at his levees. He heard about the betrothals, marriages, pregnancies, and separations among the upper classes. Sometimes he was asked to intervene in a matrimonial dispute, as in 1788 in that between Lord and Lady Bellamont. When Lord Huntingdon and Lord De La Warr quarrelled in 1767 and were about to fight a duel, the King ordered their arrest and made up the quarrel. He knew all the foibles of those who came to his levees: how George Selwyn was reputed to be fond of watching public executions and how Lady Mary Coke delighted to consort with royalty. He tried to impose on society his own standards of morality, for example by discouraging people from going to masquerades, but found no public support. He had a shrewd insight into character and was not easily deceived. Some of his remarks about the politicians he had known are not only true but sometimes have a touch of wit, as in his comment on Lord Camden who the King said had a fine voice but was no great judge – 'vox et praeterea nihil'. Auckland was 'a man of deep intrigue', Sandwich 'barring his Huntingdon jobs' had been a good First Lord of the Admiralty, Addington had proved himself 'not equal to the government of this country' – the historian of the period will appreciate the insight behind these remarks. The King told Rose in 1804: 'It had, from his entrance into life, been an invariable rule with him to store in his memory carefully every right and proper action of others, and, as far as possible, to forget instances of a contrary conduct.' He was more disposed to forgive than people have imagined, but he did not always succeed.

Drawing rooms were attended by the royal children, even when quite young. In September 1765 the company was invited to see Prince William (less than a month old), in his cradle with his two elder brothers standing one on each side. The Sunday drawing room was held after morning service in the Chapel Royal and no presentations were made. At the first drawing room of the year the Poet Laureate read his New Year's Ode to the accompaniment of music from the King's band. People used to order new clothes for the drawing rooms on the King's and Queen's birthdays, but the King took so little notice of them that this went out of fashion. There were no court days during Passion Week or Whit Week. The number of people attending varied according to the season. During the height of the parliamentary session the levee was invariably full and might last as long as three hours. In summer, when Parliament had adjourned, the numbers fell, and on one occasion in 1790 there were no more than ten present.

Court was the place where the King transacted public business. Those appointed to office, to a regiment in the army, a command in the navy, a bishopric, newly-created baronets and peers, attended to kiss the King's hand for their honour or appointment. Investitures were held on court days, addresses presented, and their bearers knighted. Those in the King's service who wished to go abroad came to ask the King's permission. Courtiers and ministers were expected to ask the King's leave to marry, and to present their future bride or bridegroom. Old-fashioned people attended to announce the birth of their children; members of the diplomatic corps came to inform the King when they were about to go on vacation and also after they got back. Young people marked their arrival at adult age by being presented to the King and Queen. These formalities followed from the King's being the head of society as well as the head of state and government. But after 1788 when court days were reduced and especially after 1805, old customs began to change and gradually the court ceased to be the centre of society. The only survival of the eighteenth-century court today is the Queen's garden party.

A court day was a convenient occasion to arrange a meeting of the Privy Council. It was also the day on which the King saw his ministers and discussed with them the business of their departments. Sometimes if a minister was pressed to attend Parliament he would see the King before the levee but more usually afterwards. These audiences were held in the King's closet, the private room beyond the state bed-chamber. Before the rise of the cabinet, the distinction between the grades of minister was between those who had or had not the right of access to the closet. The First Lord of the Treasury, the Secretaries of State, the leader of the House of Commons, and the Secretary at War attended the closet regularly; other ministers only occasionally or not at all. In the nineteenth century the Prime Minister assumed responsibility for all government business, and apart from the Foreign Secretary there was rarely need for any other minister to see the sovereign in private. But during King George III's reign the right of access to the King was a jealously guarded prerogative. In 1801, after his second illness, the King wished to give audiences only to Addington and to do business with other ministers by correspondence or through Addington. 'This is the notion of a Prime Minister as known formerly sometimes under the French government', wrote Lord Glenbervie; and he did not think the public or the ministers would approve of it. The King was the effective head of government, and ministers were responsible to him, not to a Prime Minister.

Others besides ministers obtained access to the closet, not as a right but as a favour. The King never refused a private audience to a man or woman of rank. He even allowed Lord George Gordon, who was out of his mind, to lecture him for an hour on the dangers of Popery. Most people who sought a private audience were after some job or favour and believed they were more likely to get it by applying to the King than to his minister. The Duchess of Hamilton wanted a British peerage for her son, the Earl of Huntingdon wanted a dukedom, Lord Percy wanted a regiment, the Marquess of Granby wanted the daughter of one of his borough-mongering friends to be appointed maid of honour to the Queen (these are all actual examples taken from within a few months). Those who could not apply in person did so by letter. Lord Cowper, who had lived twenty years in Italy, and had applied successively for the Bath, the lord lieutenancy of Kent, the Garter, the Thistle, and a dukedom, at last announced his intention of returning home to solicit the King in person. 'I shall finish my letter', he wrote, 'with the words of the male-factor to our saviour, "Lord, remember me when I come into thy kingdom", and am with all submission and respect . . .' And just in case the King had not taken the hint he added a further paragraph to say that he would like the Garter.

The King could not satisfy everybody, and for each suitor who went away from the closet rejoicing there would be half a dozen disappointed. What had they done, they would ask plaintively, to receive this mark of His Majesty's displeasure which had lessened them in the opinion of the world; and a few months later they would try again. It is no wonder the King talked of the greed and selfishness of the age.

It was the aim of all, high and low, to be noticed personally by the King. Glenbervie complained in 1804 that he must be out of favour because he was never ordered to attend the closet on the business of his office (Surveyor-General of Woods and Forests, which did not require attendance in the closet). Lady Mary Coke was hurt when she met the King riding and he did not take off his hat, and Dr Burney was disappointed when the King only bowed to him on the terrace at Windsor but did not speak. Lady Mary tells a story about a drawing room in 1770:

Lord Hertford [Lord Chamberlain] told me a woman applied to him this morning at St James's to intercede with the King to allow her to kiss his hand, that having for some time taken it so strongly into her head that she could not be brought to bed if she did not obtain that favour, she was now convinced it would be the death of her child, if he did not procure it for her. Lord Hertford said he was afraid of giving her too much encouragement, as it was possible he might not have succeeded, but having related the story to the King, and told him there was a precedent of his late Majesty having complied with a similar request, the King granted it in one of the rooms as he passed to the drawing room, to the great joy of the woman.

Audiences in the closet were conducted with both parties standing. This helps to explain why the King liked ministers who did their business quickly. If we are to follow the King's daily routine during the first twenty-eight years of his reign we must imagine him at St James's four or five days of the week. From about eleven in the morning, when the dressing began, to four or five in the afternoon, when the last private audience was over, he was on his feet, without anything to eat or drink since breakfast, talking to people. In July 1788, when ordered to Cheltenham for his health, he wrote to Prince Augustus: 'I am much recovered and doubt that the efficacy of the waters . . . the change of scene, privation of long conversations at St James's, and above all the exercise of riding and good mutton will do what may be at present wanting.' One can sympathize with his feelings.

Throughout history it has been the province of monarchs to encourage learning and the arts. Some have done it because it was expected of them, others through vanity. King George III did it because he really cared. He was interested in art, music, literature, and science, and spent freely in these fields. He was also a born collector, and his collections have enriched both his family and the nation.

The King was not a great collector of pictures, though he made one outstanding purchase. In 1762 he acquired for £20,000 the collection of Joseph Smith, for many years British consul in Venice. This was mainly of coins, antiques, and Italian paintings, and included the largest group of Canalettos in the world. After this the King bought few pictures, except for commissioned portraits of his family. His favourite painter was Benjamin West, whose attraction for the King lay more in the nature of his subjects than his skill as a painter. The King admired West's picture of Agrippina with the ashes of Germanicus, and commissioned from him a picture of the departure of Regulus. He called for a copy of Livy and read to West the story of how Regulus implored the senate not to make peace with Carthage even though his own death should be the consequence (which incidentally shows how well King George knew his Roman history). The King liked paintings which pointed a moral and adorned a tale. He did not care for pictures of lovers in bucolic surroundings or nude women reclining on divans but for scenes of virtue and heroism. He valued paintings as an aid to morality. The constant contemplation of Benjamin West's classical and heroic canvases – so the King hoped – would make men better and wiser. Once again we can recognize the influence of Bute.

Unlike his father and eldest son he had little appreciation of painting as an art. 'His Majesty', wrote Sir William Hamilton, himself a connoisseur, 'who is certainly a great lover of the arts, and had given them great encouragement, for want of having formed his taste early and on works of the first class, has never arrived at being sensible of what is properly called the sublime in the arts.' This was a diplomat's way of saying that the King had no artistic taste. As an art collector he reminds one of Roebuck Ramsden – he believed in the fine arts with all the earnestness of the man who does not understand them.

The best thing he did for art was to found the Royal Academy. This was the idea of Sir William Chambers, the King's tutor in architecture, and the King responded to it eagerly. He paid the initial expenses, amounting to over £5,000, out of his Privy Purse, and provided rooms for the Academy at Somerset House. The Academy was planned not only as a place where artists could exhibit their work but as a training school for future artists, and perhaps it was through the King's influence that professors were appointed for history and literature as well as for technical instruction. The King supervised the drafting of the Academy's charter, reserved to himself the appointment of Treasurer (Chambers was the first Treasurer), and regularly visited the Academy's annual exhibitions.[49]

'A love of music to distraction runs through our family', wrote the Princess Royal in 1788. The King said to Fanny Burney at their first meeting: 'To me it appears quite as strange to meet with people who have no ear for music, and cannot distinguish one air from another, as to meet with people who are dumb.' The King's father had been fond of music, and music was one of the many tastes shared by the King and Queen. Each had their own band and each played and sang. The King played at least three instruments: flute, harpsichord and pianoforte; and may also have played the organ. He collected music, and was able to provide Dr Burney, Fanny's father and the historian of music, with the scores of Handel's earlier and unpublished operas. Oratorio was his delight and Handel his passion. He had met Handel as a boy, and took pride in possessing a harpsichord which had once belonged to the composer. In 1784 he attended the concerts in Westminster Abbey to commemorate the centenary of Handel's birth and read in manuscript Dr Burney's account of the event. To Burney's annoyance the King insisted on revising some of his judgments on Handel, giving the composer more praise than the historian of music thought was his due.[50]

We do not know what other composers the King admired. According to Haydn, he admired none. It would be particularly interesting to know what he thought of Mozart. The King and Queen had heard Mozart play when he visited England in 1764 as a boy of eight, and Mozart had dedicated a set of sonatas to the Queen. From about 1780 to his death in 1791 was Mozart's great creative period, perhaps the finest achievement of eighteenth-century civilization. In 1786, while the King was leagued with Prussia to check the ambition of Joseph II of Austria, *Le Nozze di Figaro* was first performed at Vienna, with one of the King's subjects in the cast. One wonders if the King ever learnt of this. He certainly never saw any of Mozart's operas on the stage but he may have heard some of Mozart's orchestral and chamber music.

During the last year of the American war an event took place in England as momentous in the realm of science as the Declaration of Independence was in politics: the discovery by William Herschel on 13 May 1781 of the planet Uranus. From the dawn of history men had believed the solar system to consist of the sun and six planets, each of which can be seen with the naked eye. Herschel's discoveries, of which this was only the first, extended the boundaries of the universe: a change as significant for scientific and philosophical ideas as that introduced by Copernicus two hundred years earlier. King George played a small but essential part in this scientific revolution.

Astronomy satisfies both the scientific and aesthetic sides of man's nature: his curiosity about the material world and his desire to find beauty in it. The vastness of the universe, the mystery of how and why it came into being, in Keats's phrase tease us out of thought. It is not surprising that the King with his religious mind and intellectual curiosity should have become interested in astronomy. In 1768 Chambers built for him an observatory at Kew, and the King appointed Stephen Demainbray, formerly his tutor in science, to be its director. The King was proud of his observatory and fond of showing it to visitors. In 1769 he took the Prince and Princess of Hesse Darmstadt there and in 1786 the Duke and Duchess of Modena. In 1775 when Georg Christoph Lichtenberg, the scientist and Göttingen professor, visited England, the King spent two hours taking him round the observatory. On the occasion of the transit of Venus in 1769 the King had Demainbray draw up a paper explaining the phenomenon and stayed up to watch it.

The development of scientific thought is to some extent dependent on technological progress. By the middle of the eighteenth century astronomy had reached a point when it could advance no farther without bigger telescopes penetrating deeper into space. At this moment there came a man who combined an aptitude for theory with the skill of a craftsman. William Herschel, born in Hanover the same year as the King, came to England in 1757 to earn his living as a musician and to pursue his hobby of astronomy. He built his own telescope, and with the help of his sister Caroline, as devoted to astronomy as her brother, began a systematic survey of the heavens. On 25 May 1782, a year after Herschel's discovery of Uranus, the King gave him a private audience and ordered him to bring his telescope to Windsor. It was shown to the Royal Family and the King and Queen observed Saturn and Jupiter through it. The King gave Herschel a pension of £200 a year, commissioned him to build five 10-foot telescopes for his new observatory at Windsor, and ordered a gigantic one of 40 feet focal length and 49 inches aperture. This, the largest telescope of its time, cost the King £4,000, with an annual charge of £200 for maintenance and a pension of £50 for Caroline as her brother's assistant. Herschel was now able to devote his whole time to astronomy and had an instrument worthy of his genius. With this he made the observations which led to the theory of the galaxies and the modern concept of the universe. He could not have done it without a patron. Perhaps the biggest thing King George ever did was to patronize Herschel.[51]

Herschel's great telescope was set up in a field behind his house at Slough. The King and Queen paid frequent visits while it was building and when it was completed took a party there. Caroline Herschel herself is the authority for the story that the King helped the Archbishop of Canterbury into the observation seat, saying 'Come, my Lord Bishop, I will show you the way to heaven.' Herschel was a regular visitor to Windsor, both for music and astronomy. Fanny Burney describes one occasion in 1786:

At night, Mr Herschel, by the King's command, came to exhibit to His Majesty and the Royal Family the new comet lately discovered by his sister. ... Mr Herschel then showed me some of his newly-discovered universes.

'The King has not a happier subject than this man', she wrote, 'who owes wholly to His Majesty that he is not wretched.'

The King had no deep knowledge of science – that could not be expected of him – but a lively mind and a wide-ranging curiosity. He invited scientists to Windsor to demonstrate their experiments, and continued his mother's interest in the botanic gardens at Kew. He collected scientific instruments (his collection is now in the Science Museum),[52] was interested in clocks and watches, and together with Chambers designed the case for an astronomical clock by Christopher Pinchbeck. He followed closely the latest ideas in scientific farming, and conducted experiments to evolve a breed of sheep which would be equally good for mutton as for wool. He imported sheep from Spain, and played a key role in breeding the ancestors of the Merino sheep of Australia and New Zealand.[53]

His farms at Windsor were named according to the different forms of crop cultivation practised, and it is said that under an alias the King corresponded with Arthur Young on farming topics. Nor was he unaware of the changes taking place in industry. Thomas Bentley, Josiah Wedgwood's partner, wrote in 1770 after a private audience: 'The King is well acquainted with business, and with the characters of the principal manufacturers, merchants, and artists, and seems to have the success of all our manufactures much at heart, and to understand the importance of them.'

The King was one of the great book collectors of the age and a founder of the British national library.[54] His first step in collecting was taken in 1762 when he purchased the Thomason collection which he presented to the British Museum. This collection, formed by George Thomason, a seventeenth-century London bookseller, consists of over 32,000 items, mostly tracts, pamphlets, sermons, and newspapers, relating to the period of the Civil War and Protectorate. The introduction to the Museum's catalogue of the collection has this to say: 'Of the many donations which have enriched the library since its foundation in 1759 few have been of greater benefit to successive generations of scholars and students than this collection which we owe to the generosity of King George III.'

He began to collect books before he came to the throne. In 1765 he purchased for £10,000 Joseph Smith's collection of incunabula, rich in editions of the classics and Italian literature. He allotted £1,500 a year from the Privy Purse for the purchase of books, but this sum was frequently exceeded if anything exceptional came into the market. Sir Herbert Taylor, who was in charge of the King's personal finances during the period of his last illness, estimated that for some years he had been spending from £2,500 to £3,000 a year on the purchase of books.[55] His representatives attended all the great sales of the time and he bought extensively on the Continent.

The library was not acquired for his personal use but as the nucleus of a national library. The King's personal library was kept at Windsor and the Queen also had her own library. When the King came to the throne there was no national library. The British Museum had been founded as a museum and many years were to elapse before it began systematically to collect books. The King's library was designed for scholars and was open to all, to the Radical and Unitarian Joseph Priestley as well as to the Tory and High Churchman Samuel Johnson. The King would not deny the use of his library to a man of learning, however he might dislike his opinions.

At the King's death the library contained about 65,000 books and 450 manuscripts. It comprised everything that an eighteenth-century scholar could desire. Some idea of its scope can be gathered from the editions of the Bible which it contains. There are at least two hundred, including a polyglot Bible and a Gutenberg printing; versions in Arabic, Chaldaic, Greek, Hebrew, Latin, and Syriac; and the English versions, from Coverdale and Tyndale. There are translations in almost every European language, including Finnish, Hungarian, Russian, and Welsh as well as the commoner languages. There is even a version in the language of the North American Indians. Next to the Bible, Shakespeare was the most frequently collected book. The first four folios are there, the second with an inscription in the hand of Charles I. There are some thirty copies of eighteenth-century adaptations of Shakespeare's plays, including *Love in a Forest* (an adaptation of *As You Like it*) and *Sauny the Scot* (*The Taming of the Shrew*). When the King said there was 'sad stuff' in Shakespeare he may have been thinking of these contemporary adaptations.

It is fascinating to browse through the catalogue of the library – five folio volumes, at least four hundred pages each, printed in double column. There are eight columns of editions of Boccaccio; 54 columns devoted to library catalogues, including a catalogue of the sale of Queen Charlotte's books with the purchasers and prices; 26 books printed by Caxton; 19 columns of Cicero, ranging from a 1498 edition to a French translation published in 1816; Horace in 11 columns; and a first edition of *Paradise Lost*. The *Encyclopaedia Britannica* does not appear until the third edition in 1797. There are complete runs of all contemporary periodicals, in French and German as well as English; copies of state papers, the journals of the House of Commons and House of Lords, both British and Irish, the *Statutes of the Realm*, the *London Gazette*; and a magnificent collection of contemporary pamphlets, uniformly bound. These are the first books the visitor to the library sees as he approaches it from the King Edward VII gallery.

How did contemporary writers fare? Boswell would have rejoiced to learn that almost every first edition of his books was bought for the King's library. Everything by Johnson was bought as soon as it came out, and the library includes the original manuscript of *Irene*. Burke did not fare so well, and it was not until the outbreak of the French Revolution that the King began systematically to collect Burke's writings. Gibbon would have been mortified at the King's failure to acquire the first volume of the *Decline and Fall* (though he read it), but consoled by the knowledge that all his works were eventually acquired. There is a deal of Gray, including the 1765 edition of his poems, but no copy of Mason's biography. Richardson, Fielding, Smollett, and Sterne appear only after they had become established classics. All Scott's poems and early novels are included, but no Jane Austen. Despite the King's dislike of Frederick the Great, he acquired copies of his books; and even Rousseau and Voltaire (whom the King thought 'a monster') appear in the library. One wonders if Horace Walpole would have revised his opinion of King George had he known that his works were to be listed in the catalogue of the King's library in two columns. It is not surprising that the King collected the first writings of Lavoisier in French, but it is to find two novels by Restif de la Bretonne. The King's library is a guide to what contemporaries thought valuable in the learning and literature of their time.

The books were kept at the Queen's House in four rooms: the Great Library, the Octagon, the South Library, and the East Library (built in 1768). John Adams, first American minister to Great Britain and Washington's successor as President of the United States, has left a description of the library as it was in 1783:

The King's Library struck me with admiration. I wished for a week's time, but had but a few hours. The books were in perfect order, elegant in their editions, paper, binding, etc., but gawdy and extravagant in nothing. They were chosen with perfect taste and judgment; every book that a king ought to have always at hand, and as far as I could examine, and could be supposed of judging, none others. . . .

In every apartment of the whole house, the same taste, the same judgment, the same elegance, the same simplicity, without the smallest affectation, ostentation, profusion, or meanness. I could not but compare it, in my own mind, with Versailles, and not at all to the advantage of the latter.

There were also galleries for coins and drawings, for the King's collections of ships' models and of maps. The Queen's House was less a royal palace than a museum and library, with a flat for the King and Queen when they wished to pass the night in London.

Payments for the library continued to be made out of the Privy Purse during the King's last illness, and in accordance with the King's wish a catalogue was compiled. This was published between 1820 and 1829 at a cost to the King's estate of £5,000. With an average annual expenditure of £2,000, the cost of the library could not have been less than £120,000, which sum does not include the expenses of binding and the salaries of the librarians.

485

Its value today is incalculable. The King bequeathed the library to his successor, who in 1823 presented it to the British Museum. It is strange that the trustees of the Museum have never commemorated this gift by a bust of King George III in the gallery which houses his collection. There are in the King's Library busts of four benefactors to the Museum; in the Grenville Library there is a bust of Thomas Grenville, who was enabled to collect books because of a sinecure given him by the King; and in the manuscript reading room there is a fine portrait of King George II, in whose reign the Museum was founded. But in no public room of the British Museum is there a bust or portrait of King George III.

The King's well-known remark to Fanny Burney – 'Was there ever such stuff as great part of Shakespeare? only one must not say so!' – is sometimes cited as evidence that he was a literary philistine. Yet as a comment on the Shakespeare idolatry of the period it is not unfair and the subsequent conversation at least shows that the King knew Shakespeare well. Nor are his remarks on the 'extreme immorality' of the old comedies unjust as regards the post-Restoration dramatists. In truth the King was well read, especially in contemporary literature. A man who could hold his own in literary conversation with Johnson was no philistine. He read Johnson and Boswell, Gibbon and Burke. His remarks to Glenbervie on Gibbon's posthumous works are shrewd and sensible. 'He remarked on the egotism and vanity which he had found in them, and the uniform bias towards infidelity [and] observed on the strong proof of intense and methodical study to be found in these posthumous works of Gibbon's.' He was fond of Fielding. When he became blind his daughters used to read him books by other novelists and he was always pleased when he found anything which reminded him of Fielding.

He loved the theatre, especially farces; and the Queen had sometimes to restrain him from laughing too loud.

Mrs Siddons was his favourite actress. 'I am an enthusiast for her', he told Fanny Burney, 'quite an enthusiast. I think there never was any player in my time so excellent – not Garrick himself.' She used to give dramatic readings to the Royal Family.

To conclude this review of the King's collections and his interests in art and science, two points must be made. First, the King's interests were his own but in the particular objects of his collections he was guided by the advice of experts. He did not, for example, decide personally what books were to be bought for his library. He was not a scholar, but he had the good sense to consult those who were. Stephen Demainbray, Richard Dalton, Frederick Augusta Barnard, and Sir William Chambers advised him well.

Secondly: everything the King did for learning and the arts – the foundation of the Royal Academy, his patronage of Herschel, his library – was paid for out of the Privy Purse. It was his own money not the money of the nation.

King George believed that the British constitution was 'the most excellent form of government' that had ever existed. So also did his subjects. The eighteenth-century Englishman as he saw the way other countries conducted their affairs felt smug and complacent. Most of Europe, so he had been taught to believe, was sunk in Popery and despotism, and the only way to escape from these twin evils seemed to be into a wild democracy. Great Britain alone, thanks to the Protestant succession, maintained the true spirit of freedom. 'I am an Englishwoman', cries Blonde in Mozart's *Il Seraglio*, 'and am born to freedom.'

In later ages it became commonplace to contrast Great Britain's unwritten and flexible constitution with that of other nations such as the United States. This was not the view of the eighteenth century. The British constitution was enshrined in several documents – Magna Carta, the

Habeas Corpus Act, the Bill of Rights, the Act of Settlement, the Act of Union between England and Scotland – all of which were held to be immutable. The first duty of the sovereign was to preserve the constitution, this inestimable blessing, from attempts at innovation.

Thus the King saw the role of the Crown as essentially conservative. There was no place for a reforming monarch in the British system of government. Changes, if they had to come, must come from Parliament, and must not affect the essential principles of the constitution. It was the duty of the King to act as a restraint on change. Even administrative improvements must come from ministers. As early as 1771 the King suggested that the office of Secretary of State should be reorganized into a home and foreign department 'which is the case in every other court'. But North did not accept the suggestion and this very sensible change was delayed until 1782. It is not surprising therefore that the King should have opposed such measures as Grenville's bill to change the method of trying election petitions, Burke's economical reform bill, or Pitt's plan of parliamentary reform. But if these measures received the assent of Parliament the King would not refuse his own. The royal veto over legislation had not been exercised since the reign of Queen Anne but the King regarded it as still in force, to be used however not after a bill had passed both houses of Parliament but to prevent its being introduced.

In theory the King had a free choice of his ministers: in practice he rarely had any choice. The number of men willing to accept political responsibility was few, and the King's business had to be carried on by those who could win the approval of Parliament. Had the King been able to choose freely for himself he would never have taken Rockingham in 1765 or Shelburne in 1782. The King's right to choose his ministers really amounted to no more than a veto, under favourable political circumstances, against any politician who was personally obnoxious to him. The King was unwilling to accept Sandwich as Lord Lieutenant of Ireland in 1769 but had to take him as Secretary of State a year later. The King was able to exclude Fox from office between 1783 and 1806 only because Pitt and later Addington were prepared to stand by him. But when Pitt died and Addington had proved his incapacity the ban on Fox had to be lifted. He had to accede to Pitt's demand for the dismissal of Thurlow in 1792. In general the King concerned himself only about court appointments and those ministers with right of access to the closet. The nomination to minor offices was the prerogative of the Prime Minister, and the King's approval little more than a formality.

For most of King George II's reign a closet system of government had prevailed, the vital decisions being taken by a small knot of ministers in close consultation with the King. The cabinet as a regular organ of government dates from the Seven Years War. King George III fostered its growth, and during his reign the centre of power shifted from the closet to the cabinet. He invariably referred matters of policy to the cabinet and accepted their advice even against his own opinion. He referred to the cabinet the question of an honour for Rodney in 1782 and on at least one occasion accepted its recommendation to a pardon. 'In all my experience of the King or knowledge of his measures', Horace Walpole wrote in 1769, 'he never interfered with his ministers. . . . the moment he took them, he seemed to resign himself entirely to their conduct for the time.' Policy had to conform to the will of Parliament, and the King left the determination of policy to ministers who were responsible to Parliament.

Apart from his general conservative attitude, the King had definite political views only on foreign policy. He was at heart a pacifist and wished to avoid war whenever possible. Great Britain should avoid becoming entangled in the affairs of the Continent, but should pursue a maritime and colonial policy designed to foster and increase

489

commerce, the true source of her wealth. He distrusted France – 'that dangerous and faithless nation' – and regarded her as Great Britain's natural enemy. He was pro-Austrian and anti-Prussian, though as Elector of Hanover he collaborated with Prussia in 1786 against Austria's designs in Germany. 'I confess my political creed', he wrote in 1771, 'is formed on the system of King William. England in conjunction with the house of Austria and the republic [of Holland] seems the most secure barrier against the Family Compact.' All this was orthodox old Whig policy, in contrast to the new Whiggism of Chatham and Charles Fox who favoured alliances with Prussia and Russia. But King George was no doctrinaire, and was prepared according to circumstances to accept any ally who might be of service. He told John Adams, on presenting his credentials as minister from the United States in 1783:

I wish you, Sir, to believe, that it may be understood in America, that I have done nothing in the late contest but what I thought myself indispensably bound to do by the duty which I owed my people. I will be very frank with you. I was the last to consent to the separation; but the separation having been made, and having become inevitable, I have always said, as I say now, that I would be the first to meet the friendship of the United States as an independent power.

Two aspects of government were the King's personal concern: the enforcement of the law and the distribution of honours and patronage.

The British like to think of themselves as a peaceful and law-abiding people. They were certainly not so in the eighteenth century. Riots, protests, and disturbances were a constant feature of life, especially in the urban areas, and were only kept within limits by the use of the army. In Ireland, wrote North in 1775, 'they depend so much upon the protection and assistance of the military force, who are in constant employment under the command of the civil magistrate for the carrying on every part of the internal police of the kingdom, which would not be carried on at all without it.' As well as a police the army acted as a tax-gathering force. A large part of the public revenue was derived from import duties and smuggling was an organized and lucrative business. In 1776, when most of the regular army had been sent to America, the Duke of Argyll, commander-in-chief in Scotland, warned the government that there were not more than 600 soldiers in that kingdom. 'The revenue will suffer very considerably', wrote the Duke, 'for want of military assistance, so frequently called for by the officers of customs and excise.' The King exercised personal control over the use of the army, and in 1765, 1768, and 1780 directed what were virtually military campaigns against rioters in London.

One other type of decision concerned with the enforcement of the law was also the personal responsibility of the King: the prerogative of pardon. The common law of England did not err on the side of lenity. All felonies were punishable with death, and to a twentieth-century mind it is appalling to read the catalogue of offences that came within that category: murder, rape, and other sexual offences; assault against the person; burglary; larceny to the value of more than forty shillings; forgery of documents (forgery of money was treason); and a great many other offences against property. The King's correspondence is full of appeals for mitigation of the death sentence. In the case of criminals convicted at the Old Bailey (where the sessions for London and Middlesex were held) these were considered by the 'nominal' cabinet – the ordinary cabinet augmented by the Archbishop of Canterbury, the Speaker of the House of Commons, the Lord Chief Justice of the King's Bench, and the four great court officers – sitting in the presence of the King. The 'hanging committee' as it was once irreverently styled, or 'that unpleasant business' as the King described it, was guided by its legal members. For offences outside London and Middlesex the decision was taken by the King.

Appeals against capital sentences were submitted through the Secretary of State, who would sometimes add his recommendation. 'Hines's case may perhaps deserve a respite', wrote Lord Rochford in 1775, 'but pardoning anybody in these times is a cruelty instead of an act of justice.' But the decision was the King's. Here is one example, from a letter from the King to Conway in 1766:

I have examined the case of the unhappy convicts lately transmitted from Scotland. As to the young man, I am very willing to shew mercy. As to the woman, I cannot see it quite in the same light but think it may not be improper to send to the proper officer in Scotland for a report with regard to the woman, as I am ever desirous to be perfectly convinced there is no room for mitigating the rigour of the law before it takes its course.

The King gave careful consideration to each case and whenever possible wished to exercise his prerogative. If the judge who tried the case submitted a recommendation that the death penalty should be commuted to transportation for life the King always accepted it. If there was any doubt, he would grant a respite until a report had been received from the judge. He would not go contrary to the judge's report but neither would he go beyond it. Nor would he be influenced by political pressure. The law had prescribed the death penalty for felony and unless there were extenuating circumstances the law must be enforced. It was not for the Crown to change the law.

From about 1770 there arose a movement for penal reform in Great Britain. The King had a small share in this. He was interested in the welfare of people sent to prison for debt and contributed towards their relief as an act of charity.

The distribution of patronage and honours was half the business of an eighteenth-century government. The King's attitude was that 'merit is the only line for preferment', while the politicians considered that political allegiance was also a strong claim. The regius chairs at Oxford and Cambridge, he wrote in 1771, 'having been instituted for promoting learning in the universities, ought not to be given by favour but according to merit'. They were not to be sinecures and their holders were to deliver lectures. A bishop should be 'a man of exemplary character'; and he disliked the non-residence of the clergy – 'an evil', he wrote in 1782, 'I shall ever wish to be the foremost in preventing'. He did not object to accepting the recommendations of ministers for ecclesiatical preferments provided they recommended proper persons. On the death of the Bishop of Ely in 1781 he wrote to North: 'I wish to confer the bishopric on the clergyman who for private character as well as orthodoxy and learning may seem best qualified to be brought on the bench.' He was adamant against anything that looked like a job, and in 1805 refused to accept Pitt's recommendation of his former tutor and private secretary for the archbishopric of Canterbury.

The same principles applied to promotion in the army and navy. Merit and seniority alone should decide. 'I wish to take the man best qualified', the King wrote in 1782 about the colonelcy of a Highland regiment. Rules had been laid down for promotion in the lower ranks and they must be observed. 'It is impossible for me to act contrary to known rules', he wrote in 1772. Commands in the field during time of war were made according to the advice of the cabinet. It hurt the King sorely in 1794 when the cabinet recommended the recall of the Duke of York from the command of the army in Flanders, but he accepted their advice. He reserved for himself the choice of commander-in-chief of the army, though he accepted the recommendations of his ministers in 1766 and 1782. In 1809 on the resignation of the Duke of York the King appointed Sir David Dundas to the command of the army without consulting his ministers, and the Duke of Portland, then Prime Minister, did not object.

There was always a struggle for patronage between the King and his ministers. Certain specially favoured ministers (Bute in 1762, the Duke of Cumberland in 1765, and Chatham in 1766) were allowed to have virtually their own way in the disposal of patronage, but usually an unspoken compromise existed. Places tenable with a seat in the House of Commons were always bestowed according to the advice of the leader of the House, and to a large extent political considerations influenced the choice of other appointments. In 1782 the King was even prepared to waive the claims of his librarian in favour of a recommendation from North. 'Lord North knows very well', he wrote, 'that I carefully avoid wishing to distress him for employments in favour of persons only attached to myself.' When the minister felt himself insecure in Parliament (Grenville in 1763, Rockingham in 1782, Pitt in 1804) he tended to demand a larger share of patronage than was his due in order to demonstrate that he possessed the entire confidence of the Crown. Tension between the King and his ministers usually arose over the disposal of patronage, rarely on questions of policy.

Honours were usually given according to the advice of the ministers, though the King tried to reserve the Garter and the creation of peerages for himself. He rarely gave the Garter unasked, and when he did it was a sign of special favour. On the Duke of Cumberland's death in 1765 the King gave his Garter to Lord Albemarle, the Duke's friend, as a tribute of respect to his uncle. He gave the Garter to North in 1772 as a reward for his exertions on the Royal Marriage Bill and offered it to Pitt in 1790 (Pitt declined in favour of his elder brother). But there were occasions (when the Rockinghams came in in 1782 and when the Portland Whigs joined Pitt in 1794) when the Garter was given for political considerations on the advice of the minister. Pressure from the landed gentry and the need to reward naval and military commanders during the French Revolutionary and Napoleonic wars

494

led to an increase in the peerage. After 1784 peerages were granted much more frequently on ministerial advice, but the King managed to retain control. Thus he refused Pitt's recommendation of Shelburne for a dukedom, intending to reserve that distinction for members of the Royal Family. In 1807 Lord Malmesbury said there were fifty-three applications for the peerage, none of which the King would accept.

The eighteenth century was a great age for laying down rules for sport. The first laws of cricket date from 1744. Horse racing became organized with the foundation of the Jockey Club in 1756, the general stud book in 1771, and the first three classic races (the St Leger, the Oaks, and the Derby) between 1776 and 1780. Hugo Meynell and Peter Beckford changed hunting from the slaughter of wild animals into something between a sport and a science. Football as yet had no rules, but a type of football was played in the House of Commons. There were two sides with their star players and supporters, a set of rules, an impartial referee, and all the excitement of gregarious conflict. The change in politics from a form of war as it had been in the seventeenth century to a form of sport as it was in the eighteenth was a refining and civilizing influence in British life. But for the King politics was not a game and he never felt the fun or excitement of the parliamentary conflict.

He was impatient at the dilatory way Parliament appeared to do business. 'In these days keeping to the matter before the House is little practised', he wrote in 1773; and in 1776: 'Real business is never so well considered as when the attention of the House is not taken up by noisy declamations.' He liked Parliament to start early and to finish early. He was punctilious in his support of the privileges of the House, 'without which', he wrote in 1771, 'it must soon degenerate and in lieu of the bulwark of liberty become contemptible'. He supported the right of the House to prevent publication of its debates, though advising North to take no action against the printers responsible – a caution North ignored, with the result that the House made a foolish exhibition of itself. He was knowledgeable about parliamentary procedure. He liked to give the royal assent to bills in person as soon as they were ready, but private bills were always passed by commission.

The King had all the prejudices of an hierarchical society based on the ownership of land. He felt it right that the nobly born and the broad acred should govern and receive the rewards of government. He was a good Whig. He wrote in 1780 about the disposal of an office in the House of Commons: 'Lord North cannot seriously think that a private gentleman like Mr Penton is to stand in the way of the eldest son of an earl. Undoubtedly if that idea holds good it is diametrically opposite to what I have known all my life.' 'Gentlemen of landed property' were the only fit and proper people to sit in the House of Commons; and he disliked 'stock jobbers', 'money-lenders', 'nabobs', and *nouveaux riches* of all descriptions.

He liked to deal with his papers early in the morning. 'I can read papers of consequence to more effect in an early period of the day than in the evening', he wrote in 1782. Diplomatic despatches, reports of colonial governors and service commanders, and copies of intercepted correspondence, were sent to the King as soon as opened. He read them carefully and his remarks are often shrewd. He disliked fine or affected writing just as he did elaborate or rhetorical speech. To write or speak plainly in as few words as possible was for King George an ideal. Until he went blind in 1805 he had no private secretary. He wrote all his letters himself, often preparing a draft beforehand (most of his letters in the Royal Archives are drafts) or keeping a copy. He liked to reply to letters as quickly as possible. He copied himself any state papers he wished to preserve, though in later years he occasionally enlisted the Queen's help. Most of his early letters to Bute are undated, but when he came to the throne he was careful to date his letters with the exact time (to the nearest minute) at which they were written.

Hanover ceased to be a cause of political contention during the King's reign. The King governed Hanover through a regency with whom he corresponded via the Hanoverian chancery in London. British and Hanoverian affairs were kept entirely separate. In 1786 when in his capacity of Elector he joined the Furstenbund, his British ministers were kept informed but were not consulted. He had begun his reign with pronounced anti-Hanoverian sentiments which were crystallized in his well-known declaration, 'Born and educated in this country, I glory in the name of Britain.' But as Bute's influence receded the King remembered with pride his German origins. All his children were taught German, his sons were sent to Hanover for their military training, and the King and Queen spoke German in their familiar conversation. (Incidentally, the King also spoke French and wrote it at least as grammatically as some Frenchmen of the period.) He took particular interest in the welfare of Göttingen University, founded by his grandfather, and sent four of his sons there. Sophie von la Roche, who visited London in 1786, describes how the King 'laid his hand upon his breast with fine, manly frankness, saying, "Oh! my heart will never forget that it pulses with German blood." ' In 1783 he was prepared to abdicate the throne of Great Britain but not that of Hanover. It is surprising therefore that he never visited Hanover though he contemplated doing so after his illness in 1789. The reason probably was that he was discouraged by the Hanoverian regency. The government of Hanover was in the hands of a few leading families who ran the state quietly and without any bother and did not wish for the presence of their sovereign.

There were two attempts to assassinate King George, both by people who were mentally unbalanced.

497

On 2 August 1786 as the King was alighting from his horse at St James's for the levee a woman named Margaret Nicholson made an attempt to stab him. Fanny Burney, who was told the story by the King himself, wrote:

While the guards and his own people now surrounded the King, the assassin was seized by the populace ... when the King, the only calm and moderate person then present, called aloud to the mob, 'The poor creature is mad! Do not hurt her! She has not hurt me!'

Then he came forward, and showed himself to all the people, declaring he was perfectly safe and unhurt; and then gave positive orders that the woman should be taken care of, and went into the palace, and had his levee.

Afterwards he rode to Windsor and broke the news to the Queen. 'Here I am', he said, coming into the room, 'safe and well as you see! But I have very narrowly escaped being stabbed.' During the next few days people poured into Windsor to pay their respects to the King, and Fanny writes about the Royal Family's visit to Kew on 8 August:

Kew Green was quite filled with all the inhabitants of the place – the lame, old, blind, sick, and infants, who all assembled, dressed in their Sunday garb, to line the sides of the roads through which their Majesties passed, attended by the band of musicians, arranged in the front, who began 'God save the King' the moment they came upon the Green and finished it with loud huzzas.

The Queen, in speaking of it afterwards, said, 'I shall always love little Kew for this!'

The second attempt was on 15 May 1800 when James Hadfield tried to shoot the King at Drury Lane Theatre. This was more serious, as Hadfield's bullet penetrated the pillar of the King's box. Michael Kelly, the singer (Don Basilio in the first performance of *Le Nozze di Figaro*), who was on the stage at the time, wrote in his memoirs:

Never shall I forget His Majesty's coolness. The whole audience was in an uproar. The King on hearing the report of the pistol retired a pace or two, stopped, and stood firmly for an instant, then came forward to the front of the box, put his opera glass to his eye, and looked round the house without the smallest appearance of alarm or discomposure.

Sheridan hastily improvised an additional verse to 'God save the King', which Kelly sang from the stage to immense applause:

> From every latent foe,
> From the assassin's blow,
> God save the King!
> O'er him thine arm extend,
> For Britain's sake defend,
> Our father, Prince, and friend,
> God save the King!

The King took little notice of plots against his life. In 1794 when informed of a conspiracy to assassinate him, which had been betrayed to the Home Office by an informer, he wrote:

On the idea of plots of the nature supposed I have ever had but one opinion, that any informer that comes voluntary forward is not to be entirely neglected, yet that he must be looked at with a jealous eye, he being most frequently actuated alone by the object of obtaining money. We are all with the utmost caution open to events of the most fatal kind if men will at any hazard prosecute their plans, therefore anyone would be ever miserable if, not trusting in his own honest endeavours to act uprightly, and trusting in the protection of Providence, he did not banish the thought that men will be found to harbour such wicked intentions.

The interest of these attempted assassinations is that they reveal the King's immense popularity with his subjects. It is difficult at any time to gauge the popularity of royalty or to know what popularity in this sense means. People will assemble in thousands to gaze at a king merely as a spectacle or curiosity, and demonstrations of public sympathy, as for King George II during the

Jacobite rebellion of 1745, may not be for the man himself but for what he symbolizes. But the evidence is overwhelming that King George III was held in affection by his subjects. In 1791, when the King and Queen were at Weymouth, Fanny Burney met an old woman. 'There was such a holiday then as the like was not in all England', said the old woman. She had baked a hundred penny loaves for the poor, the gentry had roasted a bullock, there had been 'such a fine sermon', 'the finest band of music in all England singing God save the King and every soul joined in the chorus' – and all, said the old woman, 'not so much because he was a king, but because they said he was such a worthy gentleman, and that the like of him was never known in this nation before'. No doubt the poor would have rejoiced at being given bread and beef no matter the occasion – to say nothing of a sermon and the finest band of music in all England – but why should the gentry have gone to this expense and trouble had not the King been popular?

The King's popularity was an important factor in the general election of 1784. He was unpopular in London at the beginning of the reign, probably a reflection of the unpopularity of Bute as a Scot. But London was not Great Britain and even Londoners came round as was shown by the reception they gave to the news of his recovery in 1789. In the provinces and in Scotland and Wales he was always popular. Ireland was an exception. No King of Great Britain could be anything but a remote figure to the people of Ireland.

At first sight it is difficult to account for this popularity. No King of Great Britain in modern times has seen less of his kingdoms. He never visited Ireland, Scotland, or Wales, and in England he never travelled north of Worcester or west of Plymouth. He is the only monarch of the Hanoverian dynasty who never saw Hanover, the only British monarch during the last two hundred and fifty years who has never visited the Continent. He certainly did not broaden his mind by travel. He told George Rose that he did not like 'mountains and other romantic scenery' or 'the fine wild beauties of nature'. No wonder: he had never seen anything more mountainous than the New Forest or wilder than Bagshot Heath.

Perhaps the explanation is to be found in the silent transformation in British social life during the King's reign. The evangelicals among the upper and middle classes, the Methodists among the lower classes, brought about a revolution in manners. Great Britain acquired a social conscience, illustrated in the movement to abolish slavery and the slave trade, factory legislation, the education of the poor, penal reform, and the modernization of government. There was a dichotomy in the social life of the upper classes. There were those who gambled and got drunk, lived in adultery and debt, the high spenders and the high livers – the type of the Prince of Wales and his friend the Duchess of Devonshire: unattractive and boring in reality but fascinating to romantic novelists. There were others, the type of the King's last two Prime Ministers Spencer Perceval and Lord Liverpool, religious, sober, frugal, careful, and dull; and the middle class who saved their money and provided the capital and convictions that made Great Britain the first industrial nation of the modern world. It was to them that the future belonged.

There was no doubt to which type King George belonged. Without any attempt to make himself cheap or popular in a common way, he appealed to the most vital of his subjects. In character and convictions he was the average Briton of his day or what the average Briton aspired to be. He was John Dull.

Chapter 8

THE KING'S ILLNESS

The general election of 1784 gave Pitt a commanding majority in the House of Commons and appeared to solve all the King's political problems. He had successfully defended the constitution and asserted his right to choose his first minister. His difficulties in the next few years were not in the field of politics but concerned his own family, and especially the conduct of his eldest son.

Both the Duke of York and Prince William had warned their brother to keep out of politics. 'Take care what you are about', the Duke wrote on 9 April 1784, '. . . beware doing those things which you may hereafter repent every day of your life.' The Prince protested that he was pledged to support Fox, that he acted from principle and could not desert his friends. It is difficult to see what his principles were. He could hardly agree to Fox's demand that the Crown should surrender control of government to a group of politicians without standing in the country. There had been some political principle behind King George III's opposition to his grandfather in 1756 and even Frederick, Prince of Wales, had believed himself to be acting from public motives. But what were the Prince of Wales's motives in 1784 except to annoy his father, please his friends, and gratify his vanity? However, it was his private conduct that gave the King most concern.

After indulging in half a dozen affairs with women, more or less serious at the time, the Prince really believed that he had fallen in love. His choice was Maria Anne Fitzherbert, six years older than the Prince and twice a widow. She was also a Roman Catholic and an honest woman. Had she been willing to become the Prince's mistress, perhaps he would have tired of her after a year

502

or two, as he had done with Lady Melbourne and Madame Hardenberg, and the affair would have had no political effects. But she refused to consider any illicit relationship; and in his despair the Prince staged a mock suicide attempt and extorted from her a promise that she would become his wife. Neither Mrs Fitzherbert nor her friend the Duchess of Devonshire held that an engagement obtained in this way was binding, and to escape the Prince's importunities Mrs Fitzherbert left for the Continent. The Prince wished to follow her, and in August 1784 informed the King that he was so distressed in his finances that he would have to go abroad.

The King knew more about the Prince's affairs than the Prince realized. He knew that the Prince was friendly with the Duke of Chartres (the future Duke of Orleans, 'Philippe Egalité' of the French Revolution), and that Chartres had found him credit in Paris. He knew about Mrs Fitzherbert and that it was because of her that the Prince wished to go abroad. 'I shewed an inclination of contributing to the discharge of his debts', the King wrote to the Lord Chancellor on 31 August 1784, 'if he would give up the idea of a plan so highly improper.' On 2 September the King learnt the Prince was to set out next day, and issued an order 'as his father and his sovereign . . . not to leave the realm without having obtained my particular leave'. Lord Southampton, who conveyed the order to the Prince, told him the King was not angry and begged him to confide in his father.

The Prince dared not disobey this order. Whether the King had a legal right to forbid his son from leaving the kingdom might be a matter of doubt (in fact he had been advised by the Lord Chancellor that he had). But there can be no doubt that had the Prince left the country against the King's command in order to marry a Roman Catholic, with money supplied by a foreign prince, and leaving debts of more than £100,000 behind him, he would have imperilled his succession to the throne. He could not contract a legal marriage with Mrs Fitzherbert. By the Royal Marriage Act a marriage contracted without the King's consent was void, and by the Act of Settlement if the Prince of Wales married a Roman Catholic he forfeited his right to the throne. The Prince would have done well to put Mrs Fitzherbert out of his mind and she to have remained upon the Continent.

'He cried by the hour', wrote Lord Holland, who derived his information from his uncle Charles Fox, '. . . rolling on the floor, striking his forehead, tearing his hair, falling into hysterics, and swearing that he would abandon the country, forgo the Crown, sell his jewels and plate, and scrape together a competence to fly with the object of his affections to America.' If he could not go to Mrs Fitzherbert then she must come to him. He told her (which was possibly true) that Pitt had offered to pay his debts and give him 'an immense increase of income' if he would abandon her and marry the Prince of Orange's daughter. He also told her (which was certainly false) that the King had said that if he would renounce his right to Hanover in favour of the Duke of York the King would acknowledge Mrs Fitzherbert as his wife. He told her that their children could not succeed to Hanover: he did not tell her that they could not succeed to Great Britain. By a mixture of half truths, downright lies, and protestations of eternal devotion he persuaded her to return to England; and on 15 December 1785, in the presence of her uncle and brother, they went through a marriage ceremony according to the rites of the Church of England. It was performed by a clergyman released from the Fleet prison on payment of his debts and bribed by the promise of a bishopric in the next reign. Why Mrs Fitzherbert consented to the marriage or whether she realized it was legally no marriage, we do not know. The Prince told his brothers and it was not long before the newspapers knew.

Before undertaking to settle his son's debts, the King had to know how much they were. On 27 October 1784,

Colonel Hotham, the Prince's treasurer, estimated them at £147,293. Most of this appears to have been incurred in respect of Carlton House. The Prince had given lavish orders for the improvement of his residence and had never bothered to ask how much it would cost. 'Your Royal Highness', wrote Hotham, is 'totally in the hands and at the mercy of your builder, your upholsterer, your jeweller, and your tailor . . . these people act from your Royal Highness's pretended commands, and from their charges there is no appeal.' On 5 January 1785 this estimate was submitted to the King together with an explanation as to how it had been incurred. 'The chief part of the debt . . .', the Prince wrote, 'has been in objects which, in general, have been deemed necessary, and which from their nature cannot be again repeated.' He claimed it was impossible to reduce his expenses and laid the blame on the King for not allowing him a sufficient income.

At least one of the Prince's friends knew that this was not true. Charles Fox was concerned about his patron's conduct. The Prince, he told Lord Southampton on 28 March 1785, 'was very apt in his statements to keep back parts of a case that did not exactly make for the opinion he wished to receive'. Fox had warned him not to become entangled with Mrs Fitzherbert. He knew that even if the Prince had been given the income which the coalition had proposed for him in 1783 he would still have been in debt. Fox realized how much damage had been done to his own reputation by carelessness about money and that the Prince's debts were so large it was impossible to pay them without application to Parliament. And what would Parliament think if it knew that the Prince was about to contract an illegal marriage with a Roman Catholic? 'No man', said Fox of himself, 'saw more strongly the mischief of the King and Prince of Wales being at daggers drawn.' Lord Malmesbury also advised the Prince to give up politics, but he replied that he was pledged to Fox!

This was the first of two attempts which Fox made to effect a reconciliation with the King. Both were ignored by King George.

The King demanded that the Prince should give a full explanation of how his debts had been incurred and 'a reasonable security against the continuance of his extravagance'. It is doubtful if the Prince could have explained even had he wished, and he certainly did not wish to tell his father that he was making an allowance to Mrs Fitzherbert. By the summer of 1786 the sum amounted to £269,878, and the Prince could no longer carry on. He was compelled to dismiss his establishment and live as a private gentleman. Fox advised him to consign the greater part of his income into the hands of trustees for the payment of his debts.

The letters between the King and his son make sorry reading. Each tried to put the other in the wrong. The Prince was unrepentant: the King was unconciliatory. Malmesbury described the King's letters as harsh and unkind, yet how otherwise could he write? The Prince's debts amounted to more than a quarter of the annual civil expenditure of the realm. What a fuss the House of Commons had made in 1769 and 1777 when asked to pay the debts on the Civil List! Yet these had been incurred for national purposes, were fully accounted for, and had amounted on an average to no more than £60,000 a year. The Prince was exceeding his income at the rate of £80,000 a year purely on his own pleasures. The King had taken care from the beginning to take the ministers into his confidence and Pitt had drafted his letters. All realized that it would be a ticklish business to get through the House of Commons and some of the Prince's most considerable friends tried to dissuade him from applying. The Prince and Portland quarrelled about this and did not speak to each other for more than two years. It began to dawn on the opposition that the Prince was becoming a political liability.

'What his Royal Highness most wishes', the Prince wrote on 5 May 1787, 'is an increase of £40,000 per annum to his income ... he should prefer the increase of £40,000 per annum without the payment of debts to that of payment of debts without increase of income.' This was what Pitt and the King were determined he should not have. To give him another £40,000 a year and leave him to pay his debts at his discretion would mean that they would never be paid and that he would raise additional loans on the security of his increased income. Neither Pitt nor the King trusted the Prince. Further unpleasant letters passed, more accounts were produced (neither full nor satisfactory), and eventually a compromise was arranged. The King gave the Prince an additional £10,000 a year, making his income about £73,000 (£60,000 from the Civil List and £13,000 from the Duchy of Cornwall). Parliament voted £161,000 for the payment of debts and £60,000 for the completion of Carlton House. John Rolle, M.P. for Devon, raised in the House of Commons the question of the Prince's marriage to Mrs Fitzherbert, and Fox assured him on the authority of the Prince that the story was untrue. King George IV did many mean things in his life but perhaps he never did a meaner than to tell this lie to Charles Fox.

On 21 May 1787 the Prince visited his father and mother at the Queen's House. He promised 'as far as is in human power to foresee events' that he would incur no further debts. 'The King told him that he had lost his character but might retrieve it if he would not live with such scoundrels.' This was not a reference to Fox but to the Prince's major-domo Louis Weltje. He acknowledged to Lord Ailesbury that his son and he could never be on good terms, but he hoped the Prince would now be able to pay his debts and not get into further trouble.

On 4 June 1788 the King celebrated his fiftieth birthday. The stormy years of life were over and he seemed to be passing into a serene middle age. He had solved his political problems and Pitt's ministry was established in the confidence of the nation. The settlement of the Prince of Wales's debts opened the prospect of a better relationship with his eldest son. The country had recovered from the American war and was prosperous and content. Great Britain's prestige abroad was higher than at any time since the Seven Years War. With France on the edge of bankruptcy, Austria rent by nationalist dissensions, and Prussia the ally of Great Britain, the younger Pitt bade fair to make King George III the arbiter of Europe as his father had made King George II.

These pleasing prospects soon disappeared. Instead of a serene old age, the King's last years were to be filled with sorrow and suffering. His children were to disappoint him, he was to become estranged from his wife, his youngest and favourite daughter was to die before him. He was to meet a lonely death, blind, mentally deranged, isolated from the world and those he loved. In the sphere of politics his government was to face the threat of revolution and the remaining years of his reign were to be filled with war on a scale never previously known.

On 11 June, a week after his birthday, the King was seized with what he described as 'a pretty smart bilious attack'.[1] So great was the pain in his stomach that he had to take to his bed as 'the only tolerable posture' he could find. 'I am what one calls a cup too low', he wrote to Pitt, 'but when thoroughly cleared I hope to feel equal to any business that may occur.' Sir George Baker, President of the Royal College of Physicians and one of the King's doctors, advised him to rest for a few days at Kew. At the end of the month, the complaint not having gone away, Baker recommended the King to go to Cheltenham and drink the waters which were supposed to be good for bilious complaints. Lord Fauconberg, one of the Lords of the Bedchamber (the same who had harangued against Charles Fox in the Castle Yard at York in 1784), offered the use of his house near Cheltenham, and as soon as the session of Parliament ended the royal party set off. Besides the King and Queen and their eldest daughters there were only a few courtiers and personal servants. 'A smaller party for a royal excursion', wrote Fanny Burney, who was one of the party, 'cannot well be imagined.'

The King stayed five weeks at Cheltenham. He had never been so far from London before and it was the first prolonged stay he had made outside a royal residence. The house was small and the King lived in the style he loved – as a plain country gentleman. No levees, no drawing rooms, no tiresome audiences in the closet! 'Never did schoolboys enjoy their holidays equal to what we have done our little excursion', wrote the Queen to Prince Augustus. They went to Worcester to hear the *Messiah* at the Three Choirs Festival; they visited the King's old friend Richard Hurd, Bishop of Worcester; and indulged their passion for seeing country houses. 'We have been at Gloucester, Tewkesbury, Cirencester, Painswick, Stroud, Rodbury, Worcester, Croome, Matson, Woodchester Park, and various places', wrote the Queen. 'The crowds of people were immense, and to give you a small idea of it at Rodbury the magistrates computed the number of people for that day only to have been between fifty and sixty thousand.' Each morning at six o'clock the King drank the waters. He walked through the streets of Cheltenham arm in arm with the Queen, their daughters following behind, unaccompanied by a single soldier, as if they were on the North Terrace at Windsor. He went into people's houses, saw them at work, and asked how they lived. All this he had done at Windsor for years. The importance of the Cheltenham visit is that his doings were reported in the newspapers and the whole country learnt about them.

The visit did him good. 'The waters have been most efficacious,' he wrote to Fauconberg on his return to Windsor. A month later he had an attack of pain in the

509

face and suffered a sleepless night. The King did not like the role of an invalid. 'Setting quiet, and not sufficient ease to employ myself much, is not a situation I quite admire,' he wrote to Pitt on 20 September. He continued to find difficulty in sleeping. At Kew during the night of 16–17 October he was seized with 'a spasmodic bilious attack', and the next morning summoned Baker.

I found His Majesty [Baker wrote in his diary] sitting up in his bed, his body being bent forward. He complained of a very acute pain in the pit of the stomach, shooting to the back and sides and making respiration difficult and uneasy. The pain continued all the day, though in a less degree of acuteness towards the evening. . . . His Majesty informed me . . . that of late he had been much tormented in the night by a cramp in the muscles of his legs, and that he had suffered much from the rheumatism, which affected all his limbs, and made him lame, especially on his first going out in the morning.

'Those about him hoped he was going to have the gout', wrote Lady Harcourt. The eighteenth century believed the gout to be a preventative of all other complaints, 'rather a remedy than a disease' as Horace Walpole put it. Provided it did not fly to the head it rarely killed, and at least it kept the doctor away. 'A disorder that requires no physician', wrote Walpole, 'is preferable to any that does.' The eighteenth-century doctor was often worse than the disease. The King who was to be tormented by doctors learnt the truth of Walpole's remarks.

Baker gave the King a purgative. It was almost instinctive for physicians in the eighteenth century and for long afterwards to try to relieve the bowels. Perhaps it did no good but at least it helped to establish the patient's confidence in the physician. He prescribed laudanum to kill the pain. 'I cannot boast much to Mr Pitt of my night's rest', the King wrote on 21 October, 'but since I have dressed myself and eat a very comfortable breakfast, I certainly trust it was the state of one not quite recovered, but certainly not still oppressed with illness.' He was told that his disorder had arisen from not changing his stockings when coming home wet from hunting, so that he had caught rheumatism in the legs which had flown to the stomach. 'I shall . . . certainly have for the rest of my life a flannel cloathing next to my skin', the King told Prince Augustus.

Baker was taken aback when he saw the King (for the second time that day) in the afternoon of 22 October. 'The look of his eyes, the tone of his voice, every gesture and his whole deportment, represented a person in a most furious passion of anger.' He declaimed against the use of purgatives and said the importation of senna ought to be prohibited. 'With a frequent repetition of this and similar language', wrote Baker, 'he detained me three hours.' That night Baker informed Pitt that he had left the King 'in an agitation of spirits nearly bordering on delirium'. The Queen and her daughters were alarmed. They, who lived closest to him, knew how different this was from his usual behaviour.

But the next day the King was 'calm, composed, and free from fever'. Against Baker's advice he insisted on going to the levee on the 24th 'to show I am not so ill as some have thought'. He wrote to Prince Augustus who also had been ill in Germany but was too tired to copy out the letter:

As Dr Zimmerman thinks you should after so many attacks avoid a cold winter, I send my rough draft that no time may be lost in preparing for your going to a mild climate for this winter. I am grieved to part you from your brothers and to interrupt your studies, but the first object I want you to acquire is health.

At the levee he was 'weak and somewhat lame'. It 'was an effort beyond his strength', wrote William Grenville. The next day the King wrote to Pitt:

Mr Pitt really seemed distressed at seeing my bodily stiffness yesterday which I alone exhibited to stop further lies and any

511

fall of the stocks. ... I am certainly weak and stiff but no wonder, I am certain air and relaxation are the quickest restoratives. ... Mr Pitt is desired ... to prevent all political papers being sent to me till I meet him on Wednesday at St James's.

That day the Royal Family left for Windsor, against the Queen's inclination who would have preferred to remain in easier reach of medical attendance.

During the next few days his condition varied. On 26 October he told Fanny Burney that he had hardly slept a minute all night. On the 27th the Queen sent for Baker, who saw the King at the concert:

During the whole music he talked continually, making frequent and sudden transitions from one subject to another; but I observed no incoherence in what he said, nor any mark of false perception. ... He was lame; complained of rheumatic pain, and weakness in the knees, and was continually sitting and rising.

Baker persuaded him not to go to London for the levee, and on the 29th Fanny Burney wrote: 'The dear and good King again gains ground, and the Queen becomes easier.'

Four main groups of symptoms characterized his illness. First, a weakness in his limbs. 'He walks like a gouty man', wrote Fanny Burney. 'My dear Effy', the King said to Lady Effingham, 'you see me, all at once, an old man.' He used a stick for walking but was still able to mount a horse. Secondly, an inability to sleep. He told the Queen that when they went to bed she must not speak to him 'so that he might fall asleep as he had great want of that refreshment'. It was noted that he grew worse towards evening and if he had had a bad night the next day he would be delirious. Thirdly, there was a failing in his eyesight and hearing. He told Baker on 29 October 'that his vision was confused, and that whenever he attempted to read a mist floated before his eyes and intercepted the objects', and it was with difficulty that he could hear music.

The symptom that caused the greatest concern was his delirium. He talked rapidly and incoherently until he became hoarse. 'His great hurry of spirits and incessant loquaciousness', wrote Baker, '. . . . gave great uneasiness to the Queen.' 'The Queen is almost overpowered with some secret terror', wrote Fanny Burney on 2 November. The Queen, poor woman, heard him at his worst, late at night. And she had been warned by the King as to what might happen, for he knew he was ill and was not behaving normally. 'On the Queen declaring one day in the post chaise', records Lord Ailesbury in his dairy, 'she thought everybody ought to endeavour to bear up under afflictions, and that she had a confidence in God not inflicting more than we were able to bear, he took her round the waist and said, "Then you are prepared for the worst." '

He was still able to attend to business, and on 2 November talked on army matters to the Adjutant-General 'with great acuteness and precision'. That day Baker wrote in his diary: 'The King is better and worse so frequently, and changes so, daily, backwards and forwards, that everything is to be apprehended if his nerves are not some way quieted.' Baker felt the need of assistance and William Heberden, the 78-year-old 'doyen of English physicians', was summoned. The two doctors saw the King in the evening of 3 November. 'It was now too evident', Baker wrote, 'that his mind was greatly disturbed.' Yet that day he had written a sensible and sanguine letter to Pitt:

The King thinks it must give Mr Pitt pleasure to receive a line from him. This will convince him the King can sign warrants without inconvenience. . . . He attempts reading the despatches daily, but as yet without success; but he eats well, sleeps well, and is not in the least fatigued with riding, though he cannot yet stand long, and is fatigued if he walks. Having gained so much, the rest will soon follow.

The King's assertion that he was sleeping well is not borne out by the evidence of others, and it seems that this letter was written to assure Pitt there was no need to worry. The King believed he was getting better when in fact his illness was approaching the crisis.

This came on 5 November. Baker saw him after breakfast and found him 'more composed'. His appetite was good and he had talked cheerfully 'and with very little inconsistence'. At midday Fanny Burney saw him set off for a drive. 'He was all smiling benignity', she writes, 'but gave so many orders to the postillions, and got in and out of the carriage twice, with such agitation, that again my fear of a great fever hanging over him grew more and more powerful.' The Prince of Wales had come to Windsor to visit his parents. At dinner that afternoon the King broke out into what Fanny describes as 'positive delirium'. The Queen could hardly contain herself. All the pent-up emotions of the last few days broke forth and she sobbed hysterically. The Prince burst into tears and 'the princesses were in misery'. Baker was summoned and found the King under 'an entire alienation of mind'. 'It was too evident', wrote Lady Harcourt, 'that His Majesty had not the least command over himself.' The Queen told her (and she simply had to tell someone) that the King's eyes were like 'black currant jelly': 'the veins in his face were swelled, the sound of his voice was dreadful, he often spoke till he was exhausted . . . while the foam ran out of his mouth'. She dreaded having to sleep with him that night, and he was persuaded to sleep in the dressing room next to the Queen's room. Colonel Goldsworthy, the equerry on duty, and Richard Battiscombe, the royal apothecary, kept watch, and Goldsworthy's sister, governess to the royal children, slept with the Queen. In the middle of the night the King got up and went into the bedroom to satisfy himself the Queen was there. With a candle in his hand, he opened the bed curtains. Looking earnestly at the Queen he said: 'I will confess the truth, I

thought you had deceived me, and that you was not here.'
'He stayed a full half hour', writes Fanny Burney, 'and the depth of terror during that time no words can paint.'

The next day the Prince of Wales sent for Dr Richard Warren, one of his personal physicians. Warren was a society doctor: the Sir Ralph Bloomfield Bonington of his day, skilled in administering words of consolation to a widow with a good jointure. The King disliked him and refused to see him. Warren received such information as Baker could give, posted himself outside the door, heard the King in his delirium, and without bothering to see the Queen hastened to the Castle to inform the Prince of Wales that the King's life was in danger and that 'if he did live, there was little reason to hope that his intellects would be restored'.

The first part of Warren's prognosis was certainly correct. During the next few days the King came close to death. A rumour ran round London that he was in fact dead and that the news was being concealed until the incoming Lord Mayor had been sworn into office. Jack Payne, the Prince of Wales's *éminence grise*, wrote to Sheridan during the night of 8–9 November:

The Duke of York . . . just come out of the King's room, bids me add that His Majesty's situation is every moment becoming worse. His pulse is weaker and weaker; and the doctors say it is impossible to survive it long, if his situation does not take some extraordinary changes in a few hours. . . . Since this letter was written, all articulation even seems to be at an end with the poor King.

On 10 November he was two hours in a coma, the Lord of the Bedchamber in waiting attended at St James's to answer inquiries, and the Archbishop of Canterbury ordered prayers to be said for his recovery. Pitt went to Windsor and was told by the Prince of Wales that it was the unanimous opinion of the physicians 'that His Majesty's understanding is at present so affected that

515

there does not appear to them any interval in which any act that he could do could properly be considered as done with a consciousness and understanding of what it was about'. 'There was more ground to fear than to hope, and more reason to apprehend durable insanity than death.'

This was the situation about the middle of November. Once the danger of death had passed, it was the affliction of the mind which gave most concern and dominated the picture of the King's illness. The Prince of Wales took charge at Windsor, and Pitt began to turn his thoughts towards carrying on the government by a regency.

It was natural that both the Prince and Pitt should think of their own position rather than the King. There was little they could do for the King and much that had to be done for the nation. The Prince with all his follies and weaknesses was neither hard-hearted nor calculating. He was sincerely distressed by his father's illness and concerned for his mother's unhappiness. But he could not ignore the political situation and that of the party which looked to him for a lead. If the King's illness were to be prolonged the Prince must become Regent and the Prince's friends would expect to become ministers. Those who had backed the Prince when he was out of favour would now demand their reward. Pitt knew that he would never have become minister without the support of the Crown and could not remain after it had been withdrawn. He could only play for time in the hope that the King would recover before the regency came into force. The bill placed certain restrictions on the power of the Regent, the most important being that he could not create peerages except to members of the Royal Family. Thus the King's illness led to a bitter political controversy, the Prince and his friends contending that the Regent should exercise the full powers of sovereignty as if the King were dead while Pitt maintained that Parliament must determine what those powers should be. For the student of politics the regency crisis is one of the most fascinating episodes of the reign. It was fought largely in the dark, for neither party had any rational grounds for knowing whether or when the King would recover. But it is not the concern of the biographer of King George III.

It is the drama in the King's sickroom that demands our attention. By the end of November seven doctors had been consulted. The best medical advice possible had been procured and could do nothing. The King's illness seemed to be beyond the medical knowledge of the age. All sorts of stories about the King began to circulate in London drawing rooms, some based on the truth, others largely invented. It was said that his behaviour at Cheltenham had given concern; that he had got out of his coach in Windsor Park and addressed an oak tree under the impression that he was speaking to Frederick the Great; that he had attacked the Prince of Wales who had fled for his life, etc. As one reads books about King George one gets the impression that the ordinary rules of historical criticism do not apply and that any story will be accepted provided it is sufficiently sensational.* The King's illness is well documented and there is no need to retail the inventions of scurrilous pamphleteers or the legends of London society. The truth itself is sufficiently unpleasant.

The best picture of the King from the middle of November to his recovery in February is provided by the diary of Robert Fulke Greville, one of the King's equerries, who was in almost constant attendance. Greville was not of outstanding intelligence or discernment and had no medical knowledge. He was an ordinary man of his class and time, and his diary illustrates the great value of such documents if only the writer will describe what he has personally observed and not speculate. It begins on 5 November, the day the King became delirious at dinner and when he was persuaded not to sleep with the Queen. After this the Queen was advised to move to a more distant

*See note 10, p. 614.

room, to have a companion with her at night, and to lock her door. A constant watch was kept on the King by his pages and equerries. These precautions were necessary for the Queen's sake. Her nerves were stretched to the limit and she was frightened at being alone with him. But it was not easy to convince the King that they should be separated. He had a profound contempt for medical opinion and complained to Greville of the treatment he had received from the doctors. This seemed to them one more symptom of his disease. Patients were expected to be amenable to their physicians and if they were not it was prima facie evidence of an unsound mind.

One of the surprising things about the King's illness is that no one ever seems to have thought of sending for a clergyman. A man so pious as King George might have responded to the control of a clergyman when he rejected that of a doctor. Richard Hurd, whom he liked and trusted, would have done more good than Richard Warren, whom he disliked; and the Church of England might have been a better therapeutic agency than the Royal College of Physicians. It is wrong to think of the King as deprived entirely of the use of his reason. There were times when he was perfectly sensible. On 23 November, for example, he ordered the workmen who were engaged on his buildings at Kew to be paid their wages. 'The account books having been at this time kept away from His Majesty', writes Greville, 'he made a calculation in his head', and decided that £200 would be sufficient.

He was uneasy at night and did not sleep well. During the day he talked incessantly, on 19 November 'for nineteen hours without scarce any intermission'. His talk was confused, rambling, and incoherent, a mixture of sense and nonsense. 'Every now and then', wrote Greville on 23 November, he talked 'much unlike himself, I mean indecently, which was never his practice while in possession of his reason'. In his lucid intervals he was aware that his mind was affected. He told General Budé on 22

518

November 'some phantoms of his delusion during his delirium' – that there had been a flood, that he had seen Hanover through Herschel's telescope. 'He was sensible of having been much out of order', he said to Greville on 20 November, 'and that still he stood in need of attention and care. Sometimes he doubted his own accuracy in what he was saying, and would ask me if such and such things had been so.' But these lucid intervals were never reported outside the sickroom and the impression was allowed to take root that the King was completely out of his mind. 'His complaint is a total loss of rationality', the Duke of York wrote to Prince Augustus on 3 December 1788, 'which . . . now is grown to such a pitch that he is a compleat lunatick.' This echoed Warren's belief, and perhaps the wishes of the opposition, but was simply not true.

It seems probable that from the third week of November he was on the road to recovery. There is little account of his physical condition, but he was certainly not suffering as he had done during the previous two weeks. As he felt himself getting better he tried to resume his normal life, but his efforts to assert himself and escape from the control of the physicians seemed to them further evidence of insanity. He refused to be shaved, saying he had always done it himself, and when the doctors insisted that he must not be allowed to shave himself he at first submitted. 'But when half shaved', writes Greville, 'he refused to let the other half be finished, unless certain indulgencies were granted. After continuing some time half shaved . . . he at length gave up the point.' It was believed that company excited him, and on 25 November the doctors under the direction of the Prince of Wales issued an order that he should be attended by only two persons at a time. The King was so angry that he struck the page who brought the order, 'a violence by no means usual to his natural dispositions'. That night he sent for the page, 'took him by the hand, and asked his pardon twenty times'.

519

Matters were made worse by the doctors' wish to remove the King to Kew, which would be more convenient for them and where he could take exercise without being observed. The decision was taken at a cabinet meeting summoned by the Prince of Wales at Windsor on 27 November. It was realized that the King would object, and the physicians gave an undertaking that force would not be used.

On the morning of 29 November the Queen, who thought the move unwise, left in advance, and the bait was laid that the King would be allowed to join her at Kew. Even so it took a terrible struggle, harassing to everyone concerned, to get him there. Pitt and Thurlow talked to him in vain; the equerries and doctors had no more success; and finally he was informed that if he did not go willingly he would be taken by force. It was not until a quarter to four that he entered the coach. Greville, one of the three equerries who travelled with him, describes how they saw a party of the citizens of Windsor in the Home Park:

As the King's carriage drove by them they bowed respectfully and took a melancholy leave. The King on seeing them bowed most kindly and here he felt the greatest emotion which I had yet observed. When he bowed, the big tear started in his eye, and putting his hand before his face he said with much feeling, 'These good people are too fond of me', and he then added with affecting sensibility: 'Why am I taken from a place I like best in the world?'

As the Queen had feared, the move to Kew led to a relapse. The King was not allowed to see her and complained to Greville that he had been deceived. He refused to go to bed, became violent towards his pages, and had to be held down. The next day he refused to eat his meals or take his medicine. 'Symptoms of his disorder have increased rather than diminished', wrote Greville on 1 December.

The failure of the doctors to assert their authority or even to agree how the King should be treated is shown by an incident on 3 December. Sir Lucas Pepys had promised the King he would be allowed to take a walk, but when the time came the other doctors were doubtful and tried to throw the responsibility on to the Queen. There were further discussions as to who should accompany him and after keeping the King waiting half the morning it was finally decided that he should be allowed to walk for a quarter of an hour in front of the house. 'The King rejected the offer and refused to accept of such permission; he was angry, and declared he would not stir out of his room unless he was permitted to walk ten miles. Under such dispositions the indulgence was retracted.' The excuse for moving the King to Kew had been that he should be able to take exercise unobserved, and now he was there this was deemed unadvisable. That night he became almost unmanageable and 'was obliged to be kept in his bed'. 'Altogether', writes Greville, 'this has been the worst day His Majesty has experienced.' Yet an incident in the morning showed that there was ground for hope:

From sentences which had occasionally escaped from him during his illness he had shewn that his unhappy situation was not unknown to him. An observation dropped from him this morning while drawing which marked the sense he had of his misfortune very strongly. Having drawn a line pretty firmly and strait he approved by saying to his page, 'Pretty well for a man who is mad.'

On 30 November, the first day of the King's residence at Kew, the Privy Council decided to send for further assistance. None of the doctors who had hitherto been consulted was experienced in such cases (except Dr Addington, who was old and had retired from practice), and the King appeared unlikely to recover under their treatment. The politicians wanted quick results: either a speedy recovery or an assurance that the King would

521

never recover. They decided to send for a special practitioner, and the Queen reluctantly concurred in a measure which virtually announced to the world that the King was insane.

The Rev. Francis Willis was not a physician but a clergyman, 'who, from motives of principle and charity towards his fellow creatures', had undertaken the study of insanity. For thirty years he had kept a private asylum in Lincolnshire where he received patients of good family and claimed a high rate of cure. He was looked upon by the physicians as little more than a quack, but he was the only doctor consulted who dared to say that under his treatment the King would recover. His treatment involved the use of methods the physicians had not dared to suggest.

Greville gives this account of the King's first meeting with Willis on 5 December:

His Majesty received Dr Willis with composure and began immediately to talk to him and seemed very anxious to state to him that he had been very ill, but that he was now quite well again. He told Dr Willis that he knew where he lived, and asked him how many patients he then had with him under his care. He then thus addressed Dr Willis: 'Sir your dress and appearance bespeaks you of the Church, do you belong to it?' Dr Willis replied: 'I did formerly, but lately I have attended chiefly to physicks [i.e. medicine].' 'I am sorry for it', answered the King with emotion and agitation. 'You have quitted a profession I have always loved, and you have embraced one I most heartily detest. Alter your line of life, ask what preferment you wish, and make me your friend.'

The King understood that Willis's arrival meant that he was considered to be insane, and he was overcome with shame. 'He told one of his pages, that as Dr Willis was now come he could never more show his face again in this country, that he would leave it for ever, and retire to Hanover.'

That evening Willis gave the King a foretaste of what

was in store for him. When the King became agitated,

Dr Willis remained firm, and reproved him in nervous and determined language, telling him he must controul himself otherwise he would put him in a strait waistcoat. On this hint Dr Willis went out of the room and returned directly with one in his hand. ... The King eyed it attentively and alarmed at the doctor's firmness of voice and procedure began to submit. ...

After he was gone His Majesty continued to abuse the rest of the physicians and now principally as he said for not having dealt fairly with him and by having concealed from him his real situation. After this, the poor dear King, overcome by his feelings, burst into a flood of tears and wept bitterly.

Willis was assisted by his son and a number of attendants, accustomed to dealing with refractory patients and not gentle in their methods. His belief that he could cure the King won him the confidence of Pitt and the Queen, and gradually he ousted the other doctors from the sickroom and assumed complete control.

Willis's methods of treatment are thus described by Drs Macalpine and Hunter in their book *George III and the Mad-Business*:

So began the new system of government of the King by intimidation, coercion and restraint. No account of the illness from this point on can disregard the King's treatment, and to what extent the turbulence he displayed was provoked by the repressive and punitive methods by which he was ruled. For every non-compliance – refusing food when he had difficulty in swallowing, no appetite or a return of colic, resisting going to bed when he was too agitated and restless to lie down, throwing off his bed-clothes during sweating attacks – he was clapped into the strait-waistcoat, often with a band across his chest and his legs tied to the bed.

This description is fully confirmed by Greville's diary. The story of the next few weeks makes horrible reading. Greville had approved of the firmness Willis had shown towards the King but was taken aback when he saw his methods in practice. A few examples will suffice to illustrate his methods.

Irritants had been placed on the King's legs to raise blisters which it was hoped would draw away the humours (the cause of the illness, according to the medical theory of the day). These gave the King a great deal of pain, prevented him from sleeping, and increased his irritability. He tore them off, and was confined in the strait-waistcoat. When he was released he was so weak that he could not put his legs to the ground.

On 20 December, after only two hours' sleep, he was placed in the strait-waistcoat at five in the morning and not released until two in the afternoon. 'His legs were tied', writes Greville, 'and he was secured down across his breast.' 'Oh, Emily!' the King was heard to say, 'why won't you save your father? Why must a king lay in this damned confined condition? I hate all physicians but most the Willises, they treat me like a madman.' When he was released, Greville records: 'His agitation continued in a considerable degree and he remained much disturbed. He still talked incessantly and violently, and he was quite wrong in his ideas.' He inveighed against the Queen and Pitt for calling in Dr Willis and spoke of Fox as his friend. After nine hours in this position it is perhaps no wonder his ideas were wrong.

On 16 January 1789 he was sick after being given an emetic. He knelt in his chair and prayed: 'That he had left undone those things which he ought to have done, and done those things which he ought not to have done, and he prayed that God would be pleased either to restore him to his senses, or permit that he might die directly.' In the afternoon he was allowed a visit from the Queen and the eldest princesses. Willis was present throughout and reported 'that the King had behaved with the greatest propriety and affection to the whole party, and that the Queen by the King's desire had played a game at piquet'. In the evening he was quiet 'but at times very touchy'. He

524

played with the Queen's dog and talked cheerfully to Greville, 'but not a sentence . . . like himself in his moments of sound reason'. He passed a restless night and was put into the strait-waistcoat, which Willis seemed to regard as a cure for insomnia. 'Nothing but the terror of the strait-waistcoat', he wrote about the King on one occasion, 'could compose him so as to go to sleep.'

A restraining chair was made for him in which he was strapped so that he could not move. On 30 January, after some 'improper conversation', Willis ordered him to be confined in the chair 'and gave him a severe lecture'. 'His Majesty becoming more loud and impatient under this lecture' (which may have reminded him of George Grenville). 'Dr Willis ordered a handkerchief to be held before his mouth, and he then continued and finished his lecture.' The equerries and pages were excluded from the sickroom without Willis's consent and for most of the day the King saw no one but his keepers. He grew afraid of them and imagined they were going to murder him.

It is time to make an end of this catalogue of horrors. Willis's methods were those of a sergeant-major of the old school in a detention barracks. Far from curing the King as he boasted and has been generally believed, he probably delayed his recovery. Had the King not been a man of exceptional strength of body and mind he would never have survived Dr Willis. It was a triumph of nature over medicine. Yet it would be unjust to leave the impression that Willis was a sadistic monster. He was no more cruel than an eighteenth-century dentist who extracted teeth without an anaesthetic. He was simply following the medical ideas of his time as regards treatment of the insane.

In reading contemporary accounts of the King's illness we must remember that those outside the sickroom heard only the worst of his condition. Men believe what they wish to believe, and it was to the political advantage of Fox and the opposition that the King should not recover.

It was their only chance of office. What they believed about the King's condition is no evidence at all. The doctors were professionally jealous of Willis who was not a member of the Royal College of Physicians, and after he had taken control they did not see the King regularly. Even Pitt and the Royal Family looked on the black side. They saw how far the King was from his normal state: they did not realize the progress he had made. They did not know of his lucid intervals, when he played backgammon with Willis or sang catches or sent for a copy of Cicero to brush up his Latin. The King's sense of humour did not desert him in his illness and he hit back at Willis with the only weapon he had – ridicule. When Willis said he did no more than Christ who also went about healing the sick, the King countered: 'Yes, yes, but he had not £700 a year for it.' 'I perceived', writes Greville, 'that His Majesty played a part occasionally with Dr Willis, and not ill. Tonight while he was sitting at the table, the King in a low voice (addressing himself to Sir Lucas Pepys and me) and with a wink, told us that the doctor was a great rascal and then added, "Tricking in love and in physick you know is all fair." '

Namier is responsible for the idea that the King's talk during his illness is an expression of his unconscious mind and represents thoughts and feelings which had long been repressed. His declarations of love for Lady Pembroke and of dislike for the Queen have been cited as evidence of his unconscious wish to be unfaithful to his marriage vows. Lady Pembroke was a daughter of the 3rd Duke of Marlborough (a family whom the King liked), wife of a former Lord of the Bedchamber, and mother of the King's Vice-Chamberlain. She had been treated shamefully by her husband, who had deserted her in 1762 and run away with the daughter of a highly respectable Member of Parliament. The King liked her and was sorry for her but it is most unlikely that he was in love with her. A man cannot be in love with a woman, even unconsciously, for over twenty-five years without giving some indication of his feelings, especially when he is King and every gesture of his face and intonation of his voice is noted. Had there been anything to the story of the King and Lady Pembroke we would have heard of it before the King fell ill. His remarks about her like other things he said during his illness show that his mind was disturbed, but are very doubtful evidence as to his unconscious wishes.

Greville wrote on 27 December:

He very feelingly said to one of his pages he hoped nobody knew what wrong ideas he had had, and what wrong things he had said respecting her. . . . He observed at this time that in his delirium he must have said many very improper things, and that much must have escaped him then which ought not, and that he must try and find out what had slipped from him.

On his recovery he wrote to Lady Pembroke and she replied on 8 April 1789: 'Your Majesty has always acted by me as the kindest brother as well as the most gracious of sovereigns . . . if I might presume to say that I felt like the most affectionate sister towards an indulgent brother it would exactly express my sentiments.'

On 13 December the King saw the Queen for the first time since his removal to Kew. When told he would be allowed to see her, he said: 'It made him very happy, and that he would do all he could to recover which he was indifferent about before.' Lord Ailesbury, informed by the Queen herself, wrote in his diary:

He was exceedingly affectionate towards the Queen. On Dr Willis or his son telling him he was not so attentive to his game as he used to be at backgammon he said, 'How can I, when the person I love most in the world is in the room with me?' The Queen said she did not find the King so much altered as she expected. . . . After staying twenty minutes, the doctor proposed her going, but the King would not consent until about ten minutes after he told the King it would be better for the Queen and then he consented to her going.

On 28 December the Queen paid him another visit. She thought he looked thin and ill, but 'tolerably composed'. He received her, wrote Willis, 'with much kindness', sat down beside her, kissed her hand, and cried frequently. They talked in German, which Willis did not understand, and the visit lasted for nearly an hour instead of the stipulated fifteen minutes. After the Queen had gone the King abused Willis, said he was an old fool, and complained 'of having been detained from his wife'. 'The visit certainly failed in its object', wrote Greville, 'for it has done him no good.' Yet Willis informed the Privy Council that day: 'His Majesty is considerably better with every continued appearance of recovery.'

From the middle of January 1789 there was a gradual improvement. On 3 February he was allowed to shave himself and on the 6th to use a knife and fork. On the 10th he asked to see the Chancellor and when told by Willis that such an interview might overtax his strength, replied: 'I will not do it till you think fit; but I have been ill seventeen weeks and have much to inquire about.' On the 13th he saw Vulliamy his watchmaker and Rigaud who looked after the observatory at Kew, and talked sensibly to them. He walked in Kew Gardens, and on hearing his gardener promise to make up a basket of exotic plants for Willis, turned and said: 'Get another basket, Eaton, at the same time, and pack up the doctor in it, and send him off at the same time.'

By now the King's improvement had become the talk of London. Pitt and the ministers were elated and could afford to smile when an address arrived from the Irish Parliament, always out of step with the British, offering the regency of Ireland to the Prince of Wales. It now seemed probable that there would be no regency. The Prince of Wales and the Duke of York, who had thrown in their lot wholeheartedly with the opposition, asked for an audience to explain their conduct, but Willis advised against it. The King now saw the Queen every day. Greville was still uneasy about him, and when he learnt that he had played cards with the Queen on a Sunday took this as evidence that he was not completely recovered. 'He knows it is wrong', said John Willis, 'but he says he thinks it may now be excuseable for he had no other way of entertaining the Queen.' The Willises were confident, and even Warren admitted that all he had seen of the King was favourable.

Willis wished the King gradually to resume his normal life and not to tax his strength by a too sudden transition. On 17 February he permitted the Chancellor to see the King but warned Thurlow that he was not to talk about the Regency Bill. 'His Majesty was a little nervous', wrote Greville. 'He talked with the Chancellor about the several powers of Europe; of what the Emperor and Empress were doing; mentioned the troubles of France; asked about the new King of Spain and whether he had done any thing since he had succeeded to the throne which seemed to mark his character.' The next day, when the Queen came, 'he was in good spirits and read part of Shakespeare's *Merchant of Venice* aloud in different tones of voice as suited to the characters'. In the House of Lords on 19 February Thurlow moved to adjourn the third reading of the Regency Bill on the ground that the King was so much recovered that the bill might be unnecessary. That morning Willis told Pitt that the King was capable of attending to business and it was desirable to bring him up to date with events. The task of informing the King fell to Thurlow, who had played an equivocal part during the Regency crisis. The audience lasted two hours: and Thurlow said that he never saw the King 'more composed, collected, or distinct, and that there was not the least trace or appearance of disorder'.

On 23 February the King saw the Prince of Wales and

the Duke of York. 'Care was taken', the King wrote to Thurlow, 'that the conversation should be cordial but without running into particulars.' He talked to the Prince about horses and to the Duke about his regiment, but nothing was said about politics. He asked to see Pitt,

for though I decline entering into a pressure of public business, though the nation at large, to whom I am so much indebted for the support and anxiety shewn during my illness, may not suffer by any delay of those necessary steps which the various services may require, particularly the raising the necessary supplies for the current year.

On 27 February the *London Gazette* announced that no further bulletins would be issued.

What was this mysterious illness which afflicted King George III at the age of fifty, brought him to the brink of death, vanished three months later, reappeared after an interval of eleven years, and finally engulfed him? The King's physicians were puzzled. If it was insanity, it was insanity of a kind they had never known. A contemporary newspaper reflected their opinion when it wrote that the King's illness was held to be 'not an insanity, but a delirium'. But after the illnesses of 1801 and 1804 and the King's permanent disablement in 1811 insanity appeared to be the only possible explanation. Nineteenth-century historians accepted it without question. They did not have the materials available today for studying the King's illness nor did they consider it their duty to supply an explanation for what seemed a purely medical matter. The diagnosis of insanity appealed to Whigs and Tories alike. The King had been the declared enemy of Charles Fox, the spiritual ancestor of nineteenth-century Whiggism. He had opposed parliamentary reform and Catholic emancipation, causes dear to the hearts of the Whigs. They were concerned to blacken his reputation and to represent him as unfit for the throne.

The Tories, who looked favourably on the King, readily accepted the diagnosis of insanity which enabled them to say that the quarrels of factious Whigs had disturbed his mind.

Four periods of illness were known during which the King showed symptoms of insanity. There was also a fifth, that of February–May 1765. No sign of mental disturbance had appeared then nor did it occur to anyone in 1788 to connect the King's condition with his previous illness. But after the King's death the myth was created that he had been insane in 1765 and the fact had been hushed up by the court. At first this took the form of a mere 'belief'. 'It is believed that, soon after his accesssion to the throne, the King had a slight attack of a similar indisposition', wrote the *Gentleman's Magazine* in 1820. A little later (in Wraxall's *Posthumous Memoirs*) it became a 'probability', and finally it hardened into a 'fact' whose existence had been known only to those closely connected with the court. Mrs Papendiek, whose father was the hairdresser whom Queen Charlotte brought over in 1761, wrote in her memoirs that the King's insanity in 1765 'was not known beyond the palace'. 'We have the best authority for believing', proclaimed the Tory *Quarterly Review* in 1840, 'that it was of the nature of that which thrice afflicted His Majesty.' When the Tories had 'the best authority' for this story, why should the Whigs attempt to deny it?

In fact the *Quarterly Review* had no authority at all for what was purely a supposition. Mrs Papendiek's memoirs were written in extreme old age and are valueless as a record of the early years of the King's reign. She was not born until 1765 and most of her account is simply copied from the *Annual Register*. It is an obvious form of human vanity to pretend to an intimate acquaintance with the affairs of royalty, and there have always been clever people who like to boast that they were aware of some fact before it became known to all the world. Statements about the illness of 1765 made after the King's death must be scrutinized with the deepest suspicion.

There is no mention in contemporary letters or diaries of mental disturbance in 1765. Horace Walpole, the chronicler of the age, who had close connections with the court, did not know of any; nor did Lady Charlotte Finch, governess of the royal children and the Queen's intimate friend. Though the King ceased for a time to appear in public he transacted business with his ministers as usual. Grenville's diary is an invaluable record of the events of these months and contains no hint that the King's first minister believed the King to be mentally afflicted. The person who would certainly have known was the Queen, yet it seems incredible that had it been so she should have said nothing but continued to live a normal life with the King. We know how frightened she was in 1788. Nor is it as easy to hush up court secrets as people suppose. Too many people would have known and servants talk. Those who believe the King was mentally afflicted in 1765 must produce contemporary evidence not the suppositions of later ages.

Why then was the story accepted by almost every historian who has written on the period? Partly because any historical 'fact' if repeated a sufficient number of times by scholars whose work is valued comes to be accepted as true. Namier used to quote a saying by a pre-1914 mayor of Vienna – 'Culture is what one Jew copies from another' – and he would add that the Jews are not the only people who copy one another. All historians do it. If we had to test the accuracy of every single fact for ourselves we would have no time to write our books. When *The Complete Peerage* tells me that William Pitt was created Earl of Chatham on 4 August 1766 I do not go down to the Public Record Office and check the statement from the original records. It is natural to accept as true what is generally believed on good authority. But it is sometimes a mistake. The historian should have a suspicious mind.

There is also a deeper reason. A myth is accepted because it satisfies a need. Nineteenth-century Whigs and Tories alike wished to believe that King George suffered from insanity. For different reasons the theory was acceptable to monarchists and republicans, British and Americans. It also accorded with the ideas of the twentieth century. Neuroses, repressions, and complexes had now become part of the language of biography, and the King was an ideal subject for psychological speculation. Namier, a neurotic himself, portrayed the King as a neurotic, a man of unstable temperament, unable to cope with the realities of life, who took refuge from his responsibilities in insanity. This gave the cue to other historians, and one and all embroidered the theme of the King's neurotic temperament and predisposition to insanity. Some laid the blame on feelings of inadequacy, others on sexual tensions. His virtues were paraded as evidence against him. His temperance was proof that he lacked pliability, his chastity that he was repressed. He was described as obstinate when all the evidence went to show that he was only too ready to yield his opinion, as oscillating between elation and depression when he was of sanguine and even temperament.

It was asking too much to believe that the King had suddenly toppled into insanity at the age of fifty. Obviously his previous behaviour must have given hints of his real condition. And because historians wanted to find these proofs they found them. It was said that the King had displayed signs of insanity in his boyhood, that he experienced his first attack shortly after his marriage, that his relations with Bute showed his neurotic and inadequate temperament. Hence the importance of the illness of 1765. If the King was insane in 1788 it was likely that he was in 1765, and if he was in 1765 it was certain that the diagnosis of 1788 was correct. Each 'fact' was cited as evidence of the truth of the other. A new and more scientific name was found for the King's illness. He no longer suffered from insanity but from manic-depressive psychosis.

In 1966 two British psychiatrists and historians of medicine, Dr Ida Macalpine and Dr Richard Hunter, put forward a new diagnosis of the King's illness. Largely on the evidence of the medical records, which they were the first to study, they contended that the diagnosis of manic-depressive psychosis was untenable and that King George's illness was a classic case of porphyria.

Porphyria was a disease unknown until the twentieth century. It is an hereditary disease which may take many forms. The porphyrins are pigments in the cells of the human body, essential to its proper functioning, and the disease arises when the body manufactures too many. Its symptoms include sensitivity of the skin to sunlight or even to touch, colic, weakness of the limbs, difficulty in swallowing, hoarseness, vomiting, and constipation. In acute stages it leads to irritability, excitement, sleeplessness, delirium, and delusions, so that it may be mistaken for mental illness. It takes its name from the deep red or purple colour of the porphyrins which are frequently passed in the urine.

All these symptoms appeared during the illnesses of King George. Drs Macalpine and Hunter found from the physicians' reports four occasions on which the King passed discoloured urine, described once as 'bluish' and at another time as 'bloody'. They investigated the family history, and found porphyria in four of his sons and his grand-daughter, Princess Charlotte. They traced the incidence of the disease in the King's ancestry as far as Mary, Queen of Scots, and discovered it in two of her living descendants.

We are thus confronted with two diagnoses of the King's illness: manic-depressive psychosis, the result of an unstable and neurotic temperament; and porphyria, a physical disease of hereditary origin. Which of these, if either, is correct? It is difficult for a biographer with no medical training to decide the question on medical grounds. But he can bring to bear his training as a historian and ask which diagnosis best fits the facts of history.

At first sight the King does not seem a likely victim of mental illness, and contemporaries were taken by surprise at the illness of 1788. They could think of others who were much more likely to go mad than the King. He had none of that eccentricity of behaviour which they associated with insanity. He led a regular and chaste life, admittedly no safeguard against mental illness, but at least a proof of character and resolution. There was no insanity in the line of his father or his mother.

If the King's illness was the result of psychological factors, we would expect it to happen when the pressure was greatest. If he retreated into insanity when life became too much for him, it is at those periods that we must look for signs of mental disturbance. Consider, for example, the events of 1771–2. Within the space of a few months there took place the serious illness of the Duke of Gloucester in Italy, the lingering death of the King's mother, the marriage of the Duke of Cumberland, the disgrace and divorce of the Queen of Denmark, and finally the revelation of the Duke of Gloucester's secret marriage. These events in his family put an immense strain on the King. Yet there is no sign of any mental disturbance, no 'retreat into insanity'. If he was a neurotic character, unable to face reality, why did he not break down in 1772?

The events of 1782–3 are even more striking. In March 1782 the King was compelled to accept the resignation of North and the loss of the American colonies; in July Prince Alfred died; in March 1783 there was the protracted political crisis which ended with the King's submission to Fox; in May the death of Prince Octavius; in June the dispute over the Prince of Wales's establishment; in December the dismissal of the coalition and another prolonged political crisis. Here is a combination of public and private worries such as no other British monarch has had to endure within so short a period. Twice during these eighteen months the King was reduced so low as seriously to contemplate abdication. Yet once again there is no sign of mental disturbance or 'retreat into insanity'. Why not, if he was a neurotic character unable to face reality?

Why did he fall ill in 1788? If his illness was psychological in origin, the result of intolerable pressures, what was its precipitating cause? There was no political or personal crisis. The nation was at peace, Pitt's ministry was secure, and the settlement of the Prince of Wales's debts had eased relations between the King and his son. Why did he fall ill in one of the most placid years of his life? The flaw in the theory of manic-depressive psychosis is that it asks us to believe the impossible – that the King fell ill because of psychological pressures at the very moment when those pressures were least.

It also neglects the King's physical symptoms. What was the illness that sent him to Cheltenham in July 1788? what was the acute pain in the pit of his stomach, 'making respiration difficult and uneasy', which caused Baker to be summoned on 17 October? what was the illness which the Duke of York feared would lead to the King's death on the night of 8 9 November? why did he fall into a coma? why did he thrash about in his bed? why was he unable to sleep? why were his legs so weak that he could only walk with a stick? Neither the historian nor the physician can ignore these signs of bodily illness. The proponent of the manic-depressive psychosis theory brushes them aside as invented or at least exaggerated 'to fool the public'. But the evidence of Baker, Greville, and Willis cannot be so lightly dismissed. They were not out to fool the public. Their observations of the King were confided to their private diaries and were not revealed until more than a hundred years after his death.

We must therefore conclude that the diagnosis of manic-depressive psychosis does not explain the facts of the King's illness as the historian knows them. It can only be maintained by making an assertion which is not true (that the King showed signs of mental illness in 1765) and ignoring the evidence of his physical symptoms. Its supposition that the King was neurotic is incorrect. It can be refuted on purely historical grounds. It is in fact not a diagnosis at all but a theory, a product of the intellectual climate of the 1920s and 1930s. It owes its origin to the influence of psychoanalysis on historical thinking.

The diagnosis of porphyria does not violate the facts of history. It accounts for the King's physical and mental symptoms. It explains the puzzling fact that he first showed signs of mental disturbance at the age of 50 and not again until 62. The arguments against it on medical grounds must be left for medical opinion. Doctors frequently disagree, and it is almost impossible to prove irrefutably the diagnosis of a patient who has been dead a hundred and fifty years. All the historian can decide is whether the diagnosis satisfies the requirements of historical truth. Porphyria does, and no other.

From the point of view of the historian it does not greatly matter whether King George suffered from porphyria or some other as yet undiscovered disease. As medical knowledge advances the concept of disease changes, and it may be that in two hundred years' time porphyria will be as little known as gout, that common eighteenth-century disease, is today. The biographer wishes to know whether the King suffered from a mental or a physical disease. On the basis of our present evidence we can say that the King was not mentally ill. The myth of King George III's insanity is exposed.

Gradually the King returned to his normal life. 'I shall carefully avoid every kind of bustle or fatigue', he wrote to Prince Adolphus, 'that I may thoroughly acquire my former vigour of body; that of mind I cannot wish to be more completely reinstated than at this hour.' On 3 March 1789 he slept with the Queen for the first time since his illness. Dr Willis and his men left Kew, and on 10 March Parliament presented addresses of congratulation to the King on his recovery. That night London was ablaze with illuminations. It was, writes Wraxall, 'the most brilliant, as well as the most universal exhibition of national loyalty and joy ever witnessed in England'.

It originated . . . with the people, and was the genuine tribute of their affection . . . London displayed a blaze of light from one extremity to the other; the illuminations extending . . . from Hampstead and Highgate to Clapham, and even as far as Tooting: while the vast distance between Greenwich and Kensington presented the same dazzling appearance.

On 14 March the King returned to his favourite residence, and at every village on the road crowds turned out to cheer him. He rode on horseback, and the warmth of his reception when he arrived quite overwhelmed him. 'All Windsor came out to meet the King', wrote Fanny Burney, and even the soldiers on guard at the Castle were in tears. He had a much quieter night, he wrote the next morning, than any he had experienced since his illness; 'and the joy that appears in every countenance and the good sense of my neighbours in not wishing to incommode cannot fail of having a due effect'.

The rejoicings of March 1789 were a spontaneous tribute to the King's popularity. There had never been anything like them before. One wonders however whether there was not an element of relief, at least in London, that Pitt would remain minister? For the opposition the King's recovery was a political disaster, and while they rejoiced in public they mourned in private. The promised land, once so close, now seemed as far off as ever. The Prince of Wales and the Duke of York were anxious to justify their conduct but the King refused to talk with them. 'I pro-

538

pose avoiding all discussions that may in their nature agitate me', he wrote to the Queen, in a letter meant to be communicated to the brothers, 'and consequently must for the present decline entering on subjects that are not necessarily before me.' He was particularly hurt by the conduct of the Duke of York, who had assumed that his father would not recover and had made his bargain with the opposition. The Prince of Wales could hardly avoid making a fool of himself in politics so long as he remained connected with Fox, but before his illness the King had cautioned the Duke of York against becoming involved with his brother's friends. The Queen was incensed against the Duke of York, knowing how much his father loved him, and it was some months before he was restored to favour. For the rest of his life he was careful never to be out of step with the King.

Before reading the reports of his illness, the King took the Sacrament in order to be in the mood 'to forgive those who might have acted in a manner I could not approve'. He was hurt and and angry at what he read. All on whom he depended – the Queen, his children, Pitt – had believed him insane. The proceedings in Parliament, he told the Duke of Gloucester, had been no less than taking out a commission of lunacy against him. Had the Regency Bill passed (and it would have done had the King's illness lasted a few days longer) 'no power on earth should have prevailed on him to resume the government'. He did not make allowances for the difficult position in which the Queen and Pitt had been placed. The Queen had been anxious to do nothing except on the advice of ministers and Pitt had no alternative but to introduce the Regency Bill. Nor could they well have resisted the recommendation of the physicians to remove the King to Kew. No one who saw the King at the beginning of December 1788 could foresee that in three months he would be completely recovered.

But though the King could not forget he could forgive.

He insisted against the advice of his ministers on a thanksgiving service in St Paul's Cathedral on St George's Day, 23 April 1789. When the Archbishop of Canterbury remonstrated that perhaps the occasion might be too much for him, the King said: 'My Lord, I have twice read over the evidence of the physicians on my case, and if I can stand that I can stand anything.' He was still weak and had lost weight. 'I must candidly confess', he wrote to Pitt on 21 April, 'that though now without complaint, I feel more strongly the effects of my late severe and tedious illness than I had expected . . . I mean a certain lassitude and want of energy both of mind and body, which must require time, relaxation, and change of scene to restore.' He found levees even more of a trial than before his illness and determined to get away for a 'change of scene'.

The Duke of Gloucester placed his house at Weymouth at the King's disposal, and thither in June 1789 went the King and Queen and their three eldest daughters. As at Cheltenham the previous year, they had a delightful time and Weymouth was delighted to receive them. The King made a triumphal progress, every village turning out to cheer him. Weymouth decorated itself with 'God Save the King' – over shop doors, round the caps of children, on bathing machines, even on bathing costumes. When the King took his first dip in the sea, a band concealed in a bathing machine struck up 'God Save the King'.

A frigate was stationed in Weymouth bay so that the royal party could make sea voyages. They lived much in the same style as they did at Windsor. Instead of hunting in the afternoon, the King took the Queen to visit country houses, instead of walking on the North Terrace they walked on the Esplanade. Their friends came down to visit them, they played cards in the evening or went to the theatre, and on the anniversary of their wedding they gave a ball. The King's absence from London made no difference to the conduct of government. The King received state papers and at least once held a meeting of the Privy Council at Weymouth. 'I have the pleasure to assure you', the Queen wrote to Prince Augustus on 24 September 1789, 'that the King is come home much stronger and better for the sea bathing. He began his levees yesterday and bore it very well, but little fatigued and seemed very cheerful at night, so I have hopes that we shall soon come to go on in our old way.'

Great Britain would never go on in her old way. While the King and Queen had been enjoying themselves at Weymouth the States-General of France had been meeting at Versailles. The French Revolution had begun.

Chapter 9

THE NEXT GENERATION

'For the rest of my life', the King wrote to Pitt on his recovery, 'I shall expect others to fulfil the duties of their employments, and only keep that superintending eye which can be effected without labour or fatigue.' In fact his illness made no difference to his share in the conduct of government. The number of court days was reduced and the King inaugurated the British habit of taking a summer holiday by the seaside. Each year from 1789 to 1805, with three exceptions, he went to Weymouth, generally spending from four to six weeks there during August and September. The personal power of the King was not diminished during these years and he had at least as much work after his illness as before.

One man at least understood the implications of the regency crisis and realized that the King's illness had demonstrated the respect and affection in which he was held by the nation. On 18 July 1789, four days after the taking of the Bastille, Charles James Fox asked the Prince of Wales to speak to the King on his behalf. 'Your Royal Highness knows', Fox wrote, 'that not only I am incapable of personal disrespect to His Majesty, but that my political principles are strong in favour of keeping up the royal power entire, undivided, and full of vigour.' He offered himself in any capacity in which the King cared to employ him.

We do not know whether the Prince showed this letter to his father. Probably he knew it would be of no use. Had he done so, and had the King taken it seriously, it would have been referred to Pitt and there the matter would have ended. Pitt no more than the King wished to see Fox in office. Whether the responsibility lay with the King, the

542

Prince, or Pitt, the fact remains that at the outset of the French Revolution Fox's offer of service was slighted.

The French Revolution took Europe by surprise. No throne seemed so secure as that of the King of France. Lord Malmesbury, the most experienced diplomat in the British service, had written in 1786: 'A Madame de Pompadour, or even a Madame du Barri, will never effectively diminish or hurt the grandeur of the French monarchy, which is settled on a foundation beyond the reach of the follies of the court to shake.' How wrong he was! The French were considered the most polite and cultured people in Europe, and the treatment of the King and Queen of France by the Paris mob horrified contemporaries. 'I often think', Queen Charlotte wrote on 17 October 1789, 'that this cannot be the eighteenth century in which we live at present, for antient history can hardly produce anything more barbarous and cruel than our neighbours in France.' At first the British government was not disposed to interfere in the internal affairs of France and King George III declined to advise King Louis XVI. But events forced Great Britain into war with the French Revolution. 'I confess I am of opinion', the King wrote on 6 January 1793, 'that in the actual state of things it seems the most desirable conclusion of the present crisis.' It was a war for religion, for monarchy, for the established order.

The French Revolution drew the Prince of Wales closer to his father. He could hardly fail to see that if the principles of French democracy prevailed in Great Britain he would never inherit the throne. It was time to put an end to the mimic warfare in which he had been engaged for the last ten years. Real blood was being shed in France and might soon be shed in England. On 31 May 1792 the Prince made his maiden speech in the House of Lords in support of the government's proclamation to suppress seditious publications. The news of the execution of Louis XVI, he told the Queen on 24 January 1793, had filled him with 'a species of sentiment towards my father which surpasses all description'. He asked for an audience with the King, the better 'to express my gratitude to my good and gracious father'. He broke with Fox and declared his support for the King's ministers. He was given the command of a regiment and entertained the idea of offering himself as a volunteer with the Austrian army in the Low Countries.

The French Revolution also forced the Whigs to face the facts of political life and destroyed Whiggism as an ideal. Like their royal patron the Whigs woke up to the fact that for the last twenty years they had been talking nonsense. It was not King George III but Charles Fox who was the danger to the British constitution. The man who did most to strip the Whigs of their delusions was the man who had done most to plant those delusions in Whig minds. 'You seem in everything to have strayed out of the high road of nature', Edmund Burke told the French. 'The property of France does not govern it.' This was the Whig case against the French Revolution. No one who loves the eighteenth century will ever forget the magic words in which Burke mourned the dying civilization – 'The age of chivalry is gone. That of sophisters, economists, and calculators has succeeded; and the glory of Europe is extinguished for ever.' 'A good book', said King George about Burke's *Reflections on the Revolution in France*, 'every gentleman ought to read it.'

In July 1794 that part of the opposition led by the Duke of Portland and inspired by Burke joined Pitt in a coalition to wage war against the ideas of the French Revolution. The British government was under no delusion that it could not happen in this country. National boundaries are no barriers to ideas, and after the experience of the Gordon riots there could be no doubt that the London mob could be as cruel and destructive as that of Paris. This was no time for argument about the politics of the past. The American war, the coalition, the regency crisis were forgotten; and men who had for years been the bitterest political enemies joined hands to preserve what Burke called 'the unbought grace of life'. The Habeas Corpus Act was suspended; the cause for which Shaftesbury fled into exile and Russell died on the scaffold was put out of mind; and Portland, the friend of Newcastle and successor of Rockingham, took charge of the campaign to stamp out revolutionary ideas. The Tory party of the early nineteenth century was born of the union between Pitt and Portland, when each partner renounced the principle of liberty in order to preserve the principle of order. King George III who had begun his reign with the intention to abolish party distinctions now gave his blessing to a party based on ideology.

The 1790s were troubled years for the King both domestically and politically.

The Prince of Wales claimed that he had made a bad bargain in 1787 and that not all his debts had been paid. If so, it was his own fault, and since then his extravagance had not lessened. He had used every expedient to raise money. Foreign princes had been approached – the King of Prussia, the Duke of Orleans, the Landgrave of Hesse Cassel – and the Prince had not scrupled to borrow from his major-domo Louis Weltje. He had pawned his jewels and given up his racing stable, but he still lived beyond his income. In June 1792, only five years after the last settlement of his debts, he told Malmesbury that they amounted to £370,000, and in October 1794 Pitt estimated them at £550,000. The Prince was bankrupt. It was impossible to pay his debts from the Civil List and there was no recourse but to apply to Parliament.

Parliament was not likely to view the application sympathetically. Since 1783, in addition to his regular income, the Prince had received near £500,000 of public money. Now he was asking for another £500,000, at a time when taxation was being increased in order to pay for the war.

To obtain a larger income and the payment of his debts the Prince resolved upon a desperate expedient, the last refuge of the bankrupt rake. He resolved to marry. In August 1794 he visited his parents while they were on their summer holiday at Weymouth, told them that he had broken with Mrs Fitzherbert, and asked the King's permission to marry his cousin Princess Caroline of Brunswick.

The King was delighted that his son was about to become an honest man. He told the Prince that he thoroughly approved of his choice – 'it was the only proper alliance' – but to Prince Ernest, then on leave from the army, he expressed some doubts. He hoped the Prince would be happy but he should at first be a little on his guard. 'If he found the Princess was well behaved', Prince Ernest wrote to his brother, 'he would certainly do everything in his power to make her and you live agreeably.' Both the King and Queen had heard disquieting stories about their niece which suggested that she was not always 'well behaved'. The Queen was most upset at the Prince's choice. '*She* said', Prince Ernest wrote, 'that she had resolved never to talk, no never to open her lips about your marriage, so that no one should say she had any hand in anything. Though she never liked the Duchess of Brunswick, yet she should treat the Princess very well. . . . She hoped you would be happy, and all this she said with tears in her eyes.' She was cold towards her best beloved child and vented her ill humour on her daughters. 'What can possess her to be so odd?' inquired Prince Adolphus, 'and why make her life so wretched when she could have it just the reverse?' It was the fear that her son's life was about to be made wretched, that he would regret his marriage to the end of his days, that made the Queen so 'odd'.

Meanwhile Pitt was engaged in the herculean task of cleansing the Augean stables. He had to face the fact that the Prince was unpopular, that Parliament would refuse to vote a lump sum for the payment of his debts, and that whatever was done would be out of respect to the King not his son. Pitt's first proposal, which the King accepted, was that the Prince should be given a further £60,000 a year, together with £5,000 for the Princess, making their joint income £138,000. From this the Duchy revenues plus £25,000 (in all £38,000) should be set aside for the payment of debt and interest. Parliament was also asked to vote £27,000 for plate and jewels, £25,000 for the expenses of the marriage, and £25,000 for completing Carlton House.

These proposals met with a hostile reception from all quarters of the House of Commons, and it became clear that Pitt could not carry them. 'Your Majesty may be assured', he wrote to the King on 30 May 1795, 'that the strength and credit of your government, which has rested chiefly on sincere public opinion and on Your Majesty's personal popularity, will be deeply affected.' He now proposed that £73,000, instead of £38,000, should be set aside for the payment of debt, that the Prince should commit his affairs into the hands of trustees, and that stringent regulations should be laid down to prevent the possibility of further debts.

'I do not feel myself at liberty to recede', wrote the King. He hoped that marriage would induce his son to lead a more respectable life and he wanted the Prince to get off to a fair start. Pitt's new proposals meant that the Prince and Princess would have a joint income of only £65,000 a year, £8,000 less than the Prince had enjoyed when single. The King had pledged his word to his son for the higher income and felt he could not honourably retract. It was the Prince who reluctantly gave way and enabled his father to agree to the new proposals. The King had fought hard for his son, and the Prince was grateful at least for a time.

In 1793, when the Prince was given the command of the 10th Light Dragoons and the rank of colonel in the army, he was told that he must not expect further promotion. Three years later he asked for the rank of general and was offended when the King refused it. He toyed with the idea of going into opposition and it took an earnest letter from the Queen to dissuade him from this folly. He was refused the command of the Blues, the most coveted regiment in the army, because the King remembered a thirty years' promise to the Duke of Richmond. Though the King disliked Richmond, he would not go back on his word.

'There cannot be a doubt', the King wrote to the Prince on 8 April 1795, 'that the English do view with a jealous eye any decided predilection in those on or naturally to mount the throne to military pursuits, and I certainly feel the force of that opinion as strongly as anyone.' King George II had refused to allow Frederick, Prince of Wales to serve in the army, and the King's own offer of service during the invasion crisis of 1759 had been rejected. In giving the Prince the command of a regiment the King had done more for his son than his grandfather had done for him when Prince of Wales. The King was less jealous of his heir apparent than his grandfather had been. But the Prince had received no military training, and the King would not give him rank above regular officers who had seen service. There was more to the army than wearing a fine uniform and riding at the head of a regiment.

The Prince complained that he had nothing to do. 'The chain of public affairs, whence I might have derived instruction as well as occupation, had been uniformly withheld from me . . . I have no option but to lead a life which must to the public eye wear the color of an idleness depending on my choice. . . . There ought to be some serious object to which my time should be devoted.' Thirty-five years earlier King George when Prince of Wales had complained to Bute in words which exactly described his son's situation in 1795 – 'I really cannot remain immured at home like a girl whilst all my countrymen are preparing for the field.' Sixty years after King

George III's death another Prince of Wales, the future Edward VII, complained of having to live a life of dignified idleness, and when Gladstone tried to find some employment for the Prince he came up against the undisguised hostility of Queen Victoria. It was the unavoidable lot of the heir apparent that he was excluded from all responsibility. As Bubb Dodington had reminded Frederick, Prince of Wales in 1749, he could be King and nothing else. This was perhaps the reason why the heirs apparent of the Hanoverian kings went into opposition. Politics gave them something to do and provided an outlet for their energies.

'The King is not very communicative', wrote Queen Charlotte in 1796; and the plain truth was that he could not trust his son with government secrets. Though the Prince had declared his support for the war, he and his closest advisers were hostile to Pitt. It must be said of him as was said about his grandfather: perhaps if he had behaved with greater dignity he would have deserved more responsibility. Now that he had renounced Fox, the King treated him with more kindness and sympathy than he had ever shown.

The 'amiable qualities' of the Princess Caroline, the King wrote to his son on 8 April 1795, 'will, I flatter myself, so fully engage your attention that they will divert it from objects certainly not so pleasing to the nation'. He hoped that the Prince would be 'engrossed with domestic felicity' so that 'a numerous progeny' would result, 'a comfort to me in the decline of years'. The King must have heard how the Prince and Princess had received each other at their first meeting – that the Princess had said that her bridegroom was fat and not so handsome as his portrait had led her to believe and the Prince had declared he felt ill and had called for a glass of brandy. This did not augur well for domestic felicity. Thirty years later it was widely believed that the Prince and Princess had slept together only on their bridal night.

Their daughter, Princess Charlotte, was born on 7 January 1796. In sending his congratulations to the Prince, the King said that he had hoped the child would be a girl. His next words seemed to convey that he knew all was not well with the marriage. 'You are both young and I trust will have many children, and this newcomer will equally call for the protection of its parents and consequently be a bond of additional union.' 'The dear King talks of nothing but his grandchild', wrote Princess Elizabeth on 9 January 1796, 'drank her health at dinner, and went into the equerries' room and made them drink it in a bumper.' He called her 'his little beauty'. 'He says there never was so perfect a little creature and everybody here was delighted to see him in such ecstasies of joy.' But his joy was soon marred.

The Prince's dislike of his wife turned to hatred. Six months after the birth of their child he described her to the Queen as 'the vilest wretch this world was ever cursed with, who I cannot feel more disgust for from her personal nastiness than I do from her entire want of principle'. The Princess on her part complained of ill treatment from her husband, and accused him of having appointed his mistress, Lady Jersey, as one of her Ladies of the Bedchamber. It is happily not the duty of the biographer of King Geroge III to inquire into the rights and wrongs of this affair. No doubt there were faults on both sides as there usually are in matrimonial disputes. The Prince was not an ideal husband nor was the Princess an ideal wife: she was harsh, out to domineer, and a pathological liar. They were an ill-suited pair. He wanted a woman tender, sympathetic, and soft (his whole life was a search for such a woman), and she was not prepared to adapt herself to her husband as Queen Charlotte had done to King George.

After the birth of their child the Prince refused to live with his wife, and in May 1796 she appealed to the King and begged his protection for herself and her daughter.

550

The King was reluctant to intervene and advised his son and daughter-in-law to kiss and make up. 'It is high time to put a stop to it', he wrote to the Duke of Gloucester, the Princess's intermediary, 'and if the Princess will, when he is at home, receive him with good humour and make him find that comfort not to be met with abroad, it may by degrees effect a better understanding. . . . Believe me, submission in a woman always secures esteem, she must obtain that before more can be expected.' The Prince's reply was to repeat his complaints against his wife and to demand a formal separation.

When King George came to the throne it might have been possible to have prevented such a dispute from becoming public knowledge. But in the 1790s the affairs of the Royal Family were retailed in all the newspapers and circulated throughout the country. Queen Charlotte complained that every remark she made on the terrace at Windsor or the esplanade at Weymouth (and no doubt many she did not make) appeared in the newspapers, and she was convinced that people listened to her conversation in order to report it to the press. The news that the Prince of Wales had demanded a separation from his wife appeared in *The Times* on 24 May 1796, and his conduct was castigated in the severest terms. It was fortunate for the Prince that there was no John Wilkes writing in the 1790s. On 28 May when the Princess appeared at the opera there was an immense demonstration in her favour. Public opinion was unquestionably against the Prince.

As long ago as 1781 the King had warned his son of the consequences of his conduct. The Prince had taken no notice, but had continued to offend public opinion by his extravagance, his injudicious alliance with Fox, his illegal marriage with Mrs Fitzherbert, his unfilial conduct at the time of the king's illness. Now his sins had come home to roost. In 1796 everything he did was represented in the most unfavourable light, and public support for the Princess was less due to her own merits (for the newspapers had no real knowledge of the facts) than to dislike of the Prince of Wales. On 2 June 1796 the King wrote to his son:

You seem to look on your disunion with the Princess as merely of a private nature, and totally put out of sight that as heir apparent of the Crown your marriage is a public act wherein the kingdom is concerned, that therefore a separation cannot be brought forward by the mere interference of relations. The public must be informed of the whole business, and being already certainly not prejudiced in your favour, the auspices in the first outset would not be promising. Parliament could not fail of taking part in the business, and would certainly, as no criminal accusation can be brought against the Princess, think itself obliged to secure out of your income the jointure settled on her in case of your death and which in justice she would have in such a case a right to claim. I am certainly by no means inclined to think the Princess has been happy in the choice of conduct she has adopted, but if you had attempted to guide her she might have avoided those errors that her uncommon want of experience and perhaps some defects of temper may have given rise to.

It is improbable that Lady Jersey was the Prince's mistress, as the Princess alleged, otherwise the King would not so decidedly have taken his son's part. But the Prince was weak and amenable to feminine influence, and the King insisted that Lady Jersey should retire so that there should be no bar to a reconciliation. King George had an acute insight into his son's character. The Prince would always be dependent on someone. At this time it was the Queen whose letters to the Prince, as the Queen herself remarked, were more like those of a mistress than of a mother. If only the Princess had understood how to manage him! The King repeated the advice he had given again and again – that his birth 'imposed on him more strict rules of duty than on common individuals' and that the behaviour of royalty should be the exemplar for the nation. This had been the teaching of Bute. 'I trust the same sentiment', the King wrote on 5 June 1796, 'will by degrees be awakened in you which it has been my early habit to know the value of.'

King George was the first British King since Edward III in the fourteenth century to have a family of grown-up sons. In 1789 they ranged from the Prince of Wales, then aged 27, to Prince Adolphus, then 15. What was he to do with them? The British tradition was against any devolution of the royal authority, and it was notorious that younger sons if left without an occupation lived for pleasure or what was worse tried to make mischief in politics. Look at the troubles that had been caused in the middle ages by John of Gaunt and King Edward III's other younger sons! The King was too well read in history not to be aware of the dangers arising from a large family. He wished his children to grow up as 'examples to the rising generation'. 'I can have no wish concerning them', he wrote in 1786, 'but to make them by a good education enabled to produce any talents they may possess, and as such become of credit to their family and of utility to their country.' In the eighteenth century the opportunities of service for royalty were limited to the army and navy, and to this end they were directed.

The King was resolved not to repeat the mistakes that had been made in his own education and that of his brothers. As a young man he had lived too sheltered a life. His sons should go out into the world at an early age and learn to mingle with men. They should be reared in principles of morality and religion and provided with a reliable companion to whom they could look for advice. As they grew older this support would be withdrawn. They should be given a moderate establishment, sufficient for their rank but insufficient for extravagance. Apart from the Prince of Wales, none of his sons was created a peer until he had reached the age of 21 and Prince Edward had to wait until he was 32. They would receive a good education and a thorough training in whichever service they adopted. The King had no wish to see his sons like his brothers, senior officers in the army and navy, but without training and experience and unfit to exercise command. His sons would receive promotion gradually according to the rules of the service, and only be given high command if they showed themselves worthy.

The King's educational methods can best be seen in the case of Prince William, who was sent to sea at the age of 14. 'I strongly recommend the habitual reading of the Holy Scriptures', was the King's first advice to his son, 'and your more and more placing that reliance on the Divine Creator which is the only real means of obtaining that peace of mind that alone can fit a man for arduous undertakings.'

Though when at home a Prince, on board of the Prince George you are only a boy learning the naval profession; but the Prince so far accompanies you that what other boys might do you must not; it must never be out of your thoughts that more obedience is necessary from you to your superiors in the navy, more politeness to your equals, and more good nature to your inferiors, than from those who have not been told that these are essential for a gentleman.

The Prince was accompanied by a tutor to supervise his education. Dr Majendie was to take 'every proper opportunity' of instructing the Prince in his religious duties, and 'to accompany these with moral reflexions that may counteract the evil he may have but too many opportunities of hearing'. Prince William was to continue his study of Latin so as 'to read it with ease' and 'taste its beauties', and to practise English composition. The study of British history would be 'a pleasant as well as useful occupation', and of course the Prince must learn to speak French and German. All this in addition to learning his profession. King George believed firmly in the precept that nature found mischief for idle hands to do. Here surely was sufficient to keep a boy of fourteen out of mischief.

How did these methods work out in practice? What sort of men did the King's sons become? Did they grow up to be 'of credit to their family and of utility to their country'? Let us examine each in turn and find out.[1]

Frederick, Duke of York, was destined for the army and spent seven years in Germany learning his profession – a more thorough training than almost any other officer of the day received. He longed for an opportunity of service, and on the outbreak of war in 1793 took command of the British forces acting with the Austrians and Dutch in the Low Countries. The Duke was not a great commander but he was competent and conscientious and it was hardly his fault if the campaign which had promised so favourably in the beginning ended in failure. The cabinet came to see that he lacked the experience and authority for his difficult task, and in November 1794 advised his recall. The King, though hurt, accepted this advice, and in 1795 appointed the Duke commander-in-chief of the army in Great Britain. Here he did good work, and no less a witness than the Duke of Wellington testified to the improvement in the discipline and efficiency of the army under the Duke of York's direction. The Duke followed in the footsteps of another royal army reformer, King George III's uncle William, Duke of Cumberland, and between them they changed a collection of regiments into an army.

To King George the Duke of York could do no wrong. He was 'my dearest son', 'my valuable second son'. If he had failed in the field it was because of the cowardice of the Dutch, 'that very shabby nation', or the failure of the Austrians to cooperate. The Duke had been borne down by a 'torrent of abuse'. Fanny Burney describes how he welcomed the Duke home in 1787: 'The King was in one transport of delight, unceasing, invariable; and though the newly arrived Duke was its source and support, the kindness of his heart extended and expanded to his eldest born.' The Duke's backsliding at the time of the regency crisis was soon forgiven, and what might have been serious offences in the case of the Prince of Wales were passed over in silence when committed by the Duke of York. For the Duke was as extravagant as his brother and wasted in gambling and racing the revenues of the bishopric of Osnabruck which had accumulated during his minority. Financially speaking, considering he had fewer obligations to meet, he was better off than the Prince of Wales. On his marriage in 1791 he had an income of £40,000 a year exclusive of the revenues of Osnabruck, 'which I think I can make shift to live upon' he wrote. When his debts became pressing in 1793 the King told Henry Dundas that after 'the very creditable part' the Duke had acted in Flanders it was incumbent on the government to relieve him. But the government did nothing.

William, Duke of Clarence, the future King William IV, was perhaps the most difficult of the King's sons and yet in some ways the most likeable. He was simple, naive, and honest, and whatever he did was done in the open with no attempt at hypocrisy. As a boy he tried seriously to keep to the regime the King had laid down for him, and in one of his earliest letters after going to sea (written from Spithead on 24 November 1779) he told his father that he had gone through the first six books of Euclid, had written a short account of English history from the Reformation to the Revolution, and was now reading Sully's *Memoirs*. 'I have seen the manners practised in the world', he ended his letter, 'and things begin to appear to me in a very different light from what I had seen them before.'[2] This from a boy of fourteen was perhaps ominous. As soon as the ship got to sea (it must be remembered that this was at the height of the American war), Prince William began to resent the attentions of his tutor. What was the point of a future naval officer learning Latin? Why did he have to submit drafts of his letters to Mr Majendie before forwarding them? Why was he treated as a boy when he was expected to behave like

556

a man? Majendie wrote from New York on 27 March 1782:

Prince William's aversion to Latin, which was always pretty much marked, has become unconquerable; and I have thought it at his age better to give up the point without telling him so than by persevering with little or no profit to see him discontented day after day. The violent dislike young people conceive for Latin is generally owing to their having been over-fatigued with it when children. Too much stress is usually laid upon this acquisition which I think I may venture to say has been the case with his Royal Highness.

The letter was forwarded to the King, and it says much for him that far from resenting this criticism of his educational methods he rewarded Majendie's services with a bishopric.

'William has ever been violent when controuled', the King wrote in 1783.[3] He quarrelled with his captain and was told by the King that 'to be fit to command the knowledge of obedience must first be obtained'. When appointed to the command of a ship he quarrelled with his lieutenants. He brought home some of the habits he had learned at sea and the King sent him to Hanover to acquire a little polish. 'I think he is rather improved with regard to swearing', the Duke of York wrote to his father on 18 June 1784, 'but unluckily he has taken an idea into his head that it does not signify in what manner he behaves here.' He was 'excessively rough and rude', the Duke wrote to the Prince of Wales, and addicted to practical jokes; the Prince, more charitable, described his brother as 'a very good hearted boy, lively, spirited, perhaps a little too boisterous'. The King described his behaviour as that of an inhabitant of the forecastle, and the Queen wrote to him: 'You appear rather inclined to dislike everything that you know has been thought of as necessary towards your improvement.' Poor Prince William, the honest British tar, incurred the disapproval of all his family.

'Oh! I wish I was returned!' he wrote from Hanover on 23 July 1784. 'England, England for ever, and the pretty girls of Westminster. . . .' If he did not have a girl in every port he at least had one in Plymouth and another in Portsmouth, and in 1788 he told the King that he had contracted a venereal infection. He also became hard up. 'My circumstances are very narrow', he wrote to the Prince of Wales on 27 November 1785, 'and I at present have absolutely not a farthing.' The Duke of York had a regiment and a rich bishopric in Germany and he had only £3,000 a year. It was not fair. His father did not understand him. 'My Christmas box or New Year's gift', he wrote on 27 December 1787, 'will be a family lecture for immorality, vice, dissipation, and expense'; and on 16 February 1788: 'I understand the old boy is exceedingly out of humour and I am in hourly expectation of a thunderstorm from that quarter. Fatherly admonitions at our time of life are very unpleasant and of no use; it is a pity he should expend his breath or his time in such fruitless labour.' But when the King fell ill Prince William was sincerely distressed for 'the best of kings and fathers' and for 'that dear inestimable woman' the Queen.

The Prince was head over ears in debt and was concerned in his brothers' schemes to raise money. In 1790 he left sea and settled down at Richmond to live a life of, if not exactly respectable, at least blameless domesticity with Mrs Dorothy Jordan, the actress. This lady, who had already borne children to two previous lovers, was to give the Duke ten children, some of whom were to plague him sorely when he succeeded to the throne forty years later. The Duke saw no service during the French revolutionary war, and his political activities were confined to disconcerting speeches in the House of Lords. In April 1793 he defended the slave trade and attacked Wilberforce and his friends as 'fanatics' and 'hypocrites' – 'a most incomparable speech', wrote the Prince of Wales. The Prince thought otherwise of his brother's next speech, in July

1793, which was a plea for the opening of peace negotiations. 'The Duke's idle and indiscreet abuse of the war', wrote Glenbervie, 'and the characters and conduct of His Majesty's ministers, particularly Mr Pitt . . . is a matter of scandal and discomfort.' 'How is William?' asked Prince Adolphus, then in Germany, on 14 July 1794. 'Is he just as mad as he was before? I have heard some strange things of him.' The King gave him £6,000 towards the payment of his debts and the sinecure office of Ranger of Bushey Park, but by 1795 he had contracted fresh debts to the amount of £75,000. Goodness knows how he had got into debt, since he neither raced, gambled, nor built. The King and Queen knew all about their son's ménage with Mrs Jordan, but since they could do nothing about it turned a blind eye. The Duke of Clarence was accepted as the eccentric member of the family, and in time the King was able to chaff him about Mrs Jordan.

If William was the black sheep, Edward, Duke of Kent, was regarded as the fool of the family. He was certainly the son the King esteemed least, and the Duke repeatedly complained that he never heard from his father. Yet the Duke of Kent was no fool but rather a simple soldier, with abilities no greater than those of a regimental commander, but who did his duty under trying circumstances. In 1784 at the age of 17 he was sent to Luneburg for his military training, and there followed the example of his elder brothers by falling into debt. The Duke of York pleaded on his behalf: 'People were so very absurd as to give Edward credit to any amount that he pleased, and even to offer to lend him as much money as he wanted' – a temptation too much for a young man to resist. The King rated him soundly. 'You have wilfully and knowingly added untruth to the former errors. . . . I cannot keep up a due subordination unless I make the world see my sons must not presume to alter any regulations I have made. . . . I should have flattered myself that the having placed you in the army would have opened your ideas and

559

have drawn you from spending your time in a manner so much below you . . . your absurd singularities make it absolutely requisite to prevent your exposing yourself.' 'I cannot but with shame confess', replied the Prince, 'that I have most richly deserved it by my disobedience to your express commands.' His debts were paid and he was sent to Geneva.

Here he soon became restless. 'I have been nearly two years in the dullest and most insufferable of all places', he wrote to the Prince of Wales on 17 October 1789, 'and the last seventeen months of my stay here without a single line from the King and only one letter from the Queen.' In January 1790 he gave his 'bear-leaders' the slip and in defiance of his father's orders returned to London. His debts were again paid, and he was packed off to Gibraltar from whence he could not so easily escape.

Gibraltar was worse than Geneva. There was no society except that of his fellow officers and nothing to do except his military duties. The Prince performed these punctili-ously and took pride in the appearance and conduct of his regiment. But again he spent beyond his allowance. 'He neither drinks nor games in the least', wrote one of his staff, 'but in certain points of expence such as horses, furniture, etc. he is impatient of control.' He loved music and formed his private band. He also took a mistress – perhaps it would be more correct to say that he engaged one as he might have done a servant. He sent a con-fidential friend to Geneva to find a lady who would undertake to share his bed and preside at his table, and the result of this strange commission was more fortunate than might have been expected. Mlle St Laurent and the Duke lived together in perfect amity until in 1818 he had to break the connection in order to marry and beget an heir to the throne.

In 1792 he was sent to Canada. This, though preferable to Gibraltar, was still exile, and during the next few years he repeatedly begged permission to return home. On the outbreak of war he served with credit in the West Indies, though he would have preferred to have been employed in Europe. The King did not allow him to return until 1798, when he was surprised at the warmth of his reception: though absent eight years, he had not been forgotten. His subsequent military career was unfortunate. After a further spell of service in Canada, he was appointed governor of Gibraltar in 1802; but his efforts to restore discipline provoked a mutiny and he was recalled.

The three youngest sons, Ernest, Duke of Cumberland, Augustus, Duke of Sussex, and Adolphus, Duke of Cambridge, were educated together at Göttingen University. Prince Ernest and Prince Adolphus were commissioned in the Hanoverian army and saw service under the Duke of York in the Low Countries. They received no special treatment because they were the King's sons and the King insisted that they should serve with their regiments and not at headquarters. Both experienced all the dangers and fatigues of the campaign, both were wounded (Prince Ernest twice), and Prince Adolphus narrowly escaped being captured by the French. He did not return home until the conclusion of peace in 1801, having been absent fifteen years; while Prince Ernest was allowed only one brief period of sick leave in twelve years' service.

It is difficult to form a definite impression of the character of Adolphus, Duke of Cambridge from his letters. As a boy he was the favourite, perhaps because he was the youngest; as a man he was placid and kindhearted. Ernest, Duke of Cumberland, was a more decisive, indeed truculent, person. During the reigns of King George IV and William IV he became the bogey man of the Whigs because of his ultra-Tory principles, and the most scandalous stories (entirely untrue) were told about his private life. He was the one son of the King who dared to stand up and defy his father. He wrote to the King in a more informal style than his brothers, and yet always treated him with respect.

The Duke of Cumberland suffered from bad eyesight and had he lived in the twentieth century would have, been pronounced unfit for the army. He loved the service. 'From the bottom of my soul I am a soldier', he told the Prince of Wales in 1794, 'and by heavens I know nothing else.' He certainly knew soldiering, having served the duties of every rank from private to colonel. In February 1794 he narrowly escaped losing his arm from a cannon ball, yet it was only when with his arm in a sling he was unable to carry out his duties that the King allowed him home. Then he insisted that the Duke should accompany the Queen and himself to Weymouth, probably to remove him from the influence of the Prince of Wales. Here the Duke was abysmally bored. 'Nothing in my eyes is so terrible as a family party', he wrote. On his return to the front he was downgraded in command, possibly because of his health, and threatened to throw up his commission. He was in fact in no state to go campaigning. 'He is, I think, better in health and spirits now than when he first came', wrote his cousin Prince William of Gloucester on 24 November 1794, 'but complains of a great deal of pain at night, so much as to hinder his sleeping, but he constantly rides out in the cold and never misses being on horseback for five or six hours every day.' When the army went into winter quarters the King insisted that he should stay with his regiment and refused him leave to go to Hanover. It was a kind letter, the Duke wrote to the Prince of Wales, but 'I would rather be damned than remain as I am now'. 'You may recollect, Sir', he wrote to the King on 27 September 1795, 'from the unlucky wound I received last campaign, my left eye was merely weakened, but now, Sir, instead of its being recovered . . . I am in the horrid apprehension of losing it.' And on 11 December to the Prince of Wales:

Is it not hard to have lost the use of an eye in doing my duty and exposing myself for my country, and not to have got as yet an answer from His Majesty, though I have wrote four

562

times for leave to return to my country? . . . Now I am determined, if I do not get an answer from His Majesty, to return without leave, for I have already sacrificed enough and will not sacrifice my eye for any whim of others.

In January 1796 the King yielded to the pleas of the Prince of Wales and the Duke of Gloucester and gave the Duke leave to return.

Augustus, Duke of Sussex, was the most unfortunate of the King's sons. Debarred by ill health from a career in the navy, he had to leave Göttingen and travel in Italy and France. He was an intelligent young man, with a taste for science and attached to religion, and his letters are the most interesting of those written to the King by his sons. The other boys wrote dutiful 'bread and butter' letters, replete with the sort of sentiments they thought would please their father, but Prince Augustus's descriptions of his travels are really worth reading. He fell into debt a little at Göttingen and received the mildest reproof from the King – 'You seem so sensible to the impropriety of such a conduct that it is not necessary for me to enlarge upon it.' After three years' travelling he told the King he would like to marry and enter the Church. The King seems to have raised no objection, but replied that the Prince must remain abroad until he had recovered his health.

'Every man must be occupied', the Prince wrote to his father on 9 August 1792, 'and if he is not about something good, he will certainly be doing mischief.' It is ironical that he should have written these words in view of what was shortly to happen to him. For the Prince was bored and lonely. He rarely heard from his family (he complained in May 1793 that though he wrote to the King once a fortnight he had not heard from him for nearly three years), and was tired of travelling round Europe under the charge of a bear-leader. He wanted to come home, the physicians had advised his return, yet not a word had been received from the King. It being now undesirable to stay any longer in France, he went to Rome for the winter of 1792–3.

There he met Lady Dunmore, the wife of a Scottish peer, and her daughter Lady Augusta Murray. The Prince was only twenty while Lady Augusta was some ten years older (her mother afterwards declared she did not know her exact age). The poor boy, who had no experience of women, stood no chance against a matchmaking mamma and a daughter ripe for matrimony. Lord Bruce, son of Lord Ailesbury, the Queen's Treasurer, who had spent the winter at Rome, wrote to his father on 17 June 1793:

The Dunmores will, I am afraid, chase him everywhere as they have cut such a conspicuous figure at Rome and wish, I believe, to do the same wherever he goes. I am happy to find he behaved very properly with regard to that and they very ridiculously. There are, I know, a thousand reports, both here and in England, but don't give credit to any, as I am persuaded no connection has ever or will ever take place. He has too much sense, I am sure, ever to do so foolish a thing.

Of course the King was informed and hastily recalled his son. It was too late. On 4 April the Prince and Lady Augusta had been married at Rome by a clergyman of the Church of England.

The Dunmores arrived in England soon after the Prince. There had been no witnesses to the ceremony in Rome, and as Lady Augusta was now pregnant it was desirable to put the fact of the marriage beyond doubt. A second ceremony was gone through at St George's Hanover Square on 5 December (the Prince styling himself Mr Augustus Frederick), and a month later Lady Augusta gave birth to a son. The Prince returned to Italy at his own request, and Lady Augusta and her child remained in England.

The Prince had said nothing to his father and mother about the marriage, and it is possible the King first heard of it through the newspapers. He ordered the Privy

Council to inquire into the circumstances and the marriage was formally pronounced null and void in the ecclesiastical court. Under the Royal Marriage Act of 1772 it was no marriage at all.

Meanwhile the Prince was miserable in Rome. 'I want nothing and never shall ask for any favour but that of being left alone', he wrote to the Prince of Wales on 15 November 1794. 'My whole disposition is totally altered, that I hate society, and only feel less uncomfortable when alone.' His brothers showed little sympathy. The King refused to allow Lady Augusta to leave the country, and the Prince believed (incorrectly) that he was forbidden to correspond with his sisters. He was cheered by a 'very gracious and friendly' letter from the King (in which he was addressed as 'my dear Augustus'), and conceived the idea that the marriage might be acknowledged on the Continent though illegal in Great Britain. This the King refused to admit, but he promised if the Prince would abandon the connection to make a provision for Lady Augusta and the child. 'Whoever thinks', wrote Prince Augustus to the Prince of Wales on 20 April 1796, 'I will give up the partner of my misfortunes and my child insult my feelings.' He remained abroad, an unhappy wanderer with debts piling about him, until in 1801 he submitted to the King and separated from Lady Augusta.

It is impossible not to feel sympathy for the Prince or to deny that King George bears a heavy share of responsibility for his son's misfortunes. The King should not have allowed the Prince to remain abroad so long and at least he should have kept in touch with him. Everyone who is separated from his family loves to receive letters from home and this simple pleasure was denied the Prince. That the Prince at the age of twenty, lonely and far from home, should have contracted an imprudent and illegal marriage appears not surprising. We remember the struggle the King had between 'the boiling youth of 21 years and prudence'. Did he remember that he also might have contracted an imprudent marriage had it not been for the advice of Bute? Had he forgotten Lady Sarah Lennox? But there was no Bute to advise Prince Augustus. It behoved the King to be charitable towards his son. There, but for the grace of God, went he.

Yet there is some justification for the King's harshness. Both the Prince and Lady Augusta must have known that their marriage was illegal. How was it possible for the King to dispense with the provisions of an Act of Parliament? The Royal Marriage Act was designed to protect members of the Royal Family who were peculiarly liable to the designs of ambitious women. It is no coincidence that all those who contracted marriages without the consent of the Crown did so with women older and more experienced than themselves. Both the King's brothers had married widows; the Prince of Wales married a widow twice over; Prince Augustus married a woman ten years older than himself. Had the Prince been content to live with Lady Augusta without demanding recognition of her as his wife (as the Prince of Wales did with Mrs Fitzherbert), the King would have had to condone the affair. Nor would he have been too harsh. However much he disapproved of his son's irregular relationships, he recognized that these involved obligations which could not easily be renounced. He provided for the Duchess of Cumberland after her husband's death, and he promised the Prince of Wales that in the event of his death he would provide for Mrs Fitzherbert. And he would have done the same by Lady Augusta Murray. He could condone his son's taking a mistress: he could not condone his defiance of an Act of Parliament.

The King came to see the unreality of Bute's political ideas but never forgot his moral teaching. If Providence had placed him in an elevated situation, he wrote to the Prince of Wales on 5 June 1796, it had also imposed on him 'more strict rules of duty than on common individuals'. This was the lesson which he tried to teach his sons and which guided his conduct towards them. But high-spirited young men could not be kept in tutelage for ever. They complained of the small allowances they received from the King and of his delay in granting them their establishments. Ernest, Duke of Cumberland, who was not extravagant, was so short of money in 1797 that he was reduced to sell his equipage and every other article he could dispose of. He was then given £3,000 a year from the Civil List (at the age of 26), but it was not until 1799 that he received his establishment. Then he had £12,000 a year (increased in 1801 to £18,000), from which he had to meet the expenses of his household. There were many of the King's subjects who enjoyed much larger incomes.

The difficulty was that the King could not provide for his sons out of the Civil List. Their incomes had to come from Parliament. As the money came from the nation, the nation had some interest in how it was spent. The spectacle of the Royal Dukes keeping mistresses out of public money while another two had left-handed wives offended the sober part of the nation. They were failing in their fundamental duty of providing for the succession. Forty years after King George had succeeded to the throne, only two of his sons were married (one living apart from his wife) and he had only one legitimate grandchild. The Civil List was over-burdened (almost every politician now claimed a retirement pension) and taxation had never been so high. It was unseemly to have actions for debt brought against members of the Royal Family. One of the causes of the fall of the French monarchy was its failure to retain the respect of the French people. It seemed from the behaviour of the Royal Dukes that the British was going the same way. The strength of the Crown at the turn of the century was the character of the King, now in his seventh decade. What would happen when he died? The Prince of Wales was held in contempt, and there had already been hints in the newspapers that he should be excluded from the succession. The house of Hanover had been summoned to Great Britain by Act of Parliament, and what Parliament had decreed Parliament could revoke.

The monarchy had little to fear from pseudo-Jacobins plotting a revolution on the French model. So long as it could command the confidence of the propertied classes it was in no danger. To do this it must conform to their ideals in politics and in morals. This King George understood well. The Crown must pay its way; it must be conservative, but not opposed to change when change was the will of the nation; and it must set an example of duty and religious observance. These precepts were forgotten during the reigns of the King's two successors when the prestige of the Crown reached its nadir. 'They are the damndest millstones about the necks of any government that can be imagined', the Duke of Wellington is reported to have said about King George III's sons. This was hard on the Duke of York and unfair on the Duke of Cambridge; but if an aristocratic Conservative could speak like this what must a middle-class Radical have thought?

By reverting to the precepts of King George III Queen Victoria and the Prince Consort restored the prestige of the Crown. If we would wish to know what King George would have been like had he lived in the days of Peel and Palmerston, we have but to study the conduct of the Prince Consort. There is the same devotion to duty, frugality, concern for religion and morality, interest in the arts and science, which won for the Crown the confidence of the middle class. In ideas and precepts, though not in character, the Prince Consort might have been a reincarnation of the King. King George III was the first of the Victorians.

The King had six daughters. In age they ranged from Charlotte, Princess Royal, born in 1766, to Princess Amelia, born in 1783.

Their life was like that of novices in a well-regulated convent. The Royal Dukes, as they came of age, went out into the world and mingled with their contemporaries. The Princesses stayed at home. They attended court, they went with their parents to and from Windsor, and accompanied them on their visits to country houses and to Weymouth. Most of their days were spent with the Queen in walking, needlework, and reading. Their pleasures were card parties, visits to the theatre and concerts, and balls. 'Working, reading, writing, walking, etc. fills up our day', wrote Princess Elizabeth in 1796. This may seem a dull life, but it was the life of upper-class ladies of the period. And the Princesses had opportunities of seeing things which other ladies had not. Jane Austen's heroines, who spent all their time in the country with only occasional visits to London and Bath, would have envied the life of the King's daughters. Few ladies in the eighteenth century, for example, ever had the opportunity of sailing on the sea which the Princesses did at Weymouth. Financially they were provided for by the Queen, and she was cramped for money. In 1786 the King told Pitt that the Queen was exceeding her income by £8,000 a year in order to support her daughters, and was maintaining six daughters 'for less than four were forty-nine years ago when every article of life was cheaper than now'. Ten years later the Queen was only able to allow the Princesses Mary and Sophia £1,000 a year each. The Princesses suffered from the extravagance of their elder brother, which made it difficult for the King to ask more money for them.

In one respect their life differed from that of Jane Austen's heroines. They saw no men except their brothers and the King's courtiers. Consequently their devotion was lavished on their brothers, especially on the Prince of Wales, and the Prince's affection for his sisters is one of the most pleasing traits in his character. But a favourite brother is no substitute for a husband. Only three of the

King's daughters married: the Princess Royal at the age of 31, Princess Elizabeth at 48, and Princess Mary at 40; and none had children who survived infancy. The King enjoyed their society (we remember how he preferred daughters to sons) and was not anxious to have them marry and leave home, and perhaps the unfortunate experiences of his sisters led him to think his daughters would be happier unmarried. It seems never to have occurred to him that they would wish to have a home and family of their own. The Duke of York hoped that his own marriage to a daughter of the King of Prussia would lead to matches between the King's sons and the Duke's sisters, but the Prussian Princes married into Queen Charlotte's family of Mecklenburg Strelitz. Apart from offers from Denmark and Sweden (which the King rejected) and Wurtemberg, there were no proposals for the hand of any of King George's daughters.

The Princess Royal resented her convent life. In 1791 she complained to the Prince of Wales of 'the manner in which she was treated on all occasions, particularly by her mother, the constant restraint she was kept under, just like an infant, the perpetual tiresome and confined life she was obliged to lead' and worst of all 'the violence and the caprice of her mother's temper'. She had the wild notion of a match with the Duke of Bedford, one of Charles Fox's friends, but her brother told her the King would never give his consent. In 1794 she was described as 'fallen into a kind of quiet, desperate state, without hope, and open to every fear', and the King is said to have promised his consent to any match which was not a mésalliance. But when the Princess's suitor, the Hereditary Prince of Wurtemberg, presented his proposals in 1796 the King at first would have nothing to do with him. He had heard unpleasant stories of how the Prince had treated his first wife, a daughter of King George's sister Augusta, Duchess of Brunswick. 'I have sent abroad for information', he wrote, 'whether my opinion on the Prince of

Wurtemberg is well founded, which, if it is, no power on earth can get me to admit of his marrying any daughter of mine.' He must have been satisfied by his inquiries for the marriage took place the following year. It was not an unhappy marriage, although the Princess's only child was still-born and she and her husband suffered severely from the French occupation of Wurtemberg. After her departure for Germany, she corresponded regularly with her father but they never saw each other again.

In the nineteenth century it was rumoured that two of the King's daughters, Princess Elizabeth and Princess Sophia, had gone through ceremonies of marriage, and that Princess Sophia had given birth to a child. There is no reliable evidence for these stories. But there is no doubt about the love affair of Princess Amelia.[4] Almost everyone in the Royal Family knew about it except the King and everyone took precautions to prevent him from knowing.

Princess Amelia, born in 1783, was the King's youngest daughter and for that reason his favourite. The King 'dotes' upon her, wrote Fanny Burney in 1786, and she describes how he 'took her up in his arms, and began kissing and playing with her'. The Princess was delicate and had to spend long periods by the sea for her health, and perhaps the King paid less attention to her after the birth of his grand-daughter. About 1800, when she was only 17, she fell in love with one of the King's equerries Charles Fitzroy, son of Lord Southampton. Like Prince Augustus, she found her life depressing and fell in love with the first presentable young man that came her way. Although she knew she could not marry Fitzroy (at least during the King's lifetime), she regarded herself as betrothed to him and in her will (in which she left him all her property) wrote: 'Nothing but the cruel situation I am placed in of being the daughter of the King and the laws made by the King respecting the marriages of the Royal Family prevents me being married to him, which

I consider I am in my heart.' The King never knew of her feelings until after death.

The last twenty years of the King's reign were occupied with war with France, beginning in 1793 and with the exception of two years (1801–3) continuing until the battle of Waterloo in 1815. Like the American conflict this was for the King an ideological war – a war, he wrote in 1794, 'that every tie of religion, morality and society not only authorises but demands'. At the same time it was a war in the old Whig tradition against Great Britain's natural enemy. 'Now is the hour to humble France', he wrote on 1 June 1793, 'for nothing but her being disabled from disturbing other countries, whatever government may be established there, will keep her quiet.' Two years later he preferred to attack France's West Indian colonies rather than support the attempt of the émigrés on the coast of France, and when Holland entered the war under French direction he approved of the takeover of the Dutch colonies. The war was a conflict of principles but the King saw no reason why the British Empire should not make a profit from it.

The King's part in the war differed little from that he had taken during the American war. Although he appointed a commander-in-chief of the army (in 1793 Lord Amherst, succeeded in 1795 by the Duke of York), he exercised close supervision and control over army affairs. Returns were regularly sent to him, he decided on promotions, and even such a trivial matter as a pension of four shillings a day for a retired officer was referred to the King for his approval. The King tried to insist as he had done during the American war that in recruiting the old regiments should be completed before new ones were raised. But such was the extent of the war and the difficulty of getting soldiers that the government had to take men as it could. The King repeatedly warned Dundas as he had done North against trying to do too much. 'We

572

must not have too many irons in the fire', he wrote on 16 November 1793; and on 19 August 1795: 'The truth is we attempt too many objects at the same time.' Finally the cabinet came round and a minute of 7 September 1795 recorded this advice: 'His Majesty's British troops are inadequate to all the objects in which the interests of this country are essentially involved' – exactly as King George had told North nearly twenty years before.

The ghost of Lord North (he had died in 1792) must have chuckled at the way Pitt conducted the war. Every mistake Great Britain had made between 1775 and 1782 was repeated between 1793 and 1801, and Pitt was no more successful in suppressing French democracy than North had been in dealing with the American variety. North had had to wage war against colonies three thousand miles away, with France and Spain allied against Great Britain and the rest of Europe hostile: Pitt's theatre of war was only across the North Sea, and he had most of the powers of Europe – Austria, Prussia, Spain, and Holland – on his side. North had a formidable opposition against him in the House of Commons: Pitt's opponents could never muster so many as a hundred votes. If North was a failure as a war minister, what shall we say of Pitt?

In 1794 the French occupied the Austrian Netherlands and Holland and in 1795 Spain and Prussia made peace with France. The British army retreated into Germany and was evacuated home. 1795 was a bad harvest and there were food riots all over the kingdom. The government, with the example of Paris in mind, made arrangements that London would be well supplied with corn; and in order to save flour and give an example to his subjects the King gave orders that brown bread only was to be served in his household. On 29 October, on his way to open Parliament, the King was surrounded by a hungry mob clamouring for bread and peace, and a stone was thrown into his coach. At first it was assumed that the

King had been shot at. 'Sit still, sir', he said to an attendant, 'let us not betray any fear of what may happen.' 'At night', wrote Princess Elizabeth to a friend, 'when mamma wished him a good night, he said, "I doubt not I shall sleep; and only wish the man to sleep as well who made the attack on me." ' A second attack followed on 1 February 1796 as the King and Queen were returning from the theatre, and a stone struck Queen Charlotte in the face. There were fears that the London mob was about to rise as in 1768 and 1780.

The difference between North and Pitt as war ministers was that North was a pessimist who saw nothing but disaster round the corner while Pitt always hoped for and expected success. The British were successful at sea and outside Europe but the effort was immense, and there seemed no possibility of achieving the aims for which Great Britain had gone to war. Pitt did not think of resigning as North had done but turned his thoughts towards the possibility of a compromise peace. The King as during the American conflict was for continuing the war. 'Unless the French are thoroughly reduced', he wrote on 25 October 1795, 'no solid peace can be obtained.' War should not be lightly undertaken nor should it be lightly abandoned. In January 1796 he wrote a paper for the cabinet against opening peace negotiations with France, but did not put his veto on the attempt and was neither surprised nor sorry that it failed.

In 1797 an acute financial crisis forced the government to suspend cash payments at the Bank of England and go off the gold standard. The same year there took place the naval mutinies at Spithead and the Nore, and for some months the King's correspondence with Lord Spencer, First Lord of the Admiralty, is concerned with little else than the verdicts of courts martial. Again the cabinet proposed peace negotiations and again the King reluctantly agreed. Pitt was as optimistic about the possibility of peace as he had been about success in war and with little justification for either. The King knew that any negotiation would prove humiliating and would cause great discontent at home. 'Though an Englishman is soon tired of war', he wrote, possibly with the peace of 1783 in mind, 'he is not easily satisfied with peace.' He recognized one of the great truths of international relations – that it is easier to make war than to make peace.

The King became dissatisfied with the government's plans yet could suggest no improvement. He disliked operations on the Continent, distrusted Great Britain's European allies, and hoped that the French people would eventually overthrow their revolutionary government. This was crying for the moon. If the French monarchy was to be restored it would have to be by force of arms and this looked less and less likely. Pitt came to see that if Great Britain did not make peace she would make war alone, and like North twenty years earlier he had lost faith in the cause for which he had gone to war. As the turn of the century approached King George faced the prospect of a peace which he knew would be no peace at all.

Meanwhile the state of Ireland was causing the British government grave concern. The loss of the American colonies, as the King had feared, had weakened the British hold over Ireland. Whig civilization assumed British supremacy over Ireland just as it had assumed British supremacy over America; and the Whig hero William III, who had been a liberator in Great Britain, had been a conqueror in Ireland. While North was occupied with the American war the Irish had pushed their pretensions so far that in 1782 the Rockingham ministry was compelled to grant the Irish Parliament complete legislative independence. Henceforth Ireland was no longer dependent on Great Britain. The Irish could make what laws they pleased, subject to the assent of the King's Lord Lieutenant.

This 'very unfortunate' change in the relations between

the two countries, as the King described it, encouraged Irish nationalism and stimulated the movement for Roman Catholic emancipation. This was supported by many Protestants, no longer obsessed by memories of 1688 and anxious to prove themselves good Irishmen. In 1793 the Protestant Parliament of Ireland passed an Act which gave the franchise to Roman Catholics and allowed them to hold civil and military offices. But Catholics had still to take an oath to preserve the system of property in Ireland (that is, not to reverse the confiscations of William III's reign), and not 'to disturb and weaken the Protestant religion and Protestant Government'.

The Act of 1793 was the first crack in the edifice of the Protestant establishment in Ireland. For the Roman Catholics it was a halfway stage between servility and freedom. They were no longer treated as outcasts, yet they were not treated as responsible citizens. The supreme mark of responsible citizenship – the right to sit in Parliament – was still denied them. It could hardly be denied them long. The French Revolution like the American rebellion stimulated Irish nationalism among Protestants and Catholics alike. Patriotic Irishmen began to realize that they could never be free of Great Britain until Catholics had the same rights as Protestants. If Great Britain would not accord this to reason, she must yield to force. What America had achieved, Ireland would achieve. In 1798 there was a rebellion of the Ulster Presbyterians and of the Catholics in Wexford, and the French, who had already tried to land troops in Ireland, were preparing for a full-scale invasion. Pitt could see no way of governing Ireland except by the union of the two kingdoms and the emancipation of the Roman Catholics. The Reformation settlement was to be undone in Great Britain: the Revolution settlement in Ireland.

King George was not intolerant. In Canada, which like Ireland had a majority of Roman Catholics, he supported the right of the French Canadians to the free exercise of their religion. 'Those who have the strongest claim on the attention of this country', he wrote at the time of the Canada Act of 1791, 'are the old inhabitants, whose rights and usages ought by no means to be disturbed.' He even gave a secret service pension to a cardinal of the Roman Catholic Church, the pretender to his Crown, who had fallen on evil days after the French occupation of the Papal States. But he was too loyal to his Whig upbringing to sanction a reversal of the Revolution settlement. The house of Hanover had been summoned to Great Britain to preserve the Protestant establishment and the King had taken a solemn oath at his coronation to maintain the rights and privileges of the Church of England. To the King an oath was sacred. 'Where is that power on earth', he asked, 'to absolve me from the due observance of every sentence of that oath?... I had rather beg my bread from door to door throughout Europe than consent to any such measure.' Roman Catholic emancipation was contrary to the first principles of the constitution. It was a question 'beyond the decision of any cabinet of ministers', he told Pitt in 1795. The King reached this conclusion after consulting the highest authorities in Church and State, and from what we know of his character we can be sure that he had prayed earnestly about it.

It was suggested by some contemporaries that the King had been influenced by sources hostile to Pitt; while latter-day Whigs, hostile to him, believed that his scruples arose from sheer stupidity and obstinacy. Neither is correct. The oath had been prescribed by statute in the first year of the reign of William and Mary for the express purpose of keeping Roman Catholics from positions of authority under the Crown. The plain truth is that no King of Great Britain could conscientiously give his consent to Roman Catholic emancipation. It was also true that the oath had ceased to be relevant. When it was enacted James II was preparing with a French army to regain his throne and fears of a Roman Catholic monarch were real. No such fears were entertainable in 1801. Roman Catholicism had lost its political bite and the Pope himself was in exile. It could be argued that the Roman Catholics, if placed on a position of equality with their Protestant fellow subjects, would be the strongest supporters of King George III's throne against a Jacobinism which was equally dangerous to King and Pope. Was it not the part of true statesmanship to set aside an oath, no matter how solemnly taken, which had ceased to be relevant and was in fact a positive danger to the State? Was not a little equivocation, a little fraud, sometimes necessary in the government of men? Pitt might have said with Bassanio:

> 'And I beseech you,
> Wrest once the law to your authority,
> To do a great right, do a little wrong.'

Pitt used no such arguments. They would have been of no avail. He knew the King's mind. The King was no statesman, no equivocator, but a plain man determined to keep his word. 'None of your Scotch metaphysics', he said to Dundas, when Dundas tried to argue the oath was binding only in his executive and not in his legislative capacity. King George had no head for fine distinctions but he knew right from wrong.

Pitt took little trouble to prepare the King for his proposal (the King afterwards complained that he had been taken by surprise). There was no need, for even with the support of the Crown he could not have got it through Parliament. Catholic emancipation in 1801 was no more a practical proposition than freedom for America had been twenty-five years earlier. The King's veto was the will of his subjects.

Gladstone in extreme old age, reflecting on his failure to pass a measure of Home Rule for Ireland, concluded that this was because the idea of Home Rule had not been sufficiently long before the public. Parliamentary reform had been debated for nearly fifty years before it was introduced by the Whigs in 1831, and the repeal of the Corn Laws took place after a prolonged period of public agitation. People can get used to any idea in politics, to any reversal of opinion, provided they are given sufficient time. Catholic emancipation in 1801 like Home Rule in 1886 was sprung upon the public before they were prepared for it. It could only have been accomplished in defiance of public opinion.

'English government ought well to consider before it gives any encouragement to a proposition which cannot fail sooner or later to separate the two kingdoms', the King had written when Catholic emancipation was suggested in 1795. It is doubtful if Pitt was correct in his assumption that Catholic emancipation would strengthen the British hold over Ireland. When it came in 1828 it stimulated Irish nationalism and increased agitation for repeal of the union. So also it might have done in 1801. The denial of civil rights to Roman Catholics was only one of the grievances of Ireland. During the period of the French Revolution the Irish Protestants offered a greater threat than the Catholics to the British connection. Like the taxation of America, Catholic emancipation symbolized the complaint of a subject nation against an imperial power. It was not an ultimate cause. When it was eventually conceded, the British found that their troubles with Ireland had only just begun.

The King made no secret of his opinions and on 28 January 1801 said at his levee (in almost the same words he had used about Fox's India Bill) that he would regard any man who voted for Catholic emancipation as his personal enemy. No formal advice had yet been submitted and he seems to have hoped that Pitt would drop the proposal as he had done parliamentary reform. He wrote to Pitt on 1 February:

My opinions are not those formed on the moment, but such as I have imbibed for forty years, and from which I can never depart; but, Mr Pitt once acquainted with my sentiments, his assuring me he will stave off the only question whereon I fear from his letter we can ever agree – for the advantage and comfort of continuing to have his advice and exertions in public affairs I will certainly abstain from talking on this subject . . . I cannot help if others pretend to guess at my opinions, which as yet I have never disguised; but if those who unfortunately differ with me will keep this subject at rest, I will on my part most correctly be silent also. . . .

Pitt was annoyed at the King having declared his views, and perhaps was not sorry to leave office. Eighteen years as the King's first minister had almost worn him down. The King commissioned Henry Addington, Speaker of the House of Commons, to form a ministry. He told Rose that Pitt's conduct was 'infinitely more honourable on retiring than that of any of his predecessors . . . and that he possessed his highest esteem and good opinion'. In a letter of 18 February the King addressed his former minister as 'My dear Pitt', a familiar form he had never used to any other minister; and he offered to pay Pitt's debts. On 15 March he told Pitt he hoped 'he would allow him to consider him as his friend and that he would not hesitate to come to him whenever he might wish it'. King George and Pitt parted on the best of terms.

Throughout the 1790s the King had enjoyed good health.[5] 'It would do your heart as much good as it does mine', wrote Princess Augusta to her brother Prince Augustus on 9 March 1791, '. . . to see him come home from a late day at St James's or a long hunt, the least fatigued of the party and always so good-humoured and cheerful.' 'He is quite an altered man', wrote Lord Auckland on 12 December 1791, 'and not what you knew him even before his illness. His manner is gentle, quiet, and when he is pleased, quite cordial. He speaks even of those who are opposed to his government with complacency and without either spleen or acrimony.' He had a brief 'bilious attack' in 1795 but nothing to give concern. More serious was the deterioration in his eyesight. He now wore spectacles for reading and found it difficult to read by candlelight.

On 13 February 1801, while Addington was forming his ministry, the King was suddenly taken ill. He complained of a chill and cramp which affected his whole body, and the next day did not go out. All the symptoms of his first illness recurred: hoarseness, constipation, nausea, and colic; and soon there came evidence of mental disturbance. On 17 February Addington found his 'manner more hurried and his countenance more heated than usual', though he talked sensibly; and on the 19th his conversation was 'very extravagant' a nd his mind 'not in a proper state'. On the 20th Lord Eldon, who had been appointed Lord Chancellor in the new ministry, had a two-hour conversation with the King 'during the whole of which time he was as rational and collected as he had ever seen him'. He spoke about his previous illness, 'and especially dwelt on his feelings during some lucid intervals'. He took from the shelf a copy of Blackstone's *Commentaries* and showed Eldon the passage on the Catholic question.

The King's illness could hardly have happened at a more delicate moment. The new ministers had not yet kissed hands and the old ministers retained their offices *pro tempore*. There were some unique cabinet meetings attended by both the incoming and outgoing ministers, and one at which there were two Prime Ministers and two Lord Chancellors present. But there was no political crisis as in 1788 and no debates in Parliament. Pitt told the Prince of Wales that if the King did not recover the government would propose a restricted regency on the model of 1788, and the Prince offered no objection. Fox deliberately absented himself from Parliament.

It was to be expected that after their apparent success

in curing the King in 1788, the Willises would again be summoned. Dr Francis Willis was now over eighty and had retired, and his son Thomas, who had also attended the King in 1788, had taken over his father's practice. The King told Thomas Willis on 21 February:

I do feel myself very ill, I am much weaker than I was, and I have prayed to God all night that I might die, or that he would spare my reason . . . if it should be otherwise, for God's sake keep me from your father and a regency.

He subsequently said to Addington that he had felt his illness coming on and had told the Queen and his daughters that they would not see him for some time. Mercifully his second illness, though dangerous, did not last as long as in 1788.

The acute phase began on 23 February when the King lay all night in a coma. The regular physicians, who attended as well as the Willises, gave it as their opinion that owing to his age (he was 62) his death was more likely than in 1788. But Thomas Willis as before was optimistic, and believed that the King would recover at the outside within three weeks. There was a relapse at the beginning of March, and on the 2nd the physicians feared he would not last the day. The Queen and the Prince of Wales were summoned to the sickroom in expectation of his death. But at five o'clock in the afternoon, so Pitt told Rose, the King fell into a sleep from which, with a short interval, he did not wake until four in the morning. He awoke 'quite tranquil, asked what bed he was in (being sensible of its not being the one he usually slept in), and how long he had been ill. On being told eight days, he said he felt himself much better than he had before.' For two days he lay in a state of insensibility and stupor, but on 5 March he was able to feed himself. On the 6th he saw the Queen, asked about matters in the House of Commons, and told John Willis to inform Addington that he was getting better. On the 7th he saw the Duke of York and ques-

582

tioned him about politics. He was anxious to discover if there had been any proposals for a regency. 'Sir', said the Duke, 'it would take us too much time to tell you all this now.' 'Frederick', replied the King, 'you are more nervous than I am. I really feel quite well, and know full well how ill I have been.' On 11 March the public was informed of the King's recovery and the bulletins were discontinued. His illness had lasted almost four weeks. At no time had the Willises used physical restraint as in 1788. There had been no occasion, for the illness had been more bodily than mental.

As in 1788 there were problems about his convalescence. Either the King had recovered and was fully able to attend to the business of the nation, or he had not. There was no half-way stage and no opportunity for him gradually to resume his normal life. He was twelve years older than he had been on the occasion of his first illness and his complete recovery took much longer. He slept badly, he had lost weight, his eyes were affected, and he was pale. In July Glenbervie found him 'very much altered indeed' with 'an emaciate face and person with his clothes hanging upon him'. There were arrears of business, cabinet minutes to be read and over 800 warrants to be signed, which severely taxed the King's strength. On 17 March, little more than a fortnight from the day when the physicians had almost given him up, he attended at a meeting of the Privy Council, and afterwards gave audience to his ministers. 'He had a great deal to say to each', wrote Thomas Willis, 'and the more he talked the more he was fatigued and had the less power of restraining himself.' When he over-taxed his strength he became irritable.

To the Willises all this was evidence that their presence about the King was still necessary, and both the ministers and the King's family were reluctant to dispense with them. A unique situation arose. The Willises aspired to the position held in Roman Catholic courts by the King's

583

confessor. The doctor, who cures the ills of the body, is to the Protestant what the priest, who cures the ills of the soul, is to the Catholic. The Willises claimed the right to decide what business the King should undertake. On 18 March Addington consulted Thomas Willis about the propriety of making an overture of peace to France, and Willis undertook to obtain the King's consent. The King told Willis it was what he had long wished. 'It was some time before I could get the King to write the answer which I was anxious for', wrote Willis in his diary, 'for, as I knew, the Cabinet Council would sit at a certain hour for the purpose of receiving it.' During the next few days the King was 'extremely nervous and low spirited' and 'unequal to business'.

What King George really needed was rest and relaxation at Windsor (he had been in London throughout this second illness), without doctors or ministers to vex him. This of course he could not get. The ministers were anxious for him to appear in public and the Willises undertook to get him into proper condition. They put blisters on his legs and gave him emetics to reduce his vitality, so that when he went to court he would not appear 'hurried' or 'extravagant' or have 'wrong ideas'. All this annoyed the King and caused him to break out into expressions of anger against his doctors, and as in 1788 the Willises took this as evidence that his mind was not yet sound. (We might conclude that the King's dislike of the way he was treated by his doctors was evidence that his mind was perfectly sound.) John Willis undertook to set the King right:

The King received him very coldly and asked him why he came. Dr John answered in order to prevent His Majesty from dealing so liberally in unfounded abuse and misrepresentation. He assured the King that . . . abuse of men who had brought him out of very severe and dangerous fever was a proof of the remnant of the disorder. The King said in reply that it was no proof, for that he had abused him ever since his former illness.

Then said Dr John, you was not perfectly cured or you could not have abused where you ought to have justly extolled.

We are reminded of the way in which George Grenville had lectured the King almost forty years earlier. The King's refusal to submit himself to a politician was evidence of political unsoundness: his refusal to submit himself to a doctor was evidence of mental unsoundness. Most of the King's biographies have been written round these two themes.

The King told the Willises to pack up and go, and set off with the Queen and his daughters for Kew. But the Willises had not yet done with him. 'Besides never having fairly altogether quitted him', wrote Thomas Willis, 'and unwilling to forsake the task we had undertaken where great credit was at stake and the completion of which was confidently seen . . . these considerations were what induced and determined us, frightful as it was, to execute this cruel scheme.' The Willises were not to be baulked of their exclusive demand to dictate to the King on medical matters. With the connivance of the Queen and the tacit consent of the ministers, they carried out their 'cruel scheme' – no less than that of kidnapping the King and detaining him by force. The policy of restraint advocated by their father was applied under different circumstances. The first plan, to catch him as he went for his early morning ride, failed; and then the Willises, together with their men, went boldly into the King's room and told him why they had come. Thomas Willis wrote:

On the King getting sight of me he seemed surprized and would have hastily passed and escaped out of the room but I prevented him . . . I spoke to him at once of his situation and the necessity there was that he should be immediately under controul again. His Majesty sat down, turning very pale . . . and exclaimed, 'Sir, I will never forgive you whilst I live.'

They took him to the White House where he lived for a month under the supervision of the Willises, isolated

from the Queen and his family. They watched his correspondence, so that he had to send a letter to Prince
Adolphus (who was but two rooms off) to the Foreign
Secretary in London and ask Hawkesbury to forward it
to the Prince. All this time he continued to carry out his
functions as sovereign, corresponded with his ministers
(his letters are perfectly sensible), created at least one
peerage, and gave his assent to Acts of Parliament. He
took walks under the supervision of the Willises, played
at chess and cards, and planned his summer holiday to
Weymouth.

The end of this episode is no less extraordinary than the
beginning. Tired of his confinement, the King threatened
to go on strike – the only time in the history of the
monarchy that a King of Great Britain has contemplated
what is now called 'industrial action'. He told Lord
Chancellor Eldon, who visited him on 19 May, that 'he
had taken a solemn determination, that unless he was
that day allowed to go over to the house where the Queen
and his family were, no earthly consideration should induce him to sign his name to any paper or to do one act
of government whatever'. At this the Willises conceded
defeat, and the King walked across the road to the Dutch
House where the Queen was living.

The authors of *George III and the Mad-Business* (where
there is a full account of this extraordinary affair, on
which the above is based) rightly describe it as unique in
the history of the monarchy. Either the King was in his
right mind or he was not. If he was, by what right did the
Willises presume to detain him? If he was not, why was
he allowed to perform such acts of sovereignty as the
creation of a peerage or the royal assent to an Act of
Parliament? What would have been the reaction in
Parliament and in the nation had the full story been told?
The strong position of the Willises arose from the belief
that the King was subject to insanity and that only they
could cure him. The regular physicians had failed and the

586

mad doctors had it all their own way. The King obtained the period of convalescence he required; nature did its work; and the Willises got the credit. But nature might have worked more quickly had she not been hampered by the doctors. And the legend of insanity would not have clung so closely to the King.

Perhaps the most interesting reflection on this episode is the light it throws on the King's character. He maintained his good humour under conditions which would have strained the patience of men with less strength of character. Once again we see the absence of any sense of false pride and recognize how well he knew himself. Lord Malmesbury, who had a private audience of two hours with the King in November 1801, wrote: 'He appeared rather more of an old man, but not older than men of his age commonly appear; he stopped rather more, and was apparently less firm on his legs, but he did not look thinner, nor were there any marks of sickness or decline in his countenance or manner.' They talked about the peace treaty with France (the Peace of Amiens), which Addington had just concluded. The King said Great Britain had been compelled to make peace because she had no allies but it was only an 'experimental peace'.

I thought the subject might agitate the King [Malmesbury wrote] and therefore tried to lead him from it: he perceived my drift, and said: 'Lord Malmesbury, you and I have lived on the active theatre of this world these thirty years: if we are not wise enough to consider every event which happens quietly and with acquiescence we must have lived very negligently.'

He told Eldon he had gained one advantage from his illnesses, 'namely, the means of knowing his real from his pretended friends'.

Chapter 10

OLD AGE AND OBLIVION

The King's first illness, because of its sudden onset and the political crisis which it occasioned, has received most attention from historians. Yet the illness of 1801 was of greater significance in his life. After his recovery in 1789 the King remained in good health for almost twelve years and it came to be assumed that he was unlikely ever again to be afflicted in the same way. But after 1801 no one could be sure. It was now clear that the King was subject to a disease that might break out at any time. Henceforth the Royal Family and the ministers lived in fear of the King's insanity.

As a result the mental rather than the physical symptoms of his illness were emphasized. In 1788 it was believed that the King's illness had been caused by failure to change his wet stockings. In February 1801 the weather was extremely cold, there was snow on the ground, and the King caught a chill. But no one suggested these as the precipitating causes of his second illness. Instead it was believed that his mind had been disturbed by the proposal for Catholic emancipation, and this theory was encouraged by the Willises. 'As was usually the case with George III', wrote John Heneage Jesse, his nineteenth-century biographer, 'in times of great excitement, distress of mind induced disease of the body.' Against all the evidence, the King himself came to believe this. 'What has he not to answer for;' the King said to the Duke of York about Pitt, 'who is the cause of my having been ill at all?' Pitt saw John Willis, and with Addington as witness authorized Willis to tell the King that he would never again, either in or out of office, raise the Catholic question. Everything that was thought likely to disturb the

King's mind must be kept from him. The ministers would have preferred him not to go to Weymouth in the summer of 1801 but did not dare to tell him so. When Princess Amelia quarrelled with her governess in 1803 she was told that the King must not know. It would only make him unhappy, said the Queen, and he had quite sufficient to worry him in politics without the Princess adding to his cares.

On 15 April 1801 the Prince of Wales had a cordial conversation with the King. 'He continually and repeatedly talked of himself as a dying man', runs the Prince's account, 'determined to go abroad to Hanover, to make over the government to the Prince.'[1] If this was a serious thought, and not merely the effect of a post-illness depression, it was soon abandoned. The Prince had again been playing politics and had become an advocate for Catholic emancipation. Now he was a party leader in his own right, independent of Fox or Grenville or Pitt, and engaged in the pleasant task of forming his future cabinet. It reminds one of the state of affairs sixty years earlier when Frederick, Prince of Wales, had engaged in the opposition to King George II. It is possible that the King might have abdicated the throne of Great Britain in 1801 had he felt any confidence in the Prince of Wales. But the Prince showed every year less and less reason for confidence. He was no longer living with the Princess, who had now removed to Blackheath. He refused to gratify the King by allowing Princess Charlotte to be brought up by her grandparents. He had accumulated fresh debts in defiance of the Act of 1795 so that another parliamentary settlement had to be made (the fourth time in twenty years that Parliament had granted money for the payment of his debts). He pressed his demand for high rank in the army, and when this was again refused quarrelled with the King and the Duke of York and published his correspondence with them in the newspapers. The King was so offended at this that for nearly a year he refused to have any communication with his son and paid marked attention to the Princess of Wales. 'I do not like the footing the Royal Family are on with each other', wrote one observer in September 1803, 'which I fear the nation may one day or other suffer by.'[2] Things indeed were in a sad state.

The King recovered slowly from his illness. 'He has been very quiet, very heavy, and very sleepy all the evening,' Princess Elizabeth wrote to Thomas Willis on 9 June 1801, 'and has said two or three times, yesterday was too much for him.'[3] A week later he came back after hunting with 'a great thirst upon him' (not surprisingly after six hours on horseback), and the Queen was in 'great fear'. 'His Majesty still talks much of his prudence', wrote Thomas Willis to Eldon, 'but he shows none.' If only he would give up hunting and sit at home and do what the doctors told him! Another impression of the King at this time is that of Lord Auckland (16 August 1801), whose brother lived near Windsor and was a frequent visitor at the Castle:

He might at times appear to those who have always seen him in high spirits to be rather low; but the case really is, that his manner is much more composed and he is always ready to enter into conversation when it is going on though he does not always start it. He is become also more moderate in his exercise, and admits that it is possible to be fatigued.

Thomas Pelham on 6 October wrote: 'I never saw the King in apparently better health and spirits'; and the Archbishop of Canterbury in June 1802 gave Auckland a 'most satisfactory account' of the King's health. 'The King is perfectly well', Auckland reported on 27 January 1803, 'but less hardy, or at least more prudent than heretofore.'

In the autumn of 1803 the King began to suffer from pain in his legs. He found it difficult to mount a horse, and took to hunting with the harriers instead of the staghounds. In January 1804 he was unable to attend the Queen's birthday drawing room, and at the party in the evening walked with a crutch. Lord Pelham noticed that the Queen 'never left her eyes off the King during the whole time the party lasted'. A month later he was again stricken with his old complaint.

The illness of 1804 was less serious than those of 1788 and 1801. It lasted little more than a week and the King's life does not seem to have been in danger. Nor was his mind affected to the same extent. But Addington was taking no chances. He sent for the Willises, who refused to come unless they were given official authority from the cabinet. Armed with this, they presented themselves at the Queen's House, and were refused access to the patient. The Duke of Kent and the Duke of Cumberland informed Addington that they had given a solemn promise to their father that 'in the event of its being the will of Providence that he should again be afflicted . . . we should use every means in our power to prevent anyone of the Willis family from being placed about him'. The Royal Family were anxious to escape responsibility for the King's treatment. This was an affair of state and should be decided by the cabinet. A declaration to this effect, signed by the Queen and nine of her children, was sent to Addington. The ones who did not sign were the Duke of Sussex and the Duchess of Wurtemberg, who were living abroad; the Duke of Clarence, who was not in London; and the Prince of Wales, who refused to declare his opinion.

In place of the Willises Addington summoned Dr Samuel Simmons, physician to St Luke's Hospital for Lunatics, who followed the medical fashion of the day and put the King into a strait-waistcoat. This at the very moment when he was recovering! On 21 February the physicians declared him 'as well in understanding as before the illness'. On the 26th Addington declared in the Commons that the King was perfectly competent to assume the government but that 'it would be prudent for some time to spare him all unnecessary exertion of mind'.

This was common sense. As in 1789 and 1801 it was the period of convalescence that caused most uneasiness to the Royal Family and the ministers. The King's recovery from his illness was like that of a man awaking from a heavy sleep. He struggled to shake off the effects of sleep, to get out of bed, to dress himself and go about the business of the day. At the same time there was the temptation to settle back into bed and have another half hour's nap. He was neither asleep nor awake – or to drop the metaphor, neither ill nor well. His first thought was indignation at the way he had been treated during his illness by 'that horrible doctor' Simmons. Then came the struggle to assert himself, to get well, to resume his normal life. And all this time he was being pestered by doctors with their medicines, their blisters, their advice to take matters carefully. He saw doubt and anxiety in the faces of those he loved. They believed he had been mad. That is what they had been told by the doctors. He knew he had not been mad but desperately ill. He was now trying to get better: he was now trying to do what he had been told to do. He looked for sympathy and understanding and found fear and distrust.

It was natural for those about the King to be afraid. They had vivid memories of the horrible days of November 1788. They did not understand his illness and had to rely on the advice of the doctors. It would have been rash for any minister in 1804 to have advised the King to dismiss the doctors. Had there been a relapse, such advice might have led to an impeachment or at least to the charge of making political capital out of the King's sufferings. What was the real state of the King? He was well enough to exercise the highest prerogative of the Crown – to appoint Pitt Prime Minister on the resignation of Addington. He was not well enough to decide for himself his own treatment and convalescence.

Pitt endorsed the doctors' recommendation that the King should not go to Cheltenham and should submit himself 'for a short time longer to proper management'. The King was told by his doctors that he must 'strictly and uniformly exert himself to correct those ideas which occasionally shew themselves in his less guarded moments' and 'to avoid as much as possible any hurry or excess of fatigue'. The idea was instilled into him that if he fell ill again it would be his own fault because he had not taken the doctors' advice. The poor King, who really did not want to be ill if he could help it, endorsed the doctors' advice: 'Opinion of the five physicians, July 7th 1804, to be deposited with the former ones with the Queen of my heart.' She would be witness that he would follow the doctors' advice.

All who saw him in the summer and autumn of 1804 agree that he looked thin and emaciated. Yet his mind was perfectly clear. In October 1804 he stayed with George Rose at Cuffnells in the New Forest, and Rose's report of their conversations show how sensibly he talked and how he retained his memory. Yet Thomas Willis was correct when he told Auckland in September 'that things would never be quite right'. It would have saved an immense amount of suffering both for King George and his family had he died in 1804.

The first change was in his relations with the Queen. Queen Charlotte liked a quiet life. 'My taste', she wrote, 'is for a few select friends whose cheerfulness of temper and instructive conversation will pass the time away without leaving any remorse for what is passed, and creating a desire of renewing the meeting.' She was happy with her books, music, needlework, and evening card parties, she did not enjoy the constant to-ing and fro-ing between London and Windsor; and she begged the King to release her from the fatigues of court.

She was terrified when the King fell ill in 1801 and dreaded a breach between him and the Prince of Wales.

What she had to endure during the King's illness may be seen from a letter by Thomas Willis to Lord Eldon, 25 May 1801:

His Majesty . . . told me, with great seeming satisfaction, that he had had a most charming night, 'but one sleep from eleven to half-past four', when alas! he had but three hours sleep in the night, which, upon the whole, was passed in restlessness, in getting out of bed, opening the shutters, in praying at times violently, and in making such remarks as betray a consciousness in him of his own situation, but which are evidently made for the purpose of concealing it from the Queen. He frequently called out, 'I am now perfectly well, and my Queen, my Queen has saved me.' Whilst I state these particulars to your lordship, I must beg to remind you how much afraid the Queen is, lest she should be committed to him; for the King has sworn he will never forgive her if she relates anything that passes in the night.

His pathetic attempts to assure the Queen that all was well may have been due to suspicion of her. For the Queen trusted the Willises and would have had the King submit himself to their care. She maintained a secret correspondence with Thomas Willis via Princess Elizabeth, and it was at the Queen's instigation that the Willises had kidnapped the King at Kew in April 1801. 'God grant that his eyes may soon open', Princess Elizabeth wrote to Thomas Willis on 9 June 1801, 'and that he may see his real and true friends in their true colours.' Hence the Queen's anxiety not to have the King committed to her care and her relief when the cabinet assumed responsibility for his treatment in 1804. She trembled to think what the King would say if he found out that she favoured the Willises. Is it possible that the King had some inkling of this when he told Eldon that his illness had given him the advantage of knowing his real from his pretended friends?

In May 1804 Mrs Harcourt told Malmesbury that the King was perfectly well when talking to his ministers upon

594

matters of business, 'but in his family and usual society his manners and conversation were far from steady'. He made an effort to control himself when dealing with the business of the nation (as his doctors had told him to do) and felt the strain in familiar society. The Queen saw him at his worst. It is no wonder she almost broke down under the strain. Such an illness as the King had affects not only the sufferer but also his immediate family. There is nothing worse than to see someone we love suffer and yet be unable to relieve them. The Queen can hardly be blamed for trusting to the Willises or for her outbreaks of ill-temper. 'The Queen's temper is become intolerable', Glenbervie wrote on 27 June 1804, 'and that the Princesses are rendered quite miserable by it'; and on 22 August he learnt from one of the Queen's servants that she had 'lately shown great peevishness and tartness of behaviour to the King'.

On their return from Weymouth in the autumn of 1804 their manner of life changed. 'He never mentions her with disrespect', wrote Auckland on 11 September, 'but he marks unequivocally and by many facts that he is dissatisfied with her, and is come to a decided system of checking her knowledge of what is going forward and her interference between him and his heir.' On their return to Windsor Castle the King and Queen lived separately in their own apartments, and she took precautions to prevent him from sleeping with her. 'The Queen will never receive the King without one of the Princesses being present', wrote Malmesbury in December 1804, '... and when in London locks the door of her white room (her boudoir) against him.' If we are to believe Sir Robert Wilson, the King even threatened to take a mistress. This is almost certainly not true, but typical of the type of story whispered round London society. One needs to have a large bump of credulity to believe any story told by Sir Robert Wilson.

In October 1804 the King told Rose that he had almost

lost the sight of his right eye and it was only with difficulty and the aid of the strongest spectacles that he could read a newspaper by candlelight. 'His sight has suffered much', the Duke of Sussex wrote to the Prince of Wales on 4 November 1804, '. . . so much so that he distinguishes no one across the room and is constantly forced to ask who the persons present are.' In July 1805 cataract was diagnosed; and the Duke of York told Lord Henley in October that the King had lost entirely the sight of one eye and 'sees but ill of the other'. An operation was suggested but never attempted. In the autumn he took Herbert Taylor, who had been secretary to the Duke of York, as his private secretary. He was no longer capable of conducting his correspondence; and Taylor had to read all letters to the King and write the replies at the King's dictation. 'The patience, resignation, and unutterable good humour', wrote Taylor on 19 June 1806, 'with which he submits to so great a calamity daily increase . . . It is impossible to be with our good King without finding every hour fresh cause to love and admire him.'

A description of him at this time, in his 68th year, comes from Lord Henley, who saw him frequently at Windsor:

Our good King continues, mind and body, the sight excepted, better than I have seen him for years. . . . He plays at commerce without any further assistance than he derives from his spectacles. . . . This morning I met him in the park at ten o'clock and rode with him until a quarter past one. He was cheerful, and we had more than one of his hearty laughs, which I have not heard before for some time. . . . Lady Henley says that he presented the muffins to the ladies last night in his old jocose and good-humoured manner.

In 1803 war had broken out again between Great Britain and France, now ruled by Napoleon, a war which was to involve all the great nations of Europe (and the United States), and of which King George did not see the end. It is curious that while contemporaries bemoaned the rapid

596

change of ministries at the beginning of the King's reign and attributed this as a cause of national weakness, hardly anyone noticed that the same situation existed at the end of the reign without apparently weakening the nation in the slightest degree. Between 1801 when Pitt resigned and the onset of the King's final illness in 1810 there were five Prime Ministers, to be followed by a sixth during the years of the King's incapacity. Apart from Pitt, they are the forgotten Prime Ministers of British history. It is difficult for well-read people, even for historians who are not experts on the period, to name the Prime Minister who sent Wellington to the Peninsula or to say who was Prime Minister at the time of the battle of Waterloo. Everybody knows Asquith and Lloyd George in connection with the First World War, Chamberlain and Churchill with the second, but who remembers the Duke of Portland and the Earl of Liverpool? Yet these men, together with a blind King, helped to defeat the greatest politico-military ruler of the century.

In the autumn of 1803 the King made plans against a threatened invasion. 'The King is really prepared to take the field in case of attack', a courtier wrote on 13 November, 'his beds are ready and he can move at half an hour's warning.'[4] To his old friend Bishop Hurd, the King explained his plans in more detail:

Should his troops effect a landing, I shall certainly put myself at the head of mine, and my other armed subjects, to repel them: but as it is impossible to see the events of such a conflict, should the enemy approach too near to Windsor, I shall think it right the Queen and my daughters should cross the Severn, and shall send them to your episcopal palace at Worcester. By this hint I do not in the least mean they shall be any inconvenience to you, and shall send a proper servant and furniture for their accommodation. Should such an event arise, I certainly would rather that what I value most in life should remain during the conflict in your diocese and under your roof, than in any other place in the island.

The King was to move to Chelmsford if the landing took place in Essex or to Dartford if in Kent; Cornwallis was to take command of the reserve army; the Bank of England books to be sent to the Tower and the treasure to Worcester Cathedral; the Stock Exchange was to be closed; and the Privy Council to direct affairs from London. The press was to be prohibited from publishing news of troop movements and official government communiqués were to be issued. It all reads like 1940. Even the idea of the Home Guard was anticipated. As in 1779 there is a touch of the Churchillian spirit in King George III.

But old feuds were not forgotten even during Great Britain's darkest hour. Despite Pitt's pleadings, the King said 'he had taken a positive determination not to admit Mr Fox into his councils even at the hazard of a civil war'. These words need not have been taken too seriously for on Pitt's death the King was compelled to admit Fox to office. 'At the period of Mr Fox's return to power', Princess Augusta wrote, 'the King . . . showed for several days considerable uneasiness of mind. A cloud seemed to overhang his spirits. On his return one day from London the cloud was evidently removed, and His Majesty, on entering the room where the Queen and Princess Augusta were, said he had news to tell them. "I have taken Mr Fox for my minister, and on the whole am satisfied with the arrangement."'

When Fox entered the closet for the first time (with one exception) since 1783, the King said to him: 'Mr Fox, I little thought you and I should ever meet again in this place. But I have no desire to look back upon old grievances, and you may rest assured I never shall remind you of them.' Fox bowed, and replied: 'My deeds and not my words shall commend me to Your Majesty.' Each had been unjust to the other, each had failed to understand the other, and now it was too late. Six months later Fox was dead. If he had not set his face against the King, what might he not have achieved? The King sent a simple acknowledgment of the news of Fox's death but in private expressed his sorrow and said the country could ill afford to lose such a man. 'Little did I think', he told Addington, 'that I should ever live to regret Mr Fox's death.'[5]

The King continued to be afflicted with the troubles of his children. The Prince of Wales accused the Princess of adultery and demanded an investigation into her conduct; the Duke of Sussex broke with Lady Augusta Murray and quarrelled with her relations; the Duke of Kent continued to live happily with Mlle de St Laurent and the Duke of Clarence with Mrs Jordan. The debts of the royal Dukes were a never-ending source of worry. In 1808 £20,000 was required to relieve the Duke of York from 'some very urgent and extraordinary demands', and the Duke of Sussex was faced with an execution on his property for £1,500. None of the royal Dukes was deemed capable of exercising high command in the war against Napoleon, except the Duke of York, and even he, the most trustworthy, got into trouble. Charges were brought against him in the House of Commons in 1809 that he had allowed his mistress to sell commissions in the army. The King refused 'to doubt for one moment the Duke of York's perfect integrity and his conscientious attention to his public duty'. But the Duke had been foolish. Wilberforce expressed the opinion of the House when he acquitted the Duke of any corrupt intentions but demanded his resignation. The King accepted it reluctantly.

Despite these scandals, or perhaps because of them, the nation's affection for the King never waned. 'His popularity is very great', Lord Bulkeley wrote on 3 October 1809, 'for the mass of the people look up to his good moral character, and to his age, and to a comparison with his sons'; and on 7 November 1810: 'The personal popularity of the King is as great as it possibly can be.' When he made his visits to Weymouth, every village on the route turned out to welcome him. London had never witnessed any celebrations like those for the fiftieth anniversary of the King's accession on 25 October 1810. 'The number of people in the street . . . was immense', wrote Rose, who attended the dinner given by the bankers and merchants of London, '. . . and the illuminations remarkably beautiful.'

No one knew that this was virtually the end of King George III's reign.

The onset of the King's last illness was manifested on that day, 25 October.[6] It began as the others had with the King having caught a cold. The Royal Family were assembled at Windsor. Sadness hung over the Castle, for Princess Amelia lay dying. 'As he went round the circle as usual', a witness wrote, 'it was easy to perceive the dreadful excitement in his countenance. . . . When the King was seated, he called to him each of his sons separately, and said things to them equally sublime and instructive but very unlike what he would have said before so many people had he been conscious of the circumstance.' The next day the doctors were summoned, headed by Sir Henry Halford, physician extraordinary to the King and medical 'confessor' to the Royal Family. On 1 November it was decided to send for Dr Simmons.

The King had regularly attended Princess Amelia's sickbed and had prayed and talked with his daughter. 'His Majesty supports himself with becoming resignation', Herbert Taylor had written on 9 October, 'and is determined to meet the melancholy event with that fortitude which a confidence in the inestimable blessings of Christian faith can alone inspire.' It was naturally concluded that 'the overflowing of his heart for his youngest and dearest child', as Princess Elizabeth put it, had precipitated his illness. Again, no one seems to have paid much attention to his physical condition except to note that the chances of recovery were less at 72 than they had been earlier.

Simmons demanded complete control over the patient. But at the onset of his illness the King had extracted a promise from the physicians that he should never be left alone with a mad doctor, and had expressed particular antipathy to Simmons and his son. It was with extreme reluctance that the doctors ordered restraint, and they were annoyed when Spencer Perceval, the Prime Minister, called in Robert Willis. About the middle of November the King began to improve, and in reply to a formal request by the physicians agreed to submit himself entirely to their directions. But the improvement was not maintained, and on Christmas Eve he was thought to be dying. Again he rallied, and as always when past the crisis of the disease he became subject to delusions and delirium. He saw Perceval and Eldon and asked about the war, but could not keep his mind long on the subject. He spent much of his time playing the harpsichord, and on 18 January 1811 walked on the North Terrace for the first time since his illness.

In December the physicians were examined by select committees of the Lords and Commons. They admitted they were puzzled by the King's illness. It had 'never borne the characteristics of insanity', said Robert Willis, 'it never gets beyond derangement'. He was like a person talking in his sleep. Dr Reynolds said 'the King's memory is entire, his perceptions are entire, and his acuteness is considerable', though his judgment was perverted. All agreed that there was a good chance of his recovery.

The government decided to introduce a regency bill with restrictions on the model of 1788 which were to lapse if the King had not recovered within twelve months. On 29 January Perceval saw the King for over an hour and explained the provisions of the bill. The King asked questions about the examination of the physicians and the debates in Parliament, and wondered how the government had managed for money since he had been unable to sign Treasury warrants.[7]

The King said he had no doubt everything had been done for the best, and with the best intentions. He was ready to sign or do anything that Perceval should recommend. Perceval to this replied that His Majesty's physicians did not think him at present sufficiently recovered to be troubled with public business; upon which the King observed that they knew best, and he should conform to their advice.

He then dwelt upon his own advanced age of seventy-two, that it was time for him to think of retirement. That he must still, however, be 'King'; he could not part with that name, but *otium cum dignitate* etc was the most suitable to his age etc.

Upon representation to him of the duties which a religious sense of his situation would still require him to discharge. He listened with some unwillingness, and said, 'He should always be at hand to come forward if he was wanted', and, upon the whole was rather impatient of any pressure upon the subject of resigning his power.

The King was committed to the care of the Queen, who was to be advised by a committee of Privy Councillors headed by the Archbishop of Canterbury. On 6 February 1811 the Prince of Wales took the oaths of office as Regent and assumed charge of the government. Though he disliked the ministers he refused to dismiss them on the ground that he was only acting *pro tempore* for his father.

Sir Henry Halford undertook to inform the King of the news of Princess Amelia's will. She had left her property to Colonel Fitzroy who had renounced the inheritance, and the Prince of Wales had divided her jewels amongst his sisters. The Royal Family were apprehensive of the effect this would have on the King's mind, for the Princess's feelings for Fitzroy had been concealed from him for nearly ten years. The revelation did not disturb him, and he was pleased at the Prince's disposal of his sister's property. 'Thank God!' he said, 'for so fine a trait. The Prince of Wales has a heart. I always knew he had. I will never call him anything but George in future. . . . How thankful I ought to be to Providence for giving me such a son in the hour of my trial.' He was even more pleased when the Prince re-appointed the Duke of York Commander-in-Chief. 'He desired me to return you his thanks', the Queen wrote to the Prince on 23 May 1811, 'for having employed me to convey such agreeable news, and to assure you that he never could forget your conduct upon this occasion.' The reconciliation between the King and his son is the most pleasant event in the tragic story of George III's last years.

On 8 February the Queen saw the King for the first time since his illness. 'He received me very kindly', she wrote, 'and talked much of his family with great affection. He looks better than I have seen him after any one of his other illnesses and seems not to be so much fallen away as I expected.' The King's sons paid him regular visits, he walked on the terrace with them, and even rode in the park. He played backgammon and was read aloud to (one of the books for which he asked was Boswell's *Life of Johnson*). He looked forward to his freedom, and was disappointed when the Queen's Council informed him in April that he must submit to medical control for a little longer. Apart from occasional delusions he was perfectly sensible and nobody doubted that he would recover. The physicians thought it would take twelve months at the outside.

In the middle of July 1811 there was a sudden and startling relapse, and the King became so violent that restraint had to be used. He could not sleep even when given laudanum, and refused his meals. He was irascible and confused, talked incoherently, and appeared to have no consciousness of his situation. At one time he thought that Prince Octavius was alive, and yet he was able to give a correct account of his conversation with the American minister in 1784. Pressure was put upon the Queen by her council to recall the Willises. She complained of 'the hard task I am put to by them and how cutting it is to my feeling to do that which if the King recovers may perhaps forever make me forfeit his good opinion'. She insisted that the council make their demand in writing and yielded 'with the greatest reluctance and almost with a broken heart'. The council asked Robert Willis, 'Do you think that by throwing buckets of water upon your patient's head he would be cured?' Willis 'quite shuddered at it when he told it to us', wrote Princess Elizabeth. In spite of the protests of Halford and Heberden, the old system of restraint and seclusion was used. The King was left alone all day with his keepers, and if he became violent he was put into the strait-waistcoat. Little attempt was made to try to make contact with him, and he gradually lost touch with the world.

Possibly it made no difference from the point of view of curing the patient what system of treatment was adopted. The King was now in his 74th year, he had been blind for seven years, and in addition to his disease he was becoming senile. He ceased to ask about his family, ceased to recognize those about him; and by the beginning of 1812 he was living in a world of his own. He became more tranquil though he continued to talk incessantly, and spent hours each day playing the harpsichord. 'We do not expect the King's recovery', the physicians reported to the Queen's council on 2 April 1814, 'but it is not impossible'; and on 11 August: 'He never wants amusement and it is always satisfactory.' He was allowed to grow a beard, but was shaved at least five times between 1812 and 1818 (in November 1817 at his own request). The Queen paid him regular visits. He did not recognize her and her reports are always the same: 'The King is quiet and composed' (26 December 1814); 'the King thank God in a very calm state' (21 January 1816); 'the dear King very comfortable in every sense' (20 January 1817).[8] His family knew they would never see him again.

When the Prince of Wales assumed the regency the property of the Crown devolved upon him as if the King were dead. But the King's private property was administered on his behalf by Colonel Taylor, who sub-

604

mitted regular reports to the Queen's council and the Treasury. Taylor drew the allowance for the King's Privy Purse (£60,000 a year), from which he had to make payments for the King's library, the maintenance of his private property, and pensions and allowances to his servants. The biggest source of expense was remuneration to the physicians. The three physicians (Halford, Baillie, and Heberden) each attended two days a week; John and Robert Willis attended each day in turns; and David Dundas, the Windsor apothecary, came two days a week. The physicians and the Willises each received 30 guineas per visit and Dundas 15 guineas, plus their travelling expenses and the expenses of the Willises' men. Taylor informed Lord Liverpool, the Prime Minister, on 22 August 1812, that the medical expenses for the previous year had amounted to £33,998 and asked if they could not be reduced.[9]

The King and Queen had each made wills leaving their private property to be shared by their daughters (with the exception of the King's library, which was bequeathed to the Prince of Wales as an heirloom). The more that was spent on medical expenses, the less there would be for the Princesses when the King died. When it became clear that the King would never recover, Taylor, supported by Liverpool, pressed the Queen's Council to consider a reduction in medical attendance. Was it really necessary, he asked, that both the Willises should attend together as they sometimes did? That a physician should attend every day merely to shake his head and say the King was no better? Could not Dundas be restricted to one visit per week? If the council refused to sanction these reductions, could not Parliament make some provision? But the council would not make any reduction and the Treasury would not make any provision. Each year Taylor called attention to the high cost of medical attendance and each year he was rebuffed. When the King died, it appeared that the total cost of medical attendance since 5 January

1812 had been £271,691 18s – about £35,000 a year.[10] The doctors made a good thing out of George III. We are reminded of the lines in Hilaire Belloc's poem:

'They murmured, as they took their fees,
There is no cure for this disease.'

Queen Charlotte died at Kew on 17 November 1818 and the Duke of York assumed responsibility for the care of the King's person. 'Without any apparent illness', the physicians reported in November 1819, 'His Majesty appears declining fast.' He developed a rupture, spent most of the day in bed, and could take nothing but liquid food. The Duke of York wrote to the Prince Regent on 20 January 1820:[11]

It is with the sincrest regret that I take up my pen to inform you of the melancholy state in which I found our beloved father and King yesterday. Though the reports which I received daily from Windsor mentioned his increasing weakness, yet there was nothing in them which led one to imagine that there existed any immediate cause of alarm. But alas, upon going into the room yesterday, I never was more shocked than in perceiving the melancholy alteration which has taken place in him during the ten days that I have not seen him. The degree of weakness and languor in his looks and the emaciation of his face struck me more than I can describe.

On 27 January he was unable to rise from his bed, ceased to speak, and had to be fed with a spoon. The end came on 29 January. The Duke of York wrote to his brother, now King George IV:[12]

Dearest brother, It is my melancholy duty to inform you that it has pleased Providence to take to himself our beloved King and Father; the only immediate consolation under such a calamity is the almost conviction that his last moments were free from bodily suffering and mental distress. He expired at 38 minutes past 8 o'clock P.M.

The room in which he died, overlooking the North

Terrace and facing towards Eton, is described by a contemporary:[13]

The King occupied three compartments, two of which formed
one sitting-room, having a sort of arched open communication
between and a bedroom between the sitting-room and a large
apartment of the suite, which was allotted to his personal
attendants. All these rooms contained furniture of the most
homely description. . . . His Majesty's bed, in which he died,
stands in a little recess and is hardly larger or more luxurious
than the commonest kind of officer's camp bed. There is only
a simple mattress, one bolster and no pillow. . . . Everything
we saw and everything we heard of the late King was calculated to inspire love and respect. To have a notion of his
domestic qualities, his humility, moderation, affability, charity
and goodness, you must go to Windsor and converse with his
old servants and the old inhabitants of that place. I came away
. . . fully convinced that the monarch had not a subject in his
dominions whose private conduct and character through life
could stand a scrutiny with so much credit as his own. He was
indeed a true English King . . .

After two days' lying in state, the King was buried in
St George's Chapel on 16 February 1820.* The Duke of
York was the chief mourner. Mrs Arbuthnot, who
attended the funeral, wrote in her journal:

And thus has sunk into an honoured grave the best man and
the best King that ever adorned humanity; and it is consoling
to the best feelings of the human heart that *such* a sovereign
was followed to his last home by countless thousands of
affectionate subjects drawn to the spot by no idle curiosity to
view the courtly pageant, but to pay a last tribute of respect
and to shed the tear of affection and gratitude over the grave
of him, who, for sixty long years, had been the father of his
people.

* See note 11, p. 614.

NOTES

1. *The King and Macaulay on the revolution of 1688* (p. 111). The King's youthful essay on the revolution of 1688 concludes: '... but however this Convention with all its blemishes saved the nation from the iron rod of arbitrary power. Let that palliate all defects ... let us still remember we stand in debt for our liberty and religion to the success of 1688' (RA Add. 32/1292). Compare with this Macaulay's glorification of the revolution, written ninety years after the King's essay: 'For the authority of law, for the security of property, for the peace of our streets, for the happiness of our homes, our gratitude is due, under Him who raises and pulls down nations at his pleasure, to the Long Parliament, to the Convention, and to William of Orange.'

2. *The King and Richardson's 'Pamela'* (p. 122). We know little of the books Bute prescribed for the King's reading, but we may wonder if Samuel Richardson's *Pamela* was not among them. *Pamela* was published in two parts in 1740 and 1741, and exercised great influence over contemporaries. It is the story of a servant girl who resists the attempts of her master to seduce her, wins him in marriage, and reclaims him to a life of virtue. The book is almost unreadable today, but it is a book Bute would have enjoyed and might have recommended to the King. The following passage from the King's essay on the British political system (RA Add. 32/818–819) seems to be a paraphrase from *Pamela*:

> Let the day once come in which the banner of virtue, honour and liberty shall be displayed, that noble actions and generous sentiments shall lead to the royal favour, and prostitution of principle, venality, and corruption meet their just reward, the honest citizen, the zealous patriot, will lift up their heads, all good men will unite in support of a government built on the firm foundations of liberty and virtue, and even the degenerate mercenary sons of slavery will suppress their thoughts, and worship outwardly the generous

608

maxims of a prince, while they in secret detest his maxims and tremble at his virtues.

Compare with this the words Richardson puts into the mouth of Pamela in her observations on education (Part II, letter xciv):

For, let but the land be blest with a pious and religious prince, who makes it a rule with him to countenance and promote men of virtue and probity; and to put the case still stronger, let such a one even succeed to the most libertine reign, wherein the manners of the people are wholly depraved: yet a wonderful change will be immediately effected. The flagitious livers will be chased away, or reformed; or at least will think it their duty, or their interest, which is a stronger tie with such, to appear reformed; and not a man will seek for the favour or countenance of his prince, but by laudable pretences, or by worthy actions.

3. *Hannah Lightfoot* (p. 132). There is no British King of modern times of whom so many legends exist as King George III. One of the most ridiculous is the story of his alleged marriage to Hannah Lightfoot, 'the fair Quaker'. According to the different versions of this story, the King, while Prince of Wales, married (*or* became the lover of) Hannah Lightfoot, a girl of Quaker extraction. The marriage resulted in a son (*or* a son and daughter), who emigrated to South Africa (*or* the United States), took the name of Rex, and founded a family.

The reader may take his choice which of these alternatives he prefers. It makes no difference since both are false. Hannah Lightfoot certainly existed, but there is no evidence that the King so much as heard of her let alone married her. Royalty is peculiarly prone to legends of this nature, and there have always been people who profess to believe on the flimsiest evidence that they are descended from royalty.

4. *Where was the King when he received the news of King George II's accident?* (p. 133). The King writes in his memorandum of the events of the first day of his reign: 'The Prince of Wales was riding at a little after eight between Kew Bridge and the six milestone when a messenger stopped Mr Breton and told him an accident had happened to the King.'

609

I am obliged to Miss Marion Ward, who undertook research to find where the King was when he received the news of his grandfather's accident. Miss Ward writes:

> The six milestone (i.e. six miles from Hyde Park Corner) stood in what is now the Chiswick High Road, just south of the opening into Wellesley Road; if it still existed, its site would be between a launderette and a butcher's shop.
>
> In 1760 this portion of the Chiswick High Road was known as Gunnersbury Lane, for most of its length a country road which bordered the confines of Gunnersbury Park. At that date Wellesley Road was London Stile Lane (or in Roque's map, Turnham Green Lane), running roughly north-west between fields and market gardens to join Gunnersbury Lane opposite London Stile Farm from which it took its name. Not far beyond the six milestone the Great West Road branched off through Brentford, and straight ahead was the newly built Kew Bridge leading to Kew Palace.
>
> This area has been so altered by the construction of railway lines, and more recently by the Chiswick fly-over, that it would be quite unrecognizable to the King if he rode that way today. The maps from which its past appearance has been constructed were most kindly made available by the Chiswick Public Library. Of these the most useful were Roque's map, 1741–5; turnpike map, 1769; and 'Historical Map of the Parish of Ealing', 1777 (revised 1822 and 1828).

5. *The King's style* (p. 142). The King's style at his accession, as proclaimed by the Privy Council, was: 'George the Third, by the Grace of God, King of Great Britain, France, and Ireland, Defender of the Faith, and so forth'. The claim to the throne of France was a formal survival from the Hundred Years War, and was dropped on the union with Ireland. From 1 January 1801 the style was: 'George the Third, by the Grace of God, of the United Kingdom of Great Britain and Ireland King, Defender of the Faith'.

In Germany he was Duke of Brunswick and Luneburg, Archtreasurer of the Holy Roman Empire and Elector. The office of Archtreasurer was one of the great offices of state of the Empire which were associated with seats in the Electoral

College. On 6 August 1806 Francis II, the last Holy Roman Emperor, renounced the title, and the Empire ceased to exist. The King remained Duke of Brunswick and Luneburg until the Treaty of Vienna (9 June 1815), when the duchy was erected into a kingdom. Henceforth his style in Germany was King of Hanover.

It is said that at the time of the union with Ireland the King was advised to assume the style 'Emperor of the British and Hanoverian Dominions', but 'felt that his true dignity consisted in his being known to Europe and the world by the appropriated and undisputed style belonging to the British Crown'. See the passage from A. G. Stapleton's *Political Life of Canning*, quoted in *English Historical Documents, 1783–1832*, edited by A. Aspinall and E. Anthony Smith, page 83.

There was a further objection to this style. The crown of the United Kingdom is in remainder to the heir general, that of Hanover to the heir male; and thus the two crowns were not necessarily united. The personal union was broken in 1837 when the crown of the United Kingdom was inherited by Queen Victoria, granddaughter and heir general of King George III, while that of Hanover went to his eldest surviving son and heir male, Ernest, Duke of Cumberland.

6. *'George, be a King!'* (p. 152). The story that the King as a boy was told by his mother 'George, be a King!', with the implication that he was to assume a more personal authority than had been the case under his grandfather, was once a favourite of school text-books. It derives from *Recollections and Reflections*, the autobiography of John Nicholls, a Foxite Member of Parliament, published in 1820. Nicholls was only fifteen when the King came to the throne and could have had no personal knowledge of his upbringing. The story is not found in Lord Waldegrave or Horace Walpole and must be regarded as dubious. It probably owed its popularity in text-books to its being quoted in the article on the King in the *Dictionary of National Biography*.

Namier used to say that if this story were true it probably had reference to the King's table manners – that what the Princess really said was something like this: 'George! sit up straight! take your elbows off the table! don't gobble your food! do you want to look like your uncle Cumberland? George, be a King!'

7. *The King's Speech to his first Parliament* (p. 156). The King's Speech to his first Parliament contained the famous phrase: 'Born and educated in this country, I glory in the name of . . .' Of what? 'Britain'? or 'Briton'?

The Speech was drafted by Lord Hardwicke, and was returned by the King with this passage to be inserted. The document containing the insertion, in the King's hand, has long been on exhibition at the British Museum. There can be no doubt that the King wrote 'Britain'.

When the Speech was published in the *London Gazette*, 'Britain' had become changed into 'Briton'. 'Briton' also appears in the text of the Speech as printed in the *Journals of the House of Commons*. How had this change come about? Was it made deliberately, and if so by whom and why? Or was it simply a mistake by the clerk who transcribed the Speech?

Whether the King said 'Britain' or 'Briton' does not greatly matter as the meaning is the same. The incident is interesting because it shows how legends accumulate and how difficult it sometimes is to ascertain historical truth.

8. *The King's last meeting with Bute* (p. 228). There is another version of the King's last meeting with Bute in Jesse's *Memoirs of the Life and Reign of King George III*. According to this, on the authority of Brougham, it was Princess Amelia, the King's aunt, who arranged the meeting which took place at her house at Gunnersbury. I find it difficult to believe that Princess Amelia would have concerned herself in such a matter, and in any case the Duke of York is a better authority for what his father said than Brougham.

9. *The King's later relations with Chatham* (p. 240). Chatham after his recovery made some strange speeches. In the House of Lords on 2 March 1770 he spoke of Bute as 'the secret influence of an invisible power . . . who, notwithstanding he was abroad, was at this moment as potent as ever'. By 'an invisible power' he meant his hearers to understand the Princess. He went on to say about his ministry:

He himself had been duped, he confessed it with sorrow; that he had been duped when he least suspected treachery, at a time when the prospect was fair, and when the appearances of confidence were strong; in particular, at the time when he was taken ill, and obliged to go to Bath for a short week; he had, before he set out, formed with great pains, attention, and deliberation, schemes highly interesting and of the utmost importance to this country; schemes which had been approved in Council, and to which the King himself had given his consent. But when he returned, he found his plans were all vanished into thin air.

Most of this, as Chatham's audience knew, was wholly untrue. There had been no treachery or duplicity. His scheme for an alliance with Prussia and Russia failed because it was disliked by Frederick the Great; his scheme for an inquiry into the East India Company was carried out, and if it failed in its ultimate objectives it was because Chatham never condescended to explain these either to the King or the cabinet. Far from permitting intrigues against him, the King gave Chatham loyal support and waited patiently for his recovery. After having charged the King with duplicity, Chatham next proceeded to compare him unfavourably with King George II in respect of veracity and fair dealing (speech of 14 March 1770). The best comment on these speeches is that of the Duke of Grafton, who said they were 'the effects of a distempered mind brooding over its own discontents'.

When Chatham died, the King wrote to North (12 May 1778):

I am rather surprised the House of Commons have unanimously voted a address for a public funeral and a monument in Westminster Abbey for Lord Chatham; but I trust it is worded as a testimony of gratitude for his rousing the nation at the beginning of the last war, and his conduct whilst at that period he held the seals of Secretary of State, or this compliment if paid to his general conduct is rather an offensive measure to me personally.

He agreed to North's proposal that Chatham's pension, originally granted for three lives, should be extended for a further life.

The King should be given credit for being more charitable towards Chatham than Chatham had been to him.

10. *The legend of the oak tree* (p. 517). One of the most persistent legends about the King's illness in 1788 is the story that he got out of his coach in Windsor Great Park and shook hands with an oak tree under the impression it was Frederick the Great.

This legend derives from a pamphlet, *History of the Royal Malady, by a Page of the Presence*, published in 1789. From a note opposite the title page it has been assumed that the author was one Philip Withers. There was no one of this name in the Royal Household in 1789.

The pamphlet is not a history of the King's illness but a collection of anecdotes about various persons, presented under the guise of events at the court of Henry IV of France. It is obvious that these have been invented. There are, for example, accounts of conversations between the Prince of Wales and Mrs Fitzherbert and between the Archbishops of Canterbury and York which are so ridiculous that they could have deceived nobody. The story of the King and the oak tree falls into the same category.

11. *The story of King George's ghost* (p. 607). The story of the King's ghost is told by Sir Owen Morshead in his book *Windsor Castle*.

The rooms in which the King lived during the last years of his life overlook the North Terrace. When the guard was relieved the King would sometimes hear the tramp of soldiers' feet and would go to the window. As the guard passed, the ensign in command would give 'Eyes right' and the King would raise his hand in acknowledgment. One day after the King's death the ensign saw a bearded figure standing at the window and automatically gave the word of command. The figure raised its hand as the King had been accustomed to do.

The ensign was Sir William Knollys, subsequently Comptroller of the Household to King Edward VII as Prince of Wales, who told the story to King George V.

SOURCES

The chief materials for the life of King George III are the papers in the Royal Archives at Windsor Castle. Most of these have been published. *The Correspondence of King George III from 1760 to December 1783*, edited by the Honourable Sir John Fortescue, 6 volumes, contains all the political correspondence for this period. Unfortunately the text is not always reliable (see *Additions and Corrections to Sir John Fortescue's Edition*, by L. B. Namier). It is usually possible, however, to correct Fortescue's errors of transcription without reference to the original documents. *The Later Correspondence of George III*, edited by A. Aspinall, 5 volumes, contains virtually all the correspondence, public and private, from the Royal Archives from December 1783 to the King's final illness, together with many letters from sources outside the Royal Archives. The notes are full and informative. There is also a great deal about the King in Professor Aspinall's edition of *The Correspondence of George, Prince of Wales, 1770–1812*, 8 volumes. Professor Aspinall's editions of these papers are models of scholarship and every historian of the period is in his debt.

The following papers in the Royal Archives are unpublished:

1. The essays and exercises the King did for his tutors as a boy and youth.

2. Private correspondence, 1760–83. Some of this has been published by Professor Aspinall as an appendix to the fifth volume of *The Later Correspondence of George III*. Letters as yet unpublished are between the King and his brothers and sisters and relate mostly to their marriages and the Royal Marriage Act of 1772.

3. Accounts for different periods of the reign.

Documents printed in the above editions of correspondence will be found by reference to their dates. Unpublished documents from the Royal Archives are referred to by their numbers. RA=Royal Archives; RA Add.=Additional Manuscripts acquired by the Royal Archives since 1939.

615

Of the hundreds of books which I have consulted, one deserves special mention: John Heneage Jesse's *Memoirs of the Life and Reign of King George III*. Though written more than a hundred years ago, this is still the best biography of the King and contains a wealth of information not easily found elsewhere.

CHAPTER 1

1. For King George II, Queen Caroline, and Frederick, Prince of Wales: John Lord Hervey, *Some Materials towards Memoirs of the Reign of King George II*, edited by Romney Sedgwick.
2. The King's nurse: Fortescue, iii, 2. Mrs John Campbell's account of the King: National Library of Wales MS. 1352, ff. 59–60 (a reference given to me by Dr P. D. G. Thomas). Frederick, Prince of Wales's political testament: Sir George Young, *Poor Fred, the People's Prince*.
3. The best account of Frederick, Prince of Wales is Betty Kemp's essay in *Silver Renaissance*, edited by Alex Natan.
4. Averyl Edwards, *Frederick Louis, Prince of Wales*.
5. The King's first extant letter: Add. MS. 32684, f. 78. Printed in *The Letters of King George III*, edited by Bonamy Dobrée.

CHAPTER 2

1. RA 54237.
2. For the events following Frederick, Prince of Wales's death: Horace Walpole's *Memoirs of the Reign of King George II*; the Newcastle Papers; 'Leicester House Politics 1750–60', edited by Aubrey N. Newman, *Camden Miscellany*, volume xxiii.
3. The most important source for Frederick, Prince of Wales's later life: *The Political Journal of George Bubb Dodington*, edited by John Carswell and Lewis Arnold Dralle.
4. For this section see Romney Sedgwick's introduction to *Letters from George III to Lord Bute, 1756–1766*, and the sources there quoted.

5. *Memoirs, from 1754 to 1758,* by James, Earl Waldegrave.
6. Lady Louisa Stuart's memoir, printed in *The Letters and Journals of Lady Mary Coke,* edited by the Honourable J. A. Home.
7. RA Add. 32/2211–2250, 'Book of Latin words and phrases'; 2251, 'Beginning of translating Latin into English, July 9th 1753'; 2299, translation from Sallust; 2353–2374, translations from Caesar; 2361, drawings in the margin; 2375, 'Monsieur Cesar'; 2376–2423, Latin translations, corrected by Scott; 2484, two small notebooks containing Greek exercises.
8. RA Add. 32/2120, 'Abstract of the history of England. By Mr G. L. Sc[ott]'; 2131, 2174–2186, with corrections in Scott's hand.
9. RA Add. 32/1786–1807. The examples quoted in the text are questions 10, 20, and 49.
10. The payment to Demainbray for the course in science is recorded in Waldegrave's Privy Purse accounts, RA 55670–55704, under date 13 May 1755.
11. RA Add. 32. About 2,500 sheets, folio and quarto, together with some notebooks.
12. The character of Bute: Waldegrave's *Memoirs*; Shelburne's fragment of autobiography in Lord Fitzmaurice, *Life of William, Earl of Shelburne.*
13. RA Add. 32/5–74, Robert, son of William the Conqueror (an essay on the history of England from the Norman Conquest to the death of King John); 302, 303, Henry II of France and Catherine de Medici (an essay on the history of France to the time of Louis XIII); 63, Edward III and Bute's correction.
14. For the relations between Pitt and Bute, see their correspondence published by Romney Sedgwick in *Essays presented by Sir Lewis Namier,* edited by Richard Pares and A. J. P. Taylor.
15. The relevant documents are in Add. MSS. 32866, 32868, 33045, 35870.
16. The essay on the history of France to the time of Louis XIII, RA Add. 32/273–325, is on 104 sides; those on the reign of William III and Mary II extend from 1195 to 1530: 336 sheets.

17. RA Add. 32/1919–1952, 'Problems of practical geometry useful in fortification', has additions and corrections by Bute on 1942.
18. RA Add. 32/70–86, corrections to the essay on Richard II. The use of the ampersand was corrected in an essay on the origins of Europe, 32/914–916.
19. The following are the references to quotations from the King's essays (all RA Add. 32): Francis I of France, 290; 'the pride, the glory of Britain', 800; Andrea Doria, 291; freedom of speech, 822; the British constitution, 815; Edward III, 69; James I, 165–168; Charles I, 183, 195, 200; James II and William III, 1199–1216; the Convention Parliament, 1292; Bute's comment on royal ingratitude, 1281, 1282; the navy and army, 825.
20. The King's letters to Bute are among the manuscripts of the Marquess of Bute. They were edited by Mr Romney Sedgwick, *Letters from George III to Lord Bute, 1756–1766*. Bute's letters to the King, with few exceptions, seem to have been destroyed. If they existed one would expect them to be at Apsley House, where the King's papers were kept until they were removed to the Royal Archives, but the late Duke of Wellington assured me they are not there.
21. References to the Prince of Wales's concern for the national debt: RA Add. 32/179, 893–4, 1199, 1222, 1292; Bute's addition to the Prince's essay on Henry V, 95.
22. RA Add. 32/818–819.
23. Prince Edward's letters to the Prince of Wales are RA 54252–54280. The letter of 13 July 1759 is 54254–5.
24. The Prince's offer of service in 1759: Add. MS. 32893, and his correspondence with Bute.

CHAPTER 3

1. For the events of the first day of the King's reign: Sir Gilbert Elliot's memorandum, Minto MSS., National Library of Scotland (quoted in Namier, *England in the Age of the American Revolution*); the King's letters to Bute; Newcastle to Hardwicke, 26 October 1760 (P. C. Yorke, *Life of Lord Chancellor Hardwicke*); Fox's memorandum (Lady Ilchester and Lord Stavordale, *Life and*

Letters of Lady Sarah Lennox); Walpole's *Memoirs of the Reign of King George III*.

2. Sir Lewis Namier, *England in the Age of the American Revolution*, contains a detailed account of the political events of the first three years of the King's reign, based on all available manuscript sources.

3. The account of the King's marriage is based on Romney Sedgwick's article in *History Today*, June 1960, itself based on the Bute MSS. and documents in the Hanoverian State Archives.

4. This anecdote is recorded in Queen Victoria's journal for 22 November 1839, and was communicated to me by Miss Jane Langton.

5. RA 15671–15673.

6. For the Grenville ministry see Grenville's diary (Add. MSS. 42083), printed in *The Grenville Papers*, edited by William James Smith. J. R. G. Tomlinson in his book *Additional Grenville Papers, 1763–1765*, has shown that the diary was kept by Mrs Grenville from information supplied by her husband.

7. Mr Derek Jarrett allowed me to see the typescript of his article on the Regency Bill (*English Historical Review*, 1970) before it was published. I disagree with some of Mr Jarrett's conclusions but I learnt much from his article and am grateful for his kindness.

8. The expression 'Viceroy Cumberland' was coined by Sir Lewis Namier.

CHAPTER 4

1. The Rockingham ministry: Newcastle's papers, in particular his letters to John White (*A Narrative of the Changes in the Ministry*, edited by Mary Bateson); Grafton's papers, most of which are published in his autobiography; Walpole's *Memoirs*; the King's correspondence in volume I of Fortescue; the King's letters to Bute. The Rockingham papers are disappointing for this period; few of Conway's papers have survived; and there is little of any political consequence in the papers of the Duke of Cumberland in the Royal Archives. For this ministry, as

619

for so much else in the eighteenth century, the Duke of Newcastle is our main source.

2. For the period 1766–8: John Brooke, *The Chatham Administration*.
3. The eighteenth-century view of the Scot is best illustrated from Mrs Dorothy George's *Catalogue of Personal and Political Prints in the British Museum*.
4. Grafton's *Autobiography*; Fortescue, volume II.
5. *Memoirs of a Conservative*, edited by Robert Rhodes James.

CHAPTER 5

1. This and the next two sections are based on the King's correspondence in Fortescue, volumes III–V.
2. Sir Herbert Butterfield, *George III, Lord North, and the People, 1779–80*.
3. On the finances of the Crown in the eighteenth century see the important article by E. A. Reitan, 'The Civil List in eighteenth-century Politics', *Historical Journal*, 1966. The Civil List accounts for the early part of the reign are printed in the *Journals of the House of Commons*: 1752–69, under date 12 January 1770; 1769–76, 9 April 1776. For later accounts see *Reports from Committees of the House of Commons*, xi, 193–226, and the reference in Mr Reitan's article.
4. Historical Manuscripts Commission, *Bathurst MSS*.
5. This section is based on the Privy Purse accounts and relevant documents in the Royal Archives. The Privy Purse accounts exist only for the period 1763 to 1772, when Sir William Breton was Keeper (RA 17105–17290). Precise references to statements in the text are given below.
6. RA 50454–50459.
7. RA 16843.
8. RA 50306, 50307.
9. RA 17291–17297.
10. RA 16169, 17170.
11. RA 17296.
12. Regular payments for these services appear in the Privy Purse accounts.

13. RA 36836–36948.
14. RA 50195–50196.

CHAPTER 6

1. Ian R. Christie, 'Economical Reform and "The Influence of the Crown"', *Myth and Reality*.
2. For events from 1780 to the resignation of North, I have drawn heavily on Ian R. Christie, *The End of North's Ministry, 1780–1782*.
3. For the period 1782–4 I am indebted to John Cannon's scholarly account, *The Fox-North Coalition*. The fact that I disagree with Mr Cannon on some points does not lessen my debt to him.
4. For North's election debt, see Ian R. Christie's essay in *Myth and Reality*.
5. RA 15903–15905.
6. For the youth of the Prince of Wales and Prince Frederick, see the first volume of Professor Aspinalls' edition of *The Correspondence of George, Prince of Wales, 1770–1812*.
7. RA 16048, 16049.
8. The King to Lord Bruce, 2 June 1776, RA 16074.
9. North to the King, 3 June 1776, RA 16085.
10. The King's draft of a letter to Lord Suffolk, 3 June 1776, RA 16078.
11. RA 16079.
12. RA 16110.
13. RA 46387–46390.
14. For the quarrel over the Prince's establishment, see *The Correspondence of George, Prince of Wales*, volume i.
15. Pitt's conduct in December 1783 has long been a mystery. The mystery was solved by Mr Cannon.

CHAPTER 7

1. RA 16222.
2. For the royal children, see Lady Charlotte Finch's diary (Northamptonshire Record Office).
3. Only a handful of letters exist between the King and Queen, because few were written. They are published in appendix iii to the fifth volume of Professor Aspinall's edition of the King's later correspondence.

4. RA 15941.
5. RA 15942.
6. RA 15943.
7. The King to the Duke of Gloucester, 11 February 1772, RA 15957–15959.
8. RA 51973.
9. The King to the Duke of Gloucester, 27 December 1771, RA 15947.
10. RA 52346.
11. RA 52218.
12. RA 52257, 52258.
13. RA 15810, 15811.
14. The Duke of Gloucester to the King, 4 August 1769, RA 54310–54311.
15. RA 15975.
16. RA 15980.
17. RA 15992.
18. RA 16030.
19. RA 52351.
20. Lady Louisa Stuart's memoir, *The Letters and Journals of Lady Mary Coke.*
21. RA 54288.
22. Historical Manuscripts Commission *Carlisle MSS.*
23. RA 15939, 15940.
24. Ibid.
25. RA 15900.
26. The King's memorandum, RA 15948–15949. The Duke of Cumberland's letter to the King is RA 54427–54428.
27. 9 November 1771, RA 15938.
28. 3 November 1771, RA 15934.
29. 6 November 1771. The King's memorandum, RA 15948–15949.
30. 10 November 1771, RA 54471.
31. The King to the Princess Dowager, 28 November 1771, RA 15944.
32. RA 54323–54324 (from Pisa, 22 November 1771); 54329 (from Pisa, 20 December 1771).
33. RA 54333.
34. 11 October 1772, RA 52058–52059.
35. The King to North, 9 May 1780, RA 54443.

36. RA 54354.

37. RA 54359.

38. From Coppet, near Geneva, 22 June 1787, RA 54382–54383.

39. RA 54463–54464.

40. H. Clifford Smith, *Buckingham Palace*; John Harris, Geoffrey de Bellaigue, and Oliver Millar, *Buckingham Palace*.

41. Howard Colvin, *Royal Buildings*. The RIBA Drawing Series.

42. Manning and Bray, History of Surrey; E. Beresford Chambers, *Antiquities of Richmond*; W. J. Bean, *The Royal Botanic Gardens*; John Charlton, *Kew Palace* (Ministry of Public Works and Buildings guide).

43. RA 16734.

44. W. H. St John Hope, *Windsor Castle*; Sir Owen Morshead, *Windsor Castle*; Antony Dale, *James Wyatt*.

45. See the various editions of eighteenth-century guides to Windsor: *Les Délices de Windsor*, published by J. Pote, and *The Windsor Guide*, published by C. Knight.

46. Sir H. C. Maxwell Lyte, *A History of Eton College*.

47. Information about the King's daily life has been obtained from the diaries and journals of those who knew him. I have found the journals of the following to be the most useful: William Eden, 1st Lord Auckland; Fanny Burney; Lady Mary Coke; George Rose; James Harris, 1st Earl of Malmesbury; Sylvester Douglas, 1st Lord Glenbervie; Thomas Brudenell Bruce, 1st Earl of Ailesbury; and above all Queen Charlotte. There are two diaries of Queen Charlotte in the Royal Archives: August–December 1789, and 1794. They are invaluable for the King's daily routine.

48. Hugh Murray Baillie, 'Etiquette and the Planning of the State Apartments in Baroque Palaces', *Archaeologia*, volume 101; E. Shepphard, *Memorials of St James's Palace*.

49. Oliver Millar, 'The Queen's Pictures', *Horizon*, 1963; J. E. Hodgson and Frederick A. Eaton, *The Royal Academy and its Members*.

50. Percy A. Scholes, *The Great Dr Burney*; Roger Lonsdale, *Dr Charles Burney*.

51. Constance A. Herschel, *The Herschel Chronicle*.

52. The Science Museum have published an illustrated popular guide to the King's collection (*Physics for Princes*, by V. K. Chew), and there is a catalogue by J. A. Chaldecott.

53. H. B. Carter, *His Majesty's Spanish Flock*.

54. Seymour de Ricci, *English Collectors of Books and Manuscripts (1530–1930) and their Marks of Ownership*; Sir George F. Warner and Julius P. Gilson, *Catalogue of Western Manuscripts in the Old Royal and King's Collections* (British Museum); *Catalogue of the George Thomason Collection of Books, Pamphlets, and Newspapers, 1640–1661* (British Museum); Frederick Augusta Barnard, *Bibliothecae Regiae Catalogus*.

55. 'Memorandum of the King's receipts and disbursements', 20 September 1818, RA 50325–50330.

CHAPTER 8

1. My account of the King's illness in 1788–9 is based on Ida Macalpine and Richard Hunter, *George III and the Mad-Business*, and the sources there quoted. I wish to point out that the value of this book is independent of the diagnosis of porphyria. Even if it could be proved that this diagnosis is wrong, this would not diminish the value of the book as the only scholarly account of the King's illnesses.

CHAPTER 9

1. This account of the Royal Dukes is based on their correspondence with the King and the Prince of Wales. The early letters of the Duke of York and the Duke of Clarence are printed in appendix iii to volume v of *The Later Correspondence of George III*.

2. RA 16288–16292.

3. To Lord Hood, 16 April 1783, RA 16346, 16347.

4. William S. Childe-Pemberton, *The Romance of Princess Amelia*.

5. For the King's illness of 1801, see chapter 6 of Ida Macalpine and Richard Hunter, *George III and the Mad-Business*.

CHAPTER 10

1. Historical Manuscripts Commission, *Carlisle MSS*.
2. Thomas Dodd to Robert Wright, 22 September 1803, RA 46112–46118.
3. *Letters to Princess Elizabeth of England*, edited by P. C. Yorke.
4. Dodd to Wright, 13 November 1803, RA 46128–46130.
5. John Heneage Jesse, *Memoirs of the Life and Reign of King George III*.
6. On the King's last illness, see chapter 8 of Macalpine and Hunter, *George III and the Mad-Business*. The reports of the King's physicians are in the Queen's Council's papers in Lambeth Palace Library.
7. *The Diary and Correspondence of Charles Abbot, Lord Colchester*, edited by his son Charles, Lord Colchester.
8. These quotations are taken from letters to the Prince Regent by the Queen and Princess Mary: RA 49895–49896, 36763–36764, 36797.
9. RA Add. Geo. 2/15.
10. Final statement of the trustees of the King's real and personal estate, RA 50449–50453.
11. RA 44330.
12. RA 44331.
13. Lieut-Colonel Reynell to Denis Pack, 21 February 1820, Pack MSS. in the possession of Mr S. P. G. Ward.

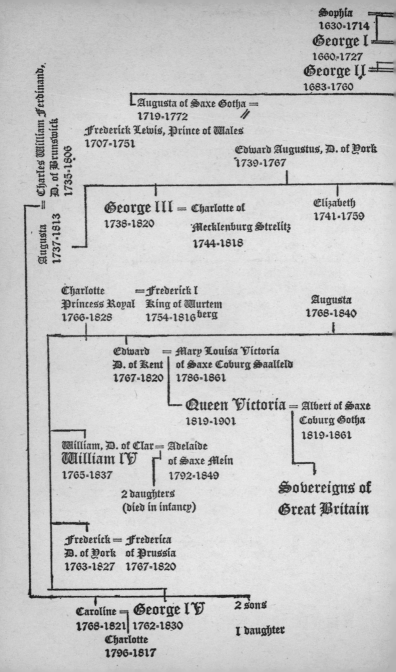

Sophia
1630-1714
George I
1660-1727
George II
1683-1760

Augusta of Saxe Gotha =
1719-1772
Frederick Lewis, Prince of Wales
1707-1751

Edward Augustus, D. of York
1739-1767

Charles William Ferdinand,
D. of Brunswick
1735-1806

Augusta
1737-1813

George III = Charlotte of
1738-1820   Mecklenburg Strelitz
              1744-1818

Elizabeth
1741-1759

Charlotte   = Frederick I
Princess Royal   King of Wurtem
1766-1828   1754-1816 berg

Augusta
1768-1840

Edward   = Mary Louisa Victoria
D. of Kent   of Saxe Coburg Saalfeld
1767-1820   1786-1861

Queen Victoria = Albert of Saxe
1819-1901   Coburg Gotha
                 1819-1861

William, D. of Clar = Adelaide
William IV   of Saxe Mein
1765-1837   1792-1849

2 daughters
(died in infancy)

**Sovereigns of
Great Britain**

Frederick = Frederica
D. of York   of Prussia
1763-1827   1767-1820

Caroline = George IV
1768-1821 1762-1830
Charlotte
1796-1817

2 sons

I daughter

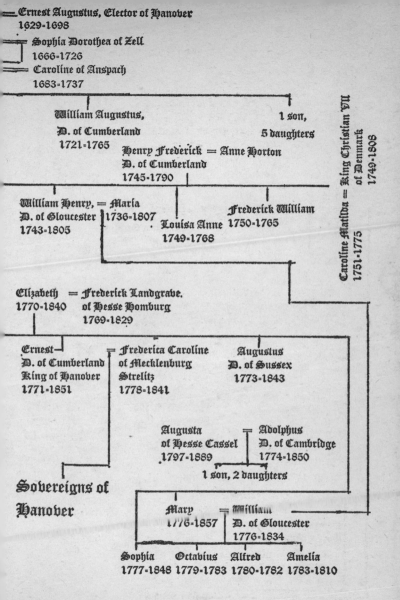

Ernest Augustus, Elector of Hanover
1629-1698

Sophia Dorothea of Zell
1666-1726

Caroline of Anspach
1683-1737

William Augustus,
D. of Cumberland
1721-1765

1 son,
5 daughters

Henry Frederick = Anne Horton
D. of Cumberland
1745-1790

Caroline Matilda = King Christian VII
1751-1775   of Denmark
                   1749-1808

William Henry, = Maria
D. of Gloucester 1736-1807
1743-1805   Louisa Anne
                 1749-1768

Frederick William
1750-1765

Elizabeth = Frederick Landgrave.
1770-1840   of Hesse Homburg
            1769-1829

Ernest   = Frederica Caroline
D. of Cumberland of Mecklenburg
King of Hanover   Strelitz
1771-1851   1778-1841

Augustus
D. of Sussex
1773-1843

Augusta   Adolphus
of Hesse Cassel   D. of Cambridge
1797-1889   1774-1850

1 son, 2 daughters

Sovereigns of
Hanover

Mary   = William
1776-1857 D. of Gloucester
           1776-1834

Sophia   Octavius   Alfred   Amelia
1777-1848   1779-1783   1780-1782   1783-1810

The Family of King George III

INDEX

In this index King George III is referred to both before and after his accession as G III. King George I and King George II are referred to as G I and G II, and the future King George IV as Prince of Wales.

Cabinet, 489

Cambridge, Duke of, *see* Adolphus, Prince

Camden, 1st Earl, and the formation of Chatham's ministry (1766), 224; as Lord Chancellor, 226; and the Middlesex election, 252, 258; G III's assessment of, 472

Campbell, Mrs (wife of John Campbell, MP), on G III as a child, 51

Carlton House, 397, 398, 505, 507, 547

Carmarthen, Lord, 409–10

Carnarvon, Lord, 449

Caroline, Princess, of Brunswick (wife of Prince of Wales, later Queen Caroline), 546, 549–52

Caroline, Princess, of Hesse Darmstadt, 145–6

Caroline, Queen (wife of G II), 37; and Frederick Prince of Wales, 46–7, 48–9; her death, 51

Caroline Matilda, Queen of Denmark (sister of G III), 427–30; on her sister Princess Augusta, 426

'castellated palace' (at Kew), 451

Catherine, Empress, of Russia, 293–4

Catholic emancipation, 575–9, 588

Cavendish, Lord George, 170–1

Cavendish, Lord John, 374, 397, 413

Chambers, Sir William, 107, 478, 480

Charles I, 35; G III's view of, 110

Charles II, 35

Charlotte, Princess (daughter of G III, Princess Royal), 568, 570–1

Charlotte, Princess (daughter of Prince of Wales), 550

Charlotte, Queen (Princess Charlotte of Mecklenburg Strelitz, wife of G III), 417–

20; her marriage, 144–51; and the Regency Act (1765), 190–3; her finances, 347–9; her appearance, 421; her death, 450; and Windsor, 452–3; and G III's illness (1788–9), 512–29 *passim*, 539; (1801), 585–6, 593–5; (1804), 593, 594–5; (1810–20), 603; and Prince of Wales's marriage, 546; on the visit to Cheltenham, 509; on the French Revolution, 543

Charlton, Mr John, on the 'castellated palace', 451

Chatham, 1st Earl of (formerly William Pitt, the elder, *q.v.*), his ministry, 226–40; and Bute, 227; G III's submission to, 229; his illness, 230, 232–4, 235, 237–8, 239; his literary style, 231–2, 233, 239; in opposition, 258–9, 261; and America, 280, 308

Chelsea water works, 334

Cheltenham, G III's visit to, 508–9

Chesterfield, 5th Earl of, 73; on gentlemanliness, 33; on Frederick Prince of Wales, 48; on quarrel between King and heir apparent, 99

Christian VII, of Denmark, 427–8

Churchill, Sir Winston, G III compared to, 359

Cinque Ports, Lord North appointed Warden of, 315

Civil List, 157, 326–36, 370; Civil List Act, 368, 370–1

Clarence, Duke of, *see* William, Prince

Clarendon, 1st Earl of, 404

Coke, Lady Mary, believes Duke of York to be in love with her, 432; and rumoured marriage of Duke of Gloucester, 440; hurt by G III's apparent discourtesy, 475; on the birth of Princess Augusta, 422; on Prince Edward and the bishopric of Osnabruck,

Papendiek, Mrs, 531
Parliament, 34, 35, 36, 284, 285; *see also* House of Commons; House of Lords
party politics, G III and, 159–61
patronage, 187, 490, 492–4; Scottish, 176–7, 187, 202, 227
Payne, Captain John, on G III's illness, 575
peerages, G III's power to create, as a political weapon, 386, 409; G III retains control of, 494–5
Pelham, Henry, 52, 91
Pelham, Thomas, 590
Pembroke, Countess of, 526–7
Pepys, Sir Lucas, 521
Perceval, Spencer, 601, 602
'personal rule' of G III, 152; *see also* constitution
Peterborough, Bishop of, *see* Thomas, John
Pimlico, G III's property in, 342
Pinchbeck, Christopher, 481
Pitt, Thomas, 185
Pitt, William, the elder (later 1st Earl of Chatham, *q.v.*), his position on death of Pelham, 91–3; and Hanover, 98–9, 111, 114, 160; and Bute, 98–100, 101–2, 111–15, 118–19, 125–7, 134–41, 198–9; Leader of the Commons, 102; war minister, 112–13, 118, 136, 162; defends Duke of Cumberland, 112–13; and G III, 125–7, 134–40, 141, 180–1, 196, 198, 201, 205–6, 210–11; and the Tories, 159–61; and Grenville, 180–2; and Rockingham, 210, 213–14, 215–16, 220–1, 226–7; becomes Earl of Chatham, 226; and America, 273, 275–6
Pitt, William, the younger, his fear of the London mob, 174; opposes Fox's India Bill, 402; becomes first minister, 404–6; forms his cabinet, 408–9; his ministry, 409–12, 516, 544–5, 547, 573–80; his India Bill,
410; and Prince of Wales, 507, 546–7; and the regency (1788), 516; and the French Revolution, 544–5; as war minister, 573, 574; and Ireland, 576–80, 588; becomes Prime Minister on resignation of Addington, 592
porphyria, 534, 537
Portland, 3rd Duke of, succeeds Shelburne as first minister, 381, 383, 385; and the Prince of Wales's income, 397–8; supports Pitt against revolutionary France, 544–5
Portsmouth dockyard, G III's visit to, 319
Prime Minister, concept of, 36–7, 256–7, 263–6, 474
Prince of Wales, constitutional position of, 41–2
Privy Purse, 333–4, 341, 342–7
Protestantism, 26–8, 270; *see also* Catholic emancipation
psychoanalysis, G III and, 420

Queen's House (Buckingham House), 156, 449, 450; houses built overlooking, 186; King's Library at, 485
Queen's Lodge (at Windsor), 452–3

Ravensworth, 1st Lord, 81
regency, Regency Acts: (1751), 63, 65, 67, 72, 92–3; (1755), 93; (1765), 189–96; (1788), 516–17, 529, 539; (1811), 601–2, 604
Reynolds, Dr, 601
Richmond, G III's farm at, 341
Richmond, 3rd Duke of, 223, 368
Richmond Lodge (at Kew), 450
Robinson, John, 314–15, 404
Robinson, Mary, 391–2
Robinson, Sir Thomas, 92
Rockingham, 2nd Marquess of, becomes head of the Treasury in 1765, 207; his ministry, 208–24; and Bute, 208–9,

637